Scholarly Religious Libraries in North America

A Statistical Examination

John F. Harvey
with the assistance of
Jo Ann Mouridou

The Scarecrow Press, Inc.
Lanham, Maryland, & London
1999

SCARECROW PRESS, INC.

Published in the United States of America
by Scarecrow Press, Inc.
4720 Boston Way
Lanham, Maryland 20706

4 Pleydell Gardens, Folkestone
Kent CT20 2DN, England

British Library Cataloguing in Publication Information Available

Library of the Congress Cataloging-in-Publication Data

Harvey, John F. (John Frederick), 1921–
Scholarly religious libraries in North America : a statistical examination / John F. Harvey ; with the assistance of Jo Ann Mouridou.
p. cm.
Includes bibliographical references (p.) and index.
ISBN 0-8108-3341-7 (alk. paper)
1. Religious libraries—United States—Statistics. 2. Religious libraries—Canada—Statistics. I. Mouridou, Jo Ann. II. Title.
Z675.R37H47 1999
027.6′7′0973—dc21 97–8405
CIP

™ The paper used in this publication meets the minimum requirements of American National Standard for Information Sciences—Permanence of Paper for Printed Library Materials, ANSI Z39.48-1984.
Manufactured in the United States of America

To Understand God's thoughts we must study statistics, for these are the measure of His purpose.

—K. Pearson, *Life . . . of Francis Galton*
Vol. II, Chapter XIII, Section 1

Thou shalt not sit with statisticians nor commit a social science.

—W. H. Auden

CONTENTS

PREFACE

This book has been prepared for all North American religious libraries and librarians in academic, special, school, and public libraries. It analyzes religious libraries, particularly academic libraries, and suggests that religious librarianship is to some degree a discrete occupational field.

Seminary librarians and faculty members should welcome a friendly opinion of their field. Religious library association leaders and their workshop and conference instructors will find useful material here. Library school faculty members may be interested in the description and analysis of a relatively new and developing field and of a proposed publication program. Religious publishers and journalists should welcome a discussion of the libraries that serve as their primary market. The best contribution that the work could make would be to draw attention to the religious library field and to spark an interest in research on it.

Data Collection and Analysis Policy and Procedure

There is little detailed data available on religious libraries, except the annual American Theological Library Association (ATLA) statistics report, which represents only a small fraction of the entire religious library population. A questionnaire sent to several thousand libraries to obtain information probably would have realized a 20 to 25 percent rate of return, at best, since in the scholarly religious library field, the percentage return on once-only mail questionnaire surveys has generally been poor. Martin Ruoss received 39 percent return in 1966 from a scholarly library target group, for instance.[1] In his directory, as a way of compensating for the lack of return, Ruoss printed the names and addresses of both those libraries that returned questionnaires and those that did not.

Therefore, the author decided to take advantage of the fact that the *American Library Directory (ALD)* (published by R. R. Bowker) carries out a North American mail survey annually, which includes several hundred popular and most scholarly religious libraries. Analyzing data from the *ALD* printed volumes was simpler, cheaper, and more satisfactory than relying on personally constructed mail questionnaires.

This book draws on data in two *ALD* editions, the 31st (1978) and the 41st (1988), thereby enabling the author to carry out a longitudinal study as well as an analysis of the information provided for each library. Wayne State University library, Detroit, purchased one book (1988) and donated the other (1978), for which the author is grateful. About 1,550 scholarly religious academic libraries are listed in each edition. The author neither visited any library nor made direct contact with any librarian.

The data collection form used for the *ALD* study is shown in Appendix D. An attempt was made to include all information found in the fuller *ALD* library listings that would be useful in understanding these libraries. The following outline lists the library information and subject areas covered by the derived questionnaire that became the *ALD* study data form and the basis for the data collected and reproduced in this book:

- I. Basic institutional and library information
  - A. *ALD* edition
  - B. Library number (research serial for longitudinal analysis purposes)
  - C. Institutional name
  - D. Library name
  - E. Questionnaire returned?
  - F. Repeat library?
- II. Geographic and demographic factors
  - A. Nation
  - B. State or province
  - C. City
  - D. City population
- III. Academic libraries
  - A. Highest degree offered
  - B. Accreditation status
  - C. Enrollment
  - D. Faculty size

IV. Denomination
V. Formal denominational affiliation
VI. Library type
  A. Junior college
  B. Senior college
  C. University
  D. Seminary
  E. Convent/monastery
  F. Denominational headquarters
  G. Historical or archival center
VII. Founding date
VIII. Personnel
  A. Professional
  B. Clerical and student assistant
  C. Total
IX. Director
  A. Name
  B. Gender
  C. Religious order membership
  D. Religious order status
X. Finance
  A. Material expenditures
  B. Personnel expenditures
  C. Other expenditures
  D. Total expenditures
XI. Collections
  A. Volumes
  B. Periodical Titles
  C. Vertical files
  D. Microforms
  E. Media
  F. Maps
  G. Art reproductions
XII. Extended collections
  A. Religious subject interests
  B. Special collections
XIII. Service
  A. Consortium memberships
  B. Local automation projects
  C. Publications

D. Departmental library?
E. Circulation restrictions
F. Reference use restriction

The author completed questionnaires from the two *ALD* editions, and then the data was keyboarded and validated with assistance first from the Fachhochschule für Bibliothekswesen in Stuttgart, Germany, under the supervision of Saiedeh and Wolfgang von Keitz and later in Nicosia under the supervision of Jo Ann Mouridou. Each chapter of this publication gives information that shows the religious libraries' distinctive character: for certain types of these libraries or for special interests for other reasons. The distinctive attributes, strengths, and weaknesses of each type of library are considered here also. They allow the author to develop the outlines of a profile in the field of North American scholarly religious libraries and its subdivisions. This profile should also help to establish acceptable working parameters for future studies.

The *American Library Directory:* Its Strengths and Its Limitations

Since 1923 the *ALD* has enjoyed a long and honorable history among North American reference books. It provides the best-known and most comprehensive collection of information about scholarly and popular religious and nonreligious libraries. It covers public, academic, and special libraries. The most notable *ALD* limitation is its almost complete disregard for school libraries. As far as this author is aware, there is no comprehensive school media center or library directory for the United States or Canada, although certain states and provinces may have their own specific directories.

The *ALD,* however, does contain an occasional printing error affecting its factual integrity, e.g., in the forty-first edition, on page 1300, the Maria Regina College Library total expenditure figure is one zero deficient. Working with the forty-third edition (1990) on another project suggested to me that the latter edition may have contained more frequent errors than the earlier one. All directory editions suffer from the tendency for a certain proportion of the libraries to be inconsistent in completing the annual questionnaire form and mailing it to the publisher. For that reason, as the years go by some smaller libraries, including many scholarly religious libraries, apparently move in and out of the directory. This creates the appearance of smaller libraries' springing up and dying with startling speed. Perhaps it is thought, erroneously, that a library which has reported to the *ALD* once need not report regularly in the future. The *ALD*'s present policy is to include all libraries returning questionnaires and all of the information reported on them.[2]

The principal denominations covered in this book are the following:

The *Baptists* (about 22 million members in North America) are numerous, the Southern Baptist Convention being the largest non-Catholic religious denomination in the United States. This evangelical group displays fragmentation among local communions; it is not a hierarchical group. In the United States alone there are at least twenty-five different Baptist bodies differing in various ways, including the expression of fundamental tenets, and representing historical subdivisions. The first Baptist church in North America was opened by Roger Williams in Providence, Rhode Island, in 1638. Current leaders in this group include the Southern Baptist Convention (strong in house of worship media centers), which was organized in 1845 in Georgia. Southern Baptist churches are located in all fifty states and most Canadian provinces. The convention exists in order to help the churches lead people to God through Jesus Christ.

Other leading Baptist groups include the Baptist Bible Fellowship International, which was organized in 1950 in Texas; the National Baptist Convention of America, organized in 1880 and composed primarily of African-American members; the Canadian Baptist Federation, which was founded in Ontario in 1763 but was reworked into its present form in the maritime provinces in 1888; and the National Association of Free Will Baptists founded in the late eighteenth century in New Hampshire by one of this author's lineal ancestors, Benjamin Randall, along with Paul Palmer, who founded an earlier group with the same principles (but no connection) in early eighteenth-century North Carolina.

The *Christian Church* (Disciples of Christ) (U.S. membership about 1.1 million persons) was born on the American frontier in the early nineteenth century. It developed from two branches originally located in western Pennsylvania and Kentucky that later united in Kentucky in 1932. This group has existed in Canada since 1810. The church is known for its informality, openness, individuality, and diversity. It has no official doctrine, such as the Church of England's Thirty-nine Articles of Faith, though it calls for the reunion of the church on the basis of a return to New Testament faith and order.

The *Churches of Christ* (1.6 million members) share a common fellowship with the Christian churches in the nineteenth century, but this fellowship was abandoned with the introduction of instrumental music into the worship services. Its individual churches are autonomous, and the Bible alone guides their faith and practice. Members believe in the divinity of Jesus Christ and immersion into Christ for the remission of sins. The New Testament pattern is followed in worship and church organization. There are no central denominational offices or church publications. The church organized in Canada in the central provinces around 1800.

The *Congregationalists* (0.4 million members) became prominent in England during the civil war of the 1640s and later were among the seventeenth-century migrants to New England seeking freedom from European state control of their religious worship. The group became a recognized denomination by the 1850s. They were influenced by the Calvinist Puritans and Separatists of the early seventeenth century. This group united with the Christian Churches in 1931 and later joined with the German Reformed Church and the Evangelical and Reformed Church in 1957 to become the United Church of Christ in Ohio. However, Congregational churches are still allowed to use the Congregational name and to lead a somewhat separate existence. The church recognizes two sacraments—Baptism and the Eucharist.

Episcopal/Anglican churches (total North American membership about 3.6 million) took on separate expressions north and south of the forty-ninth parallel. The Church of England was represented in the Jamestown colony in Virginia in 1607 and soon developed representation in other colonies also. The church became autonomous as the Protestant Episcopal Church in 1789 after the American Revolution. Church beliefs are both catholic and reformed (as distinct from Reformed, below). The historic creeds of Christianity (as they developed from the time of the early church fathers to the present day) represent the essential elements of faith, along with Holy Scripture and the two chief sacraments of Baptism and the Eucharist. Anglicanism arrived in Canada about the year 1700 in Newfoundland and Nova Scotia and has been self-governing in that country for more than a century.

Independent religious institutions are Christian yet have no specific formal or informal denominational affiliation.

Much of what was said above about Baptists applies equally well to *Lutheran* churches (with around 12 million members), at least as far as size and fragmentation are concerned. Eighteen or more separate Lutheran denominational groups exist in the United States and Canada, including the Evangelical Lutheran Church in America, Lutheran Church—Missouri

Synod, and the Wisconsin Evangelical Lutheran Synod. Their predecessor organizations can be traced back to the mid-seventeenth century in New York and the early eighteenth-century German migrations to Pennsylvania, New York, and North Carolina.

Most Lutheran groups still adhere to the beliefs inherited from their European predecessors, particularly those from Germany and the Scandinavian countries. The Wisconsin Evangelical Lutheran Synod believes that the Bible is the infallible word of God, and the Synod does not promote ecumenism. Latvian Evangelical Lutherans adhere to the Apostles, Nicene and Athanasian Creeds, the Augsburg Confession, and Martin Luther's Small and Large Catechisms. Lutherans are strong in publishing and in media use (as well as house of worship libraries). Women are important in professional church activities though they do not occupy clergy positions.

The *Mennonite Church* (combined membership may reach 0.3 million in the United States and Canada) groups are relatively small in membership numbers but are large in numbers of separate subdenominations, Canada and the United States accounting for at least twenty-eight. The Mennonite Church traces its beginnings to sixteenth-century Europe, the Protestant Reformation, and the Anabaptists. Groups arrived in the United States as early as 1683. Mennonites believe that the Word of God is central and that a new life in Christ is available to all who believe.

Mennonites generally refuse to serve in military forces, but are strong in missionary work. They try to follow the way of Jesus in their daily lives. The church is evangelical, guided by the Bible and led by the Holy Spirit. The General Conference Mennonite Church was formed in 1860 and includes persons of many different ethnic backgrounds. Canadian Mennonites are represented in all provinces and trace their history back to the European Anabaptists of the early sixteenth century. The pioneer Mennonites arrived in Canada in the early eighteenth century.

The *Methodist Church* (at least 12 million members) too is fragmented and is represented in North America by at least seventeen distinct groups, of which several are good-sized. The individual subdenominations include the United Methodist Church (formed in 1968 in Texas), the African Methodist Episcopal Zion Church, the African Methodist Church, the Christian Methodist Episcopal Church, the Free Methodist Church of North America, and, rather distantly, the Wesleyan Church. The Methodist Church originated in eighteenth-century England under John Wesley, but the American branch was established at the Christmas Conference of 1784 in Baltimore. The Methodists arrived in Canada in the late eighteenth century. The church stands for human freedom and simplicity in worship. It teaches the sanctification of one's entire life by means of grace through faith.

Other Denominations is a term that refers to all denominations with only small membership representations. It includes a great variety of faiths and denominations and even certain artificial subgroupings of its own. Several of the larger of these groups will be described briefly in order of size. The *Unknown* group includes all libraries for which no specific denominational affiliation, Christian or otherwise, could be identified by the author. The *Friends* (Quakers) group arrived in the United States in the mid-seventeenth century from English roots. Only five subgroups are listed for this small but vocal and well-educated denomination. The group stresses Inner Light, rejects the sacraments and an ordained ministry, and opposes war.

Reformed churches owe their existence to various Calvinist churches formed in European countries. The group arrived in the United States early—in 1628—with a primarily Dutch heritage. The *Seventh-day Adventist* church grew out of a worldwide religious revival in the mid-nineteenth century. The church is strong in missions, parochial schools, and publications (as well as healthful vegetarian living!). The *Church of the Brethren* and related groups date from 1708 with the Pietists and Anabaptists in Germany. Their creed is spelled out in the New Testament. The evangelistic *Church of Jesus Christ of Latter-day Saints* was organized in 1830 in New York State by Joseph Smith. Several of its prominent Mormon genealogical libraries (but none of its many smaller meetinghouse libraries) will feature repeatedly in the tables in later chapters. The *Assemblies of God* is a modern pentecostal and evangelical group and dates from a worldwide religious revival during the World War I period. It was started in Canada in 1919 and is part of the charismatic renewal movement. There are at least three million persons in the group, and it is growing rapidly. The *Church of God,* a holiness church, unlike the Assemblies of God, has many splinter groups. Nevertheless, it has at least five million members. The *Church of the Nazarene* is a holiness and pentecostal group that arose soon after the American Civil War. It stresses the importance of a devout and holy life and is Wesleyan Arminian in theology, representative in church government, and warmly evangelistic.

Eastern Orthodox, Theosoph 1st, Unitarian-Universal, United Church of Canada, Moravian, Christian Science, Salvation Army, Shaker, Bahai, Church of Scientology, International Church of the Four-Square Gospel,

Jehovah's Witnesses, Islam, Pillar of Fire, Rosicrucian, and Schwenkfelder are among the remaining component denomination-type groups, many of them represented in this study by no more than one or two libraries each.

A large group, the *Presbyterians* (about four million members) claim a dozen separate subdenominations in Canada and the United States. Leading subgroups include the Presbyterian Church in America, the Cumberland Presbyterian Church, and the Second Cumberland Presbyterian Church. The Presbyterian Church in Canada is one of the largest Protestant groups in that country. The first Presbyterian group was organized in Philadelphia in 1706. Strongly ecumenical in outlook, the present church represents the result of many mergers, some reflecting the Great Revival of 1800.

Different divisions of the church maintain different beliefs. Only some of them profess the Westminster Confession of Faith and Catechism. Presbyterianism is part of the Reformed tradition, and one of its Canadian denominations is committed to world evangelization. Canadian officers and members must subscribe to the Westminster Confession of Faith. Other subdenominations believe that the Bible is the only infallible rule of faith and practice. Its missionary interest is strong.

The *United Church of Christ* (1.7 million members) dates its existence from a 1957 conference in Ohio. However, its predecessor organizations are numerous and date back to the civil wars of the 1640s in England and even to the Heidelberg Catechism of 1563. It has a strong Lutheran and Reformed heritage also. Its immediate precursors were the Congregational Church, the Christian Churches, the German Reformed Church, and the Evangelical and Reformed Church. At the present time, apart from the semi-independence of the Congregational Church, there seem to be no splinter groups, although the various Reformed churches are closely related to the UCC. There seems to be no Canadian counterpart of the United Church of Christ. The church acknowledges its debt to the Protestant Reformation and stresses an evangelistic approach. It recognizes two sacraments, Baptism and Holy Communion, and combines the unity of the church with liberty of conscience.

Membership in all *Jewish* religious denominations totals about 6.1 million persons in Canada and the United States. Judaism existed in New York City by 1654. Jewish synagogues can be divided into four major subgroups: Orthodox, Conservative, Reformed, and Reconstructionist, according to their degree of adherence to ancient religious customs and dietary laws. Jews trace their history back to the year 1800 B.C. in Palestine.

They read from the Torah (five books of Moses), the rest of the Old Testament, and its commandments. Jews believe in God and his oneness, in the changeless Torah, the words of Moses and the later prophets, reward and punishment, the coming of the Messiah, and the resurrection of the dead. This is the only separate non-Christian religious group of any size among the fourteen leading denominations in this study. The Jews are well represented in Canada, especially in Montreal and Toronto. The history of the Canadian Jewish community began in 1760 in Quebec.

The *Roman Catholic Church* constitutes the largest single religious body in the United States and Canada (about seventy-one million members) and works presently under the spiritual leadership of Pope John Paul II. Catholics trace their history back to St. Peter, St. Paul, and the apostles of Rome. Catholic priests arrived in the new world with Columbus on his second voyage in 1493. The first continuing church was established at St. Marys, Maryland, in 1634. In Canada the church began in 1534 when the first Mass was celebrated on the Gaspé peninsula. The Canadian hierarchy is divided along linguistic lines between French and English and also along ethnic lines. Roman Catholic belief stresses the authority of the pope and other officers of the hierarchy of the church and the tenet that their church is the one holy, catholic, and apostolic church. Their faith is a reflection of the Bible. The two Vatican councils of 1869–70 and 1962–65 have further defined Roman Catholic beliefs. Sacraments include the celebration of the Mass, Baptism, Confirmation, Confession, Matrimony, Ordination, and Extreme Unction. The Virgin Mary and the saints are highly venerated. The church is not divided into separate denominations, although there are many priestly, monastic, and sisterhood orders including the Benedictines, Dominicans, Franciscans, Jesuits, Carthusians, and others.

Notes

1. John F. Harvey, *Church and Synagogue Libraries* (Metuchen, N.J.: Scarecrow, 1980); G. Martin Ruoss, *A World Directory of Theological Libraries* (Metuchen, N.J.: Scarecrow, 1968).

   Since they were studied together, the *American Library Directory's* scholarly and popular religious libraries are covered in several of this book's analyses and tables. The latter group of libraries is analyzed in detail in this book's companion volume, *Popular Religious Libraries in North America: A Statistical Examination,* to be published by Scarecrow Press in 1998.
2. As a way of providing a concise background for both the author and the

reader, a capsule (and therefore considerably oversimplified) summary follows of the history and beliefs of the fourteen North American religious denominations that figure prominently in this study. All information was taken from the *Yearbook of American and Canadian Churches,* edited by Kenneth B. Bedell (Nashville: Abingdon, 1993). The author is aware that certain of these denominations are no longer completely independent but instead work in cooperation with certain other groups.

ACKNOWLEDGMENTS

The author would like to thank a large number of people for their many contributions to this book, especially Jo Ann Mouridou of Nicosia, whose contributions were multitudinous, Susan Zambakides (the entire book was in her word processor's memory unit at one point!), Anne Gale, Carol Georgiou, Memna Hadjiharou, Donna Koulinos, Lorna Shearman, Karen Stephanou, Marie Claude Vidaillet, Janet Assadourian, Maria Damianou, Anthi Ellinidou, and Sahar Yanekian, all of Nicosia; the late Theodore Samore of Milwaukee and the late Frank Schick of Washington, D.C.; Richard Snyder of Philadelphia; Saiedeh and Wolfgang von Keitz, information scientists from Stuttgart and Unkel, Germany; and Wendy Scott of the Library Development Centre at the National Library of Canada.

Special thanks to Jo Ann Mouridou for her helpfulness in applying statistical research methods as well as for her computer analyses. However, only this intrepid author from outside the scholarly religious library and information field is responsible for any misconstructions, misstatements, or poor judgments

Two separate attempts were made to secure the active participation and advice of ATLA committees in the preparation of this book. However, a working liaison with them was found to be impractical. On the other hand, the author appreciates the interest, cooperation, and advice of former ATLA executive secretary F. Simeon Daly, O.S.B.

1

AN INTRODUCTION TO THE RELIGIOUS LIBRARY WORLD

Before beginning to discuss aspects of the religious library picture, we must clarify this book's use of several key words and phrases and of several acronyms. The reader is advised to study the glossary in Appendix B carefully to obtain an understanding of specialized words and phrases that are used in the text.[1,2] Some terms may cause confusion, such as *congregational,* which can refer to either a specific denomination or a type of library organization, and *denomination,* which may be used to describe all Baptists, for instance, or else only one of many North American Baptist groups, such as the Southern Baptists.

Scholarly Religious Libraries and the Larger World

The primary objective of this book is to describe and to analyze the fundamental characteristics of prominent groups of North American scholarly religious libraries. The characteristics to be examined are relatively basic, since this is a pioneering study and the groups of libraries are delimited and evaluated through the use of samples (in some cases large and in others small) of the population in each religious library subfield.

The emphasis is on identification and measurement of primary characteristics because even these have not yet been firmly established as existing to any degree for the religious library groups under discussion. The study methodology is by sample because only samples of each population are available to the researcher without requiring unreasonable effort and expense. Nevertheless, in general the samples that are used clearly mirror the many dimensions of the targeted subfields.

The religious library field has not previously been identified by library and information leaders as making up a distinct group sharing common characteristics. The field, therefore, needs to be defined as samples of the relevant subfields that are described and analyzed here. This book takes the religious library field seriously. While the typical general library staff member may believe that the religious library field is small, specialized, and localized, it is actually large and extensive. Work in the field is practiced in at least forty thousand North American libraries and in at least 220 countries around the world.[3] In most of these countries, both scholarly and popular religious libraries can be found.

The author hopes that the book will make a distinct contribution to library literature in seven separate dimensions:

1. In addition to the traditional list of four basic types of libraries—public, school, academic, and special—this book proposes for consideration a *new type* of North American library based on library affiliation with or sponsorship by a religious institution or organization. It divides the proposed category into two major subfields, scholarly and popular, plus five subdivisions for scholarly and three for popular religious libraries. Table 1.1 shows the author's classification. Careful study of this classification and its examples is essential to a clear understanding of the library categorization used in this book.
2. This book examines the characteristics of most North American scholarly religious academic, Bible college, seminary, convent/monastery, denominational headquarters, and history/archive libraries. A later book will examine the characteristics of most North American popular religious libraries.
3. All of this book's analyses and most of its conclusions are *founded on objective library data obtained from two questionnaire surveys.*
4. To the limited extent possible with the data available, the analysis carries out an *international library comparison* between Canada and the United States.
5. It carries out a *ten-* or, in certain cases, a *thirteen-year longitudinal comparison* of these sample libraries.
6. It compares and contrasts several *types* of scholarly religious libraries.

7. It concludes by proposing *a program of professional literature development* for the entire religious library field.

Much of the book's discussion is based on the author's analysis of the information provided by the 1978 and 1988 editions of the *American Library Directory (ALD).*[4] Some of the material discusses and develops concepts already introduced by the author in previous books and papers.[2,3]

The Larger Religious World

Generally speaking, religious libraries appear to be little discussed, written about, or researched in the North American library world. Every issue of *Library Literature (LL)* contains a few citations to material about religious books and libraries, but the list is usually short.[5] Further, religious librarians seem to maintain few ties with other kinds of libraries and contribute only rarely to the significant journal paper and book literature of their own field. They seldom hold positions of authority in general academic or special library associations, and they seldom publish papers on religious library management.

Certain religious academic librarians, e.g., those heading large libraries, seem to be active in the large national academic and general library associations but seldom in any religious library connection. Some seminary librarians are active in seminary library associations, but only a small minority of these people merit notice. Certain Roman Catholic and Jewish librarians are active in both local and national associations, such as the Catholic Library Association (Cath LA) and the Association of Jewish Libraries (AJL), but again these are small groups of leaders already active in parochial associations.

Even the larger religious world sees relatively few of these librarians.[6] This world is the world of "the cloth"—ministers, priests, rabbis, and sisters—of the denominational hierarchy and of lay religious groups with their respective sets of clergy. The denominations become the libraries' sponsoring groups and their leaders are the ones to whom the librarians must look for guidance and inspiration. The larger religious world takes its theological beliefs, practices, architecture, ceremonies, sacraments, and honors very seriously, and so must the librarian practicing therein.

This is a world of doctrine and dogma, of pomp and pageantry, of denominations and administrative divisions, of actors and politicians. Each library is an emissary in the religious world, an organization standing between the world of the institutionalized church and synagogue and the library user and is expected, to some extent at least, to represent each one to the other with integrity and fidelity. Of course, library representation is usually carried out as a unit of a larger institution, of a seminary or a synagogue, of a college or a parochial school. The library's material collection has been selected at least in part to enable it to bridge the gaps between the secular and clerical worlds. This outlook and behavior describes all kinds of religious libraries to a greater or lesser extent.

Religious adherents may be subdivided among the various faiths, such as Christian, Jewish, or Muslim—the three largest North American religious systems.[6] Within each faith exist larger or smaller denominations or sects, such as Shiite Muslims and Reform Jews. These groups differ somewhat among themselves in their forms of organization and in the articles of their faith. In most cases, their insistence on the importance of these differences sets off the related groups from each other.

In other cases, groups, denominations, and subdenominations have arisen out of regional, cultural, linguistic, or historical affinities and variations. Subdivision and further subdivision has been the rule among North American Protestants, but in the present century several mergers have occurred also, e.g., between the Universalists and the Unitarians, among several cooperating Lutheran groups, and among the groups that formed the United Church of Christ. Merely keeping track of who is aligned with or separate from whom among certain Christian groups, such as the Baptists, Lutherans, and Mennonites, requires continuing attention.

The larger American religious world contains a considerable variety of local, regional, and national administrative offices, organizations, and persons, both clerical and lay, male and female. Much of each denomination's power lies in the headquarters of the many small and large denominations that are represented in Canada and the United States. The many central offices serve the clergy, who are representatives of the denominations, and the lay members, who belong both to the worldwide denomination and to their own local houses of worship. It is not possible to be more specific than this since so many different organizational forms occur.

The denomination's headquarters not only supervises the clergy out in the local churches and synagogues but also influences the many colleges and universities that may be directly sponsored by the denomination, be affiliated closely with it, or else be affiliated with a specific house of worship. The central or regional office, such as a diocesan headquarters among Anglican churches, for example, also supervises directly or influences various of its charitable organizations, such as hospitals, orphanages, retreat houses, benevolent societies, and other social service agencies, as well as its North American or foreign missions. Headquarters officials may exercise much hierarchical authority over these organizations and the people who work in them, depending on the nature of the relationship between the supervisor and the supervised.

A few examples of the hierarchical system include the Church of Jesus Christ of Latter-day Saints (LDS, or Mormons), the Church of Christ, Scientist (Christian Science), Episcopal/Anglican, the Southern Baptist Convention, and the Roman Catholic Church, all of which are large and well organized. Denominational organization may take either a centralized, decentralized, or congregational form.

Clergy and laypeople come together in individual houses of worship. Certain aspects of their relationship will be discussed later in this chapter. Most of the denomination's income is derived from the individual house of worship, but in many cases its ecclesiastical authority is derived from the district, diocese, or archdiocese, which is presided over by a bishop or archbishop, e.g., the provincial elders of the U.S. Moravian Church. In the end, however, the larger religious world consists primarily of individual house of worship members, most of whom consider themselves to be free agents taking what they need and returning the same to their local, regional, national, or worldwide church or synagogue groups.

The sometimes more and sometimes less formally educated and ordained ministers, pastors, priests, rabbis, mullahs, emams and other "holy" men make up another important part of the religious world. These religious leaders are further subdivided by rank into cardinals, archbishops, bishops, district superintendents, vicars, deans, and ministers (among Protestant groups), and deacons, elders, presiding elders, and other titles used sometimes for religious and sometimes for lay figures, making this a rank-and-title conscious segment of North American society.

These ranks show the hierarchical, conservative, and traditional nature of the religious world and of most clergymen and clergywomen. While denominations vary, and some have no formally appointed clergy (Mormons and Christian Scientists, for instance), apparently few laymen have more than a minimal amount of political influence in the affairs of most denominations, especially in the areas of doctrine and theological importance. The full-time professional clergy are the most powerful factors in local religious affairs, though a few laypersons exert influence in certain areas.

Outside the ministerial hierarchy yet not very distant from it are the religious orders of priests, monks, and nuns, such as the members of the Society of Jesus and the Order of Friars Minor in the Roman Catholic Church. The priestly functions of religious orders may be similar to those of diocesan priests in serving churches, or they may work primarily on special missionary, publication, educational, or charitable projects.

In addition to the clergy and orders, several denominations have full-time religious professionals such as monastery and convent members, priests' assistants, or charity administration assistants. They may have such titles and fill such roles as monks, priests, brothers, sisters, and nuns or deaconesses. Denominations with these special professionals include Roman Catholics, Anglicans, Lutherans, the Salvation Army, Mennonites, and Greek Orthodox, among others. In addition, many denominations have full- or part-time lay administrative-religious employees with titles such as director of religious education, Sunday school superintendent, sacristan, verger, organist, or director of music, for instance.

The clergy are persons, predominantly men, who have entered the service of their deity, generally as a permanent vocation. They have a vested interest in institutionalized religion and represent library sponsors as well. They can be expected to push forward the religious aspect of library service and to regard a religious college library, for instance, as being primarily an organization with the basic mission of propagating religious philosophy through reading and viewing material chosen to inspire students and faculty members to lead more devout lives.

The basic mission of the religious library is to provide reading and viewing collections on religion and the devout life. Regardless of level, the primary focus is on spiritual development and on encouraging the spiritual and ethical development of the institutional and personal members. Apparently the fundamental objective of the North American religious world is to assist the laity in saving their souls. The denominational clergy get together frequently in conferences for serious business discussions to try to improve the status of their organizations as well as to discuss such practical aspects as job reassignment, building construction, and budgets.

Many laypersons participate in one or more of the many permanent or temporary religious subgroups such as a Chicago Baptist Men's Breakfast Prayer Group, the Dominican Laity, or an Anglican Holy Land pilgrimage group. Local youth clubs provide the house of worship with a continuing focus for its activities and a source of new memberships. Those of the Greek Orthodox Church in Cyprus provide good examples.

Opportunities for devoted leadership are numerous in all denominations, houses of worship, and lay groups. The conscientious library leader who is sufficiently resourceful can find many occasions to press library use and service on religious leaders. The librarian's leadership role in the library, as well as his or her specialized function in the church, necessitates this. A strong internal and external public relations program is needed to take the library ministry's service, as some congregations call it, to the largest number of persons.

The Importance of Libraries in the Religious World

Religion has a longer history than most other recognized fields of study. Several of the major faiths have existed for many centuries, such as the Hindu religion, dating from 1500 B.C. Other religions also have ancient roots. Many of the modern seminary library's titles were produced in the medieval, Reformation, or post-Reformation periods, certainly long before the twentieth century. Contrast the antiquity of the average chemistry library's holdings!

In the scripture-oriented and conservative world of religion, where books and reading are thought to present the sacred word and where daily reading is almost a requirement, the religious library and librarian ought to enjoy great importance and widespread respect. Both North American Christians and Jews are called "people of the book." At some time in most daily or weekly religious services part of the holy scripture used by the denomination or faith is read, and in other sections of the service psalms and hymns are sung that depend on or are inspired by the same holy writings.

Religion depends on the written word more than most other subject fields, so surely this should be an ideal field in which to be a librarian. The written word is all-important and the library has it! Libraries are significant in the religious world not only because they house the sacred books of the faith or the denomination but also because they provide service for the many theological commentaries and explanations, exhortations, and treatises that support and interpret the sacred works.

Few persons teaching, preaching, or performing other tasks within the religious world can function properly without access to a good selection from the extensive literature of the field. Many of its main practitioners—the clergy—have small private book collections to assist them in carrying out their responsibilities. Most other occupational fields are less book bound, especially in practical fields such as engineering and chemistry, so presumably they need fewer titles in their libraries.

Certain categories of persons use religious libraries heavily. Seminary students study the large output of religious presses and their own holy book by day and by night in course work preparation, while the clergy is expected to prepare ideas and quotations for weekly if not daily talks and sermons. Synagogue and church school teachers must regularly prepare the library material supporting their lessons, and seminary professors must read both religious and nonreligious material extensively in order to support their class and research work.

A large proportion of laypersons (including a few librarians) are conscientious in reading their holy books regularly. Librarians in all kinds of religious libraries must read through the library's new additions in order to catalog them or to carry out reference work. Certain of these persons write reviews or annotations for publication about the new books arriving each month.

As a consequence of its pivotal role, the library occupies an honored place in the religious world and should receive strong funding from officials representing houses of worship and academic and other religious organizations. However, this is not always the case, as we shall see in later chapters.

In what types of religious world institutions should libraries be found? Denominational institutions may include one or more libraries each in the national and lower-level headquarters offices, in each seminary, college or university, private synagogue or parochial school, monastery or convent (if the religious group has such institutions), and a few libraries to service historical and archival material. Perhaps the largest library category will consist of libraries serving denomination members directly in individual houses of worship. Mormon churches may support genealogical libraries, Catholic parishes may develop public libraries, and Christian Science churches have reading rooms.[7,8] Larger denominations and those whose beliefs encourage wide reading will boast many more libraries than small or more exclusively holy book-oriented groups.

What special services should a library provide for its religious constituency? Functions differ according to type of denomination and type of library. Certain denominational libraries have the obligation to preserve significant religious material of all kinds originating within the denomination, and for the individual house of worship there is a need to preserve and service its own archives and publications. In addition, each library is obligated to select, acquire, organize for use, and service a collection of appropriate recent material representing its own faith and denomination and perhaps material from the historical and wider religious world as well.

Religious academic and school libraries of all kinds, including church and synagogue schools, are expected to follow closely their parent organization's curricula, which may be either slightly or more extensively religious. In addition, on certain college and university campuses, some students take noncredit religion courses in denominational centers, such as a Jewish Hillel center or a Roman Catholic Newman center. At all levels these libraries can include recreational reading material that may or may not be religious. Of course, religious libraries may have further obligations, and may be required to provide service for research material in universities and seminaries, this year's Sunday school material in Protestant churches, and practical texts to assist daily operations in religious organization administrative office libraries.

In chemistry libraries a pressing need often exists for the most current information to be made available immediately, whereas in religious libraries there may be pressure to assemble an extensive collection but usually not for either rush service or for new book service. Only in a seminary, religious college, or university library serving a theological department is there need for a truly extensive collection. Most religious libraries are small and have modest reputations locally, much less so in the larger religious world. The popular religious library almost never boasts a large collection, ten thousand volumes being large for a congregational or a religious school library. Most parochial, convent/monastery, and religious public libraries consequently develop collections of this size or smaller.

Books and libraries vary greatly in their centrality to the religious institution that they serve and in religious officials' recognition of their value. Seminary libraries probably receive more attention and respect than any other religious libraries, but typically they serve one of the smallest user groups. North American colleges and universities support their libraries relatively well, though centrality to the curriculum and research program is seldom of a high order. Individual houses of worship vary greatly in respect to funding, with the vast majority of them providing only a quiet supplementary service.

When a Presbyterian church library, for example, is able to influence the local minister or the women's Sunday school class through its librarian's personality or its judicious selection policies, then it may achieve some local recognition. Certain other religious libraries provide superior service, also, with useful material collections. As an example, the Cambridge, Ontario, Forward Baptist Church library circulated an average of 166 volumes each Sunday morning in 1983 and must have held a position of respect in that community.[9] Certain scholarly libraries have widely recognized and well-used collections also, such as the Union Theological Seminary on Morningside Heights in New York City and Loma Linda University in Loma Linda and Riverside, California.

Religious libraries of all kinds typically possess relatively small serial collections, such as the Wisconsin Lutheran Seminary Library, which listed thirty-seven thousand book volumes but only seventeen hundred bound periodical volumes, a 21.8-to-1 ratio. Their book volume to serial volume ratio is in contrast to that in chemistry, for instance, where the ratio is relatively low. Therefore, religious libraries need a good card or computerized catalog or index much more than they need extensive serial indexes. A good theology library requires a larger collection to cover essential material than that needed for most other subject fields simply because the theological literature is so vast in quantity.

Partly as the result of so much book writing, the religious field includes more printed bibliographies than do most other fields. Bibliographies are needed to guide the reader through the extensive literature of religion. As another result of past publishing and bibliography making, the American Theological Library Association (ATLA) members' attention is directed toward reprinting and microfilming older but still useful monographic material as well as certain indexing projects for recent serial material.[10]

In certain denominations, many clergymen do not read extensively in their field, in some cases because their beliefs are holy book centered, i.e., extensive reading of the holy book is enough to answer their questions. In other cases reading widely is not essential for them professionally or spiritually. And in still other cases reading is not essential to them because they are illiterate or semiliterate. In addition, the range of literature relevant to their faith may be difficult to locate or pay for. Therefore, even though religious institutions may value libraries, they are not necessarily used heavily or funded adequately. They may be important for a few leaders and students, while other persons may endorse their role without personally feeling the need to use them.

In fact, in many places religious libraries seem to be treated like repositories rather than living, active, and helpful information centers. Few library users desire to read extensively on a religious topic, though some nonlibrary users read religious material extensively that they have obtained from other sources. No leadership role is expected of the librarian in such a library, merely quiet, dedicated, and often modestly paid or even volunteer service. In general, the library seems to occupy a place at the edge of the North American religious world, of central importance in a few cases, but often no more than an optional or little-used service in others.

The greater religious world has much power over the library and its sponsoring institution. For the librarian to become acquainted with that world and eventually to develop some degree of familiarity with various parts of it would be beneficial for both sides. The outside religious world also provides opportunities to further the goals of the house of worship or academic institution in carrying out useful projects. The dedicated religious librarian should seek fulfillment in both the outside library and the external religious arena.

The library staff may promote cooperative projects and involve the library more fully in the mainstream of religious activities. Such activity can demonstrate that the religious field and the library field are both strongly service oriented. Such an orientation is common to them but is unusual in many other professional or business fields. Both library and religious practitioners are expected to approach their tasks in such a user- or clientele-oriented spirit.

Many religious academic librarians seem to have few close, direct, working contacts with the *religious* leaders under whom they serve. Partly due to their passive nature (in some cases), few library staff members have played a strong and forceful role in the religious world. As far as this author can tell, few religious library staff members are active in formal religious library or nonlibrary organizations or associations, and an even smaller number seeks leadership roles in them. Often the activists seem to be clergy or religious order members working from an academic or parochial school library base.

The Larger Library and Information Service World

This section will indicate briefly something about the general outline and extent of the library and information service world, and provide a basis for certain religious and other library world comparisons. The *larger library and information world* is a phrase used in this book to contrast it with the more modest religious library field, and to refer to all North American libraries and library and information activities. This is the world of some large and many thousands of small libraries, of library associations both general and specialized, and of library schools both with and without doctoral programs.

Though smaller than the broader religious world, the library and information world is also rich in variety and of considerable size. It includes a range of libraries from the specialized, such as the Ames Orchid Library of Harvard University, to such heterogeneous collections as the New York Public Library. It is a world of much routine clerical and semiprofessional work and occasional scholarship, at least in a few of the leading library schools, such as the University of Illinois Graduate School of Library and Information Science.

In contrast to the religious world of doctrine and faith in abstract and unprovable concepts, the information world is one of pragmatism and technique. In contrast to the religious institution's considerable independence, the library and information service institution is heavily dependent on a local parent institution, such as a university or a house of worship. It is a world in which the large public and university library directors and department heads customarily play a major role, while the role of the small elementary school and public librarians is relatively minor. It is a world of many politicians but only a few statesmen and women.

This world is one of large and small associations, several with thousands of members (e.g., the Canadian Library Association [CLA] with over 4,500 members and the American Library Association [ALA] with over 55,000 members), while others are specialized and small (e.g., the Theatre Library Association with 500 members). Association memberships are generally growing, especially as these groups move further into continuing education. Certain large national associations take positions on national political, educational, and social issues, and their conferences attract hundreds of exhibitors and thousands of library staff members.

Several larger libraries have staffs of over a thousand persons (e.g., the Chicago Public Library has more than 2,000 staff members), yet many other libraries have single member staffs (e.g., the Center for Computer Law Library in Manhattan Beach, California). Most large libraries are not adding staff, while the number of one-person libraries is growing. Gender participation varies from the all-male administrative staff (e.g., at the Coastal Plain Regional Library, Tifton, Georgia), to the all-female administrative staff (e.g., at the Alsip-Merrionette Park Library, Alsip, Illinois). Staff members' educational specializations can vary widely both in nature and in scope, with practical subjects increasing slowly in popularity, e.g., more MBA and MPA degrees and more social science and computer science majors.

The larger library and information world includes the library press, which issues periodicals and reports of many kinds as well as books. Its influence on the field is growing. There are hundreds—if not thousands—of small North American university and congregational, association, and chapter newsletters and acquisitions lists, periodicals, and continuations, such as the *International Leads,* most of them ephemeral and aimed at local or denominational audiences. Many of the most substantial publications, such as the University of Illinois's *Library Trends,* are produced by universities. A surprising number of book publishers concentrate in this field—Dekker, Greenwood (in part), Haworth, JAI (in part), Libraries Unlimited, McFarland (in part), Neal-Schuman, Oryx, K. G. Saur, Scarecrow, Shoe String, the University of Illinois, and Wilson, as well as the American Library and the Special Libraries Associations.

In North America are concentrated more libraries, including religious libraries, than can be found on any other continent. The larger North American library and information world is one in which school libraries predominate in terms of separate units followed by numerous public libraries. School libraries in Canada and the United States outnumber all of the other kinds of libraries combined.[11,12] The total number of scholarly Canadian and U.S. libraries is about 17,640, as table 1.2 shows, of which about 14.1 percent have previous or present religious affiliation or sponsorship. Most of them are special libraries. Probably many institutions and libraries that are now largely secular had religious affiliations at some point in the past. There are about 5,160 Canadian and U.S. public and private tertiary-level colleges and universities of all kinds. These are unremarkable figures comparable to those shown in the *ALD.*[13]

Religious Library Importance in the Library and Information World

As a discrete group, religious libraries are important for several reasons, one of which is the sheer number of them in North America and elsewhere. In addition, religious librarians and their libraries form an interesting and distinctive group. Religious topics occupy an entire section in most book classification schemes (e.g., the Dewey 200s). Additionally, for several years seminary library users have been moving into interdisciplinary material use on university campuses, thereby bridging the gap to other subject fields. The policies and procedures followed in most large or small religious libraries differ little from those followed in similar libraries elsewhere. Their user groups differ little also and are characterized by persons working with or studying religious matters, as house of worship members or students in church or synagogue parochial schools or in higher education departments of religion.

In spite of their profusion, the religious libraries of most nations form a relatively small and less important segment of the national library and information world. Even in a nation with a state religion, such as the Democratic Republic of Cyprus, religious libraries are few and of minor importance, little more than depositories. Especially if we judge by median sizes of budget, staff, and collection, their rank is surprisingly low. For instance, most religious libraries have one to three staff members per library, as shown in the later chapters, and in some of the scholarly religious libraries all of these staff members are volunteers.

The largest religious libraries in this study are those located in universities (e.g., the University of Notre Dame library in Indiana, with 200 staff members). On the other hand, in Canada and the U.S. the occupational specialty of scholarly religious librarianship is a small one, smaller in numbers of persons participating than legal, musical, medical, science and technology, art, rare book, archival, media, serial, government publication, armed forces, and government agency librarianship.

Religious academic libraries range from the grossly inadequate to the superior. In the college and university departmental library field, religious libraries occupy a respectable but hardly outstanding place, in part because their collections are relatively large, but their user groups are usually small. Monastery and convent libraries, such as the St. Benedict's Monastery Library in Colorado, are certainly religious, if any libraries are, but they are usually small and may not always be fully professionalized.

Religious librarians seem to pay attention primarily to their own small "sideshows" within the larger library and information world. They do not mingle very much with other kinds of librarians. Religious library leaders seldom reach high office in national associations, except in national religious library associations. As far as this author can determine, no American Library Association (ALA) president in the past half-century has come from a religious library. Religious librarians are more likely to attend a conference that is sponsored by a religious library group, especially a group from the librarian's own denomination, than one by a general library group.

The only groups of religious librarians known to this author that attend conferences regularly or frequently are those from seminaries and parochial schools. A small group of U.S. and Canadian seminary librarians attend ATLA conferences faithfully, no matter how distant they are. However, this group constitutes only 1–2 percent of the entire North American seminary librarian population. Of course, ATLA seminary librarians may be considered to be the "cream" of the religious library world in terms of educational background (many of them have both graduate theology and graduate library and information science degrees), prestigious positions, and salary, and so we should expect much of them.

Full-time parochial school librarians turn out in large numbers for *local* parochial school library conferences, such as a Cath LA Brooklyn-Long Island chapter meeting, much less so for general school and other kinds of local conferences, and in small numbers for more distant affairs. Many popular religious librarians are part-time nonprofessional volunteers who lack sufficient time and interest (and sometimes funds) to attend general conferences where, in addition, religious library matters are seldom discussed.

Another characteristic of religious librarians is that they almost invariably have a humanities-oriented educational background. Therefore, to that extent they are qualified for work in a religious library, but they may have a poorer background for management and be less comfortable in front of a computer terminal than are business librarians. Nor, apparently, do the majority of them have religious educational qualifications, and some lack library science qualifications also.

Religious librarianship has an additional distinction. A common historical thread runs through all of theology and through the work of all religious librarians. Certain other fields have similar historical threads or frameworks to follow also. An entire curriculum can be hung on an outline of the history of religion. While the social sciences, "hard" sciences and technical fields have their histories, too, course work and curricula design, however, pay scant attention to such frameworks. Religion and theology librarians do pay attention to such frameworks.

In the author's mind, religious librarians share one other common characteristic. Many of them are surprisingly cooperative, agreeable, and humble persons. In the process of editing nine collections of other people's papers on chapter topics of his own choosing in the past quarter century, the author has become aware of the difficulty of finding well-qualified persons who will agree to prepare these papers. Sometimes he must go through a dozen names before finding one who is both well qualified and amenable. So far, the one exception to this generalization was the only book among the nine that used a group of popular religious librarian authors. Almost without exception, the first choices agreed to prepare the chapters soon after being asked.[14]

In addition to the library press, there is a religious library press that publishes mostly thin, insubstantial, and bland newsletters with usually favorable book review sections, plus thin pamphlets and bibliographies. This group too is growing in size and market penetration. Several examples are listed in appendix A. Few full-length religious library and information science books are produced by the religious library press (except for Cath LA), but the general library press publishes one or two books in the religious category each year.

Religious Versus Secular Libraries: Similarities and Differences

Based on the data available for this book, which will be discussed in detail later, in most areas religious libraries seem to be similar to nonreligious libraries of the same type. In fact, they seem to bear many more similarities than differences to corresponding nonreligious libraries. They use the same cataloging rules and classification schemes (for most of the collection); they buy from several of the same book and serial publishers and dealers; the staff organization and work assignment principles are similar; financial policies are similar and their charging systems are similar. However, certain differences and contrasts should be mentioned.

Not surprisingly, most religious library material collections of all kinds, except those of colleges, universities, and schools, are composed primarily of religious material. The Central Baptist Seminary Library, Gormley, Ontario, for example, probably contains little other than religious material, most of it Baptist. Typical nonreligious college, university, and school libraries devote only a small percentage of their collections to religious material, however. It would be surprising to find a large religious collection in the Texas A & M University library, College Station, for instance. So religious material dominates certain library collections, but others concentrate on nonreligious material.

Many monastery, convent, congregational, and religious history libraries maintain no active selection or acquisition programs. When no book funds are available, they depend on gifts to enlarge the library. Others order a few books each year from a local religious bookshop with the small funds provided by their supervisors (e.g., St. Paul's Anglican Cathedral Library, Nicosia, Cyprus).

Both seminary and congregational libraries patronize certain religious book and serial publishers, in many cases denominational. Classification activities in most religious libraries are similar to those in secular libraries except for the problem of the many Bible editions contained in the seminary library, and the special classification schemes that are used for certain special religious collections.

Seminary libraries may have their own buildings (Ruoss found that 68 percent of them did in 1968), and religious college and university libraries usually do have, but other kinds of religious libraries seldom have separate buildings.[15] In general, religious library circulation is small. Most Church and Synagogue Library Association (CSLA) congregational libraries averaged no more than twenty-five loans per week. On the other hand, certain parochial school libraries circulated one book per student per week.

Before completing the discussion of how religious and secular libraries differ, we must ask how the group of religious institutions and their libraries vary among themselves in emphasis on religion within the curriculum and in campus life. Many of them vary considerably. It is probable that Laval University in Quebec, French-speaking and Roman Catholic, strongly emphasizes Catholic viewpoints; Bishop's University, also in Quebec, English-speaking and Anglican, probably emphasizes Anglican viewpoints much less than one might suspect.

On certain campuses the particular denominational affiliation is strong and its influence permeates campus life, such as at Seton Hall University (Roman Catholic) in New Jersey and most independent Bible colleges, such as the Mennonite Brethren Bible College in Manitoba. On certain evangelical campuses a religious approach permeates daily life from breakfast prayers to evening religious services. However, on many other campuses, religious connections are weak and so is the religious influence on faculty and students, e.g., at the University of the Pacific (Methodist) in California. On some campuses, many students spend four years studying without ever entering the campus chapel or the central library. Generally, on Roman Catholic, Jewish, Mormon, Baptist, Adventist, charismatic, evangelical, and Bible college campuses the religious presence is relatively strong, whereas on many other religiously affiliated campuses it is weak, often very weak.

After having discovered differences among religious colleges and universities, we can conclude that these differences may be their greatest contrast, since, for the most part, North American religious and nonreligious academic libraries are much alike. However, the religious libraries generally have more religious library material in the collection than do nonreligious libraries. Further, the religious library may possess additional and specialized collections, at least in its own denomination or faith. In addition, religious order nuns, priests, and brothers may work on the faculty and library staff, and probably the student body contains more than the usual share of religiously committed or "saved" persons also.

Roman Catholic, Lutheran, Quaker, Episcopal, and other parochial *school* libraries are similar to public school libraries in their book and serial collections, in using the Dewey Decimal Classification, in using standard cataloging policies, and in providing the same variety of public services in curriculum support to students and faculty members.[16] However, as parochial schools they differ primarily in the following ways: (1) the curriculum contains a stronger religious element, (2) the collection may reflect a broader emphasis on religious material and probably highlights material from the school's own denomination, (3) the librarian may belong to a religious order, and (4) certain members of the faculty, library staff, and student body share a common religious heritage.

Many private parochial schools try to maintain a common frame of reference, which is not found in nonreligious private schools—a uniformity of denominational emphasis affecting the material collection, library staff, student body, and faculty. A Roman Catholic library such as that at the St. John Neumann High School in Pennsylvania, for instance, has many books written or edited by Catholics and a section or more of books on Catholic thought and leaders, avoids church-proscribed books, and buys most of its material from Catholic publishers and agents.

In certain important ways, religious *public* libraries are exceptions to the above generalizations, and they may also differ sharply from government-sponsored public libraries. They have no tax support and usually offer no children's service. The religious public library book collection is heavily slanted toward the publications of the sponsoring religious group, and most of them are Christian Science or Roman Catholic libraries.

Christian Science reading room books and periodicals seem to be almost entirely restricted to those published by the Mother Church in Boston, as found, for instance, in the First Church Reading Room in Guadalajara, Mexico.[17] All of these libraries contain copies of the current and back issues of the fine *Christian Science Monitor* newspaper, the *Christian Science Journal,* and the book writings of Founder Mary Baker Eddy. These reading rooms are always sponsored by a local church or group of churches and may often be found nearby in a storefront location on a busy business street. The material available can be either read there or purchased and taken away.

A large city may have a half-dozen or more Christian Science libraries, such as are found in Oklahoma City. Hours of service vary from two to sixty. Sponsoring the library seems to be a major church activity. Each library closely resembles the others, but they seem to be unrelated to each other in synergistic terms. Instead they relate closely to their specific parent churches. They seem to be used by different groups of people but are used primarily by Christian Science church members. Often the reading rooms are very small. Although their operation is simple when compared with that of other congregational libraries, Christian Science reading rooms have access to an office at the church headquarters in Boston, which assists new churches in establishing their libraries and in educating relevant personnel.

Roman Catholic reading rooms differ from those in Christian Science libraries in that they have a greater variety of books and publishers represented and are less singlemindedly evangelistic. Most Catholic public libraries, however, seem to emphasize familiarity with Catholicism, Catholic thought on contemporary issues, and Catholic best-selling biographies and fiction, such as are found in the Catholic Information Center on East Market Street in Philadelphia. Catholic libraries are not part of a coordinated international system as, to a certain extent, are Christian Science reading rooms. Most Roman Catholic reading rooms are supported by their fee-paying members, by a group of financial sponsors, and by healthy discounts obtained when buying their stock.

There is no nonreligious group with which to compare congregational libraries, such as the large Blumenthal Library of Sinai Temple in California. However, those libraries which serve primarily a church Sunday school or a synagogue school may be compared with those in a private religious elementary or secondary preparatory school. Most congregational libraries serve a part-time one-morning-a-week school in which all staff work is volunteer. Typically, these libraries are smaller than private or public school libraries, they concentrate primarily on religious material, especially denominational material, and they may serve all house of worship congregation members, including children and young adults, whereas private religious school libraries serve full-time curriculum, faculty, and student groups. Of course, most nonreligious school libraries probably have fewer religious materials, staff members, and users.

Religious history and archive centers, such as the Oregon Province Society of Jesus Archives Library, Spokane, Washington, differ little from nonreligious history and archive centers except for the nature of the parent organization and the focus of the material stored. Most of them are either national or regional denominational centers.

Religious organization administrative office libraries, such as the Anglican Church of Canada Harris Memorial Library in Toronto, differ little from other special libraries, but, as one would expect, they contain a large percentage of religious material since they serve a religious organization.[18] Much practical religious and nonreligious reference and historical material about a particular denomination is stocked. Many of them relate to the publishing, communication, or public relations arm of a particular denomination. In most cases, they are staffed by religiously affiliated persons who provide service to religiously affiliated users.

Is Religious Librarianship a Cohesive and Narrowly Focused Field?

What can be said about the cohesiveness of religious librarianship? Does religious librarianship show the single-minded focus and unity of a unique or discrete professional field? But first, can we define a cohesive or uniform library field? The following can be considered to be criteria for examining the cohesion of a group of religious libraries: (1) shared religious institutional sponsorship, (2) shared library objectives, (3) shared material collection emphases, and (4) shared nature of the user group. Also, the field should be served by (5) a limited number of specialized religious library associations. If all five of these criteria are unfailingly required as criteria, perhaps religious librarianship will have difficulty in qualifying as an organized and cohesive field. However, if the standard to be applied is not quite that rigorous, then perhaps religious librarianship might qualify as being generally cohesive.

Perhaps common religious institutional sponsorship is the criterion most broadly applicable to the group of libraries discussed in this book. All (or almost all) of their parent institutions have formal religious denominational sponsorship or affiliation, although their degree of closeness to the denomination or to religious observance in daily affairs varies. With religious sponsorship or affiliation, parent institutions should be to some degree religious. In all cases, therefore, these libraries have objectives that include religious material service to users for primarily religious purposes, meeting the second criterion, although in many academic libraries this objective is included only in a blanket service statement covering all kinds of library services and users.

House of worship, convent, and monastery libraries strongly emphasize religious books, as required by the third criterion, but many of the former, such as the Carmel Presbyterian Church, Glenside, Pennsylvania, also contain a proportion of nonreligious children's books for their public library-type users. Most religious college and university and parochial school libraries contain collections in which religious books constitute only a small proportion of the whole: (1) a modest number of books directly in the religious field, (2) some books in specific subject fields that were produced by a denominational author or press, and (3) many books with no religious connection but a relationship to the institution's educational programs.

The fourth criterion, uniformity in the nature of the clientele, applies to many libraries in the present book but not to all. Most academic libraries have only a few religiously affiliated users, but house of worship, monastery, and convent libraries serve almost no other kind. Parochial school libraries serve varied proportions of religiously oriented users.

Concerning organization of librarians into a number of library associations, the criterion is fairly met by scholarly and popular librarians though most of the associations are small and limited by nation, sometimes even by region, certainly by denomination and even by scholarly vs. popular library focus. Of course, organization into one large association or even into three by faith (Christian, Jewish, and Islamic), would show greater cohesion, but a fragmented picture is better than having nonexistent library associations.

Naturally, cohesiveness is a stiff requirement for any group of libraries, and each religious library subfield is more cohesive than the whole. We can conclude that the religious libraries in this book are uniform in having religious institutional sponsorship and affiliation, largely uniform in fitting themselves into library associations, and partially uniform regarding each one of the three other criteria. The entire field has a strong focus on religion, and cohesiveness varies somewhat for each subfield and each subfield varies for each criterion.

A problem with this situation is that the group of American academic religious librarians in this study (and perhaps other religious librarian subgroups as well) does not perceive itself as being composed of religious librarians in general. Rather, these individuals see themselves as being general academic librarians who work in a strongly or weakly religiously affiliated institution. In many cases, they display little religious group consciousness. In most instances, they are well aware of the institution's religiosity and are happy to be there but consider only rarely their parent institution's religious status.

Usually the lack of religious interest is due, at least in part, to the lack of campuswide religious emphasis or interest. By contrast, other kinds of religious librarians feel that they are happiest when working in a religious institutional administrative office, a Bible college, monastery, house of worship, parochial school, or religious public library. In any case, few academic library employees appear to feel any kind of religious library solidarity with the staff members of another library of the same denomination.

Certain related groups face a similar dilemma for somewhat different reasons. They recognize the religious nature of their positions without difficulty, but they think of themselves primarily as being Mormon librarians, for instance, or Jewish, or Congregational librarians, rather than general or broadly religious librarians. In these cases the particular denomination takes precedence over the general religious status in their thinking. In fact, most religious librarians are very conscious of denominational differences, even of factional differences within the denominations, such as the Independence Mormons vs. the Salt Lake City Mormons, or the Free Baptists vs. the American Baptists, and this concern often outweighs feelings of affinity with other religious librarians. Even ATLA annual conference participants are well aware of the diverse denominational interests.

The Methodist seminary librarian probably feels relatively little affinity with the Episcopal/Anglican church librarian, let us say. In this illustration, not only have we jumped to a different denomination, a different library level, and probably a part-time vs. full-time librarian, but also most Methodist seminary head librarians are men, while most Episcopal/Anglican church head librarians are women. Such feelings of narrow differences negatively influence the religious library group's thinking and inhibit its recognition of its cohesiveness as a body of general religious librarians. Many religious librarians prefer to emphasize the differences distinguishing them from other religious groups rather than the similarities binding them all together. For these and other reasons, in certain ways it is difficult to identify religious librarians as a fully cohesive group.

Criteria for Study Inclusion

The reader may wish to ask, How did the author choose the libraries to be covered in this religious library study? Cohesive or not, where did he find more than two thousand North American religious libraries? This is an especially cogent question since, in certain of the study's academic libraries, for instance, the percentage of religious material held was less than 0.5 percent, it was little used, and no staff member devoted more than a few hours a year to technical or public service for it. In reply, the author would stipulate that every library is a religious library to the extent that its sponsorship, collection, and user group come from that subject field. The libraries in this study represent both ends of the scale, from being religious to only a small degree to being almost entirely religious, i.e., wholly classified in the Dewey Decimal Classification 200s, for instance.

When organizing the study, the author saw that it would be unproductive to attempt to quiz ten thousand libraries about the size of their religious material collections and the amount of staff time, funds, and use devoted to them before deciding to include or reject the library from the study. Ascertaining the exact degree of attention a library gave to religious material may have been the best way to learn its degree of religiosity, but that method was too impractical and expensive to use in this study. Probably neither religion nor any other single subject field would occupy more than a small percentage of the library's collection, time, and funds, except in congregational, monastery, convent, or seminary libraries. Nor was there any logical and practical way of deciding what standard should be established as a minimum parameter against which to measure religious collection size, use, staffing, and funding.

The criterion of sponsorship was used because of the reasonableness of the assumption that a religiously related institution's library had an obligation to see that both collection and service contained some representation of religion, no matter how small, and particularly that of the sponsoring denomination. Such faiths and denominations as were mentioned in the previous section—Catholic, Jewish, Mormon, Baptist, charismatic, evangelical, and Bible-oriented—constituted a sizeable percentage of all academic libraries studied. They customarily made their religious influence felt throughout the parent institution and therefore could be included in the religious library group without reservation. Certain other denominations were less demanding in terms of religious activity and so were included primarily on the basis of their formal, informal, or sometimes historic affiliation.

Religious Library Contacts with Scholarly Library Groups

Certain religious libraries have contacts with scholarly library groups that should strengthen the intellectual character of their work and lead to closer library coordination on major projects. Unfortunately, in many cases these contacts seem to be relatively superficial. The ATLA is the only independent association within the North American scholarly religious library field. It is a small group composed of seminary librarians, male and female, with about 760 personal and 220 institutional members in 1992.[19] Any Christian seminary library is eligible to join, though apparently most members are Protestant. A few are Roman Catholic, and Charismatic and Pentecostal seminaries seem to be underrepresented.

Males make up about 50 percent of the membership, high for a North American library organization, and committee and board membership is about 55 percent male, though recent lists suggest that women are asserting themselves and a few of them have become president in recent years. Members are divided into six categories: honorary (surprisingly, in 1992 six out of seven honorary members were women), retired, individual, student, institutional and regular. Institutional membership is reserved for libraries representing institutions accredited by the Association of Theological Schools (ATS) in Canada and the United States.[20,21]

The ATLA is a group without close connections to other organizations except those few discussed here. The small number of contacts through representatives to other library associations, either religious or ministerial, publishing or bibliographic, is surprising. The author suggests that ATLA consider relating itself closely to several additional scholarly associations, among them the American Society of Information Science (ASIS), which could help its members to survive the ongoing computer revolution. In addition, ATLA could gain much by relating closely to a data analysis or research group that deals with the challenge of writing statistical reports. ATLA publishes statistical data on member libraries annually without publishing its terms of reference or definitions and using no specifically defined published categories.

ATLA meets annually for five days in national conference. Much business needs to be carried out during that time period since most of the more active members see each other only once annually. To this author, the conference denominational meetings are among the most interesting of the ATLA's activity areas. Eight groups met in 1986, 1987, and 1992: Anglican-Episcopal, Baptist, Campbell-Stone, Lutheran, Methodist, Presbyterian, Reformed, Roman Catholic, and United Church of Christ. These meetings should have been among the most profitable held at each conference since they enabled each librarian to discuss problems and opportunities with other members of the same denomination. Another interesting series of ATLA conference meetings was the discussions of the special interest groups: automation and technology, bib-base users, collection evaluation, college and university, OCLC users, public services, publication, rare books and special collections, and technical services. A newsletter and annual conference proceedings are published also.[10,22]

Although one hundred other library organizations are formally affiliated with the fifty-five-thousand-member American Library Association in one way or another, as far as this author can ascertain, no ALA committee relates closely to any religious library association. The one exception may be the ALA Committee on Cataloging Description and Access, of which ATLA, AJL, and Cath LA are among the forty members. When the *Anglo-American Cataloging Rules* were being revised several years ago, CSLA, Cath LA, and ATLA were represented on the advisory committee. CLA (Canadian Library Association) seems to bear much the same relationship to religious libraries that ALA does. Certain religious librarians are CLA members, but most of them play a relatively minor role in CLA affairs, and that probably through the Canadian Association of College and University Libraries Section (CALCUL).[23–26]

Religious library group contacts with the Association of College and Research Libraries (ACRL), the largest North American academic library association with ten thousand members, seem to be minimal, though some seminary library staff members are active members of it. No current ACRL or section committee is working on any religious library or bibliographic project, with one exception, as far as this author can tell.[27] There is now an ACRL philosophy, religion, and theology discussion group. Much the same thing can be said about CALCUL. Several religiously affiliated universities are members of the prestigious Association of Research Libraries (ARL): Brigham Young, Duke, Emory, Georgetown, Miami, Notre Dame, and Queen's in Ontario, for instance.

Undoubtedly they participate on an equal basis with nonreligious universities. However, ARL seems not very often to have pressing religious library problems.

AJL is divided into two sections: scholarly and popular. The Research and Special Libraries Section consists primarily of research library and rabbinical school library staff members. While it maintains connections with rabbinical schools, the section seems to have few contacts with other scholarly groups. The meetings of this section should provide excellent opportunities to discuss common problems with other rabbinical school and research library colleagues and to launch major scholarly Jewish library projects.[28] Section books, annual conference programs, and other activities are discussed on the pages of AJL publications.

This author knows of only four religious library serials that might be considered scholarly: *Judaica Librarianship,* published by AJL more or less semiannually, the ATLA annual conference *Proceedings,* the *Catholic Library World,* and the *Journal of Religious and Theological Information. Judaica Librarianship* serves all Jewish library groups with scholarly articles on a variety of subjects.[29] Frequently it deals with Jewish librarianship in other countries, especially Israel. Automation, cataloging and classification, children's literature, major book reviews, reference books, and synagogue libraries are major subject areas.

Judaica Librarianship has improved and extended its coverage measurably in recent years and is now a first-class religious library periodical. Its primary problem is its infrequent publication. Two-thirds of the *Judaica Librarianship* editorial staff members are women. Similarly, the ATLA conference *Proceedings* annually prints the feature papers of the recent conference, and they constitute a glimpse of current professional thought in this interesting and independent field.

The Cath LA has several scholarly library sections. The academic library section involves many religious institution librarians. Almost any issue of the *Catholic Library World* contains pictures and text of these libraries, and many Cath LA presidents have come from the scholarly Catholic library world.[30] This is one of the Cath LA's larger sections and a suitable place for scholarly Catholic librarians to be active.

The Cath LA, seventy years old now, publishes the *Catholic Periodical and Literature Index* covering 142 titles, the bimonthly and semischolarly *Catholic Library World,* and fifteen books and pamphlets useful for Catholic librarians—bibliographies of several kinds, a Cath LA history, and even a Catholic librarian's cookbook![31] The *Catholic Library World,* basically a news bulletin, has (or at least had until Cath

LA's recent financial setback) a large circulation—about twenty-five hundred copies—and prints some useful articles. In addition, the Cath LA has an archive section, a library education section for Catholic library and information school faculty members, a bibliographic instruction round table, and a cataloging and classification round table. They provide contact points for much scholarly religious library activity. In addition, there is a metropolitan Catholic College libraries chapter for the greater New York City area.

Perusal of the Cath LA *Annual Handbook and Membership Directory* revealed several facts about late twentieth-century Catholic librarians. A large percentage of the recent officers and committee members were (a) nuns, priests, or brothers; (b) Catholic parochial or private school, college, or university library staff members; or (c) both. A number of the clergy and nuns were sufficiently dedicated to their occupational field to have made extra membership fee contributions and were listed as Life or special personal members. This is praiseworthy! The author found that the *Handbook* also contained a necrology section.

Groups of specific Roman Catholic clerical order academic and research librarians meet formally or informally once a year for discussions. For instance, a group of Jesuit librarians gets together regularly and informally at ALA conferences, and certain of these groups meet at Cath LA conferences. In addition, in certain metropolitan areas the seminary librarians not only cooperate closely on interlibrary loans but also have formed a network for cooperation in several other service areas, e.g., Chicago and Philadelphia.

A relatively new semischolarly journal serving primarily the scholarly religious library field and worthy of the reader's attention is the *Journal of Religious and Theological Information.* It is unclear at this point whether or not this journal plans to serve the popular religious library field. The editorial board and authors for its first issues were chosen entirely from the scholarly religious library world. One of the contributions by an early paper of this journal is to point out the indexing and abstracting services currently being published in the religious field.[32]

The ATLA, AJL, Lutheran Church Library Association (LCLA), the Association of Christian Libraries (ACL), Cath LA, and CSLA have had seats on the Council of National Library and Information Associations (CNLIA), a cooperative and advisory group interested in several national projects, such as the *Bowker Annual,* national library and information field standards, and association administration. These seats brought their representatives in contact with other religious as well as nonreligious library associations and should have helped to bring new ideas and methods to the six religious library associations. Alas, CNLIA has recently died.

Lack of Other National and International Level Contacts

We have described the major national level religious library contacts for scholarly religious libraries. Several of them exist. While many scholarly and popular libraries have national contacts within their own religious library associations, as we have remarked before, few of them relate closely to the larger and more general national library associations, i.e., the CLA, ACRL, or the Special Libraries Association (SLA), for instance, or even to the regional, state, or provincial library associations, e.g., the Atlantic Provinces Library Association or the Delaware Library Association.

Contacts with leading American and Canadian professionals in library associations should expose religious librarians to a variety of useful ideas and techniques and will encourage them to participate in major national library projects as well. In consequence, both the religious librarian's viewpoint and range of first- and secondhand experience would be broadened. Certain of the ideas and viewpoints acquired when attending national conferences can be useful in the religious library setting. Certainly, more can be learned about effective library computer use at an SLA conference than at a small religious library conference, for example.

Parochial school library staff members can learn from large public and parochial school librarians. These groups are well represented at American Association of School Librarians (AASL) meetings held in conjunction with ALA summer and winter conferences. In much the same way, school of religion librarians should be able to learn useful policies and techniques from the staff members of general university schools and departments attending ACRL-ALA conferences. Religious organization administrative office librarians should participate actively in SLA activities as well. And for that matter, many Catholic and Christian Science reading room librarians should attend Public Library Association (PLA) conferences for the same sort of professional education and updating.

North American religious librarians show a lack of international library involvement, as well as a limited amount of national general library association involvement. Canadian and American librarians see each other each year at North American conferences, but they seldom visit religious libraries on other continents. A persistent problem with library attendance at international conferences is that the sponsoring institution can seldom pay the librarian's travel expenses. Many libraries experience travel budget problems for both national and international conferences. However, the situation should not rule out attendance completely, at least, not at intervals of three or four years.

While the International Federation of Library Associations and Institutions (IFLA) and the International Federation for Documentation (FID) hold annual conferences attended by as many as four hundred North American librarians, probably few of these conferees represent religious libraries. Of course, neither organization has any section or committee on religious libraries, but both maintain sections and committees for more general and for other specialized kinds of libraries, which may be relevant and useful in imparting new ideas and techniques.

European religious libraries should be interesting to North American librarians in the scholarly religious field. Several of the world's largest scholarly religious libraries are in Europe. There are professional associations of seminary libraries in at least five countries: the Association of Theological Libraries (Belgium), the Association of French Theological Librarians (France), the Association of Theological Librarians (Netherlands), and the Working Group of Theological Library Associations of Germany (Germany).[33] The United Kingdom has its Association of British Theological and Philosophical Libraries also.[34,35] Each group represents several dozen or even several hundred active librarians. Finally, there is the International Council of Theological Library Associations covering several European countries.

For popular religious librarians there are active European associations in at least three countries. They include the Working Group for Archives and Libraries in the Lutheran Church (Germany), the Working Group of Catholic Theological Libraries (Germany), the Working Group of Libraries of the Catholic Church (Germany), the German Association of Protestant Libraries (Germany), and the Dutch Center for Public Libraries and Literature (partially religious) (Netherlands).

While there are many house of worship libraries in Europe, probably there are even more parochial school and religious public libraries. Church-sponsored public libraries are especially numerous in Belgium, Netherlands, France, and Germany. Usually they are small in collection size and depend heavily on part-time volunteer staff members; they are strong in children's and media material and in providing personal service. Although sponsored by private church groups and supported in part by user fees, surprisingly, certain of these libraries also receive local government tax support.

In addition to the associations listed above, there is the National Association of Culture and Public Libraries, which has a network of eighteen hundred private Roman Catholic public libraries (France).[36] This system publishes its own journals devoted to collection development, carries on an interlibrary loan service, and has several full-time paid professional librarians in charge. In England, some popular religious libraries are similar to those in North America, but others resemble religious history or archive centers and contain medieval, eighteenth-, and nineteenth-century manuscripts and books.

Many European religious libraries differ in various positive and negative ways from North American libraries. Among scholarly libraries one can expect to find less useful card catalogs, fewer on-line databases to search, fewer computer-based catalogs, fewer circulating collections, and a smaller number of well paid professional staff members per library. Use of word processors and computers is less common than in North America, but the ability to read the languages represented in the library collection is decidedly more common there. Holdings of European religious material are stronger, of course. An enjoyable study tour of religious libraries can be taken in Europe. If the religious librarian searches for them, interesting scholarly and popular religious libraries can be found in many Asian, African, and Latin American countries also.

The Problems and the Advantages of Partial Isolation

We may conclude from the discussions in the preceding sections of this chapter that staff members in scholarly North American religious libraries appear to suffer from at least partial isolation from both the larger religious and the larger library worlds. The problems of partial isolation include potential intellectual and professional poverty, and religious librarians' associating primarily with local persons in other small and specialized religious libraries who are often as poorly informed about the field in general and about other information fields, especially those operating at a high level, as they are themselves.

As it is practiced now, popular religious librarianship (except for the parochial school field) is only somewhat professional in most locations. Due to isolation, the more important issues before the general library world, such as national and state library and book legislation, government library policies, library and information field definitions, standards, and research are almost completely outside the purview of the religious librarian.

Thus scholarly and popular religious library personnel groups may be educationally or otherwise deprived relative to many nonreligious library personnel groups. Many religious librarians leave themselves open to the criticism that they are not necessarily capable of enriching the field but merely of maintaining the status quo therein. Isolation produces uninvolved persons without inspirational and educational opportunities as well as without an understanding of the most current ideas, which close and active involvement with a more aware and experienced library group could provide.

Persons in limited circumstances do not customarily dream large dreams or launch large projects. This restricted status makes it difficult for the religious library group to improve itself, to move its members forward in knowledge and sophistication toward professional or at least paraprofessional status. In isolation from both the larger religious and the general library fields, without strong and well-focused effort, religious librarians are likely to remain at a relatively low awareness level relative to both worlds and to be largely out of touch with the most sophisticated and effective thinking in the larger worlds.

As far as this author knows, few bold national initiatives have been taken by religious library groups. Several of the ATLA bibliographic and other projects, as well as certain AJL projects, represent the exceptional few. Attempts should be made to lift sights, to make religious fields more demanding and professional and more sensitive to developments elsewhere. This is one of the most important current challenges of the religious library field.

Several rather obvious upgrading suggestions can be thrown out briefly for consideration to scholarly and popular religious librarianship. The reader will recognize that certain of these ideas are more practical than others at this time. Apparently no attempt has yet been made to (1) convert ATLA into a theological library section of the much larger and culturally richer ACRL, (2) establish within ACRL (or CALCUL) a religiously affiliated college and university library section with at least one thousand (CALCUL-200) potential religious library numbers, (3) establish within the Cath LA a section for convent and monastery librarians, (4) establish a congregational library section within either ALA, CLA, SLA or IFLA, or all four, (5) establish a parochial school library section in the American Association of School Librarians, the Canadian School Library Association, or the IFLA School Libraries Section, or all three, and (6) establish a religious public library section or committee in the U.S. Public Library Association or the Canadian Association of Public Libraries, or both.

Probably the reader will see that these suggestions contain a certain amount of logic, and that they would serve both to bring these groups of religious librarians more nearly into the mainstream of national library association activities and to surround them with positive influences from related groups. However, several of the ideas may not be entirely feasible. For instance, associations that are composed primarily of professionals, such as ALA and its divisions, may not sympathize with a group composed primarily of para- or quasi-professionals from congregational libraries to the extent of inviting them to form a new section. Further, few nonprofessional religious librarians are likely to have a strong interest either in participating in general library meetings at distant conferences or in any job activity that pays most of its participants nothing.

Much the same thing can be said about religious librarians joining national religious associations, usually denominational, such as the Dominican Laity or the Jewish National Federation of Temple Sisterhoods. They are welcome in these groups and can make useful contributions, but probably only a modest number of religious librarians, except certain academic, seminary, and parochial school library clergy and sisters, have the strength of professional convictions and interest needed to sustain such involvement.

Without the contacts and the sheer necessity to join the existing larger professional groups, and with the need to pitch most programming at the nonprofessional level for popular librarians, North American religious librarians have been obliged to join their own small and specialized scholarly and popular associations. The religious library field's initial isolation gave shape and individuality to the organizations, denominational offices, and religious contacts that arose at each level. We can hope that the success of their own small religious library associations will encourage these librarians to move toward closer cooperation with larger and more professionalized groups in the future. Perhaps a partial step in that direction can be made by providing professional-level programming at national popular library conferences for the no-longer-so-small group of professionals working in popular religious libraries.

Of course, partial isolation is less damaging than full isolation—having contact with no national, local religious, or library associations, and no denominational offices to which the religious librarian could relate. So there is some advantage in having access in these fields to the existing infrastructure upon which improvements can be made. Much freedom to maneuver is held by groups without strong ties elsewhere. Perhaps, after some decades of partial isolation they will begin to reach out, to move toward cooperation or even eventual amalgamation with other scholarly and popular groups in the two areas comprising religious librarianship, library and information service, and organized religion.

A Religious Library Service Development Plan

The development of an existing professional field and its institutions, services, and literature is an interesting study in social history. The author undertook such a study once in the past with reference to a particular country.[37] In a previous paper (for Iran), he laid out a systematic and basic list of the many professional services and publications that a country should establish before it can be said to have achieved a comprehensive and fully developed professional library and information science field. The author will undertake something similar here, but this exposition is adapted not to a country but to the occupational field of scholarly and popular religious library and information service in Canada and the United States. Such a program relates closely to the religious library upgrading program which was discussed in the previous section.

The present section will discuss the services and publications needed before North American religious librarianship can become a mature professional field. The plan is intended to include all facets of a reasonably extensive development, to provide most of the material and service needed by conscientious professionals in order to operate well in this field. A field's literature is necessary in order for its practitioners to understand its theory and practice and to grasp its complexities and extensiveness, its present and past activities. The significant literature develops as the field's intellectual development, its administrative structure, and its operational policies move forward. Each required service type (the core activities) is listed in table 1.3, and examples from the library and information field are given in the explanation. Of course, the general plan can be adapted for any library subfield.

Obviously the list constitutes a set of standards or criteria or even ideals for the extensiveness and the level of library and bibliographic services. The items listed must not only exist, but must exist in well-organized, fully rationalized, and first-class form. The author does not assume that the thirty items are necessarily of equal importance nor are they listed in any priority order. Nor does the author assume that these are the only items needed in the full development of religious libraries and their literature. Far from it! This list assumes the existence of a full infrastructure of basic and general library, religious, and bibliographic services on which the religious library development plan can be built.

There is also no assumption that a service would necessarily be practical or financially profitable to establish, now or later; merely that its establishment would be helpful to the user. Nor does the listing of a service necessarily imply that it does not now exist in some form; a few of them may exist in the religious field but most do not. The entire list represents personal thought and opinion rather than the result of any carefully planned research project. No attempt will be made to specify the nature of each item in detail. The section takes an ecumenical and global view of its subject and applies to all types of religious libraries. The items will be taken up in table 1.3 order.

In the first item, *a sizeable market of users is needed* who are ready to demand professional religious library material reference and circulation service before the establishment of these services will be practical. This situation exists now among many seminary faculty members and students, and, to some extent, with great variations, among some congregational library users. Many parochial school libraries also have such users. Concerning religiously affiliated academic libraries, the situation is more questionable and varies greatly by institution and denomination, with many evangelical campuses being ready now for such use.

Few accredited North American graduate library and information science schools have ever offered *religious library science courses.* Even elective courses in scholarly or seminary librarianship have rarely been given, presumably because the market for them in any one school's service area is so small. In several existing library and information science schools—Catholic University, Drexel, University of North Carolina, University of Texas, Texas Woman's University, and probably others—masters theses have been carried out on popular religious libraries. Probably theses have been written at certain library and information science schools about seminary libraries and their book collections too.

In 1988 AJL organized a series of Jewish library courses for Queens College in New York. However, the courses were given in the Queens continuing education division rather than in the graduate school of library and information studies. Drexel and a few other schools have offered religious-service-oriented workshops or conferences also, but most library schools have provided the field with almost no direct service on any level.[38]

The lack of leadership from library education professionals has left the religious library education field largely in the hands of its own professionals and paraprofessionals who probably are ill prepared to move it ahead as rapidly as professional library educators would have done. Both scholarly and popular fields need close contact with formal library and information education through credit and continuing education courses. Educational programs should be developed to supplement and extend upward the present program of religious library conference continuing education by attendance at religious library association conferences. Both graduate library education and undergraduate library technician programs should be developed for the religious field, the former for supervisory and academic librarians and the latter for assistants and congregational librarians.

An elective course in scholarly religious librarianship should introduce the student to that field, its library policies, and its more significant literature. Several recent trends affecting all specialized library fields should be explained and their application to religious librarianship discussed. Certain of the larger and better organized scholarly and popular libraries should host internship training programs also. Parochial and other private school librarians need either bachelor's or master's degree programs plus appropriate education courses and an introduction to denominational library literature. Library technician or paraprofessional education departments should attract many available congregational library staff members who wish to learn more about what they are doing. In all of these cases, some freedom should be allowed for the student to use his or her religious library background in preparing course work.

Short continuing education courses have been offered at ATLA annual conferences in recent years, three being given in 1987 in one preconference day on preservation, microcomputers, and the *Religious Index* database, and six were given in 1992. CEUs (continuing education units) were not offered for them, but they can be recommended to ATLA for the future. AJL has regularly offered CEU short courses at its conferences, and CSLA began continuing education courses several years ago. The intrastructure for continuing education needs to be upgraded and formalized for both scholarly and popular librarians and CEUs given for satisfactory work.

In addition to their annual national conferences, the Cath LA, CSLA, AJL, Baptists, and LCLA have extensive chapter networks that provide *local library programming*. Altogether, in various denominations, several hundred of these local chapter meetings are held each year in many North American regions. This is one of the few items in table 1.3 that is carried out extensively now, at least by the popular librarians. The scholarly librarians, however, enjoy few such local programs. They are thinly distributed by state and province, and each seminary curriculum emphasizes its own theological viewpoint, which makes cooperation difficult. Further, ATLA maintains no chapters nor is there any other national, regional, state- or provincewide seminary library association in North America, as far as this author knows. While a few of these programs are held in large metropolitan areas for greater convenience in attracting visiting lecturers, they are rare.

Religious library education should be closely coordinated for the scholarly and popular library groups at all four levels described here—graduate credit course work, technical and paraprofessional courses, continuing education courses, and local and national conference programs, in order to derive optimal educational and information gains from it.

The fifth item on table 1.3 recommends that a *comprehensive international religious library association* be established. The international council mentioned above serves only half a dozen European countries, and the chances of its expanding in the short term seem to be poor. Instead, an IFLA religious libraries section could be established. An international religious library association should be divided into two main sections—scholarly and popular—or else two separate associations should be formed. Probably the chances of establishing an international scholarly group are better than those of establishing an international popular group.

An international association is needed to carry out member services on a global basis that are similar to those now offered by the U.S. national and the Canadian regional and provincial library associations and headquarters offices. These services include providing awards for superior work, book reviews, chapter activities, conference programs, continuing education, guidance, promotion of religious library interests, and serial book publications. The recommended group should be able to provide these services for many countries that have no religious library associations. International cooperation should be facilitated by denomination as well as by type of library. In addition, the association should be able to assist the publishers of several countries in producing the kinds of material most useful to concerned libraries.

North American religious library associations, discussed in a previous section, can be divided by level between scholarly and popular, by denomination among Catholic, Jewish, and several Protestant groupings, by national vs. provincial and regional, and by country between Canada and the United States. All have annual conferences. What is needed to improve the present situation? A primary problem is the associations' lack of members and funds. On the popular level this is due at least in part to the constant shifting in and out of membership by the volunteer members. Building into the association features that will attract more members and hold them longer is much needed, and many of these features must be extended to local chapter service.

Since Canada has no national scholarly or popular religious library associations, perhaps Canadian librarians should start them. Canadian attendance at U.S. library association conferences seems to be small—only eight persons per year at the 1986 and 1987 ATLA conferences and seven in 1992! In addition, there is no scholarly North American association that makes special provision for the staff members of either (a) religiously affiliated general colleges and universities or (b) non-ATS member scholarly religious seminary libraries. Large gaps exist in present association coverage.

Interest by non-ATS member seminary and Bible college library staff members needs to be articulated and focused. A national association of all scholarly religious libraries could become a meeting place for seminary and religiously affiliated college and university librarians, and it could carry out many of the same kinds of projects for the religious group that ACRL carries out for all academic librarians. In addition, if a denomination can provide better service to its congregational librarians than the ecumenical CSLA provides for many different denominations, primarily Protestant, perhaps more denomination-specific organizations should be established.

Already three denominations provide *headquarters library advisory service*—LDS, Christian Science, and Southern Baptist, at least on the popular level. Such offices can carry out many of the services provided by the library associations for other denominations also. The library's service in support of the Sunday school and other departments of the church can best be understood and carried out on a denominational level. Advisory offices can facilitate coordination between denominational Sunday school publication programs and library service programs. A denominational group can provide a unified approach to congregational library service as no other group can. All major denominations and several minor ones should consider this idea for both the scholarly and popular library levels.

The eighth to the thirteenth table 1.3 items reflect the desirability of identifying a number of *"good" or superior or even leading libraries in each subfield to serve as models of excellence.* Study of their operation should be instructive for other libraries. A crucial question becomes, Who will name these leading libraries? The national and regional denominational library associations and library advisory offices as well as ATLA can do this. Those library associations with award programs (such as CSLA and Cath LA) already identify the kinds of libraries that fit into these select groups by establishing criteria to be met. After selection, model library identities and attributes should be well publicized. The idea of selecting a sizeable number in each category is to distribute them across various denominations, scholarly vs. popular levels and areas of each country so every librarian can identify one near enough to visit and to learn from.

Table 1.3, item 14, indicates the need for current and comprehensive *adult and children's* book and serial *bibliographies.* There is no separate, current, and comprehensive bibliography of religious material, only the general Library of Congress MARC list, *Books in Print,* the *National Union Catalog* and the Bowker, Faxon, and EBSCO international periodical and serial directories being available and well known. Such a list could be a spin-off product of one of the comprehensive bibliographies and could be used primarily as a convenient selection and acquisition tool in libraries with large religious collections.

Development of national union catalogs of religious books, serials, and manuscripts, a related idea, would also be helpful in sharing library holdings to support interlibrary loan service. Of course, these catalogs should be located in databases with wide library access. To some extent the Online Computer Library Center (OCLC) database solves this problem, at least for scholarly libraries, but many scholarly and most popular religious libraries have no direct access to it. Only a small percent of the *ALD* study libraries were part of the 1988 OCLC database. The small and independent library is seldom a member of such a system, yet it may need to consult a union catalog occasionally. Computer printouts of certain religious book, serial, and manuscript union catalogs could be duplicated for small library use.

More work should be done to prepare *comprehensive bibliographies of "good" or significant books* for each library subfield, item 15 on table 1.3. An example would be a list of current books on Pope John Paul II recommended for Roman Catholic convent reading or a list of Unitarian-Universalist biographies for academic library use. Presenting titles on a religious subject in a special bibliography should enable the library to focus user attention on its most useful titles and thereby enhance reading profitability. If such lists are well publicized, they can encourage relatively wide distribution and usage of material. What books should be included in such a basic list for each denominational field? Note that CSLA and AJL have already published such lists.[39,40]

A related and larger selection tool project would be cooperative compilation of a standard catalog of recommended titles for the two combined religious library levels. Of course, the present popular library bulletin book review sections, the ALA *Booklist* and *Choice* are available already, but they cover few religious titles. The popular library bulletin reviews are brief, superficial, denominational, and are only temporarily useful. On the other hand, Catholic parochial school librarians can profit from efforts to produce Catholic supplements to certain national school library publications.

Bill Katz identified three thousand religious periodical titles, so a *comprehensive index is needed to religious periodical literature*.[41] Such an index should cover all faiths, denominations, and sects. Among the present group of indexes, the *Index to Jewish Periodicals, Index to Articles on Jewish Studies, Catholic Periodical and Literature Index,* and especially the *Religion Index One: Periodicals* can be recommended. *Religion Index One: Periodicals* and *Two: Books* are two of ATLA's triumphs. We may be better off now in providing this item than we are for the other items on this list. Coverage of religious periodicals by existing indexes is still relatively superficial, however, and is aimed too often at the general rather than the religious library reader. Religious libraries and large public library religion departments should find an improved comprehensive index invaluable.

A subject, author, and title *index to religious library periodicals* is needed by religious librarians and students. It should cover both scholarly and popular fields and perhaps be published semiannually. Of course, we have *Library Literature* and *Library and Information Science Abstracts* already, but their religious field coverage is small, and a supplementary index is needed that covers domestic and foreign religious library and information science titles extensively and abstracts the material covered. Students will be able to study the religious library field more satisfactorily when such an index is available.

Comprehensive scholarly and popular religious librarianship

bibliographies are generally lacking. The 1986 ATLA Annual Conference *Proceedings* contains a useful conference proceedings index from 1947–86, useful partly because the literature about other scholarly religious library areas is so sparse. The ATLA index must record some of the major papers of the subfield in that time period. The *Catholic Periodical and Literature Index* covers useful bibliographies on the various types of Catholic librarianship. Both the present and the previous religious librarianship volumes by this author contain useful chapter bibliographies. There is an annual index to *Church and Synagogue Libraries* (Bulletin) also. J. Larry Murdock compiled a bibliography of early church and synagogue librarianship in 1970.[42] A comprehensive and definitive bibliography of North American religious librarianship would eliminate many gaps and assist students in these fields.

Another cooperative bibliographic project, to publish a combined *critical religious book review journal,* item 18, should be undertaken. It should target both the scholarly and popular library levels. We have the first class ATLA *Index to Book Reviews in Religion,* but this index is not always current and focuses on only one subfield.[43] In certain ways it is unfortunate that several popular denominational library groups publish their own book annotation or review bulletins—CSLA, AJL, LCLA, Baptist, ACL and to some extent Catholic—when all of the publications reviewed annually could be put into one comprehensive bulletin with denominational labels and critical evaluations!

It is likely that this enhanced journal could be published for less than the present combined cost of the separate existing bulletins. In a combined journal the annotations or short reviews would not necessarily be tailored for a particular denomination, however, but is such a narrow focus always essential? Such an ecumenical plan might blur denominational lines, and many partisan persons might be offended if it were implemented insensitively.

If the popular denominational bulletins stopped publishing their own book annotations or published fewer of them (they constitute 50 percent of their present bulletin page space), there would be more space for substantive articles, a desirable development. Of course, critical reviews are already available for many religious titles through the general scholarly book review journals, though these journals may be slower to appear than the denominational bulletins. Perhaps reviews of religious books in the general press might simply be reprinted in two journals, scholarly and popular.

All major and some minor denominations should publish a *religious library journal, bulletin, or newsletter* to communicate with their libraries and assist in improving service. Popular-level bulletins are common (see Appendix A for examples), but scholarly libraries should be served also. We need more substantial journals; the field's journals should try to make either significant contributions to its bibliography or to its religious library thought, policy, and practice. This sort of contribution may not come immediately from the popular library group, however, which seems currently to be happy with its small newsletters.

Several comprehensive surveys and analyses, item 20 on table 1.3, should be undertaken to identify the characteristics of the North American religious library and information field and to supplement the two scholarly library surveys described in chapters 2–4 of this book and the four popular library surveys to be described in a later book. Despite these six surveys, much is presently unknown about these fields. Several more surveys and analyses are needed in order to delimit and define the characteristics of the major facets of each subfield. Apparently no other comprehensive national survey of scholarly and popular religious libraries has been undertaken to date.

Denominational and geographic analyses should be made, as well as analyses by such variables as library age, staff and collection size, budget, and use per student or per house of worship member, not to mention the policies followed in selection, acquisitions, cataloging, classification, and preparation for the shelves. Analyses should attempt to clarify the relationships between denomination and library or collection size and between the types of religious groups being studied, such as evangelical vs. mainline and the various geographic areas. Analyses of both inputs and outputs should be revealing. The best of the house of worship libraries should be cardinal examples of low dollar input (an all-volunteer staff!) and both high circulation and reference service output.

We need *comprehensive scholarly and popular religious library directories* for both North American countries. Such directories are needed in the same way as for censuses of individual people in order to learn more about the composition of the population, to learn what is out there, so that generalizations can be drawn that are based on facts rather than speculation. No directory with extensive coverage lists religious academic, theological, organization administrative office, parochial or private school, public, convent, or monastery libraries. We have the 1968 Ruoss volume listing 1,788 seminary and other scholarly libraries worldwide, but it is now out of date and was never fully comprehensive. The present author is working on a new and greatly expanded edition of that directory.

The directory that covers most North American scholarly libraries is the *ALD*, but it is also substantially incomplete for convent, monastery, congregational, and parochial schools and somewhat incomplete for all other scholarly library categories. No directory covers parochial, private school, or religious public libraries comprehensively, except for the Christian Science reading room directory within its own denomination.[8] No recent congregational library directory exists.[44] The author hopes to produce a new edition of such a congregational library directory in the future.

The next item recommends compilation of *biographical directories of religious library personnel.* This author has never seen a biographical directory of religious librarians with the one exception of AJL. Who are these people?[45] Probably a few religious library leaders appear in *Who's Who in America* or at least in its regional editions. Of course, the ALA *Who's Who in Library and Information Service* presumably includes many scholarly and perhaps even certain popular American and Canadian religious librarians, but it is both more than a decade old and incomplete for the religious library field, due in part to the "second job" nature of certain of the religious library positions and to their paraprofessional status.

We need biographical directories in order to identify the field's leaders, to study their characteristics, and to recognize and honor them. The information is needed to facilitate analyses to discover the distinctive characteristics of these professional and technical groups. Often this information is useful to group chairpersons also. Compiling such a directory may turn out to be a task for the individual denominational library associations or offices.

A series of essays is needed that define and explain the nature of a scholarly or popular religious library and discuss the most important concepts involved. This is item 23. The essays should clarify the relationships of these fields to other distinctive library fields and to organized religion. Some existing essays take these fields a certain distance toward this goal.[46–50] Apparently several recent essays have provided steps forward in ATLA thinking.

Several of the titles cited in this chapter should be useful to any author who wishes to provide an appropriate explanation of the scholarly or popular library fields. Other chapters should also provide useful data. An essay is especially needed in popular religious librarianship since that field seems to be poorly understood around the world.[51] In many countries, professional librarians seem either not to understand the field as being different in important ways from scholarly librarianship, or, if they do grasp that, then they have a high opinion of the one and a low opinion of the other, which is illogical and unfair, since the two fields serve different purposes and user groups and deserve equal respect for their own unique contributions.

Full sets of *religious library standards* or guidelines should be written for all scholarly and popular library subfields.[52] Standards set guidelines or criteria for libraries to meet in order to be considered acceptable, or "good," or even superior in service when compared with other libraries of the same kind. Of course, scholarly libraries, colleges, and universities can use one of ACRL's sets of standards unless the librarian believes that the standards need to be modified for a religious (versus a secular) institution. Organization administrative office and convent and monastery libraries need their own sets of guidelines and standards.

Surprisingly, ATLA has never had its own set of theological library standards. However, a good many years ago, apparently a group of seminary librarians cooperated in preparing the ATS library accrediting standards section. According to the ATLA *Proceedings* there has been no discussion of standards since 1981. That seems to be a long interval without discussion of an important and evolving topic, and the recent news is that ATLA is now considering the idea of standards. Perhaps ATLA has assumed that a library which has met the ATS accrediting standards will hold its satisfactory service level indefinitely, or else that the ATLA member libraries differ so much from each other that too little uniformity exists to justify preparation of a fair set of national standards.

However, if leading North American university libraries, which also differ widely, find a set of guidelines or standards, or at least a set of minimums per student useful, then perhaps many ATLA members would find appropriate guidelines useful if not binding. Standards should address questions of good quality service in every library area and should be a continually evolving statement reconsidered at regular intervals. The British, Australian, and New Zealand Theological Library Associations do maintain sets of scholarly religious library standards or guidelines.[53]

Among popular religious library groups, CSLA has a statement of desirable practices in the form of a staff self-assessment program that leads to a certificate of commendation. This statement was developed by Claudia Hannaford and the Continuing Education Committee. These practices were calculated to be fairly simple for most libraries to implement, though not many members have done so thus far. AJL adopted synagogue, school, and center library standards in 1968 and published a revised edition in 1970. In turn, these standards have been superseded by a 1989 set.[54] The Cath LA published standards for parish and lending libraries in 1971. Again, these standards seem to need updating. Of course, parochial school libraries can use the AASL media center guidelines if they wish to do so. The reader will find a brief listing of certain suggested congregational library standards in my Popular Religious Libraries book.

Item 25 is *model scholarly and popular religious library policy and procedure manuals,* which are essential to guide practice.[55] They are especially useful in situations with changing procedures or large and fluctuating staffs. The word *model* means that the library is adapting another and similar library's ideas for its own use or that it is using a manual written as a "standard," one designed to be adaptable for others to use. College and university library policy and procedure manuals are available from many institutions, e.g., the Arizona State University library. Many university library manuals cover only one large department per volume. Consult *Library Literature* for other listings.

Congregational library manuals have been produced by such organizations as the Southern Baptist Convention, the Jewish Book Council of America, and the Abingdon, Augsburg, Bethany, Cokesbury, Drexel, Moody, Westminster, and Zondervan presses. CSLA has a 1980 model manual written by Martin Ruoss. While many house of worship and parochial school libraries possess such manuals, this is a management area that needs upgrading or completion for many religious libraries.

Setting *a standard for library income or expenditure* is especially difficult. To do so with justification requires the analyst to calculate what is required to stock, staff, and pay for the service level demanded by an individual library's sponsoring institution in a specific place and year. Developing a standard for an entire group of libraries can be done primarily by generalizing from many examples for which full statistical information is available, or by estimation, since the large volume of supporting data needed for an objective analysis is seldom available, or else by arbitrary assignment.

Neither of the latter two methods can be recommended. In the present case, the 5 percent of sponsoring institution's total budget (5 percent of the educational expenditures for academic institutions) recommended for the library is essentially a first guess about what may be adequate, since we know too little about these libraries to be more specific.

Five percent is a common academic library budget baseline standard, so it may fit some seminary and religious academic libraries reasonably well. The 5 percent figure may be less useful in other areas. For congregational libraries, since their present "slice of the pie" is so small, it can be suggested that one percent of congregational income be chosen as a reasonable standard. In any case, the figure being sought is one designed to provide a "reasonably adequate" income for the typical religious library of a specific type. Certainly individual library situations vary a great deal.

A comprehensive *book classification schedule* and a comprehensive *subject heading list or thesaurus* are needed for North American religious libraries to replace the present piecemeal approach to solving the book indexing problem (items 27 and 28). Or perhaps three classification schedules and thesauri are needed: Christian, Jewish, and Muslim. Such schedules should spell out expansions of the religious sections (such as the Dewey 200s) in considerable detail. In addition to religion, they should cover religious biography, bibliography, sociology, art, music, literature, mythology, history, fiction, philosophy, and several other subject fields. Subject headings should deal comprehensively with the same subject fields.

That we have schedules and lists, certain of them having been published in several successive editions, means that this area of need is met to some extent now. Whether or not the schedules listed below solve these classification and subject heading publication problems ideally is unclear to this author, however. Probably certain ones do and others do not. In addition to the Library of Congress, Dewey, Universal Decimal, Bliss, and Pettée Classifications, all general, we have the following religious library classification schedules and subject heading lists:

1. ATLA publishes its own list of current and useful Library of Congress Subject Headings.[56]
2. AJL sells Mae Weine's *Classification,* which includes subject headings. Also, the Elazar, Bolub, and Celnik classification schedules serve Jewish libraries.[57–60]
3. The Cath LA has published *Catholic Subject Headings* and *The Dewey Decimal Classification 200 Schedules Expanded.*[61,62]
4. LDS churches use their own library classification schedule for Mormon material.[63]
5. Erwin John's classification schedule is used by certain Lutheran libraries.[64]
6. Many libraries use a special or borrowed classification schedule for certain special collections.
7. Other libraries use a locally made schedule for part or all of the collection, especially for local material.

The idea of special and local schedules is that they may accommodate sizeable collections which emphasize specialized subjects, such as the Holocaust, Canadian Methodist history, or local archives, much better than does a standard classification schedule. A comprehensive subject heading list or thesaurus is needed and special subject thesauri should be compiled for specialized situations. Some literature has appeared in the ATLA *Proceedings* and in *Judaica Librarianship* on religious library cataloging and subject headings. Standard book and periodical sources can be cited for scholarly library cataloging and classification information, though not very much of it is available for the religious library field.

An annual systematic scholarly and popular *religious library data collection, analysis, and publication program* is needed. Such a program has been carried out for its members by the ATLA since 1962. Let us hope that the number of ATLA statistical categories can be expanded in the coming decade, that their definitions will be clarified and published, and that the privilege of participating in this (or a new) annual survey can be extended to a much larger and more varied group of seminary and department of religion libraries in the future. We may note the annual ALD publication of information as well.

No such annual survey is presently available for popular religious libraries, again excepting the largely incomplete *ALD*. Each denomination and headquarters may carry out its own survey if it wishes, but most of them now show little interest in any kind of library statistics. We are still in a rudimentary stage of statistical development for all kinds of religious libraries, and in the absence of such information the question must be asked, How are we to understand these libraries and their functions?

At several seminaries and graduate library and information science schools, there should be ongoing *research programs in scholarly and popular religious library and information service,* item 30 in table 1.3. These programs should enhance present scattered and sporadic efforts to study the two fields. Certain faculty members and students should focus their attention on specific current religious library and information problems and situations, especially in connection with student thesis preparation. Only through research programs can we achieve full understanding of religious librarianship. A religious library research agenda should be developed around which research projects can work. Some of these projects could be carried out in cooperation with the university school of religion faculty and with university library staff members. A few years of activity should yield progress in several areas of knowledge.

Notes

1. Several definitions were adapted from *Webster's New Collegiate Dictionary* (Springfield, Mass.: G & C Merriam, 1977) and *Harrod's Librarian's Glossary* (Aldershot, U.K.: Gower, 1987).
2. For a further definitional discussion, see John F. Harvey, "Scholarly and Popular Religious Libraries," *International Library Review* 19 (October 1987): 359–86. The close student of the author's religious library publications will realize that a few of his definitions have been modified or elaborated over time and that certain of them are still evolving.
3. See John F. Harvey, "An Introductory World Survey of Popular Church and Synagogue Libraries," *International Library Review* 18 (October 1986): 347–72.
4. *American Library Directory* (New York: R. R. Bowker). Published annually.
5. *Library Literature* (New York: H. W. Wilson Company). Published six times a year.
6. *Yearbook of American and Canadian Churches* 1988, ed. Constant H. Jacquet Jr. (Nashville: Abingdon, 1988). *Statistical Abstract of the United States* (Washington, D.C.: Government Printing Office, 1984), pp. 134–36.
7. David M. Mayfield, "The Genealogical Library of the Church of Jesus Christ of Latter-day Saints," *Library Trends* 32 (Summer 1983): 111–27.
8. ". . . Christian Science Reading Rooms," *Christian Science Journal* 106 (May 1988): pp. 9–30 (directory).
9. Report dated 20 December 1983 from Mrs. Anita Dalton, 41 Aberdeen Road North, Cambridge, ON, N1S 2X1, Canada.
10. American Theological Library Association, *Summary of Conference Proceedings* (Evanston, Ill.). Published annually.
11. *Statistical Abstract,* pp. 156–57.
12. L. Jones Milbrey, "NCES Survey of Private School Library Media Centers 1979," *Bowker Annual* (New York: R. R. Bowker, 1983), pp. 352–55. The 1979 U.S. National Center for Education Statistics survey found about 14,200 private school libraries with approximately 28,400 employees (2 employees per library). In this study, incidentally, the NCES found that Catholic schools were most likely to have a library (97 percent), schools with any other religious affiliation were next most likely (68 percent), and schools without religious affiliation least likely to have libraries (62 percent).
13. *American Library Directory,* library count.
14. John F. Harvey, ed., *Church and Synagogue Libraries* (Metuchen, N.J.: Scarecrow, 1980).
15. *The World Directory of Theological Libraries,* ed. L. Martin Ruoss (Metuchen, N.J.: Scarecrow, 1968).
16. The *World Almanac 1988* (New York: Pharos Books) listed the denominations of private U.S. religious and parochial elementary and secondary

schools. While the vast majority of them were Roman Catholic, the following denominations were well represented, (in order): Baptist, Lutheran, Christian, Jewish, Seventh-day Adventist, and Episcopal/Anglican.

17. Personal letter from Nathan A. Talbot, manager, Committees on Publication, First Church of Christ, Scientist, 175 Huntington Ave., Boston, Mass. 02115, dated May 13, 1988.
18. Alice Hedderick, "Library Spreads Gospel Truth," *Canadian Library Journal* 44 (June 1987): 183–85.
19. Stephen L. Peterson, "Theological Libraries for the Twenty First Century: Project 2000 Final Report," *Theological Education* 20 (Supplement 1984): 1–114. This report is an interesting and significant one and should be read by all persons interested in theological education libraries. It attempts to identify these libraries' primary problems and to suggest approaches to their amelioration. It is limited to Christian theological libraries. While all of its recommendations can be applauded, the report suffers from too much vagueness and ungrounded generalization and too few practical implementation suggestions.

    One of the publication's most interesting aspects is the section reporting the results of an ATLA member survey. Certain of the ideas mentioned in the present chapter are supported there, e.g., the painfully small staff size of most of these theological libraries and their late start in computer use. Particularly revealing was the members' evaluation of ATLA effectiveness at that time. They found most ATLA activities to fall into the area between being moderately effective and being ineffective. The index board, periodical exchange, and annual conferences were rated as most effective, and the consultation and placement services at least so. ATLA has moved strongly ahead in several areas since that time.
20. Association of Theological Schools in the United States and Canada, *Membership List* (Vandalia, Ohio: ATS, 1988).
21. *Fact Book on Theological Education, 1986–87,* ed. William L. Baumgaertner (Vandalia, Ohio: Association of Theological Schools, 1986).
22. American Theological Library Association *Newsletter* (Evanston, Ill.). Published quarterly.
23. *Canadian Library Yearbook* (Toronto: Micromedia, 1987).
24. *Christian Resources Handbook,* comp. Marc Canada Ministries (Mississauga, Ont.: Marc Canada, 1986).
25. Michel Theriault, "State of Religious Bibliography in Canada," *Prairie Religious Library Association Newsletter* 2 (March 1981): 2–3.
26. *Directory of Canadian Universities,1986–87*, ed. Kimberley Allen (Ottawa: Association of Universities and Colleges of Canada, 1986).
27. *College and Research Libraries* (Chicago: Association of College and Research Libraries). Published bimonthly.
28. Association of Jewish Libraries, *Index to Convention Proceedings, 1966–80* (New York: AJL, 1980).
29. *Judaica Librarianship* (New York: Association of Jewish Libraries). Pub-

lished semiannually. See vol. 5, no. 2, which includes (1) a useful and detailed history of AJL, 1965–90, and (2) one of the few who's whos of religious librarians, in this case limited to AJL members.

30. *Catholic Library World* (Haverford, Pa: Catholic Library Association). Published bimonthly.
31. *Catholic Periodical and Literature Index* (Haverford, Pa.: Catholic Library Association). Published bimonthly.
32. *Journal of Religious and Theological Information* (Binghampton, N.Y.: Haworth). Published quarterly. This title began publication in late 1992.
33. J. R. Fang, *International Guide to Library, Archive, and Information Science Associations* (New York: R. R. Bowker, 1976).
34. *Association of British Theological and Philosophical Libraries Bulletin* (Oxford: New College Library). Published three times a year.
35. *A Guide to the Theological Libraries of Great Britain and Ireland* (London: ABTAPL Publishing, 1986). See also *Collections of Religion and Theology in Australia and New Zealand* (Adelaide: Auslib Press, 1992).
36. Harvey, "An Introductory World Survey," pp. 354–58.
37. John F. Harvey, "Core Activities for National Library and Bibliographic Development," *UNESCO Bulletin for Libraries* 28 (March/April 1974): 79–86.
38. In this connection it is heartening to see a recent public relations announcement that Drexel University and Gratz College (of Jewish studies), both in Philadelphia, have inaugurated a cooperative certificate program in synagogue librarianship. Bravo!
39. *A Basic Book List for Church Libraries: A Core Collection,* comp. Bernard Deitrick, 4th ed. (Portland, Ore.: Church and Synagogue Library Association, 1991).
40. *Creating a Collection: A Resource Booklist for a Beginning Judaic Library* (New York: Association of Jewish Libraries, 1983).
41. William Katz, comp., *Magazines for Libraries* (New York: R. R. Bowker, 1986), p. 857.
42. J. Larry Murdock, "The Literature of Church and Synagogue Libraries," *Drexel Library Quarterly* 6 (April 1970): 166–75.
43. American Theological Library Association, *Index to Book Reviews in Religion* (Evanston, Ill.). Published bimonthly. See also *Books and Religion* (New York: Trinity Church). Published quarterly.
44. See the *Directory of Church and Synagogue Libraries,* ed. Dorothy Rodda and John F. Harvey (Philadelphia: Drexel, 1967). Includes 3,240 libraries. Was the most complete national U.S. directory of its field in 1975, according to *Guide to Reference Material,* by A. J. Walford (London: Library Association, 1975), p. 85.
45. However, see the recent Association of Jewish Libraries *Membership Directory* (New York: AJL, 1992).
46. Joyce White, "Church Libraries," in *Encyclopedia of Library and Information Science* (New York: Marcel Dekker, 1970), 4: 662–73.

47. Joyce White, ed., "Church and Synagogue Libraries," *Drexel Library Quarterly* 6 (April 1970), entire issue.
48. Stephen L. Peterson, "Life Begins at 40? The Institutional Context of ATLA," *American Theological Library Association Proceedings* (St. Meinrad, Ind.: ATLA, 1987), pp. 148–55.
49. Robert Wood Lynn, "The Future of Theological Research and Theological Libraries," American Theological Library Association *Proceedings* (St. Meinrad, Ind.: ATLA, 1986), pp. 145–47.
50. Claude Welch, "The Theological Library—Servant or Partner?" *American Theological Library Association Proceedings* (St. Meinrad, Ind.: ATLA, 1987), pp. 156–69.
51. Harvey, "An Introductory World Survey," pp. 368–71.
52. Joanne Klene, "Standards for Parish and Lending Libraries," *Catholic Library World* 42 (May/June 1971): 574.
53. See the *Association of British Theological and Philosophical Libraries Bulletin* 2 (June 1990): 1–31 and the *Australian and New Zealand Theological Library Association Newsletter* 6 (December 1988): 3–10.
54. Jewish Book Council of America, *Standards for Jewish Libraries in Synagogues, Schools, and Centers* (New York: Jewish Book Council of America, 1970). Superseded by *A Guide to Excellence: Standards for School, Synagogue, and Jewish Community Center Libraries,* ed. Merrily Hart (New York: AJL, 1990).
55. See also John T. Corrigan, *Guide for the Organization and Operation of a Religious Resource Center* (Haverford, Pa: Catholic Library Association, 1987).
56. *ATLA Current LC Subject Headings in the Field of Religion* (Denver: Iliff School of Theology). Published quarterly.
57. See Rebecca Dassa, "LC Subject Headings of Interest to Judaica Librarians," *Judaica Librarianship* 4 (Fall 1987): 40–45 and Paul Maher, *Hebraica Cataloging: A Guide to ALA/LC Romanization and Descriptive Cataloging* (Washington, D.C.: Library of Congress, 1987).
58. Mae Weine, *Weine Classification Scheme for Judaica Libraries* (New York: Association of Jewish Libraries, 1982).
59. David H. Elazar, *A Classification Scheme for Libraries of Judaica* (Ramat Gan, Israel: Turtledove, 1978).
60. Jewish Library Association of Greater Philadelphia, *Subject Headings for a Judaica Library* (New York: Association of Jewish Libraries, 1982).
61. Catherine M. Pilley and Matthew R. Wilt, eds., *Catholic Subject Headings* (Haverford, Pa.: Catholic Library Association, 1981).
62. Mary Celia Bauer, *Dewey Decimal Classification: Two Hundred Schedules Expanded for Use* (Haverford, Pa.: Catholic Library Association, 1988).
63. See Harvey, "An Introductory World Survey," p. 350, footnote 2.
64. Erwin E. John, *The Key to a Successful Church Library* (Minneapolis: Augsburg, 1967), pp. 7–11.

TABLE 1.1
A Religious Library Classification Scheme with Examples

SCHOLARLY LIBRARIES

COLLEGES AND UNIVERSITIES (ACADEMIC)

Al Ashar University Central Library, Cairo, Egypt
Catholic University of Louvain Library (French-speaking), Louvain, Belgium
Haigazian College Library (Armenian), Beirut, Lebanon
International Christian University Library, Tokyo, Japan
University of Minnesota Newman Center Library, Minneapolis, MN, USA

SEMINARIES, DIVINITY SCHOOLS AND RABBINICAL COLLEGES

Baltimore Hebrew College Library, Baltimore, MD, USA
Catholic Higher School Faculty of Theology Library, Tilburg, The Netherlands
Heythrop College Library (Jesuit), London, United Kingdom
Islamic University Faculty of Theology Library, Cereban, Indonesia
Ontario Theological Seminary Library, Willowdale, Ontario, Canada

MONASTERIES, ABBEYS AND CONVENTS

Bibliothèque du couvent des Dominicaines, Toulouse, France
Kykkos Monastery Library, Kykkos, Cyprus
Monastery of St. Savior Library, Saida, Lebanon
St. Anthony's Friary Library, Bangalore, India
St. Benedict's Monastery Library, Rio de Janeiro, Brazil

RELIGIOUS HISTORY LIBRARIES AND ARCHIVE CENTERS

Benedictine Order Central Principal Library, Pannonhalma, Hungary
Canadian Baptist Archives, Hamilton, ON, Canada
Gulbenkian Armenian Patriarchate Library, Aurelias, Lebanon
United Methodist Historical Society Library, Baltimore, MD, USA
United Society for the Propagation of the Gospel Library, London, United Kingdom

DENOMINATIONAL HEADQUARTERS AND ADMINISTRATIVE OFFICES

American Congregational Association Library, Boston, MA, USA
Anglican Church in Canada Library, Toronto, ON, Canada
Baptist Missionary Society Library, London, United Kingdom
Ecumenical Patriarchate Library (Greek Orthodox), Istanbul, Turkey
Lutheran Evangelical Association Library, Helsinki, Finland

TABLE 1.1 (continued)
A Religious Library Classification Scheme with Examples

POPULAR LIBRARIES

HOUSES OF WORSHIP (CONGREGATIONAL: CHURCHES AND SYNAGOGUES)

Baptist Church Library, Tripoli, Libya
Church of Jesus Christ of Latter-day Saints Meetinghouse Library, Taipei, Taiwan
Congregation Kenesseth Israel Library, Allentown, PA, USA
Eman-e-zamin Mosque Library, Tehran, Iran
Lutheran Church Library, Swift River, SK, Canada

PAROCHIAL SCHOOLS

Allayyah Girls School Library (Episcopal), Amman, Jordan
Baptist Temple Academy Library, Fairfax, VA, USA
Catholic Education Office Library, East Melbourne, Victoria, Australia
École Saint-Florent Library, Saverne, France
Seventh-day Adventist Parochial School Library, Nicosia, Cyprus

PUBLIC LIBRARIES

Canberra Catholic Library, Watson, ACT, Australia
Christian Science Reading Room, Bulawayo, Zimbabwe
Evangelische Öffentliche Buchereien (Lutheran), Bremen, W. Germany
Senor de los Malagros Parochial Public Library, Comas, Peru
Union Nationale Culture et Bibliotheques Pour Tous (Roman Catholic Public Library), Lille, France

Source: John F. Harvey, "Scholarly and Popular Religious Libraries," *International Library Review* 19 (October 1987), pp. 359–86.

TABLE 1.2
1988 Estimate of the Number of North American Religious and Nonreligious Libraries

Kind of Library	Number of Libraries	Source of Information See Footnotes Below
Nonreligious		
Canadian		
College and University	510[1]	2,3
Special	1,450	2,3
United States		
College and University	3,000	2
Special	10,500	2
Total	15,460	
Scholarly Religious		
Canadian		
College and University	150[1]	2,3
Seminary	20	2,3
Convent and Monastery	50	2,3
Religious History and Archive	10	2,3
Religious Organization Administrative Office	20	2,3
United States		
College and University	1,500[1]	2
Seminary	110	2
Convent and Monastery	200	2
Religious History and Archive	20	2
Religious Organization Administrative Office	100	2
Total	2,180	
GRAND TOTAL	17,640	

1. Includes branches
2. *American Library Directory* (New York: R. R. Bowker). Published annually. Library count
3. *Canadian Library Yearbook* (Toronto: Micromedia, 1987)

TABLE 1.3

Core Activities Required for Full Scholarly and Popular Religious Library and Bibliographic Development in Canada and the United States

1. Existence of a market ready to demand modern and professional religious library reference and circulation service.
2. Religious library education available at graduate and undergraduate technician levels.
3. Short continuing education courses for introductory education and practitioner updating.
4. Local and national library conference programs.
5. A comprehensive international library association.
6. National library associations by level and denomination.
7. National advisory library offices for major and minor denominations.
8. At least one hundred superior academic libraries named to serve as models.
9. At least two dozen superior seminary and two dozen superior Bible college libraries named to serve as models.
10. At least a dozen superior convent and a dozen superior monastery libraries named to serve as models.
11. At least a dozen superior religious organization administrative office libraries named to serve as models.
12. At least a dozen to one hundred superior congregational libraries of each denomination named to serve as models.
13. At least one hundred superior parochial and private school libraries named to serve as models.
14. Current and comprehensive adult and children's book and serial bibliographies.
15. Comprehensive bibliographies of significant books useful in each library type.
16. A current and comprehensive religious periodical index.
17. A current and comprehensive religious library periodical index.
18. One or more critical book reviewing periodicals.
19. A library journal, bulletin or newsletter published by each major denomination.
20. Several comprehensive surveys of library characteristics.
21. Comprehensive directories of the various types of libraries.
22. National biographical directories of religious librarians.
23. Several essays clearly defining and explaining the nature of religious librarianship.
24. Guidelines or performance standards for each type of library.
25. Model library policy and procedure manuals for each type of library.
26. Annual library budgets equaling at least 1–5% of the total institutional budget.
27. Comprehensive book classification schedules adapted for these libraries.
28. Comprehensive subject heading lists or thesauri.
29. Comprehensive library statistical collection, analysis and publication programs.
30. Library and information service research programs.

2

THE GEOGRAPHY AND DEMOGRAPHY OF SCHOLARLY RELIGIOUS LIBRARIES

This is a chapter of facts that are basic to an understanding of scholarly religious libraries. In this work, the geography of religious libraries refers to urban and rural areas, cities, states, provinces, regions, and countries in which the North American libraries are located. The demography of these libraries refers to statistical data concerning their basic social characteristics, such as age and income level.[1] The chapter's discussion answers such questions as, In what states and provinces were these libraries found? How many of them existed? What were their denominational affiliations? Their founding dates? Their chief city centers? Often these facts need to be broken down by type of library, region, denomination, and sometimes by total expenditure, volumes, or chief librarian's gender before we can understand them clearly.

It is important for this study to examine the geography and demography of religious libraries thoroughly because these are among the most basic characteristics of libraries in a field about which little is known. While the study will certainly not bring to completion our knowledge of the field either in whole or in part, it should advance knowledge and understanding of it, at least for the population covered by the databases being examined here—the *American Library Directory (ALD)* 31st edition (1978) and the two-volume 41st edition (1988). An analysis of library density, distribution, deaths, and other characteristics will enable us to understand these libraries more fully, especially if we can thereby obtain some understanding of the differences among them.

The present chapter provides only basic geographic and demographic information and analyses. The information here sets the stage for the study of more specialized scholarly religious library characteristics in later chapters. More intensive analyses will be performed in these later chapters and in the longitudinal comparisons included therein, and additional variables will be taken up there also. This chapter will discuss the following aspects of the scholarly library geographic and demographic pictures:

I. Geography
   A. Library Density
   B. Religious vs. Nonreligious Library Geography and Demography
   C. National Comparison: Canada vs. the United States
   D. Canada vs. the United States: A Further Comparison of Forty-five Variables
   E. Regional Comparison
   F. State and Province Comparison
   G. City Comparison
   H. Chief Population Centers
   I. Geography Section Summary and Conclusions

II. Demography
   A. Library Deaths and Births
   B. Library Age
   C. Chief Librarians
   D. Demography Section Summary and Conclusions

III. Decade Projections

IV. Subject Areas Needing Further Study

Geography: Where Are Scholarly Religious Libraries Located?

After an initial discussion of library density and religious vs. nonreligious library data, this section will take up the various subsections of geography in descending order from nation to city.

Library Density

ALD religious libraries were found almost everywhere, in most but not quite all North American states and provinces and in a great many cities and towns. But perhaps it is more expedient to ask where the scholarly religious library density is greatest. In general, geographic library density followed density of congregations, since there could hardly be institutional libraries of any kind present without reaching a certain density in number of houses of worship and congregation membership.

Similarly, academic institutions of all kinds were concentrated primarily in high population density states. This means specifically that religious academic institutions of a particular denomination were found in areas with large concentrations of the houses of worship of that particular denomination. So, to a considerable extent the location of religious colleges and universities followed the population density of the houses of worship and the congregations of the college's own denomination. Presumably this not very profound idea was a fundamental influence on library location.

This phenomenon ensured that denominational colleges were usually located in places of high general population density as well as areas of strong denominational support. So we are saying that Pittsburgh, Pennsylvania, probably contains more religious colleges of all kinds than does Pittsburg, Kansas, because of the difference in overall population density. Similarly, several Reformed church colleges are to be found in Michigan, which has many Reformed churches, and few or none are to be found in Mississippi, where there may be few or perhaps no churches belonging to that denomination.

The proximity of denominational population density centers with a large supply of potential students was presumably an important reason for establishing a denominational college nearby, but of course such an influence varies in strength according to denominational policy, the presence of competing colleges, and by other locational characteristics, such as rates of regional and denominational growth. We are speaking of the conditions existing when colleges are founded, not necessarily those pertaining a century later, by which time the particular denominational constituency may have moved elsewhere. Although the degree of correlation was not perfect, a heavily populated state like Pennsylvania had more congregations and libraries per square mile than did the sparsely populated state of Wyoming, for instance. Sparsely populated areas, of course, lacked houses of worship, congregations, and libraries.

North American denominational density and location varied greatly from one denomination and one locality to another. Certain groups were found in only a limited number of areas. For instance, the Mormons were strong in the Rocky Mountain area of Idaho and Nevada, but weak in the White Mountain area of New Hampshire. However, certain other denominations were represented in almost all regions of North America with a reasonably high degree of density. In fact, several of them, e.g., the Methodists and the Presbyterians, were so widely distributed that local concentrations could be found for them in almost every state and province.

Probably we can extend the argument to speculate further that college library distribution varied, as did the density of denominations, with or without a strong emphasis on books and libraries. We have mentioned this idea before. For instance, Lutheran and Jewish libraries may have emphasized religious books and libraries more strongly than did religiously conservative groups, such as the Assemblies of God and Church of the Nazarene. The latter groups were more likely to be holy book-centered with discipleship training courses than to favor more general religious reading. The latter denominations had few academic libraries. Consequently, many religious libraries were presumably to be found in cities with strong Lutheran or Jewish populations but fewer in cities with prominent Assemblies of God or Church of the Nazarene populations. Or at least that is how the theory goes.

Finally, density of religious libraries varied according to type of library. Junior college religious libraries were much less dense or common than senior college religious libraries: many towns had one of the latter but none of the former. Density of convent and monastery libraries was even lighter yet, although this study's *ALD* list of convent and monastery libraries must have been far from complete. Evidence will be found in later sections of this and later chapters that tends to support these generalizations.

A detailed answer to the location question (where were the scholarly religious libraries located?) is provided by table 2.1 (1978) and table 2.2 (1988) showing Canadian and U.S. scholarly and popular library concentrations by state and province together with a short list of the most popular denominations there.[2] The percentage of libraries in each state or province is added as well as a regional code.

Religious vs. Nonreligious Library Geography and Demography

In practical terms, how do religious and nonreligious library geography and demography differ? The answer to this question is largely outside the scope of this study. All the author can do is to make a guess based on experience. Overall, there would seem to be little difference between them beyond a few obvious points. Naturally, there are many more nuns and priests working in the religious than in the nonreligious libraries, and probably the religious libraries have more religious library material than do most of the nonreligious libraries. The comparison of the two varieties of academic libraries in chapters 3–4 may suggest that religious libraries are smaller and that they grow more slowly than secular libraries. However, these ideas cannot be validated and constitute only the author's brainstorming.

The author knows of no body of nonreligious library data structured so as to facilitate comparison with this book's religious library geographic and demographic data. It is hard even to compare the *ALD* seminary libraries as a whole with ATLA seminary libraries in particular, though both were listed in the *ALD,* because the latter was an elite group, while the former was a more general and only somewhat selected group. See chapter 4 for these attempts at comparisons. Another handicap in comparing the libraries is that their frequency in many of the subcells of various tables was so small as to make detailed comparisons unreliable. Only gross comparisons could validly be made with other libraries. On certain tables the no response column (no questionnaire response received from the library) was unacceptably large, thereby leaving few positive responses to be counted.[3]

The study contains little data in any subfield that would enable it to analyze these institutions' quality as distinct from their size. Desirable as that sort of analysis might be, it could not be one of the objectives of this study, since the appropriate quality information and standards were not available beyond the quantity of information per library to be found in this and later chapters. Further, the author has no way of comparing these statistics usefully at this point in the development of the field.

National Comparison: Canada vs. the United States[4]

This chapter section will discuss national geographic comparisons for the 1978 and 1988 scholarly libraries together and also individually. First we will discuss the basic and general information and then we will discuss the more specialized variables. How many scholarly libraries existed in each country—Canada and the United States—and where were they located?

While the regional tables in this and other chapters included Canadian national data from which a comparison could be made with U.S. national data, such a comparison would be more easily understood by the reader if it were made separately and directly between the two nations on several variables rather than merely deriving it from other regional comparisons. Several analyses can be made to show the nature of the national comparisons and the significant differences between the two countries. Of course, the basic difference between the U.S. and Canadian religious library databases was that the former was so much larger than the latter.

Tables 2.1 (1978), 2.2 (1988), 2.3 (1978), 2.4 (1988), 2.5 (1988), and longitudinal 2.6 covered each database as a whole and clarified its relative size and certain of its changes between 1978 and 1988. Several of these tables included not just the scholarly but also the popular libraries in the database. The longitudinal analyses will discuss change rates in tabular information between the 1978 and the 1988 databases, changes in variable scores over time. Certain of the 1988 results were similar to those in 1978 and so need not occupy our attention in a longitudinal analysis. They will already have been covered in the basic description of each variable on which the analysis will build. Certain other variables, however, changed significantly during the course of the decade, and this fact will be brought to the reader's attention.

We will also examine the scholarly library group with the help of tables 2.6 for 1978 and 1988, 2.7 for 1978, and 2.8 for 1988. The total number of scholarly and popular libraries in the *1978* database was 2,062. Of those, 1,375, or 66.7 percent, were scholarly and 687, or 33.3 percent, were popular. In addition, 1,937, or 93.9 percent, were American and 125, or 6.1 percent, were Canadian. Twelve hundred seventy-seven, or 92.9 percent, of the scholarly libraries were American and ninety-eight, or 7.1 percent, were Canadian.

The total number of scholarly and popular libraries in the *1988* database was 2,074. Of them, 1,432 or 69.0 percent, were scholarly and 642, or 31.0 percent, were popular. Of the total, 1,888, or 91.0 percent, were U.S. and 186, or 9.0 percent, were Canadian. Of the 1,988 scholarly libraries, 1,267, or 88.5 percent, were American and 165, or 11.5 percent, were Canadian. The ratios between the two nations were therefore 1,277 to 98 for 1978 and 1,267 to 165 for 1988. These ratios boiled down to 13.0 to 1.0 and 7.7 to 1.0 for 1978 and 1988, respectively.

The United States:Canada ratios between these two database sets of libraries, including both scholarly and popular, were 15.5 to 1.0 in 1978 and 10.2 to 1.0 in 1988, quite a significantly reduced contrast. In all cases, however, 88 percent, or more of the *ALD* databases, were libraries located south of the forty-ninth parallel—the U.S.-Canadian border. This study was primarily one of U.S. scholarly libraries in both databases. U.S. dominance was so great that it unbalanced the study. The scholarly domination over the popular library group was enough that certain database analyses were possible for scholarly but not for popular libraries.

For another comparison, the total number of *all kinds of libraries* listed in Canada and the United States in the 1988 *ALD*, religious plus nonreligious, was 34,366. Therefore, the religious libraries portion of this *ALD* total, that proportion which was analyzed in this book, 2,074 libraries, equaled only 6 percent of the entire *ALD* list, a small fraction of the total population.

If we look at tables 2.3 for 1978 and 2.5 for 1988 for scholarly libraries only, we see the contrasting totals. We can see the ratio between scholarly U.S. libraries and scholarly Canadian libraries to have decreased after 1978. This change represented an increase in the number of Canadian libraries and a slight decrease in the number of U.S. libraries over the decade.

For each year, the scholarly religious library world was larger in United States than Canada. In fact, the U.S. national scholarly religious library group was the largest in the world, according to Ruoss.[5] Apparently Mexico, Central America, and the Caribbean added about one hundred scholarly religious libraries to those of Canada and the United States, but this addition may not have been enough, however, to bring the combined continental North American total up to the European total level.

The number of scholarly libraries in Canada grew in the decade under study from 98 to 165, or by 70 percent. This growth can be contrasted with the overall scholarly "growth" of the U.S. libraries in the decade, which was −4 percent. Consequently, the Canadian percentage of the total number of North American libraries grew from 6 percent to 9 percent. Obviously, Canadian scholarly libraries gained substantially in number in the *ALD* during this decade, while American libraries remained essentially static.

The Canadian surge forward occurred primarily in Quebec and secondarily in Ontario, Alberta, and Manitoba. This rise must have been due to greater financial support being available to scholarly institutions and their libraries during the decade and perhaps also to increased questionnaire distribution in Canada by the *ALD* editors. Furthermore, it may have revealed that the number of scholarly religious libraries in existence grew faster by percentage in Canada in the 1980s than it did in that period in the United States. However, the evidence is much too meager to support such a generalization, intriguing though it may be.

Another longitudinal table, 2.9, shows the size of scholarly institutional student enrollment for Canada vs. the United States in matched pairs of libraries (the same library appearing in both the 1978 and 1988 databases). It shows Canada to have been well ahead of the United States in both 1978 and 1988. The ratios were 1.0 to 1.5 and 1.0 to 1.7. Percentage change was also somewhat higher for Canada than for the United States. This indicates that each Canadian academic unit handled half again as many students as did its U.S. counterpart library in each year. Furthermore, the number of students per institution was growing faster in Canada than in the United States.

Another indication that Canadian higher institutions were operating somewhat differently from American institutions was that Canadian institutions were 13 percent ahead of the United States in 1978 and 27 percent ahead in 1988 in the *students per faculty member* ratio. See longitudinal table 2.10. And the Canadian margin was growing. Another table showed student enrollment per library staff member. Canada was ahead in both 1978 and 1988. The scores were 78 to 118 students in 1978 and 70 to 115 students in 1988. See longitudinal table 2.11.

Scholarly longitudinal table 2.12 compares institutional faculty members between the two countries. Mean figures per institution favored Canada again with 1978–88 scores of 71 to 98 and 81 to 104, or ratios of 1.00 to 1.38 and 1.00 to 1.28. The longitudinal change percentage favored the United States, however, by 14 percent over the decade. We have much the same statistical outcome for matched pairs for the two countries, in which the scores were similar and favored Canada.

Of course, these findings can be interpreted as showing either that Canada was more efficient in handling more students with the same size faculty or else that the Americans offered more individual service to students with smaller faculty teaching loads than Canada did. Two more tables involved faculty members. In the first one, Canada showed a third more *faculty members by number of degree years awarded.* In the second, for matched pairs, Canada showed more total *faculty members* per institution by 45 percent for 1978 and 53 percent for 1988. We should note that Canadian institutions maintained a large number of student teaching assistants at that time.

Total material holdings was the subject of the next examination of the relationship between Canada and the United States. Total or cumulative holdings included the summed totals for library holdings of volumes, periodical titles, vertical files, and microforms. This may be a case of mixing apes, apples, and accordions, but let us examine the results in longitudinal table 2.13. Holdings in 1978 were 122,500 material units for Canada vs. 104,900 material units for the United States, a ratio of 1.17 to 1.00. The 1988 ratio favored the United States, however, 0.87 to 1.00. The change rate favored the United States proportionately by 34 percent. Another longitudinal table for scholarly libraries covered cumulative media holdings—media, maps, and art reproductions. This table showed identical trends for the two countries. Each nation scored a mean of 2.0 units in 1978 and 1.6 units in 1988. Both countries displayed negative change percentages here of −20 percent.

Overall Canada vs. United States mean total scholarly library expenditure was $194,400 for Canada and $134,800 for the United States for 1978. For 1988 the two figures were $240,400 and $244,500. While Canada led by a large margin in 1978, the United States had crept ahead by 1988. Change percentages 1978–1988 were 24 percent for Canada and 81 percent for the United States (longitudinal table 2.14).

The next longitudinal table showed the results of comparing the two nations on twenty-two growth variables (longitudinal table change percentages) for matched pairs of academic libraries. Longitudinal table 2.15 shows scholarly library distribution for 1978 and 1988 for the United States and Canada. It indicates, for instance, that U.S. junior colleges shrank in number 1978–1988, while Canadian junior colleges grew in number. The same phenomenon occurred for senior colleges and seminaries. Canadian scholarly libraries increased strongly during the decade while U.S. scholarly libraries were static. In total, Canadian library frequency grew during this decade by 49 percent overall, and U.S. libraries shrank by 2 percent. Table 2.6 for 1978 and 1988 summarizes these longitudinal findings.

Table 2.6 is a curious kind of summary table. It attempts to show ratios and percentages between Canada and the United States for each *ALD* edition. The scholarly library to popular library ratio grew larger and the Canada to United States ratio was smaller in 1988 than it was in 1978.

The reason for this change was that the frequencies of both Canadian scholarly and popular libraries increased to a greater extent in 1988 than did the number of U.S. scholarly and popular libraries for that year.

Now we have several more studies of national comparisons to consider. First, we will examine library age, city population, and staff sizes. Tables 2.16 (for 1978) and 2.17 (for 1988) show library age for the scholarly and popular databases combined with mean library ages of 72.9 years and 71.0 years. A Canada vs. United States longitudinal table, table 2.18, shows scholarly library age as contrasted by the two countries. The U.S. libraries were considerably older than the Canadian libraries, 80 to 75 and 80 to 68 years, 1978 to 1988, respectively. In terms of changes, the Canadian library mean went down during the decade, while U.S. libraries were stationary in age.

Table 2.19 presented a longitudinal table dealing with *city population size* for Canada and the United States for scholarly libraries. The table showed population to be much higher in Canadian cities, by 29 percent for 1978 and 32 percent for 1988. Decade-long population growth was a minus figure for both countries, however. In fact, the United States vs. Canada city population difference was even greater here: in 1978 the difference was 49 percent and in 1988 it was 83 percent.

We have arrived at the *library staff* section now. For professional staff members the results were almost even between the two countries. In 1978, longitudinal table 2.20 shows that they were even, 3.8 professionals a piece, but by 1988 the United States had moved slightly ahead, 4.0 vs. 3.7 professional staff members. In continuation, table 2.21 shows a longitudinal study of scholarly library clerical staff members for Canada vs. the United Sates. In both years Canadian libraries averaged more clerks than U.S. libraries, 6.6 to 4.6 clerks in 1978 and 5.9 to 5.0 in 1988. We should remember that Canadian scholarly libraries were larger and served more faculty members and students than did their U.S. counterparts. However, the U.S. clerical group was growing 20 percent faster than the Canadian group during this period.

Another staff longitudinal table compared the United States and Canada and favored the United States. This table studied student assistant staff members in scholarly libraries. For 1978 the means were 6.0 and 11.0, and for 1988 they were 8.0 and 15.0 student assistants, both with the United States significantly ahead. Percentage change was strong for both groups. Thus this series of national paragraphs showed that each nation was ahead on several variables.

Table 2.22 is another scholarly cumulative longitudinal table. It examines the institutional educational activity for Canada vs. the United States for matched pairs. The term *educational activity* refers to the cumulative scores of degree years offered, student enrollment and faculty size added together. Note how small were the no response column totals. The mean number of activity units showed Canada to have been slightly ahead in 1978 and to have drawn further ahead by 1988. The ratios were 1.03 to 1.00 and 1.49 to 1.00, indicating that the Canadian libraries were more active per library concerning educational activities. The change percentage was much higher for Canadians, so they were not only ahead of the United States in educational activities but were moving forward rapidly. This shows primarily that Canadian scholarly libraries served larger institutions than did U.S. scholarly libraries.

To summarize the national comparisons so far: U.S. libraries outnumbered Canadian libraries 1,937 to 125 in 1978 and 1,888 to 186 in 1988. While the U.S. database was divided about 2 to 1 between scholarly and popular, the Canadian database was divided about 3 to 1 in 1978 and 9 to 1 in 1988, scholarly to popular. At least 91 percent of the entire database belonged to the United States. In the field, by contrast, the ratio of scholarly libraries to popular libraries was probably more like 1 to 20. By count, the United States was ahead for certain of these tables, but Canada was ahead for a larger number of them.

Canada vs. the United States: A Further Comparison of Forty-five Variables

In comparing the two nations in this study, a large number of variables were analyzed internationally to locate interesting or revealing relationships. This subsection will mention some of the findings briefly and then discuss the results. In order to save pages, most of the tables on which this discussion is based will not be reproduced here. The section will cover library age, city population size, consortium memberships, staff size, and material holdings for scholarly libraries.

In terms of *scholarly library age* for matched pairs, which country had the oldest libraries? In 1978 the U.S. libraries were 6 percent older than the Canadian, 83 to 78 years on the average. In 1988 the two were about the same. This contrasts with the finding discussed above for the majority of libraries.

Next was *city population size* for scholarly libraries. Longitudinal table 2.19 shows Canadian libraries to have been located in cities that were larger than those in which U.S. libraries were located. The population of Canadian library cities was 29 percent larger than their counterpart U.S. cities in 1978 and 35 percent in 1988. Another table showed similar results for matched pairs of libraries. In this case, the Canadian city populations were 39 to 45 percent larger than the cities of comparable U.S. libraries. In terms of the number of *consortium memberships,* the situation was similar. In 1978 Canada was 30 percent ahead of the United States, but in 1988 the situation reversed, with the United States leading Canada by 30 percent in mean number of memberships.

For *total staff size* the library means were thirteen and sixteen staff members for 1978, with the United States well ahead. In 1988 it moved ahead even further to lead thirteen to twenty, or by 54 percent. So the United States did well on both library material and staffing. Even for *total staffing by degree years awarded* the United States came out ahead. Longitudinal table 2.23 shows that the American libraries led in 1978 by 15 percent, and since they improved faster than the matching Canadian libraries, by 1988 the U.S. group led by 37 percent.

Another longitudinal table (United States vs. Canada) showed total staff size for 1978 vs. 1988 for scholarly libraries. Where were the larger library staff sizes in North America? The two nations had dissimilar scores for mean total staff size, thirteen (1978) and thirteen (1988) for Canadian and sixteen (1978) and twenty (1988) for the United States. Again the United States showed a positive change for the decade and Canada did not, and again the positive decade growth belonged to the United States, whereas Canada showed a 35 percent decade disparity.

Now we can look at *library material holdings* in detail, United States vs. Canada. For book volume holdings the Canadian libraries led in 1978 by 13 percent, but the Americans increased their collection sizes by 23 percent and overtook the Canadians by 1988. Periodical title subscriptions came next. In 1978 the United States was only one percent ahead of Canada, but by 1988 it was 14 percent ahead. For vertical file holdings, the two nations were even in 1978 with a mean of twenty-five vertical file drawers per library, but by 1988 the United States had pulled ahead by 41 percent. Surely microform holdings was a field in which the United States should lead, also, but that was not the case. Canada led by 112 percent in 1978, but by 1988 the United States had pulled almost even so that Canada was only 9 percent ahead in these holdings.

Our final section in this series of national comparisons deals with scholarly library *expenditures*. For material expenditure in longitudinal table 2.24 we see that the two nations reversed their standing over the decade. In 1978 Canada was ahead by a third, but then the U.S. grew at a much faster rate—70 percent vs. 8 percent. So for 1988 the United States was 19 percent ahead of Canada in material expenditure. For personnel expenditure, on the other hand, Canada led all the way; see longitudinal table 2.25 for this information. Canada led by 57 percent in 1978 but by only 10 percent in 1988. Again the United States made a run during the decade but fell short this time in equaling the Canadian per library personnel expenditure.

Total expenditure can be seen in longitudinal table 2.14 in an instance in which the United States was well behind in 1978 but passed Canada by 1988. In 1978 Canada led by 44 percent, but by 1988 the United States led by 2 percent in mean total expenditures, but not in degrees awarded. If we divide these expenditure totals by degrees awarded, we find Canada ahead all of the way, by 45 percent in 1978 and by 15 percent in 1988. In the final table of this series we can study the two nations' scores in additional activities. Additional activities was a specific set of three variables and included consortium membership, OCLC membership, and local automation projects. This table provided another example of the late U.S. run for leadership. In 1978 Canada led by 13 percent, but in 1988 the United States led by 81 percent after Canada dropped by19 percent from its 1978 level.

When we consider *library material,* we can start with library volumes in longitudinal table 2.26. In 1978 the Canadian book collections were 13 percent larger than those in the United States, and in 1988 they were 9 percent smaller. However, U.S. libraries grew during this period by 23 percent and Canadian libraries lost by the equivalent of 23 percent.

A final longitudinal table, 2.27, showed the national comparison for both scholarly and popular libraries in terms of the mean number of the author's *ALD* questionnaire questions answered per library. The United States won this one. The United States/Canada numbers were 23 to 20, or 1.15 to 1.00 and 24 to 22, or 1.09 to 1.00. This meant that for 1978, for instance, typically, the Canadian libraries answered twenty and the U.S. libraries twenty-three of the questions on the author's *ALD* questionnaire. For change percentage, both nations were low. For 1988 the number of questions answered was twenty-two for Canada and twenty-four for the United States.

How did the two nations compare overall? For all variables covered in this subsection, Canada led in 1978 scores, 7 to 23 while in 1988 the two were almost tied, 15 to 17, Canada being slightly ahead. The pattern of Canada leading in 1978 and then being almost tied or else surpassed by the U.S. in 1988 occurred many times. Just what was happening can be seen in the Canada vs. U.S. discussion in the footnotes below. Either the U.S. institutions made strong improvements in their scores, or Canadian institutions ran into extensive financial problems and so improved only moderately during the decade. Probably some of both of these things happened. These scores include all US/Canada comparisons made so far in this chapter.

We can see the battle of the sexes joined with the battle of the nations in longitudinal table 2.28, and perhaps combined with the battle of 1978 vs. 1988 as well. This is a combined table that shows in concise form many of the subjects we have discussed in other sections of the book. Notice the contrast of the sexes between the U.S. and Canada. Finally, two master national comparison tables were made which listed all of the variables used in the analysis for scholarly libraries. They are not reproduced here, however, because each table is five pages long.

Regional Comparison

The need to explore the nature of the database when viewed from a regional perspective justified a large group of special analyses. Under the regional section the discussion will begin with scholarly libraries and will conclude with a further comparison of region and denomination. Tables 2.29 for 1978 and 2.4 for 1988 provide examples of these analyses. At the same time these tables will introduce the database analyses by state and province as well as by region.

The scholarly analysis by region is in certain ways even more complex than the analysis by nation. Each North American *ALD* database was divided into eight regions, as seen in Table 2.29. In all, fifty-one states (including the District of Columbia) and twelve provinces were covered. For scholarly libraries the two tables showed us that the largest regions by number were the Middle West and the Middle Atlantic, which together contained half the libraries in each database. If we add the Southeast, third largest, then we have reached two-thirds of the total. The smallest regions were the Rocky Mountains and the Northeast, totaling only 6–8 percent of the two databases.

In the Canadian, Rocky Mountains, and Southeast regions, about three-fourths of the 1978 libraries were scholarly, while in the Middle Atlantic and Southwest regions only three-fifths were scholarly. The same percentages applied to the 1988 database, with the exception that Canadian libraries rose in 1988 to be 89 percent scholarly, as pointed out before.

In tables 2.29 and 2.4 the state and provincial composition of each region is shown. The *Northeast* contained a strong representation from Massachusetts, which constituted almost half of the total. Connecticut was also strong and provided more than a quarter of the total number of libraries. Rhode Island grew in size during the decade of the study. The remaining states together constituted only a fourth to a fifth of the total. The *Middle Atlantic* was composed primarily of Pennsylvania and New York, together making up almost three-fourths of the region. New Jersey made up an eighth and the remaining three states the rest.

The *Southeast,* another major region, was less focused than the two regions described above. Its leading states numbered six and were not entirely the same ones from one database to the other: North Carolina, Tennessee, Florida, Kentucky, Georgia, and Virginia. Together they constituted more than two-thirds of the total. The *Southwest,* one of the smaller regions, was dominated by Texas, which supplied almost three-fifths of the region's libraries. Five more states contributed to the list. The *West,* another small region, was dominated by California with almost two-thirds of the total. Six more states completed the list with small contributions. The *Rocky Mountains* region was large in physical space but small in number of religious libraries, containing only three states with libraries. One state, Colorado, dominated it, with more than 70 percent of the total.

The largest region, the *Middle West,* was less narrowly focused than several of the other regions. It also contained more individual states, twelve, than any other region. Ohio, Illinois, Michigan, and Missouri contained more than half of the libraries in this region. In general, in the north central plains a low population density existed and few religious libraries could be found. The *Canadian* region was small and was focused primarily on two provinces with the largest populations—Quebec and Ontario—equaling two-thirds of the Canadian library total. Seven other provinces filled out the rest of the table. Only the Canadian region grew substantially between the databases, but the Southwest grew by 5 percent during the period. The Middle Atlantic, Rocky Mountains, and Middle West lost libraries during the decade.

We can now look at regions by type of library. Most regions were heavy on senior colleges but the Middle Atlantic and Middle West were also heavy on seminaries, the Southwest and Canada were heavy on universities, and the Southeast was heavy on junior colleges.

What scholarly religious denominations were most prominent in each region? In each Canadian province was a majority of the scholarly libraries Roman Catholic, for instance? Tables 2.30 (1978) and 2.31 (1988), plus table 2.32, answer these questions. For 1978, table 2.30 showed the population density for Canada and the United States by denomination. It showed the heavy emphasis on Roman Catholics in Canada and the heavy emphasis on both Protestants and Catholics in the United States.

In these tables, northeastern scholarly libraries were three-fifths Roman Catholic. Other denominations and independent libraries added together contained almost a fourth of the total number of libraries. Middle Atlantic and Canadian libraries were half Roman Catholic, with the Middle West being one-third Catholic.

When we examine region by denomination, we find that in 1978 the southeastern libraries were primarily Baptist and Methodist, and the southwestern libraries had Baptist and Roman Catholic as their most common denominations. The western and Rocky Mountains regions had Other Denominations and Roman Catholic as their most common denominations. So we found some variety in denominational leadership, although the Roman Catholic scholarly library groups were prominent in almost all regions. For the 1988 library database the breakdown by denomination was similar. The Roman Catholic group dominated the regional picture, with Baptists being important in the South. In terms of regional denomination, Roman Catholic libraries constituted 50 percent of the list in New England and Canada, and 47 percent in the Middle West.

In tables showing which regions were most popular for each library type, the Middle West led the scholarly libraries. Another table showed which regions were most popular for each denomination. The Southeast and Middle West scores tied for the lead in popularity, the Middle West led in the second priority column, and the Middle Atlantic led the third priority column. Tables 2.3 (1978) and 2.5 (1988) show the regional dispersion of the scholarly libraries. The two tables are similar except for Canada's sharply forward move in 1988. Thirty percent of the libraries were located in the Middle West and almost a fifth each in the Middle Atlantic and the Southeast.

Tables 2.30 and 2.31 for 1978 and 1988 are helpful scholarly library tables for us to continue with, as we analyze denominations and regions by several variables. We can see in the northeastern, middle Atlantic, and Canadian regions that the Roman Catholic group dominated each region again with more than half of the total. Baptist and Roman Catholic together accounted for almost half of the southwestern region. Other Denominations was important in the Middle Atlantic, West, Rocky Mountains, and Middle West.

Age by region can be seen in table 2.33 (1988). Oldest were the southeastern and middle western libraries (85–88 years old), while youngest were the western and southwestern (65–66 years old), as might be expected. There were two decades of difference between the oldest and the youngest denominations, a considerable disparity. Table 2.34 breaks down each type of library by denomination. We see that Roman Catholics led all types again except history/archives. Other Denominations was a strong second in several library types.

Table 2.35 (1978–88) showed a summary longitudinal table for regional distribution. While Canada, the West, and the Southwest grew in proportional representation during the decade, every other region shrank or remained static, the Rocky Mountains, Middle West and Middle Atlantic losing the most libraries for the table as a whole. Canada's growth was found in the scholarly type of library only.

In a further summary by region, the Middle West, Southeast, and Middle Atlantic were largest, and the Rocky Mountains and Northeast were smallest in numbers of scholarly libraries. Roman Catholic denominational groups were leaders in almost all scholarly regions. The Southeast and Middle West were oldest, and the West and Southwest were youngest. Table 2.6 showed the ratios between the United States and Canada.

State and Province Comparison

The next analysis concentrates on the states and provinces in the study. Tables 2.1, 2.2, 2.4, and 2.29 for 1978 and 1988, seen before, will be helpful in this section also. Tables 2.1 and 2.2 show the number and the leading denominations of Canadian and U.S. libraries in each state and province. This is a comprehensive set of tables that shows fundamental information on the databases. Tables 2.4 and 2.29 for 1988 and 1978 show the number of libraries per state, province, and region as well as the percent that each one represented for all of the U.S. and Canadian libraries.

In general, the states and provinces with the largest number of religious libraries had the largest overall population base, and the states and provinces with the smallest number of libraries had the smallest population base. We can see the state and provincial breakdowns of the two databases if we examine the tables listed just above. The states and provinces with the largest number of scholarly religious libraries in 1978 were, in order, Pennsylvania, New York, California, Ohio and Texas. The next largest states and provinces were Illinois, Mississippi, Missouri, North Carolina and Tennessee. In 1988, for the most part, the same states and provinces were the leaders again but in a somewhat different order: Pennsylvania, New York, Texas, California and Ohio with Illinois, Quebec, Wisconsin, Missouri and North Carolina following. These states and provinces were the chief centers of U.S. and Canadian religious library concentrations.

In terms of the entire database for each year, the five states listed first above (one-twelfth of the entire list by number) contained almost a third of the total number of libraries, and the first ten states and provinces (one-sixth by number) contained almost three-fifths of the total number of libraries. Or, to put it another way, a third of the libraries were found in only five states and provinces and almost three-fifths of them were found in only ten states and provinces!

In each database, one state and three provinces contained no libraries. The eight states and provinces with the smallest number of libraries in 1978 contained only eight libraries, or 0.4 percent, of the total. For 1988, the nine states and provinces that contributed least had twelve libraries, or 0.6 percent, of the total. The smallest dozen and a half states and provinces (29 percent) contained only eighty-six libraries, or 4 percent, of the total for each year.

Tables 2.1 for 1978 and 2.2 for 1988 give additional details about the states and provinces with scholarly and popular libraries combined. The last column to the right provides a concise summary of the religious denominations to which the largest number of libraries in each state or province belonged. We can see there such state emphases as the prominence of the Anglicans in British Columbia, the Baptists in Georgia and Alabama, the Congregationalists in Connecticut, Independents in New York, Jews in Pennsylvania, Delaware, and New York, Lutherans in Minnesota, Mennonites in Kansas and Manitoba, Reformed in Michigan, and Roman Catholics in Vermont. However, we can see also the prominent and widespread presence of Roman Catholics, who were the leaders in thirty-nine states and provinces in addition to those in which they were tied for the leadership with other denominational groups.

In addition, the Presbyterians (prominent in sixteen 1978 states and provinces), the Baptists (prominent in nineteen 1978 states and provinces) and the Methodists (prominent in twenty 1978 states and provinces) were, along with the Roman Catholic denomination, to a considerable degree national or even continental denominations with good representation in most regions. On the other hand, a few states and provinces had no strong concentration, e.g., Alaska, Hawaii, Ohio, Nevada, and New Brunswick, where a number of denominations were tied for numerical leadership. And, as we see in tables 2.36 (1978) and 2.37 (1988), many denominations were so small that their representation was limited to a few local institutions.

Examining the picture by state and province, five states gained libraries by 1988 while three lost in number. Changes in library totals by specific state and province between the two directory years were largest for Pennsylvania (down), Mississippi (down), Ohio (down), Texas (up), Quebec (up), Ontario (up), Alberta (up) and Manitoba (up). Quebec rose from forty-two to seventy-two libraries in 1988, by 71 percent, to top the list of changes. Texas moved up from 107 to 116 libraries, 8 percent. The regional emphasis between 1978 and 1988 changed very little, except for the 60 percent increase in Canadian libraries mentioned above.

Which states and provinces were largest in producing scholarly libraries? Generally, those with the largest total number of libraries also generated the largest number of scholarly libraries. Tables 2.38 (1988) and 2.39 (1978–88) answer this question. Table 2.39 encourages study by state or region and comparison between the two types of libraries.

In summary, for states and provinces the richest in libraries were Pennsylvania, New York, California, Ohio, and Texas for 1978 and Pennsylvania, New York, Texas, California, and Ohio for 1988. These states made up about a third of the total in each database. Three-fifths of the libraries were found in only one-sixth of the states and provinces. State emphases were brought out by denomination. Roman Catholic, Methodist (in 20 states), Baptist (in the South), and Presbyterian (in 16 states) were found in most of the states and provinces. On the other hand, several states and provinces either had no libraries or else produced very few of them.

City Comparison[6]

If we analyze the 1978 and 1988 *ALD* databases by city, what do we find? We would like to know several things about cities and scholarly religious libraries. For instance, does a difference exist in the average city population level by type of library? Which cities were the leading religious library centers in North America? The city population analysis will examine the entire situation first, then city vs. rural locations, then city population size by denomination, region, library type, total library expenditure, chief librarian's gender, and then specific cities, and finally a section summary will be presented. The overall 1978 mean city population size for scholarly libraries was 343,467 people, 2.2 percent larger than the 1988 mean size, 335,832, as seen in longitudinal table 2.40.

Several interesting things can be learned from frequency charts by city population size (not shown). First there were size differences between the mean and *median* figures, the latter being much smaller than the former. In this case, the *median* was the more useful measure where large numbers were used because the mean was more influenced by the few libraries in disproportionately large metropolitan centers of over 1 or 2 million persons. The *median* was 57,800 population for 1978 and 61,400 for 1988. In both cases, the trends were not the same as those displayed by the means. Table 2.41 for 1988 shows distribution by city population size. There was a large proportion of scholarly libraries in smaller population centers.

We may note further in these tables that a quarter of the scholarly libraries were located in small villages. The midpoint of the mean population of the smallest size category was five thousand persons. Those libraries falling into this category, under ten thousand people, were located in centers that were primarily rural villages, or, in other cases, rural-suburban villages. The largest proportion of scholarly libraries (47 percent) was found in centers with between 1 and 50,000 persons. Then the number of scholarly libraries in larger cities tapered off dramatically so that only 7 percent of scholarly libraries were found in cities of over 1 million persons.

We can express a rural-urban ratio by showing the number of libraries in (1) the village population category and then (2) all higher population categories. For scholarly libraries this ratio was 1 to 3 and for popular libraries it was 1 to 7. For scholarly libraries this means that there was one scholarly library in a village for every three scholarly libraries in cities.

Tables 2.42 and 2.43 show small and large cities for scholarly libraries by state for both 1978 and 1988. They reveal such information as that New Jersey contained many small cities and that the mean library was located in a city of about 335,000 population, small. On the other hand, typical Texas libraries were located in cities of 353,000 or over for 1978. Overall ratios for small city libraries varied from 27 percent for scholarly libraries in 1978 to 24 percent in 1988.

Another table shows scholarly libraries in small and large cities by *denomination* and by region for both 1978 and 1988. Again we can identify denominations and regions that were usually composed of libraries located in small cities. For instance, 55 percent of the scholarly Mennonite 1988 libraries were located in small cities. Overall means were 24–27 percent for scholarly libraries located in small cities.

Another analysis by *region* and city population can be seen for 1978 (not shown) and for 1988 (in table 2.44) covering scholarly libraries. Largest city population was found in the middle Atlantic region in 1978 at 716,800 persons. The smallest was in the Northeast at 120,000 persons. In 1988 the largest regional city population was in the Middle Atlantic, with 639,400, but the smallest had slipped to the Southeast at only 118,400 people. The Middle Atlantic region contained several large cities with many religious libraries, e.g., Philadelphia and New York. The regional ratio of the largest mean city population to the smallest was 5.4 to 1.0, a large ratio.

Now we can examine the libraries by *type* for both database years in longitudinal table 2.40 and in table 2.45 for 1978 and 1988. Scholarly convent/monastery and junior college libraries were located in the smallest cities, 51 percent and 44 percent respectively, the former with a mean of less than 110,000 and the latter with a mean approaching 100,000 to 200,000 population.

Longitudinal table 2.40 shows scholarly overall population means of 343,467 for 1978 and 335,832 for 1988, revealing a small decline or shift. Denominational headquarters libraries were located in the largest cities with means of 1,099,448 population in 1978 and 780,000 in 1988. History/archives libraries were next largest at the 549,000 population level. These were special libraries often connected to religious group headquarters which in turn were often located in large cities. Smallest city locations were 89,044 and 101,800 for 1978 and 1988 in population for convents/monasteries. Scholarly library change was 14 percent for convent/monasteries, −2 percent overall. Largest (positive) population change was +14 percent for convent/monastery, and smallest was −29 percent for denominational headquarters.

To table 2.40, we can add the broad scholarly denominational library analysis to the picture. The effect of this change is primarily to enlarge the size of certain scores, not to reduce them. For 1978, the scholarly Jewish library city population size stood at almost 2 million people, and Independent libraries came second in size at 600,000, smaller cities. United

Church of Christ libraries were located in the smallest cities with a mean of only 114,000 people.

City population level was shown in scholarly tables 2.46 (1978) and 2.47 (1988) by denomination and provided an instance when the Jewish and Roman Catholic institutional scores were well above those of the Other Denominations group. The 1988 city population picture changed little. The mean ratio between the largest and the smallest cities was 19.8 to 1.0, even larger than the 1978 city population ratio. In the 1988 tables, the largest library city population level was the place to find the Jewish group, with the Independent group coming second again. Smallest were the Mennonite (often a rural group) and the United Church of Christ groups.

Which scholarly denominations were those of large and which ones were those of small city libraries? For 1978, Jewish libraries at 1,967,000 population and Independent at 648,400 were largest, while UCC at 114,000 population were smallest. That was a ratio of 17.3 to 1.00, large. For 1988 again Jewish and Independent libraries were located in the largest cities at 1,553,000 as before, while Mennonites as well as the United Church of Christ were located in the smallest cities at 77,730 population. That was a ratio of 19.9 to 1.0, even larger. Obviously the latter two denominations were small city oriented. The ratio of the largest to the smallest city population levels by denomination was 20 to 1, a considerable contrast.

Clearly the Independent, Roman Catholic, and Jewish groups were oriented around large cities, while the Baptist, Christian, Congregational, Mennonite, Methodist, and United Church of Christ denominations were oriented around small cities or large towns. The popular Jewish/Roman Catholic library group city population level was significantly larger than the Protestant library group city population level also.

Now we can study the relationship between total library expenditure and mean city population for the libraries in 1978 (table 2.48) and 1988 (table 2.49). For both years we see an uneven progression upward for mean city population as annual library expenditure moved up also. For chief librarian's *gender*, longitudinal table 2.50 shows population groups by size. It shows for scholarly libraries that males gained during the decade in the ratio between males and females. We see that the smallest population group had the highest percent of males and the medium-large group had the smallest, but the difference was small in 1978. By 1988 the figures were almost even.

Chief Population Centers

Now we will turn to the final aspect of city population and its relation to the number of religious libraries. What are the main city population centers of scholarly religious librarianship in North America? Longitudinal table 2.51 answers that question for 1978 and 1988. In 1978, New York City led the list of largest religious library cities by a comfortable margin with Philadelphia, Washington, D.C., and Chicago following in being the locations for the largest numbers of libraries. For 1988, the table answered the question with a few changes from 1978. Montreal became the leader with the largest number of library locations and the next ranking library cities were the same as for 1978. Of course these were some of the largest cities in North America. Table 2.51 shows that cities contained 61 percent of all 1978 scholarly libraries and 65 percent of all 1988 scholarly libraries. A final comprehensive look at the most popular cities can be gained in longitudinal table 2.52 for scholarly libraries. Several cities showed dramatic changes during the decade while others appeared to be stable.

Over 60 percent of all scholarly libraries were found in cities containing two or more scholarly libraries. Table 2.53 shows scholarly libraries by denomination in large cities. It shows certain cities to be dominated (in this database) by a single denomination—e.g., Independent in the city of New York. We now turn to a final analysis of specific city populations, this time by denomination. By denomination we look at lists of cities that reported two or more libraries per denomination. See table 2.53 again for 1988 for scholarly libraries. For instance, the cities most popular with Christian scholarly libraries were Lexington and Fort Worth.

In summary of this section for cities and towns, the mean 1978 city population was 347,000 and the mean 1988 city population was 341,000. These were relatively large numbers, the population level of medium-sized cities. But note the discussion of mean vs. median figures. The rural-suburban figures suggested that scholarly libraries were located in slightly larger cities than were popular libraries in both 1978 and 1988. The Middle Atlantic and Canadian libraries were located in the largest cities.

Denominational headquarters libraries were located in the largest cities, while convent/monastery libraries were located in the smallest cities. Jewish, Roman Catholic, and Independent denominations were located in the largest cities, while Congregational and Mennonite libraries were located in the smallest cities. There was a direct and positive correlation between library expenditure level and mean city population size.

The chief cities by number of religious libraries were New York City, Washington, Philadelphia, Dallas, and Montreal.

Geography Section Summary and Conclusions

Where were the scholarly and popular religious libraries located? After a preliminary discussion of library density and nonreligious library geography, the discussion in this section continued by pointing out that all data collected originated in Canada or the United States. Of the two nations, the United States accounted for 88 percent or more of all data collected and so dominated the study. The total number of scholarly and popular libraries covered in 1978 was 2,062 and in 1988 was 2,074.

On the other hand the ratio *in the field* was probably more like 1 to 20, scholarly to popular libraries. American libraries shrank slightly in number in 1978–88, but the Canadian library group grew by 59 percent. In addition, the scholarly library sample as a whole grew by 4 percent in 1978–88. Scholarly libraries were strong in the United States and grew stronger in Canada by 1988. The study compared the United States and Canada on several variables, and Canada was the stronger of the two on most of them.

In general, the states and provinces with the largest overall population provided the largest numbers of libraries. By region the Middle West and the Middle Atlantic were the largest, and the Rocky Mountains and the Northeast were the smallest. By state and province, a third of the libraries were located in Pennsylvania, New York, Texas, California and Ohio in both databases. State or province longitudinal increase in sample size between 1978 and 1988 was largest in Quebec.

Mean city population level was rather small for scholarly libraries. Libraries in the middle Atlantic and Canadian regions were located in the largest cities on average and in the Northeast and Southeast in the smallest cities. *Median* population level was about 60,000 for scholarly libraries. Scholarly libraries were primarily a city and suburban phenomenon with few of them being located in small towns distant from cities.

Demography: What Are the Demographic Characteristics of Scholarly Religious Libraries?

This section on the demography of Canadian and U.S. religious libraries will discuss several basic and specialized variables by population composition. They include the following: library deaths and births, library age, and the characteristics of chief librarians. Other demographic information has already been reviewed in the previous section on geography. We will begin appropriately with the apparent *ALD* "deaths" and "births" of religious libraries.

Library Deaths and Births[7]

Library *deaths* is a subject appropriate for a demographic discussion, but one that was not covered directly in this study. Nor was the attempt to analyze the groups of scholarly libraries that died within the 1978 *ALD* edition entirely productive. Religious libraries die, of course, just as other libraries and other social institutions do, but evidence of these deaths is hard to find in this or any other scholarly study known to the author. Of course, the death rate must be universally low; once started, almost all libraries keep on operating, year after year, as far as we know.

When a library dies, its collection of material is either dispersed to a variety of locations, discarded, sold, donated to another library, or burned. An intermediate step would be to put the collection into inactive storage in its own quarters or elsewhere and release all library staff members. Whenever a seminary or monastery dies, for instance, its library usually dies also, although in certain cases the material collection (not the library) may be transferred or sold to another institution and then merged with that institution's library. If no previous library existed, it becomes the new institution's new library.

The study produced evidence suggesting that some library deaths may have occurred between the 1978 and 1988 *ALD* data collection periods. See longitudinal table 2.54. Certain libraries (422, or 20 percent) reported their questionnaire information for the 1978 edition but did not do so for the 1988 edition. Of course, in most of these nonrepeat cases, the library probably continued to exist but simply did not report its information for the 1988 edition, although it may have reported to earlier or later *ALD* editions. In certain other cases, however, the library may actually have ceased to exist.

Most libraries die because their parent institutions die, and that must have been what happened in certain of these *ALD* cases. Of course, we have no idea how many of the 1978 libraries that failed to appear in the 1988 edition actually died, as opposed to simply failing to report or undergoing some other change. We know that these 1978 libraries failed to report in 1988, and that is all. Or at least their data was not published in the 1988 edition.

In a few cases, we suspect, the nonrepeating library did not die but simply moved with its parent institution to another location, or the institution may have changed its official name. In certain of those cases, perhaps the change was not recognized by the author. Probably in almost no cases did the library die while the parent institution lived on. In conclusion, we know little about North American religious library deaths, but a few must have occurred every year in the decade studied. We can report only on the nonrepeat group, which is identified here as the "no longer listed" group. These libraries' characteristics will be described in fuller detail in chapters 3–4.

A similar demographic subject is library *births,* and again we know little about them for religious or any other kind of library. Births occurred every year, almost certainly more of them than deaths, but no measure of them was available to this author. A number of libraries (434, or 21 percent) appeared in the 1988 database that had not been listed in the 1978 database. There were more young libraries newly reported in the 41st edition than old libraries that were deceased in the 31st edition. The matched pairs totaled 1,640 libraries in each database and were neither part of the formerly listed nor the newly listed groups.

However, it is impossible to tell whether these newly listed libraries were new libraries or merely older libraries that failed to complete the 1978 edition questionnaire. Probably most of them were the latter, but certain of them must have been the former. It is interesting to note that 12 percent of the newly listed libraries were between eleven and twenty years old, and 39 percent were even older, many of them over fifty! See table 2.55 and table 2.56 for 1988. While the *ALD* marked each library that appeared for the first time with an asterisk, that does not mean that all astericks necessarily represented new libraries, merely that they were new to the *ALD*.

Library Age

In this subsection the chapter continues its demographic analysis of North American religious libraries by studying their ages. How old were the scholarly religious libraries in these databases? What was their geographic distribution by age? And their age distribution geographically? Age was discussed in an earlier section of this chapter, but tables 2.57,

2.58, and 2.59 for 1978 and 1988 showing both raw numbers and percentages deal with certain additional aspects of the age questions. Age is a significant variable in terms of the existence of religious libraries.

In certain cases age affects variables such as collection size. In other cases age itself is a function of parent denominational group maturity. In still other cases it may relate to the vigor of the parent organization. The author assumed generally that the older the library was, the stronger its scores on other variables (or correlations with them) were likely to be. We will study age by geographic region, by type, by denomination, by total expenditure, and then summarize the results to see not just whether or not the correlation holds true but to ascertain the strength of the correlation and under what circumstances it is most salient.[8]

For scholarly libraries tables 2.55 and 2.58 for 1988 and longitudinal table 2.59 show junior colleges to be young, fifty-nine years old on the average, and denominational headquarters libraries to be even younger, about forty-nine years old on the average. University libraries were oldest at ninety-four years in 1988.

But first we notice that differences between the 1978 and 1988 scholarly databases were modest, the latter being generally somewhat younger than the former. There were many more young (5–15 years old) libraries in the 1988 database than in the 1978 database. The ratio for this age group was 2.6 to 1.0 between the two databases by age, whereas the ratio between the two databases as a whole by number of libraries was 1.01 to 1.00. Of course, the range in ages was large in each database, from libraries that were less than a dozen years old to libraries dating back before the U.S. Revolutionary War period, at least 215 years old.

We have several analyses of scholarly no longer listed (dead) libraries by age for 1978. What were the distinctive ages of these libraries? Their mean age was sixty-three, which made them 21 percent younger than the scholarly libraries for the entire 1978 database. See table 2.60. We also have several analyses of scholarly newly listed (newly born) libraries by age for 1988. What were the distinctive age characteristics of these apparently new (to the *ALD*) libraries? Their mean age was quite young, forty-four years, even younger than the dead libraries, and 45 percent younger than the scholarly libraries for the 1988 database as a whole. See table 2.60 again. So while the newly listed libraries were younger than the no longer listed libraries, nineteen years younger, they were hardly new libraries.

We can study age by denomination in tables 2.61 and 2.62, which show mean ages in 1978 and 1988. Which libraries were oldest by denomination? The overall mean ages of the scholarly databases were eighty years for both 1978 and 1988. Therefore, these libraries were started on the average about 1908. The surprising thing about these tables is that the mean age for the total was similar in each database, even though the information was collected ten years apart. The 1988 libraries were somewhat more numerous than the 1978 libraries, but on the whole, library age is an unexpectedly stable variable.

We note that the 1978 Protestant libraries were much older than Jewish and Roman Catholic libraries as evidenced by these tables. Presbyterian and UCC libraries averaged 116 and Episcopal/Anglican 114 years and were the oldest denominations. The same denominations were also found to be among the oldest in the 1988 database. Youngest were the Churches of Christ and Jewish libraries at fifty-three and sixty-one years respectively. Notably, the Churches of Christ libraries were less than half as old as the Presbyterian libraries. This age tendency may be a reflection of the maturity of their respective denominations.

By 1988 the mean age was unchanged and Protestant libraries were still older than Jewish and Catholic libraries. The 1988 United Church of Christ libraries were oldest at an average of 115, and the Presbyterian libraries were next at an average of 113 years. Youngest were the Churches of Christ and Jewish libraries at fifty-two and fifty-three years. So we see that Presbyterian libraries were consistently among the oldest, while Churches of Christ and Jewish libraries were consistently among the youngest libraries.

Among scholarly libraries in both databases by region, the oldest libraries were located in the Southeast, but this was true to the extent of only a few years over the Middle Atlantic and the Middle West regions. The youngest group of libraries was found in the West, with the Southwest not far behind. Of course, we are accustomed to thinking of the West as being a young part of the continent. See tables 2.63 and 2.33 for 1978 and 1988.

We may examine the age data by scholarly type of libraries in longitudinal table 2.64 for 1978 and 1988. This table shows mean ages for all types. Which among the various types were youngest and oldest in these databases? Scholarly university and senior college libraries were seen to be oldest at ninety-eight and eighty-three years of age respectively. Denominational headquarters and convent/monastery libraries were youngest at fifty-five, little more than half as old. Largest decade gain in years was 14 years for convent/monastery and largest loss in years was −13 years for history/archives.

Tables 2.65 and 2.66 for 1978 and 1988 show age by library expenditure for scholarly libraries. They show mean age to be closely correlated with mean library expenditure. The 1978 libraries with under $1,500 annual expenditure were only forty-five years old on the average, but those with annual expenditures of $510,000 or more averaged 109 years of age. For 1988 the correlation was just as direct—increasing annual library expenditure correlated directly with increasing library age.

The ages of specific libraries were also interesting. We will look at the oldest scholarly libraries from all denominations in the 1978 and 1988 databases, as seen in tables 2.67 and 2.68. They include many of the oldest scholarly libraries in North America. All of the scholarly libraries in these two tables were founded before the year 1800. Note also that eight of the twenty-eight libraries were Roman Catholic (almost 30 percent), six were Presbyterian (21 percent), and four were affiliated with Other Denominations (three of them being Moravian). Therefore eighteen out of twenty-eight (or two-thirds) of the most venerable libraries were supplied by these three long-established denominations.

By state, eight of these libraries were located in Pennsylvania and three in Maryland, thereby contributing a total of ten or more than a third of the total in the two databases over 180 years old. For the most part, these were older higher education libraries: thirteen senior college, six university, and six seminary libraries or almost seven-eighths of the total. It should be noted further that ten of the thirteen libraries from 1978 were repeated in the 1988 list.

Why were a proportion of the libraries in certain regions and certain types much older than those in other regions and types? What this analysis of denominational ages tells us is not conclusive because a definitive history of scholarly religious library development is not available to this author. Perhaps it tells us simply that certain North American denominations were older than others, or at least their institutional library development started earlier. No doubt the history of early religious denominational settlement in each region, state and province had great influence on the founding of early religious academic institutions.

Certain denominations began to develop libraries in specific colleges earlier and others later for reasons that relate primarily to the development of their educational and book publishing programs and to their financial situations. While we can speculate about the causes of the rise of early religious libraries, these causes are only superficially understood and probably differed to some extent by denomination and region of North America.

The development of seminaries and colleges must have counted heavily among scholarly institutions. In any case, certain denominations did not develop and prosper until long after other denominations had become well established. For instance, the Quakers founded libraries and colleges in the seventeenth and eighteenth centuries, while the Churches of Christ were much later founders. A student should study the scholarly denominational library ages (separately!) to evaluate the question of why they differed so much.

Now we can study age by *denomination* for specific scholarly libraries. For *Baptist,* two separate tables for 1988 listed the oldest libraries, and the Colgate Rochester Theological Seminary Library was the only one among them to be 180 or more years old.[9,10] These older libraries were located in different states, and most states were located in the southeastern region. The oldest *Christian* libraries are shown for 1988 in table 2.69. Oldest by far was Transylvania University in Kentucky. Missouri and Kentucky constituted half of the older library locations, and most of the Christian institutions were senior colleges.

The oldest *Churches of Christ* libraries in the 1988 database were listed also. Note that the years of establishment were much more recent than those of the previously examined Baptist and Christian denominational lists. Though relatively young in years, the Chicago Theological Seminary was the oldest library in the table. California and Tennessee were the favorite locations by state for these long established libraries. We have a *Congregational* denomination list, table 2.70, for 1978 only. This short list included four regions and its libraries were relatively young, also, running from 40 to 140 years old.

Episcopal/Anglican libraries show that one library was much older than the others, the University of King's College in Halifax, one of Canada's oldest higher institutions, at 225 years old. In general, the libraries in this table were located in the Northeastern and Southwestern United States and in eastern Canada. Three New York libraries led by state. This group was quite miscellaneous by type of library.

Independent scholarly libraries are shown for 1988 in table 2.71. Again we have one library that was much older than the others on the list, Brown University, a pioneer institution. No regional emphasis was identified, though more than half of the libraries were located generally in eastern Canadian, Northeast and Middle Atlantic regions. New York and Massachusetts led the list by state. The presence of three seminary libraries made the list somewhat distinctive.

The most surprising thing about the 1988 *Lutheran* libraries was that they contained no Minnesota or Wisconsin libraries, surprising since these states were traditional Lutheran strongholds. Four of the five libraries were those of seminaries, and they displayed considerable geographic spread. However, none of the libraries in *Mennonite* 1988 table 2.72 were seminary libraries. Further, these latter institutions were young and some served the Middle West, especially Kansas and Indiana. Most libraries on this table served undergraduate colleges.

The 1978 *Methodist* library list represented another instance in which one library, Dickinson College, was much older than the others, 225 years old. This short list was followed on the printout by fourteen more libraries at 160 years of age! A third of these Methodist libraries were located in Pennsylvania, but a wide geographic spread was shown. Most of them served undergraduate colleges.

The miscellaneous denominational group called *Other Denominations* revealed strong representation from both Quaker and Moravian libraries. A peculiarity of this group was that the age of two of its oldest libraries, Salem and Moravian Colleges, jumped thirty-five years in 1978–88, according to the *ALD*! The four oldest in 1988 table 2.73 were among the oldest libraries in the entire study, 225 or more years old. And two of them were located in the same city, Winston-Salem. North Carolina and Pennsylvania contained all but two of this short list of libraries.

For *Presbyterian* libraries, the 1978 and 1988 lists of the oldest libraries were identical. The 1988 list included three rather old libraries, and half of the list was composed of seminaries. The states of Tennessee, Pennsylvania, and Virginia accounted for three-fourths of the list. Table 2.74 lists the oldest 1988 *United Church of Christ* libraries. One was an old undergraduate college library, Franklin and Marshall. Most of them were located in the Northeastern and middle Atlantic regions, and half of them were located in Pennsylvania and Ohio.

In the *Jewish* library list for 1988, we have another example of a library that grew younger over the decade, at least in the *ALD;* the Jewish Theological Seminary was one hundred years old in 1978 but only eighty years old in 1988. Remarkable! The libraries on the lists for the Jewish faith were usually younger than most of the other denominational lists. Three New York City, two Pennsylvania, and two Massachusetts libraries constituted most of the list.

Last came the *Roman Catholic* list for 1988. The 1978 and 1988 lists differed to some degree. Three of these libraries were among the oldest in the study. Of the fifteen library listings, five were located in Maryland, three in Missouri, and two each in California and the District of Columbia; altogether four states provided four-fifths of the libraries. Seven of the fifteen were located in the U.S. capital area of Baltimore and Washington, D.C. See table 2.75.

In summary, for scholarly library age, seventeen libraries were listed in the top category, 225 years old or older. The denominations with the largest number of old libraries were Other Denominations, Presbyterian, and Roman Catholic. Among the oldest libraries the states of Pennsylvania, New York, Missouri, California, Tennessee, and Massachusetts led in popular locations. Scholarly institutions needed libraries and founded them as soon as the institution was founded.

Chief Librarians[11,12]

Often the only staff member listed in the *ALD* for a library was the chief librarian. So analyses of staff members' characteristics should include certain analyses of the chief librarians. Chief librarians' gender was identifiable (usually!) and could be studied. We can examine this matter by type of library, region, and city population size and then look at named chief librarians. Chief librarians' gender by type of library tells us several interesting things, as revealed by tables 2.76 (1978) and 2.77 (1988). We notice a difference between these two tables in that many of the 1978 "no response" libraries moved to either the male or the female column by 1988, mostly toward the female side. Overall, the 1988 scholarly libraries were led by men (1.0 to 0.8).

Females were clearly dominant in junior college libraries, but in no other type of scholarly library. This result follows the recent findings of other scholarly studies of women librarians' leadership roles, which show that women were numerous as heads of small libraries but not as heads of larger libraries.[13] Although for denominational headquarters libraries females made up less than half of the total, they were significantly more numerous than the number of either males or no responses. Senior college libraries were in the middle, half headed by women and half by men. Males had a commanding lead as heads of university, seminary, monastery, and history/archive libraries.

In summary, men dominated several scholarly library types, women dominated one and led in another type. These facts are displayed in tables 2.7 (1978) and 2.8 (1988). Much the same picture can be seen in table 2.76 (1978 database) and table 2.77 (1988 database). Table 2.78 for 1978–88 is a master or summary chief librarian's gender table, which is also longitudinal. It shows both the heavy male emphasis in the scholarly group and the areas of overall strength for the female group. It illustrates also the apparently slow growth rate for the male group contrasted with the much faster growth rate for the female group. What was the ratio between the chief librarians' gender by region? Table 2.8 for 1988 scholarly libraries shows that Canadian and western region libraries were more heavily male, while northeastern and southeastern libraries were more heavily female.

Now we can look at mean city population level by chief librarian's gender for scholarly libraries in 1978 and 1988 in table 2.79. And what we see is the most unusual scholarly chief librarian's gender table of them all, since in both years mean city population size was slightly higher for females than for males. Remarkable, especially for scholarly libraries in which the gender ratio was almost even. The mean male to female ratio was 0.96 to 1.00 for 1978 and 0.88 to 1.00 for 1988.

In this scholarly study, there were two definite tendencies concerning the distribution of men and women as chief librarians in city vs. town centers. There was a trend for chief librarians (mostly males) to gravitate toward small city population sizes, toward cities of less than 300,000 population. This trend developed after 1978 and may have related to the findings in the previous paragraph. Further, there was a tendency for chief female librarians to head city libraries.

In summary, for chief librarians, women led in number for junior college and denominational headquarters libraries, while males led in senior college, university, seminary, convent/monastery, and history/archive libraries. Table 2.54 is another master table, a summary of changes for scholarly libraries for 1978 and 1988 that lists each entire database, matched pairs, no longer listed, and newly listed libraries. Notice also that the numbers of newly listed and history/archive libraries were larger for 1988, so that their 1978–88 growth rate was large. University libraries also grew strongly. Scholarly newly listed vs. no longer listed libraries grew in the 1978–88 decade (260 to 206) as did scholarly libraries generally, 1,432 vs. 1,375 libraries or an increase of 4 percent. Convent/monastery libraries shrank between the no longer listed and the newly listed. More than half of the scholarly matched pairs were senior college libraries.

Demography Section Summary and Conclusions

The demographic section undertook to describe the databases in terms of basic population characteristics—library deaths and births, age, and chief librarian's gender. While deaths were numerous in the *ALD* (20 percent of the total number of libraries) in terms of dropout from one edition to the next, it is almost certain that a much smaller proportion of the libraries ceased to exist in the real world. No firm information was available on the larger population, however, so little that was definitive could be said about it. Much the same was true for library births, though it seems likely that they were numerous in the real world. But speculation was all the author could offer on the appearance of 434 *ALD* libraries in 1988, which had not appeared in the 1978 edition. However, the proportion of new libraries to the greater population was around 2 to 3 percent per year.

Age was analyzed for scholarly libraries, which were found to average eighty years of age. University, Southeast, Presbyterian, United Church of Christ and seventeen specific libraries were identified as containing (or being) the oldest scholarly libraries. The youngest scholarly libraries were in the West, in denominational headquarters, and in Churches of Christ groups. The chief librarian's gender was male for most but not all scholarly libraries. Canadian and university or seminary libraries dominated the female scholarly group. The longitudinal study by chief librarian's gender focused on the changes in database composition by nation and by library type from the earlier to the later period.

Decade Projections

In conclusion, this chapter provides not only the readings from the 1978 and 1988 *ALD* databases but also projections for the same variables for 1998 as well as a short list of subject areas needing further study. These projected figures address the question of what level will have been attained for each variable by the year 1998 and are based on extrapolations from the 1978 and 1988 data. Tables 2.80 through 2.83 should be consulted. They are derived from the statistical discussion that constitutes appendix C.

The projections show varied results. For instance, table 2.83 indicates that mean U.S. scholarly library age cannot be expected to advance beyond age eighty-one by 1998, which was its mean figure for 1988. Mean city population size may shrink for the decade 1988–98 by as much as

3.9 percent, from 336,600 people in 1978 to 311,400 people in 1998. Probably total staff size will grow by 20 percent to a mean of twenty-four staff members if current trends continue. Institutional enrollment will grow by only 1.0 percent in the decade. A large decade's growth can be expected for institutional expenditures, however, by 44.7 percent if financial policy changes do not occur after 1988. Volume holdings will grow rapidly from a mean of 92,630 volumes in 1978 to 134,970 in 1998. Microform holdings will grow rapidly also, by 43.5 percent for the decade if we assume that microforms will not be replaced by CD-ROMs by that time. These figures apply to the United States alone.

For Canada, the scholarly library projections are similar but are based on the much smaller Canadian database. Mean age should sink from 75 in 1978 to about 61 in 1998. Total staff may remain the same as before. Annual library expenditure will rise rapidly from a mean of $213,500 all the way to $311,700 in 1998. Volume holdings may sink slightly from a mean of 104,300 volumes in 1978 to 103,700 volumes in 1998. Periodical titles and microform holdings should both sink, also. Mean consortium memberships can be expected statistically to drop rapidly from 2.6 in 1978 to 1.4 memberships in 1998, but just why is hard to understand. Total mean change 1978–98 showed a rise of 19.4 percent for the decade for the United States, but a drop of 105 percent for the decade for Canada, due primarily to the unstable nature of the Canadian sample.

In conclusion, this section for the United States and Canada extrapolated the data available for fourteen variables from 1978 to 1988 and on as far as 1998. Some of the variables were predicted to rise, while others were predicted to fall. In all cases, however, variable change was based on the trend obtained between 1978 and 1988 and was only as valid and reliable as the data samples from which it was drawn.

Subject Areas Needing Further Study

This chapter has a concluding section of suggestions for further study in its subject subfield. Additional studies are needed to replicate this study and to examine certain aspects of it more closely. The chapter leaves many useful and reasonable questions unanswered or even unmentioned. They should be attacked, one by one. On the other hand, the following list is far from being complete for the research needed. We have here a brief list of suggested research or exploration and analysis projects on these scholarly religious libraries:

1. Within the states and provinces a further study of religious library geography would be helpful. Where within a specific state or province or group of them are its scholarly religious institutions concentrated? Where are its chief religious centers located?
2. Correlation or regression studies should be made between congregational density, house of worship density, and library density, all within the same denomination. To what extent and under what conditions is it true that denominational density in a particular location determines the density of its libraries there?
3. From a geographic perspective, an analysis should be made to describe the location of religious libraries by denomination within several metropolitan areas in order to reach generalized conclusions.
4. Study library deaths and births. Learn why several hundred religious libraries dropped out of the *ALD* each decade and several hundred more were added, which were not there the decade before. How many of them actually died and how many were actually newly born each year? Just how healthy and growing is the scholarly religious library field? And just how complete for certain cities are the *ALD* academic and special library listings?
5. Work out correlations between institutional founding dates and library founding dates for each one of the ten types of libraries and see how these findings relate to library size, development, and services offered.
6. The researcher should attempt to identify the reasons why certain states or certain denominations are strongly represented in the religious library world and others are not, beyond the number of university students.
7. Ethnicity should be considered in the religious library world. To what extent do the scholarly religious libraries in this study represent the North American Anglo-Saxon tradition vs. a Hispanic-American, African-American, or French-Canadian tradition?
8. In 1998 a graduate student should carry out a further longitudinal study of the libraries in this study to reevaluate variable trends and determine the status of the leading libraries of 1978 and 1988.[14]

Notes

1. The difference between geography and demography is real and should be apparent to the reader. However, the two fields overlap in that demographers study not only population statistics but also the distribution of populations throughout geographic areas. The various subtopics under these two main subject fields have been distributed between them here in such a manner as to facilitate chapter organization. As a result, the distribution of the religious library population has been assigned to geography, for instance, and other subtopics also may have been assigned to one or the other main field in rather arbitrary fashion.

   In fact, much of the entire book might fit into an extended chapter on demography. Much demographic information is covered in the geographic portion of the chapter, also. Further, certain subtopics are discussed that do not fit well into either main field but fit even less well anywhere else in the book. The author hopes the reader will forgive such arbitrary subject assignments.
2. The reader will note in this and later chapters that 1988 tables are used extensively whereas 1978 tables are used less often: the reader might, however, have expected the study to employ the data from both years with the same frequency and consistency. There are two reasons for our policy: (1) often the 1978 (31st edition) picture was much like that of the 1988 (41st edition) one. Thus the earlier table was omitted to avoid unnecessary repetition, which would confuse and bore the reader and add little to the argument; and (2) a simplified presentation was preferred.
3. Nonresponse may be the result of any one of several factors. Each factor has a different effect on the libraries that do respond. Therefore, a high nonresponse rate may or may not be catastrophic. For example, nonresponse due to

   1. Deliberate suppression of facts
      Number of Volumes held

Mean	*No Response*
27,483	61 percent

      Result: *Mean Too Low* or too high depending on the bias of the nonrespondents
   2. Non-applicability (e.g., they have no holdings of this type)
      Number of Films

Mean	*No Response*
129	71 percent

      Result: *No Effect on Mean* as zero responses were omitted from means calculations
   3. Ignorance or lack of data
      Congregational Budget

Mean	*No Response*
1,625,450	39 percent

Result: *Slight Effect on Mean,* usually in an upward direction since ignorance is generally associated with small budgets.

4. The task of profiling for Canadian and U.S. scholarly libraries is relatively simple because the scholarly sample sizes are large. For the two editions, 1978 and 1988, the numbers of U.S. scholarly libraries were 1,277 and 1,267; of them 1,086 were the same libraries repeated in both editions. For Canada, of course, the scholarly numbers were much smaller, only 98 and then 164 for the two editions respectively. However, at least the second of these two latter figures is respectable as a sample and speaking statistically. The overlap from edition to edition for Canada is 83 and 85—or about 84 of the original sample of 98. Therefore, for both Canada and the United States there is strong stability provided through 85 percent of the samples containing the same libraries in both editions.

   For the United States for both 1978 and 1988, the largest part of the scholarly samples comprised senior colleges and seminaries, approximately 50 percent and 17 percent respectively. The next largest group was universities, accounting for 10 percent and 13 percent in the two years. Added together, senior colleges, universities, and seminaries comprised close to 80 percent of the samples for each one of the two years. For Canada, on the other hand, the distribution was different. Senior colleges and universities together accounted for 69 percent and 64 percent of the totals for the two editions. If seminaries are added into the cumulative totals (8 percent and 15 percent), we find 77 percent and 79 percent of the totals to be accounted for.

   Therefore, the proportions accounted for are comparable for the two countries (approximately 80 percent). The major difference is that seminaries were more prominent in the United States (after senior colleges by proportion), whereas universities were dominant in Canada. In both countries the proportion of junior colleges was 9 percent or less. It is worth noting, however, that the proportion of seminaries in Canada rose somewhat in 1988 as the proportion of universities decreased. Therefore, over time the two countries' profiles tended to converge.

   Since Canada had slightly more universities as a proportion of the total samples, we need to expect that Canadian scholarly libraries will somewhat outshine their American counterparts on the average. This phenomenon is the logical concomitant of seminaries tending on the average to be smaller and less well supported than universities. As we will see later, this trend is certainly true for the 1978 edition, but it reverses itself by 1988. Therefore, for the United States, the composite growth score over the decade was 60 percent, while the matching rate for Canada was only 28 percent.

   Hence, although Canada had a composite score in 1978 that was 2.5 percent *ahead* of the U.S. on average, by 1988 this lead had dropped to an 18 percent *lag*. In fact, Canada's 26 percent of the universities in 1978 fell by eight percentage points to only 18 percent by 1988. This fall was accompanied by a larger proportion of seminaries, as mentioned above; however, it was *also* accompanied by an increase in the total number of senior colleges (from 42 to 76 or an increase of 34 new libraries), many of which were relatively small and less well supported than were the older universities.

The summary profiles for these scholarly libraries, then, show us two slightly different pictures. The U.S. library samples tend to be composed (80 percent) of the large-scale scholarly types (senior colleges, universities, and seminaries). They tend to be more or less the same libraries over a period of ten years, and they experienced rapid growth in support per library. The picture for Canada started out differently, with Canada leading in proportion of universities—many of which were larger and more prominent than those in the United States. By 1988 the balance of component libraries had approximated the U.S. configuration, with the proportion of seminaries increasing.

However, the introduction of thirty-four new, smaller senior colleges in the latter edition threw out the growth rate for Canada somewhat and produced an apparent setback for the Canadian sample as a whole relative to its U.S. counterpart sample.

Looking at the denominational breakdown, we find that within the U.S. samples only three denominations predominated: Baptists, Methodists, and Other Denominations. These three groups together accounted for 38 percent of the totals of both samples, and there was no distribution shift among the three between the two editions. All Protestant accounts for 65 percent and 67 percent of the totals respectively for 1978 and 1988. Roman Catholic libraries composed 32 percent of the sample in 1978 and fell slightly to 29 percent by 1988. For Canada we find that only Episcopal/Anglican, Independent, and Other Denominations were prominent within the Protestant groups.

However, none of the three accounted for more than 16 percent of the total, and All Protestant within the Canadian groups ranked only 41 percent in 1978 and 46 percent in 1988. This was considerably lower than that for the U.S. libraries, which were mostly Protestant. For Canada, Jewish scholarly libraries accounted for only 2 percent of all libraries, as in the United States. The large difference between countries was Roman Catholic libraries, which contributed 57 percent of the total in 1978 and 52 percent in 1988—in other words, more than half for each scholarly edition.

We can say, then, that the U.S. scholarly samples were largely Protestant with a little less than one-third of the total being Roman Catholic. Canada, on the other hand, was almost equally split between Roman Catholic and Protestant denominations, but with Roman Catholic leading. It is interesting, as an aside, that the new libraries within the 1988 sample were five Independent, seven Mennonite, sixteen Other Denominations, and thirty Roman Catholic. Therefore, it is easy to see that new Roman Catholic libraries contributed about one-half of all the new libraries in 1988. By deduction, then, the less well-supported new libraries tended to be mostly smaller senior colleges split equally between Protestant and Roman Catholic! Notably, and in general, neither the Roman Catholic libraries nor their Mennonite counterparts tended to be either large or relatively wealthy.

5. G. Martin Ruoss, *A World Directory of Theological Libraries* (Metuchen, N.J.: Scarecrow, 1968), pp. 13–18.
6. The questionnaire query concerning whether or not the scholarly library was a *departmental library* elicited little in terms of response. For the United States for the two editions of the *ALD,* the percentage of libraries responding yes was a constant 3 percent. For Canada the percentage of libraries responding, either yes or no was 7 percent in 1978 and then 3 percent, as in the United States. However, for Canada there was a low number of no responses for both editions.

   Questionnaire returned produced somewhat more interesting results. Almost all libraries could be assigned a response to the question, either yes or no. The percentage of libraries that returned their questionnaires in 1978 was considerably lower than that in 1988—about three-quarters of all libraries for both countries. By the time of the 1988 edition almost all libraries *did* return the required information—99 percent for the United States and 100 percent for Canada. Although it would be interesting to try to analyze this outcome as the result of Canada-U.S. activity, it seems more reasonable to conclude that the difference between the two editions may have been the result of a change in the *ALD* editorial policy.

   Library director named produced identical results for both countries for both editions. All libraries could be assigned either a yes or a no answer to this question on the basis of whether or not the name of the director appeared in the directory. In 1978 both countries produced directors' names for approximately 90 percent of their respective libraries. By 1988 this had risen to almost 100 percent. In contrast to the preceding inquiry, the outcome of this question appears to have been the result of a spontaneous tendency among librarians to submit the desired names. Why this change occurred is unknown.

   Religious order status among scholarly libraries was another question that produced ambiguous results. For the United States the percentage of libraries responding as having directors who were members of religious orders fell from 11 percent in 1978 to 8 percent in 1988. It is interesting that the proportion within the number who were *female* rose slightly over the decade. In Canada over the decade there was no change in terms of percentage of "religious" among library directors—only 3 percent for both editions. However, for Canada the tendency was reversed relative to that in the United States; there were slightly more male religious proportionately in Canada in 1978 than in the United States, and by 1988 this male propensity had increased somewhat.

   For both countries, however, and for both years, there tended to be more women than men; about four-fifths of all the religious who appeared as library directors were women. It is possible that the slightly larger percentage of men among the Canadian library directors who were members of a religious order was *simply a reflection of the larger percentages of male library directors within the Canadian subsamples generally*. In fact, there were at least 20 percent more male directors in Canada for both editions. This surplus more than covered the tendency toward larger numbers of priests and brothers versus nuns and sisters in Canada. Similarly, the trend over the decade was the same for both variables—toward a slightly larger proportion of men in both cases. In this case, then, *library director's gender* is the more determinative of the two variables.

The average scholarly library *city population size* for the United States was close to 337,000 in 1978 and fell somewhat by 1988 to about 324,000. For Canada there was also a slight tendency toward smaller cities and residential centers, but the mean city size for Canada was nearly 100,000 persons larger than that for the United States in both editions. The tendency toward smaller cities was weaker in Canada than the United States—a mean fall of 12,000 persons in the United States versus a decrease of only about 4,000 persons for Canada. Therefore, given that city population size was a rock-hard variable to analyze statistically (and there can be no "missing cases" or "no responses" among the libraries), we can conclude that in both countries there was a slight tendency toward smaller urban centers, but that this tendency was roughly three times as strong in the United States as in Canada—and slight for both, less than 4 percent in any case.

Library age produced some curious results. The scholarly library response rate for the United States was steady at over 90 percent, and the mean age was roughly eighty or eighty-one years old (measuring from the time of the 1988 survey). For Canada, on the other hand, the response rate was lower, 82 percent and only 71 percent for the two editions respectively. The mean also fell from seventy five to sixty-eight years. It is to be assumed from this information that the change in both the mean Canadian age and the Canadian response rate was the result of the new libraries' appearing on the *ALD* scene in 1988, almost all of which were located in senior colleges, and, we must assume, many of which were "younger" than the mean of sixty-eight years. This is not unreasonable, as many Canadian academic institutions were relatively recent in origin, and there is no reason to suppose that many older institutions should suddenly wish to appear on the *ALD* list.

It is clear enough, at any rate, from a comparison of the Canadian and the U.S. results that (1) the penetration rate of the *ALD* among U.S. libraries was reasonably steady; (2) the penetration rate in Canada was on the rise between 1978 and 1988 with the most appeal being felt among younger institutions; and (3) the average Canadian scholarly library was younger absolutely than its U.S. counterpart. The fact that the response rate fell in Canada for the 1988 edition suggests that the average Canadian library was *more than thirteen years younger* than its U.S. counterpart, as the statistics suggest, simply because older libraries would have no reason to suppress their age and "venerability," and for younger, rapidly changing libraries, library age would not have been perceived as being important enough to waste valuable librarian time attempting to track it down accurately.

Scholarly *institutional degrees awarded* rose for the United States over the ten-year period and fell for Canada. For the United States four-fifths of all libraries produced this information for both editions. For Canada, however, the response rate fell from 70 percent to slightly less than 50 percent in 1988. The only sure conclusion here is that the average institution in both countries offered more than the standard four-year baccalaureate program. For the United States, the mean number of years for degrees awarded rose from 4.3 to 4.7; this was in accordance with the large preponderance of senior colleges and universities in the United States. In Canada the mean fell from 4.6 to 4.4, which is also in accordance with the falling percentage of universities and increasing number of senior colleges in that country. However, the no response rate for Canada in 1988 (over 50 percent) was so high that we must conclude that probably a large number of the new institutions listed in the 1988 directory offered less than the mean 4.4 years—perhaps only a four-year bachelor's degree or even a three-year bachelor's degree, which is still common in Canada depending on the field of study.

The number of *staff members per degree year* is a revealing variable, although it may be related to the fact that *Canadian scholarly institutions on the whole were much larger than were their American counterparts*. This relates also to the fact that Canadian senior colleges and universities were located in significantly larger cities, and this will probably remain so for the indefinite future. In the United States the mean number of staff members per degree year rose from 3.9 to 4.8—an increase of almost one person on average over the ten years. For Canada, on the other hand, there was a slight rise, from 3.4 to 3.5 persons over the decade. Again the Canadian response rate was a little lower, but not overwhelmingly so—only about as much as would be explained by the missing responses for the "number of degree years awarded" variable.

The differential in the means for Canada and the U.S. can be explained in two ways: (1) Canada had a large number of incoming senior colleges in 1988, at least some of which were not highly staffed, and (2) it might be argued that Canadian scholarly institutions, being larger than the average U.S. institution, practiced a form of "economy of scale" with their staffing policies. Certainly a 1988 U.S. mean of 4.8 persons was significantly higher than was the Canadian mean of 3.5, so whether the Canadian economy was a false one might be a matter of debate—no doubt for professional library administrators. Another consideration, however, might be budgeting, which was not entirely in the hands of library administrators. A quick look at the following compound scholarly variable table might be instructive.

Percentage Differentials between the United States and Canada

	1978		1988	
	Canada	U.S.A.	Canada	U.S.A.
Entire staff membership size	13	16	13	20
Differential	−19		−35	
Percentage change, 1978–1988			0	25
Staff members per degree year	3.4	3.9	3.5	4.8
Differential	−13		−27	
Percentage change, 1978–1988			3	23
Institutional faculty size	98	71	104	81
Differential	38		28	
Percentage change, 1978–1988			6	14
Institutional student enrollment	1,588	1,041	1,637	1,160
Differential	53		41	
Percentage change, 1978–1988			3	11
Total expenditure per annum	213,500	136,900	262,600	247,700
Differential	56		6	
Percentage change, 1978–1988			23	81
Expenditure on personnel	141,000	89,890	154,200	140,200
Differential	57		10	
Percentage change, 1978–1988			9	56
Value of relevant dollar (approx.)	0.9	1.0	0.8	1.0
	−10		−20	

We can conclude our discussion of these scholarly libraries with a close look at the summary data shown above. We know three things about Canadian scholarly libraries, based on the foregoing analysis of U.S. libraries: (1) the Canadian sample had a decreasing proportion of universities and a rising proportion of both senior colleges and seminaries; (2) Canadian libraries tended to appear to be the "better" or more elite of their kind, more so than was true of the U.S. sample; and (3) the Canadian library profile in 1988 began to resemble that of the United States quite closely in terms of proportionate distribution (meaning that about the same proportions of the different types of scholarly libraries were listed in the *ALD* and incidentally made our subsamples more comparable). To this list we can now add a fourth point, which completes the country profiles: Canadian scholarly institutions were highly and significantly *larger* than their U.S. counterparts. In a moment we will see that they were not necessarily better off, however.

We know that Canadian scholarly libraries were located in larger cities, on the average, than were their U.S. counterparts. The effect has been that the scholarly institutions to which they were attached became proportionately larger. In fact, we can say that the city differential between U.S. and Canadian city sizes was 29 percent for 1978 and 32 percent for 1988. If we look at the matching figures for institutional student enrollment, we find that the average Canadian institution (within our samples) was 53 percent larger in 1978 and 41 percent larger in 1988 than for the comparable U.S. institution. The average "faculty size" differential was 38 percent and 28 percent.

These numbers raise some qualms, however, which on investigation are justified. Students per faculty member in the United States were fifteen and fifteen for the two editions, versus seventeen and nineteen for Canada, with the ratio worsening for Canada over the ten-year period. Library staff members per hundred students for the United States were 2.2 and 2.6. For Canada the figures were 1.5 and 2.0 for every hundred students enrolled. At least both countries appear to be moving in the right direction and to about the same extent.

However, it is clear from the above paragraph that while Canadian institutions were larger, they were larger than their city size warranted in terms of student body (if size of city is thought to justify larger institutions), and both the number of faculty members per student *and* the number of staff members per student were lower than was the case for U.S. institutions. This is more or less the same type of relationship that exists with faculty members per degree year awarded. It could certainly be argued on the basis of these figures alone that the quality of education in Canada, on the average, was likely to be compromised by overstretching.

A glance at the expenditure variables tells us that in 1978, while the average Canadian institution was about 50 percent larger in terms of enrollment, the average total library expenditure was approximately 56 percent greater—large enough to cover the extra institutional size, but not large enough to cover the differential in spending power of the U.S. dollar over the Canadian dollar. Therefore, although even the library personnel expenditure for Canada was 57 percent larger than that for the United States, given the larger size of Canadian institutions, the extra budgetary monies could not quite cover the additional size plus the dollar discrepancy. The result of this, as might be expected, was larger class sizes per faculty member, and not quite as many library staff members per hundred students.

It is interesting, in light of 1988 developments, that the number of library staff members per hundred students rose from 1.5 to 2.0 within the Canadian subsample. In 1978 the Canadian libraries lagged behind U.S. libraries in spending power per student by a few percentage points (say about 10 percent or 11 percent). However, by 1988, while student enrollment per institution was still about 40 percent higher, the total annual library expenditure differential was only 6 percent in favor of Canada (in Canadian dollars). Also, the annual library personnel expenditure differential was a mere 10 percent higher; neither the 6 percent nor the 10 percent came even close to covering the difference between the Canadian and U.S. dollars at this point, which was about 15 to 20 American cents per dollar in spending power.

Obviously, as the mean number of library staff members remained stable over the period (13 and 13 for 1978 and 1988), the average Canadian library staff member's salary proceeded to fall further behind that of his or her U.S. matching staff member. Looking at matters from another angle, we can see that the average scholarly library expenditure in the United States rose by 81 percent between 1978 and 1988—enough to cover both increased staffing (from 16 to 20 members) *and* the inflation level. In Canada, although the average enrollment rose from 1,588 to 1,637 students over the same period, the mean annual scholarly expenditure rose by only 23 percent—enough to cover the fall in the Canadian dollar value, but not enough to cover more than the start of the value of inflation plus the increase in student enrollment.

Considering that cumulative inflation during this decade was about 60 percent (roughly), the fall in the value of the Canadian dollar was approximately 10 or 11 percent (depending on how it is calculated), the increase in enrollment was about 3 percent, and given the expenditure level per student in 1978 of $154.00 (based on the 30 Canadian libraries reporting this data), it would have been necessary for the average Canadian library in 1988 to spend about $372,000 just to keep up with rising costs and allowing nothing for real growth.

The rise in Canadian library expenditure was to $262,600—more than $100,000 short. No wonder then that extra staff members could not be added to improve the student-staff ratio, and additional faculty members were added at just about the rate of increase in student enrollment (6 percent versus 3 percent). Even accepting that some of the institutions entering the 1988 subsample were smaller and younger (hence reducing the means for the overall subsample), it is hard to picture Canadian scholarly institutions, and their corresponding libraries, as doing anything but falling behind in the 1980s.

The interesting point is that while the mean entire library staff size in Canada grew not at all over the decade, and student enrollment increased, on average, by 3 percent in Canada and 11 percent in the United States, the staff members per hundred students rose from 1.5 to 2.0 in Canada! Growth in mean staff members in the United States increased from sixteen to twenty per library—enough to cover the calculated increase in the student-staff member ratio from 2.2 members to 2.6 members and a little more. However, in Canada this is not the case, and the explanation is almost certainly to be found in the high no response rates among Canadian libraries on variables such as library staff size, institutional student enrollment, number of library professionals, institutional faculty size, etc.

For these variables the no response rate may be as high as 65 percent (although this is rare), which makes valid comparison between Canada and the United States difficult. It also makes it almost impossible to calculate the extent of the bias in favor of larger and better-off libraries that is built into the 40 percent to 60 percent of the Canadian subsample that provided accurate responses to the questionnaire queries. The apparent increase in staff members per hundred students enrolled for Canada was an *accurate figure for only those libraries submitting data on the two relevant variables,* i.e., for the 39 percent in 1978 and the 43 percent in 1988 that responded substantially to the questions. We can easily see, however, based on data for questions to which the no response rate was lower (e.g., student enrollment and total expenditure) that an important part of the picture was missing—the part relating to libraries that did not respond.

Thus I think it is fair to conclude that by 1988 Canadian institutions were feeling the dollar squeeze much more than were corresponding institutions in the United States. Similarly, in terms of important ratios such as students per faculty member, library professionals per hundred students, total library staff members per hundred students, faculty members per degree year, dollar expenditure per student, and dollar expenditure per faculty member, Canadian institutions had fallen into a seriously disadvantaged position.

The extent to which this was true is difficult to calculate due to the opposing influences of the large no response rates among Canadian libraries (generally about 10 percent higher than for U.S. libraries, and probably affecting the means for their respective countries in an upward fashion) and the influx of a number of newer (and probably smaller) libraries into the Canadian subsample (affecting the Canadian means in a downward direction).

To achieve an *accurate* estimate of the degree of the Canadian disadvantage based on these conflicting trends would be impossible (unless a close appraisal of the relevant variables for only the *matched pairs* of libraries were undertaken), but based on the mean annual library expenditure figures alone ($372,000 needed versus the subsample mean of $262,600) we can calculate that the mean shortfall in budget was about 30 percent—enough to hurt, and enough to be hurtful in terms of Canadian higher educational goals.

7. *Scholarly Libraries: Matched Pairs, No Longer Listed and Newly Listed Libraries.* When we examine the proportional distribution of matched pairs of scholarly libraries, we find little significant difference from the distribution within the entire samples except that Canada's resemblance to the U.S. pattern becomes more marked. That is, in 1978 for U.S. libraries a total of 83 percent of all the matched pairs were either senior college, university, or seminary in type. By 1988 this proportion had risen to 84 percent. Note that for the entire sample these proportions were somewhat lower—around 80 percent for both editions. This indicates that the core of the samples, i.e., the matched pairs, tended even more heavily to be of the same three types listed above and were stable in terms of their representation in succeeding *ALD* editions. For Canada the tendency was similar except that the proportion of universities in 1988 jumped to constitute 28 percent of the matched pairs (only 18 percent of the entire Canadian sample). In 1978 the three types listed in the paragraph above absorbed 80 percent of the Canadian matched pair sample, 77 percent of the entire sample, and by 1988 this proportion had risen to 82 percent—no doubt as a result of the heavy proportion of universities. This

is a 3 percent increase over the matching figure (79 percent) for the entire Canadian sample.

The result of these twin tendencies in the United States and Canada is that any analysis of the matched pairs (exclusive of libraries that were referred to as either "no longer listed" in 1978 or "newly listed" for 1988) will show an even more distinct tendency toward an elitist or "better" characteristic configuration than did the entire samples for the two countries. The reason for this is quite clear. As the proportion of senior colleges, universities, and seminaries increased, so did the trend toward diversified-holding, better supported, larger, and more wealthy libraries.

Although not without many exceptions, senior colleges, universities, and seminaries were better endowed with funds, volumes, and staff than were convents, denominational headquarters libraries, and history or archival centers. The latter may have been intended for only limited or specialist use and were almost certain to concentrate on specialized holdings of only restricted appeal.

An analysis of the type distribution for the *unmatched libraries* produces a different perspective and illuminates (to some extent) changes in the library environment. For the "no longer listed" libraries in the United States and Canada (for the 1978 edition), we find that the senior colleges, universities, and seminaries accounted for only 64 percent of the total for the United States and 60 percent of the total for Canada. What this means is that in the United States sixty-nine senior colleges, four universities, and forty-nine seminaries had dropped out of the *ALD* by 1988. For Canada a total of nine senior colleges that were listed in 1978 had dropped out by 1988.

Precisely why there should have been such a loss of senior colleges between editions is hard to imagine. It is interesting that the magnitude of attrition within types matches closely the magnitude of the types proportionately within the samples. Therefore, the largest loss was among senior colleges, which were the largest group within the 1978 sample. This was followed by the loss among the seminaries, which made up the second largest group, etc. Probably we can conclude from this finding that the attrition rate was natural and sprang from failure to publish data for libraries that simply did not return their questionnaires to the *ALD* publisher regularly, or more specifically in 1988, and perhaps some of these colleges and their libraries died.

In the Canadian sample it is interesting that nine senior colleges dropped out, as did five denominational headquarters libraries, and there was almost no other library loss. Certainly within Canada the group of senior colleges was the largest group (43 percent in 1978), but it is hard to guess why 60 percent of the loss should be in this category—unless there was a trend toward a smaller *absolute* number of senior colleges in Canada. This possibility was effectively ruled out, however, by the fact that in the 1988 *ALD* edition, 57 percent (forty-five libraries) of those newly listed were senior colleges, replenishing the loss from 1978 by 500 percent!

Among the newly listed libraries we find that 28 percent of the new U.S. libraries were senior colleges (fifty new libraries), and 14 percent were seminaries (twenty-six libraries). Therefore, the *ALD* added a total of seventy-six new libraries within the "better-off" types. Only seven new universities appeared, which more than offset the four that were lost from the 1978 edition. In Canada 13 percent of the incomers were junior colleges (ten libraries) and 57 percent, or forty-five new libraries, were of the senior college type. Altogether, the junior colleges, senior colleges, universities, and seminaries represented 87 percent of all new Canadian libraries. Senior colleges, universities, and seminaries combined to account for 74 percent of the newcomers (compare only 46 percent for the United States for the same three library types).

The distribution breakdown above suggests strongly that the proportion of "better-off" libraries coming into the *ALD* in 1988 (and probably in other years close to that time) was somewhat lower than the proportion of well-off libraries within the *ALD* in previous years. We have already found that about 80 percent of the *ALD* scholarly institutions were of the larger, diversified-holding, senior scholarly types. The incoming proportions were 74 percent for Canada and only 46 percent for the United States. This confirms the fact that for Canada only the better libraries managed to achieve *ALD* representation, but it also confirms the fact that the U.S. trend in representation was changing from previous years.

The question then becomes, If the proportion of senior scholarly libraries was falling off, what new types were replacing (or augmenting) them? The answer to this question is summarized below:

Proportions of Libraries Listed in the 1988 *ALD* (in percentages)

	Entire Sample		Newly Listed Libraries	
	Canada	U.S.A.	Canada	U.S.A.
Junior colleges	9	7	13	5
Convents/monasteries	2	2	1	4
Denominational HQ	5	6	6	21
History/archives	4	6	5	24
Total (of these types)	20%	21%	25%	54%
Senior scholarly	79%	79%	74%	46%
Total (of all types)	99%	100%	99%	100%

For the United States a small part of the "augmentation" was performed by convents/monasteries, but this increase was small. However, the increase in denominational headquarters and history/archive libraries was more significant. In 1988 the total proportions of these two types accounted for only

12 percent. But in the "newly listed" group the proportion had risen to 45 percent—or almost half of all new listings. For Canada the picture was different. There was a small additional number of junior colleges (some of which would no doubt like to "grow up" to become senior colleges some day, a total of ten libraries), and no other significant increase in any other library type. Notably there was a small increase in denominational headquarters and history/archive libraries, but this increase was not significant in any sense.

Concluding from the above, it can be seen that in the United States there was some move toward more "democratization" of *ALD* library representation—a gross move of 33 percent in terms of proportional representation. In Canada, however, this move was to the tune of only 5 percent and was limited to junior colleges. It appears that in this area at least the United States established a trend that Canada had yet to follow.

A larger number of smaller, more specialized U.S. libraries were submitting information for publication; in Canada it was still the larger, better, and probably more prestigious libraries that were listed with the *ALD* and hence appeared in the Canadian sample. There is little reason to suspect that these trends will not continue until the turn of the century. However, if a change does occur, then it is reasonable to predict that Canada will conform to the U.S. pattern after an indeterminable time lag.

For institutional accreditation we find a large difference between Canada and the United States. For the two editions three-quarters of all U.S. libraries responded that they had acquired a mean of 1.5 accreditations each with outside accrediting organizations. In Canada, on the other hand, in 1978 one quarter of all scholarly institutions reported a mean of 2.1 accreditations. By 1988 this proportion had fallen to only 8 percent, although the mean was stable at 2.2 accreditations each (in the two editions the same institutions responded with their accreditations). In Canada, it would seem, outside accreditation by those organizations considered important in the United States was either difficult to obtain or largely by-passed. See table 2.84 for U.S. figures.

The fact that the percentage of Canadian institutions with U.S. accreditation dropped significantly, from twenty-three to thirteen, hints that accreditation did not come easily or automatically to newer or smaller Canadian institutions. That there were sixty-six new institutions in the Canadian sample in 1988 and that a total of ten out of twenty-three institutions among the entire sample either "lost" or failed to report their accreditation status strongly indicated that this status itself was of little perceived value in Canada.

This fact was especially telling when we reflect that most of the Canadian sample institutions were of the senior scholarly type serving larger public institutions (such as McGill University) and were primarily responsible to the board of governors rather than to a professional organization external to (and in some ways irrelevant to) the operations and standards of the library. What *other* measures were taken to ensure professionalism within and communications among the larger Canadian institutions remained unrevealed by the *ALD* data.

Formal denominational affiliation as a variable was neither useful nor interesting except concerning one small anomaly in the United States for 1978. Generally speaking, there was a slight decline in data concerning affiliation over time: from 97 percent and 96 percent for the United States and Canada in 1978 to 95 percent and 91 percent respectively in 1988. The anomaly appears in that for the United States in 1978 the number of no responses was quite significant—approaching 10 percent of all responses. This can probably be taken as meaning very little as, presumably, those who responded no in 1978 (or were published as having no formal denominational affiliation) simply became no responses in the subsequent edition.

The tendency toward a greater percentage of no responses was of almost sufficient magnitude to justify the above conclusion. At any rate, there was a small but general trend within both countries to *downplay formal affiliation with religious denominations*. Whether or not this boded well for the religious library field as a separate subdivision of librarianship generally is another question.

8. The author must point out that this discussion of ages is an analysis of the founding dates of the libraries, not of their parent institutions. Sometimes the parent institution and the library were founded in the same year or even at the same time, but sometimes several years elapsed before the parent institution managed to establish its library. Therefore, parent institution founding dates should not be confused with library founding dates.
9. In each table, for the same variable value the libraries were listed in exact alphabetical order by the name of the state or province and then by city, with all Canadian libraries following all U.S. libraries.
10. Individual library scores on each variable were expressed in terms of the midpoint of each group within the entire group of scores. This fiction facilitated statistical analysis and data collection. The figure of 225 years of age is used because it represents hypothetically the midpoint of the range of ages of those libraries founded in the year 1800 or before.
11. The following were among the book titles that were helpful to the author in preparing the chapters in this book:

Accredited Institutions of Postsecondary Education 1980–81 (Washington: American Council on Education);

Accredited Institutions of Postsecondary Education 1987–88 (Washington: American Council on Education);

American Association of Bible Colleges, *Directory 1987–88* (Fayetteville, Ark.: 1987);

Ash, Lee, *comp., Subject Collections* (New York: R. R. Bowker, 1985);

Association of Advanced Rabbinical and Talmudic Schools. *List of All Accredited Schools* (New York: 1988);

Christian Resources Handbook (Mississauga, ON: Marc Canada, 1987);

Directory of Canadian Universities (Ottawa: Association of Universities and Colleges of Canada, 1986);
Education Directory, Colleges and Universities 1980–81 (Washington, D.C.: U.S. National Center for Education Statistics);
Fact Book on Theological Education (Vandalia, OH: Association of Theological Schools, 1986);
Graduate Programs in the Humanities and Social Sciences 1988 (Princeton, N.J.: Peterson, 1987);
Index of Majors, 1986–87 (New York: College Entrance Examination Board, 1986)
Information Please Almanac (Boston: Houghton Mifflin, 1986), p. 315;
Frank S. Mean, *Handbook of Denominations in the United States* (Nashville: Abingdon, 1980);
Philosophy, Religion, and Theology: A Catalog of Selected Doctoral Dissertation Research (Ann Arbor: University Microfilms International, 1985);
Readers Digest Almanac (Pleasantville, N.Y.: 1980).

12. Chief librarian's gender is an interesting variable where scholarly libraries are concerned. For the United States in both 1978 and 1988 the samples were almost equally split between males and females with males leading slightly (by exactly 6 percentage points in each case)—with 50 percent and 52 percent of the samples by proportion. In Canada, on the other hand, the proportion of males was somewhat higher than in the United States, 62 percent and 63 percent for the two editions. The proportion of females was curious, however, in that it rose from 28 percent in 1978 to 35 percent in 1988. There was virtually no change whatsoever in the proportions of male heads between 1978 and 1988 for either the United States or Canada for scholarly libraries.

If the configuration of proportions has been interpreted correctly above, then we are forced to conclude that there has been little swing in library leadership toward either male or female library heads. There has, however, been a distinct tendency for female chiefs to "come out of the woodwork," so to speak. The no response rate for the United States in 1978 was 6 percent followed by only one percent in 1988. The matching figures for Canada were 10 percent and 2 percent. Here again, Canada gave evidence of following the U.S. lead.

The interesting point about the question of gender is twofold: (1) there was no significant change toward more females—in fact over the decade there was a 2 percent increment toward males in the United States accompanied by a one percent growth in Canada; and (2) Canada had an 11 percent or 12 percent lead in terms of male over female heads. These figures were stable over the ten-year period. How to explain this pair of facts is difficult. It is clear that there was no *trend* in the United States that might be followed in Canada after an appropriate lag of a few years. And it is equally clear that Canada had more males than females and that the situation was not changing—except toward a larger proportion of males!

A study of the data at the end of the 1990s is necessary to resolve this interesting riddle. At the moment it looks as if the trend in both the United States and Canada was toward slightly more males and that Canada was leading in the race. An alternative explanation might simply be that the larger, better libraries attracted male librarians—and that as the Canadian *ALD* libraries tended to be quite a lot "better" (larger) than the average library within the population, the percentage of males in the sample was even higher than in the United States.

13. See John F. Harvey and Elizabeth M. Dickinson, *Librarians' Affirmative Action Handbook* (Metuchen, N.J.: Scarecrow, 1983), p. 24, table 9.
14. It should be clear to all readers that the author produced more tables for this study than could be used in the published version of it. Photocopies or telefaxes of additional tables are available for inspection by any reader on request to John F. Harvey, Suite 1105, 82 Wall Street, New York, N.Y. 10005, (telephone 212-509-2612 or fax 212-968-7962). Please specify the exact tables desired or the primary focus of interest.

TABLE 2.1
Total 1978 *American Library Directory* Questionnaires by State and Region

State or Province	State or Province Abbreviation	Regional Abbreviation	Useable Questionnaires Obtained	Percentage	Most Popular Denomination(s)
Canada					
Alberta	AB	CA	8	0	Lutheran, Roman Catholic
British Columbia	BC	CA	2	0	Anglican
Manitoba	MB	CA	6	0	Roman Catholic
New Brunswick	NB	CA	3	0	3 tied
Newfoundland	NF	CA	1	0	Anglican
Northwest Territories	NT	CA	0	0	—
Nova Scotia	NS	CA	9	0	Roman Catholic
Ontario	ON	CA	36	2	Roman Catholic, Anglican
Quebec	PQ	CA	51	2	Roman Catholic, Jewish
Saskatchewan	SK	CA	11	1	Roman Catholic
Prince Edward Island	PE	CA	0	0	—
Yukon	YT	CA	0	0	—
United States					
Alabama	AL	SE	27	1	Baptist, Methodist
Alaska	AK	W	4	0	4 tied
Arizona	AZ	SW	13	1	Baptist, Jewish, Roman Catholic
Arkansas	AR	SW	15	1	Baptist, Methodist
California	CA	W	116	6	Roman Catholic, Jewish, Baptist, Presbyterian
Colorado	CO	RM	27	1	Lutheran, Roman Catholic, Congregational, Methodist
Connecticut	CT	NE	36	2	Roman Catholic, Congregational, Jewish
Delaware	DE	MA	4	0	Jewish
District of Columbia	DC	MA	36	2	Roman Catholic, Methodist
Florida	FL	SE	42	2	Baptist, Jewish, Presbyterian, Independent, Roman Catholic
Georgia	GA	SE	38	2	Baptist, Methodist, Presbyterian

TABLE 2.1 (continued)
Total 1978 *American Library Directory* Questionnaires by State and Region

State or Province	State or Province Abbreviation	Regional Abbreviation	Useable Questionnaires Obtained	Percentage	Most Popular Denomination(s)
Hawaii	HI	W	11	1	9 tied
Idaho	ID	W	5	0	5 tied
Illinois	IL	MW	92	5	Roman Catholic, Methodist, Presbyterian, Jewish
Indiana	IN	MW	54	3	Roman Catholic, Methodist
Iowa	IA	MW	33	2	Roman Catholic, Lutheran, Methodist
Kansas	KS	MW	31	2	Roman Catholic, Mennonite, Methodist
Kentucky	KY	SE	39	2	Baptist, Roman Catholic, Christian
Louisiana	LA	SW	21	1	Roman Catholic, Baptist, Methodist
Maine	ME	NE	5	0	Roman Catholic
Maryland	MD	MA	31	2	Roman Catholic, Jewish, Presbyterian
Massachusetts	MA	NE	55	3	Roman Catholic, Jewish
Michigan	MI	MW	86	4	Roman Catholic, Jewish, Reformed, Presbyterian
Minnesota	MN	MW	51	2	Lutheran, Roman Catholic, Baptist
Mississippi	MS	SE	23	1	Baptist, Methodist
Missouri	MO	MW	69	3	Baptist, Roman Catholic, Christian
Montana	MT	RM	5	0	Roman Catholic
Nebraska	NE	MW	20	1	Methodist, Lutheran
Nevada	NV	W	2	0	2 tied
New Hampshire	NH	NE	6	0	Roman Catholic
New Jersey	NJ	MA	51	2	Roman Catholic, Jewish, Presbyterian
New Mexico	NM	SW	13	1	Presbyterian, Roman Catholic

TABLE 2.1 (continued)
Total 1978 *American Library Directory* Questionnaires by State and Region

State or Province	State or Province Abbre- viation	Regional Abbre- viation	Useable Question- naires Obtained	Percent- age	Most Popular Denomination(s)
New York	NY	MA	137	7	Roman Catholic, Jewish, Independent
North Carolina	NC	SE	60	3	Baptist, Presbyterian, Methodist
North Dakota	ND	MW	9	0	Roman Catholic, Presbyterian
Ohio	OH	MW	108	5	Roman Catholic, Methodist, Jewish, Presbyterian
Oklahoma	OK	SW	21	1	Baptist, Christian
Oregon	OR	W	22	1	Baptist, Presbyterian, Roman Catholic
Pennsylvania	PA	MA	173	8	Roman Catholic, Jewish, Presbyterian, Methodist
Rhode Island	RI	NE	7	0	Roman Catholic, Jewish
South Carolina	SC	SE	24	1	Baptist, Methodist
South Dakota	SD	MW	14	1	Baptist, Lutheran, Roman Catholic
Tennessee	TN	SE	59	3	Baptist, Methodist, Presbyterian
Texas	TX	SW	106	5	Baptist, Roman Catholic, Methodist, Presbyterian
Utah	UT	RM	5	0	Mormon
Vermont	VT	NE	5	0	Roman Catholic
Virginia	VA	SE	37	2	Baptist, Methodist, Episcopal, Presbyterian
Washington	WA	W	22	1	Roman Catholic, Methodist
West Virginia	WV	SE	9	0	Presbyterian
Wisconsin	WI	MW	58	3	Roman Catholic, Lutheran
Wyoming	WY	RM	0	0	—
Total			2062	100	

TABLE 2.2
Total 1988 *American Library Directory* Questionnaires by State and Region

State or Province	State or Province Abbre- viation	Regional Abbre- viation	Useable Question- naires Obtained	Percent- age	Most Popular Denomination(s)
Canada					
Alberta	AB	CA	21	1	Roman Catholic, Lutheran, United Church Canada
British Columbia	BC	CA	6	0	6 tied
Manitoba	MB	CA	15	1	Mennonite, Roman Catholic
New Brunswick	NB	CA	3	0	3 tied
Newfoundland	NF	CA	1	0	Episcopal
Northwest Territories	NT	CA	0	0	—
Nova Scotia	NS	CA	8	0	Roman Catholic
Ontario	ON	CA	47	2	Roman Catholic, Jewish, United Church Canada
Quebec	PQ	CA	72	3	Roman Catholic, Independent, Jewish
Saskatchewan	SK	CA	13	1	Roman Catholic, Lutheran
Prince Edward Island	PE	CA	0	0	—
Yukon	YT	CA	0	0	—
United States					
Alabama	AL	SE	23	1	Baptist, Presbyterian, Methodist
Alaska	AK	W	4	0	4 tied
Arizona	AZ	SW	15	1	Baptist, Jewish, Lutheran, Roman Catholic
Arkansas	AR	SW	13	1	Baptist, Methodist
California	CA	W	116	6	Roman Catholic, Jewish, Presbyterian
Colorado	CO	RM	21	1	Roman Catholic, Congregational, Methodist
Connecticut	CT	NE	30	1	Roman Catholic, Jewish
Delaware	DE	MA	6	0	Jewish, Methodist
District of Columbia	DC	MA	30	1	Roman Catholic, Methodist

TABLE 2.2 (continued)
Total 1988 *American Library Directory* Questionnaires by State and Region

State or Province	State or Province Abbre-viation	Regional Abbre-viation	Useable Question-naires Obtained	Percent-age	Most Popular Denomination(s)
Florida	FL	SE	48	2	Jewish, Baptist, Methodist, Presbyterian
Georgia	GA	SE	31	2	Methodist, Baptist, Presbyterian
Hawaii	HI	W	7	0	Independent, plus 5 tied
Idaho	ID	W	6	0	Roman Catholic
Illinois	IL	MW	87	4	Roman Catholic, Methodist, Jewish
Indiana	IN	MW	58	3	Roman Catholic, Methodist
Iowa	IA	MW	35	2	Roman Catholic, Methodist, Lutheran
Kansas	KS	MW	28	1	Roman Catholic, Mennonite, Methodist
Kentucky	KY	SE	41	2	Baptist, Roman Catholic, Christian, Methodist
Louisiana	LA	SW	16	1	Baptist, Roman Catholic
Maine	ME	NE	3	0	3 tied
Maryland	MD	MA	33	2	Roman Catholic, Jewish, Presbyterian
Massachusetts	MA	NE	53	3	Roman Catholic, Jewish, Independent, Methodist
Michigan	MI	MW	71	3	Roman Catholic, Jewish, Reformed
Minnesota	MN	MW	55	3	Lutheran, Roman Catholic, Baptist
Mississippi	MS	SE	22	1	Baptist, Methodist, Presbyterian
Missouri	MO	MW	70	3	Baptist, Roman Catholic, Christian
Montana	MT	RM	3	0	Roman Catholic
Nebraska	NE	MW	22	1	Christian, Lutheran, Methodist

TABLE 2.2 (continued)
Total 1988 *American Library Directory* Questionnaires by State and Region

State or Province	State or Province Abbreviation	Regional Abbreviation	Useable Questionnaires Obtained	Percentage	Most Popular Denomination(s)
Nevada	NV	W	2	0	Mormon, Salvation Army
New Hampshire	NH	NE	7	0	Roman Catholic
New Jersey	NJ	MA	46	2	Jewish, Roman Catholic, Presbyterian
New Mexico	NM	SW	17	1	Baptist, Methodist
New York	NY	MA	140	7	Roman Catholic, Jewish, Independent, Episcopal
North Carolina	NC	SE	63	3	Baptist, Methodist, Presbyterian
North Dakota	ND	MW	8	0	Roman Catholic, Presbyterian
Ohio	OH	MW	96	5	Jewish, Roman Catholic, Methodist
Oklahoma	OK	SW	21	1	Baptist, Methodist
Oregon	OR	W	19	1	Baptist, Roman Catholic
Pennsylvania	PA	MA	162	8	Roman Catholic, Jewish, Presbyterian
Rhode Island	RI	NE	12	1	Roman Catholic, Jewish
South Carolina	SC	SE	21	1	Baptist, Methodist
South Dakota	SD	MW	13	1	Baptist, Lutheran, Roman Catholic
Tennessee	TN	SE	57	3	Methodist, Baptist, Presbyterian
Texas	TX	SW	117	6	Baptist, Methodist, Roman Catholic, Presbyterian
Utah	UT	RM	5	0	Mormon
Vermont	VT	NE	6	0	Roman Catholic
Virginia	VA	SE	43	2	Baptist, Methodist, Presbyterian
Washington	WA	W	24	1	Roman Catholic, Lutheran, Methodist
West Virginia	WV	SE	10	0	Presbyterian
Wisconsin	WI	MW	52	3	Roman Catholic, Lutheran
Wyoming	WY	RM	0	0	—
Total			2,074	100	

TABLE 2.3
Total 1978 *American Library Directory* Scholarly Libraries by Region

Region	Number	Percentage
Northeast	76	6
Middle Atlantic	264	19
Southeast	267	19
Southwest	112	8
West	119	9
Rocky Mountains	27	2
Middle West	412	30
Canada	98	7
Total	1,375	100

TABLE 2.4
1988 *American Library Directory* Regional Scholarly and Popular Library Composition by State/Province

Region and State/Province	Libraries	Percentage	Percentage of Total
Northeast	111	100	5
Massachusetts	53	48	
Connecticut	30	27	
Rhode Island	12	11	
New Hampshire	7	6	
Vermont	6	5	
Maine	3	3	
Middle Atlantic	417	100	20
Pennsylvania	162	39	
New York	140	34	
New Jersey	46	11	
Maryland	33	8	
District of Columbia	30	7	
Delaware	6	1	
Southeast	359	100	17
North Carolina	63	18	
Tennessee	57	16	
Florida	48	13	
Virginia	43	12	
Kentucky	41	11	
Georgia	31	9	
Alabama	23	6	
Mississippi	22	6	
South Carolina	21	6	
West Virginia	10	3	
Southwest	199	100	10
Texas	117	59	

TABLE 2.4 (continued)
1988 *American Library Directory* Regional Scholarly and Popular Library Composition by State/Province

Region and State/Province	Libraries	Percentage	Percentage of Total
Oklahoma	21	11	
New Mexico	17	9	
Louisiana	16	8	
Arizona	15	8	
Arkansas	13	6	
West	178	100	9
California	116	65	
Washington	24	13	
Oregon	19	11	
Hawaii	7	4	
Idaho	6	3	
Alaska	4	2	
Nevada	2	1	
Rocky Mountains	29	100	1
Colorado	21	73	
Utah	5	17	
Montana	3	10	
Middle West	595	100	29
Ohio	96	16	
Illinois	87	15	
Michigan	71	12	
Missouri	70	12	
Indiana	58	10	
Minnesota	55	9	
Wisconsin	52	9	
Iowa	35	6	
Kansas	28	5	
Nebraska	22	4	
South Dakota	13	2	
North Dakota	8	1	
Canada	186	100	9
Quebec	72	39	
Ontario	47	25	
Alberta	21	11	
Manitoba	15	8	
Saskatchewan	13	7	
Nova Scotia	8	4	
British Columbia	6	3	
New Brunswick	3	2	
Newfoundland	1	1	
Total	2,074	100	100

TABLE 2.5
Total 1988 *American Library Directory* Scholarly Libraries by Region[1]

Region	Number	Percentage
Northeast	76	5
Middle Atlantic	261	18
Southeast	266	19
Southwest	117	8
West	128	9
Rocky Mountains	21	1
Middle West	398	28
Canada	165	12
Total	1,432	100

1. One library from the 1988 sample fell into both the scholarly and popular categories. For this reason, scholarly tables sum to either 1,431 or 1,432 libraries. Either total may be correct depending on the variable being studied.

TABLE 2.6
1978 and 1988 *American Library Directory* Longitudinal Scholarly Library Geographical Data Summary

	1978				1988			
Basic Data	U.S.A.	Canada	Entire Sample	Ratios	U.S.A.	Canada	Entire Sample	Ratios
Number of Libraries	1,277	98	1,375	1277:98 13.0:1.0	1,267	165	1,432	1267:165 7.7:1.0
Percentage	92.9	7.1	100		88.5	11.5	100	

TABLE 2.7
1978 *American Library Directory* Scholarly Chief Librarian's Gender by Region

Region	Male	%	Female	%	No Response	%	Number of Libraries
Northeast	37	48	32	43	7	9	76
Middle Atlantic	145	55	105	40	14	5	264
Southeast	112	42	139	52	16	6	267
Southwest	49	44	57	51	6	5	112
West	56	47	57	48	6	5	119
Rocky Mountains	18	67	8	30	1	4	27
Middle West	223	54	168	41	21	5	412
Canada	61	62	27	28	10	10	98
Total	701	51	593	43	81	6	1,375

TABLE 2.8
1988 *American Library Directory* Scholarly Chief Librarian's Gender by Region

Region	Male	%	Female	%	No Response	%	Number of Libraries
Northeast	37	49	38	50	1	1	76
Middle Atlantic	138	53	120	46	3	1	261
Southeast	128	48	134	50	4	2	266
Southwest	63	54	50	43	4	3	117
West	75	59	53	41	0	0	128
Rocky Mountains	12	57	9	43	0	0	21
Middle West	211	53	183	46	4	1	398
Canada	105	64	57	35	3	2	165
Total	769	54	644	45	19	1	1,432

TABLE 2.9
1978 and 1988 *American Library Directory* Longitudinal Study Scholarly Institutional Student Enrollment for Canada and the United States for Matched Pairs

	---------------1 9 7 8---------------				---------------1 9 8 8---------------				
Region	Number of Libraries	No Response	Total Libraries	Mean Students	Number of Libraries	No Response	Total Libraries	Mean Students	Percentage Change 1978–88
Canada	43	40	83	1,701	48	37	85	2,058	21.0
U.S.A.	917	169	1,086	1,107	926	160	1,086	1,213	9.6
Total	960	209	1,169	1,134	974	197	1,171	1,255	10.7

TABLE 2.10
1978 and 1988 *American Library Directory* Longitudinal Study Scholarly Institutional Student Enrollment per Faculty Member for Canada and the United States

	---------------1 9 7 8---------------				---------------1 9 8 8---------------				
Region	Number of Libraries	No Response	Total Libraries	Mean Students	Number of Libraries	No Response	Total Libraries	Mean Students	Percentage Change 1978–88
Canada	34	64	98	17	63	101	164	19	12.0
U.S.A.	992	285	1,277	15	945	322	1,267	15	0.0
Total	1,026	349	1,375	15	1,008	423	1,431	16	6.7

TABLE 2.11
1978 and 1988 *American Library Directory* Longitudinal Study
Scholarly Student Enrollment per Library Staff Member for Canada and the United States

	---------------1 9 7 8---------------				---------------1 9 8 8---------------				
Region	Number of Libraries	No Response	Total Libraries	Mean Students	Number of Libraries	No Response	Total Libraries	Mean Students	Percentage Change 1978–88
U.S.A.	653	624	1,277	78	735	532	1,267	70	−10.0
Canada	38	60	98	118	70	94	164	115	−2.5
Total	691	684	1,375	80	805	626	1,431	74	−7.5

TABLE 2.12
1978 and 1988 *American Library Directory* Longitudinal Study
Scholarly Institutional Faculty Members for Canada and the United States

	---------------1 9 7 8---------------				---------------1 9 8 8---------------				
Region	Number of Libraries	No Response	Total Libraries	Mean Faculty	Number of Libraries	No Response	Total Libraries	Mean Faculty	Percentage Change 1978–88
Canada	34	64	98	98	66	98	164	104	6.1
U.S.A.	994	283	1,277	71	947	320	1,267	81	14.1
Total	1,028	347	1,375	72	1,013	418	1,431	83	15.3

TABLE 2.13
1978 and 1988 *American Library Directory* Longitudinal Study
Scholarly Total Library Holdings (Cumulative) for Canada and the United States[1]

	---------------1 9 7 8---------------				---------------1 9 8 8---------------				
Region	Number of Libraries	No Response	Total Libraries	Mean Holdings	Number of Libraries	No Response	Total Libraries	Mean Holdings	Percentage Change 1978–88
Canada	82	16	98	122,500	157	7	164	122,700	0.2
U.S.A.	1,193	84	1,277	104,900	1,232	35	1,267	140,800	34.2
Total	1,275	100	1,375	106,100	1,389	42	1,431	138,800	31.8

1. The holdings variable equals the sum of holdings for book volumes, periodical titles, microforms, vertical files, media, maps, and art reproductions.

TABLE 2.14
1978 and 1988 *American Library Directory* Longitudinal Study
Scholarly Library Total Annual Expenditure (Cumulative) for Canada and the United States[1]

	---1978---				---1988---				
Region	Number of Libraries	No Response	Total Libraries	Mean Dollars	Number of Libraries	No Response	Total Libraries	Mean Dollars	Percentage Change 1978–88
Canada	52	46	98	$194,400	108	56	164	$240,400	24
U.S.A.	970	307	1,277	$134,800	993	274	1,267	$244,500	81
Total	1,022	353	1,375	$137,800	1,101	330	1,431	$244,100	77

1. This variable equals the sum of material plus personnel plus other expenditures OR total annual library expenditure, whichever was greater, as in some cases, a total expenditure figure was given by the *ALD*, but with no indication of component expenditures.

TABLE 2.15
1978 and 1988 *American Library Directory* Longitudinal Study
Academic Library Distribution for Canada and the United States

	Canada			United States			Canada/U.S. Ratio Value		Totals		
Library Type	1978	1988	% Change	1978	1988	% Change	1978	1988	1978	1988	% Change
Academic	82	144	76	1,134	1,088	−4	.07	.13	1,216	1,232	1.3
Junior College	7	15	114	118	93	−21	.06	.16	125	108	−14
Senior College	42	76	81	662	629	−5	.06	.12	704	705	0
University	25	29	16	129	160	24	.19	.18	154	189	23
Seminary	8	24	200	225	206	−8	.04	.12	233	230	−1

TABLE 2.16
1978 *American Library Directory* Scholarly and Popular Libraries by Age

Founding Date	Number of Libraries	Percentage
1981+	0	0
1971–1980	38	2
1961–1970	183	9
1941–1960	435	21
1921–1940	236	11
1901–1920	171	8
1881–1900	180	9
1861–1880	124	6
1841–1860	126	6
1821–1840	49	2
1801–1820	16	1
0–1800	13	1
No Response	491	24
Total	2,062	100
Mean		Year: 1905.1 or 72.9 Years Old

TABLE 2.17
1988 *American Library Directory* Scholarly and Popular Libraries by Age

Founding Date	Number of Libraries	Percentage
1981+	9	0
1971–1980	87	4
1961–1970	210	10
1941–1960	422	20
1921–1940	233	11
1901–1920	163	8
1881–1900	183	9
1861–1880	125	6
1841–1860	120	6
1821–1840	60	3
1801–1820	17	1
0–1800	16	1
No Response	429	21
Total	2,074	100
Mean		Year: 1917 or 71 Years Old

TABLE 2.18
1978 and 1988 *American Library Directory* Longitudinal Study of Scholarly Library Age in Years for Canada and the United States

	1978				1988				
Region	Number of Libraries	No Response	Total Libraries	Mean Years	Number of Libraries	No Response	Total Libraries	Mean Years	Percentage Change 1978–88
Canada	80	18	98	75	117	47	164	68	−9
U.S.A.	1,172	105	1,277	81	1,155	112	1,267	81	0
Total	1,252	123	1,375	80	1,272	159	1,431	80	0

TABLE 2.19
1978 and 1988 *American Library Directory* Longitudinal Study Scholarly Library City Population Size for Canada and the United States

	1978				1988				
Region	Number of Libraries	No Response	Total Libraries	Mean Persons	Number of Libraries	No Response	Total Libraries	Mean Persons	Percentage Change 1978–88
Canada	98	0	98	432,600	164	0	164	428,800	−0.9
U.S.A.	1,277	0	1,277	336,600	1,266	1	1,267	324,000	−3.7
Total	1,375	0	1,375	343,500	1,430	1	1,431	336,100	−2.1

TABLE 2.20
1978 and 1988 *American Library Directory* Longitudinal Study Scholarly Library Professional Staff Members for Canada and the United States

	1978				1988				
Region	Number of Libraries	No Response	Total Libraries	Mean Members	Number of Libraries	No Response	Total Libraries	Mean Members	Percentage Change 1978–88
Canada	47	51	98	3.8	83	81	164	3.7	−3
U.S.A.	712	565	1,277	3.8	813	454	1,267	4.0	5
Total	759	616	1,375	3.8	896	535	1,431	4.0	5

TABLE 2.21
1978 and 1988 *American Library Directory* Longitudinal Study
Scholarly Library Clerical Staff Members for Canada and the United States

	1978				1988				
Region	Number of Libraries	No Response	Total Libraries	Mean Members	Number of Libraries	No Response	Total Libraries	Mean Members	Percentage Change 1978–88
Canada	44	54	98	6.6	88	76	164	5.9	−11.0
U.S.A.	677	600	1,277	4.6	770	497	1,267	5.0	8.7
Total	721	654	1,375	4.7	858	573	1,431	5.1	8.5

TABLE 2.22
1978 and 1988 *American Library Directory* Longitudinal Study
Scholarly Institutional Educational Activity Variable for Canada and the United States for Matched Pairs[1]

	1978				1988				
Region	Number of Institutions	No Response	Total Institutions	Mean Units	Number of Institutions	No Response	Total Institutions	Mean Units	Percentage Change 1978–88
Canada	65	18	83	1,180	55	30	85	1,882	59
U.S.A.	950	136	1,086	1,144	951	135	1,086	1,264	10
Total	1,015	154	1,169	1,146	1,006	165	1,171	1,298	13

1. This variable contains the scores for faculty members, student enrollment, and degrees awarded.

TABLE 2.23
1978 and 1988 *American Library Directory* Longitudinal Study
Scholarly Institution Total Library Staff per Degree Year Awarded for Canada and the United States

	1978				1988				
Region	Number of Libraries	No Response	Total Libraries	Mean Ratio Value	Number of Libraries	No Response	Total Libraries	Mean Ratio Value	Percentage Change 1978–88
Canada	40	58	98	3.4	62	102	164	3.5	3
U.S.A.	648	629	1,277	3.9	733	534	1,267	4.8	23
Total	688	687	1,375	3.9	795	636	1,431	4.7	21

TABLE 2.24
1978 and 1988 *American Library Directory* Longitudinal Study
Scholarly Libraries with Material Expenditure for Canada and the United States

	1978				1988				
Region	Number of Libraries	No Response	Total Libraries	Mean Dollars	Number of Libraries	No Response	Total Libraries	Mean Dollars	Percentage Change 1978–88
Canada	39	59	98	$64,810	98	66	164	$69,780	7.7
U.S.A.	710	567	1,277	$48,580	959	308	1,267	$82,700	70.0
Total	749	626	1,375	$49,430	1,057	374	1,431	$81,500	65.0

TABLE 2.25
1978 and 1988 *American Library Directory* Longitudinal Study
Scholarly Libraries with Personnel Expenditure for Canada and the United States

	1978				1988				
Region	Number of Libraries	No Response	Total Libraries	Mean Dollars	Number of Libraries	No Response	Total Libraries	Mean Dollars	Percentage Change 1978–88
Canada	34	64	98	$141,000	91	73	164	$154,200	9.2
U.S.A.	642	635	1,277	$89,890	904	363	1,267	$140,200	56.0
Total	676	699	1,375	$92,460	995	436	1,431	$141,500	53.0

TABLE 2.26
1978 and 1988 *American Library Directory* Longitudinal Study
Scholarly Library Volume Holdings for Canada and the United States

	1978				1988				
Region	Number of Libraries	No Response	Total Libraries	Mean Volumes	Number of Libraries	No Response	Total Libraries	Mean Volumes	Percentage Change 1978–88
Canada	81	17	98	104,300	156	8	164	104,000	−0.2
U.S.A.	1,177	100	1,277	92,630	1,225	42	1,267	113,800	23.0
Total	1,258	117	1,375	93,380	1,381	50	1,431	112,700	20.7

TABLE 2.27
1978 and 1988 *American Library Directory* Longitudinal Study Entire Sample Libraries Answering Questions for Canada and the United States

	1978				1988				
Region	Number of Libraries	No Response	Total Libraries	Mean Questions Answered	Number of Libraries	No Response	Total Libraries	Mean Questions Answered	Percentage Change 1978–88
Canada	125	0	125	20	186	0	186	22	10.0
U.S.A.	1,937	0	1,937	23	1,888	0	1,888	24	4.3
Total	2,062	0	2,062	22	2,074	0	2,074	24	9.0

TABLE 2.28
1978 and 1988 *American Library Directory* Longitudinal Study of Scholarly Chief Librarians' Gender by Nation

	1978			1988			Totals		1978–1988 % Change		
Region/ Nation	Male	Female	No Response	Male	Female	No Response	1978	1988	Male	Female	No Response
U.S. Scholarly	640	566	71	664	587	16	1,277	1,267	4	4	−77
Percentage	50	44	6	52	46	1	100	100			
Canada	61	27	10	104	57	3	98	164	70	111	−70
Scholarly	62	28	10	63	35	2	100	100			
Percentage											
Total	786	923	353	851	1,150	73	2,062	2,074	8	25	−79
All Scholarly	701	593	81	768	644	19	1,375	1,431	10	9	−77
Percentage	51	43	6	54	45	1	100	100			
U.S. Total	716	885	336	739	1,079	70	1,937	1,888	3	22	−79
Percentage	37	46	17	39	57	4	100	100			
Canada Total	70	38	17	112	71	3	125	186	60	87	−82
Percentage	56	30	14	60	38	2	100	100			

TABLE 2.29
1978 *American Library Directory* Regional Scholarly and Popular Library Composition by State/Province

Region and State/Province	Libraries	Percentage	Percentage of Total
Northeast	114	100	6
Massachusetts	55	48	
Connecticut	36	32	
Rhode Island	7	6	
New Hampshire	6	5	
Maine	5	4	
Vermont	5	4	
Middle Atlantic	432	100	21
Pennsylvania	173	40	
New York	137	32	
New Jersey	51	12	
District of Columbia	36	8	
Maryland	31	7	
Delaware	4	1	
Southeast	358	100	17
North Carolina	60	17	
Tennessee	59	16	
Florida	42	12	
Kentucky	39	11	
Georgia	38	11	
Virginia	37	10	
Alabama	27	8	
South Carolina	24	7	
Mississippi	23	6	
West Virginia	9	3	
Southwest	189	100	9
Texas	106	56	
Louisiana	21	11	
Oklahoma	21	11	
Arkansas	15	8	
Arizona	13	7	
New Mexico	13	7	
West	182	100	9
California	116	64	
Oregon	22	12	
Washington	22	12	
Hawaii	11	6	
Idaho	5	3	
Alaska	4	2	
Nevada	2	1	

TABLE 2.29 (continued)
1978 *American Library Directory* Regional Scholarly and Popular Library Composition by State/Province

Region and State/Province	Libraries	Percentage	Percentage of Total
Rocky Mountains	37	100	2
Colorado	27	73	
Montana	5	14	
Utah	5	14	
Middle West	625	100	30
Ohio	108	17	
Illinois	92	15	
Michigan	86	14	
Missouri	69	11	
Wisconsin	58	9	
Indiana	54	9	
Minnesota	51	8	
Iowa	33	5	
Kansas	31	5	
Nebraska	20	3	
South Dakota	14	2	
North Dakota	9	1	
Canada	125	100	6
Quebec	49	39	
Ontario	36	29	
Saskatchewan	11	9	
Nova Scotia	9	7	
Alberta	8	6	
Manitoba	6	5	
New Brunswick	3	2	
British Columbia	2	2	
Newfoundland	1	1	
Total	2,062	100	100

TABLE 2.30
1978 *American Library Directory* Scholarly Libraries by Region and Leading Denominations[1]

Region	Number of Libraries	Percentage
Northeast		
Roman Catholic	47	63
Independent	8	11
Other Denominations	8	11
Middle Atlantic		
Roman Catholic	133	51
Other Denominations	39	15
Jewish	18	7
Independent	15	6
Southeast		
Baptist	64	24
Methodist	64	24
Presbyterian	34	13
Roman Catholic	24	9
Southwest		
Baptist	26	23
Roman Catholic	25	22
Methodist	15	13
Other Denominations	12	11
West		
Other Denominations	33	28
Roman Catholic	33	28
Baptist	12	10
Independent	12	10
Rocky Mountains		
Other Denominations	10	38
Roman Catholic	7	27
Methodist	3	12
Middle West		
Roman Catholic	144	35
Other Denominations	78	19
Lutheran	42	10
Methodist	42	10
Canadian		
Roman Catholic	56	63
Episcopal/Anglican	11	12
Other Denominations	11	12
Total	1,026	50

1. Only the most common denominations are listed for each region.

TABLE 2.31
1988 *American Library Directory* Scholarly Libraries by Region and Leading Denominations[1]

Region	Number of Libraries	Percentage
Northeast		
Roman Catholic	41	54
Other Denominations	12	16
Independent	8	11
Methodist	5	7
Middle Atlantic		
Roman Catholic	121	47
Other Denominations	37	14
Jewish	20	8
Independent	16	6
Southeast		
Baptist	66	25
Methodist	59	22
Presbyterian	34	13
Other Denominations	24	9
Southwest		
Baptist	31	26
Roman Catholic	23	20
Methodist	16	14
Other Denominations	11	9
West		
Roman Catholic	36	28
Other Denominations	33	26
Independent	12	9
Baptist	10	8
Rocky Mountains		
Other Denominations	7	33
Roman Catholic	6	29
Methodist	3	14
Middle West		
Roman Catholic	125	31
Other Denominations	67	17
Methodist	43	11
Lutheran	40	10
Canadian		
Roman Catholic	87	53
Other Denominations	26	16
Independent	11	7
Baptist	9	5
Total	1,039	50

1. Only the most common denominations are listed for each region.

TABLE 2.32
Canadian and U.S. Religious Pies: Distribution of the National Populations by Denomination: 1986 and 1990

Canadian House of Worship Membership

Religious Faith or Denomination	Estimated Number of Persons	% of Total
Roman Catholic	12,288,000	48.0
United Church of Canada	4,352,000	17.0
Episcopal/Anglican	4,352,000	17.0
Lutheran	768,000	3.0
Baptist	640,000	2.5
Presbyterian	640,000	2.5
Orthodox, Jewish, Islamic, Sikh, Hindu, or Buddhist	896,000	3.5
No religion listed	1,664,000	6.5
All Protestant	10,752,000	42.0
Total	25,600,000	100.0

Source: J. S. Moir (Knox College), "Canadian Religious Historiography: An Overview (for 1990)," American Theological Library Association Proceedings (Winter 1991): 95–119.

U.S. House of Worship Membership

Religious Group	Members	% of Total
Protestant Bodies and Others	77,253,700	54.9
Roman Catholic	52,392,934	37.2
Jewish	5,728,075	4.1
Eastern Orthodox	4,033,668	2.9
Old Catholic, etc.	1,149,687	0.8
Buddhist	70,000	0.0
Miscellaneous	188,321	0.1
Total	140,816,385	100.0

Source: Information Please Almanac (New York: Houghton Mifflin, 1986), p. 413.

TABLE 2.33
1988 *American Library Directory* Scholarly Library Age by Region

Region	Number of Libraries	No Response	Total Number of Libraries	Mean Age
Northeast	67	9	76	77
Middle Atlantic	232	29	261	82
Southeast	245	21	266	88
Southwest	106	11	117	66
West	113	15	128	65
Rocky Mountains	20	1	21	75
Middle West	372	26	398	85
Canada	117	48	165	68
Total	1,272	160	1,432	80

TABLE 2.34
1988 *American Library Directory* Scholarly Libraries by Denomination

Denomination	Number of Libraries	Percentage
	Junior College	
Roman Catholic	44	41
Methodist	18	17
Other Denominations	14	13
Lutheran	9	8
Baptist	7	6
Churches of Christ	5	5
Presbyterian	5	5
Mennonite	3	3
Episcopal/Anglican	2	2
Christian	1	1
Total	108	100
	Senior College	
Roman Catholic	203	29
Other Denominations	118	17
Methodist	81	11
Baptist	78	11
Presbyterian	62	9
Independent	40	6
Lutheran	36	5
Christian	30	4
United Church of Christ	15	2
Churches of Christ	13	2
Mennonite	12	2
Jewish	9	1
Episcopal/Anglican	8	1
Total	705	100

TABLE 2.34 (continued)
1988 *American Library Directory* Scholarly Libraries by Denomination

Denomination	Number of Libraries	Percentage
	University	
Roman Catholic	74	39
Baptist	28	15
Methodist	25	13
Other Denominations	17	9
Independent	11	6
Lutheran	7	4
Presbyterian	7	4
Churches of Christ	5	3
Jewish	5	3
Episcopal/Anglican	4	2
Christian	3	2
United Church of Christ	3	2
Total	189	100
	Seminary	
Roman Catholic	75	32
Other Denominations	32	14
Independent	26	11
Baptist	25	11
Methodist	15	7
Lutheran	12	5
Presbyterian	12	5
Episcopal/Anglican	10	4
Jewish	10	4
Christian	5	2
Churches of Christ	4	2
United Church of Christ	4	2
Mennonite	1	0
Total	231	100
	Convent/Monastery	
Roman Catholic	24	96
Lutheran	1	4
Total	25	100
	Denominational Headquarters	
Roman Catholic	23	27
Other Denominations	18	21
Independent	17	20
Jewish	10	12
Baptist	5	6
Lutheran	5	6
Episcopal/Anglican	3	3
Presbyterian	2	2
Christian	1	1

TABLE 2.34 (continued)
1988 *American Library Directory* Scholarly Libraries by Denomination

Denomination	Number of Libraries	Percentage
Mennonite	1	1
Methodist	1	1
Total	86	100
	History/Archives	
Other Denominations	18	21
Roman Catholic	16	18
Jewish	11	12
Baptist	9	10
Methodist	9	10
Lutheran	6	7
Episcopal/Anglican	5	6
Mennonite	5	6
Independent	3	3
United Church of Christ	3	3
Presbyterian	2	2
Christian	1	1
Total	88	100
Grand Total (All Scholarly)	1,432	100

TABLE 2.35
1978 and 1988 *American Library Directory* Scholarly Library Demographics: Regional Distribution by Edition Showing Percentage Change[1]

	1978	Percentage of Sample	1988	Percentage of Sample	Percentage Change
Northeast	76	5.5	76	5.3	0
Middle Atlantic	264	19.2	261	18.2	−1
Southeast	267	19.4	266	18.6	0
Southwest	112	8.1	117	8.2	4
West	119	8.7	128	8.9	8
Rocky Mountains	27	2.0	21	1.5	−22
Middle West	412	30.0	398	27.8	−3
Canada	98	7.1	165	11.5	68
Total	1,375	100.0	1,432	100.0	4

1. Percentage change in the final column is based on the change in library frequencies shown in columns 1 and 3 and not in columns 2 and 4.

TABLE 2.36
Total 1978 *American Library Directory* Denominational Breakdown

Rank	Denomination	Number of Libraries	Percentage
1	Roman Catholic	513	25
2	Baptist	223	11
3	Presbyterian	205	10
4	Methodist	202	10
5	Jewish	198	10
6	Lutheran	123	6
7	Independent	87	4
8	Episcopal/Anglican	74	4
9	Christian/Disciples of Christ	59	3
10	Unknown	51	3
11	United Church of Christ	37	2
12	Congregational	33	2
13	Churches of Christ	27	1
14	Friends	25	1
15	Reformed	19	1
16	Mennonite	17	1
17	Adventist	16	1
18	Brethren	16	1
19	Church of Jesus Christ of Latter-day Saints	16	1
20	Assemblies of God	13	1
21	Church of God	13	1
22	Church of Nazarene	12	1
23	Christian and Missionary Alliance	7	0
24	Eastern Orthodox	7	0
25	Theosophy	7	0
26	Unitarian-Universalist	7	0
27	United Church of Canada	7	0
28	Swedenborgian	5	0
29	Moravian	4	0
30	Pentecostal	4	0
31	Christian Science	3	0
32	Evangelical Covenant	3	0
33	Salvation Army	3	0
34	Shaker	3	0
35	Missionary Church	2	0
36	Open Bible Standard	2	0
37	Unity	2	0
38	Wesleyan	2	0
39	Bahai	1	0
40	Bible Fellowship	1	0
41	Christian Evangelical Church of America	1	0

TABLE 2.36 (continued)
Total 1978 *American Library Directory* Denominational Breakdown

Rank	Denomination	Number of Libraries	Percentage
42	Church of Scientology	1	0
43	Evangelical Free	1	0
44	Grace Gospel Fellowship	1	0
45	International Church of the Four Square Gospel	1	0
46	Jehovah's Witnesses	1	0
47	Muslim	1	0
48	Pentecostal Holiness	1	0
49	Pillar of Fire	1	0
50	Rosicrucian	1	0
51	Schwenkfelder	1	0
52	Spiritual Frontiers Fellowship	1	0
53	United Church of Religious Science	1	0
Total		2,062	100

TABLE 2.37
Total 1988 *American Library Directory* Denominational Breakdown

Rank	Denomination	Number of Libraries	Percentage
1	Roman Catholic	490	24
2	Jewish	232	11
3	Baptist	223	11
4	Methodist	213	10
5	Presbyterian	187	9
6	Lutheran	118	6
7	Independent	100	5
8	Episcopal/Anglican	66	3
9	Christian/Disciples of Christ	58	3
10	Unknown	43	2
11	United Church of Christ	38	2
12	Churches of Christ	29	1
13	Mennonite	26	1
14	Congregational	23	1
15	Friends	23	1
16	Reformed	19	1
17	Adventist	17	1
18	Church of Jesus Christ of Latter-day Saints	17	1
19	Church of God	15	1
20	Brethren	14	1

TABLE 2.37 (continued)
Total 1988 *American Library Directory* Denominational Breakdown

Rank	Denomination	Number of Libraries	Percentage
21	Church of Nazarene	14	1
22	Assemblies of God	13	1
23	Eastern Orthodox	11	1
24	United Church of Canada	11	1
25	Swedenborgian	6	0
26	Theosophy	6	0
27	Christian and Missionary Alliance	5	0
28	Moravian	5	0
29	Salvation Army	5	0
30	Unitarian-Universalist	4	0
31	Buddhist	3	0
32	Christian Science	3	0
33	Missionary Church	3	0
34	Muslim	3	0
35	Shaker	3	0
36	Evangelical Church of Canada	2	0
37	Evangelical Covenant	2	0
38	Evangelical Free	2	0
39	Pentecostal	2	0
40	Pentecostal Holiness	2	0
41	Rosicrucian	2	0
42	Unity	2	0
43	Atheism	1	0
44	Bahai	1	0
45	Bible Fellowship	1	0
46	Christian Evangelical Church of America	1	0
47	Church of Scientology	1	0
48	Grace Gospel Fellowship	1	0
49	International Church of the Four Square Gospel	1	0
50	Jehovah's Witnesses	1	0
51	Open Bible Standard	1	0
52	Pillar of Fire	1	0
53	Schwenkfelder	1	0
54	Spiritualist	1	0
55	United Church of Religious Science	1	0
56	United Missionary	1	0
Total		2,074	100

TABLE 2.38
1988 *American Library Directory* Number of Libraries by State/Province for the Scholarly Group by Order of Occurrence

State or Province	Region	Scholarly Libraries 1988	% of Sample
PA	MA	107	66
NY	MA	94	67
TX	SW	67	57
CA	W	77	66
OH	MW	58	60
IL	MW	61	70
PQ	CAN	64	89
MI	MW	36	51
MO	MW	52	74
NC	SE	51	81
IN	MW	40	69
TN	SE	48	84
MN	MW	34	62
MA	NE	39	74
WI	MW	30	58
FL	SE	23	48
ON	CAN	38	81
NJ	MA	21	46
VA	SE	34	79
KY	SE	32	78
IA	MW	31	89
MD	MA	17	52
GA	SE	21	68
DC	MA	18	60
CT	NE	17	57
KS	MW	26	93
WA	W	18	75
AL	SE	13	57
MS	SE	17	77
NE	MW	16	73
SC	SE	20	95
CO	RM	14	67
OK	SW	16	76
AB	CAN	18	86
OR	W	18	95
NM	SW	2	12
LA	SW	11	69
AZ	SW	9	60
MB	CAN	15	100
AR	SW	12	92
SD	MW	9	69
SK	CAN	12	92

TABLE 2.38 (continued)
1988 *American Library Directory* Number of Libraries by State/Province for the Scholarly Group by Order of Occurrence

State or Province	Region	Scholarly Libraries 1988	% of Sample
RI	NE	7	58
WV	SE	7	70
NS	CAN	8	100
ND	MW	5	63
NH	NE	5	71
HI	W	5	71
ID	W	6	100
VT	NE	5	83
BC	CAN	6	100
DE	MA	4	67
UT	RM	4	80
AK	W	4	100
ME	NE	3	100
MT	RM	3	100
NB	CAN	3	100
NV	W	0	0
NF	CAN	1	100
TOTAL		1,432	100

TABLE 2.39
1978 and 1988 *American Library Directory* Number of Libraries by State/Province for the Scholarly Group in Alphabetical Order by Region

State or Province	Region	1978	% of Sample	1988	% of Sample	% Change
CT	NE	18	50	17	57	−6
MA		43	78	39	74	−9
ME		4	80	3	100	−25
NH		4	67	5	71	25
RI		3	43	7	58	133
VT		4	80	5	83	25
DC	MA	22	61	18	60	−18
DE		1	25	4	67	300
MD		14	45	17	52	21
NJ		24	47	21	46	−13
NY		98	72	94	67	−4
PA		105	61	107	66	2
AL	SE	14	52	13	57	−7
FL		23	55	23	48	0
GA		27	71	21	68	−22
KY		31	79	32	78	3
MS		18	78	17	77	−6

TABLE 2.39 (continued)
1978 and 1988 *American Library Directory* Number of Libraries by State/Province for the Scholarly Group in Alphabetical Order by Region

State or Province	Region	1978	% of Sample	1988	% of Sample	% Change
NC		48	80	51	81	6
SC		22	92	20	95	−9
TN		51	86	48	84	−6
VA		26	70	34	79	31
WV		7	78	7	70	0
AR	SW	12	80	12	92	0
AZ		6	46	9	60	50
LA		11	52	11	69	0
NM		3	23	2	12	−33
OK		17	81	16	76	−6
TX		63	59	67	57	6
AK	W	3	75	4	100	33
CA		75	65	77	66	3
HI		4	36	5	71	25
ID		5	100	6	100	20
NV		0	0	0	0	
OR		18	82	18	95	0
WA		14	64	18	75	29
CO	RM	19	70	14	67	−26
MT		4	80	3	100	−25
UT		4	80	4	80	0
IA	MW	32	97	31	89	−3
IL		68	74	61	70	−10
IN		36	67	40	69	11
KS		28	90	26	93	−7
MI		39	45	36	51	−8
MN		31	61	34	62	10
MO		52	75	52	74	0
ND		6	67	5	63	−17
NE		16	80	16	73	0
OH		58	54	58	60	0
SD		10	71	9	69	−10
WI		36	62	30	58	−17
BC	CAN	2	100	6	100	200
AB		8	100	18	86	125
MB		6	100	15	100	150
NB		2	67	3	100	50
NF		1	100	1	100	0
NS		9	100	8	100	−11
ON		30	83	38	81	27
PQ		30	61	64	89	113
SK		10	91	12	92	20
Total		1,375	67	1,432	69	4

TABLE 2.40
1978 and 1988 *American Library Directory* Longitudinal Study
Scholarly Library City Population Size

	1978				1988				
Library Type	Number of Libraries	No Response	Total Libraries	Mean Persons	Number of Libraries	No Response	Total Libraries	Mean Persons	Percentage Change
Scholarly	1,375	0	1,375	343,467	1,431	1	1,432	335,832	−2
Junior College	125	0	125	191,895	108	0	108	192,916	1
Senior College	704	0	704	210,447	705	0	705	222,518	6
University	154	0	154	497,403	189	0	189	439,272	−12
Seminary	233	0	233	470,129	231	0	231	447,045	−5
Convent/Monastery	35	0	35	89,044	25	0	25	101,800	14
Denominational HQ	77	0	77	1,099,448	85	1	86	780,000	−29
History/Archives	47	0	47	549,043	88	0	88	542,386	−1

TABLE 2.41
Total Number of 1988 *American Library Directory* Scholarly Libraries in Each City Population Size

City Population Size Group	Number	Percentage
1,000,001+	107	7
500,001–1,000,000	142	10
300,001–500,000	139	10
100,001–300,000	208	15
50,001–100,000	155	11
10,001–50,000	332	23
0–10,000	348	24
Not classified	1	0
Total	1,432	100
Median	61,600	
Mean	335,800	

TABLE 2.42
1978 *American Library Directory* State/Province City Population Data: Number of Scholarly Libraries in Small Cities and Mean City Size by State/Province

State or Province	Small Cities	Percent	Other Cities	All Libraries	Mean City Size
NY	28	29	70	98	1,240,969
DC	0	0	22	22	850,000
PQ	6	20	24	30	821,833
TX	9	14	54	63	353,532
ON	2	7	28	30	327,667
PA	43	41	62	105	397,929
IL	13	19	55	68	727,757
AZ	0	0	6	6	379,167
WI	10	28	26	36	282,500
WA	3	21	11	14	218,036
CA	8	11	67	75	392,905
HI	1	25	3	4	300,625
MI	10	26	29	39	360,128
OH	11	19	47	58	179,009
OK	0	0	17	17	224,706
MO	11	21	41	52	301,490
CO	2	11	17	19	425,000
IN	13	36	23	36	165,764
KY	17	55	14	31	105,565
TN	11	22	40	51	223,480
MD	1	7	13	14	441,607
MN	5	16	26	31	210,081
OR	4	22	14	18	218,889
IA	16	50	16	32	52,969
NV	0	0	0	0	0
RI	0	0	3	3	146,667
UT	0	0	4	4	168,750
AL	2	14	12	14	221,429
LA	2	18	9	11	455,455
FL	8	35	15	23	112,391
GA	10	37	17	27	145,000
MA	13	30	30	43	156,337
KS	9	32	19	28	55,089
NC	22	46	26	48	73,542
VA	9	35	17	26	79,712
NE	4	25	12	16	156,563
SC	6	27	16	22	67,727
NM	1	33	2	3	80,833
CT	5	28	13	18	87,361
AR	6	50	6	12	47,500

TABLE 2.42 (continued)
1978 *American Library Directory* State/Province City Population Data: Number of Scholarly Libraries in Small Cities and Mean City Size by State/Province

State or Province	Small Cities	Percent	Other Cities	All Libraries	Mean City Size
DE	0	0	1	1	20,000
ME	2	50	2	4	16,250
MT	1	25	3	4	44,375
NB	1	50	1	2	41,250
MS	11	61	7	18	41,806
WV	5	71	2	7	14,643
ND	2	33	4	6	30,000
NH	0	0	4	4	61,250
SD	2	20	8	10	33,500
AK	2	67	1	3	8,333
VT	1	25	3	4	21,875
NJ	9	38	15	24	39,271
SK	4	40	6	10	121,000
BC	0	0	2	2	300,000
ID	3	60	2	5	21,500
AB	1	13	7	8	260,313
MB	1	17	5	6	500,417
NF	0	0	1	1	75,000
NS	4	44	5	9	95,000
Total	370	27	1,005	1,375	343,467

TABLE 2.43
1988 *American Library Directory* State/Province City Population Data: Number of Scholarly Libraries in Small Cities and Mean City Size by State/Province

State or Province	Small Cities	Percent	Other Cities	All Libraries	Mean City Size
NY	23	24	71	94	1,181,942
PQ	9	14	54	63	656,389
IL	7	11	54	61	1,012,582
DC	0	0	18	18	600,000
AB	3	17	15	18	374,861
TX	5	7	62	67	406,903
ON	2	5	36	38	337,500
AZ	2	22	7	9	540,000
CA	8	10	69	77	403,571
IN	15	38	25	40	203,813
OK	1	6	15	16	172,031

TABLE 2.43 (continued)
1988 *American Library Directory* State/Province City Population Data: Number of Libraries in Small Cities and Mean City Size by State

State or Province	Small Cities	Percent	Other Cities	All Libraries	Mean City Size
TN	11	23	37	48	232,656
NM	1	50	1	2	21,250
WA	4	22	14	18	171,389
OH	13	22	45	58	155,991
WI	7	23	23	30	188,750
MO	11	21	41	52	208,221
HI	1	20	4	5	244,500
NC	18	35	33	51	93,725
NV	0	0	0	0	0
UT	0	0	4	4	168,750
MI	10	28	26	36	290,000
CO	1	7	13	14	240,893
PA	44	41	63	107	346,215
MN	6	18	28	34	146,912
VA	11	32	23	34	79,926
MA	11	28	28	39	202,115
LA	1	9	10	11	420,227
GA	8	38	13	21	141,190
NE	4	25	12	16	140,333
FL	5	22	18	23	164,239
MD	3	18	14	17	415,441
KY	15	47	17	32	78,203
RI	0	0	7	7	148,571
IA	14	45	17	31	55,968
CT	3	18	14	17	113,088
AL	1	8	12	13	133,654
AR	4	33	8	12	50,000
OR	2	11	16	18	213,056
ND	2	40	3	5	21,000
MS	7	41	10	17	58,088
WV	5	71	2	7	14,643
DE	0	0	4	4	61,250
NH	2	40	3	5	48,000
SD	2	22	7	9	34,444
VT	2	40	3	5	18,000
NJ	8	38	13	21	29,762
SK	3	25	9	12	123,958
KS	9	35	17	26	54,519
SC	6	30	14	20	37,500
AK	4	100	0	4	3,750

TABLE 2.43 (continued)
1988 *American Library Directory* State/Province City Population Data: Number of Libraries in Small Cities and Mean City Size by State/Province

State or Province	Small Cities	Percent	Other Cities	All Libraries	Mean City Size
BC	2	33	4	6	140,833
ID	1	17	5	6	80,417
ME	2	67	1	3	15,000
MB	5	33	10	15	401,500
MT	0	0	3	3	56,667
NB	1	33	2	3	40,833
NF	0	0	1	1	75,000
NS	3	38	5	8	106,563
Total	348	24	1,083	1,431	335,832

TABLE 2.44
1988 *American Library Directory* City Population Size by Region for Scholarly Libraries

Region	Number of Libraries	No Response	Total Libraries	Mean Number of Persons
Northeast	76	0	76	147,600
Middle Atlantic	261	0	261	639,400
Southeast	266	0	266	118,400
Southwest	117	0	117	343,100
West	128	0	128	310,300
Rocky Mountains	21	0	21	200,800
Middle West	397	1	398	293,600
Canada	165	0	165	426,400
Total	1,431	1	1,432	335,800

TABLE 2.45
1978 and 1988 *American Library Directory* Longitudinal Study
Scholarly Libraries in Small Cities by Type of Library[1,2]

Library Type	Number of Libraries in Small Cities 1978	Percentage in Small Cities 1978	Number of Libraries in Small Cities 1988	Percentage in Small Cities 1988	Percentage Change 1978–1988
Scholarly	370	27	348	24	−6
Junior College	55	44	46	43	−16
Senior College	210	30	185	26	−12
University	22	15	25	13	14
Seminary	46	20	47	20	2
Convent/ Monastery	18	51	14	56	−22
Denominational HQ	9	12	15	17	67
History/Archives	10	21	16	18	60

1. Small cities have populations of ten thousand persons or fewer.
2. The percentage change column is calculated from the increase/decrease in raw frequencies from 1978 to 1988, i.e., columns 1 and 3.

TABLE 2.46
1978 *American Library Directory* City Population Size by Denomination for Scholarly Libraries

Denomination	Number of Libraries	No Response	Total Libraries	Mean Number of Persons
Baptist	140	0	140	182,900
Christian	40	0	40	161,000
Churches of Christ	27	0	27	271,400
Congregational	5	0	5	161,500
Episcopal/Anglican	32	0	32	359,900
Independent	82	0	82	648,400
Lutheran	70	0	70	284,400
Methodist	147	0	147	148,000
Other Denominations	214	0	214	265,600
Presbyterian	90	0	90	184,200
U.C.C.	24	0	24	113,500
Summary				
Jewish	35	0	35	1,967,000
Roman Catholic	469	0	469	385,300
All Protestant	871	0	871	255,600
Total	1,375	0	1,375	343,500

TABLE 2.47
1988 *American Library Directory* City Population Size by Denomination for Scholarly Libraries

Denomination	Number of Libraries	No Response	Total Libraries	Mean Number of Persons
Baptist	152	0	152	199,400
Christian	41	0	41	153,700
Churches of Christ	27	0	27	307,300
Episcopal/Anglican	32	0	32	348,800
Independent	97	0	97	576,100
Lutheran	76	0	76	220,500
Mennonite	22	0	22	77,730
Methodist	149	0	149	137,100
Other Denominations	217	0	217	275,500
Presbyterian	90	0	90	138,600
U.C.C.	25	0	25	116,100
Summary				
Jewish	44	1	45	1,553,000
Roman Catholic	459	0	459	405,700
All Protestant	928	0	928	243,500
Total	1,431	1	1,432	335,800

TABLE 2.48
1978 *American Library Directory* City Population Size by Total Annual Library Expenditure for Scholarly Libraries

Library Expenditures	Number of Libraries	No Response	Total Libraries	Mean Number of Persons
Under $1,500	19	0	19	187,800
$1,501–$20,000	109	0	109	390,900
$20,001–$95,000	375	0	375	235,400
$95,001–$220,000	286	0	286	229,400
$220,001–$410,000	110	0	110	273,200
$410,001–$510,000	17	0	17	521,000
$510,001 and over	53	0	53	500,800
No response	406	0	406	509,300
Total	1,375	0	1,375	343,500

TABLE 2.49
1988 *American Library Directory* City Population Size by Total Annual Library Expenditure for Scholarly Libraries

Library Expenditures	Number of Libraries	No Response	Total Libraries	Mean Number of Persons
Under $1,500	12	0	12	666,000
$1,501–$20,000	65	0	65	211,200
$20,001–$95,000	203	1	204	285,200
$95,001–$220,000	296	0	296	219,200
$220,001–$410,000	218	0	218	314,900
$410,001–$510,000	49	0	49	234,400
$510,001 and over	204	0	204	391,900
No response	384	0	384	458,400
Total	1,431	1	1,432	335,800

TABLE 2.50
1978 and 1988 *American Library Directory* Longitudinal Study Scholarly Library City Population Size by Chief Librarian's Gender

City Population Size	1978 Male	1978 Female	1978 No Response	1978 Total	1988 Male	1988 Female	1988 No Response	1988 Total	Percentage Change Male	Percentage Change Female	Percentage Change No Response	Percentage Change Total
SMALLEST	202	155	13	370	187	158	3	348	−7	2	−77	−6
1–10,000 persons (actual percentage)	55%	42%	4%	100%	54%	45%	1%	100%				
MEDIUM–SMALL	218	187	30	435	262	215	9	486	20	15	−70	12
10,001–100,000 persons (actual percentage)	50%	43%	7%	100%	54%	44%	2%	100%				
MEDIUM LARGE	224	205	29	458	266	217	7	490	19	6	−79	7
100,001–1,000,000 persons (actual percentage)	49%	45%	6%	100%	54%	44%	1%	100%				
LARGE CITIES	56	45	9	110	53	53	1	107	−5	18	−89	−3
1,000,001 & over persons (actual percentage)	51%	41%	8%	100%	50%	50%	1%	100%				
No response	1	1	0	2	0	1	0	1	−100	0	N/A	−50
(actual percentage)	50%	50%	0%	100%	0%	100%	0%	100%				
Totals	701	593	81	1,375	768	644	20	1,432	10	9	−77	4
(actual percentage)	51%	43%	6%	100%	54%	45%	1%	100%				

TABLE 2.51
1978 and 1988 *American Library Directory* Longitudinal Study Scholarly Libraries Located in Specific Cities

City	State or Province	Region	1978 Libraries in City	1978 Number of Scholarly Libraries	1978 Percentage Scholarly Libraries	1988 Libraries in City	1988 Number of Scholarly Libraries	1988 Percentage Scholarly Libraries	Percentage Change 1978–88
NEW YORK	NY	MA	36	26	72%	36	23	64%	−12%
PHILADELPHIA	PA	MA	42	23	55	26	21	81	48
WASHINGTON	DC	MA	36	22	61	30	18	60	−2
CHICAGO	IL	MW	23	19	83	19	15	79	−4
NASHVILLE	TN	SE	18	17	94	19	15	79	−16
ST. LOUIS	MO	MW	22	16	73	21	15	71	−2
MONTREAL	PQ	CAN	23	16	70	31	26	84	21
DENVER	CO	RM	14	11	79	9	7	78	−1
MILWAUKEE	WI	MW	19	11	58	16	8	50	−13
TORONTO	ON	CAN	14	10	71	18	13	72	1
PORTLAND	OR	W	11	9	82	8	8	100	22
ST. PAUL	MN	MW	10	9	90	11	9	82	−9
BOSTON	MA	NE	10	8	80	14	11	79	−2
ATLANTA	GA	SE	12	8	67	9	6	67	0
NEW ORLEANS	LA	SW	9	8	89	7	7	100	13
CINCINNATI	OH	MW	13	8	62	14	7	50	−19
BALTIMORE	MD	MA	11	7	64	10	8	80	26
PITTSBURGH	PA	MA	11	7	64	10	7	70	10
AUSTIN	TX	SW	8	7	88	12	9	75	−14
DALLAS	TX	SW	20	7	35	19	8	42	20

TABLE 2.51 (continued)
1978 and 1988 *American Library Directory* Longitudinal Study Scholarly Libraries Located in Specific Cities

			1978			1988			
City	State or Province	Region	Libraries in City	Number of Scholarly Libraries	Percentage Scholarly Libraries	Libraries in City	Number of Scholarly Libraries	Percentage Scholarly Libraries	Percentage Change 1978–88
SAN ANTONIO	TX	SW	12	7	58	14	9	64	10
LOS ANGELES	CA	W	10	7	70	12	8	67	−5
DETROIT	MI	MW	16	7	44	8	5	63	43
KANSAS CITY	MO	MW	8	7	88	10	8	80	−9
MEMPHIS	TN	SE	8	6	75	8	7	88	17
OKLAHOMA CITY	OK	SW	8	6	75	6	3	50	−33
MINNEAPOLIS	MN	MW	16	6	38	15	7	47	24
BUFFALO	NY	MA	8	5	63	8	5	63	0
ROCHESTER	NY	MA	10	5	50	12	5	42	−17
LANCASTER	PA	MA	5	5	100	6	5	83	−17
LOUISVILLE	KY	SE	9	5	56	11	6	55	−2
BIRMINGHAM	AL	SE	9	5	56	6	3	50	−10
HOUSTON	TX	SW	9	5	56	10	3	30	−46
GRAND RAPIDS	MI	MW	12	5	42	10	5	50	20
INDIANAPOLIS	IN	MW	10	5	50	15	8	53	7
SPRINGFIELD	MO	MW	7	5	71	7	5	71	0
EDMONTON	AB	CAN	5	5	100	9	7	78	−22
WINNIPEG	MB	CAN	5	5	100	10	10	100	0
ERIE	PA	MA	9	4	44	6	3	50	13
RICHMOND	VA	SE	6	4	67	8	6	75	13

TABLE 2.51 (continued)
1978 and 1988 *American Library Directory* Longitudinal Study Scholarly Libraries Located in Specific Cities

			1978			1988			
City	State or Province	Region	Libraries in City	Number of Scholarly Libraries	Percentage Scholarly Libraries	Libraries in City	Number of Scholarly Libraries	Percentage Scholarly Libraries	Percentage Change 1978–88
WINSTON-SALEM	NC	SE	5	4	80	6	5	83	4
FORT WORTH	TX	SW	6	4	67	8	6	75	13
SAN FRANCISCO	CA	W	6	4	67	6	4	67	0
CLEVELAND	OH	MW	11	4	36	8	4	50	38
LINCOLN	NE	MW	6	4	67	7	4	57	−14
DAYTON	OH	MW	7	4	57	4	3	75	31
MIAMI	FL	SE	6	3	50	7	4	57	14
LEXINGTON	KY	SE	5	3	60	6	5	83	39
PHOENIX	AZ	SW	7	3	43	7	5	71	67
SEATTLE	WA	W	7	3	43	7	4	57	33
HONOLULU	HI	W	9	3	33	4	3	75	125
COLUMBUS	OH	MW	8	3	38	8	4	50	33
PROVIDENCE	RI	NE	6	2	33	8	5	63	88
YONKERS	NY	MA	3	2	67	6	4	67	0
ALBUQUERQUE	NM	SW	5	1	20	10	0	0	−100
TERRE HAUTE	IN	MW	9	0	0	5	0	0	N/A
TOLEDO	OH	MW	8	0	0	4	0	0	N/A
QUEBEC	QU	CAN	2	0	0	7	5	71	N/A
Total libraries in specific cities			660	405	61%	648	424	65%	7%

TABLE 2.52
1978 and 1988 *American Library Directory* Longitudinal Study: Change in Most Popular Cities for Scholarly Libraries

City Name	State or Province	Edition 31	Edition 41	Percentage Change
ALBUQUERQUE	NM	1	0	−100
ATLANTA	GA	8	6	−25
AUSTIN	TX	7	9	29
BALTIMORE	MD	7	8	14
BIRMINGHAM	AL	5	3	−40
BOSTON	MA	8	11	38
BUFFALO	NY	5	5	0
CHICAGO	IL	19	15	−21
CINCINNATI	OH	8	7	−13
CLEVELAND	OH	4	4	0
COLUMBUS	OH	3	4	33
DALLAS	TX	7	8	14
DAYTON	OH	4	3	−25
DENVER	CO	11	7	−36
DETROIT	MI	7	5	−29
EDMONTON	AB	5	7	40
ERIE	PA	4	3	−25
FORT WORTH	TX	4	6	50
GRAND RAPIDS	MI	5	5	0
HONOLULU	HI	3	3	0
HOUSTON	TX	5	3	−40
INDIANAPOLIS	IN	5	8	60
KANSAS CITY	MO	7	8	14
KINGSTON	ON	1	1	0
LANCASTER	PA	5	5	0
LEXINGTON	KY	3	5	67
LINCOLN	NE	4	4	0
LOS ANGELES	CA	7	8	14
LOUISVILLE	KY	5	6	20
MEMPHIS	TN	6	7	17
MIAMI	FL	3	4	33
MILWAUKEE	WI	11	8	−27
MINNEAPOLIS	MN	6	7	17
MONTREAL	PQ	16	26	63
NASHVILLE	TN	17	15	−12
NEW ORLEANS	LA	8	7	−13
NEW YORK	NY	26	23	−12
OKLAHOMA CITY	OK	6	3	−50
OTTAWA	ON	4	5	25
PHILADELPHIA	PA	23	21	−9
PHOENIX	AZ	3	5	67

TABLE 2.52 (continued)
1978 and 1988 *American Library Directory* Longitudinal Study: Change in Most Popular Cities for Scholarly Libraries

City Name	State or Province	Edition 31	Edition 41	Percentage Change
PITTSBURGH	PA	7	7	0
PORTLAND	OR	9	8	−11
PROVIDENCE	RI	2	5	150
QUEBEC CITY	PQ	1	5	400
RICHMOND	VA	4	6	50
ROCHESTER	NY	5	5	0
SAN ANTONIO	TX	7	9	29
SAN FRANCISCO	CA	4	4	0
SEATTLE	WA	3	4	33
SPRINGFIELD	MO	5	5	0
ST. LOUIS	MO	16	15	−6
ST. PAUL	MN	9	9	0
TERRE HAUTE	IN	0	0	0
TOLEDO	OH	0	0	0
TORONTO	ON	10	13	30
TROIS-RIVIERES	PQ	1	1	0
WASHINGTON	DC	22	18	−18
WINNIPEG	MB	5	10	100
WINSTON-SALEM	NC	4	5	25
YONKERS	NY	2	4	100
Totals		412	431	5

TABLE 2.53
1988 *American Library Directory* Most Popular Cities for Scholarly Libraries in Alphabetical Order by Denomination

City Name	State or Province	Region	Denominational Libraries in City	All Scholarly Libraries in City
Baptist Libraries				
Phoenix	AZ	SW	2	5
Atlanta	GA	SE	2	6
Indianapolis	IN	MW	2	8
Louisville	KY	SE	2	6
New Orleans	LA	SW	2	7
St. Paul	MN	MW	2	9
Kansas City	MO	MW	2	8
Winston-Salem	NC	SE	2	5
Rochester	NY	MA	2	5
Nashville	TN	SE	4	15
Dallas	TX	SW	4	8
Fort Worth	TX	SW	2	6
Richmond	VA	SE	5	6
Christian Libraries				
Lexington	KY	SE	2	5
Forth Worth	TX	SW	2	6
Episcopal/Anglican Libraries				
Austin	TX	SW	2	9
Toronto	ON	CAN	2	13
Independent Libraries				
Chicago	IL	MW	2	15
New York	NY	MA	7	23
Portland	OR	W	2	8
Nashville	TN	SE	2	15
Toronto	ON	CAN	2	13
Montreal	PQ	CAN	2	26
Lutheran Libraries				
St. Paul	MN	MW	2	9
St. Louis	MO	MW	3	15
Columbus	OH	MW	2	4
Philadelphia	PA	MA	2	21
Milwaukee	WI	MW	2	8
Mennonite Libraries				
Winnipeg	MB	CAN	2	10
Denver	CO	RM	2	7
Washington	DC	MA	2	18
Atlanta	GA	SE	2	6
Indianapolis	IN	MW	2	8

TABLE 2.53 (continued)
1988 *American Library Directory* Most Popular Cities for Scholarly Libraries in Alphabetical Order by Denomination

City Name	State or Province	Region	Denominational Libraries in City	All Scholarly Libraries in City
Boston	MA	NE	3	11
Lincoln	NE	MW	2	4
Nashville	TN	SE	3	15
Dallas	TX	SW	2	8
Other Denominations Libraries				
Chicago	IL	MW	3	15
Boston	MA	NE	4	11
Grand Rapids	MI	MW	3	5
Springfield	MO	MW	3	5
Winston-Salem	NC	SE	3	5
Philadelphia	PA	MA	3	21
Winnipeg	MB	CAN	4	10
Toronto	ON	CAN	3	13
Presbyterian Libraries				
Pittsburgh	PA	MA	2	7
Memphis	TN	SE	2	7
United Church of Christ Libraries				
Lancaster	PA	MA	3	5
Jewish Libraries				
Los Angeles	CA	W	5	8
Baltimore	MD	MA	3	8
New York	NY	MA	9	23
Philadelphia	PA	MA	4	21
Roman Catholic Libraries				
Denver	CO	RM	3	7
Washington	DC	MA	14	18
Chicago	IL	MW	8	15
Indianapolis	IN	MW	3	8
New Orleans	LA	SW	4	7
Baltimore	MD	MA	4	8
Detroit	MI	MW	4	5
St. Paul	MN	MW	3	9
St. Louis	MO	MW	6	15
Buffalo	NY	MA	5	5
New York	NY	MA	3	23
Yonkers	NY	MA	3	4
Cincinnati	OH	MW	4	7
Cleveland	OH	MW	3	4
Erie	PA	MA	3	3

TABLE 2.53 (continued)
1988 *American Library Directory* Most Popular Cities for Scholarly Libraries in Alphabetical Order by Denomination

City Name	State or Province	Region	Denominational Libraries in City	All Scholarly Libraries in City
Philadelphia	PA	MA	8	21
San Antonio	TX	SW	7	9
Milwaukee	WI	MW	6	8
Ottawa	ON	CAN	4	5
Toronto	ON	CAN	3	13
Montreal	PQ	CAN	21	26
Quebec City	PQ	CAN	5	5

TABLE 2.54
1978 and 1988 Demographics: *American Library Directory* Library Type by Edition Showing Percentage Change for All Sample Divisions Except Popular Only

	-------Scholarly and Popular Combined-------								
	----Matched Pairs----			No Longer Listed	Newly Listed		-----Scholarly Only---		
	1978	1988	% Change	1978	1988	% Change	1978	1988	% Change
Scholarly	1,169	1,172	0	206	260	26	1,375	1,432	4
Percentage	71	71		49	60		67	69	
Junior College	109	89	−18	16	19	19	125	108	−14
Percentage	9	8		8	7		9	8	
Senior College	626	610	−3	78	95	22	704	705	0
Percentage	54	52		38	37		51	49	
University	150	177	18	4	12	200	154	189	23
Percentage	13	15		2	5		11	13	
Seminary	184	196	7	49	35	−29	233	231	−1
Percentage	16	17		24	13		17	16	
Convent/Monastery	16	17	6	19	8	−58	35	25	−29
Percentage	1	1		9	3		3	2	
Denominational HQ	46	43	−7	31	43	39	77	86	12
Percentage	4	4		15	17		6	6	
History/Archives	38	40	5	9	48	433	47	88	87
Percentage	3	3		4	18		3	6	

TABLE 2.55
1988 *American Library Directory* Scholarly Library Age by Library Type[1]

Year Opened	Type of Library: Junior College	Senior College	University	Seminary	Convent/ Monastery	Denom. HQ	History/ Archives	Total %
Before 1800	0	38	25	19	0	0	13	95
1801–20	0	29	12	47	0	6	0	94
1821–40	0	49	19	24	0	2	5	99
1841–60	3	51	26	13	1	2	4	100
1861–80	4	60	17	11	0	1	4	97
1881–1900	7	55	16	13	2	1	2	96
1901–20	8	55	15	10	2	1	2	93
1921–40	6	48	5	15	1	6	4	85
1941–60	5	28	5	9	2	3	3	55
1961–70	10	22	8	9	0	6	3	58
1971–80	3	23	8	14	1	9	10	68
1981 onward	11	22	0	0	0	22	11	66
No response	3	10	2	8	2	6	7	38
Total	5	34	9	11	2	4	4	69

Note: Total number of libraries is 1,431.

1. Scholarly libraries represent 69 percent of the entire sample for 1988. It is quite clear that almost all older libraries, however, especially those established before 1900, fall into the scholarly category.

TABLE 2.56
1988 *American Library Directory* Library Age by Library Type for Newly Listed Scholarly Libraries

Library Type	1–10	%	11–20	%	21–50	%	51 and over	%	No Response	%	Number of Libraries	Mean Years
Scholarly	6	2	39	15	68	26	46	18	101	39	260	44
Junior College	1	5	1	5	10	53	3	16	4	21	19	41
Senior College	2	2	14	15	33	35	18	19	28	29	95	41
University	0	0	3	25	6	50	0	0	3	25	12	25
Seminary	0	0	5	14	2	6	11	31	17	49	35	71
Convent/ Monastery	0	0	1	13	0	0	3	38	4	50	8	54
Denominational HQ	2	5	7	16	8	19	4	9	22	51	43	34
History/ Archives	1	2	8	17	9	19	7	15	23	48	48	47

TABLE 2.57
1978 and 1988 *American Library Directory* Longitudinal Study Entire Sample Age for No Longer Listed and Newly Listed Scholarly Libraries by Library Type

	No Longer Listed 1978				Newly Listed 1988				
Library Type	Number of Libraries	No Response	Total Libraries	Mean Years	Number of Libraries	No Response	Total Libraries	Mean Years	% Change 1978–88
Scholarly	155	51	206	63	159	101	260	44	−30.0
Junior College	15	1	16	53	15	4	19	41	−23.0
Senior College	68	10	78	63	67	28	95	41	−35.0
University	2	2	4	38	9	3	12	25	−34.0
Seminary	36	13	49	77	18	17	35	71	−7.8
Convent/ Monastery	12	7	19	46	4	4	8	54	17.0
Denominational HQ	17	14	31	53	21	22	43	34	−36.0
History/Archives	5	4	9	73	25	23	48	47	−36.0

TABLE 2.58
1988 *American Library Directory* Scholarly Libraries by Age (Actual)

	Type of Library								
Year Opened	Junior College	Senior College	University	Seminary	Convent/ Monastery	Denom. HQ	History/ Archives	Total	%
Before 1800	0	6	4	3	0	0	2	15	1.0
1801–1820	0	5	2	8	0	1	0	16	1.1
1821–1840	0	29	11	14	0	1	3	58	4.1
1841–1860	3	61	31	15	1	2	5	118	8.2
1861–1880	5	75	21	14	0	1	5	121	8.5
1881–1900	13	100	30	24	3	2	4	176	12.3
1901–1920	13	90	25	16	3	2	3	152	10.6
1921–1940	13	112	12	34	2	13	9	195	13.6
1941–1960	23	117	22	38	8	14	12	234	16.4
1961–1970	21	46	16	18	0	13	7	121	8.5
1971–1980	3	20	7	12	1	8	9	60	4.2
1981 & after	1	2	0	0	0	2	1	6	0.4
No response	13	42	8	34	7	27	28	159	11.1
Total	108	705	189	230	25	86	88	1,431	100.0
Mean Birth Years	1929	1906	1894	1906	1925	1939	1918	1,908	

TABLE 2.59
1978 and 1988 *American Library Directory* Longitudinal Study of Scholarly Library Age by Library Type

Library Type	1978 Number of Libraries	1978 No Re-sponse	1978 Total Libraries	1978 Mean Years	1988 Number of Libraries	1988 No Re-sponse	1988 Total Libraries	1988 Mean Years	Percentage Change 1978–88
Scholarly	1,252	123	1,375	80	1,272	159	1,431	80	0
Junior College	118	7	125	63	95	13	108	59	−6.3
Senior College	674	30	704	83	663	42	705	82	−1.2
University	146	8	154	98	181	8	189	94	−4
Seminary	197	36	233	79	196	34	230	82	3.8
Convent/ Monastery	24	11	35	55	18	7	25	63	15
Denomina-tional HQ	55	22	77	54	59	27	86	49	−9
History/Archives	38	9	47	81	60	28	88	70	−14

TABLE 2.60
1978 and 1988 *American Library Directory* Longitudinal Study Scholarly Library Age by Denomination for No Longer Listed and Newly Listed Libraries

Denomination	1978 Number of Libraries	1978 No Re-sponse	1978 Total Libraries	1978 Mean Years	1988 Number of Libraries	1988 No Re-sponse	1988 Total Libraries	1988 Mean Years	Percentage Change 1978–88
Baptist	13	1	14	63	16	11	27	40	−37.0
Christian	2	1	3	33	3	0	3	35	6.1
Churches of Christ	2	0	2	40	3	0	3	38	−5.0
Episcopal/Anglican	3	2	5	92	5	3	8	73	−21.0
Independent	9	5	14	83	18	10	28	35	−58.0
Lutheran	6	4	10	101	8	8	16	49	−51.0
Mennonite	0	0	0	0	6	2	8	45	0.0
Methodist	8	1	9	57	6	3	9	63	11.0
Other Denominations	31	7	38	46	30	22	52	39	−15.0
Presbyterian	3	1	4	127	2	1	3	78	−39.0
U.C.C.	1	0	1	25	1	1	2	60	140.0
<u>Summary</u>									
Jewish	2	4	6	40	7	8	15	19	−52.0
Roman Catholic	75	25	100	63	54	32	86	48	−24.0
All Protestant	78	22	100	63	98	61	159	44	−30.0
Total	155	51	206	63	159	101	260	44	−30.0

TABLE 2.61
1978 *American Library Directory* Library Age by Denomination for Scholarly Libraries

Denomination	1–30	%	31–50	%	51 and over	%	No Response	%	Number of Libraries	Mean Years
Baptist	16	11	31	22	85	61	8	6	140	82
Christian	3	8	13	33	22	55	2	5	40	74
Churches of Christ	2	7	15	56	10	37	0	0	27	53
Congregational	0	0	1	20	4	80	0	0	5	108
Episcopal/Anglican	4	13	1	3	21	66	6	19	32	114
Independent	14	17	16	20	43	52	9	11	82	69
Lutheran	8	11	3	4	52	74	7	10	70	98
Methodist	10	7	16	11	113	77	8	5	147	94
Other Denominations	27	13	46	21	121	57	20	9	214	69
Presbyterian	1	1	7	8	79	88	3	3	90	116
U.C.C.	2	8	0	0	22	92	0	0	24	116
Summary										
Jewish	2	6	10	29	18	51	5	14	35	61
Roman Catholic	53	11	100	21	261	56	55	12	469	71
All Protestant	87	10	149	17	572	66	63	7	871	86
Total	142	10	259	19	851	62	123	9	1,375	80

TABLE 2.62
1988 *American Library Directory* Library Age by Denomination for Scholarly Libraries

Library Type	1–10	%	11–30	%	31–50	%	51 and over	%	No Response	%	Number of Libraries	Mean Years
Baptist	0	0	20	13	33	22	80	53	19	13	152	79
Christian	0	0	3	7	14	34	22	54	2	5	41	76
Churches of Christ	0	0	3	11	14	52	10	37	0	0	27	52
Episcopal	0	0	5	16	1	3	21	66	5	16	32	108
Independent	0	0	23	24	21	22	41	42	12	12	97	60
Lutheran	1	1	9	12	4	5	52	68	10	13	76	96
Mennonite	0	0	2	9	5	23	13	59	2	9	22	63
Methodist	0	0	8	5	12	8	120	81	9	6	149	102
Other Denoms.	2	1	31	14	32	15	120	55	32	15	217	73
Presbyterian	0	0	3	3	7	8	78	87	2	2	90	113
U.C.C.	0	0	1	4	0	0	23	92	1	4	25	115
Summary												
All Protestant	3	0	108	12	143	15	580	63	94	10	928	85
Jewish	1	2	7	16	9	20	17	38	11	24	45	53
Roman Catholic	2	0	66	14	82	18	254	55	55	12	459	71
Total	6	0	181	13	234	16	851	59	160	11	1,432	80

TABLE 2.63
1978 *American Library Directory* Scholarly Library Age by Region

Region	Number of Libraries	No Response	Total Number of Libraries	Mean Years
Northeast	68	8	76	72
Middle Atlantic	231	33	264	85
Southeast	250	17	267	85
Southwest	104	8	112	70
West	112	7	119	68
Rocky Mountains	22	5	27	71
Middle West	385	27	412	83
Canada	80	18	98	75
Total	1,252	123	1,375	80

TABLE 2.64
1978 and 1988 *American Library Directory* Longitudinal Study of Scholarly Library Age by Library Type

Library Type	1978 Number of Libraries	1978 No Response	1978 Total Libraries	1978 Mean Years	1988 Number of Libraries	1988 No Response	1988 Total Libraries	1988 Mean Years	Percentage Change
Scholarly	1,252	123	1,375	80	1,272	160	1,432	80	0
Junior College	118	7	125	63	95	13	108	59	−6
Senior College	674	30	704	83	663	42	705	82	−1
University	146	8	154	98	181	8	189	94	−4
Seminary	197	36	233	79	196	35	231	82	4
Convent/Monastery	24	11	35	55	18	7	25	63	15
Denominational HQ	55	22	77	55	59	27	86	49	−11
History/Archives	38	9	47	81	60	28	88	70	−14

TABLE 2.65
1978 *American Library Directory* Library Age by Total Annual Library Expenditure for Scholarly Libraries

Library Expenditures	Number of Libraries	No Response	Total Libraries	Mean Number of Years
Under $1,500	18	1	19	45
$1,501–$20,000	104	5	109	58
$20,001–$95,000	368	7	375	76
$95,001–$220,000	284	2	286	94
$220,001–$410,000	110	0	110	103
$410,001–$510,000	17	0	17	121
$510,001 and over	53	0	53	109
No response	298	108	406	66
Total	1,252	123	1,375	80

TABLE 2.66
1988 *American Library Directory* Library Age by Total Annual Library Expenditure for Scholarly Libraries

Library Expenditures	Number of Libraries	No Response	Total Libraries	Mean Number of Years
Under $1,500	7	5	12	46
$1,501–$20,000	48	17	65	53
$20,001–$95,000	188	16	204	63
$95,001–$220,000	285	11	296	79
$220,001–$410,000	217	1	218	94
$410,001–$510,000	49	0	49	105
$510,001 and over	202	2	204	101
No response	276	108	384	65
Total	1,272	160	1,432	80

TABLE 2.67
1978 *American Library Directory* Oldest Scholarly Libraries by Denomination

Library	Denomination	Age (in years)
1. Santa Barbara Mission Archive, Santa Barbara, CA	Roman Catholic	225
2. Georgetown University, Washington, DC	Roman Catholic	225
3. Transylvania University, Lexington, KY	Christian	225
4. St. Mary's Seminary and University, Baltimore, MD	Roman Catholic	225
5. St. Mary's Seminary College, Catonsville, MD	Roman Catholic	225
6. Dickinson College, Carlisle, PA	Methodist	225
7. Franklin and Marshall College, Lancaster, PA	United Church of Christ	225
8. Diocese of Pennsylvania, Philadelphia, PA	Roman Catholic	225
9. Pittsburgh Theological Seminary, Pittsburgh, PA	Presbyterian	225
10. Brown University, Providence, RI	Independent	225
11. Tusculum College, Greenville, TN	Presbyterian	225
12. Hampden Sydney College, Hampden Sydney, VA	Presbyterian	225
13. University of King's College, Halifax, NS	Episcopal/Anglican	225

TABLE 2.68
1988 *American Library Directory* Oldest Scholarly Libraries by Denomination

	Library	Denomination	Age (in years)
1.	Santa Barbara Mission Archive, Santa Barbara, CA	Roman Catholic	225
2.	Georgetown University, Washington, DC	Roman Catholic	225
3.	Transylvania University, Lexington, KY	Christian	225
4.	St. Mary's Seminary and University, Baltimore, MD	Roman Catholic	225
5.	New Brunswick Theological Seminary, New Brunswick, NJ	Other Denominations	225
6.	Moravian Church in America, Winston-Salem, NC	Other Denominations	225
7.	Salem College, Winston-Salem, NC	Other Denominations	225
8.	Moravian College, Bethlehem, PA	Other Denominations	225
9.	Dickinson College, Carlisle, PA	Methodist	225
10.	Franklin and Marshall College, Lancaster, PA	United Church of Christ	225
11.	Pittsburgh Theological Seminary, Pittsburgh, PA	Presbyterian	225
12.	Tusculum College, Greenville, TN	Presbyterian	225
13.	Brown University, Providence, RI	Independent	225
14.	Hampden Sydney College, Hampden Sydney, VA	Presbyterian	225
15.	University of King's College, Halifax, NS	Episcopal/Anglican	225

TABLE 2.69
1988 *American Library Directory* Oldest Scholarly Christian Libraries

	Library	Age (in years)
1.	Transylvania University, Lexington, KY	225
2.	Bethany College, Bethany, WV	160
3.	Eureka College, Eureka, IL	140
4.	Culver-Stockton College, Canton, MO	140
5.	Columbia College, Columbia, MO	140
6.	Hiram College, Hiram, OH	140
7.	Lexington Theological Seminary, Lexington, KY	120
8.	Tougaloo College, Tougaloo, MS	120
9.	William Woods University, Fulton, MO	120
10.	Texas Christian University, Fort Worth, TX	120

TABLE 2.70
1978 *American Library Directory* Oldest Scholarly Congregational Libraries

Library	Age (in years)
1. American Congregational Association, Boston, MA	140
2. Olivet College, Olivet, MI	140
3. Washburn University, Topeka, KS	120
4. Piedmont College, Demarest, GA	100
5. Evangelical Congregational School of Theology, Myerstown, PA	40

TABLE 2.71
1988 *American Library Directory* Oldest Scholarly Independent Libraries

Library	Age (in years)
1. Brown University, Providence, RI	225
2. Harvard University, Cambridge, MA	180
3. American Bible Society, New York, NY	180
4. Hartford Seminary, Hartford, CT	160
5. Union Theological Seminary, New York, NY	160
6. McGill University, Montreal, PQ	160
7. Wheaton College, Wheaton, IL	140
8. General Theological Seminary, Boston, MA	140
9. Berea College, Berea, KY	120
10. Shaw University, Raleigh, NC	120

TABLE 2.72
1988 *American Library Directory* Oldest Scholarly Mennonite Libraries

Library	Age (in years)
1. Goshen College, Goshen, IN	100
2. Bethel College, North Newton, KS	100
3. Bluffton College, Bluffton, OH	100
4. Goshen College Mennonite Historical Library, Goshen, IN	80
5. Hesston College, Hesston, KS	80
6. Tabor College, Hillsboro, KS	80
7. Freeman Academy, Freeman, SD	80
8. Eastern Mennonite University, Harrisonburg, VA	80

TABLE 2.73
1988 *American Library Directory* Oldest Scholarly Other Denominations Libraries

Library	Age (in years)
1. New Brunswick Theological Seminary, New Brunswick, NJ	225
2. Moravian Church in America, Winston-Salem, NC	225
3. Salem College, Winston-Salem, NC	225
4. Moravian College, Bethlehem, PA	225
5. Guilford College, Greensboro, NC	160
6. Haverford College, Haverford, PA	160
7. Church of Jesus Christ of Latter-day Saints, Salt Lake City, UT	160

TABLE 2.74
1988 *American Library Directory* Oldest Scholarly United Church of Christ Libraries

Library	Age (in years)
1. Franklin and Marshall College, Lancaster, PA	225
2. Bangor Theological Seminary, Bangor, ME	180
3. Andover-Newton Theological School, Newton Center, MA	160
4. Lancaster Theological Seminary, Lancaster, PA	160
5. Catawba College, Salisbury, NC	140
6. Defiance College, Defiance, OH	140
7. Heidelberg College, Tiffin, OH	140
8. Pacific University, Forest Grove, OR	140

TABLE 2.75
1988 *American Library Directory* Oldest Scholarly Roman Catholic Libraries

Library	Age (in years)
1. Santa Barbara Mission Archives, Santa Barbara, CA	225
2. Georgetown University, Washington, DC	225
3. St. Mary's Seminary and University, Baltimore, MD	225
4. Mt. Saint Mary's College, Emmitsburg, MD	180
5. St. Louis University, St. Louis, MO	180
6. College de St. Boniface, Winnipeg, MB	180
7. St. Mary's University, Halifax, NS	180

TABLE 2.76
1978 *American Library Directory* Chief Librarian's Gender by Library Type for Scholarly Libraries

Type of Library	Male	%	Female	%	No Response	%	Number of Libraries
Scholarly	701	51	593	43	81	6	1,375
Junior College	35	28	84	67	6	5	125
Senior College	331	47	349	50	24	3	704
University	108	70	45	29	1	1	154
Seminary	160	69	55	24	18	8	233
Convent/Monastery	16	46	9	26	10	29	35
Denominational HQ	22	29	36	47	19	25	77
History/Archives	29	62	15	32	3	6	47

TABLE 2.77
1988 *American Library Directory* Chief Librarian's Gender by Library Type for Scholarly Libraries

Type of Library	Male	%	Female	%	No Response	%	Number of Libraries
Scholarly	769	54	644	45	19	1	1,432
Junior College	37	34	71	66	0	0	108
Senior College	361	51	332	47	12	2	705
University	112	59	76	40	1	1	189
Seminary	157	68	69	30	5	2	231
Convent/Monastery	14	56	11	44	0	0	25
Denominational HQ	29	34	56	65	1	1	86
History/Archives	59	68	29	32	0	0	88

TABLE 2.78
1978 and 1988 Demographics: *American Library Directory* Chief Librarian's Gender by Edition Showing Percentage Change for Scholarly Libraries

	1978	% of Sample	1988	% of Sample	% Change
Male	701	51	769	54	5.9
Female	593	43	644	45	4.7
No Response	81	6	19	1	7.0
Total	1,375	100	1,432	100	

TABLE 2.79
1978 and 1988 *American Library Directory* Longitudinal Study City Population Size by Chief Librarian's Gender for Scholarly Libraries

1978

Chief Librarian's Gender	Number of Libraries	No Response	Total Libraries	Mean Number of Persons
Male	700	1	701	334,800
Female	592	1	593	347,000
No Response	81	0	81	393,200
Total	1,373	2	1,375	343,500

1988

Chief Librarian's Gender	Number of Libraries	No Response	Total Libraries	Mean Number of Persons
Male	769	0	769	316,600
Female	643	1	644	359,900
No Response	19	0	19	299,100
Total	1,431	1	1,432	335,800

TABLE 2.80
American Library Directory Statistical Information and Projections on All Major Variables: 1978, 1988, and 1998[1]

	Profile of Means and Mean Deviations All Scholarly Libraries								
	+ − 1.65 Standard Deviations (90% accuracy)	Percentage Growth (ten yrs.)	Projected Growth (1st year)	P.A. Projected Unit Change	Projected Variable Minimum	Projected Variable Maximum	Actual 1978 Mean	Actual 1988 Mean	Extrapolated 1998 Mean
Library age	72	.0	.0	.00	77	83	80	80	80
Library city population size	1,147,804	−2.2	−.2	−740.00	284,549	372,851	343,500	335,800	328,700
Institutional degree years offered	2	4.3	.4	.02	4	5	4	5	5
Total library staff size	23.2	15.8	1.6	.30	20.4	23.6	16.0	19.0	22.0
Library professionals	5.0	5.0	.5	.02	3.6	4.8	3.8	4.0	4.2
Library clerks	6.6	7.8	.8	.04	4.7	6.3	4.7	5.1	5.5
Library student assistants	16.9	26.7	2.7	.40	17.6	20.4	11.0	15.0	19.0
Faculty size	123.7	13.3	1.3	1.10	87.8	100.2	72.0	83.0	94.0
Students enrolled	1968	11.0	1.1	13.00	1,237	1,417	1,065	1,196	1,327
Total annual library expenditure	233,269	43.6	4.4	10,850.00	345,359	369,842	140,600	249,100	357,600
Annual expenditure on material	80,006	39.3	3.9	3,207.00	109,301	117,839	49,430	81,500	113,570
Annual expenditure on personnel	140,089	34.7	3.5	4,904.00	182,793	198,287	92,460	141,500	190,540
Annual expenditure on 'other'	11,634	22.6	2.3	390.00	20,487	21,873	13,380	17,280	21,180

TABLE 2.80 (continued)

American Library Directory Statistical Information and Projections on All Major Variables: 1978, 1988, and 1998[1]

	Profile of Means and Mean Deviations All Scholarly Libraries								
	+−1.65 Standard Deviations (90% accuracy)	Percentage Growth (ten yrs.)	Projected Growth (1st year)	P.A. Projected Unit Change	Projected Variable Minimum	Projected Variable Maximum	Actual 1978 Mean	Actual 1988 Mean	Extrapolated 1998 Mean
Library volume holdings	174,958	17.1	1.7	1,932.00	124,657	139,383	93,380	112,700	132,020
Library periodical subscriptions	715	.7	.1	.40	522	587	546	550	554
Library microform holdings	97,695	41.0	4.1	1,926.00	60,295	72,065	27,660	46,920	66,180
Library vertical file drawers	48	19.4	1.9	.60	34	40	25	31	37
Library consortium memberships	2	23.1	2.3	.06	3	4	2	3	3
Library subject interests	2	26.3	2.6	.05	2	3	1	2	2
Library special collections	2	.0	.0	.00	1	2	2	2	2
Library publications	2	.0	.0	.00	1	2	2	2	2
Total	1,888,442	350	35	22,485	1,129,455	1,294,438	762,245	987,096	1,211,947
Averages	89,926	17	2	1,071	53,784	61,640	36,297	47,005	57,712

1. Minor deviations between this table and previous tables arise from slightly different methods of handling missing data and responses well above the category maxima.

TABLE 2.81
American Library Directory Statistical Summaries for Determining the Extent of Statistical Reliability: Scholarly Libraries

	Variable Range from 0 and above	Value of 1 Standard Dev'n	Percentage of Range	Value of 1 Standard Error of the Means
All Scholarly Libraries				
Total	7,092,256	1,144,510	418.90	82,492
Average	337,726	54,500	19.90	3,928
All Scholarly Libraries: Matched Pairs				
Total	7,092,256	1,116,526	421.3	88,573
Average	337,726	53,168	20.1	4,218
Percentage Difference: All versus Matched pairs				
Average		−2.4	.6	7.4

TABLE 2.82
American Library Directory Statistical Summaries for Scholarly Libraries and Matched Pairs

	+−1.65 Standard Deviations (90% accuracy)	Percentage Growth (ten yrs.)	Projected Growth (1st year)	P.A. Projected Unit Change	Projected Variable Minimum	Projected Variable Maximum	Actual 1978 Mean	Actual 1988 Mean	Extrapolated 1998 Mean
All Scholarly Libraries									
Total	1,888,442	350	35	22,485	1,129,455	1,294,438	762,245	987,096	1,211,947
Average	89,926	17	2	1,071	53,784	61,640	36,297	47,005	57,712
All Scholarly Libraries: Matched Pairs									
Total	1,842,267	372	37	25,970	1,198,639	1,375,785	767,808	1,027,510	1,287,212
Average	87,727	18	2	1,237	57,078	65,514	36,562	48,929	61,296
Percentage difference: All versus Matched Pairs									
Average	−2.4	6.3	5.7	15.5	6.1	6.3	.7	4.1	6.2

TABLE 2.83
American Library Directory Scholarly Library Variable Projections for Canada and the United States

	CANADA							
Variable	No. of Libraries 1978	No. of Libraries 1998	Mean 1978	Mean 1988	Projection 1998	10-Year % Change	1st Year % Change	P.A. Unit Change
Library age	80	117	75	68	61	−10.3	−1.0	−7
City population size	98	164	432,600	428,800	425,000	−0.9	−0.1	−3,800
Total library staff	47	94	13	13	13	0	0	0
Library professionals	47	83	3.80	3.70	3.60	−2.7	−0.3	−0.1
Institutional faculty size	34	66	98	104	110	5.8	0.6	6
Institutional enrollment	47	83	1,588	1,637	1,686	3.0	0.3	49
Total annual library expenditure	46	96	213,500	262,600	311,700	18.7	1.9	49,100
Annual library expenditure on material	39	98	64,810	69,780	74,750	7.1	0.7	4,970
Annual library expenditure on personnel	34	91	141,000	154,200	167,400	8.6	0.9	13,200
Library volume holdings	81	156	104,300	104,000	103,700	−0.3	−0.0	−300
Library periodical subscriptions	55	107	541	487	433	−11.1	−1.1	−54
Library microform holdings	28	59	55,790	50,620	45,450	−10.2	−1.0	−5,170
Library consortium memberships	13	33	2.60	2	1.40	−30	−3	−0.6

TABLE 2.83 (continued)

American Library Directory Scholarly Library Variable Projections for Canada and the United States

Variable	No. of Libraries 1978	No. of Libraries 1998	Mean 1978	Mean 1988	Projection 1998	10-Year % Change	1st Year % Change	P.A. Unit Change
	CANADA							
Subject ints + Special coll'ns + publications	53	97	2.10	2.30	2.50	8.7	0.9	0.2
Totals	702	1,344	1,014,324	1,072,317	113,031	−14	−1	57,994
Averages	50.1	96	72,451.7	76,594.1	80,736.5	−1.0	−0.1	4,142.4
Percentage of U.S. averages	−94.3	−90.1	38.4	12.1	−4.3	−105.0	−105.0	−74.1
	UNITED STATES							
Library age	1,172	1,155	81	81	81	0	0	0
City population size	1,275	1,266	336,600	324,000	311,400	−3.9	−0.4	−12,600
Total library staff	728	851	16	20	24	20	2	4
Library professionals	712	813	3.80	4	4.20	5	0.5	0.2

TABLE 2.83 (continued)
American Library Directory Scholarly Library Variable Projections for Canada and the United States

	CANADA							
Variable	No. of Libraries 1978	No. of Libraries 1998	Mean 1978	Mean 1988	Projection 1998	10-Year % Change	1st Year % Change	P.A. Unit Change
Institutional faculty size	994	947	71	81	91	12.3	1.2	10
Institutional enrollment	1,009	993	1,041	1,160	1,279	10.3	1.0	119
Total annual library expenditure	924	952	136,900	247,700	358,500	44.7	4.5	110,800
Annual library expenditure on material	710	959	48,580	82,700	116,820	41.3	4.1	34,120
Annual library expenditure on personnel	642	904	89,890	140,200	190,510	35.9	3.6	50,310
Library volume holdings	1,177	1,225	92,630	113,800	134,970	18.6	1.9	21,170
Library periodical subscriptions	911	1,072	546	556	566	1.8	0.2	10
Library microform holdings	594	718	26,330	46,620	66,910	43.5	4.4	20,290
Library consortium memberships	572	793	2	2.60	3.20	23.1	2.3	0.6
Subject ints + special coll'ns + publications	826	920	2.10	2.60	3.10	19.2	1.9	0.5
Totals	12,246	13,568	732,693	956,927	118,116	272	27	224,234
Averages	874.7	969.1	52,335.2	68,351.9	84,368.7	19.4	1.9	16,016.7

TABLE 2.84
1978 and 1988 *American Library Directory* Longitudinal Study
Scholarly Libraries Accreditation by Library Type

Library Type	1978 Number of Libraries	1978 No Response	1978 Total Libraries	1978 Mean Accreditations	1988 Number of Libraries	1988 No Response	1988 Total Libraries	1988 Mean Accreditations	Percentage Change
Scholarly	978	397	1,375	1.5	974	457	1,431	1.5	0.0
Junior College	89	36	125	1.1	78	30	108	1.0	−9.0
Senior College	594	110	704	1.2	585	120	705	1.2	0.0
University	129	25	154	1.1	152	37	189	1.2	9.0
Seminary	158	75	233	3.2	156	74	230	3.0	−6.2
Convent/ Monastery	0	35	35	0.0	0	25	25	0.0	0.0
Denominational HQ	2	75	77	2.0	0	86	86	0.0	−100.0
History/ Archives	6	41	47	1.0	3	85	88	1.0	0.0

3

SCHOLARLY RELIGIOUS LIBRARIES, Part I

What are the essential characteristics of North American scholarly religious libraries? How do these libraries differ among themselves for 1978 and 1988? This chapter and the following one seek to provide the answers to these questions to the extent that they were discovered in the data collected and analyzed for this study. Chapter discussions will emphasize findings that establish positive relationships between variables and are of some significance for scholarly libraries.

Chapters 3–4 have two aims: (1) to describe and analyze scholarly religious libraries as a discrete group and (2) to compare 1978 libraries with 1988 libraries. The chapters will display statistical findings and also relationships among the variables' findings and their implications for study of the field.

To refresh the reader's memory, scholarly religious libraries are either attached to an adult, college, or university-level institution or in any case to an institution primarily devoted to encouraging serious study and research work, as opposed to popular religious congregational, school, and public libraries that provide primarily recreational and instructional service for young adults and children. See appendix B for further definitions.

In all, 39 variables and 265 questions and answers plus open-ended questions about these libraries were examined. The more fundamental questions with their maximum ranges were the following, listed as they occurred on the questionnaire:

American Library Directory:	Edition 31 (1978) or Edition 41 (1988)
Nation:	United States or Canada

Region:	Northeast, Middle Atlantic, Southeast, Southwest, West, Rocky Mountains, Middle West, or Canada
State or province:	Sixty-three included
City population size:	0–3+ million
Library type:	Scholarly—junior college, senior college, university, seminary, convent/monastery, denominational headquarters, or history/archives Popular—congregational, parochial school, or public
Denomination:	Thirty-two listed, plus others
Library age or Founding date:	0–1981+
Highest degree awarded:	associate, bachelor's, master's, or doctoral
Accreditation:	Regional, AABC, ATS and ATLA, U.S. Office of Education
Enrollment size:	0–5001+
Staff size:	Professional 0–10+; clerical 0–10+; student assistant 0–29+
Expenditures:	Material \$0–\$162,001+; personnel \$0–\$300,001+; other \$0–\$1,800+; total \$0–\$510,001+
Faculty size:	0–341+
Holdings:	Book volumes 0–540,001+; periodical titles 0–1,601+; microforms 0–180,001+; vertical files 0–131+
Consortium memberships:	0–8
Religious special collections:	0–9
Religious subject interests:	0–9
Publications:	0–9

This chapter opens a discussion of the scholarly religious libraries listed in the *American Library Directory*. The reader should also examine the questionnaire form (appendix D) to understand the sequence of investigation. It is important to note that a complete set of data was obtained for only a small percentage of the libraries, some of which failed to provide part (or even a little) of the requested *ALD* information. Certain discussions in later chapters attempt to identify statistically the probable characteristics of libraries that failed to answer many of the questionnaire questions.

The chapters assume that the *ALD* list of scholarly religious libraries is largely complete for most of the study categories. Therefore, this is an analysis of something close to the North American scholarly religious library population (see chap. 1). The chapter provides a basic statistical and table-driven analysis and interpretation of key information. What is distinctive or unique about scholarly religious libraries? They may be essentially similar to scholarly nonreligious, privately supported, or popular religious libraries, but this is not the experience of the author. We should have some idea about their nature by the end of chapter 4.

In the discussions, the author will emphasize findings that establish positive or negative relationships between variables and are significant for specific library groups, though many of the findings may be hard to interpret beyond the fairly obvious. All answers to pertinent questions were derived from multiple cross-variable comparisons, and special attention was given to fundamental variables by crossing them against a consistent set of background independent variables—country, edition, type of library, denominations, volume holdings, region, librarian's gender, and total annual library expenditure. Causal factors were distinguished from effects and cross-correlations, at least to some extent. On the basis of the explanatory or independent variables, the dependent variable distribution could be evaluated for aspects of special interest. Examples are staff size, library holdings, accreditation status, and other library activities.

Chapter 3 includes the following sections:

I. Institutional types, denominations, and regional distribution
  A. Introduction
  B. Library type
  C. Denominations and tables
  D. Institutions by denomination
  E. Scholarly matched pairs analysis
  F. Highest degrees awarded by the academic institutions
  G. Interim summary
II. Institutional accreditation
  A. AABC accredited college libraries
  B. ATLA and other seminary libraries
III. Institutional student enrollment levels
IV. Institutional faculty size and library staff size levels
  A. Student enrollment per library staff member and per faculty member
  B. Summary of the student, faculty, and library staff member sections

V. Library service
   A. Library cooperation and automation
   B. Cooperative library consortium membership
   C. Membership in the Online Computer Library Center, Inc.
   D. Local library automation projects
VI. Miscellaneous service topics
   A. Questionnaire returned
   B. Questions answered
   C. Repeat question
   D. Chief librarian named
   E. Departmental libraries—I
   F. Departmental libraries—II
   G. Subject interests and special collections
   H. Publications
   I. Circulation and reference service to members only

Institutional Types, Denominations, and Regional Distribution

Readers of much general academic library literature are accustomed to seeing discussions and analyses of public and private college and university libraries. But they are not accustomed to seeing discussions of *religious* college and university libraries. In order to adopt the proper mindset for appreciating these chapters, it is necessary to refocus the mind on religious libraries as a discrete group. Though these libraries may resemble other scholarly libraries in many ways, they are different in one way: all of them are *religious* libraries.

At the very least, these libraries are in certain ways unusual, and the reader must distinguish them from other scholarly libraries so they can be studied carefully. They are a subset of private scholarly institutions and organizations existing largely because of religious sponsorship. They are not restricted to academic libraries (which constitute the majority of them, however) but include special libraries in addition to the four levels of academic libraries. As such, they have seldom been studied in North American scholarly library literature. It is true that North American seminary libraries have been examined previously, at least in part, but this fact does not extend to other kinds of scholarly religious libraries as far as this author can find. This makes the present study unusual and (the author hopes) intriguing for many readers.

Scholarly religious institutions may be unfamiliar to the reader who has not previously read the literature of religious libraries. Since little of it exists in systematic form, except for bibliographies (which are numerous and often very helpful), generalized thinking is understandable, but now is the time to focus attention on the religious library subfield as a unique entity, especially on management and statistical aspects of it that are critical for encouraging library growth and more effective service-oriented development.

All North American libraries are supported by (1) the citizens of a nation, state, province, or city through public tax funds; (2) private organizations or institutions, such as nondenominational schools, colleges, and business firms; and for this study (3) private religious institutions, such as religious orders, universities, or houses of worship.

Examples of these three types of institutions are (1) the University of California, Los Angeles, a public institution; (2) the University of Southern California, Los Angeles, a private institution; and (3) the Hebrew Union College, Los Angeles, a private *religious* institution. A private religious institution is an organization controlled by a board of directors with certain distinctive religious or moral objectives that are inseparably related to its overall mission and rationale.

In retrospect, the decade 1978–88 was one of relatively generous North American academic institutional funding, though at the time few of the concerned academic librarians would have admitted it. It was also a period when librarians attempted to increase service as well as material access and staff coverage without the major budget additions required to carry out the task effectively. A few budgets moved forward boldly, a few others edged forward modestly, and many others were "steady state."

During the period there was an increasing need for service enhancement to keep up with burgeoning bibliographic and research pressures. Cataloging uniformity increased as card catalog use diminished and computerized database use increased. Budgets were uninspiring for the most part, and the beginning of a recession could be predicted from increasingly frequent budget cuts, "restructuring," "repositioning," "less is more," and "downsizing," some of the terms that library administrators were reluctantly adding to their vocabularies and strategies.

In an effort to understand the library's parent institution, this section will examine the characteristics of the scholarly institutions that acted as sponsors. Their libraries will then be described in detail in the remainder of this and the following chapter.

This section describes the scholarly institutions of both *American Library Directory* editions and examines them against several variables. In certain cases the description given will show information in detail on a particular variable, while in other cases the description will provide merely summary information. The discussion will concentrate on the scholarly libraries. In general, the depth of the information collected on a variable depended on its intrinsic importance or interest and also on the types and depth of data available for it. For instance, denominational affiliation was a variable of prime importance, while restriction on circulation was one of less importance.

Library Type

First we will examine the institutions by library and institutional type, then by region, then by denomination, and finally broken down by all three variables. Seven *types* of scholarly institutions (not primarily of libraries but of institutions) were represented. They were listed in the introduction above. See also chapter 1 for a discussion of definitions and the institutional and library classification systems used for them. How many institutions of each type were shown in each *ALD* edition? See longitudinal table 2.54, which shows 1978 and 1988 totals for the seven subtypes of scholarly institutions to be studied in later chapters.[1,2]

Essentially the seven scholarly institutional types were composed of academic (junior and senior college, university and seminary) and other institutions (convents/monasteries, denominational headquarters, and history/archive centers). The four kinds of academic institutions together made up 85–88 percent of the scholarly institutions, while convent/monasteries, denominational headquarters, and history/archive centers made up only 12–15 percent of the total. Senior colleges by themselves constituted one-half of the entire scholarly group; together with the seminaries, they equaled two-thirds of the entire scholarly sample.

While scholarly institutions as a whole rose in number by 5 percent in 1988, among specific scholarly institution types, junior colleges, and convents/monasteries diminished in size during this period, by 13 percent and 28 percent respectively. It is easy to imagine convents and monasteries shrinking in number because of the decreasing size of Roman Catholic religious orders during the study period, but it is difficult to imagine junior colleges diminishing also, since this was a growing educational field at that time. In addition, the rates at which the three growth fields—university, denominational headquarters, and history/archives—expanded were surprisingly strong.

Which institutional types were most popular for each denominational group? Table 3.1 presents a breakdown for 1978. Nine denominations listed senior colleges as being most popular, while the other four listed popular congregational libraries as most popular. That was column 1, or first most popular. Seminary libraries led column 3, or third most popular.

For type of library by denomination, table 3.2 gives us a different view when we look at the columns vertically. It points out that junior colleges were mostly Roman Catholic, Methodist, and Other Denominations. Senior colleges were made up of Roman Catholic, Other Denominations, Methodist, and Baptist. Universities were Roman Catholic, Baptist, and Methodist. Seminaries were Roman Catholic plus a mixture of other denominations. Convents/monasteries were Roman Catholic. Denominational headquarters libraries were Roman Catholic, Other Denominations, and Independent. History/archives were Other Denominations, Roman Catholic, and Jewish.

If we look at the table horizontally, we see that Baptist institutions were mostly senior colleges, as were Christian and Churches of Christ. Episcopal/Anglican were seminaries and senior colleges. Independent libraries were senior colleges and seminaries, Lutheran were senior colleges (as were Mennonites, Methodists, Other Denominations, Presbyterians and UCC). Jewish institutions were history/archives, seminaries, and denominational headquarters, while Roman Catholic institutions were senior colleges, universities, and seminaries.

Another type of library table was 3.3 for 1988, which introduced a different variable: type of library by *region*. It shows that libraries in the Northeast were primarily senior college but almost as often seminaries or history/archives. Canada was mostly senior colleges but had large numbers of universities and seminaries. The reader can work out the other relationships privately. Table 3.4 for 1988 shows which regions were most popular by denomination. In column 1, the Southeast and Middle West tied for the lead in popularity, by denomination. The Middle West led column 2 in the second most popular regions, and the Middle Atlantic led column 3. In another table for 1988 showing which regions were most popular for each library type, the Middle West led the scholarly libraries in columns 1 and 2, and there was no clear leader in column 3.

Yet another table, 3.5 for 1978 and 1988, showed region by denomination. Notice concentrations by region for horizontal rows and by denomination for vertical rows. In this way we can see the highlights for each group—1988 Southeast and Southwest for Baptist and Independent, Other Denominations, and Roman Catholic for Canada, for instance.

Tables for region by type of library showed that junior colleges were heavy in the Southeast and senior colleges were heavy in every region. Universities were significant in Canada and the Southwest and seminaries were widely distributed. Convents/monasteries were heavy in the Northeast, while denominational headquarters were heavier in Canada, the Middle Atlantic, and the West. History/archives were heaviest in the Northeast and Rocky Mountains. Another table shows 1978 and 1988 denominations by region. The domination of Roman Catholic libraries is clear, as is the importance of the Middle West here. However, the Rocky Mountains and Northeast and the Mennonite and UCC groups were small. Regarding change, the Roman Catholic column contained more minuses for lower scores in 1988 than in 1978. See table 3.6 for 1978 and 1988.

In summary, the seven types of scholarly libraries were introduced in this section and basic information was provided on each one. Growth rates were mentioned, as well as the libraries' denominational affiliations, and regional locations were explained.

Denominations and Tables

The author gave some thought to the problems of tabular presentation of the denominational data. Since it was impractical to make thousands of tables covering the fifty-five or sixty denominations included in the study, a selection was made of the twelve largest denominations in each database (excluding "unknown") in order to develop a uniform tabular presentation for all denominations (they can be seen above in table 3.1). After selecting the largest twelve, the remaining denominations were pooled (including "unknown") into a new and artificial composite called "Other Denominations" to form the thirteenth denomination, thereby permitting assignment of every denominational group and every library to a consistent place on each one of the denominational tables.

Certain of the denominations within the Other Denominations group were only a little smaller than the denominations in the original group of twelve, but the majority of these groups were quite small, both in their own denominational membership sizes and in the numbers of institutions included in this study. The denominational breakdowns are shown in alphabetical order for both the leading denominations and the other denominations separately, as well as in frequency order for the Other Denominations in tables 3.7 and 3.8 (1978) and 3.9 and 3.10 (1988), which include both scholarly and popular libraries.

Eleven of the thirteen groups were Protestant and Christian, leaving two (Jewish and Roman Catholic) that were not.[3] Protestants constituted roughly two-thirds and Jewish/Roman Catholic one-third of the membership in each database. Tables 3.7 through 3.11 (1978 and 1988) clearly show the distribution of denominations for both entire samples and scholarly libraries as a group.

Institutions by Denomination

We must discuss the denominations in relation to a large number of separate variables before we can claim to understand thoroughly the scholarly institutions or their libraries. The denominational affiliation of the library always matches that of the sponsoring institution, and it belongs primarily to the institution and only secondarily to the library.

Tables 2.1, 2.2, and 2.32 show the national denomination breakdowns for both Canada and the United States, and the heavy Canadian emphasis on Roman Catholics with secondary emphasis on Episcopal/Anglican and United Church of Canada. When the three denominations are combined, they constitute 82 percent of the Canadian population. Such large U.S. denominations as the Methodists are poorly represented, and Baptist and Lutheran are only modestly represented on the table. For the United States, Protestants rule, with Roman Catholics running a strong second.

Naturally the data sorted itself into many different American and Canadian religious denominations. To continue this discussion properly we should look at longitudinal table 3.12, which is a composite or comprehensive table for scholarly libraries, and at longitudinal table 3.13, which shows all denominations. Denominational changes during the study decade can be pinpointed here. The denominations are shown in scholarly and popular combined tables 2.36 for 1978 and 2.37 for 1988 arranged by frequency from the most popular, Roman Catholic, with 513 (1978) and 490 (1988) libraries, to fourteen or fifteen different denominations, a fourth of the total, which had only one library representative. These two tables cover the entire database for each year.

Notice that the four most numerous denominations listed in each database contained more than half of its total. In all, fifty-five (1978) and fifty-six (1988) different denominations were represented in the two samples.

Note that 2–3 percent of each database belonged to institutions for which the denominations could not be identified from the evidence available in the *ALD* or elsewhere. They became the Unknown group.[4]

Denominational ratios (percents) are also shown in tables 2.36 and 2.37. In each year, the Roman Catholic group constituted a fourth of the entire database and contained more than twice as many institutions and libraries as the Baptist and Jewish groups, which ranked second in 1978 and 1988 respectively. The Roman Catholic, Baptist, Presbyterian, and Methodist groups led the 1978 table in popularity, while in 1988 it was the Roman Catholic, Jewish, Baptist, and Methodist groups in order, since the Jewish group grew in numbers by 1988 while the Presbyterian group declined during that period. Smallest were the Churches of Christ group in 1978 table 3.14 and the Mennonite group in 1988 table 3.15, which was still increasing its *ALD* membership and was thus added to the list when Congregational was dropped. Both tables 3.14 and 3.15 include scholarly and popular library groups.

When we separate the scholarly institutions from the popular institutions, we have new denominational ratios and therefore a new scholarly denominational rank order: Roman Catholic (a *third* of each scholarly database here!), Other Denominations, Methodist, and Baptist for 1978 and Roman Catholic, Other Denominations, Baptist, and Methodist in order for 1988. The Other Denominations group made up the second largest of the thirteen scholarly denominational groups in each year. The change in the scholarly institutional order was due to a Baptist surge forward in the 1980s. Notice that for such denominations as Jewish and Congregational, most of their institutions were located in the popular classification group, not the scholarly. On the other hand, the Mennonites were more numerous in the scholarly group.

We can ask, To which denominations did the junior and senior colleges and the other scholarly types of libraries belong? Table 2.34 for 1988 provides an answer. Roman Catholics constituted two-fifths of the junior colleges and the universities, three-tenths of the senior colleges and seminaries, a fourth of the denominational headquarters group, a fifth of the history/archive libraries, and almost 100 percent of the convents and monasteries! The remaining components or members of each list were scattered among all other denominations but were especially clustered around Other Denominations, Methodist, Baptist, Independent, and Jewish. To reverse the analysis, we see also that history/archive libraries were often Mennonite and Episcopal/Anglican and the denominational headquarters libraries were often Independent. Junior college libraries were heavily Mennonite and Church of Christ.

A series of scholarly tables starting with table 3.16 for 1988 *Baptist* libraries shows the specific libraries located in the largest cities by denomination. The libraries located in Philadelphia and Houston lead this table. A *Christian* table shows a group of libraries from various regions that were located in smaller cities than were the Baptist libraries. Much the same thing can be said for table 3.17 for 1988, *Church of Christ* libraries. The next table for 1988 contained three Canadian libraries and seven libraries from *Episcopal/Anglican* seminaries or else diocesan offices. We have already noticed that *Independent* scholarly libraries are concentrated in city locations. Table 3.18 for Independent libraries shows that the ninth largest library was located in Chicago, with four million people. In fact, the entire table is a series of New York City and Chicago locations.

Another table is for *Lutherans* and covers only five states and provinces for eight libraries. *Mennonite* libraries in table 3.19 for 1988 were located in smaller cities that went down to twenty thousand population by the seventh listed library. A *Methodist* table for 1988 locates its libraries in larger cities. Various small scholarly libraries appear for the first time in the text in certain of these tables. Table 3.20 for 1988 shows *Other Denominations* and is concentrated entirely among cities of 1.5 million population and above. A table for 1988 shows *Presbyterian* libraries in a variety of large cities.

Again we see a denomination whose libraries are located in smaller cities. *United Church of Christ* in table 3.21 for 1988. By the eighth entry we are already down to a population of seventy-five thousand. A 1988 table shows primarily one city, New York City, and all entries are listed at the four million population level for *Jewish* libraries. The *Roman Catholic* library list in table 3.22 for 1988 concentrated primarily in Chicago, with three libraries added from New York City. In conclusion, all denominations had libraries located in large North American cities, perhaps with the exception of the Mennonites, whose libraries were located in small cities, and this series of tables enabled us to see a small sampling of them.

The databases' denominational frequency may have differed in several ways from the frequency of the scholarly religious institutions and their libraries as actually found in the North American population (reality). However, no comprehensive or directly comparable religious institution and library data was available from the field against which to correct the two databases. The reader can be referred to the discussion of American Theological Library Association and Association of College and Research Libraries information at the end of chapter 4 for an attempt at such an evaluation.

The author believed that the present study's scholarly database was probably (1) weaker than reality in having too few Baptist, Christian Science, Jewish, Lutheran, Mormon, and United Church of Canada institutions and (2) stronger than the field in displaying a large proportion of Friends and Mennonite institutions or organizations. At any rate we have introduced the institutional and library types, regions, and denominations so now we can analyze the present databases to see what we have in more detail for the 1,637 or so scholarly 1978 and 1988 institutions.

Scholarly Matched Pairs (Paired Libraries) Analysis

Longitudinal table 2.54 shows the membership in the entire scholarly database (100 percent), the matched pairs groups (85 percent of the entire database for 1978 and 82 percent for 1988), the no longer listed (15 percent for 1978) and the newly listed (18 percent for 1988) libraries. This subsection will describe certain characteristics of the scholarly matched pairs, no longer listed and newly listed libraries, some characteristics of which differ from those of the database as a whole.

There were 1,169 and 1,171 matched pairs of scholarly libraries in each database, 1978 and 1988. Senior colleges constituted more than half of the matched pairs, with seminaries coming next in size. If we look at table 2.54 closely, we see some incongruous but explainable figures. For instance, look at the seminary numbers under matched pairs for 1978 and 1988. Presumably in the case of matched pairs we should have exactly the same number of seminary libraries in 1978 as we have in 1988, in fact the same libraries. There is, however, a discrepancy.

Instead, we have 184 seminaries in 1978 and 196 in 1988. The reason for this change is that the twelve libraries in question, which were classified as seminaries in 1988, were previously considered to be colleges, but they changed their nature or at least their emphasis by 1988. Note the overall gain in numbers by seminaries, convents and monasteries, universities and history/archive libraries. In certain cases they were junior or senior colleges in 1978 and became universities by 1988. Note also that matched pairs made up as much as 97 percent of the university libraries but only 46 percent of the convents and monasteries in 1978, the remainder obviously being no longer listed.

This finding points to the fact that the 1978 convent/monastery group was composed of libraries more than half of which later dropped out of *ALD*. Obviously convent/monastery was a relatively if only apparently unstable group. On the other hand, only 3 percent of the 1978 university libraries fell into the no longer listed group. Clearly universities, being high-investment and high-profile organizations, maintained relatively stable library questionnaire-answering policies.

Other tables showed that the matched-pairs group was strong and had relatively high quality scores when compared to the other three groups—the entire database, the no longer listed and the newly listed groups. For instance, table 3.23 shows that 48 percent of the matched-pair libraries in 1988 were OCLC members, while only 28 percent of the entire 1988 scholarly database were OCLC members. Further, table 3.24 tells us that the matched pair mean annual total library expenditure was $267,700 for 1988, while the mean annual total expenditure for the entire database was only $249,100, 7 percent less.

Now we will look at the scholarly no longer listed and newly listed libraries. In general, 16 percent of the entire 1978 database dropped out (were no longer listed). However, the percentages for specific parts of the list differ. For junior colleges the no longer listed group registered at 13 percent. Senior college no longer listed were 11 percent of the entire database. On the other hand seminaries provided 21 percent of the no longer listed group and denominational headquarters, 40 percent. Were no longer listed libraries strong or weak as a group?

Further on the same subject, table 3.25 for 1988 shows that scholarly libraries averaged 46,672 microforms per library in general, whereas table 3.26 for 1988 shows scholarly libraries to average only 4,969 microforms for newly listed libraries only. For table 3.27, no longer listed 1978 scholarly libraries, the mean number of microform holdings was only 1,367, in comparison with the 46,672 figure for the database as a whole. The point is that in no longer listed and newly listed libraries the scores were small or weak, suggesting that these libraries were among the smaller and weaker ones in the entire database. Alternatively, they might also be classified as the infants in their groups (depending on age) or as small service institutions.

Newly listed libraries were somewhat more numerous, perhaps by a quarter, than no longer listed libraries, as table 2.54 shows. The only remarkable change here was the frequency of the history/archives newly listed group, which showed a 433 percent surplus over the 1978 no longer listed frequency. There is no evidence to suggest, however, that the 1988 newly listed group was stronger or of better quality than the 1978 no longer listed libraries. Now we can look at table 3.28 for 1978–88, which concentrates on no longer listed and newly listed libraries by region. For scholarly libraries the percentage distribution varies roughly by the percent for the entire database, but look at Canada 1978–88, a strong growth. The Middle West and the Rocky Mountains changed significantly in the decade, also.

Highest Degrees Awarded by the Academic Institutions

In continuing the section on institutional characteristics, the first variable to be studied addresses the highest degree offered question. We will look at degrees by type of institution, region, total expenditure, and denomination. The questionnaire brought replies that are summarized in table 3.29 for 1988. The author's assumption was that a high degree level represented a desirable institutional characteristic. In 1988, the bachelor's degree offered by the senior colleges made up somewhat under half of the degrees offered (44 percent). Neither junior college associate (6.5 percent) nor university doctoral degrees (16 percent) constituted more than a fraction of the total. So, regarding highest degrees awarded, the undergraduate colleges led the way quantitatively.

To a limited extent, later findings are reflected in evidence that shows mean degree level by *type of institution.* In unreproduced tables the degree levels shown are the same in 1988 as they were in 1978 for all types of institutions except for seminaries, for which the average moved up in 1988 from the master's to the doctoral level. Of course, the means for junior and senior colleges were the expected two- and four-year levels. Also, the entire 1988 sample's average highest degree awarded moved up one notch to the master's degree level.[5]

As for institutional degrees awarded by *region,* considerable academic progress was shown during the decade. In 1978 scholarly institutions in the Northeast, Middle Atlantic and West averaged master's degree programs, while the bachelor's degree was the mode in the other regions. By 1988 the mode was the master's degree for six out of eight regions, only the Southeast and Canada still being at the bachelor's degree level. Clearly the advance was made primarily in the western regions. Just why one region differed from another in terms of level was not clear. It was clear, however, that these differences in degree levels awarded were small. The high level of no response figures lent some degree of doubt to the validity of the regional fluctuations.

A trend can be observed here that reflects the real world. All graduate degrees combined equalled only a third of the 1978 total, but this proportion increased to almost half by 1988. Correspondingly, bachelor's and associate degrees decreased their ratio from two-thirds to somewhat above half (53.5 percent) of the total during that time period.

We have several tables on *institutional degree years offered* by *total library expenditure*. The table mean for 1988 was 4.6 years, and the difference between the categories was small. However, there was clearly a positive correlation between the rise in library expenditure and the number of years of higher education provided. Those libraries in the highest category of expenditure were located in institutions that offered master's or doctoral degrees.

A separate table for the matched pairs on this variable showed most of them to be slightly higher, 4.7 years, than the 4.6 year mean of the entire database. As suggested earlier, the matched pairs were thought to be the "cream of the crop" of libraries in most ways, and their cumulated and mean scores on variables were often somewhat higher than those of the databases as a whole. For both the "no longer listed" or dead libraries and the "newly listed" or newly born libraries, the mean scores were lower on this variable, 4.1 and 4.2 years.

Mean institutional degree level is shown for denominations in two unreproduced tables for 1978 and 1988. The highest average 1978 degree levels were those in the Independent, Episcopal/Anglican, and United Church of Christ denominations—they reached the master's degree level.[6] These denominational groups seemed to lead the database in producing graduates of a somewhat higher educational level than those of the other denominations. The Jewish group fell out of consideration in 1978 due to the large no response category, but in 1988 its scores were quite high. Lowest were eight denominations at the bachelor's degree level.

In 1988 the Independent, Episcopal/Anglican (both apparently at the top level in 1978!), and Mennonite groups were at the minimum degree level. It should be pointed out that the number of denominations moving up from the bachelor's mean to the master's mean degree level in the decade from 1978 to 1988 was five. Of course the institutions at the master's degree level were presumably preparing graduate students with higher average education and competency levels than were the bachelor's degree level institutions.

Interim Summary

To summarize chapter progress thus far, after setting the stage by describing the scholarly databases and the types of institutions to be found there, this section found that the Roman Catholic institutions were most numerous, with the Baptist and Jewish groups ranking second for the databases as a whole. One-third of the total were Jewish and Roman Catholic libraries, and two-thirds were Protestant. The Other Denominations group was formed from the large number of smaller denominations. In terms of highest institutional degrees awarded, the bachelor's degree was most popular, but graduate degrees increased in number in 1988. Half of all degree-awarding institutions were senior colleges. Five denominations apparently raised the level of the highest degree that they awarded between 1978 and 1988.

Institutional Accreditation

The next major variable to be examined is higher education institutional accreditation, to which this chapter will devote considerable attention. Presumably accreditation separated the stronger from the weaker institutions. The author's assumption was that accredited higher education institutions were more mature and offered generally better quality education than did unaccredited institutions, at least in the United States; accreditation or approval in Canada is more a provincial government responsibility than it is a matter of accrediting body concern.

Accreditation has been a common feature of American (but to a much lesser extent of Canadian) secondary school and higher education for several generations. It provides assurance for the incoming student and his or her parents that the institution meets minimum quality standards when compared with other institutions of the same kind. The best-known type is regional accreditation, for which the United States is divided into several regions. In each region an organization has been established by the member schools, colleges, and universities to supervise and regulate accreditation, such as the North Central Association of Colleges and Secondary Schools, which covers and regulates several states in the Middle West.

After an institution applies for accreditation, a visit to the institution is scheduled by the association, and a committee is appointed to carry out the visit, make the evaluation, and prepare the evaluation report and recommendations. After a self-evaluation study, the institution itself is asked to submit a detailed report on its present activities. The regional association's committee is made up of higher education leaders from its area.

Such a committee may include a professional academic library leader to supervise consideration of the institution's library, or else the library evaluation task may be assigned to another committee member who is familiar with library evaluation. The final committee report forms a basic document for the association's evaluation of the institution.

After the visit is made and the evaluations are considered, a final report is sent to the institution. After full accreditation is achieved, the institution will be revisited by a new association committee and an evaluation will be made anew concerning the continuation or suspension of accreditation. Such reevaluations are carried out at approximately ten-year intervals.

Professional accreditation complements and supplements regional accreditation. Both regional and professional accreditation programs are carried out by associations or organizations recognized by an officially designated office of the U.S. Department of Education. The professional organization approaches its task in much the same fashion as regional associations do, and visiting evaluation committees are used for professional education accreditation also. In certain subject fields Canadian institutions participate in U.S. professional accreditation, e.g., in library and information science education, but they do not participate in U.S. regional accreditation.

Let us examine regional and professional accreditation along with other variables. Accredited vs. unaccredited institutions and libraries will be examined by type, age, total expenditure, chief librarian's gender, region, and denomination. Tables 3.30 and 3.31 for 1978 and 1988 will help us in this area.

Not only was common regional higher educational accreditation included in these tables but also the professional theological school accreditation provided by AABC for Bible colleges and by ATS for Christian seminaries. The number of libraries distributed by type for each database and accredited by the various accrediting agencies studied was shown in tables 3.30 and 3.32 for 1978 and 1988. We also derived an analysis of regional accreditation by institutional or library type for matched pairs, which showed senior colleges to contain more than half of the accredited institutions in the scholarly 1978 database: 513 of them. Universities were next with 119 institutions: smallest was the junior college group with 81 libraries. For 1988 the numbers were somewhat different, but the internal ratios were similar.

AABC accreditation was primarily focused on senior colleges, while ATS accreditation was focused on graduate seminaries. USOE accreditation affected only a few new and small institutions. Regional accreditation included all four types of higher institutions. Note further that only about half of the junior colleges, 50–60 percent of the seminaries, three-fourths of the senior colleges, and six-sevenths of the universities were accredited by any group on this table. It is especially interesting that almost half of the *ALD* seminaries were neither regionally nor ATS accredited. We may note that the mean number of accreditations per academic institution was one for junior and senior colleges and universities and three for seminaries. We may note further that the total number of all accreditations was 976 in 1978 and 974 in 1988, or 1.5 per institution.

Accreditation and *age* are examined for 1978 and 1988. The analysis showed consistently that the accredited institutions were more likely to be the older relative to the unaccredited and the younger institutions. So old age and accreditation go together here. A seemingly contrary finding, however, was shown for senior colleges. It showed that the AABC-accredited institutions were younger than residual unaccredited institutions. Since AABC was a relatively young organization accrediting primarily Bible and Christian colleges, this finding added another dimension to earlier findings.

Several other analyses were made of regional accreditation. The overall mean *annual total expenditure* of regionally accredited academic institution libraries was $94,000 for 1978 and $280,000 for 1988. Only 22 percent were above $220,000 in 1978 and only 53 percent were above that figure for 1988! The mode was in the $20,001–$95,000 category for 1978 and the $95,001–$220,000 category for 1988. If we look at the regionally accredited institutions for 1978 and 1988 by annual total library expenditure for no longer listed and newly listed libraries, we find that the newly listed were somewhat smaller in expenditure than the no longer listed libraries, but both were small. When we look at regional accreditation by *chief librarian's* gender, we see that males outranked females for academic libraries again with ratios of 1.2 to 1.0 for each year.

For institutions accredited by *region*, the leaders in numbers were the Middle West (265 institutions) and the Southeast (191). The smallest numerically was in Canada (none; regional accreditation did not exist there) and the Rocky Mountains (12). That was for 1978. For 1988 the largest numbers of regionally accredited institutions were again in the Middle West (271) and the Southeast (200). Smallest numbers were again in Canada (0) and the Rocky Mountains (12) for matched pairs only. Regional accreditation can be seen to be a stable and slowly progressive variable with a strong foothold in the Southeast and Middle West.

Our next set of analyses dealt with all kinds of accreditation combined and included library type, volume holdings, annual total library expenditure, and library staff. Let us start with *type of library,* where we find that senior colleges constituted 60 percent of the entire accredited group with junior colleges being least numerous, about 8–9 percent. Table 3.30 shows accredited libraries by type for 1978 and 1988 in numbers. Most academic institutions in this database (seminaries excepted in 1978) were accredited by a regional agency.

Variations on previous themes relating to accreditation and a new variable—*volume holdings*—are shown in tables 3.33, 3.34, 3.35, and 3.36 for 1978 and 1988. Table 3.33 shows ATLA membership for seminary libraries by mean volumes held. Again we see that the accredited seminaries averaged twice as many volumes as the unaccredited seminaries. The same theme was carried forward in table 3.34 for regional accreditation only and for all four types of academic libraries. The volume ratio between the accredited and the unaccredited ranged from 1.1 to 1.0 for junior colleges to 2.9 to 1.0 for senior colleges, all accredited groups being larger than the unaccredited groups on the average.

We can see the findings for AABC accredited libraries and volume holdings in table 3.37 for 1978 and 1988. Here, the nonaccredited libraries had more than twice as many volumes as did the AABC-accredited libraries (this table divided all senior colleges between the AABC-accredited and the non-AABC-accredited institutions). We have established the fact that AABC-accredited academic libraries scored lower on volume holdings than did the other academic libraries. Junior colleges were also either equal—accredited and unaccredited—by staff size or else the unaccredited group occasionally scored higher. Table 3.38 for 1978 and 1988 was similar to table 3.39 for 1978 and 1988, but table 3.38 confirmed the results shown in the other tables in this section with reference to total annual library expenditure.

A trio is formed for mean number of volumes for accredited institutions which is similar to the one seen earlier for matched pairs, no longer listed and newly listed total expenditure, and the results were similar to those achieved earlier, also. Note that the AABC-accredited senior college libraries had fewer volumes than the non-AABC (but regionally) accredited libraries. Seminary libraries showed the volume holdings of ATS-accredited institution libraries to be about twice as large as those of the unaccredited institutions. A table for all four types of academic libraries showed the expected distribution of results, table 3.34.

The analysis of accreditation in terms of *total expenditures* was carried out, also. It showed about a 2-to-1 ratio between the expenditures of accredited institutions and those of unaccredited institutions, on the average. By types of libraries, in all cases, the accredited institutional libraries had the higher expenditures. For instance, in 1978 the overall mean was $154,300 for accredited and $73,220 for unaccredited libraries. For seminary libraries the accredited score was $93,680, while the unaccredited score was $28,480. In the case of matched pairs, that situation just emphasized the difference, except in one category. In several tables the unaccredited junior college expenditure was higher than the accredited junior college expenditure because of a few well-funded and unaccredited libraries (see table 3.40 for 1988).

The table dealing with seminary libraries and their ATLA membership and with regional accreditation and library type showed the expected results. So far so good, but when we study the table closely, we see contradictory evidence for junior colleges and a near miss for universities. For the latter the ratio of mean expenditures per library between the accredited and the unaccredited was only 1.08 to 1.00, almost even. However, for junior colleges the ratio was 0.54 to 1.0; the unaccredited institutions spent almost twice as much on the library as did the accredited! The unaccredited figure represented only a small sample, however, and was also questionable due to a high no response rate.

Additional information on the accreditation situation and expenditures is provided by other tables for 1978 and 1988. The evidence goes in the expected direction until we again come to AABC Bible college accreditation. First, we notice that only about 10 percent of the religious senior colleges were accredited by AABC and, second, that AABC-accredited institutions were much lower in mean total annual expenditures than were the AABC unaccredited ones. So again we see that AABC accreditation was associated with small budgets and limited service when compared with the other senior colleges in this study. Only a small proportion of the senior colleges were Bible colleges, which differ somewhat from other senior colleges.

A further analysis seems to justify the initial assumption of superior status, since it shows that regionally accredited institutions had larger *library staffs* than did unaccredited institutions. Yet another table shows staff size by regional accreditation, table 3.41 for 1978 and 1988. The table shows a wide gap between staff size for accredited and for unaccredited institutions, the ratios being 3.1 to 1.0 and 3.2 to 1.0 for the two years. In fact, the unaccredited institution library staff membership number was so small as to suggest that those libraries were providing no more than minimum user services. Seminary libraries showed the expected larger number of staff members for the accredited libraries. However, the two ratios found did not reach the usual 2-to-1 level and were seriously compromised by the large no response scores of the unaccredited institutions.

Four further analyses show much the same results for accredited libraries that we have seen in the previous series of tables, but with a few interesting exceptions. The new set of tables dealt with the mean number of staff members per library and per accreditation. Again we found a roughly 2-to-1 ratio between the accredited and the unaccredited libraries except for junior colleges. Junior colleges were the only type of library that might also have been eliminated due to a high no response rate. Further analysis shows the expected results for AABC, that it accredited only a limited number of senior level institutions which turned out to be modest-sized Bible and Christian colleges.

Now we may turn to other aspects of accreditation for academic libraries in general. We will examine accreditation by region, chief librarian's gender, denomination, matched pairs, no longer and newly listed libraries. By *region,* the Middle West led in number of accredited libraries, the Southeast was next, and Rocky Mountains was last. For *chief librarian's gender* the ratios by edition were both 1.2 to 1.0, less than the usual male dominance. Is this noteworthy?

Which *denomination's* institutions had the highest percentage of these indicators of status and respect (accreditation) in 1978 and 1988? Table 3.42 for 1988 showed the regional accreditation denomination picture for academic libraries. With an average of 70–72 percent accredited, we see that the leading denominations in terms of percentage of institutions accredited were the United Church of Christ, the Methodist Church, and the Presbyterian Church, three denominations that were strong on many variables. Poorest were the Episcopal/Anglican, Mennonite, Independent, and Other Denominations for both years plus Christian for 1988. Longitudinal table 3.43 shows standings for all kinds of accreditation by denomination.

Based on different variables from those in table 3.42, another table shows the percentage of denominational institutions that were accredited for both 1978 and 1988 with all levels of higher educational institutions being included. By percentage the following three denominations were high in both years: United Church of Christ, Presbyterian, and Methodist, the same picture as we saw above. Accreditation was low in both years for Roman Catholic, Other Denominations, Episcopal/Anglican, and Jewish.[7] Ratios between the highest and lowest denominational accreditation percentages were 1.4 to 1.0 for 1978 and 1.6 to 1.0 for 1988. For *matched pairs* there was nothing noteworthy in addition, though clearly the Protestants again dominated strongly. Matched pair chief librarians were strongly for males for the entire database, 1.25 to 1.00.

When we arrive at the chief librarian male vs female analysis for *no longer listed* and *newly listed* libraries, we encounter some new ratios. Male-female was 1.00 to 1.26, females dominating the 1978 nonrepeat group. But also the male-female ratio for the 1988 group was only 1.07 to 1.00, a small male margin. So both old and new groups showed reduced male dominance. This is not quite the same old story. Again we see among the no longer listed and the newly listed that few libraries listed their financial information and most of them were relatively low expenditure libraries. And of what library types were the no longer listed and the newly listed—we have already seen that they were largely senior college and seminary libraries.

We have several additional analyses of scholarly no longer listed (dead) libraries for 1978. What were the distinctive ages of these libraries? Their mean age was sixty-three, which made them 21 percent younger than the scholarly libraries for the entire 1978 database. We also have several analyses of scholarly newly listed (newly born) libraries for 1988. What were the distinctive age characteristics of these libraries? Their mean age was quite young, forty-four years, younger than the dead libraries, and 45 percent younger than the scholarly libraries for the 1988 database as a whole.

AABC Accredited College Libraries

Next in the accredited vs. unaccredited comparisons, we come to a full set of analyses devoted to the academic libraries with AABC accreditation only. There were only seventy-nine (1978) and eighty-four (1988) of them, so we must be prepared for minimum table cell size. The libraries were analyzed by type of library, region, chief librarian's gender, total annual expenditure, denomination, and matched pairs. We can start with the type of library group that was heavily devoted to senior colleges,

85 percent. Regionally, these libraries were located primarily in the Middle West, Southeast, and West, accounting for 72 percent of the group.

Chief librarian female-male ratios were 1.45 to 1.00 and 1.08 to 1.00 for the small number of AABC-accredited libraries in 1978 and 1988. Female domination was reduced by 1988. See tables 3.44 and 3.45 for 1978 and 1988. Annual total expenditure was heavily centered in the three or four lowest questionnaire expenditure categories ($95,000 and less), a small budget group. By denomination, they were even more heavily Protestant than other accredited groups, 99–100 percent. Other Denominations, Independent, Baptist, and Christian led the denominational list. The matched pairs group presented nothing unique in this analysis. Matched pairs for males vs. females and for total annual expenditures had the same scores as for the entire database. See table 3.46 for 1978, for instance.

Before concluding this series of accreditation analyses, we need to look at regional accreditation and age for each type of academic library. For 1988 junior colleges, 70 percent of which were accredited, we note that the mean age was sixty-five years compared with forty-three years for the unaccredited group; this represents a mean age differential of twenty-two years. For senior colleges in 1988, 76 percent accredited, their mean age difference was thirty-eight years, ninety years old for the accredited vs. fifty-two years for the unaccredited, a wide gap. For universities, 80 percent accredited, mean age difference between the two groups was nineteen years, ages ninety-seven to seventy-eight. For seminaries, 51 percent accredited, mean age difference was twenty-one years, ninety-one to seventy years. In all cases the accredited group was significantly older and presumably better established.

ATLA and Other Seminary Libraries[8]

We have several analyses of seminary libraries in institutions that were ATS members and whose libraries therefore belonged to ATLA. What were their distinctive characteristics? The number of accredited libraries was 143 in 1978 and 123 in 1988. They were analyzed by type of library, region, total annual expenditure, chief librarian's gender, denomination, matched pairs, no longer listed, and newly listed. First, by *library type,* almost all of them were classified as seminaries, naturally, though 7–9 percent were classified as senior colleges.

By *region,* the Middle West and Middle Atlantic led the list in number of institutions with the Southeast coming in third. The Middle West dominated the group with 34–35 percent of each database. For total *library expenditure* the mean was about $220,000 in 1978 and $410,000 in 1988 showing a strong financial position and a real money gain over time. Both years produced larger figures than the overall scholarly academic library mean. *Male-female ratios* for ATLA member libraries were 1.1 to 1.0 and 1.3 to 1.0 for 1978 and 1988, relatively modest in favoring males, but moving toward greater male dominance.

By *denomination,* the largest groups of accredited higher institutions were Roman Catholic, Other Denominations, Methodist, and Baptist. That was for 1978. In 1988, the leaders were Roman Catholic (266), Methodist (125), and Other Denominations (104), as before. Smallest were Congregational (4), Episcopal/Anglican (11), Mennonite (8), and Churches of Christ (23). Note that the Protestant percentage was 74–75 percent, larger than usual. In the *matched pairs* tables we see some difference from those comparisons based on the entire database. The Protestant percentage fell off to a third of the total due to increased Catholic stability of representation. As for the no longer listed and the newly listed, both were quite small groups of little importance in the ATLA accredited group.

For ATLA accreditation only, as listed in the *ALD* for 1988, the leading denominations were Roman Catholic, Methodist, Other Denominations, and Independent (table 3.47 for 1988). For annual expenditure, table 3.48 for 1988 shows their numbers. The mean was about $200,000 per year. Only about ten no longer listed and newly listed libraries were accredited.

For *ALD* seminary libraries only we may study total volume holdings for ATLA- and ATS-accredited libraries in 1978. For the accredited, mean number of volumes was 101,444, and for the unaccredited the mean was 50,422, less than half as many. For 1988, the corresponding figures were 132,736 and 60,793, again more than a 100 percent difference. For the same libraries we can see the mean number of staff members by accredited vs. unaccredited for both *ALD* editions. Accredited libraries ranged from 27 percent to 44 percent better off in mean number of staff members. See table 3.49 for 1978 and 1988.

In an attempt to bring the study closer to other reports of scholarly library statistics and to extend the accreditation discussion, a special analysis was made of certain ATLA and other seminary data. ATLA publishes annually (1) a report of its members' statistical data, so this data can be compared with (2) the *ALD* ATLA member seminary library data reports, and (3) with the *ALD* non-ATLA member seminary library data, to the extent that the three sets of data were comparable.

Tables 3.50 for 1985–86 and 3.51 for 1978–88 summarize certain data taken from the *ALD* and from the ATLA annual conference proceedings statistical report, about which a remark was made in chapter 1 and an analysis in footnote 8 of this chapter. Now we see two tables of cumulative and mean data. These tables summarize the standings of the ATLA members and the seminary libraries in the *ALD*. While this is not a perfect comparison, it is the best we can do with the data available.

Please note in table 3.50 that the ATLA data is organized to facilitate a Canada-United States comparison. In this comparison, although Canadian seminaries averaged more students, U.S. seminaries averaged more faculty members. Canadian libraries averaged more staff members per student and spent more funds per student. In addition, American seminaries more often were affiliated with a university or other institution (1.3 to 1.0) than were Canadian seminaries, which were more likely to be independent.

If we turn to tables 3.33 and 3.51, we can note first the differences between the ATLA member seminary libraries in the *ALD* database and the non-ATLA member seminary libraries in the same database. The included ATLA member libraries were much stronger than the non-ATLA seminary libraries, often by 2-to-1 or even 3-to-1 ratios in their variable scores. Which one of the two groups seemed to be changing and growing faster? This picture was less clear cut, but on most variables, the ATLA members in *ALD* seemed to be growing faster than were the non-ATLA members. For instance, the volume holdings for the former were growing faster than those of the latter—34.7 percent to 21.3 percent per decade. However, on both total annual library expenditure and enrollment per faculty member, the advantage favored the non-ATLA member *ALD* seminary group!

What can we learn from the comparison of the official ATLA member data for the group as a whole, the *ALD* ATLA members, and the non-ATLA member group in the *ALD*? Of course, we must realize that we are comparing somewhat unlike quantities here, groups of data collected with somewhat different definitions and at different times. In any case, we may begin by comparing the three enrollment levels for 1988 (and 1986): *ALD* ATLA data, *ALD* non-ATLA seminary data, and official ATLA data.

Obviously, the group highest in enrollment was the ATLA statistics group, with a mean of 708 students. The ATLA group in *ALD* had about

375 students, on the average, and the non-ATLA group in *ALD* had only 259 students. Just why the two ATLA groups differed from each other so much is unclear. Perhaps the first figure represented full-time enrollment and the other, head count enrollment. The ATLA's own data contained no explanatory or interpretive notes. For volume holdings, the ATLA proper averaged 125,000 volumes in 1986, ATLA in *ALD* 152,700, and non-ATLA in *ALD* 61,200 volumes in 1988 (and 1986). Clearly the ATLA group in either source year was stronger than the non-ATLA group. The reader can make other comparisons, but these remarks have introduced the subject and have shown where the three groups stood.

What can we conclude from our various studies of accreditation as a whole or in part in these databases? The accredited higher institutions differed from the unaccredited institutions on all six or more of the variables tested. The accredited nearly always scored higher on the criterion variable than did the unaccredited institutions. The only exception to this generalization occurred in connection with the AABC accreditation of senior colleges—and there it turned out that even the best Bible colleges were weaker than the average regionally accredited senior colleges, in this study at least.

In summary and conclusion, the study found that the United Church of Christ, Presbyterian, and Methodist institutions were somewhat stronger in proportional accreditation frequency than the remaining denominational institutions. It is obvious from the tables presented here that a description of unaccredited institutions would simply stress their generally lower scores on all variables than those scores obtained for the accredited institutions. However, the unaccredited may improve their status markedly by 1998. It is also possible that by 1998 there will be an entirely new group of young, unaccredited and growing scholarly libraries.

Institutional Student Enrollment Levels[9]

Let us examine still another aspect of religious institutional life. What were the full-time equivalent student enrollment levels of the four types of scholarly academic institutions in this study? And what were the enrollment ratios among the universities, seminaries, junior, and senior colleges? For student enrollment we will examine first undergraduate vs. graduate enrollment, then type of library, region, expenditure per library staff member, specific libraries by denomination, analyses per faculty member, per professional staff member, and denomination. At the end we will make a final summary. Presumably the larger the student enrollment the greater the magnitude of the institution's service to its clientele.

Undergraduate and graduate enrollment information can be seen in tables 3.52 and 3.53, 3.54, and 3.55 for 1978 and 1988. Initially, the no response figures may seem to be large, but they included many institutions without student bodies, such as churches, denominational headquarters, and convents/monasteries, leaving sizeable residual figures for the academic institutions (1,216 institutions total for 1978 and 1,233 total for 1988).

Overall academic student enrollment means were 1,065 and 1,196 students per institution for 1978 and 1988, a growth of 12 percent (an eighth) between *ALD* editions, or 1.2 percent per year. However, certain categories of institutions (types) rose faster than others. Junior college enrollment rose by a fourth and seminary enrollment by a fifth between 1978 and 1988, though there were fewer junior colleges by the later year due to reclassification rather than to sample loss.

These tables show also that most institutions were small in enrollment size. Only 6 percent of the institutions reported more than four thousand students and only 28 percent reported more than twelve hundred students. About 38 percent of the institutions had six hundred or fewer students. Table 3.56 for 1978 and 1988 shows additional student enrollment levels. Mean enrollment totals ascended regularly from junior college to university. Seminary enrollments were about half of those for junior colleges. No table listing university library names was prepared, since forty-two libraries were tied for the enrollment lead within the 5,250-student category, that is, within the category running 5,001 students and above per institution.

We can study mean institutional enrollment by *region* also. Table 3.57 for 1988 shows scholarly institution enrollment by region. Highest enrollment by region in 1978 was in the Canadian, Middle Atlantic, and Southwest regions and lowest in the Southeast and the Middle West, a difference of 41 percent between highest and lowest regions. For 1988, the largest mean enrollments were 1,595 in Canada and 1,363 in the Rocky Mountains. Smallest were 1,023 in the Southeast and 1,065 in the Middle West, a difference of 56 percent. Just what these mean institutional enrollment differences between regions meant is not clear. Clearly in 1978, Southeast institutions were smaller, on average, than those in other regions, however, the author does not know why. Perhaps it was just coincidence? And perhaps it relates to regional tradition, need patterns, population density, or economic viability.

Table 3.58 for 1988 shows mean degree level by region. This indicates that those scholarly institutions in the Northeast, Middle Atlantic, Rocky Mountains, and West averaged master's degree programs, while in the other regions the bachelor's degree was the mode. For 1988 the mode was the master's degree for four out of eight regions, only the Southeast, Southwest, Middle West, and Canada still being at the bachelor's degree level. This represents an unmistakable advance during the decade. Clearly in 1978, Southeast (rural) institutions were smaller on average than those of any other regions, but again this author does not know why.

We have two tables on institutional student enrollment by total *annual library expenditure*. An analysis shows a strong positive correlation between institutional enrollment and library expenditure. Institutions spending under $1,500 per year on the library averaged 150 students, while those spending over $510,000 on the library averaged 3,172 students. See table 3.59 for 1988. Note from the same table that the estimated expenditure per student also rises in precisely the same fashion. Hence are larger institutions more expensive per head?

Now we can look at mean student enrollment per faculty member by library type. Overall student enrollment means per faculty member were fifteen and sixteen for the 1978 and 1988 years, showing negative gain. Largest mean student enrollments per faculty member were in the junior college and university library types in 1978 and in the junior colleges in 1988. Smallest scores on student enrollment per faculty member were in the seminaries and senior colleges. However, the variation from one institution to another was small.

We can examine student enrollment by library type in table 3.60 for both 1978 and 1988. It shows the largest student enrollment per staff member (heaviest library workload) to have been in university libraries. Smallest enrollment was in seminaries and then senior colleges. A further refinement of the previous table analysis was student enrollment by professional staff member by library type. This analysis showed much the same outcome as the previous table except that 1988 junior college enrollment was larger than senior college enrollment by this analysis. Several small colleges had poor (too large) student per professional library staff member ratios. Overall means were 305 and 325 students. Largest mean student enrollments in 1978 and 1988 were in university libraries at the 387 and 416 levels. Smallest were seminaries with 164 in 1978 and 148 in 1988 (smallest workload), thereby benefiting from their graduate status.

Which institutional *denominations* had the largest and smallest mean student enrollments? The largest among 1978 higher institutions were found in the Roman Catholic, Methodist, and United Church of Christ denominations. Smallest 1978 enrollments were found in the Episcopal/Anglican, Christian, and Other Denomination groups. The Roman Catholic institutions had increased their enrollment lead even more by 1988, until they were 30 percent larger than the denomination ranking second, the United Church of Christ group, as seen in longitudinal table 3.61. Smallest in 1988 were the Mennonite and Christian denominations, the latter for a second time. The 1988 ratio of the largest to the smallest mean denominational enrollment was quite large, 4 to 1. This pattern was clearly denomination specific and could not have happened by chance.

In examining scholarly institutions by denomination we need to look at specific institutional performance levels as they relate to student enrollment, also. This information will help us to gain a fuller understanding of the parent institutions and the libraries under examination. Which specific institutions were largest in student enrollment?

As an introduction to the subject, an attempt was made to develop general tables that listed by name the specific institutions which led all others in enrollment levels for all denominations. However, for 1978 there were forty-one and for 1988 there were fifty-three of these institutions at the top student enrollment level, so the idea was abandoned. We must use the specific denomination tables instead. Tabular construction was handicapped for several specific denominations due to this problem—the presence of large numbers of libraries (often 30–200) that were tied for the top ranking on a variable. The fault lay in the questionnaire categorization system, which needed to be broad enough to cover all institutional sizes from very small to enormous. The result was that top categories were required to include too broad a spectrum of large institutions and therefore accumulated large numbers in one category that could later no longer be sorted according to size. No useable table could be made in these cases.[10]

In order to reveal the picture of scholarly religious institutional service in detail, we must examine each denomination carefully to identify the specific institutions that were its leading North American representatives for a particular variable. When we examine each denomination separately through this series of variables, we can see in just which states they were located as a group and what level of performance they gave. The discussion will also bring out the predominating library types. Reading these recitals of facts emphasizing strengths and weaknesses will enable us to gain a knowledge of specific institutions. Frequent summaries should assist the reader in following the discussion. Normally findings will be discussed from a few tables only for each denomination on each variable.

For the discussion of specific institutions below, tables 3.62 and 3.63 list institutional *Baptist* enrollment for 1978 and 1988. Table 3.62 shows three universities to be positioned at the highest enrollment level of over 5,250 students—Temple, Baylor, and McMaster. Seven of the 1978 table's institutions were universities, three were colleges, and one was a seminary. Table 3.63 shows three institutions at the 1988 maximum level. By this date, nine institutions were universities, one was a seminary, and one a college. Two were located in North Carolina, and two, in Texas. Only one *Christian* institution is listed at the top enrollment level, Texan Christian University, well above the other 1988 institutions listed. In general, these institutions were smaller than the Baptist institutions shown above. Only two institutions were over the two-thousand student level.

Leading *Churches of Christ* institutions are listed in table 3.64 for 1988 in order of student enrollment level. Pepperdine and Abilene Christian Universities led by large numbers. Most of the institutions listed here will be seen on later Churches of Christ tables also, and most of them were small, only four institutions registering more than two thousand students. Almost two-thirds of the institutions were universities, however. Notice that three of the institutions were located in Texas and two in Tennessee, more than half of the total.

What will be a common pattern for *Congregational* institutions can be found in a 1978 analysis. Only a few of them were listed, and Washburn University led the group by a large number. It was also true that Washburn reached the maximum enrollment level, 5,250+ students.[11] The 1988 *Episcopal/Anglican* institutions seen in table 3.65 were small, also, and most of them were colleges rather than universities. Bishop's University of Quebec led in enrollment by a clear margin. Two of these institutions were located in New York State.

Independent colleges (2) and universities (7) were analyzed for 1988. Four universities were tied at the top level with maximum enrollment—Brown, Bob Jones, Vanderbilt, and McGill. *Lutheran* institutions are shown in 1988 table 3.66. They were notably larger than the Episcopal/Anglican institutions shown earlier. Wilfred Laurier University was by far the largest of them and reached the top enrollment level of 5,250+

students. More than half of this group was located in Minnesota, Iowa, and Ohio.

One of the smallest groups of scholarly institutions in 1988 was found to be *Mennonites*. Almost half of these colleges (all were colleges) were located in Kansas, and all had small enrollments. On the other hand, as we might expect from their high enrollment level, *Methodists* had more large institutions than any other denomination except Roman Catholic. Six of the eight universities in 1988 table 3.67 were at the enrollment maximum, and each institution came from a different state.

Other Denominations institutions for 1988, of which three reached the highest level, were analyzed here. The three were Ricks College, Brigham Young University, and the University of Winnipeg, two of them being Mormon. The Other Denominations group usually contained interesting information, and this table was no exception. One of the largest institutions was neither a university nor a college but instead was a junior college, Ricks. By location, three of the institutions were in Michigan. The *Presbyterian* picture is shown in table 3.68 for 1988 libraries. Queen's and Tulsa were almost twice as large as any other Presbyterian institution, but only Queen's reached the top enrollment level. Three universities were listed together with seven senior colleges, and two of them were located in Pennsylvania.

United Church of Christ institutions were also analyzed. Only one United Church of Christ institution was large, Eden Webster University, and two of them were universities, the rest being senior colleges. Missouri, North Carolina, and Pennsylvania locations dominated the table. The generally small *Jewish* institutions are shown in 1988 table 3.69. Yeshiva and Brandeis were well ahead of the other institutions by enrollment, but this table included only one large institution. Massachusetts and New York City dominated the geographic locations. No *Roman Catholic* table could be prepared because top-ranking libraries were too numerous at 217 frequency above the 5,250 enrollment level.

Student enrollment totals can be summarized now. Forty-one institutions from a variety of denominations reached the highest enrollment level, 5250+. The strongest denominations by mean student enrollment were Methodist, Baptist, Independent, Lutheran, Other Denominations, and Roman Catholic and the weakest were the Congregational and Mennonite groups. The majority of institutions with large enrollments were located in universities. By state, New York, Pennsylvania, and Texas led the way.

Institutional Faculty Size Level

Now we turn to another aspect of religious academic institutional life in this series of analyses of the institutions sponsoring the study's libraries. Identifying the number of faculty members therein will enable us to learn more about each institution, knowledge that will complement the student enrollment information discussed above. For faculty size, we will look first at the general scene, then at analyses by type of institution, by region, by 1978 vs. 1988, by expenditure, by denomination, and by lists of the largest specific libraries. Finally we will make a summary of the findings.

Faculty size in general can be examined in longitudinal tables 3.70 and 3.71 for 1988. They show institutional faculty members and their increase in number during the decade. Again we see that the mean size was small, but it advanced from seventy-two to eighty-three faculty members per institution in the decade of the study for an increase of 15 percent, about the same as the student body increase rate. Only 25 percent to 30 percent of the academic institutions had more than one hundred faculty members, while 44 percent of them had sixty or fewer faculty members. Small! Since table 3.70 is longitudinal, we may note that junior colleges grew fastest, by 31 percent and universities slowest, by 4 percent, which was to be expected. We have several variables indicating that junior colleges are a rapidly changing group relative to other institutional types.

By *type of institution,* universities had by far the largest faculty groups, their mean membership reaching almost two hundred faculty members by 1988 (table 3.72 for 1988). Seminary faculty membership was the smallest group, with less than half of the seminaries having as many as twenty-five faculty members. Senior colleges had comparatively small faculty groups, also, well below one hundred members on the average.

Notice, incidentally, in table 3.72, that, aside from the three types of scholarly libraries that had no faculty members, the largest percentage of no responses, (35–36 percent) was found among the seminary libraries. For matched pairs the mean number of faculty members for 1978 was seventy-six, compared to seventy-two for the entire database; for 1988 it was eighty-six to eighty-three. For no longer listed and newly listed libraries the mean was thirty-two in 1978 and forty-seven in 1988, for much smaller institutions.

Other longitudinal tables showed the percentage change in number of institutional faculty members 1978–88 for library type and denomination. Mean number of faculty members rose 27 percent in 1978–88 for junior colleges, 8 percent for senior colleges, 3 percent for universities, and 21 percent for seminaries. Highest positive changes were those of the Roman Catholics at 28 percent and the Lutherans at 27 percent. Negative changes were registered by the Mennonite and UCC groups. For the stable group of matched pairs we have slightly smaller figures and for the "dead-born" groups comparatively we have much larger figures, but the Ns in many data cells were small.

In two additional tables (the only ones available for 1988) we can see the lists of institutions with the largest number of faculty members, tables 3.73 and 3.74 for junior colleges and seminaries. Vanier College led the junior college table with 350 faculty members, and Southwestern Baptist Theological Seminary led the seminary table with 170 faculty members. Half of the table 3.73 libraries were Canadian, while California and Texas led table 3.74 geographically. Nine colleges led the senior college table with 350+ faculty members. Seven libraries on 1988 table 3.75 were Canadian or from New York state. For universities with thirty-seven libraries listed at the 350+ faculty member level, no table could reasonably be reproduced.

We studied institutional faculty size by degree years awarded by library type, a specialized analysis, also. University libraries were largest in table 3.76 and seminaries were smallest. This meant that seminaries were much better stocked with faculty members on a per student basis than were other higher education institutions, especially universities. If we look at table 3.77, we can see that there was some variation in faculty size by degree years awarded by denomination. In 1988 the Lutheran and Roman Catholic groups led all denominations in faculty size. At the other end of the spectrum were Christian and Mennonite at about half the scores of the leaders.

The mean number of faculty members by *region* is shown in table 3.78 for 1988. Mean for 1978 was seventy-one faculty members with a high of eighty-seven for the Middle Atlantic region and a low of fifty-seven for the Southeast, a figure more than a third lower. For 1988 the overall mean was eighty-two faculty members. The change during the preceding decade was significant. The Northeast and the Rocky Mountains changed most, by 35 percent and 25 percent respectively. Canada and the Middle Atlantic region led in number of faculty members, the Canadian figure going over one hundred for 1988. The Middle Atlantic and the Northeast were also high. Lowest were the Southeast, with sixty-five, and the Middle West, with seventy-seven. The Middle Atlantic seemed to be consistently high and the Southeast consistently low on these tables. The highest to lowest faculty numbers ratio was 1.6 to 1.0.

Table 3.79 for 1988 shows institutional faculty members by *annual library expenditure*. It shows a strongly positive correlation between mean number of faculty members and library expenditure, which was to be expected. Institutions with mean annual expenditures at $1,500 averaged only ten to eleven faculty members, but those with more than $500,000 annual expenditures averaged more than two hundred faculty members. The corresponding 1978 table (not shown) showed the same pattern of positive correlation.

For academic institutions table 3.80 for 1988 showed the mean number of faculty members by *denomination*. The largest mean numbers of faculty members were those for the Roman Catholic and United Church of Christ groups for 1978 (not shown), and Roman Catholic again plus Lutheran for 1988, as we saw above. These tables showed the correlation between the size of the institution in number of faculty members and the denomination. Obviously, Roman Catholic institutions tended to be consistently large while Christian, for instance, were consistently small. Notice further that almost three-fourths of the Churches of Christ institutions had sixty or fewer faculty members in 1988. Enrollment size and faculty size levels were comparable in the 1978 and 1988 databases.

First in the series of faculty analyses for *specific denominations* and specific institutions is that for 1988 *Baptist* institutions. All of the nine institutions listed were large, with the three at the top having reached the highest faculty size level of 350+ faculty members. All but one of them were universities—Temple, Baylor, and McMaster. Four of them were located in Texas and Virginia. *Christian* institutions were shown in table 3.81 for 1988 by size of faculty. Only one institution was large, TCU. Eight of them were senior colleges and two were from Missouri. Again we see that this was not a denomination with large institutions.

Churches of Christ institutions were analyzed for 1988. The leader, Pepperdine University, was an example of an institution which, according to the *ALD*, shrank in both enrollment and faculty size from 1978 to 1988. Faculty membership apparently shrank from 350 to 230, for instance. That was unusual, since most institutions increased in size or at least remained the same over the decade. Most Churches of Christ institutions were small in faculty size, however. Two Tennessee and two Texas locations were identified. The few *Congregational* scholarly institutions are listed by size of faculty in table 3.82 for 1978. Again, Washburn was far ahead of the other two institutions listed, and none were large.

Episcopal/Anglican institutions were listed by 1988 faculty size. Two institutions were Canadian, including Bishop's University, the leader, which was much larger than any of the others. Most of them were small colleges. Two of these colleges were located in one city, Raleigh, North Carolina, and another two were located in New York City. Table 3.83 shows 1988 *Independent* institutions. Both Oral Roberts and Brown were in the top size group with 350+ faculty members. Three of the Independent institutions were Californian.

Among the 1988 *Lutheran* institutions, four were located in Minnesota and three in Canada. The largest was a college at the University of Regina that reached the maximum level of 350+ faculty members. The only *Mennonite* table available for 1988 faculty members was table 3.84, listing eight small college institutions. Three of them were located in Kansas. *Methodist* institutions were analyzed for 1988. Six of them were listed at the maximum level, 350+ faculty members. All were large universities, none were colleges. Incidentally, the table covering the comparable 1978 Methodist figures (not shown) showed the faculty member count for these institutions to have risen not at all by 1988.

Other Denomination institutions were similar in being large (the top three of them) and being almost as large in 1978 as they were in 1988. Table 3.85 is shown for 1988. Five of the 1988 institutions were large colleges and the rest were universities, in a few cases with faculty sizes well above the 350+ questionnaire maximum. Three western institutions were at the maximum faculty size level—Laverne, Loma Linda, and BYU. Notable in this fast company was Ricks, still a junior college. Seven separate denominations were represented in this table.

Presbyterian institutions for 1988 were analyzed. Again they were little larger than the comparable 1978 Presbyterian institutions. Queen's and Tulsa were significantly larger in terms of faculty members than the remaining institutions, however. Three of them were universities and the rest, colleges. Queen's reached the questionnaire maximum level of 350+. *United Church of Christ* institutions were little larger in 1988 than those for 1978 in number of faculty members, also. In general they were small institutions, most of them colleges. Three were located in Pennsylvania and two in Missouri, as we see in 1988 table 3.86.

Scholarly 1988 *Jewish* institutions were analyzed in detail. Most of them had small faculties, except for Yeshiva and Brandeis, which reached the top level, 350+. Two were New York City and two were Massachusetts institutions. Only two were universities. Again, it was not possible to make a Roman Catholic table because twenty-nine institutions were tied for the lead at 350+ faculty members.

In summary for faculty size levels, forty-six institutions had faculty sizes at the top level, 350+, and Missouri and New York were the leading state locations. Roman Catholic, Baptist, Independent, Methodist, Other Denominations, and to a lesser degree Jewish and Presbyterian were the denominations with the largest numbers of large institutional faculties. Mennonite and Congregational were the smallest faculty size groups. These denominations were similar to those listed above as leaders for the student enrollment analysis.

Student Enrollment per Library Staff Member and per Faculty Member

Two series of tables constitute this section. The first series examines the colleges with the largest student load per faculty member, and the second examines the colleges with the smallest student load per library staff member. These two constitute the best and the worst of faculty and student workloads. Subsections of these two analyses will be studied also. In the analysis of the mean student enrollment per library staff member by library type, overall means were eighty and seventy-four students for 1978 and 1988. Enrollment was fifty and forty students for seminary libraries. What were the ratios here by library type? Students per library staff member for junior and senior colleges ranged from 46 to 1 and 61 to 1 in 1978 and for universities around 120 to 1. Obviously each university library staff member had twice as many students to serve as each junior and senior college library staff member.

Table 3.87 shows student enrollment per library staff member by region. Which region had the largest ratio of students per library staff member? Canada and the Rocky Mountains led with 115 and 114 students per library staff member, while the Southeast had the lowest ratio of fifty-seven students for 1988, a ratio of highest to lowest of 2.02 to 1.00.

When varied slightly by using the ratio of students per library professional staff member, the results were similar but about four times as large. And for clerical staff members the results were similar, also. For student staff members the ratio was similar, with about 275 students per student assistant this time. When student enrollment was examined per library consortium membership—yet another variable—the combined ratio for junior and senior colleges and universities became at least 6 to 1.

In a special analysis, a set of tables examined the highest denominational student enrollment per professional library staff member. These were libraries at the bottom end of the list in which each professional librarian had a large and heavy workload with many students to serve. By denomination these libraries were the worst of the worst, as far as enrollment per professional librarian went.

First for *Baptists,* Campbell University "led" their table with 1,083 students per professional staff member. Table 3.88 for 1988 showed that *Christian* libraries were not as badly off as Baptists. However, nine libraries were listed that had large enrollments per library professional, 450 to 350 students per library professional. For *Churches of Christ* the libraries did poorly in table 3.89. Their ratios ran from 675 to 1 to 404 to 1. Two-thirds of them were universities, and half were located in Texas. *Episcopal/Anglican* enrollment ratios were modest, with half located in Canada and half in New York.

For *Independent* libraries, Jordan College "led" with 1,950 students per professional library staff member; Luther Rice Seminary was second. For *Lutheran* libraries Suomi Junior College led with 750 students per professional librarian. Table 3.90 for 1988 shows that the *Mennonite* group had half of its members located in Kansas. Its libraries had only modest figures. For *Methodists* the University of Indianapolis "led" with 813 students per professional. These are institutions that are poor in size of library staff per student served.

Other Denominations in table 3.91 for 1988 ranged from 975 to 525 students per professional. The worst case was for Southwestern Adventist College in Texas, 975 students per professional. *Presbyterian* colleges (and these are almost all small colleges) were led (from the wrong end) by Grove City College at 2,250 students per professional librarian. *United Church of Christ* had three libraries with ratios above 500 to 1, of which two were universities (table 3.92).

In table 3.93 the *Jewish* libraries were few and had only modest and commendable student-to-professional librarian ratios. Finally, we have an even worse case in the *Roman Catholic* group in table 3.94, a table full of apparent worst cases. Collège de Maisonneuve in Montreal had one professional librarian for every 2,625 students! In conclusion, we found a considerable number of small college and some university libraries by denomination in which the student-to-professional staff member ratio was poor. However, as an ameliorating factor, the questionnaire categorization system probably distorted some of these figures, especially those for large institutions. This problem was discussed above.

We have next a series of tables that shows the institutions with the smallest student enrollment per library staff member. How many students did the academic library staff member serve? An institution with a low score here indicated a very favorable situation for the librarian. Table 3.95 for 1988 for *Baptist* colleges showed a range from nine to twenty students per library staff member. This was small. Even the twenty-student level was a light load for the library staff member, and the load of nine was ideal for the Calvary Baptist Theological Seminary. The *Christian* table (not shown) presented much the same picture. Table 3.96 for 1988 for *Churches of Christ* was short and sweet, since it presented colleges with favorable student and library staff member ratios.

The *Episcopal/Anglican* table (not shown) contained three New York State libraries, half of the total. Table 3.97 for *Independent* colleges consisted primarily of seminaries, Christian and Bible colleges, with favorable student loads. The Reformed Theological Seminary led the table. The next table showed much the same scores for *Lutheran* college libraries; the libraries served seminaries and undergraduate colleges. *Mennonite* table 3.98 was short but featured good enrollment-to-staff member ratios. More than half of them were located in Canada, including the table leader, Winkler Bible Institute. The *Methodist* analysis presented a similar picture.

Other Denominations in table 3.99 presented the range of twenty to twelve students per library staff member. Aside from two seminaries this was a table of small colleges. Tennessee, Kentucky, and North Carolina made up three-fifths of the table locations. Northwest Bible College had the lightest workload. *United Church of Christ* in table 3.100 was a short table with two seminaries, one small university, and two colleges. Cedar Crest College has been prominent in several previous UCC tables. Again the *Roman Catholic* table, in this case table 3.101, proved to be among the best (or the worst!). Its range was from twelve to eight students per library staff member. More than half of these libraries served seminaries. Saint Meinrad College staff members served only eight students apiece. Altogether, this series of tables showed the libraries working under very favorable student workload circumstances.

Now we can look at a list of institutions that had the lowest student-to-faculty ratios, e.g., those libraries serving institutions in which the most favorable enrollment per faculty member levels existed. That list is presented in long table 3.102 for 1988, arranged by denomination for the entire database. While several universities are included, most of the listings are of small colleges and seminaries. The reader can see for himself or herself what the listings were.

Which type of institution's faculty members had the heaviest student loads? Differences were small but were larger for 1988 than for 1978. Largest of these ratios was that of the universities and smallest was that of the senior colleges and seminaries. The library type with the largest 1978–88 change percentage was that of the junior colleges. As for denomination, the largest student loads per faculty member were those of the Jewish, Baptist, and Independent groups; the smallest were those of the Mennonite and Lutheran groups. The Rocky Mountains and Canada had the highest scores and Northeast, West, and Middle West were the lowest in students per faculty member.

In summary for this miscellaneous section, many higher education religious institutions were found that had favorable student-faculty and student-library staff member ratios, as well as a large number of other institutions that had unfavorable or perhaps questionable ratios.

Summary of the Student, Faculty, and Library Staff Member Sections

Now that the discussion has been completed for students, faculty members, and library staff members in scholarly religious institutions, a summary of the analysis of these institutions is in order. Institutional student enrollment levels varied greatly, but averaged 1,031 (1978) and 1,191 (1988) students. The results showed an enrollment increase of 15.5 percent for 1988 over 1978, or a 1.5 percent gain per year. The university student enrollment mean was largest, almost three thousand in 1988, and seminary enrollment was smallest, averaging about 350 students per institution. The denominations with the largest mean enrollments were the Methodist, Baptist, Independent, Lutheran, and Other Denominations.

Mean faculty size in 1988 was eighty-three per institution, with universities reaching almost two hundred per institution in that year. Most institutions were small to medium-sized colleges, probably smaller than most public colleges in the same regions. Those denominations with the largest faculties per institution were the Methodist, Baptist, Independent, and Other Denominations. These are much the same denominations that were listed just above as highest in student enrollment. Lists were provided of the institutions with the best and the worst student enrollment-to-faculty size ratios. Several special analyses were made to reveal the colleges with the largest and smallest enrollment per library staff member or per faculty member.

Library Service

This section will conclude the chapter's discussion of the variables against which the scholarly institutions and their libraries were examined. It consists of the analyses of several small and miscellaneous variables for which data could be collected on the *ALD* questionnaire and that related to library service—consortium membership, library cooperation, OCLC membership, and local automation. A summary will be provided at the end of the section.

Library Cooperation and Automation Service

We have now finished the analysis of the sponsoring institutions so we can move on to examine other aspects of the lives of the scholarly libraries that constitute our primary focus. Therefore, we will turn immediately to several studies of topics that relate to library cooperation and automation. The presence of such listings in the *ALD* entries indicated an interest in cooperation, service improvement, and modern computer use. As a consequence of increased activity, in the 1988 edition the *ALD* provided much more detail on consortia and automation than was found in previous editions.

Cooperative Library Consortium Membership

The attempt to develop a table listing the largest libraries of all denominations by number of *consortium memberships* was successful in this section. Eureka! It is table 3.103 for 1988, and it shows the top thirteen scholarly libraries with either seven or eight such memberships. Eight were universities and the rest were colleges. Three were located in Pennsylvania, three in Illinois, and two in Michigan, thereby accounting for three-fifths of the group. Six were Roman Catholic, and two were from the Other Denominations group, again accounting for three-fifths of them. These were the leading libraries in the 1988 North American database by number of consortium memberships.

Membership in a consortium enabled the scholarly library to share the resources of other scholarly libraries in order to improve service to its own users as well as to offer its own resources for use by other consortium members. The larger the number of consortia joined, the greater the service enhancement, in most cases, one would hope. We will examine consortium membership by number of memberships, library type, region, accreditation, chief librarian's gender, library expenditure, and denomination.

Type of library was an obvious variable on which to analyze library consortium memberships. Overall mean was 2.0 memberships per library for 1978. Leading in 1978 with 2.6 memberships each were university libraries. History/archives was next with 2.0 memberships. Overall 1988 mean was 2.6 memberships. For 1988, university libraries led again with 3.1 consortium memberships. Senior colleges were second and seminaries were third, with 2.6 and 2.1 memberships. Type of library and number of staff members showed history/archives and university libraries to lead in number of professional staff members. These two types of libraries also led in mean number of clerical staff members as well as student assistants. In the final analysis, these two types of libraries plus senior colleges led in mean staff members per library.

Table 3.104 for 1988 provides a view of the eight *regions* and their religious library characteristics. Overall mean number of consortium memberships per library rose from a rounded off two to a rounded off three in 1978–88, an apparent 50 percent increase, but actually a rise of 30 percent. Good! Note that our old bugaboo, the no response column, equaled somewhat more than half of the total number of libraries, however. Differences by specific region could be seen in a separate table. There Canada showed itself to be the leading region in terms of the number of memberships per library for 1978, with 2.6 of them. The Southeast had the lowest number of memberships, 1.4 per library. In 1988, the highest region was the Rocky Mountains with 3.0 and the lowest were the West and Canada (the highest in 1978!) with 2.0 memberships.

Several other analyses were made of memberships. One studied the relationship between these consortium memberships and institutional regional *accreditation*. Clearly the accredited institutions had more consortium memberships than the unaccredited institutions, by ratios of 9 to 1. Much the same picture was found in 1978 and 1988 table 3.105 for all types of accreditation. *Chief librarian's gender* and consortium membership were studied also. The analysis showed that male-led libraries averaged three memberships per library, while female-led libraries averaged only two each. This is evidence that men headed the larger and women the smaller libraries in this study.

We have additional examples of chief librarian's gender differences for scholarly libraries. There is no need to show the relevant tables since the message can be summarized in the text. Institutional student enrollment in 1978 for institutions with libraries headed by males showed a mean of 1,293 students; for institutions with libraries headed by females enrollment was 828. The comparable figures for 1988 were 1,370 and 998 students. These ratios were 1.56 to 1.00 and 1.37 to 1.00 respectively (and depressingly).

Institutions with libraries headed by males had an average of eighty-five faculty members; libraries headed by females, fifty-eight faculty members. In 1988 there were ninety-two and seventy-three faculty members. These are major differences: 47 percent and 26 percent. This difference carries through the matched pairs (eighty-nine and sixty for 1978, and ninety-five and seventy-six for 1988) and then through newly listed libraries (fifty-seven for male and thirty-nine for female). For no longer listed libraries, however, we find a surprising twenty-one faculty members for males and forty-two for females, or 1.0 to 2.0!

By total *library expenditure* the relevant table shows that the number of memberships went up as total expenditure rose, from 1.0 membership for under $1,500 library expenditure to 3.4 memberships for $510,000 expenditure and over in 1978. In 1988 the corresponding figures were 1.0 to 3.3 memberships.

Membership in cooperative library consortia was studied by *denomination* in 1988. Six denominations led with three memberships apiece. Memberships in 1988 were 2.8 apiece for Lutheran and UCC and 1.8 for Episcopal/Anglican. The Roman Catholics were more active than Protestant libraries in this kind of cooperation. Perhaps the remarkable thing about this finding is that no denomination averaged less than two memberships. So scholarly religious libraries were active in cooperative resource sharing, with not much difference by denomination. An eighth of the 1988 libraries had four or more consortium memberships.

Now we can move on to examine each denomination individually in order to identify its leading libraries by number of consortium memberships. Tables 3.106 and 3.107 for 1978 and 1988 reveal two database features for scholarly *Baptist* libraries. They show that consortium memberships grew strongly in the membership decade, the first six libraries in each table showing a 50 percent growth in consortium membership in that period. Both tables were led by libraries that were members of eight consortia, a large number.

The two tables also showed almost completely different lists of libraries, for the first time in these tables listing specific libraries. So both tables are reproduced here. Notable was the presence in the 1978 leadership table of two libraries from Sioux Falls, South Dakota, a state with few religious libraries. Note also that both of these tables were led by Canadian libraries. While McMaster led the earlier table with eight, it listed only two consortium memberships in the later year—surprising!

The 1988 scholarly *Christian* library analysis showed a modest consortium membership display for these leaders. Most of them were college libraries. For *Churches of Christ* scholarly libraries, look at table 3.108 for 1988. Harding University led with a strong six memberships. Three of these were seminary libraries and only two were universities. Two were Tennessee-based and two were Illinois libraries. Two *Congregational* libraries made the printout, too few to warrant a table. However, one, Washburn University in Topeka, participated in five consortia, a good number.

Episcopal/Anglican scholarly libraries for 1988 are shown in table 3.109. Sixty percent of them were seminary libraries. Unusual! Only one university library was involved. Three New York and two Austin, Texas, libraries were found in the table, and two libraries were on the overall leadership list. The *Independent* scholarly libraries presented a strong consortium membership picture led by Brown University, with seven memberships. Kentucky and New York state had two libraries apiece on this list. Half of the libraries were located in senior colleges.

For 1978 scholarly *Lutheran* libraries, table 3.110 presents a surprisingly good showing, with Luther College leading with five memberships. The comparable 1988 table showed more memberships but fewer libraries. Pennsylvania with four libraries and Iowa, Illinois, and Minnesota with two apiece constituted almost the entire table. For *Mennonite* libraries in 1988 the number of consortium memberships was modest. The state pattern was similar to that in previous Mennonite tables with Kansas and Indiana showing two libraries apiece.

In 1988, *Methodist* scholarly libraries can be seen in table 3.111 in a strong consortium membership showing in which Emory University leads the group and has seven memberships. Each library is located in a different state. Scholarly 1988 *Other Denomination* libraries offer another strong consortium membership picture. This time there were two libraries with seven memberships apiece—Aurora University and Principia College, both in Illinois. So Illinois with three and Missouri with two libraries constituted more than half of the table's list.

Presbyterian 1978 libraries are listed in table 3.112. Most of them were located in small colleges. By state, two came from Iowa and three from Pennsylvania. Lake Forest and Wilson Colleges were the leaders, with five memberships apiece. *United Church of Christ* libraries were strongly represented in consortia also. Table 3.113 shows these 1988 scholarly libraries to have been led by Cedar Crest College, with seven memberships. Only two of these institutions were located in universities and one in a seminary. By state, three were located in Pennsylvania and two in Missouri.

An analysis was made for *Jewish* scholarly 1988 libraries. Yeshiva University led this analysis with six consortium memberships in a generally weak Jewish showing. Two libraries were located in Massachusetts, and four of them were located in universities. For scholarly *Roman Catholic* libraries, both 1978 and 1988 tables are shown: tables 3.114 and 3.115. They represented an interesting contrast, in length and in number of memberships, but both provided strong consortium membership pictures. Growth in number of memberships was evident, also. Strangely, DePaul University, which led the 1978 table with eight memberships, reported only four of them for 1988.

In conclusion, the strongest denominations by number of consortium memberships were Independent, Methodist, Other Denominations, and Roman Catholic, with United Church of Christ following. Weakest denominations were Mennonite and Jewish. By state, the leaders were Illinois, Pennsylvania, New York, Iowa, and Missouri.

Membership in the Online Computer Library Center, Inc.

On to a related topic. How did this group of scholarly religious libraries perform in OCLC membership? We will look at OCLC membership by type of library, region, chief librarian's gender, expenditure, and denomination. What about OCLC membership distribution by *type of library*? Longitudinal table 3.116 shows the 1978 and 1988 distributions longitudinally. University libraries led in percentages in both cases, with the percentage rising in 1988 in all types of libraries. Senior colleges were next in order by membership percentages. Convents/monasteries were least often OCLC members in 1988. The longitudinal table for these variables showed large decade percentage increases for each type of library.

OCLC membership was unusual in 1978 but much more common in 1988. University libraries were members in 29 percent of the cases in 1978, but in 69 percent of the cases in 1988; senior colleges, in 17 percent of the cases in 1978 and 49 percent of the cases in 1988. However, junior colleges were OCLC members in only 2 percent of the cases in 1978 and 9 percent in 1988. Seminary libraries were OCLC members in 9 percent of the cases in 1978 and in 36 percent of the cases in 1988.

How was 1988 OCLC membership distributed by *region*? While Canada did not increase its 1988 membership, the Middle West and Middle Atlantic were already showing their leadership in this area. Table 3.117 for 1988 shows that the Middle West led the regions with more than half of its libraries being members, while the Northeast trailed the regions with only a third of its libraries being members. The no response figures were high for these tables, but presumably in many cases this meant that no membership existed.

When we look at matched pairs on this factor, we see somewhat fewer OCLC members there, and that is surprising. When we look at the no longer listed libraries, we see that only 2 percent of them were members in 1978, a very small percentage as compared with the entire scholarly 1978 database ratio of 14 percent. And what about the newly listed libraries? Their 1988 membership percent was 8 percent, small again but larger than that of the no longer listed group. As a sidelight on this situation, a separate analysis for 1988 shows that males headed OCLC member libraries more often than did females. Again female *chief librarians* came out second best in comparison with males.

In general, there was a positive correlation between level of *library expenditure* and number of 1988 OCLC members. Note that only 5 percent of the member libraries had annual incomes below $95,000. When we look at matched pairs for this variable, we see scores that were slightly below those of the entire database, surprisingly.

If we study OCLC membership by *denomination,* in longitodinal table 3.23 we can see that it totaled only 183, or about 16 percent, of the total number of libraries in 1978. Methodist and Presbyterian libraries led the denominations in percentage of membership there. By 1988 all denominations had increased their membership percentages significantly, an average of 207 percent. OCLC membership was now common among scholarly libraries in the United States and Canada. The UCC and Mennonite denominations led this list with 83 percent and 64 percent members. Forty-one percent of the 1988 libraries (44 percent of the Protestant group) were OCLC members. Jewish and Independent scholarly libraries were members of the OCLC least often. Episcopal/Anglican, Lutheran, and Methodist libraries also rated high here, 50 percent or over.

Local Library Automation Projects

A related subject was the development of local automation projects in religious libraries, which we will examine by type of library, region, expenditure, and denomination. This activity grew rapidly during the 1980s. An earlier table (not shown) showed a total of only nine such projects, or less than one percent, for the entire 1978 database. By 1988, however, in table 3.118 the picture had changed and 632 libraries, or 44 percent, of the scholarly database were listed as having automation projects. This was an increase of 6,922 percent!

A table for 1988 was examined for *type of library:* table 3.119. It showed that most of these projects were located in senior college, university, and seminary libraries, in that order, for number of libraries involved. However, 77 percent of the university libraries had automation projects to lead the list. Fifty-two percent of the senior colleges, 35 percent of the seminaries, and 19 percent of the junior colleges were involved, all in 1988. For *region* the Middle West and Middle Atlantic led in project proportions with over half of their libraries active. Only 21 percent of the Canadian libraries had these projects. See table 3.120 for 1988.

When we look at *expenditure* in table 3.121 for 1988, we see a regular progression upward on the library expenditure scale in percentage of libraries with local automation projects. Since 1988 data was often much like 1978 data, then the change since 1988 to the current date was probably small. Only 3 percent of libraries with under $20,000 annual expenditures had local automation projects, but 87 percent of the $510,000 and over expenditure libraries were involved in them. This finding yielded a strong positive correlation between expenditures and automation projects. The United Church of Christ and Presbyterian *denominations* had the largest percentage of 1988 libraries with automation projects, 60–61 percent.[12] Independent and Baptist libraries were poorest here, 32–41 percent.

If we compare the three related areas of library automation and cooperation—consortium membership, OCLC membership, and local automation projects—we find that all of them increased strongly during the decade of this study in almost all analyses. The United Church of Christ, Presbyterian, Roman Catholic, and Methodist denominations were leaders in these activities, while Jewish, Independent, and Mennonite were weak therein. The Middle West and Middle Atlantic led by region.

Miscellaneous Service Topics

The concluding subsections of this library service section cover several small and miscellaneous matters: questionnaire returned, questions answered, repeat question, chief librarian named, two subsections on departmental libraries, subject interests, special collections, publications, and circulation and reference restrictions, and concluding with a section summary and then a chapter summary.

Questionnaire Returned

What percentage of the *ALD* questionnaires sent out to libraries were returned to the publishers? The reader may believe that all questionnaires mailed out were completed and returned, or at least that all for which an entry appeared in the directory were returned, but that is not quite true. The scholarly library return record for 1978 was mediocre, but the record for 1988 was much better. In 1978 the figure was 933 scholarly religious library questionnaires returned, or 67.9 percent of the total published, and in 1988 it was 1,416, or 98.9 percent, of the questionnaires published.

The percentage of cooperation increased markedly by 1988 due in part to increased activity by the editors to ensure returns or else to locate the information elsewhere. When a questionnaire was not returned, the *ALD* editors tried to fill in the entry data cells from information sources such as the state library, local library directories, association membership lists, education directories, reference books, telephone directories, and members of the same library consortium. When the information published was not obtained directly from the library, an asterisk was inserted into the *ALD* entry to indicate that fact.[13]

With such a poor questionnaire return for 1978 it is reasonable to ask, What were the characteristics of the libraries that failed to return their questionnaires? Were they different in certain ways from the libraries that did return their questionnaires? Tables 3.122, 3.123, and 3.124 show certain answers to this question. We will examine questionnaire return by type of library, region, total expenditure, and denomination. Initially, by type of library, which ones were least cooperative? Convent/monastery, junior college, and denominational headquarters types replied least frequently, while university and history/archives replied most consistently. The latter two were only 13 percent and 19 percent delinquent. It appeared that the Rocky Mountains and Western regions were poorest in returns, but not much poorer than the other regions; Canada was most cooperative in returns.

Libraries with total expenditures of $410,000 and under had a number of no returns, but those with expenditures below $95,000 were the worst in 1978. By denomination, Congregational and Lutheran were least cooperative and Churches of Christ and Mennonite best, but again the differences between denominations were small. So, in conclusion, among scholarly libraries, the poor returns came primarily from the Rocky Mountains and Western regions, Congregational and Lutheran denominations, those libraries with smaller expenditures, and convent/monastery, junior college, and denominational headquarters types of libraries for 1978. Libraries fitting into the alternative categories for each variable were more likely to have returned their questionnaires.

Questions Answered

We may now describe several tables that analyze the author's information forms (not the *ALD*'s own questionnaires) (see appendix D) completed on the libraries in terms of the number of questionnaire questions answered per library. Few libraries answered all forty-one questions, but longitudinal table 3.125 showed that on the average, university libraries answered twenty-nine (1978) and thirty-one (1988) questions per library to lead the scholarly library types, 71 percent and 76 percent completed. Convent/monastery and history/archive libraries answered only eighteen questions apiece in 1978, however, 44 percent. Obviously the larger the library the larger the number of questions it should have been able to answer, but many libraries failed to answer all of the questions for which they had data.

Repeat Question

Repeat libraries were those represented in both of the *ALD* editions. All matched pairs were repeat libraries. No no longer listed or newly listed libraries were repeats by definition. The number of 1988 scholarly libraries that were repeats from 1978 was 1,171, or 81.8 percent of the total. Therefore, most libraries were found in both databases. Repeat libraries were similar in their table scores to the scores for the entire database.

Chief Librarian Named

We can look at *chief librarian named* by type of library. This section refers to the frequency with which the chief librarian's name was printed in the library entry. Chief librarian named for 1978 provided a relatively favorable scholarly library practice, at least when compared with that for popular libraries. For 1978, 94 percent of the chief librarians were named in the *ALD* text and for 1988, 99 percent were named, so most of the scholarly libraries can be seen to have named their chief librarians in the *ALD*. But even most of those that did not do so in 1978 complied in 1988. Poorest performances were given by the convent/monastery group and the denominational headquarters group. In 1978, 71 percent of the convent/monasteries listed the chief librarians' names and in 1988 100 percent did so. In 1978, 75 percent of the denominational headquarters libraries listed the chief librarian's name compared with 99 percent in 1988. See longitudinal table 3.126.

By denomination, Jewish, Christian, Roman Catholic, and Lutheran were poorest in 1978, below a 95 percent return. All improved by 1988. As for region, poorest in 1978 were Canada and the Northeast, again below a 95 percent return.

Departmental Libraries I

The first departmental library question asked was, Was this library a branch or a subject departmental library in a network of libraries, as we might expect to find on a university campus, for instance? In only thirty-nine cases, or 2.8 percent of the scholarly libraries in 1978, was the reply yes. For 1988 the yes replies amounted to thirty-seven, or 2.6 percent, of the total. Both percentages were quite small, so obviously most of these libraries were not departmental units in a library system.

In any case, what was the nature of these departmental libraries? Most of them were located in the Middle Atlantic or Middle West regions. They were often seminary libraries in a university system or other parts thereof, their expenditures were in the $20,000–$95,000 range for 1978 or the $95,000–$220,000 range for 1988, and they were often Roman Catholic.

Departmental Libraries II

The few notes at the end of the each *ALD* questionnaire were used for a variety of purposes. This was a catchall question used to supplement the subject heading and special collection questions as well as the denomination and the departmental library questions, especially for small groups.

This question asked for the number of departmental libraries of all kinds (both religious and nonreligious) listed for each main university library's system, whether or not they were covered in this study. This number totaled 217 departmental and branch libraries in ninety-four main library systems, or 2.3 departmental libraries in each system, for 1978 and 261 in 117 libraries, or 2.2 libraries apiece, in 1988. Certain scholarly library systems contained only one departmental library, but others contained as many as nineteen in many different subject fields.

Further, certain scholarly and popular libraries, especially senior college and congregational libraries, served not only the primary user group but also another and smaller but discrete group. For example, Grace College library in Winona Lake, Indiana, served not only the college but also the campus seminary. All of this information was included in the notes.

Subject Interests and Special Collections

Toward the bottom of the second page of the ALD questionnaire were two open-ended questions that asked for a list of the subject interests (headings) and for a list of the special collections contained in the *ALD* entry for each library. Both questions referred to the material collection, the latter one especially to the rare book or special collection holdings. Only the religious subjects were listed here.

Table 3.127 for 1978 and 1988 summarizes the number of each kind of heading found for each *ALD* edition. The number of special collections was much smaller than the number of subject interests. About 43–45 percent of the libraries had subject interests, but only 23–30 percent had special collections. The number of subject interests dropped slightly in 1988, but the number of special collections rose by a third in 1988.

Table 3.128 lists the *subject interest* frequency by topic for 1978 and 1988. General religion, theology, and the Bible led the two lists. In fact, the two lists were similar. The table showed also the change in subject interest frequency from the earlier to the later list. It showed that general religion, Jewish history, and literature, theology, missions and missionaries, the Bible, and pastoral care increased their frequency by the highest percentages. Table 3.129 for 1978 showed exactly what were the subject interests.

In 1978 714 scholarly libraries listed subject interests and in 1988 588 of them did so. These figures represented 52 percent and 41 percent of the total numbers of scholarly libraries in these databases with means of 1.4 and 1.9 interests per library having any at all. Libraries with subject interests listed were numerous. By type of library, denominational headquarters led the list with an average of 2.9 subject interest headings per library for 1978 and 2.5 for 1988. Next was convent/monasteries with 2.7 and 2.6 headings each. Number of interests was similar for each denomination, but Episcopal/Anglican led the list with 2.0 and 2.6 per library.

A study was made to learn the library types, denominational and regional characteristics of the libraries strong on subject interests. Which of the library groups were strongest in this activity? More than half of the libraries with subject interests were senior colleges. The bottom three library types had few libraries with this activity. University libraries were heavily involved. Churches of Christ were strong in subject interest lists, and so were Roman Catholics in 1978. By denomination Episcopal/Anglican and Jewish libraries, with 2.2 collections per library led in 1978, and Lutheran libraries led in 1988.

Subject interest distribution by region was studied also. The Middle West and Middle Atlantic led and included two-thirds of the libraries with an indication of subject interests. Another characteristic of the libraries listing their subject interests was that 98 percent of them were Roman Catholic. Most of these libraries were medium-sized, with annual expenditures in the $50,000–$90,000 range.

Several tables were designed to analyze change over the decade in the variables being studied. Table 3.130 is the first one of these longitudinal tables to be reproduced. It shows the change in the mean number of subject interests listed by the scholarly libraries. The number increased by 31 percent, a significant gain. Seminary libraries led the increase, with a 44 percent change, with senior colleges second. Change in a negative direction was led by denominational headquarters, with a 14 percent loss.

Many libraries listed *special collections*. By type of library, it is not surprising to find that history/archives led the list with an average of 2.2 headings per library for special collections for both years. Next was seminaries with 2.3 and 2.1 headings each. Generally, fewer headings were listed in 1988 than in 1978, but convents/monasteries were unusual in moving from 1.9 in 1978 to 2.4 in 1988. Scholarly libraries as a whole averaged 1.7 special collections in 1978 and 1.6 in 1988. Only convents/monasteries had a positive change percentage, 26 percent.

Scholarly special collections were listed by 416 of 1,375 libraries in the 1978 database and 530 of the 1,431 libraries in the 1988 database. That yields the following percentages: 30 percent and 37 percent. Means for each year were 1.7 and 1.6 special collections per library listing any at all. In table 3.131 for 1978 and 1988 and 3.132 for 1978 we have lists of the most popular subjects for special collections. We can see only that the subject interests and special collection lists were similar. And again the 1988 special collection list showed the change from the 1978 special collection list. Church history, Judaism, comparative religion, and other, miscellaneous faiths and denominations, and Bibles showed the greatest gain, and table 3.132 listed the specific special collection names.

A longitudinal table was made to describe the change in the number of special collections. As a whole, scholarly libraries remained constant at 1.7 collections per library. Convent/monastery libraries led with a 26 percent increase. University libraries led in a negative direction with a 12 percent decrease in a number of special collections.

An attempt to interpret these tables on subject interest and special collections can be seen in 1978 and 1988 table 3.133, Measures of Concentration, a concept that we have discussed before. This table attempted to show whether the data tended to focus and center itself narrowly or else to proliferate interests and collections. The data generally showed a tendency by the two databases away from concentration and toward proliferation of listings. So be it.

Publications

Also near the bottom of the second page of the *ALD* questionnaire was a question asking for listings of books and serials published by the library. Here are the results of that request for information. Scholarly library publications can be seen in tables 3.134, 3.135, 3.136, and 3.137 covering 1978 and 1988. Table 3.134 lists the leading types of publications according to their frequencies. Leaders were library newsletters, guides and handbooks, and bibliographies, and they accounted for 30 percent of the publications. Most of them were designed to facilitate library use, but monographs later in the list included many literary titles.

Table 3.135 shows a 1978 publications list. The 1988 list was too long to reproduce here. The number of Roman Catholic publications led the list, with Other Denominations second and Methodist third. See table 3.136 for 1988. Mean number of publications per library was highest in

1988 for UCC, with Lutheran and Roman Catholic next. Publications are listed by type in table 3.137 for 1988 scholarly libraries. Total number was 597 publications. Thirteen hundred seventy-five scholarly libraries had a total of fifty-eight publications in 1978, and 1,431 scholarly libraries had 366 publications in 1988, or about one for every four libraries. The average was 1.7 apiece for the libraries that had publications.

Among these libraries with publications for 1988, change during the decade was nil. The 1988 universities led in number of publications per library, with senior colleges second, 1.8 and 1.6. Their mean publication figures were 1.9 and 1.6 per library respectively in 1978 for those libraries concerned. Middle Atlantic led the list by region, with Middle West and Southeast next. For 1988 all scholarly library types had publications except convents/monasteries. Scholarly publications were few among the journals published. Obviously only a few scholarly libraries were strong in producing publications.

Circulation and Reference Service to Members Only

In 1978, fifty-six scholarly libraries, or 4 percent of the total, had a "circulation to members only" rule, while in 1988, fifty-five, or 3.8 percent of them, had such a rule, indicating little change. This rule was apparently designed to restrict library use to the members of a particular institution, student body, or user group having some sort of right to use that other borrowers lacked. Presumably, such a restriction was imposed because of the danger of leaving too few books on the shelves for member use.

In 1978, also, forty-nine, or 3.6 percent, of the scholarly libraries restricted reference service to members only, while in 1988, fifty-three, or 3.7 percent, had such a restriction, again indicating little change. This picture was similar to that for circulation restriction above. The numbers given above total 105 libraries for 1978 and 108 for 1988. The percentage now becomes 7.5 percent of the total number of libraries in each year. An attempt was made to identify the characteristics of this small group of restricted libraries. Table 3.138 for 1978 enables us to pin down one of its characteristics. It shows that 42 percent of the restricted libraries were quite small in terms of total expenditures. The 1988 table (not shown) showed no change from that generalization.

Two more statistics were helpful in pinning down this phenomenon's characteristics. When we look at the libraries restricting circulation and reference service by type, we see strong concentrations in the denominational headquarters, convent/monastery, and history/archives types, but not among the academic libraries. The three former library types account for 32 percent, 26 percent, and 15 percent of the total in these groups for both 1978 and 1988. By denomination, Roman Catholic and Other Denominations were leaders among the libraries. These libraries seemed to be located primarily in the Middle Atlantic and Middle West, but then many other kinds of libraries were located in these regions, also.

Special Studies

Two additional special studies were made, and we will look at them now. Several tables were made to analyze Additional Library Activities (cumulative). Additional Library Activities included OCLC and consortium memberships and local library automation projects. See longitudinal tables 3.139 and 3.140 and table 3.141 for 1988. First by library type, university libraries were clearly the leaders, with a 4.7 mean as compared with the overall mean of 3.7 projects for scholarly libraries in general. Next highest was senior colleges at 3.8. Smallest mean was history/archives (for 1988) at 1.8 projects. The relevant longitudinal table showed that senior colleges registered a 73 percent growth rate. As far as denomination went, UCC led with a score of 4.4. Presbyterian, Methodist, and Lutheran followed at 4.0. Smallest were Churches of Christ and Jewish, below 3.0 projects. Growth rate was highest for Presbyterians at 90 percent. For regions, highest was the Middle West at 4.2 and the Middle Atlantic at 4.0. Lowest was Canada at 3.1 projects.

Another analysis was made for Extended Services and Collections (cumulative). Extended Service and Collections included library special collections, subject interests, and publications. A high score on this measure meant high scores on its component parts. By library type, the highest score was made by history/archives at 3.8 against an overall mean of 2.5 in 1988. Junior college had the smallest score at 1.5. Growth rate was modest in all cases. By denomination, the highest score was made by Jewish libraries, with a score of 4.2, with Independent next at 3.0. Presbyterian was smallest at 2.0. By region for 1988 Northeast was highest at 3.2 and Rocky Mountains was smallest at 1.9.

Section Summary

An attempt to summarize meaningfully the many variables that this section presents may seem to be foolhardy, but here is this author's intepretation. For questionnaires returned, the percentage rose significantly 1978 to 1988—by 46 percent. A major improvement! Those libraries failing to return their 1978 questionnaires were largely Congregational or Lutheran libraries located in junior colleges, convents/monasteries, or denominational headquarters in the Rocky Mountains or the West.

For repetition of libraries between the two databases, 1,640 specific libraries were paired and appeared in both databases. Somewhat less than 3 percent of the libraries were branches in an academic library system. As for the number of branch or departmental system libraries included in these databases, the total numbers were 217 and 216 branch libraries, with mean branch figures per system of 2.2 and 2.3 libraries. In addition, certain libraries served not only the main institution and its users but also a subsidiary institution such as a seminary.

Several tables showed us the headings of the subject interests and special collections listed by these libraries. Theology, general religion, and the Bible led the subject interest list. Church history, evangelism, and Roman Catholicism led the special collections subject list. Table 3.133 for 1978 and 1988 showed the results of a study of subject interest and special collection headings in terms of concentration vs. proliferation of headings on a single topic, such as the Bible. The tendency was somewhat toward proliferation of headings.

In conclusion, book and serial publications were discussed also. Library publications were generally few in number, but some libraries published several titles annually. For another variable, circulation and reference service to users was restricted to institution members in about 3.5 percent of the scholarly libraries in each database.

Chapter Summary

This chapter introduced a variety of scholarly institutional variables. The seven types of scholarly libraries were introduced as well as such standard variables as region, total expenditure, chief librarian's gender, volumes, age, and denomination. The numbers and proportions of each type, region, and denomination of libraries were discussed. A detailed examination of religious library denominations was given. The origin of the Other Denomination group was explained, as well as the domination of the Roman Catholics in these databases.

The chapter then turned to a description of the higher education institutions sponsoring the scholarly libraries. It began with a discussion of the highest degrees awarded by these institutions. The domination of senior college bachelor's degrees was discussed. Institutional accreditation and its examination by type of library as well as the problems with AABC accreditation were explained. This discussion brought out the relationship of accreditation to several other variables. The special problems of seminary libraries were also mentioned.

Student enrollment and faculty levels were explained, as well as their relationship to several other variables. A detailed examination was made of the relationship between student enrollment and faculty size on the one hand and several other variables on the other. Student enrollment by library staff member and by faculty member was examined in special analyses.

The chapter then turned to an analysis of library service in its various aspects. The first major subsection of that heading was library cooperation and automation service. Consortium memberships were analyzed and compared with other variables, including denominations. OCLC membership was singled out for special attention. Local automation projects were examined also. All of these variables increased in size or frequency during the decade of the 1980s. The UCC, Presbyterian, Roman Catholic, and Methodist denominations were leaders here. Several other minor variables were examined also—questionnaire return, questions answered, repeat questions, chief librarians named, departmental libraries, subject interests, special collections, publications, and circulation and reference service to members only—which concluded the analysis.

Notes

1. The U.S. Bureau of the Census, *Statistical Abstract 1990* (Washington, D.C.: Government Printing Office, 1990), p. 165, listed totals of 1,249 junior colleges and 3,398 senior colleges and universities in the United States in 1988. If we compare our 1988 *ALD* U.S. figures with those in the *Statistical Abstract,* we can see that this study had about 9.2 percent of the *Statistical Abstract* junior colleges and 33 percent of the other higher institutions in the *ALD* religious sample. Of course, the large proportion of public community colleges in the field left the number of private religious junior colleges at a low proportion of the total.
2. No claim is made that the data studied here were necessarily typical of religious institutions or libraries in North America. All we can say is that they

were comprehensive for the *American Library Directory,* which was thought to be a reasonably adequate list of scholarly religious libraries. Nor did the study establish hypotheses for many of its variables, due to the lack of information on them and on their populations. In addition, no appropriate sets of general academic library statistics and means could be located for the two years of these databases. However, useful comparisons are made in chapter 4 with ATLA seminary library data and with Association of College and Research Libraries (ACRL) large university library data.

3. The author is using the designation *Protestant* loosely here. What is included is any discrete religious group (Christian or non-Christian) that is neither Jewish nor Roman Catholic. Thus the word *Protestant* is being used as a catchall category. The author does not wish to offend or misclassify any group, sect, faith, or denomination by calling it a Protestant or denominational group, though most of the groups in the Protestant category are normally called Protestant denominations in the United States and Canada. However, it is clearly much more practical to develop analyses and tables with thirteen to fourteen subgroups rather than with twenty-four or more, especially when many of the additional groups are quite small.

   Practicality has ruled here, so the author apologizes if he has given offense to any group, especially Bahai, Buddhist, Church of Scientology, Eastern Orthodox, Mormon, Muslim, Rosicrucian, Theosophist, or United Church of Religious Science. All Christian and non-Christian sects, groups, and faiths except Jewish and Roman Catholic are included in the "Protestant" group as used in this study. The category Other Denominations is used in the same way and includes about forty different religious groups.

4. The database's Independent and Unknown denominational groups should not be confused. The Independents were thought to deliberately affiliate with no other formally organized Christian group, while the Unknowns were institutions for which the denominations were not known. Probably most of the "Unknown" institutions were affiliated with some denomination, but the author was unable to identify that denomination from the information available to him.
5. Incidentally, there was occasional evidence that the chief librarians reporting to the *ALD* did not know the latest developments on their own campuses. In certain instances there was disagreement between the *ALD* and other higher education reports (no doubt sent in by other campus officials) on the institution's highest degree awarded, bachelor's or master's.
6. Both the Anglican Church of Canada and the U.S. Episcopal Church belonged to the worldwide Anglican Communion and therefore belonged to the same denominational family. Most figures given for the Episcopal/Anglican denomination included their libraries in both the United States and Canada. In certain tables, to save space, only the word *Episcopal* was used to refer to both denominational groups. In much the same way, convent and monastery on the one hand and history and archive institutions and libraries on the other hand were joined in a single listing to represent each closely related group in many tables.

7. Jewish institutions were relatively low on accreditation, due in part to the lack of a separate Jewish accrediting agency concentrating on Colleges of Judaica. The Jewish seminaries were excluded from the ATS accreditation since they were not Christian. The rabbinical seminary association, the Association of Advanced Rabbinical and Talmudic Schools, New York, seemed not to cover Judaica colleges, nor did the seminaries that they covered have libraries listed by the *ALD*. This was unfortunate.
8. Need for changes made to reported ATLA proceedings figures. The information provided for ATLA libraries in several annual ATLA conference proceedings in the late 1980s proved to contain an unidentified number of errors which could not be fully corrected due to an inability to identify the precise degree, direction, and pervasiveness of the perceived inconsistencies. In addition, it is not possible to know exactly what definitions, if any, were used for such terms as *professional, clerical, enrollment, faculty member,* etc. Therefore, given these areas of doubt, it was possible to make corrections only for errors that were most obvious, e.g., where cumulated expenditures registered significantly in excess of the "totals" shown on the printed tables.

   A secondary result of the discrepancies shows in the means, medians, and ranges calculated for the printed values. These must be regarded as approximations only as it is impossible to estimate accurately the number of errors in the data and the degree of their effect on summary statistics. This tendency is made even more severe through the fact that the statistician was not able to distinguish between values that legitimately registered a zero and those zeros which simply represented missing data. Thus, means, medians, and terminal range values were probably calculated on the basis of slightly inaccurate numbers of cases, resulting in greater deviations from the true values of these statistics. The 1996 ATLA Conference Proceedings Summary volume contains a newly expanded and improved library statistics section.
9. Student enrollment had the same problems as certain other variables in having too little space on the 8.5-by-11-inch (A4) *ALD* questionnaire to accommodate the range of categories and figures up to the top scores of the largest institutions. Therefore, the top figure in all tables was merely the level of the highest category, or more precisely, the assumed midpoint of the highest category. The tables in all chapters should be interpreted to mean not just thirteen or even thirteen+ but thirteen or more professional staff members, for instance, since the questionnaire listed the highest category as ten or more, and thirteen was the midpoint of that top-level category. Often this top level represented only a fraction of the proper size of the figures for the largest research libraries, for total volumes or total library expenditures, for example. Yet on the other hand, the questionnaire scale had also to accommodate the much smaller figures of small congregational libraries. While the majority of institutions could easily be fitted into the questionnaire parameters, a small percentage of variable scores at the top for large institutions were not well accommodated in this questionnaire.

10. Among the printouts listing the ten to twelve leading or largest libraries in various categories, most were put into table form (by denominations, types of libraries, or other variables) for use in this book, but some could not be so portrayed. In making the tables, the author's strong preference was to list only the ten to twelve largest libraries. Listing more than that seemed to be unnecessary and would have consumed more space than the table was worth in the chapter.

    An additional rule was that all libraries with a particular score had to be shown. For instance, if one library with three consortium memberships was included, then *all* libraries with three memberships had to be shown. In certain cases, no table or only a short table was made because too many libraries achieved the same score. In fact, in certain cases, more than a dozen libraries showed the highest score (sometimes as many as 200 libraries!), so no table at all could be made. This situation happened with Roman Catholic, Methodist, Presbyterian, senior college, and university libraries frequently.
11. Washburn University, seen in 1978 tables as the largest scholarly Congregational denomination library, was listed in 1988 tables as belonging among the Other Denominations libraries. Why? While Congregational libraries were numerous enough in 1978 to warrant a separate listing and set of tables, their numbers were significantly smaller in the 1988 database, too small to warrant a separate listing and table.

    For Mennonite tables the history was just the opposite. For 1978 there were few Mennonite libraries, but for 1988 there were enough to allow it to replace Congregational among the basic thirteen denominational table listings. So Congregational listings were found separately in the 1978 tables but not in the 1988 tables, and Mennonite listings were found separately in the 1988 tables but not in the 1978 tables. And further, when the Congregational and Mennonite denominations were not listed in the tables in their own names, they were always listed as part of the large Other Denomination group.
12. PresbyNet is an ecumenical, computer-accessible bulletin board and electronic mail system with conference proceedings that has five hundred or more members. See the Graduate Theological Union *Library Bulletin* 5 (Spring/Summer 1987): 2. Probably several other electronic theological library networks exist by now.
13. The reader should realize that a few of the libraries changed classifications between the 1978 and 1988 *ALD* editions. They changed from junior to senior college or from senior college to university classification, for instance, because their parent institutions changed their nature. In a few other cases, the library's classification changed between editions in other ways also. For instance, a library that served both a college and a seminary may have seemed to emphasize the former in the earlier edition and the latter in the later edition, so was classified accordingly. In a similar manner, a few libraries changed location between editions because the parent institution moved.

TABLE 3.1
1978 *American Library Directory* Most Popular Library Type by Denomination

Denomination	First	Second	Third
Baptist	Senior College	Congregational	University
Christian	Senior College	Congregational	Seminary
Churches of Christ	Senior College	Junior College	Seminary
Episcopal/Anglican	Congregational	Seminary	Senior College
Independent	Senior College	Seminary	Headquarters
Lutheran	Congregational	Senior College	Seminary
Mennonite	Senior College	History/Archives	Congregational
Methodist	Senior College	Congregational	University
Other Denominations	Senior College	Congregational	Seminary
Presbyterian	Congregational	Senior College	Seminary
United Church of Christ	Senior College	Congregational	Seminary
Jewish	Congregational	Parochial	Seminary
Roman Catholic	Senior College	Seminary	University

TABLE 3.2
1988 *American Library Directory* Scholarly Library Type (Actual) by Denomination

	----------Type of Library----------						
Denomination	Junior College	Senior College	University	Seminary	Convent/ Monastery	Denom. HQ	History/ Archives
Baptist	7	78	28	25	0	5	9
Christian	1	30	3	5	0	1	1
Churches of Christ	5	13	5	4	0	0	0
Episcopal/Anglican	2	8	4	10	0	3	5
Independent	0	40	11	26	0	17	3
Lutheran	9	36	7	12	1	5	6
Mennonite	3	12	0	1	0	1	5
Methodist	18	81	25	15	0	1	9
Other Denominations	14	118	17	32	0	18	18
Presbyterian	5	62	7	12	0	2	2
U.C.C.	0	15	3	4	0	0	3
Jewish	0	9	5	10	0	10	11
Roman Catholic	44	203	74	74	24	23	16
Total	108	705	189	230	25	86	88

TABLE 3.3
1988 *American Library Directory* Scholarly Library Type by Region (Actual)

	Type of Library						
Region	Junior College	Senior College	University	Seminary	Convent/ Monastery	Denom. HQ	History/ Archives
Northeast	5	31	6	14	4	4	12
Middle Atlantic	18	111	21	55	5	24	27
Southeast	35	153	27	29	3	11	8
Southwest	6	44	35	22	0	4	6
West	7	56	25	19	1	9	11
Rocky Mountains	2	9	2	3	1	2	2
Middle West	20	225	44	64	7	23	15
Canada	15	76	29	24	4	9	7
Total	108	705	189	230	25	86	88

Note: Total number of libraries is 1,431.

TABLE 3.4
1988 *American Library Directory* Most Popular Scholarly Library Regions by Denomination

Denomination	First	Second	Third
Baptist	Southeast	Southwest	Middle West
Christian	Southeast	Middle West	Southwest
Churches of Christ	Middle West	Southwest	Southeast
Episcopal/Anglican	Southeast	Canada	Middle Atlantic
Independent	Southeast	Middle West	Middle Atlantic
Lutheran	Middle West	Middle Atlantic	West
Mennonite	Middle West	Canada	Middle Atlantic
Methodist	Southeast	Middle West	Southwest
Other Denominations	Middle West	Middle Atlantic	West
Presbyterian	Southeast	Middle West	Middle Atlantic
United Church of Christ	Middle West	Middle Atlantic	Southeast
Jewish	Middle Atlantic	Middle West	West
Roman Catholic	Middle West	Middle Atlantic	Canada

TABLE 3.5
1978 and 1988 *American Library Directory* Scholarly Library Denominations by Region, Percentages Only

Region	Bapt	Christ	C. Ch	Epis	Indep	Luth	Menn	Meth	O. Denom	Pres	UCC	Jew	RC	Total
1978														
Northeast	0	0	0	3	11	0	0	5	12	0	3	5	62	100
Middle Atlantic	3	0	0	2	6	4	0	5	15	5	2	7	50	100
Southeast	24	6	2	3	8	1	0	24	9	13	1	0	9	100
Southwest	23	8	7	2	4	2	0	13	11	7	1	0	22	100
West	10	3	3	0	10	4	1	5	27	4	1	3	28	100
Rocky Mountains	7	0	0	0	7	7	0	11	37	4	0	0	26	100
Middle West	6	3	2	1	3	10	2	10	17	6	2	2	35	100
Canada	5	0	0	11	6	4	1	0	10	3	0	2	57	100
Total	10	3	2	2	6	5	1	11	15	7	2	3	34	100
1988														
Region	Bapt	Christ	C. Ch	Epis	Indep	Luth	Menn	Meth	O. Denom	Pres	UCC	Jew	RC	Total
Northeast	0	0	0	4	11	0	0	7	16	0	4	5	54	100
Middle Atlantic	3	0	0	2	6	6	1	6	14	5	2	8	46	100
Southeast	25	5	2	3	9	2	0	22	9	13	2	0	8	100
Southwest	26	6	6	3	7	2	0	14	9	7	1	0	20	100
West	8	4	2	1	9	5	1	5	26	4	2	5	28	100
Rocky Mountains	5	0	0	0	10	5	0	14	33	5	0	0	29	100
Middle West	7	3	2	1	4	10	3	11	17	6	3	3	31	100
Canada	5	1	1	5	7	4	5	1	16	2	0	2	52	100
Total	11	3	2	2	7	5	2	10	15	6	2	3	32	100

TABLE 3.6
1978 and 1988 *American Library Directory* Scholarly Library Denominations by Region (Actual)

	1978 Denomination													
Region	Bapt	Christ	C. Ch	Epis	Indep	Luth	Menn	Meth	O. Denom	Pres	UCC	Jew	RC	Total
Northeast	0	0	0	2	8	0	0	4	9	0	2	4	47	76
Middle Atlantic	8	0	1	6	15	11	1	13	39	13	6	18	133	264
Southeast	64	15	6	7	21	4	1	64	23	34	4	0	24	267
Southwest	26	9	8	2	4	2	0	15	12	8	1	0	25	112
West	12	4	4	0	12	5	1	6	32	5	1	4	33	119
Rocky Mountains	2	0	0	0	2	2	0	3	10	1	0	0	7	27
Middle West	23	12	8	4	14	42	10	42	70	26	10	7	144	412
Canada	5	0	0	11	6	4	1	0	10	3	0	2	56	98
Total	140	40	27	32	82	70	14	147	205	90	24	35	469	1,375

	1988 Denomination													
Region	Bapt	Christ	C. Ch	Epis	Indep	Luth	Menn	Meth	O. Denom	Pres	UCC	Jew	RC	Total
Northeast	0	0	0	3	8	0	0	5	12	0	3	4	41	76
Middle Atlantic	8	1	1	5	16	15	2	15	37	14	6	20	121	261
Southeast	66	14	6	9	23	5	1	59	24	34	4	1	20	266
Southwest	31	7	7	3	8	2	0	16	11	8	1	0	23	117
West	10	5	3	1	12	7	1	7	33	5	1	7	36	128
Rocky Mountains	1	0	0	0	2	1	0	3	7	1	0	0	6	21
Middle West	27	13	8	3	17	40	10	43	67	25	10	10	125	398
Canada	9	1	2	8	11	6	8	1	26	3	0	3	86	164
Total	152	41	27	32	97	76	22	149	217	90	25	45	458	1,431

TABLE 3.6 (continued)
1978 and 1988 *American Library Directory* Scholarly Library Denominations by Region: (Actual)

	Percentage Change, Denomination													
Region	Bapt	Christ	C. Ch	Epis	Indep	Luth	Menn	Meth	O. Denom	Pres	UCC	Jew	RC	Total
Northeast	N/A	N/A	N/A	50	0	N/A	N/A	25	33	N/A	50	0	−13	0
Middle Atlantic	0	N/A	0	−17	7	36	100	15	−5	8	0	11	−9	−1
Southeast	3	−7	0	29	10	25	0	−8	4	0	0	N/A	−17	−0
Southwest	19	−22	−13	50	100	0	N/A	7	−8	0	0	N/A	−8	4
West	−17	25	−25	N/A	0	40	0	17	3	0	0	75	9	8
Rocky Mountains	−50	N/A	N/A	N/A	0	−50	N/A	0	−30	0	N/A	N/A	−14	−22
Middle West	17	8	0	−25	21	−5	0	2	−4	−4	0	43	−13	−3
Canada	80	N/A	N/A	−27	83	50	700	N/A	160	0	N/A	50	54	67
Total	9	3	0	0	18	9	57	1	6	0	4	29	−2	4

TABLE 3.7
1978 *American Library Directory* Denominational Breakdown for Scholarly and Popular Libraries

Denomination	Number of Libraries	Percentage
Baptist	223	11
Christian/Disciples of Christ	59	3
Churches of Christ	27	1
Congregational	33	2
Episcopal/Anglican	74	4
Independent	87	4
Jewish	198	10
Lutheran	123	6
Methodist	202	10
Presbyterian	205	10
Roman Catholic	513	25
United Church of Christ	37	2
Other Denominations, Faiths, and Unknown in alphabetical order		
Adventist	16	1
Assemblies of God	13	1
Bahai	1	0
Bible Fellowship	1	0
Brethren	16	1
Christian and Missionary Alliance	7	0
Christian Evangelical Church of America	1	0
Christian Science	3	0
Church of God	13	1
Church of Jesus Christ of Latter-day Saints	16	1
Church of the Nazarene	12	1
Church of Scientology	1	0
Eastern Orthodox	7	0
Evangelical Covenant	3	0
Evangelical Free	1	0
Friends	25	1
Grace Gospel Fellowship	1	0
International Church of the Four Square Gospel	1	0
Jehovah's Witnesses	1	0
Mennonite	17	1
Missionary Church	2	0
Moravian	4	0
Muslim	1	0
Open Bible Standard	2	0
Pentecostal	4	0
Pentecostal Holiness	1	0
Pillar of Fire	1	0

TABLE 3.7 (continued)
1978 *American Library Directory* Denominational Breakdown for Scholarly and Popular Libraries

Denomination	Number of Libraries	Percentage
Reformed	19	1
Rosicrucian	1	0
Salvation Army	3	0
Schwenkfelder	1	0
Shaker	3	0
Spiritual Frontiers Fellowship	1	0
Swedenborgian	5	0
Theosophist	7	0
Unitarian-Universalist	7	0
United Church of Canada	7	0
United Church of Religious Science	1	0
Unity	2	0
Unknown	51	3
Wesleyan	2	0
Other Denominations Subtotal	281	13
Total	2,062	100

TABLE 3.8
1978 *American Library Directory* Denominational Breakdown for Scholarly and Popular Libraries

Denomination	Number of Libraries	Percentage
Roman Catholic	513	25
Baptist	223	11
Presbyterian	205	10
Methodist	202	10
Jewish	198	10
Lutheran	123	6
Independent	87	4
Episcopal/Anglican	74	4
Christian/Disciples of Christ	59	3
United Church of Christ	37	2
Congregational	33	2
Churches of Christ	27	1
Other Denomination, Faiths, and Unknown in descending order of frequency		
Unknown	51	3
Friends	25	1

TABLE 3.8 (continued)
1978 *American Library Directory* Denominational Breakdown for Scholarly and Popular Libraries

Denomination	Number of Libraries	Percentage
Reformed	19	1
Mennonite	17	1
Adventist	16	1
Brethren	16	1
Church of Jesus Christ of Latter-day Saints	16	1
Assemblies of God	13	1
Church of God	13	1
Church of the Nazarene	12	1
Christian and Missionary Alliance	7	0
Eastern Orthodox	7	0
Theosophist	7	0
Unitarian-Universalist	7	0
United Church of Canada	7	0
Swedenborgian	5	0
Moravian	4	0
Pentecostal	4	0
Christian Science	3	0
Evangelical Covenant	3	0
Salvation Army	3	0
Shaker	3	0
Missionary Church	2	0
Open Bible Standard	2	0
Unity	2	0
Wesleyan	2	0
Bahai	1	0
Bible Fellowship	1	0
Christian Evangelical Church of America	1	0
Church of Scientology	1	0
Evangelical Free	1	0
Grace Gospel Fellowship	1	0
International Church of the Four Square Gospel	1	0
Jehovah's Witnesses	1	0
Muslim	1	0
Pentecostal Holiness	1	0
Pillar of Fire	1	0
Rosicrucian	1	0
Schwenkfelder	1	0
Spiritual Frontiers Fellowship	1	0
United Church of Religious Science	1	0
Other Denominations Subtotal	281	13
Total	2,062	100

TABLE 3.9
1988 *American Library Directory* Denominational Breakdown for Scholarly and Popular Libraries

Denomination	Number of Libraries	Percentage
Baptist	223	11
Christian/Disciples of Christ	58	3
Churches of Christ	29	1
Episcopal/Anglican	66	3
Independent	100	5
Jewish	232	11
Lutheran	118	6
Mennonite	26	1
Methodist	213	10
Presbyterian	187	9
Roman Catholic	490	24
United Church of Christ	38	2
Other Denominations, Faiths, and Unknown in alphabetical order		
Adventist	17	1
Assemblies of God	13	1
Atheist	1	0
Bahai	1	0
Bible Fellowship	1	0
Brethren	14	1
Buddhist	3	0
Christian and Missionary Alliance	5	0
Christian Evangelical Church of America	1	0
Christian Science	3	0
Church of God	15	1
Church of Jesus Christ of Latter-day Saints	17	1
Church of the Nazarene	14	1
Church of Scientology	1	0
Congregational	23	1
Eastern Orthodox	11	1
Evangelical Church of Canada	2	0
Evangelical Covenant	2	0
Evangelical Free Church	2	0
Friends	23	1
Grace Gospel Fellowship	1	0
International Church of the Four Square Gospel	1	0
Jehovah's Witnesses	1	0
Missionary Church	3	0
Moravian	5	0
Muslim	3	0
Open Bible Standard	1	0
Pentecostal	2	0

TABLE 3.9 (continued)
1988 *American Library Directory* Denominational Breakdown for Scholarly and Popular Libraries

Pentecostal Holiness	2	0
Pillar of Fire	1	0
Reformed	19	1
Rosicrucian	2	0
Salvation Army	5	0
Schwenkfelder	1	0
Shaker	3	0
Spiritualist	1	0
Swedenborgian	6	0
Theosophist	6	0
Unitarian-Universalist	4	0
United Church of Canada	11	1
United Church of Religious Science	1	0
United Missionary	1	0
Unity	2	0
Unknown	43	2
Other Denominations Subtotal	294	14
Total	2,074	100

TABLE 3.10
1988 *American Library Directory* Denominational Breakdown for Scholarly and Popular Libraries

Denomination	Number of Libraries	Percentage
Roman Catholic	490	24
Jewish	232	11
Baptist	223	11
Methodist	213	10
Presbyterian	187	9
Lutheran	118	6
Independent	100	5
Episcopal/Anglican	66	3
Christian/Disciples of Christ	58	3
United Church of Christ	38	2
Churches of Christ	29	1
Mennonite	26	1
Other Denominations, Faiths, and Unknown in descending order		
Unknown	43	2
Congregational	23	1
Friends	23	1
Reformed	19	1

TABLE 3.10 (continued)
1988 *American Library Directory* Denominational Breakdown for Scholarly and Popular Libraries

Denomination	Number of Libraries	Percentage
Adventist	17	1
Church of Jesus Christ of Latter-day Saints	17	1
Church of God	15	1
Brethren	14	1
Church of the Nazarene	14	1
Assemblies of God	13	1
Eastern Orthodox	11	1
United Church of Canada	11	1
Swedenborgian	6	0
Theosophist	6	0
Christian and Missionary Alliance	5	0
Moravian	5	0
Salvation Army	5	0
Unitarian-Universalist	4	0
Buddhist	3	0
Christian Science	3	0
Missionary Church	3	0
Muslim	3	0
Shaker	3	0
Evangelical Church of Canada	2	0
Evangelical Covenant	2	0
Evangelical Free	2	0
Pentecostal	2	0
Pentecostal Holiness	2	0
Rosicrucian	2	0
Unity	2	0
Atheist	1	0
Bahai	1	0
Bible Fellowship	1	0
Christian Evangelical Church of America	1	0
Church of Scientology	1	0
Grace Gospel Fellowship	1	0
International Church of the Four Square Gospel	1	0
Jehovah's Witnesses	1	0
Open Bible Standard	1	0
Pillar of Fire	1	0
Schwenkfelder	1	0
Spiritualist	1	0
United Church of Religious Science	1	0
United Missionary	1	0
Other Denominations Subtotal	294	14
Total	2,074	100

TABLE 3.11
1978 *American Library Directory* Denominational Breakdown for Scholarly Libraries in Descending Order of Frequency

Denomination	Number of Libraries	Percentage
Roman Catholic	469	34
Other Denominations	214	16
Methodist	147	11
Baptist	140	10
Presbyterian	90	7
Independent	82	6
Lutheran	70	5
Christian/Disciples of Christ	40	3
Jewish	35	3
Episcopal/Anglican	32	2
Churches of Christ	27	2
United Church of Christ	24	2
Congregational	5	0
Total	1,375	100

TABLE 3.12
1978 and 1988 *American Library Directory* Longitudinal Study Scholarly Library Distribution for Canada and the United States by Denomination

	U.S.A.			CANADA			Canada/U.S.A. Ratio Value		Total		
Denomination	1978	1988	% Change	1978	1988	% Change	1978	1988	1978	1988	% Change
Baptist	135	143	6	5	9	80	.04	.06	140	152	9
Christian	40	40	0	0	1		0	.03	40	41	3
Churches of Christ	27	25	−7	0	2		0	.08	27	27	0
Episcopal/Anglican	21	24	14	11	8	−27	.52	.33	32	32	0
Independent	76	86	13	6	11	83	.08	.13	82	97	18
Lutheran	66	70	6	4	6	50	.06	.09	70	76	9
Mennonite	13	14	8	1	8	700	.08	.57	14	22	57
Methodist	147	148	1	0	1		0	.01	147	149	1
Other Denominations	195	191	−2	10	26	160	.05	.14	205	217	6
Presbyterian	87	87	0	3	3	0	.03	.03	90	90	0
U.C.C.	24	25	4	0	0		0	0	24	25	4
Summary											
Jewish	33	42	27	2	3	50	.06	.07	35	45	29
Roman Catholic	413	372	−10	56	86	54	.14	.23	469	458	−2
All Protestant	831	853	3	40	75	88	.05	.09	871	928	7
Total	1,277	1,267	−1	98	164	67	.08	.13	1,375	1,431	4

TABLE 3.13
Complete List of *American Library Directory* Denominations in Alphabetical Order for 1978 and 1988

Denomination	1978 Scholarly	1988 Scholarly	Percentage Change 1978–88 Scholarly
Assemblies of God	12	12	0
Atheist	0	1	0
Bahai	1	1	0
Baptist	140	152	9
Bible Fellowship	1	1	0
Brethren	14	13	−7
Buddhist	0	3	0
Christian and Missionary Alliance	7	5	−29
Christian Evangelical Ch. of America	1	1	0
Christian Scientist	1	3	200
Church of Canada	0	0	0
Church of Christ	27	27	0
Church of God	12	14	17
Church of Jesus Christ of Latter-day Saints	8	8	0
Church of Scientology	0	0	0
Church of the Nazarene	11	13	18
Congregational	5	5	0
Disciples of Christ	40	41	3
Eastern Orthodox	7	10	43
Episcopal/Anglican	32	32	0
Evangelical Church of Canada	0	2	0
Evangelical Covenant Church	2	2	0
Evangelical Free Church	1	2	100
Friends	19	17	−11
Grace Fellowship	1	1	0
Independent	82	97	18
International Church of Four Square Gospel	1	1	0
Jehovah's Witnesses	1	1	0
Jewish	35	45	29
Lutheran	70	76	9
Mennonite	14	22	57
Methodist	147	149	1
Missionary Church	2	3	50
Moravian Church	4	5	25
Muslim/Islamic	1	2	100
Open Bible Standard Church	2	1	−50
Pentecostal	3	2	−33
Pentecostal Holiness Church	1	2	100
Pillar of Fire	1	1	0
Presbyterian	90	90	0
Reformed	9	9	0

TABLE 3.13 (continued)
Complete List of *American Library Directory* Denominations in Alphabetical Order for 1978 and 1988

Denomination	1978 Scholarly	1988 Scholarly	Percentage Change 1978–88 Scholarly
Roman Catholic	469	458	−2
Rosicrucian	1	1	0
Salvation Army	2	4	100
Schwenkfelder Church	1	1	0
Seventh-day Adventist	16	17	6
Shakers	3	3	0
Spiritual Frontiers Fellowship	1	0	−100
Spiritualist	0	0	0
Swedenborgian Church	3	3	0
Theosophist	6	4	−33
United Church of Canada	7	9	29
United Church of Christ	24	25	4
United Church of Religious Science	0	0	0
United Missionary	0	1	0
Unitarian-Universalist	2	2	0
Unity	2	2	0
Unknown	31	29	−6
Wesleyan	2	0	−100
Total	1,375	1,431	
Average Change (Libraries per Denomination)			.97

TABLE 3.14
1978 *American Library Directory* Scholarly and Popular Libraries by Denomination

Denomination	Number of Libraries	Percentage
Baptist	223	10
Christian	59	3
Churches of Christ	27	1
Congregational	33	2
Episcopal/Anglican	74	4
Independent	87	4
Lutheran	123	6
Methodist	202	10
Other Denominations	281	14
Presbyterian	205	10
United Church of Christ	37	2

TABLE 3.14 (continued)
1978 *American Library Directory* Scholarly and Popular Libraries by Denomination

Denomination	Number of Libraries	Percentage
Summary		
Jewish	198	10
Roman Catholic	513	25
All Protestant	1,351	66
Total	2,062	100

TABLE 3.15
1988 *American Library Directory* Scholarly and Popular Libraries by Denomination

Denomination	Number of Libraries	Percentage
Baptist	223	11
Christian	58	3
Churches of Christ	29	1
Episcopal/Anglican	66	3
Independent	100	5
Lutheran	118	6
Mennonite	26	1
Methodist	213	10
Other Denominations	294	14
Presbyterian	187	9
United Church of Christ	38	2
Summary		
Jewish	232	11
Roman Catholic	490	24
All Protestant	1,352	65
Total	2,074	100

TABLE 3.16
1988 *American Library Directory* Scholarly Baptist Libraries Located in Large Cities[1]

City	Library	Population
1. Philadelphia, PA	Eastern Baptist Theological Seminary	1,500,000
2. Philadelphia, PA	Temple University	1,500,000
3. Houston, TX	Houston Baptist University	1,500,000
4. Phoenix, AZ	Grand Canyon University	850,000
5. Phoenix, AZ	Southwestern Baptist Bible College	850,000
6. Indianapolis, IN	Baptist Bible College	850,000
7. Indianapolis, IN	Heritage Baptist University	850,000
8. Dallas, TX	Bishop College	850,000
9. Dallas, TX	Criswell College	850,000
10. Dallas, TX	Dallas Baptist University	850,000
11. Dallas, TX	Independent Baptist College	850,000
12. San Antonio, TX	Hispanic Baptist Theological Seminary	850,000

1. City population size, as shown in these tables, represents the mid-points of a number of city population size categories. For smaller city sizes, these mid-points were reasonably accurate. However, as the categories approached the upper maxima their accuracy decreased quite significantly. Therefore, the reader would be wise to accept the category mid-points used here as approximate statistical indicators of relative city size.

TABLE 3.17
1988 *American Library Directory* Scholarly Churches of Christ Libraries in the Largest Cities

City	Library	Population
1. Chicago, IL	Chicago Theological Seminary	4,000,000
2. Memphis, TN	Harding College Graduate School of Religion	600,000
3. Calgary, AB	Alberta Bible College	600,000
4. Cincinnati, OH	Cincinnati Bible Seminary	400,000
5. Oklahoma City, OK	Oklahoma Christian College	400,000
6. Portland, OR	Columbia Christian College	400,000
7. Nashville, TN	David Lipscomb University	400,000

TABLE 3.18
1988 *American Library Directory* Scholarly Independent Libraries in the Largest Cities

City	Library	Population
1. New York, NY	American Bible Society	4,000,000
2. New York, NY	Institute of Religion and Health	4,000,000
3. New York, NY	Interchurch Center	4,000,000
4. New York, NY	Union Theological Center	4,000,000
5. New York, NY	New York Theological Seminary	4,000,000
6. New York, NY	United Church Board for World Ministries	4,000,000
7. New York, NY	YWCA National Board	4,000,000
8. Chicago, IL	Institute on the Church in Urban Industry	4,000,000
9. Chicago, IL	Moody Bible Institute	4,000,000

TABLE 3.19
1988 *American Library Directory* Scholarly Mennonite Libraries in Large Cities

City	Library	Population
1. Winnipeg, MB	Canadian Mennonite Bible College	600,000
2. Winnipeg, MB	Mennonite Brethren Bible College	600,000
3. Fresno, CA	Fresno Pacific College	200,000
4. Lancaster, PA	Lancaster Mennonite Historical Society	75,000
5. Waterloo, ON	Conrad Grebel College	75,000
6. Elkart, IN	Associated Mennonite Biblical Seminary	40,000
7. Goshen, IN	Goshen College	20,000
8. Goshen, IN	Goshen College Mennonite Historical Library	20,000
9. Lansdale, PA	Mennonite Historical Society	20,000
10. Harrisonburg, VA	Eastern Mennonite University	20,000

TABLE 3.20
1988 *American Library Directory* Scholarly Other Denominations Libraries in the Largest Cities

City	Library	Population
1. New York, NY	American Buddhist Archives	4,000,000
2. New York, NY	Salvation Army Research Center	4,000,000
3. Chicago, IL	Meadville-Lombard Theological School	4,000,000
4. Chicago, IL	North Park College	4,000,000
5. Chicago, IL	North Park College Seminary	4,000,000
6. Los Angeles, CA	L.I.F.E. Bible College	2,500,000
7. Brooklyn, NY	Watchtower Bible School of Gilead	2,500,000
8. Philadelphia, PA	Manna Bible Institute	1,500,000
9. Philadelphia, PA	Society of Friends Yearly Meeting	1,500,000
10. Philadelphia, PA	Willet Stained Glass Studios	1,500,000
11. Montreal, PQ	McGill University Islamic Studies Library	1,500,000

TABLE 3.21
1988 *American Library Directory* Scholarly United Church of Christ Libraries in Large Cities

City	Library	Population
1. Memphis, TN	Le Moyne-Owen College	600,000
2. St. Louis, MO	Eden Webster University	400,000
3. Nashville, TN	Fisk University	400,000
4. Austin, TX	Huston-Tillotson College	400,000
5. Hartford, CT	United Church of Christ	200,000
6. Springfield, MO	Drury College	200,000
7. Allentown, PA	Cedar Crest College	200,000
8. Lancaster, PA	United Church of Christ	75,000
9. Lancaster, PA	Franklin and Marshall College	75,000
10. Lancaster, PA	Lancaster Theological Seminary	75,000

TABLE 3.22
1988 *American Library Directory* Scholarly Roman Catholic Libraries in the Largest Cities

City	Library	Population
1. New York, NY	New York University Catholic Center	4,000,000
2. New York, NY	Fordham University Lincoln Center	4,000,000
3. New York, NY	Marymount Manhattan College	4,000,000
4. Chicago, IL	Catholic Theological Union	4,000,000
5. Chicago, IL	DePaul University	4,000,000
6. Chicago, IL	Felician College	4,000,000
7. Chicago, IL	Jesuit-Kraus-McCormick Seminary	4,000,000
8. Chicago, IL	Loyola University	4,000,000
9. Chicago, IL	Mundlein College	4,000,000
10. Chicago, IL	Loyola University Niles College	4,000,000
11. Chicago, IL	Saint Xavier University	4,000,000

TABLE 3.23
1978 and 1988 *American Library Directory* Longitudinal Study Scholarly Libraries Showing OCLC Membership by Denomination for Matched Pairs

	1978				1988				
Denomination	Number of Libraries	Percent-age	No Re-sponse	Total Libraries	Number of Libraries	Percent-age	No Re-sponse	Total Libraries	Percentage Change 1978–88
Baptist	14	11	112	126	58	46	67	125	314
Christian	2	5.4	35	37	17	45	21	38	750
Churches of Christ	2	8	23	25	10	42	14	24	400
Episcopal/ Anglican	2	7.4	25	27	12	50	12	24	500
Independent	8	12	60	68	26	38	43	69	225
Lutheran	9	15	51	60	36	60	24	60	300
Mennonite	4	29	10	14	9	64	5	14	125
Methodist	30	22	108	138	79	56	61	140	163
Other Denoms.	30	18	137	167	74	45	91	165	147
Presbyterian	18	21	68	86	53	61	34	87	194
U.C.C.	7	30	16	23	19	83	4	23	171
Summary									
Jewish	2	6.9	27	29	6	20	24	30	200
Roman Catholic	55	15	314	369	162	44	210	372	195
All Protes-tant	126	16	645	771	393	51	376	769	212
Total	183	16	986	1,169	561	48	610	1,171	207

TABLE 3.24
1978 and 1988 *American Library Directory* Longitudinal Study Total Annual Scholarly Library Expenditure for Matched Pairs

Library Type	1978 Number of Libraries	1978 No Response	1978 Total Libraries	1978 Mean Dollars	1988 Number of Libraries	1988 No Response	1988 Total Libraries	1988 Mean Dollars	Percentage Change 1978–88
Scholarly	875	294	1,169	150,800	909	263	1,172	267,700	78
Junior College	71	38	109	57,830	61	28	89	104,500	81
Senior College	521	105	626	137,600	512	98	610	260,400	89
University	128	22	150	351,800	156	21	177	462,700	32
Seminary	118	66	184	87,850	141	55	196	193,700	120
Convent/ Monastery	8	8	16	4,094	4	13	17	8,875	117
Denominational HQ	11	35	46	27,020	13	30	43	87,480	224
History/ Archives	18	20	38	25,400	22	18	40	133,500	425

TABLE 3.25
1988 *American Library Directory* Scholarly Library Microform Holdings by Denomination

Denomination	Microform Holdings 1–5,000	%	5,001–20,000	%	20,001–80,000	%	80,001–and over	%	No Response	%	Number of Libraries	Mean Microforms
Baptist	43	28	13	9	16	11	22	14	58	38	152	52,910
Christian	14	34	6	15	1	2	3	7	17	41	41	23,540
Churches of Christ	6	22	5	19	5	19	3	11	8	30	27	45,950
Episcopal/ Anglican	9	28	1	3	5	16	1	3	16	50	32	16,800
Independent	19	20	15	15	6	6	10	10	47	48	97	48,820
Lutheran	12	16	12	16	11	14	10	13	31	41	76	55,900
Mennonite	8	36	1	5	3	14	0	0	10	45	22	17,150
Methodist	30	20	34	23	19	13	17	11	49	33	149	43,360
Other Denominations	50	23	20	9	22	10	17	8	108	50	217	40,910
Presbyterian	15	17	21	23	16	18	10	11	28	31	90	45,770
U.C.C.	6	24	7	28	4	16	5	20	3	12	25	45,480
Summary												
Jewish	6	13	1	2	3	7	0	0	35	78	45	14,310
Roman Catholic	82	18	44	10	39	8	49	11	245	53	459	55,330
All Protestant	212	23	135	15	108	12	98	11	375	40	928	44,260
Total	300	21	180	13	150	10	147	10	655	46	1,432	46,920

TABLE 3.26
1988 *American Library Directory* Microfrom Holdings for Newly Listed Scholarly Libraries

Library Type	1–5,000	%	5,001–20,000	%	20,001–80,000	%	80,001–and over	%	No Response	%	Number of Libraries	Mean Microforms
	Microform Holdings											
Scholarly	55	21	13	5	8	3	2	1	182	70	260	12,970
Junior College	5	26	0	0	0	0	0	0	14	74	19	1,430
Senior College	23	24	11	12	1	1	0	0	60	63	95	5,323
University	0	0	1	8	3	25	2	17	6	50	12	99,170
Seminary	9	26	1	3	3	9	0	0	22	63	35	11,050
Convent/Monastery	0	0	0	0	0	0	0	0	8	100	8	0
Denominational HQ	5	12	0	0	0	0	0	0	38	88	43	1,920
History/Archives	13	27	0	0	1	2	0	0	34	71	48	4,968

TABLE 3.27
1978 *American Library Directory* Microfrom Holdings for No Longer Listed Scholarly Libraries

Library Type	1–5,000	%	5,001–20,000	%	20,001–80,000	%	80,001–and over	%	No Response	%	Number of Libraries	Mean Microforms
	Microform Holdings											
Scholarly	30	15	3	1	2	1	0	0	171	83	206	4,659
Junior College	3	19	0	0	0	0	0	0	13	81	16	217
Senior College	15	19	3	4	0	0	0	0	60	77	78	3,139
University	0	0	0	0	1	25	0	0	3	75	4	30,000
Seminary	7	14	0	0	1	2	0	0	41	84	49	8,594
Convent/Monastery	0	0	0	0	0	0	0	0	19	100	19	0
Denominational HQ	2	6	0	0	0	0	0	0	29	94	31	1,525
History/Archives	3	33	0	0	0	0	0	0	6	67	9	1,367

TABLE 3.28
1978 and 1988 *American Library Directory* Demographics: Regional Distribution by Edition and Showing Percentage Change for No Longer Listed and Newly Listed Libraries

Region	1978	% of Sample	1988	% of Sample	% Change
Northeast	16	7.7	16	6.2	0
Middle Atlantic	44	21.4	41	15.8	−7
Southeast	28	13.6	27	10.4	−4
Southwest	14	6.8	19	7.3	36
West	20	9.7	29	11.2	45
Rocky Mountains	10	4.9	4	1.5	−60
Middle West	59	28.6	45	17.3	−24
Canada	15	7.3	79	30.4	427
Total	206	100.0	260	100.1	26

TABLE 3.29
1988 *American Library Directory* Highest Academic Institutional Degree Offered for the Entire Sample

Degree	Number of Libraries	Percentage
Doctorate	174	8
Master's	331	16
Bachelor's	475	23
Associate	103	5
No Response	991	48
Total	2,074	100

TABLE 3.30
1978 and 1988 *American Library Directory* Accredited Academic Libraries by Type for Four Types of Accreditation

Edition	Type of Library	Regional	AABC	ATS	U.S. Office of Education	Total	% Each of the Type	Total Number of Libraries	% Each Type
1978	Junior College	85	5	0	0	90	8	125	10
	Senior College	532	67	22	0	621	56	704	58
	University	121	0	7	0	128	12	154	13
	Seminary	106	7	129	0	242	22	233	19
	Total	844	79	158	0	1,081	99	1,216	100
1988	Junior College	76	2	0	0	78	7	108	9
	Senior College	537	72	12	2	623	56	705	57
	University	151	1	9	0	161	15	189	15
	Seminary	117	9	117	1	244	22	231	19
	Total	881	84	138	3	1,106	100	1,233	100

TABLE 3.31
1978 and 1988 *American Library Directory* Junior and Senior College, University, and Seminary Libraries with Regional Accreditation and by Mean Staff Members

Edition	Accreditation Status	Number of Libraries	No Response	Mean Number of Staff Members
1978	Accredited	844	287	19
	Unaccredited	372	216	8
1988	Accredited	881	218	24
	Unaccredited	352	174	10

TABLE 3.32
1978 and 1988 Junior and Senior College, University, and Seminary Accreditation by Denomination[1]

Denomination	Total Number of Accredited Institutions 1978	Percentage	Total Number of Institutions
Baptist	105	82	131
Christian	33	89	37
Churches of Christ	23	85	27
Congregational	4	100	4
Episcopal/Anglican	20	71	28
Independent	54	81	68
Lutheran	51	80	64
Methodist	127	93	137
Other Denominations	133	73	183
Presbyterian	80	94	87
United Church of Christ	21	95	23
Jewish	16	80	20
Roman Catholic	279	70	407
Total	946	79	1,216
	1988		
Baptist	111	80	138
Christian	34	87	39
Churches of Christ	23	85	27
Episcopal/Anglican	15	63	24
Independent	64	83	77
Lutheran	52	81	64
Mennonite	8	50	16
Methodist	132	95	139
Other Denominations	121	67	181
Presbyterian	81	95	85
United Church of Christ	22	100	22
Jewish	15	63	24
Roman Catholic	284	72	396
Total	962	78	1,232

1. The table combines three types of American accreditation—regional, AABC, and ATS.

TABLE 3.33
1978 and 1988 *American Library Directory* Volume Holdings by American Theological Library Association Membership for Seminary Libraries

Type of Library	Number of Libraries	No Response	Mean Volumes	% Change in Volumes
		1978		
Seminary				
Members	122	10	101,400	N/A
Not Members	111	25	50,400	N/A
		1988		
Seminary				
Members	108	3	132,700	31
Not Members	123	9	60,800	21

TABLE 3.34
1988 *American Library Directory* Volume Holdings by Regional Accreditation Status by Type of Library: Academic Libraries

Type of Library	Number of Libraries	No Response	Mean Volumes
Junior College			
Accredited	76	1	39,300
Unaccredited	32	0	39,100
Senior College			
Accredited	537	2	126,900
Unaccredited	168	7	43,700
Universally			
Accredited	151	1	276,100
Unaccredited	38	1	268,000
Seminary			
Accredited	117	4	127,300
Unaccredited	114	8	61,200

TABLE 3.35
1978 and 1988 *American Library Directory* Seminary Library Volume Holdings for Accredited Institutions

Edition	Accreditation Type and Status	Number of Libraries	No Response	Mean Volume Holdings
31st	Accredited (regional)	106	10	113,900
	Unaccredited	127	25	46,700
41st	Accredited (regional)	117	4	127,300
	Unaccredited	114	8	61,200
31st	Accredited (ATS)	129	14	100,400
	Unaccredited	104	21	50,000
41st	Accredited (ATS)	117	4	129,100
	Unaccredited	114	8	59,200
31st	Accredited (all types)	158	16	97,100
	Unaccredited	75	19	34,200
41st	Accredited (all types)	156	5	117,000
	Unaccredited	75	7	47,100

TABLE 3.36
1978 and 1988 *American Library Directory* Senior College Total Expenditures for Accredited Institutions

Edition	Accreditation Type and Status	Number of Libraries	No Response	Mean Total Library Expenditure
31st	Accredited (regional)	532	57	$143,600
	Unaccredited	172	76	53,500
41st	Accredited (regional)	537	64	272,200
	Unaccredited	168	71	130,200
31st	Accredited (AABC)	67	20	52,900
	Unaccredited	637	113	135,600
41st	Accredited (AABC)	72	17	89,800
	Unaccredited	633	118	264,900
31st	Accredited (all types)	594	81	136,000
	Unaccredited	110	52	61,000
41st	Accredited (all types)	585	77	258,800
	Unaccredited	120	58	159,600

TABLE 3.37
1978 and 1988 *American Library Directory* Volume Holdings by American Association of Bible College Accreditation Status for Senior College Libraries

Type of Library	Number of Libraries	No Response	Mean Volumes	% Change in Volumes
		1978		
Senior College				
Accredited	67	6	34,600	N/A
Unaccredited	637	32	92,500	N/A
		1988		
Senior College				
Accredited	72	0	47,900	38
Unaccredited	633	9	114,600	24

TABLE 3.38
1978 and 1988 *American Library Directory* Total Expenditures for Regional and All Types of Accreditation for Junior and Senior College, University, and Seminary Libraries Combined

Edition	Accreditation Type and Status	Number of Libraries	No Response	Mean Total Library Expenditure
1978	Accredited (regional)	844	121	$162,400
	Unaccredited	372	170	71,400
1988	Accredited (regional)	881	112	286,700
	Unaccredited	352	152	174,700
1978	Accredited (all types)	970	165	153,000
	Unaccredited	246	126	71,500
1988	Accredited (all types)	971	136	273,100
	Unaccredited	262	128	204,200

TABLE 3.39
1978 and 1988 *American Library Directory* Seminary Library Total Expenditures for Accredited Institutions

Edition	Accreditation Type and Status	Number of Libraries	No Response	Mean Total Library Expenditure
31st	Accredited (regional)	106	26	$112,200
	Unaccredited	127	66	41,600
41st	Accredited (regional)	117	15	227,100
	Unaccredited	114	57	113,800
31st	Accredited (ATS)	129	34	97,600
	Unaccredited	104	58	48,700
41st	Accredited (ATS)	117	17	223,500
	Unaccredited	114	55	123,800
31st	Accredited (all types)	158	43	93,700
	Unaccredited	75	49	28,500
41st	Accredited (all types)	156	26	210,700
	Unaccredited	75	46	78,100

TABLE 3.40
1988 *American Library Directory* Total Expenditures by Regional Accreditation and Library Type: Academic Libraries

Type of Library	Accreditation Status	Number of Libraries	No Response	Mean Expenditures Per Library
Junior College	Accredited	76	17	$99,000
	Unaccredited	32	17	82,500
Senior College	Accredited	537	64	272,200
	Unaccredited	168	71	130,200
University	Accredited	151	16	464,300
	Unaccredited	38	7	430,300
Seminary	Accredited	117	15	227,100
	Unaccredited	114	57	113,800

TABLE 3.41
1978 and 1988 *American Library Directory* Staff Size by Regional Accreditation for the Entire Samples[1]

Type of Library	Number of Libraries	No Response	Mean Number of Staff Members
		1978	
Accredited	850	292	19.0
Unaccredited	1,212	878	6.2
		1988	
Accredited	883	219	23.6
Unaccredited	1,191	736	7.4

1. All popular libraries are represented in the categories shown as "unaccredited."

TABLE 3.42
1988 *American Library Directory* Libraries with Regional Accreditation by Denomination for Academic Libraries

Denomination	Libraries with Regional Accreditation	%	No Response	%	Number of Libraries
Baptist	101	73	37	27	138
Christian	22	56	17	44	39
Churches of Christ	18	67	9	33	27
Episcopal/Anglican	11	46	13	54	24
Independent	43	56	34	44	77
Lutheran	52	81	12	19	64
Mennonite	8	50	8	50	16
Methodist	130	94	9	6	139
Other Denominations	103	57	78	43	181
Presbyterian	79	92	7	8	86
U.C.C.	22	100	0	0	22
Summary					
Jewish	15	63	9	38	24
Roman Catholic	277	70	119	30	396
All Protestant	589	72	224	28	813
Total	881	71	352	29	1,233

TABLE 3.43
1978 and 1988 *American Library Directory* Longitudinal Study
Scholarly Library Accreditation: AABC, ATS, and Regional
by Denomination

	1978				1988				
Denomination	Number of Libraries	Percentage	No Response	Total Libraries	Number of Libraries	Percentage	No Response	Total Libraries	Percentage Change 1978–88
Baptist	107	76	33	140	111	73	41	152	3.8
Christian	34	85	6	40	34	83	7	41	0
Churches of Christ	23	85	4	27	23	85	4	27	0
Episcopal/ Anglican	20	63	12	32	15	47	17	32	−25
Independent	55	67	27	82	63	65	34	97	15
Lutheran	51	73	19	70	53	70	23	76	4
Mennonite	8	57	6	14	10	45	12	22	25
Methodist	128	87	19	147	132	89	17	149	3.1
Other Denom.	130	63	75	205	122	56	95	217	−6.1
Presbyterian	82	91	8	90	80	89	10	90	−2.4
U.C.C.	22	92	2	24	22	88	3	25	0
Summary									
Jewish	16	46	19	35	16	36	29	45	0
Roman Catholic	279	59	190	469	282	62	176	458	1.1
All Protestant	660	76	211	871	665	72	263	928	.8
Total	955	69	420	1,375	963	67	468	1,431	.9

TABLE 3.44
1978 *American Library Directory* Libraries with AABC Accreditation
by Chief Librarian's Gender for Academic Libraries

Librarian's Gender	Libraries with AABC Accreditation	%	No Response	%	Number of Libraries
Male	31	5	603	95	634
Female	45	8	488	92	533
No Response	3	6	46	94	49
Total	79	6	1,137	94	1,216

TABLE 3.45

1988 *American Library Directory* Libraries with AABC Accreditation by Chief Librarian's Gender for Academic Libraries

Librarian's Gender	Libraries with AABC Accreditation	%	No Response	%	Number of Libraries
Male	39	6	628	94	667
Female	42	8	506	92	548
No response	3	17	15	83	18
Total	84	7	1,149	93	1,233

TABLE 3.46
1978 *American Library Directory* AABC Library Accreditation by Total Annual Expenditure for Matched Pairs of Academic Libraries

Library Expenditures	Libraries with AABC Accreditation	%	No Response	%	Number of Libraries
Under $1,500	1	13	7	88	8
$1,501–$20,000	7	12	50	88	57
$20,001–$95,000	38	12	277	88	315
$95,001–$220,000	1	0	278	100	279
$220,001–$410,000	2	2	106	98	108
$410,001–$510,000	0	0	17	100	17
$510,001 and over	0	0	53	100	53
No response	24	10	208	90	232
Total	73	7	996	93	1,069

TABLE 3.47
1988 *American Library Directory* Libraries with ATLA Membership by Denomination for Academic Libraries

Denomination	Libraries with ATLA Membership	%	No Response	%	Number of Libraries
Baptist	12	9	126	91	138
Christian	5	13	34	87	39
Churches of Christ	1	4	26	96	27
Episcopal/Anglican	7	29	17	71	24
Independent	13	17	64	83	77
Lutheran	6	9	58	91	64
Mennonite	2	13	14	88	16
Methodist	15	11	124	89	139
Other Denominations	14	8	167	92	181
Presbyterian	11	13	75	87	86
U.C.C.	5	23	17	77	22
Summary					
Jewish	0	0	24	100	24
Roman Catholic	32	8	364	92	396
All Protestant	91	11	722	89	813
Total	123	10	1,110	90	1,233

TABLE 3.48
1988 *American Library Directory* Libraries with ATLA Membership by Total Annual Expenditure for Academic Libraries

Library Expenditures	Libraries with ATLA Membership	%	No Response	%	Number of Libraries
Under $1,500	0	0	6	100	6
$1,501–$20,000	2	6	32	94	34
$20,001–$95,000	17	10	159	90	176
$95,001–$220,000	42	15	247	85	289
$220,001–$410,000	28	13	185	87	213
$410,001–$510,000	6	13	42	88	48
$510,001 and over	17	8	186	92	203
No response	11	4	253	96	264
Total	123	10	1,110	90	1,233

TABLE 3.49
1978 and 1988 *American Library Directory* Mean Number of Staff Members for Seminary Libraries by ATLA Membership

Edition	Membership Status	Number of Libraries	No Response	Mean Number of Staff Members
1978	Member	122	46	9
	Non-member	111	82	7
1988	Member	108	34	11
	Non-member	123	83	8

TABLE 3.50
1985 and 1986 American Theological Library Association Statistical Record Report Summary[1]

	Salary	%	Materials	%	Binding	%	Total Expenses	Check Total	Educational & General	Enroll.	Expenditure Per Stud't
							Canada (14)				
Total	$2,069,190	60	$1,307,374	38	$79,322	2	$3,930,567	$3,455,886	$44,615,270	5,573	$30,277
Mean	37,348		32,350		2,160	1	118,080	113,040	1,173,625	429	2,329
							United States (134)				
Total	15,544,056	61	9,186,951	36	722,489	3	31,193,348	25,530,030	378,449,135	49,435	285,739
Mean	116,000		68,559		5,392		232,786	190,523	2,824,247	369	2,132

	Bound Volumes	%	Microforms	%	A–V	%	Others	%	Total Items	Periodicals	%	Grand Total
							Canada (14)					
Total	1,454,218	66	482,864	22	137,119	6	122,267	6	2,087,479	9,936	0	$2,216,404
Mean	103,873		34,490		9,794		8,733		149,106	710		158,315
							United States (134)					
Total	17,238,696	81	1,793,204	8	644,264	3	1,390,920	7	19,338,409	86,866	0	21,331,129
Mean	128,647		13,382		4,808		10,380		144,316	648		159,188

	ILL Sent	ILL Received	Indep Lib	Nonindep Lib
				Canada (14)
Total	2,838	1,965	8	5
Mean	203	140		
				United States (13)
Total	51,110	29,836	106	24
Mean	381	223		

	Enroll	Faculty	Stud't/Fac Ratio	Prof Staff	Prof/ 100 Stud't	Full-Time Staff	Part-Time Staff	Total Staff	Total Staff Per 100 Students
					Canada (14)				
Total	5,573	322	17.3	40.0	0.7	74.9	33.3	148.2	2.7
Mean	429	23	17.3	2.9	0.7	5.4	2.4	10.6	2.7
					United States (134)				
Total	49,435	5,087	9.7	389.9	0.79	388.1	395.1	1,173.0	2.4
Mean	369	38	10	3	0.79	2.9	2.9	8.8	2.4

Source: Summary of Proceedings, 41st Annual Conference of the American Theological Library Association (St. Meinrad, Ind.: ATLA, 1987), pp. 52–63.

1. Apparent discrepancies are merely *apparent* and arise as the results of missing values on some variables.

TABLE 3.51
1978 and 1988 *American Library Directory* Table of Means for ATLA versus Non-ATLA Seminaries Relative to Means for the Entire Samples[1]

	Entire Sample			ATLA Seminaries	Non-ATLA Seminaries
	Scholarly	Popular	All	Scholarly	Scholarly
Institutional Faculty Members					
Edition 31	72	70	72	39	19
Active *N*	1,028	2	1,030	109	57
Edition 41	83	40	83	48	18
Active *N*	1,013	2	1,015	100	63
% Change 1978–88	15.2	−42.9	15.2	23	−5.3
Institutional Student Enrollment					
Edition 31	1,065	250	1,063	548	255
Active *N*	1,056	3	1,059	113	60
Edition 41	1,196	300	1,195	708	259
Active *N*	1,076	2	1,078	110	66
% Change 1978–88	12.3	20	12.4	29.1	1.5
Institutional Student Enrollment/Faculty Ratio					
Edition 31	15	15	15	14	13
Active *N*	1,026	1	1,027	108	57
Edition 41	16	7	15	17	17
Active *N*	1,008	2	1,010	100	61
% Change 1978–88	6.6	−53.4	0	21.4	30.7
Library Expenditure on Material					
Edition 31	49,430	1,811	43,330	41,420	18,070
Active *N*	749	110	859	92	28
Edition 41	81,500	4,085	67,670	86,220	41,730
Active *N*	1,057	230	1,287	110	65
% Change 1978–88	64.8	125.5	56.1	108.1	130.9
Library Expenditure on Personnel					
Edition 31	92,460	6,029	88,320	76,470	40,000
Active *N*	676	34	710	87	22
Edition 41	141,500	21,990	132,300	133,900	72,590
Active *N*	995	83	1,078	109	56
% Change 1978–88	53	264.7	49.7	75.1	81.4

Source: American Library Directory (New York: R. R. Bowker, 1978; 1988).
1. *All* ATLA libraries are seminaries.

TABLE 3.52
1978 *American Library Directory* Academic Institutional Enrollment

Enrollment	Number of Libraries	Percentage
4001+	53	3
2401–4000	42	2
1801–2400	64	3
1201–1800	124	6
601–1200	309	15
1–600	467	23
No response	1,003	48
Total	2,062	100
Mean	1,065 students	

TABLE 3.53
1988 *American Library Directory* Academic Institutional Enrollment

Enrollment	Number of Libraries	Percentage
4001+	76	4
2,401–4,000	45	2
1,801–2,400	95	5
1,201–1,800	126	6
601–1,200	272	13
1–600	464	22
No response	996	48
Total	2,074	100
Mean	1,196 students	

TABLE 3.54
1978 *American Library Directory* Scholarly Student Enrollment per Professional Library Staff Member by Denomination

Denomination	Number of Libraries	No Response	No Response Percentage	Mean Students
Baptist	131	54	41	360
Christian	37	14	38	270
Churches of Christ	27	9	33	321
Congregational	4	2	50	563
Episcopal/Anglican	28	14	50	189
Independent	68	32	47	267
Lutheran	64	27	42	290
Methodist	137	55	40	312
Other Denominations	183	88	48	270
Presbyterian	87	32	37	304
United Church of Christ	23	9	39	263
Jewish	20	11	55	183
Roman Catholic	407	187	46	322
All Protestant	789	336	43	299
Total	1,216	534	44	305

TABLE 3.55
1988 *American Library Directory* Scholarly Student Enrollment per Professional Library Staff Member by Denomination

Denomination	Number of Libraries	No Response	No Response Percentage	Mean Students
Baptist	138	40	29	322
Christian	39	14	36	263
Churches of Christ	27	7	26	276
Congregational	24	11	46	186
Episcopal/Anglican	77	25	32	322
Independent	64	17	27	306
Lutheran	16	5	31	234
Methodist	139	33	24	302
Other Denominations	181	82	45	281
Presbyterian	86	29	34	328
United Church of Christ	22	4	18	274
Jewish	24	15	63	166
Roman Catholic	396	163	41	393
All Protestant	813	267	33	299
Total	1,233	445	36	325

TABLE 3.56
1978 and 1988 *American Library Directory* Longitudinal Study
Scholarly Institutional Student Enrollment by Library Type

	1978				1988				
Library Type	Number of Inst's.	No Re-sponse	Total Inst's.	Mean Stu-dents	Number of Inst's.	No Re-sponse	Total Inst's.	Mean Stu-dents	% Change 1978–88
Scholarly	1,056	319	1,375	1,065	1,076	356	1,432	1,196	12
Junior College	114	11	125	540	91	17	108	652	21
Senior College	646	58	704	955	649	56	705	1,010	6
University	136	18	154	2,936	173	16	189	2,977	1
Seminary	159	74	233	296	161	70	231	356	20
Convent/ Monastery	1	34	35	150	0	25	25	0	−100
Denomin-ational HQ	0	77	77	0	2	84	86	150	N/A
History/Archives	0	47	47	0	0	88	88	0	0

TABLE 3.57
1988 *American Library Directory* Institutional Enrollment by Region

Region	Number of Libraries	No Response	Mean Enrollment
Northeast	111	58	1,325
Middle Atlantic	417	234	1,342
Southeast	359	129	1,023
Southwest	199	107	1,257
West	178	84	1,232
Rocky Mountains	29	13	1,363
Middle West	595	267	1,065
Canada	186	103	1,595
Total	2,074	995	1,196

TABLE 3.58
1988 *American Library Directory* Scholarly Institutional Degree Years Offered by Region[1]

Region	-------------Institutional Degree Years Offered--------------								No Response	%	Number of Libraries	Mean Years	% of Inst's. with M.A. or above
	1–2	%	3–4	%	5–6	%	7 and over	%					
Northeast	6	8	15	20	20	<u>26</u>	12	16	23	30	76	4.9	60
Middle Atlantic	16	6	62	24	66	<u>25</u>	34	13	83	32	261	4.8	56
Southeast	34	13	119	<u>45</u>	51	19	31	12	31	12	266	4.3	35
Southwest	5	4	42	<u>36</u>	28	24	17	15	25	21	117	4.8	49
West	5	4	32	25	41	<u>32</u>	20	16	30	23	128	5.0	62
Rocky Mountains	2	10	5	24	7	<u>33</u>	3	14	4	19	21	4.7	59
Middle West	20	5	169	<u>42</u>	99	25	43	11	67	17	398	4.6	43
Canada	15	9	31	<u>19</u>	19	12	14	8	86	52	165	4.4	42
Total	103	7	475	<u>33</u>	331	23	174	12	349	24	1,432	4.6	47

1. Underlined values represent modal categories.

TABLE 3.59

1988 *American Library Directory* Scholarly Institutional Student Enrollment by Total Annual Library Expenditure[1]

Library Expenditure	Student Enrollment 1–900	%	901–1,800	%	1,801–3,000	%	3,001 and over	%	No Response	%	Number of Libraries	Mean Students	Estimated Mean Expenditure Per Student
Under $1,500	3	25	0	0	0	0	0	0	9	75	12	150	$5
$1,501–$20,000	12	18	0	0	1	2	0	0	52	80	65	404	27
$20,001–$95,000	156	76	7	3	0	0	0	0	41	20	204	308	187
$95,001–$220,000	219	74	47	16	5	2	1	0	24	8	296	652	242
$220,001–$410,000	65	30	111	51	31	14	2	1	9	4	218	1,183	266
$410,001–$510,000	9	18	23	47	10	20	3	6	4	8	49	1,508	305
510,001 and over	10	5	37	18	54	26	94	46	9	4	204	3,172	177
No Response	131	34	30	8	9	2	6	2	207	54	383	685	N/A
Total	605	42	255	18	110	8	106	7	355	25	1,431	1,196	208

1. Estimated expenditure per student is artificially low for the final category ($510,000 and over) because its top limit was assumed to be $610,000 p.a., much lower than in reality—some libraries had million-dollar budgets. Also, the mean for the entire scholarly group is probably rather low as the mean expenditure figure for all scholarly libraries including convent/monasteries and denominational headquarters was used, rather than just the mean for all academic institutional libraries.

TABLE 3.60
1978 and 1988 *American Library Directory* Longitudinal Study
Scholarly Institutional Student Enrollment by Library Type

Library Type	1978 Number of Inst's.	1978 No Response	1978 Total Inst's.	1978 Mean Students	1988 Number of Inst's.	1988 No Response	1988 Total Inst's.	1988 Mean Students	% Change 1978–88
Scholarly	1,056	319	1,375	1,065	1,076	356	1,432	1,196	12
Junior College	114	11	125	540	91	17	108	652	21
Senior College	646	58	704	955	649	56	705	1,010	6
University	136	18	154	2,936	173	16	189	2,977	1
Seminary	159	74	233	296	161	70	231	356	20
Convent/ Monastery	1	34	35	150	0	25	25	0	−100
Denominational HQ	0	77	77	0	2	84	86	150	0
History/Archives	0	47	47	0	0	88	88	0	0

TABLE 3.61
1978 and 1988 *American Library Directory* Longitudinal Study
Scholarly Student Enrollment by Denomination

Denomination	1978 Number of Institutions	1978 No Response	1978 Total Inst's.	1978 Mean Students	1988 Number of Inst's.	1988 No Response	1988 Total Inst's.	1988 Mean Students	% Change 1978–88
Baptist	121	19	140	1,109	128	24	152	1,145	3%
Christian	31	9	40	769	36	5	41	658	−14
Churches of Christ	26	1	27	988	26	1	27	942	−5
Episcopal/ Anglican	20	12	32	615	17	15	32	768	25
Independent	60	22	82	960	69	28	97	973	1
Lutheran	57	13	70	1,034	59	17	76	1,150	11
Mennonite	10	4	14	570	14	8	22	407	−29
Methodist	131	16	147	1,148	132	17	149	1,176	2
Other Denominations	144	61	205	848	145	72	217	885	4
Presbyterian	84	6	90	918	85	5	90	932	2
U.C.C.	23	1	24	1,111	22	3	25	1,255	13
Summary									
Jewish	15	20	35	770	18	27	45	767	0
Roman Catholic	334	135	469	1,257	325	134	459	1,645	31
All Protestant	707	164	871	981	733	195	928	1,008	3
Total	1,056	319	1,375	1,065	1,076	356	1,432	1,196	12

TABLE 3.62
1978 *American Library Directory* Scholarly Baptist Institutions with the Largest Student Enrollment

Library	Student Enrollment
1. Temple University, Philadelphia, PA	5,250
2. Baylor University, Waco, TX	5,250
3. McMaster University, Hamilton, ON	5,250
4. Samford University, Birmingham, AL	4,250
5. Wake Forest University, Winston-Salem, NC	4,250
6. Tennessee Temple Schools, Chattanooga, TN	4,250
7. Southwestern Baptist Theological Seminary, Fort Worth, TX	3,250
8. University of Richmond, Richmond, VA	3,250
9. Mississippi College, Clinton, MS	2,850
10. Acadia University, Wolfville, NS	2,850
11. Baptist Bible College, Springfield, MO	2,550

TABLE 3.63
1988 *American Library Directory* Scholarly Baptist Institutions with the Largest Student Enrollment

Library	Student Enrollment
1. Temple University, Philadelphia, PA	5,250
2. Baylor University, Waco, TX	5,250
3. McMaster University, Hamilton, ON	5,520
4. Wake Forest University, Winston-Salem, NC	4,750
5. Liberty University, Lynchburg, VA	4,750
6. Southwestern Baptist Theological Seminary, Fort Worth, TX	4,250
7. Samford University, Birmingham, AL	3,750
8. University of Richmond, Richmond, VA	3,750
9. Mississippi College, Clinton, MS	3,250
10. Campbell University, Buies Creek, NC	3,250
11. Acadia University, Wolfville, NS	3,250

TABLE 3.64
1988 *American Library Directory* Scholarly Churches of Christ Institutions with the Largest Student Enrollment

Library	Student Enrollment
1. Pepperdine University, Malibu, CA	5,250
2. Abilene Christian University, Abilene, TX	4,250
3. Harding University, Searcy, AR	2,850
4. David Lipscomb University, Nashville, TN	2,250
5. Faulkner University, Montgomery, AL	1,350
6. Oklahoma Christian College, Oklahoma City, OK	1,350
7. Freed-Hardeman University, Henderson, TN	1,350
8. Amber University, Garland, TX	1,050
9. Lubbock Christian University, Lubbock, TX	750

TABLE 3.65
1988 *American Library Directory* Scholarly Episcopal/Anglican Institutions with the Largest Student Enrollment

Library	Student Enrollment
1. Bishop's University, Lennoxville, PQ	2,550
2. Hobart and William Smith Colleges, Geneva, NY	1,650
3. Kenyon College, Gambier, OH	1,650
4. St. Augustine's College, Raleigh, NC	1,350
5. University of the South, Sewanee, TN	1,050
6. Bard College, Annandale-on-Hudson, NY	750
7. Voorhees College, Denmark, SC	750
8. Saint Paul's College, Lawrenceville, VA	750
9. Huron College, London, ON	750

TABLE 3.66
1988 *American Library Directory* Scholarly Lutheran Institutions with the Largest Student Enrollment

Library	Student Enrollment
1. Wilfred Laurier University, Waterloo, ON	5,250
2. Valparaiso University, Valparaiso, IN	3,750
3. St. Olaf College, Northfield, MN	3,250
4. Pacific Lutheran University, Tacoma, WA	3,250
5. Concordia College, Moorehead, MN	2,850
6. Luther College, Decorah, IA	2,250
7. Gustavus Adolphus College, St. Peter, MN	2,250
8. Capital University, Columbus, OH	2,250
9. Wittenberg University, Springfield, OH	2,250

TABLE 3.67
1988 *American Library Directory* Scholarly Methodist Institutions with the Largest Student Enrollment

Library	Student Enrollment
1. University of Denver, Denver, CO	5,250
2. American University, Washington, DC	5,250
3. Emory University, Atlanta, GA	5,250
4. Boston University, Boston, MA	5,250
5. Duke University, Durham, NC	5,250
6. Southern Methodist University, Dallas, TX	5,250
7. University of the Pacific, Stockton, CA	3,750
8. University of Indianapolis, Indianapolis, IN	3,250

TABLE 3.68
1988 *American Library Directory* Scholarly Presbyterian Institutions with the Largest Student Enrollment

Library	Student Enrollment
1. Queen's University, Kingston, ON	5,250
2. University of Tulsa, Tulsa, OK	4,250
3. Lafayette College, Easton, PA	2,250
4. Grove City College, Grove City, PA	2,250
5. Trinity University, San Antonio, TX	2,250
6. Lindenwood College, St. Charles, MO	1,950
7. Lewis and Clark College, Portland, OR	1,950
8. Macalester College, St. Paul, MN	1,650
9. College of Wooster, Wooster, OH	1,650
10. Whitworth College, Spokane, WA	1,650

TABLE 3.69
1988 *American Library Directory* Scholarly Jewish Institutions with the Largest Student Enrollment

Library	Student Enrollment
1. Yeshiva University, New York, NY	4,250
2. Brandeis University, Waltham, MA	3,250
3. Spertus College of Judaica, Chicago, IL	1,050
4. Hebrew College, Brookline, MA	1,050
5. Gratz College, Philadelphia, PA	1,050
6. Cleveland College of Jewish Studies, Beachwood, OH	750
7. Ner Israel Rabbinical College, Baltimore, MD	450
8. Jewish Theological Seminary, New York, NY	450

TABLE 3.70
1978 and 1988 *American Library Directory* Scholarly Institutional Faculty Members by Library Type

Library Type	1978 Number of Inst's.	1978 No Re-sponse	1978 Total Inst's.	1978 Mean Faculty	1988 Number of Inst's	1988 No Re-sponse	1988 Total Inst's.	1988 Mean Faculty	% Change 78–88
Scholarly	1,028	347	1,375	72	1,013	419	1,432	83	15
Junior College	111	14	125	36	83	25	108	47	31
Senior College	633	71	704	66	616	89	705	72	9
University	132	22	154	188	163	26	189	195	4
Seminary	152	81	233	21	148	83	231	23	10
Convent/ Monastery	0	35	35	0	1	24	25	10	0
Denomina-tional HQ	0	77	77	0	2	84	86	10	0
History/Archives	0	47	47	0	0	88	88	0	0

TABLE 3.71
1988 *American Library Directory* Institutional Faculty Members

Number of Faculty Members	Number of Libraries	Percentage
281+	56	3
241–280	17	1
181–240	38	2
121–180	94	5
61–120	277	13
1–60	531	26
No response	1,061	51
Total	2,074	100
Mean	83 faculty members	

TABLE 3.72
1988 *American Library Directory* Institutional Faculty Members by Library Type for Scholarly Libraries

Library Type	1–60 Faculty Members	%	61–120 Faculty Members	%	121–180 Faculty Members	%	181+ Faculty Members	%	No Response	%	Number of Libraries	Mean Faculty Members
Junior College	71	66	7	6	1	1	4	4	25	23	108	47
Senior College	305	43	223	32	58	8	30	4	89	13	705	72
University	14	7	39	21	33	17	77	41	26	14	189	195
Seminary	138	60	8	3	2	1	0	0	83	36	231	23
Convent/Monastery	1	4	0	0	0	0	0	0	24	96	25	0
Denominational HQ	2	2	0	0	0	0	0	0	84	98	86	0
History/Archives	0	0	0	0	0	0	0	0	88	100	88	0
Total	531	37	277	19	94	7	111	8	419	29	1,432	83

TABLE 3.73
1988 *American Library Directory* Junior College Institutions with the Largest Number of Faculty Members

Library	Denomination	Number of Faculty Members
1. Vanier College, St. Laurent, PQ	Roman Catholic	350
2. Cégep de Jonquière, Jonquière, PQ	Roman Catholic	270
3. Ricks College, Rexburg, ID	Other Denominations	250
4. Gwynedd-Mercy College, Gwynedd Valley, PA	Roman Catholic	210
5. Red Deer College, Red Deer, AB	Lutheran	170
6. Faulkner University, Montgomery, AL	Churches of Christ	110
7. Marianapolis College, Montreal, PQ	Roman Catholic	110
8. St. Mary's College, Minneapolis, MN	Roman Catholic	90

TABLE 3.74
1988 *American Library Directory* Seminary Institutions with the Largest Number of Faculty Members

Library	Denomination	Number of Faculty Members
1. Southwestern Baptist Theological Seminary, Fort Worth, TX	Baptist	170
2. Graduate Theological Union, Berkeley, CA	Independent	150
3. Southern Baptist Theological Seminary, Louisville, KY	Baptist	110
4. Mount St. Mary's College, Emmitsburg, MD	Roman Catholic	110
5. New Orleans Baptist Theological Seminary, New Orleans, LA	Baptist	90
6. St. Vincent's College, Latrobe, PA	Roman Catholic	90
7. Fuller Theological Seminary, Pasadena, CA	Independent	70
8. St. Meinrad College, St. Meinrad, IN	Roman Catholic	70
9. Luther Northwestern Seminary, St. Paul, MN	Lutheran	70
10. Dallas Theological Seminary, Dallas, TX	Independent	70

TABLE 3.75
1988 *American Library Directory* Senior College Institutions with the Largest Number of Faculty Members

Library	Denomination	Number of Faculty Members
1. Boston College, Chestnut Hill, MA	Roman Catholic	350
2. College of St. Thomas, St. Paul, MN	Roman Catholic	350
3. St. Peter's College, Jersey City, NJ	Roman Catholic	350
4. Manhattan College, Riverdale, NY	Roman Catholic	350
5. Mercy College, Dobbs Ferry, NY	Roman Catholic	350
6. College of New Rochelle, New Rochelle, NY	Roman Catholic	350
7. Iona College, New Rochelle, NY	Roman Catholic	350
8. College de Maisonneuve, Montreal, PQ	Roman Catholic	350
9. University of Regina Luther College, Regina, SK	Lutheran	350
10. Cégep St. Jean-sur-Richelieu, St. Jean-sur-Richelieu, PQ	Roman Catholic	290

TABLE 3.76
1978 and 1988 *American Library Directory* Longitudinal Study Scholarly Institutional Faculty Size by Degree Years Awarded by Library Type

	1978				1988				
Library Type	Number of Libraries	No Response	Total Libraries	Mean Ratio Value	Number of Libraries	No Response	Total Libraries	Mean Ratio Values	% Change 1978–88
Scholarly	1,002	373	1,375	16	980	451	1,431	18	13%
Junior College	110	15	125	18	81	27	108	23	28
Senior College	626	78	704	15	600	105	705	16	7
University	129	25	154	32	162	27	189	33	3
Seminary	137	96	233	4	136	94	230	4	3
Convent/ Monastery	0	35	35	0	0	25	25	0	0
Denominational HQ	0	77	77	0	1	85	86	2	0
History/Archives	0	47	47	0	0	88	88	0	0

TABLE 3.77
1978 and 1988 *American Library Directory* Longitudinal Study Scholarly Institutional Faculty Size by Degree Years Awarded by Denomination

	1978				1988				
Denomination	Number of Libraries	No Re sponse	Total Li- braries	Mean Ratio Value	Number of Libraries	No Re sponse	Total Li- braries	Mean Ratio Values	% Change 1978–88
Baptist	116	24	140	15	119	33	152	15	0%
Christian	31	9	40	11	35	6	41	11	0
Churches of Christ	25	2	27	13	25	2	27	12	−8
Episcopal/Anglican	18	14	32	13	14	18	32	17	31
Independent	58	24	82	14	60	37	97	12	−14
Lutheran	55	15	70	18	54	22	76	23	28
Mennonite	9	5	14	14	14	8	22	11	−21
Methodist	129	18	147	17	125	24	149	18	6
Other Denominations	133	72	205	14	129	88	217	15	7
Presbyterian	82	8	90	14	81	9	90	15	7
U.C.C.	23	1	24	19	21	4	25	16	−16
Summary									
Jewish	14	21	35	12	11	34	45	12	0
Roman Catholic	309	160	469	19	292	166	458	23	21
All Protestant	679	192	871	15	677	251	928	16	7
Total	1,002	373	1,375	16	980	451	1,431	18	13

TABLE 3.78
1988 *American Library Directory* Institutional Faculty Members by Region for Scholarly Libraries

Region	1–60 Faculty Mem- bers	%	61–120 Faculty Mem- bers	%	121–180 Faculty Mem- bers	%	181+ Faculty Mem- bers	%	No Re- sponse	%	Number of Li- braries	Mean No. of Faculty Members
Northeast	28	37	8	11	6	8	9	12	25	33	76	96
Middle Atlantic	81	31	48	18	18	7	27	10	87	33	261	97
Southeast	130	49	66	25	13	5	9	3	48	18	266	65
Southwest	43	37	27	23	8	7	9	8	30	26	117	84
West	43	34	21	16	11	9	12	9	41	32	128	92
Rocky Mountains	9	43	3	14	0	0	3	14	6	29	21	91
Middle West	158	40	99	25	33	8	25	6	83	21	398	77
Canada	39	24	5	3	5	3	17	10	99	60	165	104
Total	531	37	277	19	94	7	111	8	419	29	1,432	83

TABLE 3.79
1988 *American Library Directory* Scholarly Institutional Faculty Members by Total Annual Library Expenditure

	Institutional Faculty Members											
Library Expenditure	1–60	%	61–120	%	121–180	%	181 and Over	%	No Re-sponse	%	Number of Libraries	Mean Faculty
Under $1,500	3	25	0	0	0	0	0	0	9	75	12	10
$1,501–$20,000	14	22	0	0	0	0	0	0	51	78	65	11
$20,001–$95,000	150	74	4	2	0	0	0	0	50	25	204	22
$95,001–$220,000	187	63	62	21	6	2	1	0	40	14	296	49
$220,001–$410,000	52	24	119	55	24	11	10	5	13	6	218	85
$410,001–$510,000	7	14	25	51	8	16	3	6	6	12	49	102
$510,001 and over	8	4	36	18	50	25	91	45	19	9	204	207
No response	110	29	31	8	6	2	6	2	231	60	384	49
Total	531	37	277	19	94	7	111	8	419	29	1,432	83

TABLE 3.80
1988 *American Library Directory* Scholarly Institutional Faculty Members by Denomination

Denomination	1–60 Faculty Members	%	61–120 Faculty Members	%	121–180 Faculty Members	%	181+ Faculty Members	%	No Response	%	Number of Libraries	Mean Faculty
Baptist	68	45	35	23	9	6	9	6	31	20	152	73
Christian	24	59	9	22	1	2	1	2	6	15	41	49
Churches of Christ	20	74	2	7	2	7	2	7	1	4	27	54
Episcopal/Anglican	9	28	4	13	1	3	1	3	17	53	32	63
Independent	44	45	9	9	4	4	4	4	36	37	97	62
Lutheran	24	32	18	24	10	13	5	7	19	25	76	90
Mennonite	11	50	3	14	0	0	0	0	8	36	22	37
Methodist	68	46	34	23	13	9	11	7	23	15	149	84
Other Denominations	84	39	34	16	10	5	11	5	78	36	217	64
Presbyterian	45	50	30	33	4	4	3	3	8	9	90	68
United Church of Christ	10	40	8	32	2	8	1	4	4	16	25	78
Summary												
Jewish	11	24	0	0	0	0	2	4	32	71	45	72
Roman Catholic	113	25	91	20	38	8	61	13	156	34	459	111
All Protestant	407	44	186	20	56	6	48	5	231	25	928	70
Total	531	37	277	19	94	7	111	8	419	29	1,432	83

TABLE 3.81
1988 *American Library Directory* Scholarly Christian Institutions with the Largest Number of Faculty Members

Library	Number of Faculty Members
1. Texas Christian University, Fort Worth, TX	350
2. Lynchburg College, Lynchburg, VA	130
3. Atlantic Christian College, Wilson, NC	110
4. Chapman University, Orange, CA	90
5. Phillips University, Enid, OK	90
6. Transylvania University, Lexington, KY	70
7. Tougaloo College, Tougaloo, MS	70
8. Columbia College, Columbia, MO	70
9. William Woods University, Fulton, MO	70
10. Hiram College, Hiram, OH	70
11. Bethany College, Bethany, WV	70

TABLE 3.82
1978 *American Library Directory* Scholarly Congregational Institutions with the Largest Number of Faculty Members

Library	Number of Faculty Members
1. Washburn University, Topeka, KS	190
2. Olivet College, Olivet, MI	50
3. Evangelical Congregational School of Theology, Myerstown, PA	10

TABLE 3.83
1988 *American Library Directory* Scholarly Independent Institutions with the Largest Number of Faculty Members

Library	Number of Faculty Members
1. Oral Roberts University, Tulsa, OK	350
2. Brown University, Providence, RI	350
3. Bob Jones University, Greenville, SC	310
4. Biola University, La Mirada, CA	250
5. Azusa Pacific University, Azusa, CA	170
6. Graduate Theological Union, Berkeley, CA	150
7. Jordan College, Cedar Springs, MI	150
8. Wheaton College, Wheaton, IL	130
9. Maharishi International University, Fairfield, IA	110
10. Berea College, Berea, KY	110

TABLE 3.84
1988 *American Library Directory* Scholarly Mennonite Institutions with the Largest Number of Faculty Members

Library	Number of Faculty Members
1. Goshen College, Goshen, IN	90
2. Fresno Pacific College, Fresno, CA	70
3. Hesston College, Hesston, KS	70
4. Tabor College, Hillsboro, KS	50
5. Bethel College, North Newton, KS	50
6. Bluffton College, Bluffton, OH	50
7. Eastern Mennonite University, Harrisonburg, VA	50
8. Freeman Academy, Freeman, SD	30

TABLE 3.85
1988 *American Library Directory* Scholarly Other Denominational Institutions with the Largest Number of Faculty Members

Library	Number of Faculty Members
1. University of La Verne, La Verne, CA	350
2. Loma Linda University, Loma Linda, CA	350
3. Brigham Young University, Provo, UT	350
4. University of Winnipeg, Winnipeg, MB	270
5. Ricks College, Rexburg, ID	250
6. Washburn University, Topeka, KS	250
7. Calvin College, Grand Rapids, MI	250
8. Andrews University, Berrien Springs, MI	230
9. Anderson University, Anderson, IN	190
10. Hope College, Holland, MI	190
11. Bryn Mawr College, Bryn Mawr, PA	190

TABLE 3.86
1988 *American Library Directory* Scholarly United Church of Christ Institutions with the Largest Number of Faculty Members

Library	Number of Faculty Members
1. Eden Webster University, St. Louis, MO	250
2. Elon College, Elon College, NC	150
3. Franklin and Marshall College, Lancaster, PA	130
4. Elmhurst College, Elmhurst, IL	110
5. Hood College, Frederick, MD	110
6. Drury College, Springfield, MO	110
7. Pacific University, Forest Grove, OR	110
8. Ursinus College, Collegeville, PA	90
9. Heidelberg College, Tiffin, OH	70
10. Cedar Crest College, Allentown, PA	70
11. Fisk University, Nashville, TN	70

TABLE 3.87
1988 *American Library Directory* Scholarly Student Enrollment per Library Staff Member by Region

	-----Institutional Student Enrollment per Library Staff Member-----											
Region	1–50	%	51–100	%	101–150	%	151 and over	%	No Response	%	Number of Libraries	Mean Students
Northeast	16	21	13	17	6	8	3	4	38	50	76	76
Middle Atlantic	63	24	42	16	12	5	13	5	131	50	261	72
Southeast	103	39	47	18	19	7	4	2	93	35	266	57
Southwest	31	26	21	18	10	9	9	8	46	39	117	91
West	26	20	27	21	1	1	8	6	66	52	128	72
Rocky Mountains	2	10	3	14	2	10	2	10	12	57	21	114
Middle West	136	34	73	18	23	6	20	5	146	37	398	70
Canada	25	15	16	10	11	7	18	11	94	57	164	115
Total	402	28	242	17	84	6	77	5	626	44	1,431	74

TABLE 3.88
1988 *American Library Directory* Highest Scholarly Christian Student Enrollment per Professional Library Staff Member

Library	Ratio
1. San Jose Bible College, San Jose, CA	450
2. Midway College, Midway, KY	450
3. Ozark Christian College, Joplin, MO	450
4. Texas Christian University, Fort Worth, TX	404
5. William Woods University, Fulton, MO	375
6. Phillips University, Enid, OK	375
7. Lynchburg College, VA	375
8. Bethany College, Bethany, WV	375
9. Transylvania University, Lexington, KY	350

TABLE 3.89
1988 *American Library Directory* Highest Scholarly Churches of Christ Student Enrollment per Professional Library Staff Member

Library	Ratio
1. Oklahoma Christian College, Oklahoma City, OK	675
2. Amber University, Garland, TX	525
3. Harding University, Searcy, AR	475
4. Abilene Christian University, Abilene, TX	472
5. Ambassador College, Big Sandy, TX	450
6. Pepperdine University, Malibu, CA	404

TABLE 3.90
1988 *American Library Directory* Highest Scholarly Mennonite Student Enrollment per Professional Library Staff Member

Library	Ratio
1. Hesston College, Hesston, KS	450
2. Fresno Pacific College, Fresno, CA	375
3. Goshen College, Goshen, IN	350
4. Bethel College, North Newton, KS	250
5. Eastern Mennonite University, Harrisonburg, VA	250
6. Tabor College, Hillsboro, KS	225

TABLE 3.91
1988 *American Library Directory* Highest Scholarly Other Denominations Student Enrollment per Professional Library Staff Member

Library	Ratio
1. Southwestern Adventist College, Keene, TX	975
2. Latter-day Saints Business College, Salt Lake City, UT	750
3. University of Winnipeg, Winnipeg, MB	656
4. Hope College, Holland, MI	563
5. Washburn University, Topeka, KS	531
6. Calvin College, Grand Rapids, MI	531
7. Mount Vernon Nazarene College, Mount Vernon, OR	525

TABLE 3.92
1988 *American Library Directory* Highest Scholarly United Church of Christ Student Enrollment per Professional Library Staff Member

Library	Ratio
1. Eden Webster University, St. Louis, MO	679
2. Elmhust College, Elmhurst, IL	542
3. Elon College, Elon College, NC	542
4. Hood College, Frederick, MD	488
5. Drury College, Springfield, MO	390
6. Heidelberg College, Tiffin, OH	350
7. Pacific University, Forest Grove, OR	270

TABLE 3.93
1988 *American Library Directory* Highest Scholarly Jewish Student Enrollment per Professional Library Staff Member

Library	Ratio
1. Yeshiva University, New York, NY	327
2. Hebrew College, Brookline, MA	263
3. Brandeis University, Waltham, MA	250
4. Spertus College of Judaica, Chicago, IL	210

TABLE 3.94
1988 *American Library Directory* Highest Scholarly Roman Catholic Student Enrollment per Professional Library Staff Member

Library	Ratio
1. Collège de Masonneuve, Montreal, PQ	2,625
2. François-Xavier Garneau College, Quebec, PQ	1,875
3. St. Joseph's College, Edmonton, AB	1,650
4. College of Lévis, Lévis, PQ	1,350
5. Vanier College, St. Laurent, PQ	1,313
6. Cégep St. Jean-sur-Richelieu, St. Jean-sur-Richelieu, PQ	1,125
7. Trois-Rivières College, Trois-Rivières, PQ	1,063
8. Parks College of Aeronautics, Cahokia, IL	1,050
9. Briar Cliff College, Sioux City, IA	1,050
10. Cégep de St. Félicien, St. Félicien, PQ	1,050
11. University of Saskatchewan St. Thomas More College, Saskatoon, SK	1,050

TABLE 3.95
1988 *American Library Directory* Smallest Scholarly Baptist Student Enrollment per Library Staff Member

Library	Ratio
1. North American Baptist Seminary, Sioux Falls, SD	20
2. Franklin College, Franklin, IN	19
3. Grand Rapids Baptist College, Grand Rapids, MI	19
4. Hispanic Baptist Theological Seminary, San Antonio, TX	18
5. Atlantic Baptist College, Moncton, NB	18
6. Piedmont Bible College, Winston-Salem, NC	16
7. Morris College, Sumter, SC	10
8. Calvary Baptist Theological Seminary, Lansdale, PA	9

TABLE 3.96
1988 *American Library Directory* Smallest Scholarly Churches of Christ Student Enrollment per Library Staff Member

Library	Ratio
1. Great Lakes Bible College, Lansing, MI	19
2. Chicago Theological Seminary, Chicago, IL	18
3. Columbia Christian College, Portland, OR	17
4. Southwestern Christian College, Terrell, TX	16
5. Ohio Valley College, Parkersburg, WV	10

TABLE 3.97
1988 *American Library Directory* Smallest Scholarly Independent Student Enrollment per Library Staff Member

Library	Ratio
1. New York Theological Seminary, New York, NY	15
2. Harvard University Andover-Harvard Theological Library, Cambridge, MA	15
3. Mid-South Bible College, Memphis, TN	14
4. Christian Broadcasting Network University, Virginia Beach, VA	12
5. Yale University Divinity School, New Haven, CT	12
6. Clearwater Christian College, Clearwater, FL	11
7. Reformed Theological Seminary, Jackson, MS	8

TABLE 3.98
1988 *American Library Directory* Smallest Scholarly Mennonite Student Enrollment per Library Staff Member

Library	Ratio
1. Associated Mennonite Biblical Seminary, Elkhart, IN	25
2. Steinbach Bible College, Steinbach, MB	20
3. Eastern Mennonite University, Harrisonburg, VA	19
4. Columbia Bible College, Clearbrook, BC	12
5. Winkler Bible Institute, Winkler, MB	7

TABLE 3.99
1988 *American Library Directory* Smallest Scholarly Other Denominations Student Enrollment per Library Staff Member

Library	Ratio
1. Canadian Nazarene College, Winnipeg, MB	20
2. Olivet College, Olivet, MI	19
3. Principia College, Elsah, IL	19
4. Naropa Institute, Boulder, CO	18
5. Pinebrook Junior College, Coopersburg, PA	18
6. Huntington College, Sudbury, ON	16
7. Patton College, Oakland, CA	14
8. New Brunswick Theological Seminary, New Brunswick, NJ	14
9. Northeast Bible College, Minot, ND	12

TABLE 3.100
1988 *American Library Directory* Smallest Scholarly United Church of Christ Student Enrollment per Library Staff Member

Library	Ratio
1. Lancaster Theological Seminary, Lancaster, PA	20
2. Huston-Tillotson College, Austin, TX	18
3. Fisk University, Nashville, TN	17
4. Andover Newton Theological School, Newton Center, MA	14
5. Cedar Crest College, Allentown, PA	13

TABLE 3.101
1988 *American Library Directory* Smallest Scholarly Roman Catholic Student Enrollment per Library Staff Member

Library	Ratio
1. Cathedral College of the Immaculate Conception, Douglaston, NY	13
2. Mount Marty College, Yankton, SD	12
3. Felician College, Chicago, IL	11
4. College of St. Teresa, Winona, MN	11
5. Pontifical College Josephium, Columbus, OH	10
6. St. Mary's Seminary, Baltimore, MD	9
7. College of St. Thomas Divinity School, St. Paul, MN	9
8. St. Meinrad College, St. Meinrad, IN	8

TABLE 3.102
1988 *American Library Directory* Lowest Enrollment/Faculty Size Ratios by Institutional Enrollment Level in Descending Order[1]

Denomination	Enrollment	Faculty	Ratio	Institution
Baptist	5,250	350	15.0	Temple University, Philadelphia, PA
	4,750	330	14.4	Wake Forest University, Winston-Salem, NC
	3,750	310	12.0	University of Richmond, Richmond, VA
	2,250	210	10.7	Belmont University, Nashville, TN
	1,950	210	9.2	Wayland Baptist University, Plainview, TX
	1,050	110	9.5	Ouachita Baptist University, Arkadelphia, AR
	1,050	110	9.5	Eastern College, St. Davids, PA
	450	70	6.4	California Baptist College, Riverside, CA
	450	50	9.0	Ottawa University, Ottawa, KS
	150	30	5.0	Midwestern Baptist College, Pontiac, MI
Christian	5,250	350	15.0	Texas Christian University, Fort Worth, TX
	750	90	8.3	Phillips University, Enid, OK
	450	50	9.0	San Jose Bible College, San Jose, CA
	450	50	9.0	Ozark Christian College, Joplin, MO
	450	50	9.0	Milligan College, Milligan College, TN
	150	30	5.0	Manhattan Christian College, Manhattan, KS
Churches of Christ	150	30	5.0	Michigan Christian College, Rochester, MI
	150	30	5.0	Columbia Christian College, Portland, OR
	150	30	5.0	Southwestern Christian College, Terrell, TX
	150	30	5.0	Ohio Valley College, Parkersburg, WV
Episcopal/ Anglican	1,050	110	9.5	University of the South, Sewanee, TN
	750	90	8.3	Bard College, Annandale-on-Hudson, NY
	450	50	9.0	Saint Mary's College, Raleigh, NC
	150	20	7.5	George Mercer School of Theology, Garden City, NY
Independent	5,250	350	15.0	Brown University, Providence, RI
	4,750	350	13.5	Oral Roberts University, Tulsa, OK
	2,850	250	11.4	Biola University, La Mirada, CA
	1,050	150	7.0	Graduate Theological Union, Berkeley, CA
	750	110	6.8	Maharishi International University, Fairfield, IA
	450	50	9.0	Hawaii Loa College, Kaneohe, HI
	450	50	9.0	Washington Bible College, Lanham, MD
	150	30	5.0	Northeastern Bible College, Essex Falls, NJ
Lutheran	3,250	250	13.0	Pacific Lutheran University, Tacoma, WA
	1,650	170	9.7	Augsburg College, Minneapolis, MN
	450	70	6.4	Concordia College, Ann Arbor, MI
	450	70	6.4	Dr. Martin Luther College, New Ulm, MN
	150	30	5.0	Wisconsin Lutheran College, Milwaukee, WI

TABLE 3.102 (continued)
1988 *American Library Directory* Lowest Enrollment/Faculty Size Ratios by Institutional Enrollment Level in Descending Order[1]

Denomination	Enrollment	Faculty	Ratio	Institution
Mennonite	450	70	6.4	Hesston College, Hesston, KS
	450	50	9.0	Tabor College, Hillsboro, KS
	450	50	9.0	Bluffton College, Bluffton, OH
	150	30	5.0	Freeman Academy, Freeman, SD
Methodist	5,250	350	15.0	University of Denver, Denver, CO
	3,750	330	11.3	University of the Pacific, Stockton, CA
	2,850	290	9.8	Wesleyan University, Middletown, CT
	2,850	270	10.5	University of Evansville, Evansville, IN
	1,350	150	9.0	Drew University, Madison, NJ
	1,050	110	9.5	Southwestern University, Georgetown, TX
	1,050	110	9.5	Shenandoah College, Winchester, VA
	750	90	8.3	Randolph-Macon Woman's College, Lynchburg, VA
	450	70	6.4	Dakota Wesleyan University, Mitchell, SD
	450	50	9.0	Central Wesleyan College, Central, SC
Other Denominations	5,250	350	15.0	Brigham Young University, Provo, UT
	3,750	350	10.7	University of La Verne, La Verne, CA
	2,550	230	11.0	Andrews University, Berrien Springs, MI
	2,250	190	11.8	Hope College, Holland, MI
	1,950	350	5.5	Loma Linda University, Loma Linda, CA
	1,650	190	8.6	Bryn Mawr College, Bryn Mawr, PA
	1,350	150	9.0	Walla Walla College, College Place, WA
	1,050	110	9.5	Haverford College, Haverford, PA
	750	110	6.8	Atlantic Union College, South Lancaster, MA
Presbyterian	5,250	350	15.0	Queen's University, Kingston, ON
	4,250	310	13.7	University of Tulsa, Tulsa, OK
	2,550	250	10.2	Trinity University, San Antonio, TX
	1,350	150	9.0	Queens College, Charlotte, NC
	1,050	110	9.5	Austin College, Sherman, TX
	450	50	9.0	Jamestown College, Jamestown, ND
	450	50	9.0	Erskine College, Due West, SC
	450	50	9.0	Schreiner College, Kerrville, TX
	150	30	5.0	Sheldon Jackson College, Sitka, AK
United Church of Christ	450	50	9.0	Huston-Tillotson College, Austin, TX
	150	30	5.0	Andover-Newton Theological School, Newton Center, MA
Jewish	4,250	350	12.1	Yeshiva University, New York, NY
	3,250	350	9.2	Brandeis University, Waltham, MA
	450	50	9.0	Jewish Theological Seminary, New York, NY
	150	30	5.0	Hebrew Union College, Cincinnati, OH

TABLE 3.102 (continued)
1988 *American Library Directory* Lowest Enrollment/Faculty Size Ratios by Institutional Enrollment Level in Descending Order[1]

Denomination	Enrollment	Faculty	Ratio	Institution
Roman Catholic	5,250	350	15.0	Loyola Marymount University, Los Angeles, CA
	4,750	350	13.5	St. Louis University, St. Louis, MO
	4,750	350	13.5	Manhattan College, Riverdale, NY
	4,250	350	12.1	College of New Rochelle, New Rochelle, NY
	3,750	350	10.7	St. Peter's College, Jersey City, NJ
	3,250	270	12.0	Cégep de Jonquière, Jonquière, QU
	2,550	210	12.1	Saint Xavier University, Chicago, IL
	2,550	210	12.1	College of the Holy Cross, Worcester, MA
	2,550	210	12.1	St. Bonaventure University, St. Bonaventure, NY
	2,550	190	13.4	Diocese of Phoenix, Phoenix, AZ
	2,250	290	7.7	Cégep de St. Jean-sur-Richelieu, St. Jean-sur-Richelieu, QU
	1,950	210	9.2	Rockhurst College, Kansas City, MO
	1,950	210	9.2	Gwynedd-Mercy College, Gwynedd Valley, PA
	1,650	210	7.8	Mercy College, Detroit, MI
	1,350	190	7.1	St. Ambrose University, Davenport, IA
	1,350	170	7.9	Molloy College, Rockville Centre, NY
	1,050	130	8.0	College Misericordia, Dallas, TX
	750	130	5.7	College of St. Mary, Omaha, NE
	750	110	6.8	Carlow College, Pittsburgh, PA
	750	110	6.8	La Roche College, Pittsburgh, PA

1. The figures used for the enrollment, faculty, and ratio columns are based on the midpoints of the enrollment categories. In a few cases for large universities this led to a distortion of the institution's enrollment and faculty size levels and therefore to misleading results.

TABLE 3.103
1988 *American Library Directory* Scholarly Libraries with the Largest Number of Consortium Memberships

Library	Denomination	Consortium Memberships
1. University of Detroit, Detroit, MI	Roman Catholic	8
2. Acadia University, Wolfville, NS	Baptist	8
3. La Salle University, Philadelphia, PA	Roman Catholic	8
4. University of Ottawa, Ottawa, ON	Roman Catholic	8
5. Georgetown University, Washington, DC	Roman Catholic	7
6. Emory University, Atlanta, GA	Methodist	7
7. Aurora University, Aurora, IL	Other Denominations	7
8. Principia College, Elsah, IL	Other Denominations	7
9. Rosary College, River Forest, IL	Roman Catholic	7
10. Madonna University, Livonia, MI	Roman Catholic	7
11. Cedar Crest College, Allentown, PA	United Church of Christ	7
12. Muhlenberg College, Allentown, PA	Lutheran	7
13. Brown University, Providence, RI	Independent	7

TABLE 3.104
1988 *American Library Directory* Scholarly Library Consortium Membership by Region

	------Consortium Membership------											
Region	1–2	%	3–4	%	5–6	%	7 & over	%	No Response	%	Number of Libraries	Mean Memberships
Northeast	20	26	19	25	0	0	1	1	36	47	76	2.6
Middle Atlantic	88	34	59	23	14	5	4	2	96	37	261	2.7
Southeast	98	37	50	19	5	2	1	0	112	42	266	2.3
Southwest	38	32	23	20	1	1	0	0	55	47	117	2.3
West	44	34	17	13	3	2	0	0	64	50	128	2.0
Rocky Mountains	6	29	2	10	2	10	0	0	11	52	21	3.0
Middle West	143	36	120	30	30	8	5	1	100	25	398	2.8
Canada	26	16	3	2	2	1	2	1	131	80	164	2.0
Total	463	32	293	20	57	4	13	1	605	42	1,431	2.6

TABLE 3.105
1978 and 1988 *American Library Directory* Consortium Memberships by Regional and All Types of Accreditation for Junior and Senior College, University, and Seminary Libraries Combined

Edition	Accreditation Type and Status	Number of Libraries	No Response	Mean Number of Consortium Memberships
1978	Accredited (Regional)	844	348	2.0
	Unaccredited	372	293	1.5
1988	Accredited (Regional)	881	173	2.6
	Unaccredited	352	265	1.9
1978	Accredited (All Types)	970	447	2.0
	Unaccredited	246	194	1.3
1988	Accredited (All Types)	971	225	2.6
	Unaccredited	262	213	2.1

TABLE 3.106
1978 *American Library Directory* Scholarly Baptist Libraries with the Largest Number of Consortium Memberships

Library	Number of Consortium Memberships
1. McMaster University, Hamilton, ON	8
2. Temple University, Philadelphia, PA	6
3. Sioux Falls College, Sioux Falls, SD	4
4. Ouachita Baptist University, Arkadelphia, AR	3
5. Southern Baptist Theological Seminary, Louisville, KY	3
6. Kalamazoo College, Kalamazoo, MI	3
7. North American Baptist Seminary, Sioux Falls, SD	3
8. Bishop College, Dallas, TX	3

TABLE 3.107
1988 *American Library Directory* Scholarly Baptist Libraries with the Largest Number of Consortium Memberships

Library	Number of Consortium Memberships
1. Acadia University, Wolfville, NS	8
2. Judson College, Elgin, IL	6
3. Cumberland College, Williamsburg, KY	6
4. Temple University, Philadelphia, PA	6
5. William Jewell College, Liberty, MO	5
6. Liberty University, Lynchburg, VA	5

TABLE 3.108
1988 *American Library Directory* Scholarly Churches of Christ Libraries with the Largest Number of Consortium Memberships

Library	Number of Consortium Memberships
1. Harding University, Searcy, AR	6
2. Chicago Theological Seminary, Chicago, IL	4
3. Oklahoma Christian College, Oklahoma City, OK	3
4. David Lipscomb University, Nashville, TN	3
5. Lincoln Christian College, Lincoln, IL	2
6. Cincinnati Bible Seminary, Cincinnati, OH	2
7. Harding College School of Religion, Memphis, TN	2
8. Abilene Christian University, Abilene, TX	2

TABLE 3.109
1988 *American Library Directory* Scholarly Episcopal/Anglican Libraries with the Largest Number of Consortium Memberships

Library	Number of Consortium Memberships
1. General Theological Seminary, New York, NY	5
2. Episcopal Divinity School, Cambridge, MA	4
3. Nashotah House, Nashotah, WI	3
4. Bard College, Annandale-on-Hudson, NY	2
5. Hobart and William Smith Colleges, Geneva, NY	2
6. Kenyon College, Gambier, OH	2
7. University of the South, Sewanee, TN	2
8. Christ Seminary, Austin, TX	2
9. Episcopal Theological Seminary, Austin, TX	2
10. Virginia Theological Seminary, Alexandria, VA	2

TABLE 3.110
1978 *American Library Directory* Scholarly Lutheran Libraries with the Largest Number of Consortium Memberships

Library	Number of Consortium Memberships
1. Luther College, Decorah, IA	5
2. Concordia Teachers College, River Forest, IL	4
3. Augustana College, Rock Island, IL	4
4. Muhlenberg College, Allentown, PA	4
5. Gettysburg College, Gettysburg, PA	4
6. Wartburg College, Waverly, IA	3
7. Augsburg College, Minneapolis, MN	3
8. Concordia College, Moorhead, MN	3
9. Wittenberg University, Springfield, OH	3
10. Lutheran Theological Seminary, Philadelphia, PA	3
11. Susquehanna University, Selinsgrove, PA	3

TABLE 3.111
1988 *American Library Directory* Scholarly Methodist Libraries with the Largest Number of Consortium Memberships

Library	Number of Consortium Memberships
1. Emory University, Atlanta, GA	7
2. Spring Arbor College, Spring Arbor, MI	6
3. Randolph-Macon College, Ashland, VA	6
4. North Central College, Naperville, IL	5
5. Southwestern College, Winfield, KS	5
6. Nebraska Wesleyan University, Lincoln, NE	5
7. Drew University, Madison, NJ	5

TABLE 3.112
1978 *American Library Directory* Scholarly Presbyterian Libraries with the Largest Number of Consortium Memberships

Library	Number of Consortium Memberships
1. Lake Forest College, Lake Forest, IL	5
2. Wilson College, Chambersburg, PA	5
3. Beaver College, Glenside, PA	4
4. Westminster College, New Wilmington, PA	4
5. Hanover College, Hanover, IN	3
6. Coe College, Cedar Rapids, IA	3
7. University of Dubuque, Dubuque, IA	3
8. Tarkio College, Tarkio, MO	3
9. Davidson College, Davidson, NC	3
10. Carroll College, Waukesha, WI	3

TABLE 3.113
1988 *American Library Directory* Scholarly United Church of Christ Libraries with the Largest Number of Consortium Memberships

Library	Number of Consortium Memberships
1. Cedar Crest College, Allentown, PA	7
2. Elmhurst College, Elmhurst, IL	6
3. Eden Webster University, St. Louis, MO	6
4. Ursinus College, Collegeville, PA	4
5. Franklin and Marshall College, Lancaster, PA	4
6. Hood College, Frederick, MD	3
7. United Theological Seminary, New Brighton, MN	3
8. Drury College, Springfield, MO	3
9. Elon College, Elon College, NC	3
10. Pacific University, Forest Grove, OR	3
11. Lakeland College, Sheboygan, WI	3

TABLE 3.114
1978 *American Library Directory* Scholarly Roman Catholic Libraries with the Largest Number of Consortium Memberships

Library	Number of Consortium Memberships
1. DePaul University, Chicago, IL	8
2. University of Ottawa, Ottawa, ON	8
3. Georgetown University, Washington, DC	7
4. Barat College, Lake Forest, IL	7
5. Marquette University, Milwaukee, WI	7
6. University of Detroit, Detroit, MI	6
7. Saint Xavier University, Chicago, IL	5
8. Loras College, Dubuque, IA	5
9. Xavier University, New Orleans, LA	5
10. St. Charles Borromeo Seminary, Philadelphia, PA	5
11. Saint Joseph's University, Philadelphia, PA	5
12. Rosemont College, Rosemont, PA	5

TABLE 3.115
1988 *American Library Directory* Scholarly Roman Catholic Libraries with the Largest Number of Consortium Memberships

Library	Number of Consortium Memberships
1. University of Detroit, Detroit, MI	8
2. La Salle University, Philadelphia, PA	8
3. University of Ottawa, Ottawa, ON	8
4. Georgetown University, Washington, DC	7
5. Rosary College, River Forest, IL	7
6. Madonna University, Livonia, MI	7

TABLE 3.116
1978 and 1988 *American Library Directory* Longitudinal Study Scholarly OCLC Membership by Library Type

	1978				1988				
Library Type	Number of Libraries	Percentage	No Response	Total Libraries	Number of Libraries	Percentage	No Response	Total Libraries	% Change 1978–88
Scholarly	188	14	1,187	1,375	582	41	849	1,431	210
Junior college	2	1.6	123	125	10	9.3	98	108	400
Senior college	119	17	585	704	347	49	358	705	192
University	45	29	109	154	130	69	59	189	189
Seminary	20	8.5	213	233	83	36	147	230	315
Convent/Monastery	1	2.9	34	35	0	0	25	25	−100
Denominational HQ	0	0	77	77	4	4.7	82	86	N/A
History/Archives	1	2.1	46	47	8	9	80	88	700

TABLE 3.117
1988 *American Library Directory* Scholarly Libraries Showing OCLC Membership by Region

Region	Libraries with OCLC Membership	%	No Response	%	Number of Libraries
Northeast	24	32	52	68	76
Middle Atlantic	127	49	134	51	261
Southeast	102	38	164	62	266
Southwest	49	42	68	58	117
West	48	38	80	63	128
Rocky Mountains	7	33	14	67	21
Middle West	225	57	173	43	398
Canada	0	0	164	100	164
Total	582	41	849	59	1,431

TABLE 3.118
1978 and 1988 *American Library Directory* Longitudinal Study Scholarly Libraries with Local Automation Projects by Denomination

	1978				1988				
Denomination	Number of Libraries	Percentage	No Response	Total Libraries	Number of Libraries	Percentage	No Response	Total Libraries	% Change 1978–88
Baptist	0	0	140	140	63	41	89	152	N/A
Christian	0	0	40	40	19	46	22	41	N/A
Churches of Christ	1	3.7	26	27	11	41	16	27	1,000
Episcopal/ Anglican	0	0	32	32	16	50	16	32	N/A
Independent	1	1.2	81	82	31	32	66	97	3,000
Lutheran	0	0	70	70	44	58	32	76	N/A
Mennonite	0	0	14	14	6	27	16	22	N/A
Methodist	0	0	147	147	78	52	71	149	N/A
Other Denom.	2	1	203	205	93	43	124	217	4,550
Presbyterian	0	0	90	90	55	61	35	90	N/A
U.C.C.	1	4.2	23	24	15	60	10	25	1,400
<u>Summary</u>									
Jewish	0	0	35	35	6	13	39	45	N/A
Roman Catholic	4	.9	465	469	195	43	263	458	4,775
All Protestant	5	.6	866	871	431	46	497	928	8,520
Total	9	.7	1,366	1,375	632	44	799	1,431	6,922

TABLE 3.119
1978 and 1988 *American Library Directory* Longitudinal Study
Scholarly Libraries with Local Automation Projects

	1978				1988				
Library Type	Number of Libraries	Percentage	No Response	Total Libraries	Number of Libraries	Percentage	No Response	Total Libraries	% Change 1978–88
Scholarly	9	.7	1,366	1,375	632	44	799	1,431	6,922
Junior College	0	0	125	125	20	19	88	108	N/A
Senior College	5	.8	699	704	365	52	340	705	7,200
University	1	.7	153	154	145	77	44	189	14,400
Seminary	3	1.3	230	233	81	35	149	230	2,600
Convent/ Monastery	0	0	35	35	0	0	25	25	N/A
Denominational HQ	0	0	77	77	11	13	75	86	N/A
History/ Archives	0	0	47	47	10	11	78	88	N/A

TABLE 3.120
1988 *American Library Directory* Scholarly Libraries with Local Automation Projects by Region

Region	Libraries with Automation Projects	%	No Response	%	Number of Libraries
Northeast	28	37	48	63	76
Middle Atlantic	132	51	129	49	261
Southeast	109	41	157	59	266
Southwest	46	39	71	61	117
West	53	41	75	59	128
Rocky Mountains	8	38	13	62	21
Middle West	221	56	177	44	398
Canada	35	21	129	79	164
Total	632	44	799	56	1,431

TABLE 3.121
1988 *American Library Directory* Scholarly Libraries with Local Automation Projects by Total Annual Library Expenditures

Library Expenditures	Libraries with Automation Projects	%	No Response	%	Number of Libraries
Under $1,500	0	0	12	100	12
$1,501–$20,000	2	3	63	97	65
$20,001–$95,000	46	23	158	77	204
$95,001–$220,000	136	46	160	54	296
$220,001–$410,000	170	78	48	22	218
$410,001–$510,000	35	71	14	29	49
$510,001 and over	177	87	27	13	204
No response	66	17	317	83	383
Total	632	44	799	56	1,431

TABLE 3.122
1978 *American Library Directory* Library Questionnaires Returned by Region for Scholarly Libraries

	Questionnaire Returned?						
Region	Yes	%	No	%	No Response	%	Number of Libraries
Northeast	53	70	22	29	1	1	76
Middle Atlantic	178	67	84	32	2	1	264
Southeast	177	66	89	33	1	0	267
Southwest	71	63	39	35	2	2	112
West	78	66	40	34	1	1	119
Rocky Mountains	16	59	11	41	0	0	27
Middle West	289	70	119	29	4	1	412
Canada	71	72	26	27	1	1	98
Total	933	68	430	31	12	1	1,375

TABLE 3.123
1978 *American Library Directory* Scholarly Library Questionnaires Returned by Denomination

Denomination	Questionnaire Returned? Yes	%	No	%	No Response	%	Number of Libraries
Baptist	99	71	40	29	1	1	140
Christian	29	73	11	28	0	0	40
Church of Christ	20	74	7	26	0	0	27
Congregational	3	60	2	40	0	0	5
Episcopal	23	72	9	28	0	0	32
Independent	60	73	21	26	1	1	82
Lutheran	43	61	27	39	0	0	70
Methodist	107	73	40	27	0	0	147
Other Denominations	143	67	68	32	3	1	214
Presbyterian	63	70	26	29	1	1	90
U.C.C.	17	71	7	29	0	0	24
Summary							
Jewish	23	66	11	31	1	3	35
Roman Catholic	303	65	161	34	5	1	469
All Protestant	607	70	258	30	6	1	871
Total	933	68	430	31	12	1	1,375

TABLE 3.124
1978 *American Library Directory* Scholarly Library Questionnaires Returned by Library Type

Library Type	Questionnaire Returned? Yes	%	No	%	No Response	%	Number of Libraries
Scholarly	933	68	430	31	12	1	1,375
Junior College	69	55	56	45	0	0	125
Senior College	503	71	196	28	5	1	704
University	130	84	20	13	4	3	154
Seminary	140	60	91	39	2	1	233
Convent/ Monastery	12	34	23	66	0	0	35
Denomi- national HQ	42	55	35	45	0	0	77
History/Archives	37	79	9	19	1	2	47

TABLE 3.125
1978 and 1988 *American Library Directory* Longitudinal Study
Scholarly Libraries Reporting Pieces of Information

Library Type	1978 Number of Libraries	1978 Mean Pieces	1988 Number of Libraries	1988 Mean Pieces	% Change 1978–88
Scholarly	1,375	26	1,431	27	4
Junior College	125	25	108	26	4
Senior College	704	28	705	29	4
University	154	29	189	31	7
Seminary	233	24	230	26	8
Convent/Monastery	35	18	25	19	6
Denominational HQ	77	18	86	19	6
History/Archives	47	21	88	22	5

TABLE 3.126
1978 and 1988 *American Library Directory* Longitudinal Study
Scholarly Library Director Named

Library Type	1978 Number of Libraries	1978 Percentage	1978 No Response or "No"	1978 Total Libraries	1988 Number of Libraries	1988 Percentage	1988 No Response or "No"	1988 Total Libraries	% Change 1978–88
Scholarly	1,295	94	80	1,375	1,414	99	17	1,431	9.2
Junior College	119	95	6	125	108	100	0	108	−9.2
Senior College	682	97	22	704	694	98	11	705	1.8
University	152	99	2	154	189	100	0	189	24.3
Seminary	215	92	18	233	225	98	5	230	4.7
Convent/Monastery	25	71	10	35	25	100	0	25	0.0
Denominational HQ	58	75	19	77	85	99	1	86	46.6
History/Archives	44	94	3	47	88	100	0	88	100.0

TABLE 3.127
1978 and 1988 *American Library Directory* Listings of Subject Interests and Special Collections for Entire Samples

ALD Edition	Libraries Total	Libraries Listing Subject Interests	Percentage
31	2,062	922	45
41	2,074	892	43
		Libraries Listing Special Collections	
31	2,062	468	23
41	2,074	632	30

TABLE 3.128
1978 and 1988 *American Library Directory* Subject Interests Broken Down into Categories for Scholarly Libraries[1]

Subject Interest	--------1978------- No. of References	% of Total	-------1988------- No. of References	% of Total	For 1988 % of Subject Interests Accounted for by Scholarly Libraries
Religion: general	643	60	415	37	87
Theology	58	5	143	13	74
Bible	34	3	105	9	65
Judaica	9	1	11	1	7
Church history	58	5	82	7	68
Jewish history and literature	12	1	55	5	50
Missions and missionaries	8	2	39	4	68
Miscellaneous faiths and denominations	42	4	32	3	64
Religious education	10	1	26	2	59
Roman Catholicism	23	2	37	3	90
Christian life	12	1	13	1	33
Pastoral care	15	1	31	3	89
Church work	18	2	29	3	97
Biography and fiction	3	0	7	1	29
Baptist church	12	1	20	2	87

TABLE 3.128 (continued)
1978 and 1988 *American Library Directory* Subject Interests Broken Down into Categories for Scholarly Libraries[1]

Subject Interest	--------1978------- No. of References	% of Total	-------1988------- No. of References	% of Total	For 1988 % of Subject Interests Accounted for by Scholarly Libraries
Jewish life	15	1	13	1	62
Philosophy and psychology	28	3	17	2	89
Music	10	1	16	1	94
Devotionals	0	0	0	0	0
Mysticism	13	1	12	1	86
Sociology and religion	9	1	4	0	40
Other unclassified	31	3	3	0	75
Total	1,073	100	1,110	100	67

Scholarly Libraries	1978	1988
Number of libraries with subject interests	714	588
Number of subject interests per library	1.5	1.9

1. These figures refer only to those libraries naming their subject interests.

TABLE 3.129
1978 *American Library Directory* Scholarly Subject Interests

1. Biography (Christian biographies, ministers' biographical references, Christian autobiographies, Bible characters, lives of saints, hagiography, fiction [Christian fiction, Jewish fiction, inspirational fiction, Christian novels, theological fiction], Virgin Mary [Virgin Mary material, Josephology])
2. Bibles (biblical literature, biblical studies, Scripture, biblical works, Bible references, Christian Bible, Bible stories, biblical commentaries, biblical and inspirational, Bible study aids, Old Testament, biblical archeology, biblical science, biblical aids, Greek and Hebrew Scriptures, biblical research)
3. Baptist church (Baptist writing, Baptist history and theology, Baptist books, Baptist religion, Baptist Church life, Canadian Baptist Church life, Southern Baptist denomination, Baptistiana, Anabaptist)
4. Christian life (Christian concerns, church-related subjects, Christian living, religious practices, Christian literature, societies, Christianity, Christian influence, ecumenism, ecumenics, faith, personal faith, laity, Reformation, Reformation history, mythology, religious, women, spiritual growth, stewardship, Christian ethics)
5. Church history (Episcopal church history, Evangelical church history, Brethren history, Dutch church history, Disciples of Christ Church history, Christian history, Mormon history, Lutheran history, Quaker history, Augustinian history, Evangelical and Reformed Church, United Church of Christ, Mennonite and Amish history, English church history, Byzantine history, Church of the Brethren, Congregational-Christian archives, YWCA history, YMCA history, United Brethren church: Christian churches: genealogy, evolution, Mennonites, Mennonitica, Moravian Church, Moravian Church history, Salvation Army history, Nazarene Church history, anti-evolution polemics, scientific creationism, Anglican Church history, Methodist history, Presbyterian Church history, U.S. church history, black church, Seventh-day Adventist)
6. Church work (church school, worship, social work, church research, American churches, outreach, American communion, church art, art of the Western church, art of the Eastern church, holy days, church ministries, family worship, church renewal, church architecture, sermons, church records, family guidance, restoring the New Testament church, civil rights, multimedia, radio programs library, church and social action, altar, ecclesiology, ecclesiastical science, church growth, church and society)
7. Devotions (devotionals, devotional literature, devotional studies, pietism)
8. Jewish life (Jewish problems, Jewish issues, Canadian Jewry, Jewish social welfare, Jewish community organization, Jewish community studies, Jewish labor, Jewish immigration, Jewish sociology, Jewish holidays, Jewish art, Jewish interests, Jewish education, Jewish biography, Jewish interests of children, Jewish leaders)
9. Jewish history and literature (Hebrew literature, Hebraica, books by Jewish authors, rabbinical literature, Hebrew language, Yiddish language and literature, Jewish history and culture, Reconstructionist Judaism, Judaic history, Maryland Jewish history, Holocaust, Israel, Palestine, Zionism, Dead Sea Scrolls, the Holy Land and its people)
10. Judaica (Judaism, Jewish religion, Jewish studies, Haggadah, Talmud, English Judaica, Jewish religious practices)
11. Missions and missionaries (missiology, missionary material, apostolate, world missions, evangelical and missionary goals of the church, evangelical material, soul winning, Pentecostalism, Pentecostal Holiness Church, evangelism)

TABLE 3.129 (continued)
1978 *American Library Directory* Scholarly Subject Interests

12. Music (liturgical music, church music, Jewish music, hymnology, hymnography, sacred music, hymnals, music and religion, Moravian Church music)
13. Mysticism (occult, magic, yoga, meditation, Theosophy, Theosophical history)
14. Philosophy and psychology (Jewish philosophy, ethics, metaphysics, religious philosophy, religious psychiatry, ESP, psychiatry, temperance, character building, Rosicrucianism, Egyptology, philosophy of religion, Masons, reincarnation, agnosticism, atheism, non-Christian mythology, H. P. Blavatsky, morals)
15. Pastoral care (pastoral studies, pastoral counseling, healing, spiritual healing, inspirational reading, inspirational material, liturgy, Ukrainian liturgy, liturgical books, homiletics, visitation, spiritual life, Christian ministry)
16. Religious education (Christian education, church curriculum, education, religious school curricula, religion and Christian education, Unity school, preseminary)
17. Religion (religion in America, religious books, religious subjects, religion and science, church-oriented books, Eastern and Western religion, history of religion, Protestant religion, comparative religion, Christian religion, religious books, development, international relations, prayer, prayer books, children's material, Christian children's books, religious cults, religious symbolism, Christian symbolism, religious art and architecture, religious studies, apologetics, religious drama, world religious doctrine, faith and culture, interreligious relations, contemporary religious movements)
18. Roman Catholicism (Catholic religion, Catholic systematic thought, Catholic Church, Catholic theology, Catholic publications, Jesuitiana, Jesuit history, Franciscana, Franciscan studies, Franciscans, bishop's papers, parish archives, canon law, Carmelita, Augustinian studies, monasticism, monastic history and theology, catechetics)
19. Sociology and religion (social problems, social aspects of religion, religion and social problems, ethnic studies [Antisemitism, discrimination, African-American religious studies], utopias [utopian communities, Shakers])
20. Theology (Catholic theology, Scandinavian theology, dogmatic theology, theological studies, British theology, ecclesiastical science, biblical theology, theological subjects, doctrinal theology, moral theology, pastoral theology, Mormon theology, Christian doctrine, Shaker theology, theology and health, Jesus Christ, spirituality, Holy Spirit, patristics, women and theology, Reformed theology, ecumenical theology)
21. Miscellaneous faiths and denominations (Anglican Church [Anglican dogma, Anglican biography, Anglican faith, Anglican Church religion], Christian Science [Christian Science books, Mrs. Eddy's writings], Islam [Islamics, Islamic faith, Islamic history, Christian-Moslem relations, Islamic culture, Moslem world], Lutheran Church [Lutheran orthodoxy, Lutheranism, Lutheran Church archives], Methodism [Methodistica, United Methodist Church, Wesleyan, United Methodist publishing, Methodist archives], Orthodox churches [Byzantine Catholic, Lithuanian life, Christian East literature and theology], Presbyterian Church [Presbyterian records, Presbyterian Church archives], Quakers [Friends, Quaker life, Quaker authors, peace, peace movement history, disarmament, Evangelical Friends Church], Reformed Church [Reformed Church records, German Reformed Church], Swedenborgian Church [Swedenborgian works, Church of the New Jerusalem])

TABLE 3.130
1978 and 1988 *American Library Directory* Longitudinal Study
Scholarly Library Subject Interests[1]

	1978				1988				
Library Type	Number of Libraries	No Response	Total Libraries	Mean Interests	Number of Libraries	No Response	Total Libraries	Mean Interests	% Change 1978–88
Scholarly	714	661	1,375	1.4	588	844	1,432	1.9	31
Junior College	63	62	125	1.1	30	78	108	1.3	18
Senior College	351	353	704	1.1	253	452	705	1.5	36
University	99	55	154	1.2	71	118	189	1.5	25
Seminary	107	126	233	1.8	115	116	231	2.6	44
Convent/ Monastery	16	19	35	2.7	13	12	25	2.6	−4
Denominational HQ	45	32	77	2.9	54	32	86	2.5	−14
History/ Archives	33	14	47	2.2	52	36	88	2.1	−5

1. This table refers to all libraries showing subject interests including those reporting them but not providing the subject interest title.

TABLE 3.131
1978 and 1988 *American Library Directory* Special Collections Broken Down into Categories for Scholarly Libraries

Special Collection	--------1978------- No. of References	% of Total	--------1988------- No. of References	% of Total	For 1988 % of Special Collections Accounted for by Scholarly Libraries
Church history	44	6	107	12	89
Judaism	33	5	45	5	42
Miscellaneous faiths and denominations	69	10	102	11	96
Religion: comparative and other	69	10	92	10	95
Bibles	60	8	66	7	81
Methodist Church	48	7	64	7	97
Baptist Church	40	6	61	7	100
Theology and philosophy	44	6	44	5	79
Roman Catholicism	26	4	50	5	94
Missions and missionaries	24	3	41	4	93
Roman Catholic religious orders and groups	44	6	38	4	97
Music	28	4	35	4	95
Literature and art	23	3	22	2	79
Lutheran Church	22	3	25	3	93
Biography (Roman Catholic)	33	5	25	3	100
Quakers	17	2	21	2	95
United Brethren in Christ Church	14	2	19	2	100
Evangelism	8	1	17	2	100
Presbyterian Church	11	2	11	1	79
Adventism	12	2	13	1	100
Patristics	12	2	12	1	100
Biography and fiction	20	3	8	1	80
Other unclassified	18	3	0	0	0
Total	719	100	918	100	87

Scholarly Libraries	1978	1988
Number of Libraries with special collections	418	532
Number of special collections per library	1.72	1.73

TABLE 3.132
Names of Special Collections in 1978 *American Library Directory* Scholarly Libraries

1. Adventism (Seventh-day Adventists, Adventist black history, Adventist publications)
2. Bibles (New Testament, biblical literature, rare Bibles, Studor, Indian Bibles and hymnals, early Bibles, old Bibles, Hanoi POW Bible, Kimball Bibles, Scripture, sacred Scripture, New Testament studies, biblical commentaries, English Bible history, Bible teaching pictures, biblical studies, biblical archeology, Sewell Bible Library, Bible translations, Bible versions, biblical literature, Bible and theology, Bible texts, ecclesiology, seminary theses, Bible fellowship, New Media Bible collection, Braille Bibles)
3. Biography and fiction (all faiths) (saints, pastors, religious biographies, C. S. Lewis, Oral Roberts archives, Jesus Christ and culture, Billy Sunday, Rev. John Tabb collection, Rabbi Silver archives, life of Christ, Christian authors, Mather family, interfaith fiction, Jewish fiction, Virgin Mary [Mariology, Marian Shrines, Marian iconography, Josephology, Marianite Community Library])
4. Biography (Roman Catholic) (early Catholic Americans, Cardinal Newman, Joan of Arc, Madonna, St. Jane Chantal, St. Thomas Aquinas, Hagiography, Sir Thomas More, Archbishop Alemany Library, G. K. Chesterton, Dante, St. John Fisher, Sheeniana, Archbishop Purcell, Cardinal Mooney, St. Francis de Sales, Pope Pius XII, Thomas Merton, Ambrosian Library, Pere Brisson, St. Maria Alayuoquo, Madonna Center, St. Francis Mission, Catholic authors, St. Bernard, Flood collection)
5. Baptist Church (history, collection, Baptist General Conference, English Baptist history, Free Will Baptist history, Oklahoma Baptist history, Arkansas State Convention minutes, Texas Baptist history, Baptist yearly meetings, Virginia Baptists, Baptist archives, Mississippi Baptist history, American Baptist home missions, North American Baptist archives, New England Baptist history, *General Baptist Messenger,* Anabaptist history, Baptist Convention minutes, Baptist Association minutes, Indiana Baptist collection)
6. Church history (genealogy, ecclesiastical history, church historical records, denominational history, church records, medieval Jewish-Christian relations, church and conference records, Canadian church history, Anti-evolution polemics, Christianity, church archives, French Canadian Protestant history, Irish history, diocesan archives, Dutch in Iowa, labor and church history, Church Federation of Chicago records, Norwegian Seminary archives, American church history, evolution, Christian Church history, black church, Reformation church history, American Society of Christ history, Christian and Missionary Alliance Church history, California Council of Churches archives, Disciples of Christ Church history, Hutterites, Millerites, Nashotah House archives, Restoration, general archives)
7. Evangelism (Charismatic authors, Moodyana, Pentecostal research, Pentecostal movement, Holiness Church, Pentecostal Holiness, the Christian evangelist, Wallace Library of Evangelism, Holiness authors, Evangelical churches in Canada)
8. Judaism (Jewish art, archives, Haggadahs, Hebrew texts, Jewish history, Jewish philosophy, Jewish mysticism, Talmudic law, Holocaust, Jewish organization archives, Hebraica, Hebrew manuscripts, Hebrew books, Yiddish linguistics, Halakah, Jewish Canadiana, Hasidism, Sephardic studies, rabbinics, Jewish holidays, *Encyclopedia Judaica,* Jewish family life, Semitics, Maryland Jewish oral history, Jewish periodicals, Jewish medical ethics, Jewish communal studies, Jewish education)

TABLE 3.132 (continued)
Names of Special Collections in 1978 *American Library Directory* Scholarly Libraries

9. Lutheran Church (archives, Muhlenburg family, Lutheran Church history, Deaconness archives, American Lutheran Church, Lutheran music, Martin Luther, Luther first editions, Luther's works, Luther Bibles, early Reformation documents, Lutheran Church records, Reformation, Counter Reformation, Lutheran orthodoxy, Lutheran Brotherhood Foundation, Luther and Bible translations)
10. Literature (church magazines, hassidic and rabbinistic literature, religious literature, Puritan literature, Recusant literature, pastor's collection, liturgical books, *Christian Recorder,* French religious books, religious and historical books, religion and literature, religious authors, sermons, American sermons, pastors' sermons, denomination yearbook, journal publishers, modern Hebrew literature, Christian Church periodicals, religious reference material, *Interpreter's Dictionary of the Bible,* Hebrew newspapers, sixteenth- and seventeenth-century religious material, devotional literature)
11. Methodist Church (Methodistics, Methodist history, Wesleyana, United Methodists, New England Methodist history, British Methodism, United Methodist Church history, AME Zion Church, Free Methodism, Arkansas Methodism, Alabama Methodism, Methodistica, United Methodists Publishing, Missouri Methodism, Montana Methodist history, United Methodist Churches, Wesleyan, John Wesley, Free Methodist Church history)
12. Miscellaneous faiths and denominations (Assemblies of God Church, Bahai, Buddhist, Congregational Church, Christian Science, Church of God, Christian Church, Episcopal Church, Evangelical Church, Evangelical Covenant Church, Evangelical Free Church, Israel [Holy Land, Zionism, American Zionist history, world Zionism, Egypt, Turkey, Iberia], India [Hinduism, Krishna], Islam, Mormonism, Mennonite Church, Moravian Church, Orthodox Church, Reformed Church, Rosicrucian Order AMORC, Swedenborgian Church, Society of Shakers, Schwenkfelder Church, Theosophy, Unitarian and Universalist Church, Unification Church, United Church of Canada, United Church of Christ, Unity Church)
13. Music (hymnology, gospel, sacred music, Byzantine music, hymnals, organ music, Jewish music, church music, hymnody, liturgical music, Jewish choral music, Methodist hymnals, liturgics, Gregorian chant, psalmody)
14. Missions (China missions, missionaries, African missions, foreign missions, Texas missions, Christian missions, evangelism, American Board of Commissioners of Foreign Missionary papers, Missionary Church, China Mission 1847–1945, Board of Foreign Missions, urban missions, missionary materials, missions to Hispanics, Baptist Missionary Association, missiology, missionary research, Mexican Women's Missionary Union archives)
15. Patristics (early Christian writings, patrology, petrologia)
16. Presbyterian Church (records, United Presbyterian Church, Presbyterian college catalogs, Southern Presbyterianism, Cumberland Presbyterian Church archives, Reformed Presbyterian Church records, Calvinism)
17. Quakers (rare books, Friends' history and doctrine, Society of Friends, Friends tracts, Friends meeting minutes, records, Richard Nixon, John G. Whittier)

TABLE 3.132 (continued)
Names of Special Collections in 1978 *American Library Directory* Scholarly Libraries

18. Roman Catholic religion (Catholic Americana, American bishops' statements, archidiocese collection, *Catholic Encyclopedia,* Catholic periodicals, Catholic news, papal documents, canon law, Catholic theology, Roman Catholic dogma, sodality and Christian life community, Catholic history, Jansenism, Holy Shroud of Turin, Vatican Library, Vatican publications, Dominican dissertations, Canadian Catholic Church, nineteenth-century American Catholicism, Catholic press service, Benedictina, catechetics, Lay Catholic Movement, Official Catholic Directory, Inquisition, Texas Catholic Conference)
19. Religion (black religion, comparative religion, religion and philosophy, religious research, religious debates, religious history, women and religion, religious science, religion and sociology, religion and psychology, religious art, science and Christian faith, prayer, Christmas, religious education, Christian education, pastoral education, sanctification, Salem College, Woman's Press, pastoral psychology, World Student Volunteer Movement, church architecture, world religion, English churches, church union, religion of liberal churches, new religious movements, interaction of faith and culture, Christian social science [Population records, Christian economics, personal growth], ecumenism [Ecumenical Institute of Religious Studies], Christian ministry and homiletics [preaching, ministry, Hispanic pastoral ministry], youth work [Jewish juveniles, young people's societies, children's religious literature, World Student Christian Federation], American Sunday School Union, Catholic Association for International Peace, Fellowship of Reconciliation, National Council for the Prevention of War, World Council of Churches, Salvation Army, Church of the Nazarene)
20. Roman Catholic religious orders and groups (Knights of Malta, Dominicans, Dominicana, Franciscans, Franciscan life, Franciscana, monasticism, Handmaidens of Christ, Carmelites, Redemptorist Fathers, Benedictine Fathers, Atonement Friars, Ursuline Sisters, Christian Brothers, Vincentian Fathers, Cistercian Monastery history, Trinitariana, Jesuitica, Jesuit Order, Ephrata Cloister)
21. Theology and philosophy (pastoral theology, Protestant theology, Arminian-Wesleyan theology, Mercersberg theology, Reformation theology, English Reformed and Puritan theology, English language theology, spirituality, early American theological pamphlets, ecumenical theology, dogmatics, systematic theology, practical theology, New England theologians, Woodstock Theological Library, Holy Spirit, metaphysics, ethics, Science of Creative Intelligence, Church of Scientology, Scientology, International New Thought Alliance, Maharishi Mahesh Yogi, agnosticism, euthanasia, free thought, non-Christian mythology, atheism, pietism)
22. United Brethren in Christ Church (Evangelical United Brethren, Mennonite Brethren history and historical library, Church of the Brethren archives, Plymouth Brethren, Evangelical United Brethren Church history)

TABLE 3.133
1978 and 1988 *American Library Directory* Measures of Concentration[1,2]

Categories	Number of Libraries	Number of Different Categories Listed	Total Number of Specific Listings	Measure of Concentration	Mean Specific Listings per Library
1978 *American Library Directory*					
Subject interests	922	747	1,414	1.9	1.5
Special collections	468	710	791	1.1	1.7
1988 *American Library Directory*					
Subject interests	892	1,382	1,655	1.2	1.9
Special collections	632	947	1,011	1.1	1.6

Interpretation:

Measure of concentration shows how many libraries listed more than one subject interest or special collection in the same general subject category. For instance, listing not only Bible but also Old Testament.

Mean listings per library show how many subject interests and special collections were listed per library.

1. These are the actual numbers including the religious category for subject interests but not for interests or collections checked off without the specific label or name attached (the tendency is toward more specialized, nonrelated subject interests and more subject interests per library: see measure of concentration).
2. There is some apparent discrepancy among the numbers of total listings and the numbers of libraries reporting listings for subject interests and special collections. The reason for this is that a few libraries reported having two or more of these collections *within* specific subcategories, which accounts entirely for the measures of concentration. This is the phenomenon that produces the discrepancy and is quite separate from the fact that many libraries reported two or more subject interests or special collections each.

TABLE 3.134
1978 and 1988 *American Library Directory* Scholarly Library Publications[1]

Type	Number of Libraries	Percentage
1. Library guides and handbooks	166	23
2. Bibliographies	131	18
3. Library newsletters	84	12
4. Accessions and acquisitions lists	57	8
5. News bulletins	57	8
6. Serials and index lists	45	6
7. Monographs	33	5
8. Journals and newspapers	32	4
9. Literature and history	27	4
10. Miscellaneous	27	4
11. Annual reports	19	3
12. Friends of the library newsletter	15	2
13. Media lists	14	2
14. Exhibit catalogs	5	1
Total	712	100

1. This table includes all named publications for both years but not references to publications for which no title was provided.

TABLE 3.135
1978 *American Library Directory* Scholarly Library Publications: Exact Titles (Exclusive of Duplication)

A Classified Bibliography of the Special
About Roots, Branches and Trees
Accession List
Adventist Heritage
Audiovisual Catalog; Audio Cassette Catalog
Basic Rules of Alphabetical Sequence Simplified
Bibliog. of Spanish Borderlands in Frabarese Collec.
Bibliographia Tripotamopolitana
Books of Brown
Breviaria
Burrow Library Monograph Series
Catalog of Canadian Folk Music
Catalog of Spanish Documents Collection
Checklist of Publications Added to the Library
Cloister Door
Crown Jewels Newsletter
Dickinson College Manuscript Collections

TABLE 3.135 (continued)
1978 *American Library Directory* Scholarly Library Publications: Exact Titles (Exclusive of Duplication)

Duke Memorial Library Newsletter
Ex Libris
Focus: About Books
Foundations in Wisconsin: A Directory
Friends of the Library Newsletter
Friends of the Library Newsletter: Keepsakes
Friends of the Library Newsletter: The Loner
George Karson Folklore Archive Register
Hearing Disabilities and Mental Retardation
Heritage Hall Publications
Library Handbook
Library Happenings
Library Notes; Newsletter; Library Link
Library Wine
List of Serials; Student Guide to the Library
Master Serials List; Library Guides
McMaster University Research News; Russell
Media Newsletter
Monthly Acquisitions List
Pacific Historian
Pathfinders
Periodical Notes
Recent Acquisitions List; Student Library Handbook
Scholars Choice; Pettee Matters
Sermon on the Mount
Siena Bookshelf
Southwest Research Center Newsletter
St. Louis Statistical Abstracts
Student Library Handbook
Student Library Manual; Faculty Library Guide
Studies in Bibliography and Booklore
The Censor
The Markham Review
The Paytonian
Wofford Bibliopolist
Woman and Church
Women as We See Them in 1978
Women's Study; Guides for Research
Seventh-day Adventist Periodical Index

TABLE 3.136
1978 and 1988 *American Library Directory* Longitudinal Study Library Publications by Denomination[1]

Denomination	1978 Number of Libraries	1978 No Response	1978 Total Libraries	1978 Mean Publications	1988 Number of Libraries	1988 No Response	1988 Total Libraries	1988 Mean Publications	% Change 1978–88
Baptist	5	218	223	1.8	34	189	223	1.4	−22
Christian	2	57	59	1.5	9	47	58	1.6	6.7
Churches of Christ	1	26	27	2	3	26	29	1.7	−15
Episcopal/Anglican	0	74	74	0	9	57	66	1.3	0
Independent	2	85	87	1	28	72	100	1.6	60
Lutheran	3	120	123	1.7	22	96	118	1.8	6
Mennonite	0	17	17	0	8	18	26	1.3	0
Methodist	5	197	202	1.6	44	169	213	1.6	0
Other Denom.	7	290	297	2.1	52	242	294	1.5	−29
Presbyterian	9	196	205	1.2	29	158	187	1.4	17
U.C.C.	2	35	37	1.5	10	28	38	2.0	33
Summary									
Jewish	1	197	198	2	32	200	232	1.7	−15
Roman Catholic	21	492	513	1.7	130	360	490	1.8	6
All Protestant	36	1,315	1,351	1.7	248	1,104	1,352	1.6	−6
Total	58	2,004	2,062	1.7	410	1,664	2,074	1.7	0

1. This table includes all reported publications including those that were unnamed but reported. It calculates the mean number of publications for only the libraries that reported publications. Otherwise, the means for 1978 and 1988 respectively would become .048 and .336!

TABLE 3.137

1988 *American Library Directory* Scholarly Library Publications Broken Down into Categories[1]

Type of Publication	1988 Scholarly Libraries	% of Total
Library bulletin/newsletter	94	16
Books	82	14
Bibliography	77	13
Library handbook	77	13
Miscellaneous	70	12
Library guide	58	10
Acquisitions list	51	9
Serials list	40	7
Journal/periodical/magazine	2	0
Annual report	20	3
Catalog	15	3
Friends of the library newsletter	11	2
Total	597	100

1. The number 597 represents all the publications listed including those for libraries with several publications each. Number of libraries represented = 410.

TABLE 3.138

1978 *American Library Directory* Scholarly and Popular Libraries Restricting Reference Service to Members by Total Annual Library Expenditures

Library Expenditures	Libraries with Reference Service Restrictions	%	No Response	%	Number of Libraries
Under $1,500	27	21	102	79	129
$1,501–$20,000	12	8	138	92	150
$20,001–$95,000	4	1	375	99	379
$95,001–$220,000	1	0	285	100	286
$220,001–$410,000	0	0	111	100	111
$410,001–$510,000	0	0	17	100	17
$510,001 and over	1	2	52	98	53
No response	47	5	890	95	937
Total	92	4	1,970	96	2,062

TABLE 3.139
1978 and 1988 *American Library Directory* Longitudinal Study
Scholarly Library Additional Activities (Cumulative)[1]

Library Type	1978 Number of Libraries	1978 No Response	1978 Total Libraries	1978 Mean Activities	1988 Number of Libraries	1988 No Response	1988 Total Libraries	1988 Mean Activities	% Change 1978–88
Scholarly	586	789	1,375	2.3	892	539	1,431	3.7	61
Junior College	35	90	125	1.4	42	66	108	2.1	50
Senior College	360	344	704	2.2	514	191	705	3.8	73
University	100	54	154	3.1	167	22	189	4.7	52
Seminary	81	152	233	2	129	101	230	3.2	60
Convent/Monastery	4	31	35	1.5	3	22	25	1	−33
Denominational HQ	4	73	77	1.5	16	70	86	2.4	60
History/Archives	2	45	47	2.5	21	67	88	1.8	−28

1. Additional activities include consortium membership, OCLC membership, and local automation projects.

TABLE 3.140
1978 and 1988 *American Library Directory* Longitudinal Study
Scholarly Library Additional Activities (Cumulative) by Denomination

Denomination	1978 Number of Libraries	1978 No Response	1978 Total Libraries	1978 Mean Activities	1988 Number of Libraries	1988 No Response	1988 Total Libraries	1988 Mean Activities	% Change 1978–88
Baptist	53	87	140	2.1	88	64	158	3.8	81
Christian	14	26	40	1.6	28	13	41	3.0	88
Churches of Christ	9	18	27	2.0	19	8	27	2.8	40
Episcopal/Anglican	11	21	32	1.7	22	10	32	3.0	76
Independent	22	60	82	2.4	47	50	97	3.6	50
Lutheran	33	37	70	2.5	55	21	76	4.0	60
Mennonite	7	7	14	2.4	12	10	22	3.3	38
Methodist	78	69	147	2.3	110	39	149	4.0	74
Other Denoms.	72	133	205	2.4	126	91	217	3.4	42
Presbyterian	52	38	90	2.1	73	17	90	4.0	90
U.C.C.	17	7	24	2.7	21	4	25	4.4	63
Summary									
Jewish	7	28	35	1.3	12	33	45	2.9	123
Roman Catholic	211	258	469	2.3	279	179	458	3.8	65
All Protestant	368	503	871	2.3	601	327	928	3.7	61
Total	586	789	1,375	2.3	892	539	1,431	3.7	61

TABLE 3.141
1988 *American Library Directory* Scholarly Library Additional Activities (Cumulative) by Region

	---Consortia & OCLC Memberships and Automation Projects---											
Region	1	%	2–3	%	4–5	%	6 and over	%	No Response	%	Number of Libraries	Mean Activities
Northeast	9	12	11	14	17	22	6	8	33	43	76	3.6
Middle Atlantic	34	13	36	14	67	26	40	15	84	32	261	4.0
Southeast	33	12	52	20	63	24	19	7	99	37	266	3.4
Southwest	10	9	18	15	33	28	6	5	50	43	117	3.6
West	16	13	28	22	22	17	7	5	55	43	128	3.2
Rocky Mountains	1	5	5	24	2	10	3	14	10	48	21	4.1
Middle West	44	11	55	14	131	33	75	19	93	23	398	4.2
Canada	27	16	16	10	2	1	4	2	115	70	164	2.1
Total	174	12	221	15	337	24	160	11	539	38	1,431	3.7

4

SCHOLARLY RELIGIOUS LIBRARIES, PART II

This chapter will conclude the discussion of scholarly religious libraries. As was true for chapter 3, findings are based on the scholarly library databases in the 1978 and 1988 editions of the *American Library Directory*. Their resemblance to other databases is unknown but is thought to be limited.[1] In brief, the chapter will deal with library personnel, library material holdings, and library expenditures. Chapter 4 includes the following sections:

I. Library Personnel
   A. Introduction
   B. Professional staff membership size
   C. Clerical staff membership size
   D. Student staff membership size
   E. Total staff membership size
   F. Interim personnel summary
   G. Chief librarians: Gender
   H. Chief librarians: Clerical or Laypersons
   I. Named and unnamed chief librarians

II. Library material holdings
   A. Book volumes
   B. Periodical title subscriptions
   C. Vertical files
   D. Microform holdings
   E. Media holdings
   F. Map holdings
   G. Art reproduction holdings

H. Holdings summaries

III. Annual library expenditure
   A. Material expenditure
   B. Personnel expenditure
   C. Other expenditure
   D. Total library expenditure
   E. Special library expenditure analysis

IV. Denominational characterizations and cumulative tables
   A. Denominational characterizations
   B. Type of library
   C. Region
   D. Cumulative tables

V. Subject areas for further study

Library Personnel

What are the essential characteristics of scholarly religious library personnel? We will try to answer that question in a considerable variety of ways but in this section we will answer it by examining personnel by such variables as position level, type of library, region, consortium membership, library expenditure, and denomination. It will be answered at least in part for professionals, clerks, student assistants, and staff member totals, and for chief librarians separately.

This section will examine tables from either one or the other of the two scholarly databases, usually 1988, sometimes 1978 or even both, and often with the relevant table neither being illustrated nor cited at all. Readers should realize that the 1988 table figures are often much like those for 1978, surprisingly enough, and even that the libraries often rank in about the same order for the two separate years. When the two edition tables are strikingly different, as they sometimes are, both may be reproduced.

In certain circumstances, no table was reproduced for a denomination or other variable for a specific year since too many (or occasionally too few) libraries scored in the highest category to make a table practical. Where no average figure is given, this means that the number of libraries figure minus the no response figure was so large a proportion of the whole that no statistically significant average figure could be calculated.

Professional Staff Membership Size

We begin now a series of analyses of the scholarly libraries by the highest numbers of library professionals. They will be analyzed by library type, region, per hundred enrolled students, by library expenditure, per $10,000 total library expenditure, per consortium member, by chief librarian's gender, and by denomination.

For our study by library type let us look at longitudinal table 4.1. We see that the overall 1988 staff mean was four professionals per library, a slight rise from 1978 when the mean was 3.8 professionals. This information tells us again that we are dealing with small libraries. Largest professional staff was typically found in university libraries, with an average of 7.9 staff members. Smallest was convent/monastery libraries, where the mean was 1.3, but only 24 percent of the convent/monastery libraries had any professionals at all on the staff. Matched pairs of libraries scored slightly higher than the entire database. Both the no longer listed and the newly listed libraries had about half as many professionals as the entire database, and the latter was somewhat larger than the former.

We should identify the libraries that led the databases in number of professional staff members. The results of such an analysis arranged by *type of library* can be considered in several tables. A table (not shown) for 1988 produced the *junior college* listing of professional staff members by library. Five colleges led the table with four professionals apiece. Two-thirds of them were Roman Catholic libraries, and they were primarily from Canada and New York.

Naturally *senior colleges* had larger numbers of professionals than junior colleges did. Table 4.2 for 1988 shows sixteen libraries to have equaled the maximum with thirteen-plus professionals apiece. More than half of them were Roman Catholic. Pennsylvania, Minnesota, and New York led the table by library location. No table could be made for *universities,* since fifty university libraries were tied for the thirteen-plus professional lead.

Seminary libraries can be analyzed for 1988, also. Only one seminary library had a high score here, the Graduate Theological Union. Independent libraries led this table with one-third of the total, and Texas libraries led in location with one-fifth of the group. *Convent/monastery* libraries are seen in table 4.3 for 1988. Only one library in this group had more than one professional, Blue Cloud Abbey, in South Dakota, a Roman Catholic institution.

Another 1988 table showed the specific *denominational headquarters* libraries with the largest number of professional staff members. It was led by two Christian Science libraries, but the numbers of staff members were generally small. The last of these libraries were the ones for *history/archive* centers, as seen in table 4.4. They were generally small, but two of them reached the top questionnaire level in number of professional staff members, Yivo Institute and the Headquarters, Church of Jesus Christ of Latter-day Saints, with thirteen-plus. Other Denominations led the table in denomination, and New York state led in geographic location.

A longitudinal table was made for professional staff members by library type also. Overall professional staff change 1978–88 was small, 5.5 percent. Highest change was found in denominational headquarters, with 23 percent, and lowest was minus-six percent for convent/monastery. Another table covering 1988 scholarly professionals examined total library expenditures in relation to the mean number of professionals per library. The results were similar to those in later tables in this series. The 1988 table (not shown) for professional staff members by total annual library expenditure shows a regular increase in mean number of professionals, from one for those libraries with expenditures under $1,500 to 8.7 for those libraries above $510,000 expenditure. So the two variables correlated positively and closely.

An assessment of the tables just examined leads to the following conclusions by type and number of scholarly professional staff members. Senior college and university libraries led in number of libraries with large professional staffs; convent/monastery libraries had the fewest libraries with more than one professional.

Now we will look at professionals by *region*. The professionals in the various regions were similar in number. Mean number of scholarly professional staff members per library in 1978 ranged from three to five. The largest number of professionals was to be found in Middle Atlantic, Southeast, and West, and the smallest number was found in Southwest and Canada in both cases.

Table 4.5 shows the picture for 1988 professionals by region. While differences were small, Rocky Mountains, was apparently largest in staff size, though its *N* was low. Regions with the largest mean number of professionals per library in 1988 were the Northeast with 4.7 and the West with 4.5. Smallest were the Middle West and Canada, with 3.7 apiece, 27 percent different, not very much. Matched pairs were only 8 percent larger in overall mean. Both the no longer listed and the newly listed libraries had overall means about half as large as those for the entire database.

The next few tables dealt with the mean number of academic library professionals *per hundred students enrolled.* By type of library, the overall means were 0.6 and 0.5 professionals per hundred students for the two databases. Seminary libraries had the largest number of professionals in both cases. Specialized professional education got good staff treatment here. The lowest ratios were those of the university libraries.

Now for *total expenditure* by number of professionals in academic libraries. The largest number of professionals-per-dollar category was to be found in the smaller libraries with $1,500 to $20,000 expenditures and $1,500 and under in 1978 plus the $20,001 to $95,000 levels, which had the largest number of professionals in 1988. The lowest expenditure level was the largest personnel category in 1978 and one of the two largest categories in 1988. The largest number of professionals was found in the Jewish group in both years. The smallest number of professionals was found in the 1978 Congregational and the 1988 Baptist and Roman Catholic groups.

A series of analyses was made of professionals *per $10,000 in total library expenditures.* This section will discuss the results of these analyses by library type and by denomination. By library type the number of professionals per $10,000 library expenditures produced a 1978 mean of 0.5 professionals and a 1988 mean of 0.3 professionals. We can note immediately that all of the 1988 staff figures for the table were smaller than the 1978 figures. Apparently this difference was caused by the rise in library expenditures for 1988, which was not fully met by a corresponding rise in professional staff members.

The three lowest library types by number of library professionals were convent/monastery first, then denominational headquarters and junior colleges. Of course these three types normally had the fewest professionals in each database. Convent/monastery libraries scored 4.8 and 2.6 professionals in the two databases.

For the denominations the overall means were 0.5 and 0.3 professionals per $10,000 in total library expenditure in 1978 and 1988. The mean number of staff members dropped by 67 percent in 1988. Scoring highest were the Methodist and Roman Catholic denominations for 1978 and 1988. Lowest were the Episcopal/Anglican and Lutheran denominations for 1978, and seven denominations tied for 1988.

The next set of analyses was made for mean library professionals *per consortium membership* by library type and by denomination. Overall means for library type were 2.9 for 1978 and 2.2 for 1988 in professionals per consortium membership. Largest categories by library type were university for 1978 and history/archive and university libraries for 1988. The smallest were junior college and seminary libraries in 1978 and the same two in 1988. The final analysis showed mean library professionals per consortium membership by denomination. The largest mean number of professionals per consortium membership was found in the Methodist and Roman Catholic groups in 1978 and the Episcopal/Anglican group in 1988. The smallest was Congregational in 1978 and Christian, Lutheran, Other Denominations, and Presbyterian in 1988.

For 1988 in several tables (not shown) we can see a mean staff-member picture similar to that for 1978. And the number of scholarly *professional* male *chief librarians* was significantly larger than the number of professional female chief librarians. Further, in the tables for no longer listed and newly listed libraries, we can see that in the former, female chief librarians predominated while in the latter males predominated by a small margin. This finding may be suggestive. Table 4.6 for 1988 summarized the professional staff members in each denomination. On first impression the table shows how small these libraries were. Highest denominations were the Roman Catholic and United Church of Christ with means of about five, and lowest was Mennonite with two professional staff members.

We can study the number of library professional staff members by *denomination* here. Largest professional staffs by denomination in 1988 were the Roman Catholic with 4.7 and the UCC with 4.6 per library. Smallest were the Mennonites with 1.8 and the Christians and Churches of Christ with 3.0. Matched pairs in 1988 brought us up to 4.3 professionals. The no longer listed overall mean was 1.8, and the newly listed mean was 2.0 professionals. The longitudinal change percentage 1978–88 was small, an overall 5.3 percent. The largest longitudinal change was 41 percent for Episcopal/Anglican and the smallest was minus-22 percent for Mennonite again.

Table 4.7 for 1988 shows more detail on this subject, specifically, the number of professional staff members working in the larger libraries. This table gives an overview of the libraries leading in professional staff members. Almost every denomination had one or more libraries in the thirteen-plus professionals category. Certain denominations, such as Baptist, Methodist, and Roman Catholic, had several of these libraries.

Clerical Staff Membership Size

The percentage of scholarly libraries reporting clerks was only 52 percent in 1978, but moved up to 60 percent in 1988. Mean number of clerical staff members per library was 4.6 in 1978 and 5.1 in 1988, an 11 percent increase for those libraries having any at all. Table 4.8 for 1988 showed mean clerks per library by type of library. The leader was university libraries, with ten clerks; senior colleges were next, with five clerks. After that we have seminary libraries with four clerks. The poorest was convent/monastery libraries with no clerks.

We have the results of a series of analyses concerning clerks in scholarly libraries also by library type, region, total annual expenditure, chief librarian's gender, per hundred students enrolled, per consortium membership, and denomination. Later we will examine clerical staff members per hundred students enrolled. In a continuation by *library type,* the largest group in 1978 was university library clerks, a mean of 9.7 of them, with senior college next, averaging 4.2 clerks. Smallest group was the junior colleges for 1978. For 1988 the results were similar, with junior college clerical staffs now almost as large as seminary clerical staffs.

We can continue the type of library analysis for clerks with *junior colleges* for 1988. Four libraries led the table (not shown), two Lutheran and two Roman Catholic, each one with thirteen-plus clerks. They were Waldorf, Red Deer, and Vanier Colleges and Cégep de Jonquière, three of them Canadian. For the table as a whole almost half were Roman Catholic and a fourth were Canadian.

Since no *senior college* and *university* library tables could be made, due to the large numbers of libraries in the top categories, next came *seminary* libraries with four of them at the top level, thirteen-plus clerks: Graduate Theological Union, Hebrew Union College, Southeastern Baptist Theological Seminary, and Southwestern Baptist Theological Seminary. The seminary table was stronger than the junior college table. Six of the libraries were Independent and five were Baptist. See table 4.9 for 1988. Another table (not shown) for 1988 showed *convent/monastery* libraries that had only small clerical staffs. The Sisters of the Immaculate Conception Convent was the leader, and all were Roman Catholic.

Denominational headquarters libraries in table 4.10 for 1988 had a leader, the Canadian Center for Ecumenism, but its score was far from the top level possible. Roman Catholic and Other Denominations led this table by denomination. Three of the *history/archive* libraries equaled the top level in number of clerks per library: the Presbyterian Church Office of History, the Central Mormon Archive Center, and one of the Mormon genealogical centers. Other libraries were generally small.

By *region,* the picture was strong for Rocky Mountains, Canada, and the West (in 1988 only). Tables for 1978 and 1988 (table 4.11) showed the number of clerical staff members per library per region. With a 1978 mean of five, Rocky Mountains led all regions with six clerks per library, while the Southeast and Middle West trailed with only four clerks apiece. The 1988 table looks similar with a mean of five clerks per library, but this time the Rocky Mountains and Canada and the West lead.

In the *total annual expenditure* table there was a strong positive correlation between expenditure and the number of clerical staff members. It ranged from 1.2 clerks for the libraries with total expenditures of $1,500 or less to thirteen clerks for the libraries with expenditures of $510,000 or more. This was for 1978, but a similar picture emerged for 1988. The *chief librarian's* male-to-female ratio was 1.4 to 1.0 for 1978 and 1.3 to 1.0 for 1988. Males predominated.

Now we have two special analyses—per hundred students enrolled and per consortium member. Scholarly library clerks per hundred students enrolled was examined by library type, region, total library expenditure, and denomination. For library type we have overall means of 0.7 clerks per hundred students in both years. Largest group was again the seminary libraries in both cases, so these libraries did well here also. Smallest in clerks per hundred students enrolled were the university libraries, again.

The largest region for clerks per hundred students enrolled was the Rocky Mountains in both years; the smallest was the Southwest in 1978 and the Northeast and the Southwest again in 1988. For total expenditure, again the largest in number of clerks was the $20,001–$95,000 category in both cases. Smallest was the under $1,500 category for 1978 and largest was $510,001 and over for 1988. For denomination and clerks the largest again was the Jewish group in both years. Smallest was Congregational in 1978 and Presbyterian and Roman Catholic in 1988.

We have now two analyses of mean library clerks per consortium membership, by type of library and by denomination. For type of library the overall means were 3.3 and 2.7 clerks per consortium membership for the years 1978 and 1988 respectively. By number of clerks the largest type of library was university in both 1978 and 1988, and the smallest was junior college, in both years. For denomination, overall means were the same as for library type. Largest denominations were Baptist and Episcopal/Anglican. Smallest were Congregational and Mennonite for the two years.

By *denomination* the clerical group was largest for the UCC, Roman Catholic, and Lutheran denominations and smallest for Mennonite, Jewish, and Christian, all between 2.6 and 6.6 clerks. That was for 1978. For 1988, largest were the Lutheran and Methodist, Christian and Independent denominations.

Now we can stop to see what we have learned in the immediately previous tables about libraries with clerks on the staff. Forty-five libraries reached the top level of thirteen-plus clerks per library. Senior college, university, and seminary libraries led the group by type of library. Roman Catholic libraries led the denominations in frequency of occurrence.

Student Staff Membership Size

We can move on to the next section in which we study student staff members by type of library, region, library expenditure, per hundred student enrollment, per consortium membership, and denomination. Perhaps we should begin by reminding the reader that certain institutions counted student assistants in their total staff reporting but others did not, so the total staff figures for one group do not always reflect the same meaning as those for another group.

The percentage of libraries reporting these staff members was only 40 percent in 1978 but moved up to 47 percent in 1988, of course nearly all of them working in academic libraries. When in turn we ask the question about mean total number of student assistants per library, we get the answer of eleven for 1978 and fifteen for 1988. Table 4.12 for 1988 shows a 36 percent increase. This table breaks the analysis down and shows 1988 university libraries to have averaged twenty-four student assistants per library to lead the other types of libraries. Now we can look at each individual *library type*—tables showing the specific libraries with the largest number of student assistants.

For *junior colleges* a 1988 table shows nine libraries with more than ten student assistants apiece, but no library which reached the table and questionnaire maximum of 33.5+ student assistants. Methodist libraries were the most numerous here. A *senior college* table could not be made since there were fifty-one of these libraries at the maximum level of 33.5+ student assistants. Nor could a *university* table be made for the same reason—sixty-one libraries at the 33.5+ student assistant level. *Seminary* libraries made a strong showing also. Two libraries reached the maximum number, 33.5+ student assistants: the Graduate Theological Union and Southwestern Baptist Theological Seminary. Fine! Independent and Roman Catholic libraries dominated table 4.13 for 1988 by denomination.

Roman Catholic *convent/monastery* libraries had few student assistants. Table 4.14 1988 shows the leading *denominational headquarters* libraries by number of student assistant staff members. The leader here was the Naropa Institute which was well ahead of the other libraries in this table of small student staff members. Other Denominations led the denominations. The last table in this series dealt with the libraries staffed by student assistants in *history/archive* libraries. There, two libraries were well ahead of the rest, the American Buddhist Archive and the Concordia Historical Institute. Mennonite and Jewish libraries constituted more than half of the total number.

Longitudinal table 4.12 shows that seminaries grew most (82 percent) in number of student library assistants during the decade of the study while denominational headquarters lost the most by 80 percent. Scholarly libraries as a whole grew by 36 percent. The situation for student assistants, therefore, can be seen to be fluid, which is hardly surprising since students do not usually work under contract as do some full-time staff members. Student employment changes can be effected quickly.

By denomination we had high scores of nineteen student assistants from Lutherans and eighteen from Methodists. Smallest student staffs belonged to the Mennonites again, with nine. In another student staff member table, Churches of Christ and Methodist led the 1978 tables with thirteen apiece and Lutherans and Methodists led in 1988 with seventeen and sixteen students.

Longitudinal table 4.15 shows student assistants by denomination. Overall growth rate 1978–88 was 44 percent. However, UCC grew at a 121 percent rate and Episcopal/Anglican at a 100 percent rate. Churches of Christ grew only at a 7.7 percent rate, however. We have a longitudinal analysis of student assistants by denomination for matched pairs, and these libraries grew at a higher rate than those in the entire database. In terms of longitudinal change for academic degree years offered, by denomination in 1988, the Jewish group led with a mean of 6.0 years of higher education. The Mennonite group was weakest, with 3.9 years.

For student staff members the Southwest was the largest *region* at a mean of seventeen staff members per library in 1988. Canada was smallest at 8.3. If we look at student library assistants by *annual total library expenditure* for 1988, there was a positive correlation between number of student assistants and total expenditures also. The libraries averaging under $1,500 total expenditure averaged also 4.6 student assistants, while those spending over $510,001 averaged twenty-four student assistants. For matched pairs the overall mean number of students was slightly higher, at fifteen students. So total expenditure and number of student assistants rose together.

By total library expenditure 1978 we have a picture that is the opposite of what is to be expected. Mean number of student assistants fell from

5.0 to 0.6 as library expenditure rose. So it appears that the large libraries provided less student assistant service per enrolled student than did small libraries, or at least that was so in this table. So much for 1978. For 1988 the previous picture (1978) seemed not to apply. For 1988 the mean number of student assistants rose as expenditure rose until it reached the $95,001 to $220,000 level, then it fell sharply. Confusing!

Now we have a series of special analyses of academic library student assistants *per hundred student enrollment* by library type, region, annual expenditure, and denomination. If we begin with type of library, we see that the overall means were 1.3 and 1.9 student assistants per year per hundred students enrolled. Largest libraries per hundred students were the junior college libraries and the seminary libraries in 1978 and 1988, respectively. Smallest were the senior college and university libraries, respectively. Next comes the regional tables. Largest was the Southeast in both years. Smallest were Canada, the Northeast, and the Rocky Mountains.

The next special analysis was that of mean student library assistant *per consortium membership* by library type. Overall means were 7.1 and 7.8 student assistants, some gain being shown for 1988. The largest number of student assistants was shown for universities in each database. The smallest number of student assistants was shown for seminary libraries in each database. Now we have the same analysis by denomination. Largest denominations were Baptist and Episcopal/Anglican for the two years by mean number of student assistants. Smallest were the UCC and the Mennonites. The final tables are those of *denominations*. The largest number of student assistants belonged to the Churches of Christ and the Presbyterian academic institutions in 1978 and to the Mennonite group in 1988. Smallest were the Congregational and the Roman Catholic denominations.

Let us summarize the findings on these tables showing scholarly libraries strong in student staff members. Forty libraries reached the maximum staffing level and fourteen other libraries had more than fifteen student assistants apiece. Senior college and university libraries had most of the larger staffs. Each table had a different leading denomination.

Total Staff Membership Size

Total library staff member size information was obtained from a surprisingly small group of scholarly libraries. Only about 770 out of 1,375 scholarly libraries in 1978 reported any staff information, or 56 percent. In 1988, 944 out of 1,431 libraries reported staff information, or 66 percent. Within these two groups the mean staff sizes were 15.6 and 19.0 part- and full-time staff members. For the matched pairs the mean staff sizes were about 1.0–1.5 staff members larger than for the entire database. In all, there were 17,950 staff members working in 1,431 scholarly North American religious libraries in 1988. An eighth of the libraries had twenty-five-plus staff members, but nearly one-third had eight or less. Mean scholarly staff members increased from sixteen to nineteen per library, or by nineteen percent during the decade, as shown in table 4.16 for 1978 and 1988.

On the average how many total staff members existed in these libraries by library type, region, library expenditure, degree years awarded, per hundred students, per consortium membership, for specific libraries, and denomination in general? Longitudinal table 4.17 shows this information for *type of library*. University libraries led the 1988 table with a mean of thirty-six staff members per library, and senior colleges came next. Roman Catholic libraries led by denomination. Smallest staffs were those in convents/monasteries, which averaged a total of only two people.

Turning to *region,* we see the staff sizes varying less than in many other tables. Largest staffs were in the Southeast and smallest were in the Canadian region, 18 to 13, or a ratio of 1.4 to 1.0 for 1978. Furthermore, Canada gained only 8 percent during the decade, well under the mean advance. So Canada was not only last but fell further behind in staff size as the decade progressed. For 1988, the Southeast was again largest at twenty-one staff members and Canadian again smallest at thirteen, a ratio of 21 to 13, or 1.6 to 1.0. The Middle West rose the most, from fifteen to twenty staff members, while Canada did not rise at all. In table 4.18 for 1988 the total scholarly library mean was nineteen staff members. The highest total number of staff members was that for the Southeast, eighteen staff members in 1978 and twenty-one in 1988. Canada was the lowest in each table at thirteen staff members.

Total staff size by total *annual library expenditure* should yield a strong positive correlation, and it does for 1988. See table 4.19 for 1988. For libraries with only $1,500 or less annual expenditure, the mean staff size was 2.3. For libraries with annual expenditure of $510,001 and over mean staff size was 39.0 persons. Now we can look at several special studies of total staff members.

For total library staff members we have the same kind of analysis as above—number of staff members per $10,000 in total expenditure, but this time for type of library, region, total annual expenditure, and denomination. The pattern of staff shrinkage for 1988 continued. For type of library, the analysis showed that the largest staffs per $10,000 expenditure were those in convent/monastery, denominational headquarters, and history/archives, with 2.7 to 3.9 staff members per library. That result speaks well for libraries that have low incomes. Overall means were 2.0 and 1.2 staff members for 1978 and 1988; for region they were 2.0 and 1.2; for library expenditures they were 2.0 and 1.2; and for denomination they were 2.0 and 1.2 staff members. That was a quick summary of the per $10,000 total annual expenditure picture.

In continuation of this analysis, let us look at certain tables that examine total staff size by several variables in addition to the old familiar ones. One staff display for 1978 and 1988 was complex and showed the percentage increase in number of staff members from 1978 to 1988 by type of library. For total staff size by library type we have an overall change rate of 20 percent. Largest change was that for the seminaries at 26 percent and smallest was that for convents/monasteries at −19 percent. Before leaving this section, we will look at a regional analysis of *student enrollment per library staff member,* table 2.11 for 1978 and 1988. In this table, we see that in 1988 Canada led with 115 students (quite efficient) to 70 students for the United States. The Southeast was smallest of all regions with fifty-seven students per library staff member.

We can consider a longitudinal analysis of *total staff members by number of different academic degrees awarded* by library type. Here again we see the familiar scene of the university libraries with the largest mean score and the seminary libraries with the smallest mean score. It shows the student body and library staff size differences essentially and suggests that some seminary libraries may be understaffed, though there must certainly be others that are fully staffed. We have tables on *mean total staff size per hundred students* by library type 1978 and 1988; overall means were 2.2 and 2.6 staff members. Largest were the seminary libraries in 1978, and smallest in both years were the university libraries. Generally, the larger the staff sizes the smaller the mean number of staff members per hundred students.

This study examined the number of library staff members *per hundred students enrolled* by library type. For clerks the result was the same—seminary libraries led the list. For student assistants, seminary libraries led the list again with junior colleges second, with 2.7 and 2.4 student assistants per hundred students. University libraries were lowest, with only 1.1 student assistants per hundred students. The final analysis of total staff members showed seminary libraries to lead again with 4.3 student assistants per hundred students. Junior college, senior college, and university staff followed in that order. All of these analyses were made with 1988 data.

A set of analyses was made for mean total number of library staff members *per consortium membership* by library type, annual expenditure, and denomination. What were the results? Average means for the type of library table were twelve and eleven staff members for 1978 and 1988. Largest staff numbers were in university libraries in both years. Smallest were denominational headquarters in both years. The ratio between largest and smallest mean staff total averaged 5.9 to 1.0

The next analysis was for annual total expenditure per consortium membership. Overall means did not change from the previous analysis. Largest expenditure in both years was at the highest level. In fact, the total staff size rose as the expenditure level rose, with a strong positive correlation in both years. Therefore the smallest library expenditure level was the one that equaled the smallest staff size. Finally, denominational analysis showed the largest numbers of staff members for this group to be found in the Baptist and Episcopal/Anglican denominations. Smallest number of staff members was in the UCC and Mennonite denominations. Table 4.20 for 1988 shows the specific scholarly libraries with the highest total number of staff members by denomination.

Now we can look at tables showing the largest number of total staff members for *specific libraries* in each scholarly database. Large tables 4.21 and 4.22 for 1978 (26 of them!) and 1988 (47 of them!) show these figures. These are the individual scholarly libraries with the largest staffs selected from all denominations in the study. Roman Catholic and Methodist made up more than half of the total in both tables. By state and province, the leaders were Pennsylvania, Massachusetts, New York, California, Texas, North Carolina, Utah, and Quebec, in total making up more than half of all the libraries.

In concluding this section, tables for 1978 and 1988 showed mean numbers of staff members by type—professionals four, clerks five, and student assistants eleven, thereby giving the typical scholarly library a staff of twenty people. All of this referred to 1978. In 1988, professional and clerical staff member sizes remained constant, but the student staff rose to fifteen per library. Therefore the 1988 mean total rose to twenty-four staff members, a 20 percent increase. See longitudinal table 4.16 for size of the entire staff.

Now we have arrived at the denominations. What was the difference between the groups by *denomination*? The largest 1978 denomination was the

Methodist group, with a mean of nineteen staff members. Smallest were the Mennonite and Jewish libraries, with only ten staff members apiece on the average. By 1988 table 4.23 showed that the database mean had advanced 10 percent to nineteen staff members. United Church of Christ led the 1988 table with twenty-five staff members per library, and Lutheran was next with twenty-three. Smallest staffs were Jewish at nine and Mennonite at eleven. Ratio of largest to smallest mean 1988 staffs was 2.8 to 1.0.

Two tables (not shown) examined the total 1978 and 1988 library staff size from another direction. They showed that about three-fifths of each group of large libraries belonged to only three denominations—Roman Catholic, with about a third of the total, Baptist, and Methodist. Two-thirds of the large 1978 libraries were still included among the large 1988 libraries. See table 4.24 for 1988. Before looking at detailed denominational tables, we will look at tables 4.25 and 4.26 for 1978 and 1988, which summarize the total North American staff member situation. For scholarly libraries we can see that 26 percent of these libraries had thirteen-plus staff members in 1978 and 36 percent had thirteen-plus staff members in 1988, a significant gain.

In contrast to North American staffs we can note information from two other nations on seminary library staff size. Australian and New Zealand theological libraries were said to average total staffs of only 1.5 persons apiece and to have professionals in only one-third of the libraries in 1988.[2] British seminary libraries were said to contain professional librarians in only a minority of the cases in 1990.[3]

Personnel by Denomination for Specific Libraries

We have finished the introductory personnel discussion, so now we will look at the series of tables showing highest staff sizes for specific libraries in order by specific denomination. These are lists of the North American library staff size leaders. We will look at four staff member tables per denomination, those with the highest number of professionals, the highest number of clerks and the highest number of student staff members, as well as the highest total number of staff members.

We see the number of *Baptist* professional librarians in table 4.27 for 1988. This table shows that most of the leaders in this category were university libraries, some of them quite sizeable. Eight libraries made the highest category, thirteen-plus professional staff members, but only one seminary made the list. Clerical staff members per *Baptist* library came next. All thirteen listed here were in the top category of thirteen-plus staff members, and only half of them were 1978 university libraries. Clerical staff member libraries in 1988 were too numerous to list. Eighteen of them tied at thirteen-plus staff members

All *Baptist* student library staff member leaders for 1978 were tied for the lead with 33.5+ students each. About half of them were university libraries. We see again the Southeastern strength of the Baptists, since three-fourths of the libraries were located in that region, almost half of them in North and South Carolina and Tennessee; two were in Texas. For 1988, twenty-five Baptist libraries were tied at 33.5+ staff members, so no table could be made.

Tables 4.28 and 4.29 for 1978 and 1988, which give staff totals, were both shown here because so few repeats occurred from 1978 and 1988 in the lists of leading *Baptist* libraries. Five libraries achieved the top 1988 category, 59.5+ total staff members, and all ten on the list were university libraries. The five were Stamford, Wake Forest (in 1978 also), Temple (in 1978 also), Baylor, and Richmond universities.

A short table for 1988 showed the *Christian* scholarly libraries having the largest number of professional staff members. Only one was a university library (table 4.30). However, note that Texas Christian University was far ahead of the other libraries in size of professional staff and reached the maximum level of thirteen-plus staff members. The seven libraries came from six different states in four different U.S. regions. As for clerical staff members, table 4.31 for 1988 shows the TCU lead again by a wide margin. There were only three university libraries in the table; otherwise all were undergraduate colleges. There was much repetition of institutions between the different lists of the same denominations here and elsewhere.

Another table for 1988 listed the *Christian* libraries with the largest student staffs. Note that for many libraries the part-time student staff was larger than the full-time professional and clerical staffs combined. Only two libraries reached the top category here—Lynchburg and Bethany Colleges. Table 4.32 shows total 1988 Christian library staff members—professional, clerical, and student combined. No new institutions were listed in this table. These were the leading Christian libraries in terms of staff member size, with TCU on top again.

The leading scholarly *Churches of Christ* libraries in terms of professional staff members were listed in a small table, table 4.33 for 1988. Pepperdine University led the list by a wide margin, with Abilene Christian University second. The other libraries showed small totals.

Table 4.34 for 1988 shows the leading libraries by number of clerical staff members and contains four libraries not shown in the comparable 1978 table, while dropping four other libraries from the table. Ten of the twenty libraries listed in the two tables were located in Tennessee and Texas. Again Pepperdine and ACU led the way at the maximum level, thirteen-plus clerical staff members. Half were college and half were university libraries.

A list was made of the leading 1988 *Churches of Christ* libraries in terms of student staff members. Four reached the highest level of 33.5+ students apiece: Harding, Pepperdine, David Lipscomb, and Abilene Christian. The libraries in this table were located in states that stretched from West Virginia to California. In the final table of total staff sizes, two libraries were far ahead of the others, again Pepperdine and ACU. Note also that the four leading libraries in 1988, table 4.35, led all other libraries by a large margin.

Congregational institutions were small in number and size and were present in the 1978 tables. The initial table for 1978 showed only three libraries, of which Washburn University had a much higher score than the other two libraries. Table 4.36 plus three not shown for 1978 complete the story. The same three libraries were found in the remaining tables (except for the student staff table), also, and again with Washburn in front by a substantial margin. However, Washburn reached the highest possible staff member level in none of them.

Next came the *Episcopal* (United States) and *Anglican* (Canada) libraries combined. The University of the South led the table of the largest libraries in this denomination by number of professional librarians by a large margin and reached the top questionnaire level of thirteen-plus professionals. No two libraries were located in the same state or province. See table 4.37 for 1988 professionals. Table 4.38 for 1988 shows the size of the clerical staffs, and three libraries led by a wide margin with maximum scores of thirteen-plus clerks: Hobart and William Smith, University of the South, and Bishop's University. Only two universities were listed, and they held two of the top three places on the list. New York, Tennessee, North Carolina, and one or two Canadian provinces appeared on each list.

In the table for 1988 *Episcopal/Anglican* student staff members, Canadian libraries occupied three places and New York libraries two places to account for more than half of the list. Three libraries reached the maximum score of 33.5+ students: Bard, Voorhees, and University of the South. On the final Episcopal/Anglican table, 4.39 for 1988 for the entire staff, the University of the South led the way by a large margin and reached the maximum level of 59.5+ staff members. Again Canada had three libraries and New York two to lead the list of states and provinces.

Several leading universities and seminaries were included in the 1988 *Independent* libraries group. The Graduate Theological Union, Brown, and McGill Universities led all other libraries at the highest level, thirteen-plus professionals. The libraries were widely dispersed geographically in the United States and Canada.

Another table for 1988 showed the *Independent* libraries that were strongest in professional staff members, table 4.40. Two were located in California, and only one ranked at the top of the list, thirteen-plus professional staff members. Table 4.41 for 1988 shows the largest library clerical staffs. More than half of the institutions were universities, and the first eight of them tied for leadership at the maximum level in this personnel area, thirteen-plus clerks. The final display, 1988 table 4.42, showed total number of staff members for these libraries, of which seven were located in universities. Again four of the libraries were in California, and three libraries ranked in the highest, 59.5+, category. There was a trend for the number of universities to increase in proportion to the whole list in each one of these tables from 1978 and 1988.

The *Lutheran* libraries with the largest number of professional librarians are shown in table 4.43 for 1988. Two of the libraries were located in universities and two in Minnesota. The two leading libraries reached the top professional level and were far ahead of the remainder of the list: Muhlenberg College and Wilfred Laurier University in Canada. For clerical staff members in 1988 all eleven of the leaders scored in the top category of thirteen-plus. Generally, Lutheran libraries were located in the north central U.S. states, so we find Minnesota with three libraries but also Pennsylvania with two, thereby constituting almost half of the libraries.

Lutheran student staff member levels for 1978 are shown in table 4.44. Five libraries were in the highest category of 33.5+ and were far ahead of the other libraries listed. The final table (not shown) for 1988 showed Muhlenberg College leading the total staff list and reaching the highest level, with St. Olaf and Gettysburg Colleges at a second level. Eight of these libraries were located in colleges.

The reader may notice that certain institutions ranked high on more than one preliminary table but still failed to make the final and total denominational and personnel tables. This surprising result was caused either by the library's failure to report its figures on one or two of the personnel variables for the reporting period or else by the fact that its final score was less impressive when all subtotals were summed.

Mennonite libraries are represented in most 1988 table series. They were almost without exception small since they were supported only by small budgets and small staffs. No universities were listed on these tables, only primarily small senior colleges and historical societies. Such states and provinces as Indiana, Kansas, Pennsylvania, and Manitoba were prominent here. Most of these institutions were located in small or medium-sized cities.

Table 4.45 for 1988 shows the *Mennonite* libraries with the largest number of professional librarians, the four leaders having three professionals apiece. Four of the 1988 clerical staff member libraries were Canadian from three different provinces, plus three libraries located in Indiana. In addition there were two Kansas and two Pennsylvania libraries. Eastern Mennonite University in Virginia had by far the largest student staff for 1988. This college reached the top level in this staffing area, 33.5+. Eastern Mennonite also scored highest in total staff in 1988 table 4.46. The table showed Kansas, Indiana, Pennsylvania, and Canada to contain 90 percent of the Mennonite libraries, high in total staff members also.

As for *Methodist* libraries with the largest number of 1988 professional librarians, all except one were university libraries, most of them large and some of them prestigious, e.g., Boston, Duke, Emory, and Wesleyan Universities. All of the libraries scored in the highest category. While Methodist libraries can be found in many states, the leading libraries represented in this database seem to have been located primarily in the eastern half of the United States. Table 4.47 contains 1978 libraries located in eleven states and all regions except Canada. Again all 1988 Methodist libraries were tied at the highest category for the lead in the number of library clerks available.

We see that two libraries represented Indiana and three represented Ohio for student staff members. Twelve libraries were tied for leadership at the maximum level of 33.5+ student staff members apiece. The final table, 4.48, shows 1988 *Methodist* libraries with the largest total number of staff members. Eight libraries were tied at the highest level, 59.5+ professional, clerical, and student employees—from eight states. All but one of this table's libraries served universities.

The *Other Denominations* group contained several outstanding libraries. The number of 1978 professional staff members ranged from nine to thirteen. The table included two Mormon, three Seventh-day

Adventist, two Quaker, one Nazarene, and two United Church of Canada libraries—five denominations. Five libraries ranked in the top category, thirteen-plus professionals: Andrews, Bryn Mawr, Swarthmore, Brigham Young, and the LDS Church headquarters in Salt Lake City. All of the 1978 institutions on table 4.49 showed the maximum number of clerical staff members, thirteen-plus. California, Pennsylvania, Utah, and Canada institutions provided four-fifths of the total number. For 1988 Other Denominations listed thirteen libraries at the thirteen-plus level so no table was made.

All but one of the 1988 *Other Denominations* student staffs were large enough to be listed in the highest category, 33.5+ staff members. Note that the repetition of specific libraries between professional and student employee lists has been reduced to one: BYU in Provo. Curious. Four of the libraries were located in Illinois and Pennsylvania, and only two of the ten institutions were universities. Table 4.50 for 1988 listed the total staff members in Other Denominations libraries. Only two universities were listed, the rest being senior colleges. Pennsylvania with three libraries and Illinois with two made up more than half of the table total. Quaker libraries made up three of the nine libraries, and Adventist, two. BYU led the way with a top level staff.

The *Presbyterian* libraries listed in these tables represented strong small and medium-sized colleges, not universities. There was again little repetition of institutions between tables. Four libraries were at the top with the maximum number of professional staff members in 1988: Tulsa, Lafayette, Trinity, and Queen's. Number of clerical staff members in 1988 table 4.51 showed nine libraries to have reached the maximum of thirteen-plus clerical staff members, far ahead of the three remaining libraries in the table. Three of these libraries were located in Pennsylvania.

The leading seven *Presbyterian* 1988 libraries with student staff members were clustered at the top of the table with scores at the maximum level, 33.5+. Presbyterian seemed to be strongest in the Middle West and Middle Atlantic regions. Iowa, Illinois, and Texas had two libraries apiece, thereby constituting two-thirds of the table. The final table, 4.52, showed four university libraries and also two Illinois, two Iowa, and two Pennsylvania libraries, which made up more than half of the total. First among these 1988 libraries and clearly well ahead of all others was Trinity University in San Antonio, which had 59.5+ staff members.

Cedar Crest College was well ahead of all other *United Church of Christ* libraries and reached the top category of professional staffing in 1988. A third of these libraries were located in universities. Two Pennsylvania, two Missouri, and two North Carolina libraries made up two-thirds of this list. This denomination's libraries seemed to be located primarily in the Middle West and Middle Atlantic and included only a few universities among its leaders. Table 4.53 shows the number of *United Church of Christ* clerical staff members in 1988. The leading four libraries scored at the maximum level (13+): Elmhurst, Eden Webster, Cedar Crest, and Franklin and Marshall. Missouri and Pennsylvania contained almost half of the table's libraries.

When compared to its companion table for 1978, table 4.54, the 1988 table, 4.55, showed growth in number of *United Church of Christ* student staff members during the decade separating the two *ALD* editions. The top figure for 1978, 15.5 students (with one exception), equaled the bottom figure for 1988. Each table was composed primarily of strong senior college libraries, with no junior college and few university libraries being listed. Five libraries in the 1988 table 4.55 made the top category, 33.5+ students. Total 1988 library staff members for these colleges showed Cedar Crest College again to lead the group with the maximum number, fifty-nine-plus staff members.

Jewish 1988 libraries are shown in table 4.56 with three of them having professional librarian totals well above the rest: Brandeis, Yeshiva, and Yivo. These libraries led at the highest level, thirteen-plus staff members per library. Three of the table's nine libraries were in universities, four in colleges of Judaica; two were special libraries. In general, the Jewish libraries were in the Northeast and Middle Atlantic: two were from Massachusetts and four, from New York City. The next table for 1988 also had three libraries at the top, with thirteen-plus clerical staff members apiece, again reaching the top category: Brandeis, Yeshiva, and Hebrew College. New York and Ohio dominated this table. The reader may have noticed that the Jewish library group contained more special and nonacademic libraries than did the other denominational groups.

In table 4.57 for 1988 only the Brandeis University library had a large number of *Jewish* institution student assistants, 33.5+, at the maximum level. Total staff members concluded the Jewish section of 1988 libraries. Several of these libraries represented small colleges of Judaica, with only Brandeis reaching the highest number—59.5+ total staff members. This table showed two libraries located in Massachusetts and three in New York City, for half of the total. An unusual feature in the table was the presence of two libraries from the same parent institution, Yeshiva University.

Often there were so many *Roman Catholic* libraries scoring in the top category on a variable that it was impractical to make a table for them. So we had to take what we could get for this group, only two tables, one listing the libraries leading in student staff members and the other listing those leading in total staff members, both taken from the 1978 database. For professionals in 1988 there were thirty-three libraries tied at thirteen-plus staff members apiece. For 1988 Roman Catholic clerks the number of libraries tied at thirteen-plus staff members was seventy, so no table was produced.

The 1978 table for *Roman Catholic* student assistants was simple since sixty-five libraries made the maximum score, 33.5+. New York, Illinois, and Ohio led the table by state in number of libraries included. For 1988 Roman Catholic libraries were so numerous that no table could be made. There were thirty-seven of them at the top level, 33.5+ student staff members.

Table 4.58 for 1978 shows the *Roman Catholic* libraries having the largest total number of staff members. In the end, only five university libraries reached the highest staff member level, 59.5+: Georgetown, DePaul, Fordham, St. John's, and Dayton Universities. Eight of the table's ten libraries were located in universities; two each were located in the District of Columbia, New York, and Illinois, six altogether, in three states. For 1988, eighteen libraries scored at the 59.5+ level, so no table could be made.

Interim Personnel Summary

Now we can ask the summary question: Which denominations excelled in size of staff per library and which were weakest in this area? Staff member tables came in four parts, and here are the leading denominations in the four sets of personnel tables:

1. Professional: Baptist, Methodist, Other Denominations, and Roman Catholic, followed by Independent, Jewish, and Presbyterian.
2. Clerical: Baptist, Independent, Lutheran, Methodist, Other Denominations, Presbyterian, and Roman Catholic (primary leaders), followed by Episcopal/Anglican and United Church of Christ (secondary leaders).
3. Student assistants: Baptist, Churches of Christ, Methodist, Other Denominations, Presbyterian, Roman Catholic, followed by Independent and Lutheran.

4. Total: Methodist followed by Baptist, Roman Catholic, and Other Denominations. Weakest denominations were the Congregational and Mennonite, as we have seen before. Leading state and province locations were Pennsylvania, Illinois, New York, North Carolina, Tennessee, and Ohio.

To summarize this staff member section further and to supplement the paragraph above, here are the final scholarly denominational scores (rankings) for all four library staff member categories and for all denominations:

Baptist, 3.5 points
Christian, 0.0
Churches of Christ, 1.0
Congregational, 0.0
Episcopal/Anglican, 0.5
Independent, 2.0
Lutheran, 1.5
Mennonite, 0.0 points
Methodist, 4.0 (a perfect score!)
Other Denominations, 3.0
Presbyterian, 2.5
United Church of Christ, 0.5
Jewish, 0.5
Roman Catholic, 3.5

In order of scores, the leaders were Methodist, Baptist, Roman Catholic, Other Denominations, Presbyterian, and Independent. A perfect score required being a primary leader at all four personnel levels in order to earn one point for each level. A half-point was earned for being a secondary leader in one personnel category.

A final table can be considered. It tried to show the ratios between professional, clerical, student assistant, and total by denomination. Notice some major changes within certain denominations from one table to another, tables 4.59 for 1978 and 4.60 for 1988—for Christian, Episcopal/Anglican, and UCC, for instance. Notice also the difference between the Jewish ratio and the ratios for Christian and Roman Catholic. Notice that the percentage professional is highest in the Jewish group and lowest in the Mennonite group. Does that finding suggest that the Jewish group was therefore potentially the most sophisticated and professionalized of the denominations?

The same sort of distribution can be seen in table 4.61 for 1988 to show type of library. Denominational headquarters shows the highest percentage of professionals and the lowest percentage of student assistants. Notice that senior college, university, and junior college have a heavy emphasis on student assistant personnel.

Chief Librarian's Gender

Certain characteristics of the chief librarians of these libraries were examined, and we will explain the results here. For many libraries they were the only staff members named in the *ALD*. The characteristics examined included gender, type of library, region, total expenditure, OCLC membership, institutional and library size, and library age—variables familiar to the reader by this time. Of course the variables were limited to the information given in the directories.

Were chief scholarly librarians chiefly male or female? Not only is the *gender* of a chief librarian of some interest in itself, but we would also like to know if there were any distinguishing characteristics of those libraries headed by males vs. females. Were the libraries headed by males consistently larger than those headed by females, for instance? Note that Canada's percentage male was higher than that of the United States. The databases did suggest certain consistent differences, and we will look at them.[4]

In 1978, 701 scholarly chief librarians, or 51 percent of them, were male and for 1988, 768, or 54 percent, of them were male. In 1978 also, 593, or 43 percent, were female and in 1988, 644, or 45 percent, were female. The remaining percentages were those for no responses. For the group as a whole the percentage of each gender rose slightly in 1988, while the percent of no responses fell. Note that the percentage of males apparently grew slightly faster than that of females. So males were more numerous than females in these two groups during the decade, by a small margin. Tables 2.7, 2.8, and 2.28 for 1978 and 1988 show these results for type of library and other variables.

The next table for 1978 and 1988 looked at chief librarian figures in another way. It showed for 1978, for instance, that 89 percent of the males and 64 percent, of the females were scholarly, but only 23 percent of the no responses were scholarly (obviously most of them were for popular librarians). It showed further that the number of no responses dropped sharply in 1988 for both scholarly and popular. In a table for 1978 and 1988 we can look at the dead (1978) and the newly born (1988) libraries. How did they perform on chief librarian's gender? The table showed that scholarly male chief librarians increased in number for newly born libraries even more in the 1978–88 period than did female chief librarians.

What was the percentage male of the scholarly chief librarians by *type of library*? *Junior colleges* were from a quarter to a third male and two-thirds female, with the percentage male rising slightly for 1988. *Univer-*

sity chief librarians were 59 to 70 percent male, and 29 to 40 percent female with the percentage male falling. *Seminary* libraries were static at 2 females to 1 male, as the ATLA membership ratio suggested in chapter 1. *Convent/monasteries* were about half male and two-fifths female, with the percentage of each gender rising. *Denominational headquarters* rose over the years for both male and female, though the ratio was about 1 to 2 male to female. *History/archive* libraries were relatively static, about 2 to 1 male to female. In summary, men led four scholarly library types, and women led two of them. These and other facts are displayed in the tables listed above plus others in this and previous chapters.

By *region*, was there a difference in regard to the chief librarian's gender? Yes, see table 2.8 for 1988. The Northeast and Southeast were 50 percent female, whereas Canada was only 35 percent female. For that year Canada was 64 percent male, while the Southeast was only 48 percent male. For 1978 Canada was 28 percent female, while Rocky Mountains was 67 percent female. Table 4.62 shows for 1988 the results of analyzing chief librarian's gender by *total library expenditures*. It shows that the percentage female was high—67 percent—at the lowest expenditure level and low—27 percent—at the highest expenditure level. Correspondingly the male percentage rose from 25 percent to 72 percent as female percentages fell. The corresponding 1978 table showed the same results. Table 4.63 shows total 1988 expenditure by library type for matched pairs.

An additional table shows another factor on which males exceeded the performance of females—OCLC institutional membership. The chief librarian OCLC institutional male membership percentage was half again as high as the female membership percentage. We can see if the denominations differed by chief librarian's gender in 1978. In that year, Lutheran libraries were two-thirds male and Presbyterian were 60 percent male. Churches of Christ were two-thirds female, and UCC libraries were half and half.

Several additional tables were made concerning chief librarian's gender to test the hypothesis that they would be male. Look at table 4.64 for 1988, for instance. The percentage of graduate-level degrees awarded by the male-led institutions was 64 percent, while the percentage of graduate degrees awarded by the female-led institutions was only 35 percent. The 1978 ratio between male and female was similar. Look at table 4.65 for both 1978 and 1988 chief librarians and total library expenditure per student. It showed that the male chief librarian's library expenditure per student was higher than the female chief librarian's library expenditure per student for both 1978 and 1988, by 31 percent and 21 percent. Other tables not shown here revealed the same type of picture.

Similar pictures are presented for 1988 institutional enrollment (17 percent male vs. 6 percent female for enrollment levels above 1,800 students) and table 4.66 for 1988 and library staff members (47 percent male vs. 40 percent female in number of staff members above thirteen). And also, table 4.67 (1988) shows the number of faculty members in academic institutions in which the library was headed by a male vs. a female. Male chief librarians worked in institutions that were 26 percent larger in number of faculty members than those institutions with libraries headed by females.

And finally, we can compare library age and chief librarian's gender. Which were the older, libraries headed by males or by females? Table 4.68 shows that males were heads of older libraries in both the 1978 and 1988 databases. Libraries headed by males were eighty-nine years old on the average in 1978 and eighty-six in 1988, while libraries headed by females were only seventy-two years old, on the average, one-fifth younger.

Clerical vs. Laypersons

Were many of the chief librarians in these databases also professional religious figures—ministers, priests, brothers, sisters, or nuns? The only way in which we could identify these men and women was to look for *Pastor*, *Reverend, Father, Brother,* or *Sister* before the chief librarian's name or the initials of a religious order following the name, such as S.J., R.S.B, O.S.B., S.S.J., I.A.M., or C.M. This limitation reduced the field to Roman Catholic clergy and sisters. Probably other chief librarians in Protestant and Jewish libraries were also members of the clergy, but without some way of identifying them the author could not count them. Some of the clergy were identified, and we can look at findings by type of library, region and denomination.

In what types of libraries did these clergy work? Most of the male clergy were shown in tables 4.69 and 4.70 to have worked in senior colleges, monasteries, and seminaries, while the nuns and sisters worked in senior college, junior college, and convent libraries. In fact, 16 percent of all junior college and 11 percent of all senior college libraries were headed by the religious. Much the same picture was seen for 1988.

The 1988 clergy denominational picture can be examined now. We can count the number of 1978 priests or brothers as 30 and the number of nuns or sisters as 121. They represented 6 percent and 23 percent of the total number of Roman Catholic chief librarians. When we turn to 1988, we see a significant drop in the number of clergy for that year, by about 20 percent, due to replacement of the religious by lay chief librarians.

Where were the libraries located which were headed by these Catholic priests and nuns? The 1978 priests were located in the Middle West and Middle Atlantic, while the sisters were located in those two plus the Northeast. In 1988 the distribution of these libraries was much the same. By volume holdings, longitudinal table 4.71 shows a slight drop in number of staff members from 1978 to 1988 and suggests that the drop affected primarily priests and brothers rather than sisters. It shows also that most of these libraries had between 3,501 and 240,000 volumes, a wide range.

Named vs. Unnamed Chief Librarians

In what percentage of the cases was the chief librarian named—his or her name given—in the *ALD* library description? For 1978 scholarly libraries, 1,295 were named, or 94.2 percent. For 1988, 1,415 were named, or 98.8 percent. Again the percentage rose for the later edition. While this situation was probably not of great importance, it was sufficiently curious to be noted and for us to study the libraries not naming their chiefs. We will study them for type of library, for annual expenditure, and for denomination.

The first analysis of this matter suggested that the unnamed chief librarians were primarily scholarly convent/monastery and denominational headquarters, senior college and seminary librarians. In fact, they made up significant percentages of the convent/monastery and denominational headquarters groups. In addition, if we look at the 1978 total annual expenditure, we see that the unnamed chief librarians were found primarily in the lower expenditure categories. We can also examine this factor by denomination. In the 1978 Jewish libraries 11 percent of the chief librarians were not named and in the Christian denomination 10 percent of them were not named. All other denominations named their chief librarians more often.

Summary

In conclusion, what can we say about scholarly chief librarians? This group was somewhat more often male than female except in junior colleges and denominational headquarters, both of which were more often headed by females. It seems that scholarly religious libraries must have resembled scholarly nonreligious libraries in that males had administrative positions in institutions which were larger or more prestigious than the institutions in which the females had administrative positions. Priests and sisters headed 16 percent of the junior and 11 percent of the senior college libraries with their number on the decline. The vast majority of chief librarians were named in the *ALD* entries.

Section Summary

In the personnel section we examined the data for professionals, clerks, student assistants, and total staff. Only 56 percent and 66 percent of the libraries reported any staff information for 1978 and 1988, respectively. Almost every denomination had one or more libraries in the thirteen-plus category for both professionals and clerks and in larger figures than that for student assistants. Mean 1988 figures were approximately four professionals, five clerks, fifteen student assistants, and a total of nineteen or twenty staff members. Staffs in university and senior college libraries were larger than those in the other five kinds of libraries. The largest denominations varied, but Mennonite and Jewish often brought up the rear. Size of staff varied directly with size of library expenditure.

Variation by region was small, but the Canadian region usually had the smallest staff numbers. In longitudinal tables the total staff change percentage 1978–88 was usually small, about 20 percent. The staff sizes were examined for specific leading libraries. We were also able to examine several tables that showed the ratios of types of staff members by other variables. Among student assistants, seminary libraries excelled. When the denominations were finally evaluated, the leaders were Methodist, Baptist, and Roman Catholic.

For chief librarians, a slight majority were men, 57 percent in 1978 and 54 percent in 1988. Women led in junior college and denominational headquarters, but males led everywhere else. Further, analyses suggested that males headed the libraries that were larger in every way and more prestigious than those headed by women. Clerical or religious chief librarians, at least those who were Roman Catholic, included 16 percent of the junior colleges and 11 percent of the senior colleges. Named chief librarians included 94–99 percent of the total. Altogether an interesting group!

Library Material Holdings

This section deals with the scholarly religious library collections of reading, viewing, and listening material. Which libraries were best able to meet user demands for printed and media material? Hardly any other variable made as important a contribution to the library's potential for a strong service program as this one, so let us see what the libraries offered here. We will examine the material holdings in each scholarly library for each one of the fourteen denominational groups, as well as for several other familiar variables.

The author's assumption was that, generally speaking, the larger the material collection, the more useful it could be to its readers. Which library in each group had the largest number of books, periodical subscriptions, microforms, and other types of library material? Again we will examine the quantity of the holdings only, there being no measure of holdings quality available, though quality of service surely depended to some extent on quantity.

We will analyze the subject in the following order: book volumes, periodical subscriptions, vertical files, microforms, media, maps, and art reproductions, with each type of material being studied by type of library, sometimes by region, total expenditure level, number of consortium memberships, by chief librarian's gender, and then by each denomination separately and each large library individually before the next type of material is taken up. Then we will look at several special studies. We will look at volume holdings per student by denomination, and then the smallest volume holdings per student by denomination. Within the book volume section immediately below we will examine the data for all of these variables.

Book Volumes

In the initial study of the size of book (including bound periodical volume) collections we can look at holdings by the seven types of scholarly libraries. Longitudinal table 4.72 enables us to look at the mean volumes by type of library for both 1978 and 1988. It enables us to compare the library types, also. The 1978 scholarly mean was 93,400 volumes per library. Richest type by far was university libraries, with 246,600 mean volumes. Next largest was senior colleges. Smallest was denominational headquarters libraries with an average of only 15,663 volumes.

In 1988 the overall scholarly mean was 112,610 volumes, 21 percent higher than the 1978 figure. Largest were the university libraries again, at 276,238 volumes, a 12 percent increase over 1978. Senior colleges were again second highest. Smallest was denominational headquarters again. Largest to smallest mean 1988 ratio was 18.4 to 1.0. Growth rate was highest for senior colleges and lowest for history/archives libraries.

Let us now continue the volume holdings analysis by library type with 1978 *junior college* libraries. Of course they were small, only one library reaching 200,000 volumes. Other Denominations, Baptist and Roman Catholic libraries led the table with five-sixths of the total number of libraries. North Carolina and New York led in geographic location. *Senior college* libraries were larger than junior college libraries in table 4.73 for 1988. Three of them reached the maximum of 590,000+ volumes, one Catholic and two Quaker colleges, with a third Quaker college being fourth on the list. Pennsylvania led by state with a third of the libraries. *Universities* had many libraries at a high level, thirty-seven at 540,000+ volumes each, so no table could be made. Other evidence showed that most universities were Baptist, Independent, Methodist, Other Denominations, or Roman Catholic.

Seminary libraries came next and contained one library at the top level in volumes: Union Theological Seminary. All other libraries on the list also had strong collections. Independent institutions included 38 percent of the total. No specific state led the list in table 4.74 in 1988. *Convent/monastery* libraries were small, Roman Catholic, and were led by North Dakota libraries. *Denominational headquarters* libraries were also small and were led by four Canadian libraries, all Roman Catholic. See table 4.75 for 1988. In fact, Roman Catholic constituted 40 percent of the total number of libraries in this table. Five Canadian libraries (29 percent) led the table in location.

History and archive libraries covered a large range but were led by the Yivo Institute in table 4.76 for 1988. Other Denominations and Jewish libraries included more than a third of the total and New York state libraries had almost as many. For book collections, Roman Catholic and Other Denominations led the denominations and New York led the states.

Total library volumes per enrolled student by library type comes next. We see here a picture similar to those seen in other parts of the chapter. University library average volume levels per student are the smallest and seminary levels are the largest. While universities have many volumes they also have many students, as we have seen before. Seminaries have few students but often they have good-sized book collections. Senior colleges had more books per student than did junior colleges which were often younger as well.

We have also a longitudinal study of volume holdings by library type. What was the overall decade rate of change here? Twenty-one percent was the study's change rate. Leading type of library was senior college with a 23 percent change rate, and seminary libraries were second with 20 percent. Lowest change percentage was −23 percent for history/archives.

Scholarly library volume holdings by *region* had the Northeast with the largest number, at a mean number of 119,300 volumes, and the Southeast at 78,060 volumes—the smallest number. So much for 1978. For 1988 the Middle Atlantic was largest with 129,700 volumes, and the West was smallest with 98,400 volumes. Again, no consistency could be found in the "largest" and "smallest" regions. Largest to smallest volume ratio was 1.3 to 1.0, only a modest-sized ratio.

Table 4.77 for 1988 shows the relationship between library volume holdings and annual *library expenditure*. The positive correlation that was to be expected here was achieved, both for 1978 and 1988. Table 4.77 shows the mean volumes at the lowest expenditure level, $1,500 and under, to have been 20,130, whereas at the $510,000 and over expenditure level, the mean volume total was 321,800. We also have a table that shows the mean volume holdings by number of *consortium memberships*. It makes clear that there was a strong positive correlation between the two. For one membership the mean number of volume holdings was 103,000, but for six-plus memberships the mean holding was 292,400 volumes.

Volume holdings by *chief librarian's gender* showed the expected difference between the sexes. Institutions with male chief librarians had a mean of 117,200 volumes in their collections in 1978 and those with female chief librarians had a mean of only 71,280 volumes. The ratio was therefore 1.6 to 1.0. The 1988 table had a similar ratio.

By *denomination,* the overall view of volume holdings shows considerable variation. Highest denomination was the Methodist with a mean of 121,200 volumes per library. Lowest was Other Denominations with a mean of 66,850 volumes, 81 percent short of the highest. That was 1978. In 1988 the largest denominational book collection was the Methodists, again, with 138,800 volumes. The smallest collection belonged to the Mennonites and had 54,140 volumes, this time a disparity of 156 percent. We have another table for no longer and newly listed libraries (1978–88) combined for volume holdings by denomination. The table's means were well below those for the entire database, with Roman Catholic and Independent in the lead and Jewish at the bottom. Note that Protestant libraries were much smaller than Jewish or Catholic libraries.

The denominational subsection of the book volumes section will carry out a detailed analysis of denominations and specific libraries. Table 4.78 shows the mean volume holdings of 1988 libraries for all denominations. We begin the detailed study with the *Baptist* library group, often a leader in these denominational studies. Four libraries reached the top level for volumes, 590,000+: Wake Forest, Temple, Baylor, and McMaster. The remaining libraries were not far below them. All of the table's libraries were located in universities, an unusual feature, plus one seminary. Texas led the states with three representatives, more than a third of the total.

Christian libraries can be seen in table 4.79 for 1978. Only one library in either 1978 or 1988 reached the top level, that of Texas Christian University which was at that level in both *ALD* editions. In addition, in 1988, three more of these libraries had reached the 200,000-volume level. More than half of the libraries were located in colleges.

Table 4.80 for 1988 shows the libraries with the largest number of volumes in *Churches of Christ* institutions. No library in this table came close to the top level in volume holdings. When we compare this table with the one for 1978 (not shown), we see one remarkable change. Pepperdine University reported significantly fewer volumes for 1988 than for 1978, 390,000 compared to 290,000. Just why this happened is not clear, but it is probably significant that the library reported 206,000 bound serial volumes in 1978 but only 23,000 of them in 1988. Three of these libraries were sponsored by seminaries, and the rest were divided equally between colleges and universities. Tennessee with three, Illinois and Texas with two each led in number of libraries by location and made up almost two-thirds of the table.

Congregational libraries for 1978 enable us to welcome two new institutions to this series of scholarly library tables. However, the table was led by two of the old-timers, Washburn University and the American Congregational Association. Most Congregational libraries were modest in size.

Another denomination of modest-sized libraries was *Episcopal/Anglican*. No library in table 4.81 (1988) reached the top level, though Kenyon College and the University of the South came close. In general, the denomination with the larger universities had the larger libraries, which produced the higher levels on these denominational tables. And in most cases, if a library stood high (or low) on one table in a series, then its record on later tables was similar. This table showed four seminaries (a high number), five colleges, and only two universities. New York claimed three and Tennessee two libraries, almost half of the total.

In the *Independent* libraries for 1988 we see that four of them reached the 590,000+ volume level—Union Theological Seminary, Oral Roberts, Brown and McGill—and two more were strong in volumes among only seven libraries. Three of them were seminaries. Table 4.82 lists the 1988 libraries that led the *Lutheran* denomination. Wilfred Laurier University in Ontario led the way with a strong but not top level showing. Note that seven of the table's institutions were colleges and four were universities. Minnesota and Pennsylvania led the states with two libraries apiece.

The *Mennonite* libraries constituted one of the smallest denominational groups in the study. No library came close to the top level, but five libraries were tied at 130,000 volumes apiece in the 1988 list of leading libraries by volume holdings. All were colleges, except for one seminary. Again Indiana and Kansas led the representation by state, with two libraries apiece.

The *Methodist* denomination regularly produced a number of high-level libraries in every category. This was not only true for table 4.83 (1988) but was also true for the 1978 table (not reproduced here). The 1978 table had six libraries at 590,000+ volumes, and the 1988 table had seven of them. The 1988 libraries were all universities: Denver, Wesleyan, American, Emory, Boston, Duke, and Southern Methodist. A fine showing! These universities were located in nine states ranging from California to Massachusetts.

The small denominations making up the *Other Denominations* group provided more high-powered libraries than the reader may have expected. A 1988 table showed that four of them reached the top level in volumes—Andrews, Bryn Mawr, Swarthmore, and Brigham Young, two colleges and two universities. In addition, Haverford College had a large collection. The top five included three Quaker, one Seventh-day Adventist, and one Mormon library. Pennsylvania led the state representation with three libraries, and Michigan with two.

Presbyterian libraries are shown for 1988 in table 4.84. Six colleges and two seminary libraries dominated the table, but three university libraries led it. Tulsa, Trinity, and Queens had the largest number of volumes, and reached the top level of 590,000+ volumes here. The state and province locations ranged from Oregon to North Carolina. No large 1988 *United Church of Christ* libraries were found here. Cedar Crest and Franklin and Marshall Colleges were leaders on many of these UCC tables. Both UCC and Presbyterian institutions were small or medium-sized, and most of them were colleges, not universities. Pennsylvania with three libraries and Missouri with two led the states.

Table 4.85 lists the libraries for 1988 that led all *Jewish* institutions in numbers of volume holdings. Two of them—Brandeis and Yeshiva Universities—reached the top level of volumes. Only three of these libraries were located in universities, while four were located in colleges, two in seminaries, and three in historical or denominational libraries. Five libraries were located in New York City and two in Waltham, Massachusetts, making up almost two-thirds of the total.

Another table showed 1978 *Roman Catholic* libraries by number of volumes and suggested again the problems that plagued Catholic table making. We have eleven libraries in the table, and all of them reached the top level of the questionnaire with 590,000+ volumes. All institutions were universities except for Boston College, which resembled a university in many ways. These institutions were located in the District of Columbia (2), Quebec (2), and New York (2), as well as in five other states and provinces.

Longitudinal analysis by denomination showed an overall 21 percent increase for scholarly book volumes. The largest denominational increase was for Episcopal/Anglican at 43 percent. Next was Roman Catholic at 29 percent. Largest *decreases* were Jewish at 11 percent and Mennonite at 7 percent. Matched pairs showed a slightly larger increase than that for the entire database. Largest matched pair denominational increases in that group were Jewish at 61 percent (a small number reporting) and Episcopal/Anglican at 51 percent. The no longer listed and newly listed groups had changes well below the entire database, the former somewhat below the latter.

Several specialized studies were made of volume holdings, most of them by denomination and all of them on a per-student basis. A table was made to show what happens by volume and by denomination when we combine the curious 1978 no longer listed with the 1988 newly listed libraries. The leading denomination by this formulation was the Roman Catholic, far ahead of other denominations with a 50,160 volume mean. Second was the Independent group. Lowest were the Jewish and the Episcopal/Anglican. Overall the mean was 27,520 volumes. How does this finding compare with the figures for the database as a whole? It is much smaller than the overall mean figure.

Now come two analyses of mean library volumes per student enrolled, the first one by library type. Overall mean was 156 library volumes for 1978 and 189 volumes for 1988. Largest were the seminary libraries in both years, with 384 and 478 volumes per student enrolled. This was predictable. Smallest were 100 volumes for university in 1978 and 106 for junior colleges in 1988. Scholarly volume holdings per student by denomination can be studied for both 1978 and 1988. For 1988 the largest volume holdings were in the Jewish denominational group at 503 volumes per student. Second was the Episcopal/Anglican group at 386. Smallest holdings were those of the Baptist group at 143 volumes per student. Yet another specialized study using a composite longitudinal growth variable of twenty-three questions for volume holdings that combined scholarly and popular libraries showed a net decade growth of 36 percent.

Now we can look at volume holdings from another viewpoint, the number of volumes held per enrolled student for academic institutions. A series of tables shows these ratios per student for 1988. For a library to score above one thousand volumes per student in these tables was very good, and a few of them did.

For *Baptist* libraries all scores were modest, but two libraries were located in liberal arts colleges. *Christian* colleges were again modest in their collection sizes per student, but one university entered this table at both the top and the bottom ends, so at both top and bottom were Phillips University libraries. The seminary library approached the thousand-volume level (table 4.86 for 1988). The *Churches of Christ* denomination was filled with seminaries, Bible colleges, and Christian colleges.

Episcopal/Anglican libraries were few in number, but two of them were well above a thousand volumes per student—the Episcopal Divinity School in Cambridge with 1,933 volumes per student and the General Theological Seminary in New York with 1,333 (table 4.87 for 1988). *Independent* libraries were led by the Union Theological Seminary in New York with 1,311 volumes per student. Other Independent libraries were more modest in holdings.

The short *Lutheran* table had libraries with modest book volume levels per student (table 4.88 for 1988). Much the same thing can be said for *Mennonite* libraries, more than half of them Canadian. The level of table 4.89 for 1988 for *Methodist* libraries was good but not excellent. *Other Denominations* presented a table with good but not excellent collection sizes also. Two-thirds of them were seminaries.

We come to *Presbyterian* libraries in table 4.90 for 1988. This table is led by Union Theological Seminary in Richmond with 1,933 volumes per student, very good. A short table for *United Church of Christ* libraries had one leader, the Andover Newton Theological School in Massachusetts with 1,333 books per student. The Hebrew Union College in Cincinnati with 2,600(!) and the University of Judaism in Los Angeles with 1,333 volumes per student led table 4.91 for 1988 for *Jewish* libraries.

Roman Catholic libraries were led by St. Mary of the Lake Seminary in Illinois with 1,330 volumes per student. This full table included a long list of strong libraries. Almost a third of them were located in New York State. It seems to be true that the libraries listed in the per-student tables were primarily those serving small enrollments.

So much for scholarly library volume holdings per student! Now that we have looked at the largest volume holdings and the largest volume holdings per student, we can look at the smallest volume holdings per student by denomination for 1988. These were the scholarly religious libraries that provided the smallest book collections per student enrolled for faculty and student use. They were libraries with material collections that were very small for the size of the student body. Therefore their volume-per-student ratios were poor. We begin with *Baptist,* table 4.92 for 1988. The table ranges from fifteen to thirty-three volumes per student, small numbers. A college student body of five hundred would be served by a total collection of only seventy-five hundred volumes at the fifteen books per student rate of one college listed in this table.

The institutions listed in these tables are small colleges, for the most part. We have at least two universities, Pepperdine and Abilene Christian, which appear on both the list of the largest *Churches of Christ* collections and on the list of least volumes per student for that denomination. Curious. But we never said that those collections were large per student. The Churches of Christ library holdings range from fourteen to sixty-eight volumes per student. Sixty-eight volumes per student equals sixty-eight thousand volumes for a thousand students. Too small!

Next is *Independent* table 4.93 for 1988, which consists primarily of seminaries and Bible colleges. Its range is from three up to thirty-three volumes per student. We see some of the same names here that we saw in previous Independent lists of small libraries: Luther Rice College and Jordan College. Again we are in the presence of a list of *Methodist* college libraries with small enrollments and small book collections, twenty to forty-seven volumes per student. And again a considerable variety of state locations. The *Other Denominations* table 4.94 for 1988 has two libraries below ten volumes per student. And famous Ricks College makes yet another appearance, but this time in unfavorable circumstances.

The *Presbyterian* table had a range from six to seventy-one volumes per student, the former in the School of the Ozarks. Only one of these libraries served a university. Missouri and Iowa libraries made up more than half of the table. For *United Church of Christ* we see that Elon College had only forty volumes per student. For the most part, these were libraries at small colleges, plus a few small universities. A few of them were good quality institutions, but all had inadequate book collections (table 4.95 for 1988).

For *Jewish* scholarly libraries we had eight libraries ranging from 33 to 182 volumes per student. In defense of the low scores for certain Jewish institutions listed in this table, many of them had objectives that were quite limited. They were narrowly focused on preparing students and teachers for Jewish elementary and secondary education so could hardly be expected to have well-rounded book collections. One-fourth of the Jewish libraries were located in Ohio, and most of them were colleges.

The table for *Roman Catholic* libraries showed some of the smallest figures yet. The Roman Catholic table (4.96 for 1988) had a low range, from three to twenty volumes per student. Almost two-fifths of these libraries were Canadian and one-fourth were universities. For this series of tables as a whole, the libraries were a deplorable group in terms of collection size.

Volume holdings per faculty member by region, another approach to the study of book collections, are shown in table 4.97. For 1978, the Middle Atlantic region led the way with 2,641 volumes per member. The Southeast was weakest with only 1,742 volumes per member. The largest regions in 1988 were the Middle Atlantic at 3,255 volumes per faculty member and 3,016 volumes per faculty member for the Northeast region; the smallest was Canada with only 2,079 volumes per faculty member. The ratio of highest to lowest was 1.57 to 1.00. The no response percentage was low.

In summary, the leading denominations in volume holdings were Methodist and Roman Catholic with Baptist, Independent, and Other Denominations following. Weakest denominations were the Churches of Christ, Congregational, and Mennonite. By state and province, the leaders were New York, Pennsylvania, Tennessee, and Texas.

Periodical Title Subscriptions

Next we will take up another type of library material, periodical subscriptions. We will examine subscriptions by type of library, by region, by chief librarian's gender, by expenditure level, and finally by denomination. In beginning this discussion of subscriptions we can look at several small analyses. But first we will note that this subsection covers subscriptions only, since bound periodical volumes were counted in the book volume variable discussed above.

Longitudinal table 4.98 enables us to see the mean number of periodical titles subscribed to by each *type of library*. The scholarly 1978 database showed a mean of 546 periodical titles and the 1988 database showed a mean of 550 titles, a gain of only one percent in the decade. Largest scholarly increase was for the seminary libraries with 9 percent, still small. Largest negative figure was for the history/archives group at −15 percent. Table 4.99 for 1988 shows the mean number of subscriptions by each scholarly library denomination. Largest was the UCC group with an average of 745 titles and next was Lutheran with 679. Smallest number of titles was that of the Mennonite group with 334.

For type of library the seminary libraries gained 9.3 percent during the decade to lead the entire group. History/archives lost 15 percent to lead in a negative direction. University libraries contained the largest number of titles (of all subject fields), 1,139 in 1978 and 1,134 in 1988. Next was senior college libraries with 538 titles for 1988. Convents/monasteries held the smallest numbers: sixty-eight and sixty-three titles. Change percentage was highest for seminaries.

By type of library we have a list of the leading *junior college* libraries for 1988 in table 4.100. Half of them were Roman Catholic. Red Deer College in Alberta led with fifteen hundred subscriptions. Seven 1978 *senior colleges* led in subscriptions held, seventeen hundred-plus titles (the maximum) apiece. Eight of them were Roman Catholic or Other Denominations libraries. Pennsylvania led the states with about half of the list. Senior colleges in 1988 included nineteen libraries at the seventeen-hundred-plus level as well as ten at the fifteen hundred level, so no table was made for them. For *university* libraries the list was long—sixty-one of them—at the seventeen-hundred-plus level, so no table could be made.

Seminary libraries for 1988 are shown in table 4.101. Two libraries led in subscriptions with seventeen hundred-plus titles each, the Graduate Theological Union and the Southwestern Baptist Theological Seminary. Four of the top ten libraries were Baptist. *Convent/monastery* libraries in

1988 listed two libraries at the 150 level, the institutions in Wappingers Falls, New York, and Marvin, South Dakota. Below them were fourteen libraries at the fifty-periodical title level. This was not the kind of information that can easily be put into a table, however.

In the *denominational headquarters* table for 1988 the numbers were smaller and the denominations more varied, but New York led by location. For *history/archives* libraries again the numbers were modest and the denominations still varied. New York and Pennsylvania led by location in table 4.102 for 1988.

If we look at *regional* variations, we can see for 1988 that the Rocky Mountains averaged 548 periodical titles while the Southwest averaged only 410, a difference of a third. For both 1978 and 1988, periodical subscriptions differed *between the sexes.* Libraries headed by males subscribed to 49 percent more titles (1978) than did libraries headed by females, in spite of the fact that the two sexes headed almost equal numbers of libraries.

For *library expenditures,* the expected correlation was obtained, also. The number of titles to which the library subscribed rose regularly commensurate with the level of the total expenditure. Libraries spending $1,500 or under subscribed to fifty titles on the average, while libraries spending $510,001 or over averaged 1,632 titles in 1978 among those libraries subscribing to titles of any kind. Incidentally, a total of 82 percent of the libraries said that they subscribed to periodical titles.

Now we can look at periodical subscription totals in detailed *denominational* tables. See table 4.99 for 1988. How did *Baptist* libraries fare on this new variable? Eight of them appeared for 1988 at the highest level of subscriptions, seventeen hundred-plus titles, so they fared well. Seven of them were university and two were seminary libraries. On the full list, libraries were spread over a large geographic area, from Texas to Nova Scotia.

Most *Christian* libraries on the "largest" table, 4.103, for 1988, were much smaller than the Baptist libraries described above. The TCU library led the table and reached the top subscription level. The tables represented a good mix of library types. The 1978 and 1988 *Churches of Christ* tables were quite similar. They showed two university libraries, Pepperdine and Abilene Christian, at the top. The geographic spread of the libraries was large, from California to Tennessee, with Tennessee (Southeast) being the location of almost half of the libraries.

Table 4.104 shows 1988 *Congregational* libraries. Washburn led the table with a high score. Two of the *Episcopal/Anglican* libraries, the

University of the South and Bishop's University, were the leaders and were at the top level. They were followed by four other libraries with large periodical subscription lists. Three of the seven libraries were located in seminaries. New York and Tennessee made up more than half of the list.

Two outstanding *Independent* libraries in the 1978 table (not shown) were not repeated in table 4.105 for 1988 because their subscription total was omitted from the 1988 *ALD*. They were Union Theological Seminary and Yale University Divinity School. On the other hand four libraries equaled or exceeded the highest level of subscription totals. Six of the ten large libraries were located in universities, and two were in seminaries.

Three scholarly 1988 *Lutheran* libraries reached the highest level in subscriptions, seventeen hundred-plus titles. Three of this table's libraries were located in Minnesota and two in Pennsylvania. The entire list of (mostly college) libraries presented a strong picture (table 4.106 for 1988). *Mennonite* libraries are shown in table 4.107 (1988). None reached the top level of subscriptions. Half were located in Indiana and Kansas. All nine 1988 *Methodist* libraries reached the top end of the periodical frequency chart, seventeen hundred-plus titles. They were located in nine different states and all but one, a medical school, were located in universities, some of them sizeable. Another strong Methodist showing.

Scholarly *Other Denomination* libraries are shown in Table 4.108 (1988). All ten of them reached the top level of periodical title holdings, seventeen hundred-plus titles, an excellent showing. Six were located in universities, and two each in Michigan, Pennsylvania, and Canada, a varied geographical scene. Four *Presbyterian* libraries reached the top level by number of subscriptions, and all twelve libraries were above the thousand-title level. The four were Davidson, Tulsa, Lafayette, and Queen's. Only one of these 1988 libraries was located in a university.

Only one 1988 scholarly *United Church of Christ* library, the Franklin and Marshall College Library, reached the top level in number of subscriptions, and only half of the libraries on the list were above the thousand-title level. Only two of these libraries were located in universities. By state, Pennsylvania had three libraries, North Carolina and Missouri two each. Three separate regions were seen in 1988 table 4.109.

Among 1988 *Jewish* only two libraries reached the top level, whereas three 1978 Jewish libraries reached that level of subscriptions. How could this happen? Hebrew Union College in Cincinnati dropped from seventeen hundred to eleven hundred periodical titles during the decade, as reported in the *ALD*. Only three 1988 libraries were above the thousand-title level. Again we see that half of the Jewish libraries were located in New York City and one-fourth of them in Waltham, Massachusetts. Three-fourths of these libraries were located in Jewish religious colleges or special libraries. No table could be made for *Roman Catholic* libraries because it included thirty-seven libraries listing seventeen hundred-plus periodical titles apiece!

In summary, we can characterize the following denominations as giving a strong performance on periodical title holdings: Baptist, Methodist, Other Denominations, and Roman Catholic. The following gave fair performances: Independent, Lutheran, and Presbyterian. The following denominations were comparatively weak: Congregational, Mennonite, and Jewish. The states and provinces mentioned most often as the locations of these libraries were Pennsylvania, New York, and Tennessee.

Vertical Files

In continuing this discussion of library material collections, we can now compare the various types of libraries, regions, total expenditures, and denominations with the number of vertical file drawers possessed. Vertical file holdings of various kinds often supplemented the book and periodical collections discussed above.

Longitudinal table 4.110 shows vertical file holdings in a summary table for scholarly libraries and thereby shows several interesting things about that situation. First, it shows the no response percentage to have been high, especially for the 1988 edition. The table shows further that while the mean number of drawers per library rose between editions, the total number of drawers fell by 4.2 percent during that period of time, as fewer libraries reported holdings.

Vertical files are seen in detail for *type of library* also in longitudinal table 4.110. Scholarly libraries averaged twenty-five drawers per library in 1978 and thirty-one drawers, or seven or eight file cases per library in 1988. University and history/archive libraries averaged forty-one drawers to lead the library types. Both senior colleges and denominational headquarters averaged thirty-one drawers per library, also, strong collections. Smallest means were those of the junior college and seminary libraries, at twenty-one and twenty-three vertical file drawers. Change was largest for junior colleges at 40 percent.

The matched pairs group, the cream of the crop, so to speak, and appearing in both databases, is slightly stronger in table scores than the entire database. For 1988 matched pairs the average was slightly larger at thirty-two drawers. For both the no longer listed and the newly listed libraries, the mean was smaller, twenty drawers. Percentage change was zero on the average, with university leading with 31 percent and five library types on the negative side. Incidentally the table suggests that for both of these rather curious categories, the senior college and seminary categories accounted for half to two-thirds of the total.

On the other hand, the no longer listed and newly listed were much weaker in scores than either the matched pairs or the entire database. Just what we can conclude from this finding is not clear—perhaps that the former group of libraries did die soon after 1978 or that their staff was not capable of sustaining the *ALD* listing in consecutive years; also that the newly listed group was still new and small. At any rate, both groups were weak.

We may continue our library type analysis now. Table 4.111 shows the 1988 *junior college* libraries with the largest number of files. St. Mary's College in Missouri led the list with 123 files. Other Denominations and Roman Catholic libraries led this list by denomination. Another table showed 1978 *senior college* libraries with the largest number of vertical files. Eleven libraries had 138+ or more of them. Methodist and Other Denominations led the list of denominations. *University* libraries in 1988 table 4.112 showed all the leaders at 138+ and a third of them from North Carolina. More than half of them were Baptist or Other Denominations.

Two 1988 *seminary* libraries reached the 138+ level. Asbury in Kentucky and General in New York. Methodist, Independent, and Jewish libraries accounted for more than half of the denominations. In 1988 table 4.113 for *convent/monastery* libraries, one, the Franciscan Monastery in Washington, D.C., led with a strong 123 vertical files. Among 1988 *denominational headquarters* libraries the Jewish Educational Service in New York led the way. In fact, 40 percent of these libraries were Jewish. And in 1988 table 4.114 for *history/archive* libraries, again a Jewish and also a UCC library reached the top level of 138+ drawers: the American Jewish Historical Society and the Evangelical and Reformed Historical Society.

We can study scholarly library vertical file drawers by *region* now. Largest mean figures by region were the four thirty-two-drawer scores of the Middle Atlantic, Southeast, West, and Middle West. Smallest was the sixteen drawers of the Rocky Mountains. By total annual *library expenditure* the overall mean number of files was twenty-five in 1978 and thirty-one in 1988, as we have seen before, a 24 percent increase. We find the expected positive correlation, also, between total expenditure and number of files. For libraries with $1,500 or less total expenditures, the mean number of files was 2.5, while for libraries with $510,000 total expenditures and over the mean number of files was 42.0.

Vertical file drawers by *denomination* can be studied now. Largest 1988 denominations by files were Jewish with a mean of fifty-six and UCC with a mean of thirty-six files. Smallest were Churches of Christ with seventeen and Episcopal/Anglican and Roman Catholic with twenty-seven files. Matched pairs 1988 overall mean was thirty-two, just 3 percent above the entire 1988 database figure.

Now let us examine vertical file holdings in detail by denomination and by specific library. Table 4.115 shows this picture for 1988 scholarly *Baptist* libraries. The Baptists presented a strong vertical file showing with six of their libraries reaching the maximum level of 138+ drawers: Samford, Mobile, Grand Canyon, Southwest Baptist, Campbell, and Wake Forest.

Three-fifths of the Baptist libraries were in universities, while three of the libraries were located in Alabama and two in North Carolina. This placed half of them in the Southeast. It is of interest to note that four of the libraries listed in the 1978 table were not listed in the 1988 table either because their vertical file collections were now too small or because these holdings were not listed at all in the 1988 *ALD*.[5]

For *Christian* scholarly libraries we see a similar and perhaps even stranger picture for 1978 and 1988. The three largest 1978 libraries were larger than any 1988 library, and two of them seem to have shrunk in the decade elapsing between the two databases. Three 1978 libraries were the only ones in either Christian database to reach the top level of vertical file holdings, Manhattan Christian College and the two Phillips University libraries. Further, half of the libraries listed in 1978 were not around in 1988. Note also that the nineteen libraries in two tables included two each from Oklahoma and Missouri, three from Tennessee, a regional picture that encompasses the Middle West, Southeast, and Southwest.

Vertical files seem to have been an erratic part of the *ALD* holdings listings, since both 1978 and 1988 tables for *Churches of Christ* were strange. Listings from 1978 were notably larger than those of 1988 (see table 4.116 for 1988). Most of the 1978 libraries did not repeat for 1988 nor did any library in either table reach the top holdings level. It would appear that Tennessee and Texas led the states in numbers of libraries, Southeast and Southwest. Altogether an unusual set of tables. The *Congregational* table for 1978 showed the usual three Congregational libraries with Washburn leading them, however.

What surprises do the two *Episcopal/Anglican* tables bring? None, thank goodness. The libraries listed in 1978 were much the same as those listed in 1988, and only table 4.117 for 1988 is reproduced here. One library, General Theological Seminary, reached the maximum shown in the questionnaire, 138+ vertical file drawers. Several well-known *Independent* religious institutions were represented here for 1988, e.g., Moody, Maharishi, JBU, and LeTourneau, as well as the American Bible Society. Only Moody reached the maximum number of file drawers, 138+, however.

Short *Lutheran* table 4.118 for 1988 libraries shows only one university to be represented. Three of the institutions shown were not academic. Two libraries reached the 138+ maximum level, Valparaiso University and Concordia Teachers College. *Mennonite* libraries, none of them universities, were studied for 1988. We notice here and elsewhere the presence of historical society libraries in these vertical file tables. Most of those societies were strong in both vertical file and microform holdings. Also, almost half of this table's libraries were located in Kansas.

Table 4.119 for 1988 scholarly *Methodist* libraries and its 1978 predecessor present problems that we have seen before in these vertical file tables. The overlap of libraries between tables was small, and there was little increase in number of files over the decade's time. Curious. The problem may be in the author's expectation that 1988 should exceed 1978 vertical file totals. In any case, table 4.119 shows three libraries to have reached the highest level. The *Other Denominations* group presented the expected picture, nothing unusual. Five libraries reached the highest level, a good showing: Loma Linda, Pacific Oaks, Central, Andrews, and Ashland. Three of them were in California and two were in Iowa, a group with widespread locations.

Presbyterian libraries presented a normal picture in the 1978 table (not shown) and 1988 table 4.120, except for a lack of repeating libraries. Each table had one top-level library, but the two tables had different libraries at the top: Covenant College and Johnson C. Smith University. Only two universities were listed here. *United Church of Christ* libraries were normal and even had one of their number at the 138+ drawer level, the Evangelical and Reformed Historical Society. Again most of these were 1988 college libraries.

Jewish libraries are seen in table 4.121 for 1988. Again there were more files in the 1978 than the 1988 table, but there were several libraries at the top level in each table, eight altogether. And again many libraries failed to repeat from the earlier to the later database. Seven of the eighteen libraries were located in New York City. Only five of the eighteen libraries were in academic institutions, quite distinctive. Most of the libraries seem to have served administrative or coordinating organizations. *Roman Catholic* is another denomination that maintains several libraries with large numbers of vertical files. Six of the 1988 libraries were at the maximum questionnaire level, and all ten of the table's libraries had over one hundred files. Seven of the ten were college libraries.

We can summarize the vertical file findings for specific libraries by denomination here. Thirty-two libraries reached the top level of files, 138+. Denominations with the largest number of top-level libraries were Baptist, Other Denominations, and Roman Catholic with Christian, Jewish, Lutheran, and Methodist following. Poorest were Churches of Christ and Congregational showings. The leading state was Tennessee.

We have a final longitudinal table for vertical file holdings also. Overall mean showed a 23 percent gain. Largest gain during the decade was 40 percent with junior colleges and 31 percent with senior colleges, and smallest was a change of −25 percent by the denominational headquarters. In fact, both denominational headquarters and history/archive had negative change figures, which was surprising for these two library types. Finally, the percent change 1978–88 in the longitudinal study showed the largest gain to be 36 percent for the Other Denominations and the largest loss to be −29 percent for the Mennonite denomination. Both no longer listed and newly listed libraries scored a mean of twenty files, or 35 percent less than the entire 1988 group.

Microform Holdings

Microforms may be studied by analyzing them for type of library, region, level of library expenditure, chief librarian's gender, and denomination. See longitudinal table 4.122. The database microform collections averaged 27,658 microforms per library for 1978 and 46,925 for 1988. This represented a 49 percent sample of the 1978 group of libraries and a 54 percent sample of the 1988 group of libraries, and also represented a 69.7 percent increase in holdings over the decade. A large jump.

By *type of library* we learn that the largest libraries were the university and history/archives groups and the smallest were the convent/monastery and denominational headquarters groups with 92,717 and 91,441 microforms and 1,696 and 1,775 microforms respectively. That was for 1978. For 1988 we see university and senior colleges with the largest collections and convent/monastery and denominational headquarters groups again with the smallest groups. The overall mean is 46,925 for 1988. Growth percentage was largest for seminaries and senior colleges.

We will look at type of library further for 1988, first for *junior colleges* in table 4.123. Two of these libraries held more than 100,000 microforms: Lindsey Wilson and Ricks College. A third of the table's libraries were Roman Catholic and a fourth were located in New York. For *senior college* we see a table filled with libraries at the maximum of the 230,000+ microforms for 1978. Four of them were located in Pennsylvania and four were Roman Catholic. Senior college libraries in 1988 were too numerous at the top level to allow us to make a table. There were thirty-one of them with 230,000+ microforms. For 1988 *university* libraries the problem was the same, with fifty libraries at the 230,000+ microform level.

For *seminary* libraries in table 4.124 for 1988 two libraries led the list, the Graduate Theological Union and St. Meinrad College, with 230,000+ microform titles each. More than a third of this table's libraries were Independent. For *convents/monasteries* in 1988 we see only two small microform collections, both Roman Catholic. *Denominational headquarters* in table 4.125 for 1988 again showed small collections of which almost half were Other Denominations libraries and a fourth were from New York.

Further, we have a longitudinal table for microform holdings and library type. Largest library type change for microforms was seminary, again with a 124 percent rise, and senior colleges were next with 105 percent. The smallest library type change for microforms was history/archives with −3 percent.

And by *region,* what have we? The Rocky Mountains region led with a mean of 68,570 microforms; Canada was next with 55,790 microforms. That was 1978. For 1988 we have 96,940 for Rocky Mountains and 68,740 for Southwest at the largest and 34,940 for Middle West and 38,520 for Southeast as the smallest. If we look at microform holdings by level of *library expenditure,* we can see that the collection size rose as the level of library expenditure rose. Table 4.126 shows this picture for 1988. Mean range of holdings was from 50 to 124,400 microforms as the expenditure level rose from under $1,500 to $510,000 and over expenditures.

When matched pairs were examined for microform scores, their scores were 10 percent higher than the mean for the entire database. No longer listed libraries averaged 4,659, and newly listed libraries averaged 12,970 titles. We can also look at microform holdings by *chief librarian's gender*. For 1978, male-led libraries averaged 33,390 microforms and female-led libraries averaged 19,930 of them or a ratio of 1.7 to 1.0. For 1988 the ratio was 54,920 to 37,340, male to female, or 1.5 to 1.0. So men headed the leading libraries again.

When we move on to *denomination*, the picture becomes more complicated. Jewish scholarly libraries led with 43,430 microforms in 1978 and Episcopal/Anglican were lowest with 5,692 in 1988. In 1988, the largest was the Lutheran group with a mean of 55,900 microforms and the smallest was the Jewish group with 14,310 microforms, after having been the largest in 1978.

For another look at microform holdings we will study them in table 4.127, which takes a comprehensive approach to the mean microform holdings for the 1988 scholarly database by denomination. The Roman Catholic, Lutheran, and Baptist groups were highest with an average of more than fifty-thousand microform titles per library. The Episcopal/ Anglican, Jewish, and Mennonite groups were lowest, with less than twenty thousand titles per library. Ratio of highest to lowest denominational holdings was 3.9 to 1.0. Two denominations must be crossed off due to the no response factor: Jewish and Mennonite. Overall 1988 mean was 46,920 microforms. The reader should also notice the denominational changes in emphasis from one type of material to another.

In this section we have the beginning of a new series of analyses by denomination of the specific libraries with the largest number of microforms. In a few cases, of course, library holdings exceeded the highest level allowed by the questionnaire—230,000+ titles. In other cases, holdings were much more modest. Four 1978 *Baptist* libraries were listed at the highest level, 230,000+ microforms, all four being universities: Ouchita Baptist, Wake Forest, Temple, and McMaster. In fact, seven of the eleven libraries in the table were located in universities. Two libraries were located in North Carolina, also. The 1988 Baptist printout listed sixteen libraries at the 230,000+ level, so no 1988 table was made.

Christian libraries showed considerable growth in numbers between the databases, and one library, Lynchburg College, was the sole representative on the lists that reached the highest level of microform holdings, table 4.128 for 1988. Both Phillips University libraries in Oklahoma appeared on the list, again a positive accomplishment. The state representation showed much scatter, but Oklahoma listed two libraries. Most of the libraries were located in undergraduate colleges.

Churches of Christ libraries had two representatives at the top holdings level, Pepperdine and Abilene Christian Universities. Almost half of these libraries were located in universities, and three of them were located in Texas. Our three faithful scholarly 1978 *Congregational* libraries can be seen in the next table, and again Washburn led the list. *Episcopal/Anglican* libraries for 1988 show that the University of the South was far ahead of the rest of the list. Two libraries were Canadian, two were Texan, and two were located in universities. *Independent* libraries for 1988 are shown in table 4.129. Seven of these libraries were at the top level by size of microform collection, two of them were Californian, and six of them were university libraries. A strong showing for Independent institutions!

Again seven libraries were listed at the top level among 1988 *Lutheran* libraries. And again three of them were located in the state of Minnesota. Well done! *Mennonite* libraries were the smallest group by size of 1988 microform collections. None were located in universities, but three were located in Kansas and two in Indiana. See table 4.130 for 1988.

Scholarly *Methodist* libraries had many microforms, as seen in table 4.131 (1988). All eleven of them made the highest level! No state had more than one representative, but the states stretched from California to Connecticut and Georgia. Four-fifths of them were university libraries. A strong showing! Tables were made of the 1988 *Other Denominations* libraries with the largest number of microforms. All eleven of them were at the highest level—three Mormon, two Quaker, and two Nazarene, among them. The table had a western bias in state location. A strong effort!

Presbyterian libraries are shown for 1988 in table 4.132. The presence of a historical/archives library was unusual. Two Texas and two Pennsylvania libraries can be seen. Only three university libraries were represented in this microform listing. Five libraries reached the top level of the table: Tulsa, Presbyterian Church Office of History, Trinity, Austin, and Queen's. Three in Pennsylvania and two in North Carolina made up half of the UCC 1988 libraries. Two *United Church of Christ* libraries reached the top level—Hood and Elon Colleges—with 230,000+ microforms, but only one university library was included.

Jewish libraries for 1988 are listed in table 4.133, which represented a surprise. Only one of them, the American Jewish Historical Society, reached the top level. Brandeis University was omitted from the table because its 1988 *ALD* entry listed no microform holdings. Jewish libraries were weak in microform holdings because the institutions listed in this table were small, with quite specialized collections. Again four libraries were located in New York City and two in Massachusetts, constituting two-thirds of the table. *Roman Catholic* 1988 libraries listed thirty-two libraries at the 230,000+ level so no table could be made.

In summary, a total of eighty-three libraries reached the top level in scholarly library microform holdings. The denominations with the most impressive quantity of microform holdings were Independent, Lutheran, Methodist, Other Denominations, and Roman Catholic, followed by Baptist and Presbyterian. Weakest were the Congregational and Mennonite groups. State location strengths were primarily in Texas, California, and Pennsylvania.

Several additional special analyses were made. A further longitudinal look at microform holdings by denomination shows some interesting facts. Percentage change was highest for Mennonite scholarly libraries, perhaps because of their small overall number. Their decade percentage change was 983 percent, from 1,583 to 17,146 microforms. Next was the UCC group with a 200 percent enlargement. Lowest was the Jewish group with −67 percent, for whatever reason.

For a more comprehensive approach, longitudinal table 4.134 takes a look at total cumulative material holdings (book volumes, periodical titles, vertical files, and microforms), by type of library. The mean decade growth rate was 31 percent. Senior college libraries grew the most at 36 percent with seminary collections next at 28 percent. The poorest growth rate was a negative 17 percent for history/archive libraries. Clearly, since this 31 percent growth rate was much smaller than the 70 percent book growth rate, the addition of the other three types of material to books reduced the total.

A longitudinal table for total holdings (cumulative)—book volumes, periodical titles, vertical files, and microforms (another unholy combination!)—by region showed the Rocky Mountains and the Southwest to lead the table. In terms of decade-long longitudinal gain Canada led with 71 percent and the Southwest was second with 44 percent. Poorest growth was Middle Atlantic with 3 percent. The no response rate was low. By denomination the same analysis showed considerable variation for total holdings (cumulative). Episcopal/Anglican led the longitudinal table by change percentage with 39 percent. Smallest change was −20 percent in the Jewish group.

Media Holdings

We now move into another facet of the material holdings series by taking up the scholarly libraries' holdings of audiovisual media. This brief section will discuss media by type of library, by region, and by denomination except for those listed separately here. In the 1978 scholarly database, 958 or 69.7 percent of the libraries had some media holdings and in 1988 these numbers rose slightly to 1,066 libraries and 74.4 percent. As an additional indication of its importance in the 1988 edition the *ALD* editors provided more detail than before on media holdings. We have no tables in this media subsection that list specific libraries, however, since only possession or nonpossession was recorded for individual libraries.

Two media tables for 1978 and 1988 show holdings by *type of library,* tables 4.135 and 4.136. The first thing the author looked for was evidence of a major holdings leap forward for 1988. However, there was no evidence of such a change, and in fact the percentage of scholarly libraries having media was much the same in 1988 as it was in 1978. Senior colleges and universities had media in the largest and convents/monasteries and denominational headquarters scholarly libraries had them in the smallest proportions in both years. For 1988 senior college and university libraries, 79 percent and 75 percent had media, respectively. More than half of the libraries with media were senior colleges.

By *region*, two additional tables show how media holdings were distributed, tables 4.137 for 1978 and 4.138 for 1988. Both tables cover both scholarly and popular libraries. The Southeast had the largest percentage of libraries with media, 61 percent. Canada lagged behind the U.S. libraries here, since only 42 percent of its libraries had media. That was for 1978. For 1988, again the Southeast was the leader with 66 percent of its libraries having media, and again Canada was at the bottom of the table with only 44 percent.

Table 4.139 for 1988 shows media holdings by *denomination*. Highest percentage was held by the Churches of Christ and the Christian denominations. Lowest was held by Jewish and Episcopal/Anglican denominations. This table shows a relatively modest difference between denominations, however, the range from highest to lowest being only from 85 percent to 65 percent or 1.3 to 1.0. Note that Protestant libraries were somewhat ahead of non-Protestant libraries in this subject area.

Map Holdings

Now this analysis in library material moves on to cover map holdings in a short section. We will touch on type of library differences and denominational differences. In the 1978 database 639, or 46.5 percent, of the libraries had some map holdings and in 1988, 433 or, 30.2 percent, of them reported map holdings, a drop for the libraries or a drop in directory listings of them, at least. What was the showing for map holdings by *library type*? Tables 4.140 and 4.141 for 1978 and 1988 give an impression of this situation, though it is compromised by so many no responses. The 1988 table shows that 37 percent of university and 35 percent of senior college libraries had maps, while only 13 percent of denominational headquarters and 17 percent of seminary libraries had maps in their collections.

In tables 4.142 and 4.143 we can see 1978 and 1988 map holdings and study the sharp drop during that period. The Baptist, Churches of Christ, Independent, Lutheran, Methodist, Other Denominations, Presbyterian, UCC, Jewish, and Roman Catholic *denominations* reflected the drop in holdings while the Mennonite and Episcopal/Anglican denominations did not. Surprising!

Leading 1988 denominations in map holdings were the Other Denominations, while the weakest denominations were the Jewish and United Church of Christ. Protestant libraries were slightly stronger on maps than non-Protestant libraries. The reason for the drop in number of libraries with maps, which was obviously widespread throughout the sample, could not be ascertained nor could the author tell whether or not it related more closely to a change in reporting definitions or techniques or to a drop in holdings.

Art Reproduction Holdings

This final library material holdings category features the analysis of art reproductions by library type, region, and denomination. It will be followed by both a short backward look to draw together the main findings of the media subsection and a short final summary of the entire library material section.

In 1978, 252, or 18.3 percent, of the scholarly libraries had some art reproduction holdings, and in 1988, 147, or 10.3 percent of them, showed art reproduction holdings. This change represented a large drop in holdings or at least directory indication thereof. We can study tables 4.144 and 4.145, for 1978 and 1988 for enlightenment here. They show that all denominations dropped in 1988 for this variable. No reason is known for this change, which may represent only a change in reporting policies. So both library map and art reproduction holdings dropped significantly 1978–88.

Table 4.146 for 1978 showed sharp differences between *library types* for art reproduction holdings. Leading were junior colleges, with almost a fourth having art reproductions. Senior colleges were a strong second and history/archives a strong third. Weakest here were seminary libraries, again. By *region*, table 4.147 shows 1978 art reproduction holdings. Again the Southeast region led the group with 20 percent of holdings. Next was the Middle West with 17 percent. Poorest was the West with only 10 percent. Note that tables 4.147, 4.148, and 4.149 covered the entire scholarly and popular library groups.

Mennonite (surprisingly enough!) and Methodist libraries led the way in 1988, with 18 percent and 14 percent of their scholarly libraries having art reproduction, while Episcopal/Anglican and Independent were the weakest *denominations* on this variable with only 3 percent apiece having them. This situation provided a ratio of 6 to 1 between highest and lowest percentages. Note that Protestant and non-Protestant pulled even in holdings here.

Holdings Summaries

In general and in a short summary when all three of these types of (or total) media categories—media, maps, and art reproductions—are considered, we have little uniformity, but Churches of Christ, United Church of Christ, senior colleges, universities, and junior colleges were among the strongest denominations and library types on media holdings and Episcopal/Anglican, Congregational, Jewish, and denominational headquarters where among the weakest. Obviously maps and art reproductions faded in popularity during the decade or at least were reported in smaller numbers or in different ways, and strong denominations were difficult to find for them. See table 4.148 for 1978 holdings combined.

When we look at total media holdings—media, maps, and art reproductions—by region, for all kinds of media combined, we see again the leadership of the Southeast with the Middle West next revealing 66 percent and 64 percent of the libraries with this form of material, table 4.148 for 1978. Canada and the Northeast were at 45 percent and 54 percent, table 4.149. We also see an overall mean of 1.6 media items per library. Rocky Mountains led with 1.9 items and Middle Atlantic was weakest with 1.5 items. Generally, media holdings were lacking with all groups showing negative change percentages.

In conclusion, a final summary was provided for the entire library material section by table 4.150 for 1988, which listed the scholarly libraries most often listed on the study's tables. These are the most popular libraries in terms of "largest" number of table listings for the entire 1988 sample. Brown and Notre Dame Universities led this list. It showed half of these leaders to have been Roman Catholic, and Baptists and Methodists added another quarter of the total. By state and province, there was much scatter.

As a final library material holdings summary covering all types of material—book volumes, periodical titles, vertical files, microforms, and all three types of media—a tally showed Baptist, Methodist, Other Denominations, and Roman Catholic to be the leading denominations, with Christian and Churches of Christ in the second rank. Tennessee and Pennsylvania led the states and provinces in holdings, with New York and Texas not far behind.

Annual Library Expenditure

Now we turn to a new and fundamental variable—expenditure—which is divided into four separate parts—material, personnel, other, and total.

Material Expenditure

Annual material expenditure—expenditure for all types of library material—is an important variable for any library. It is one of the two principal divisions of a library's total expenditures, along with personnel. Let us turn to an examination of the highest expenditures on material by 1988 types of libraries, then by region, then by chief librarian's gender, then by total library expenditure and finally by denomination.

Longitudinal table 4.151 shows for 1988 an overall mean annual scholarly library material expenditure of $81,500, as compared with a 1978 figure of $49,490, and therefore a strong 65 percent increase during the decade. Highest among the scholarly *library types* was the university group with a mean expenditure of $144,352. Next was senior colleges with $82,177. Lowest were convent/monastery and history/archives libraries with $10,750 and $12,994 respectively. Again the corresponding matched pairs overall mean figure was $88,530, a little larger than the figure for the 1988 database. By the longitudinal study we see that expenditures for history/archives and denominational headquarters rose the largest amount (1978–88). University libraries, with the largest beginning figure, rose the smallest amount.

Table 4.152 for 1988 shows *junior colleges* and lists the libraries with the highest expenditure. Four libraries and five denominations led this list by spending $175,000+ per year on material: Ricks, St. Mary's, Kettering, and Red Deer. Four of the entire library list were located in Canada, and five of them were Roman Catholic.

Among *senior college* libraries in table 4.153 for 1978, twelve libraries reached the top annual level of $175,000+ spent on material. More than half were Other Denominations or Roman Catholic. Forty percent of them were located in Pennsylvania. The 1988 table was longer and included the same libraries at the same level, but twenty-two of them were tied at the $175,000+ level, so no table was made.

For 1988 *university* libraries, two hundred tied at the $175,000 level so no table could be made. The same pattern was found for 1988 for *seminary* libraries, of which fifteen were in the top category. There was much scatter by denomination as well as by geographic location. For *convent/monastery* libraries, all Roman Catholic and all shown in 1988 table 4.154, we can see that material expenditures were quite low. Passionist Monastery led with a $37,500 figure.

Material expenditure in 1988 by *denominational headquarters* libraries showed again that expenditures were small with the Southern Baptist Convention library in Richmond leading the way. Independent and Roman Catholic libraries led with half of the entire group. Much geographic scatter was found. The *history/archive* libraries shown in the 1988 table were again relatively small. No library exceeded $100,000 in expenditures. Both location and denomination showed much scatter.

We have reproduced a longitudinal table for material expenditures by library type. Although the overall percentage change was 65 percent, a strong statement of the importance of material to these libraries, it was not as strong as that made by the popular libraries that had a material expenditure percentage change twice as high. In the scholarly change, leading library types were history/archives and denominational headquarters, both well above 200 percent. Convent/monastery and seminary libraries were also strong in this area. Smallest percentage change was the university group, which had the largest initial figures.

Annual scholarly library material expenditure by *region* showed the largest region by mean material expenditure to be the Middle Atlantic, with $94,300, and the smallest to be the Rocky Mountains with $66,700, a 41 percent difference. At the outset we see that the material expenditure among libraries with *male chief librarians* was one-third higher than that among libraries with female chief librarians for 1988. By *total expenditure,* table 4.155 for 1988 shows the strong positive correlation between total expenditure and material expenditure when both scholarly and popular libraries are included. At a total expenditure level of $1,500 or less, $678 was spent on material. At a total expenditure level of $510,000 and over, however, $167,400 was spent on material. Notice that the proportions, however, were significantly different: 45 percent vs. 33 percent.

By *denomination,* Presbyterian and Methodist led with $98,960 and $95,698 annual material expenditures, and Mennonite and Christian were poorest with $33,800 and $54,150 material expenditures. The ratio between the highest and lowest expenditures was 2.9 to 1.0. We can shift to matched pairs now, and their overall mean was 8 percent larger than the entire database figure. The no longer listed and newly listed means were 81 percent lower and 57 percent lower than that for the entire database. The longitudinal matched pairs analysis in another table brought an overall change figure of 65 percent, the same as that for the 1988 database. The largest change percent was 90 percent for Independent and the smallest was 19 percent for Christians.

Let us see how the various denominations fared on material expenditure as we examine the lists of individual libraries. Among the *Baptist*, we see that five libraries reached the top level allowed by the questionnaire, $175,000+: Mississippi, Wake Forest University, Benedict, Furman, and Richmond Colleges. The 1978 table showed two seminary libraries on the list of leading libraries. Two of the libraries were located in South Carolina. Table 4.156 shows *Christian* 1988 libraries with the largest annual material expenditure. Three libraries reached the top category of $175,000+ per year: Chapman, Texas Christian, and Lynchburg. Oklahoma claimed two from this library list.

Churches of Christ libraries placed two of their number at the top annual expenditure level. They were two university libraries seen often in this denomination's tables, Pepperdine and Abilene Christian. Tennessee and Texas (Southeast and Southwest regions) provided half of the 1988 libraries. The small 1978 *Congregational* library table shows the same three libraries that dominated previous Congregational tables. Again Washburn was well ahead of the other two libraries.

Four *Episcopal/Anglican* libraries led the 1988 table at the highest level: St. Mary's, Kenyon, University of the South and Bishop's. Four of the ten libraries belonged to seminaries, an unusually high proportion for that type of library. Two Tennessee and two New York libraries led the material expenditure list. *Independent* 1978 libraries can be seen in table 4.157. Only two libraries reached the top level—Brown and McGill Universities. Three seminaries were represented here also. California libraries led the way with four representatives, followed by two Kentucky libraries.

For 1978 *Lutheran* libraries we can see no top-level libraries, but the ten high-level institutions were led by Wittenburg and Gettysburg at $152,000. Three Pennsylvania and two Minnesota locations led the table. Colleges and universities were about even in number here. *Mennonite* libraries can be seen in table 4.158 (1988). Again all Mennonite libraries were colleges, except for one seminary. Two Indiana and two Kansas libraries led the table by state, a Middle Western material expenditure focus.

Methodist 1978 libraries were impressive. There were eight top-level and four nearly top-level libraries, but there was much scatter by location. Most of these libraries represented universities. Another denominational group doing well for annual material expenditure was *Other Denominations*, table 4.159 for 1978. Six of these libraries were at the top level of $175,000+ and the rest ranked high. The table featured California, Michigan, and Pennsylvania as well as senior college and university libraries. *Presbyterian* presented a short 1978 table of senior college libraries, of which four reached the top level of annual material expenditure at $175,000+: Davidson, Lafayette, Trinity, and Queen's. Pennsylvania claimed two libraries here.

Six *United Church of Christ* libraries spent $175,000 or more per year on material to lead table 4.160 for 1988. Pennsylvania libraries constituted one-third of the entire list, a Middle Atlantic focus. Three 1988 *Jewish* libraries reached the highest category—Brandeis, Yeshiva, and Hebrew Union. Four of them were located in New York City, two in Pennsylvania, and two in Massachusetts, all in the Northeast and Middle

Atlantic regions. No *Roman Catholic* table could be made, but Catholic libraries at the top level were numerous, ninety-five of them at $175,000+.

In summary, 137 libraries reached the top annual material expenditure level. The leading denominations were Baptist, Episcopal/Anglican, Lutheran, Methodist, Other Denominations, and Roman Catholic, with Christian, Jewish, Presbyterian, and United Church of Christ following. Pennsylvania and Texas led the states in table location.

Personnel Expenditure

We can examine the highest expenditure for scholarly library personnel through tables showing library type, region, library expenditure, chief librarian's gender, and denomination in this series. Mean total number of personnel expenditures was $92,463 for 1978 and $141,520 for 1988. This showed a gain of 53 percent, substantial. These figures represented two-thirds of the 1978 database and 69 percent of the 1988 database, which listed their personnel expenditures. Again university and senior colleges led the way by *library type,* and convent/monastery was smallest in 1988. Percentage expenditure increase was highest for history/archives and lowest for university libraries.

Table 4.161 for 1988 featured *junior college* libraries. Four libraries reached the top category for personnel expenditure level of $325,000+ per year: Ricks, Red Deer, and Vanier Colleges and Cégep de Jonquière. Three of these four leaders were Canadian and two were Roman Catholic. Half of the entire table's libraries were Roman Catholic and two-thirds were Canadian, New York, and North Carolina libraries. No tables could be made for *senior college* or *university* due to the large number of libraries tied for the top position at $325,000+ per library. Senior college had fifty-eight libraries in the first rank, and university had 115.

Many *seminary* libraries had high personnel expenditures. Twelve of the 1988 libraries reached the top category of $325,000+ per year. By denomination and by location there was much scatter. For the 1988 *convent/monastery* libraries in table 4.162 there were few paid personnel and much scatter in location. Independent and Other Denominations equaled half of the total number of libraries in the 1988 table for *denominational headquarters*. There was much spread here in geographic location. *History/archive* libraries in 1988 can be seen in table 4.163. Again no library reached the top level, but several libraries had sizeable personnel expenditure totals. A fourth were Baptist, and location was again scattered.

We can see considerable difference among the library types. The largest 1978–88 difference was $27,330 for the history/archives centers. This was a difference of 652 percent. In 1988 the largest type of library was $265,400 for university libraries again. Smallest was the denominational headquarters group with an expenditure of $38,380. Matched pair levels were slightly above those of the entire database.

By *region*, we can see considerable difference in the mean personnel expenditures. The 1978 region with the largest personnel expenditure was Canada at $141,000. This was surprising, but their dollars bought less than did American dollars. Next was the West. The smallest expenditure was that in the Rocky Mountains region with $71,750, and then came the Southeast. The 1988 region with the highest expenditure was the West with $166,300, and the region with the smallest personnel expenditure was Rocky Mountains again with $109,800, improved by 53 percent from 1978.

If we examine mean personnel expenditures by total *library expenditure,* we see that the one did rise as the other rose also. At $1,500 and under total expenditure, the mean personnel expenditure was $0, while at $510,000 and over total expenditure, the mean personnel expenditure was $317,500. That was for 1978. The range for 1988 was $8,750 to $312,300, or a ratio of 35.7 to 1.0. If we examine the male to female *chief librarian ratio* for personnel expenditure we can see that for 1978 it was $109,000 to $69,260 or 1.6 to 1.0 while the ratio for 1988 was $161,000 to $116,800, or 1.4 to 1.0. Males won again. Expenditure among libraries with male chief librarians was one-third higher than among libraries with female chief librarians for 1988.

By *denomination*, what was the strongest group on mean personnel expenditure? For 1978, the Jewish group spent $142,200 per library, and the Lutheran group spent $122,400 per library. The smallest sums were spent by the Churches of Christ at $49,120 and the Christian group at $67,380 per year. So much for 1978. At the end of the decade the largest denominational expenditures were again Lutheran with $176,400 and Jewish with $175,200. Smallest were Mennonite with $70,790 (no figure available for 1978) and again Churches of Christ with $94,020. Matched pair expenditures were about the same or somewhat larger.

Now we have reached the tables showing the specific leading libraries by denomination for annual personnel expenditure. This set of tables provides one of the two other major expenditure table sets mentioned above.

The table showed the denominational standings on personnel expenditures for scholarly libraries. When we examine each denomination separately through this series of variables, we can see what level of performance it gave and in which states it was located as a group. In this set of tables we will see many libraries repeating their fine performances from previous tables.

The only *Baptist* table available represented 1978 and was not reproduced here. Five libraries reached the highest personnel expenditure level, $325,000+ per year: Wake Forest, Temple, Southwestern Baptist Theological Seminary, Richmond, and Acadia. Four university and one seminary library led by reaching the highest level of expenditure. By state, Texas and South Carolina led this table, from the Southeast and Southwest regions. Table 4.164 shows *Christian* libraries in 1988 with two of them reaching the highest level: Chapman University and TCU. Both Phillips University libraries were included in this personnel list again, as well as two Oklahoma libraries.

The 1988 *Churches of Christ* table demonstrated that the same libraries were personnel expenditure leaders in 1988 that had been leaders in 1978, usually with larger scores on the variables. Two university libraries led the table by type of library and equaled the highest expenditure level in dollars—Pepperdine and Abilene Christian. Three Tennessee libraries (Southeast region) led the list by state. *Congregational* libraries from 1978 showed again that Washburn University led with a creditable score.

Episcopal and *Anglican* libraries are seen in table 4.165 for 1988 institutions. Three of them scored at the highest level, but no state had a particularly strong showing here: Kenyon, University of the South, and Bishop's. Three seminaries were included in the list. Five seminary libraries were included in the 1978 *Independent* table. Only one library reached the highest level, $325,000+, that of Brown University. Three California and two Kentucky libraries were leaders by state and constituted half of the table. All others reached a high level, but none reached the top level in personnel expenditures.

Lutheran libraries are listed in table 4.166 for 1978, and while all were above $177,000, none reached the top level. Two Minnesota and two Ohio libraries lead the representation by state. Personnel expenditures were quite modest for *Mennonite* libraries in 1988. Again no universities can be seen, but two historical libraries and one seminary break the string of undergraduate colleges. Three Indiana and three Kansas libraries lead the list by state, a Middle Western focus.

Seven university libraries constitute the entire printed 1978 *Methodist* list for personnel expenditures, and all of them reached the highest level. Each one was from a different state, and they were from six different regions. Table 4.167 shows these figures. Very good. The number of 1978 *Other Denominations* libraries reaching the highest expenditure level was even larger, eight of them altogether. By state, California with three and Michigan and Pennsylvania with two each constituted 70 percent of this table and suggested strong and wide geographic coverage. Mormons, Seventh-day Adventists, and Quakers dominated the table of annual expenditures for personnel, and half were colleges and half universities. Another strong record!

Presbyterian libraries for 1978 are shown in table 4.168 and for 1988 are shown in table 4.169. Two of them in 1978 and all eleven libraries in 1988 spent an amount on personnel that placed them at the highest level, $325,000+. Again, the reason for showing both tables is that there was so much difference in the specific libraries listed in them, six of the 1988 libraries not being listed in the 1978 table. Four of the libraries were located in Pennsylvania and three in North Carolina, thereby emphasizing the Middle Atlantic and Southeast regions.

Four 1988 *United Church of Christ* libraries were at the top level: Elmhurst, Cedar Crest, Franklin and Marshall, and Fisk. Three of the libraries were located in Pennsylvania and two in Missouri. Table 4.170 shows the 1988 *Jewish* libraries with the largest annual personnel expenditures. Four of them reached the highest level of expenditures, $325,000+: Brandeis, Jewish Theological Seminary, Yeshiva, and Hebrew Union College. Three libraries were located in New York City and two in Massachusetts. Again no table could be made for *Roman Catholic* libraries, but it had seventy-two libraries tied at $325,000+ in 1988.

In summary, which denominations led the final list in annual personnel expenditures? One hundred nineteen libraries reached the top expenditure level and Methodist, Other Denominations, Presbyterian, and Roman Catholic led (entirely different from the material expenditure leader list!) with Baptist, Episcopal/Anglican, Jewish, and United Church of Christ following. As usual, the Congregational and Mennonite denominations were weakest. By state, locations in Pennsylvania and California led this series of tables.

Before closing this section, we have longitudinal studies of personnel expenditure by type of library and denomination. The history/archive libraries were the leaders with a 102 percent increase for the decade. Seminaries were next with an 83 percent change. Smallest change was found in the university group by type of library. Independent and Churches of Christ were the decade change leaders, with over 110 percent increases. Smallest increases were those of the Jewish at 35 percent and Methodist at 41 percent.

Other Expenditure

The Other expenditure variable was the third of four parts of the library expenditure series of variables. It covered administrative expenses such as staff travel, hospitality, library supplies, equipment, utilities, repair, remodeling, and the special expenses incurred each year. Normally it was the smallest of the four expenditure categories. Types of libraries, region, expenditure, and denominations were analyzed here. How did they look in this area?

Two general tables were made for Other expenditure. One described Other expenditures by type of library and the other by denomination. Both showed $20,000 expenditures for each category so are not reproduced here. Mean Other expenditure was $13,380 in 1978 and $17,280 in 1988, showing a modest growth of 29 percent.

Table 4.171 for 1988 shows Other expenditure by *library type*. University libraries spent the largest amount, on the average, $19,450, and covents/monasteries spent the least, $0. Matched pairs scored about the same as the entire database, and the no longer listed and newly listed groups had too few cases to warrant consideration. Longitudinal increased percentage in mean scores were highest for history/archive and smallest for convent/monastery libraries.

We have three detailed types of library tables for Other expenditures. Almost all of the *junior colleges* leading in these expenditures were at the maximum level of $20,000+, and almost half of them were Canadian. *Senior college* libraries for 1988 were quite numerous—250 of them in all at the $20,000+ level—so no table could be made for them. *University* libraries had the same problem in 1988. Ninety libraries tied for the lead at $20,000+ each, so no table could be made. *Seminary* libraries in table 4.172 for 1978 show eleven institutions to have reached the $20,000+ annual Other expenditure level. Independent claimed more than a fourth of the total, and California and Ohio claimed more than a third of them. Seminary libraries for 1988 were numerous at the $20,000+ level, forty of them, so no table could be made here.

Denominational headquarters libraries for 1988 showed three libraries to have spent at the maximum level: Seventh-day Adventists, Jewish, and Southern Baptist Convention. *History/archive* libraries can be seen in table 4.173 for 1988 and show six libraries to have spent at the maximum level.

We have a longitudinal table for Other expenditures by library type also. The type of library that moved up the most during the decade was history/archives, again with 110 percent. Seminaries did well also at 55 percent. Only denominational headquarters had a negative change and moved down by 3 percent. Other expenditure differed very little from one *region* to another. The Southwest region had the highest annual expenditure, and the Rocky Mountains region the smallest.

The author also examined the annual Other scholarly library expenditure by total annual *library expenditure*. It showed the expected strong positive correlation. For libraries with total library expenditure of $510,000 and over the average Other expenditure reached $19,790 in 1988, very high.

The *denomination* spending the most in 1988 was Lutheran, with $19,070, and the denomination spending the least was Mennonite, with $13,780. The matched pairs 1988 mean was $17,350, less than one percent larger than the entire database mean. A longitudinal table for Other expenditures by denomination showed that the largest denominational increase was Episcopal/Anglican at 70 percent and the smallest was the Other Denominations group at 15 percent.

Now we are ready for the detailed analysis of specific libraries by denomination. All twelve 1978 *Baptist* libraries reached the top level of the questionnaire range, $20,000+, shown in table 4.174, a complete success. Two libraries belonged to seminaries and the rest were equally divided between college and university. By state, North Carolina provided two libraries and so did South Carolina, a southeast regional focus. Four *Christian* 1978 libraries reached the top level—Chapman, Hiram, Phillips, and TCU—while others were below it. Two-thirds of the table were college libraries. Texas and Oklahoma provided two libraries apiece.

Churches of Christ provided two libraries at the top level—Oklahoma Christian and Abilene Christian. Others were well below that standard. Most of the libraries were located in colleges, one, in a junior college. Texas provided two libraries, as did Oregon. A modest showing in table 4.175 for 1978. Three 1978 *Episcopal/Anglican* libraries made the top score—Hobart and William Smith College, University of the South, and Bishop's University. Half of the institutions were seminaries! Three New

York and two Canadian libraries constituted the leaders by state and province.

Seven *Independent* libraries reached the highest level for Other expenditures, $20,000+, a good showing. See table 4.176 for 1978. The table was well supplied with seminaries, two of them being counted, plus four colleges. California led the states in providing three libraries. Four denominations—*Lutheran, Methodist, Other Denominations,* and *Presbyterian*—had too many libraries listed at the $20,000+ level for tables to be made. In order they listed fifteen, twenty-four, twenty-two, and fifteen libraries at maximum expenditure level.

For *United Church of Christ* two libraries can be seen in the 1978 table: Eden Webster University and Lakeland College. They made the top level on that questionnaire. Three seminaries and four colleges made up most of the table, and Wisconsin had two representatives on it. The 1978 *Jewish* libraries table showed that two libraries reached the top level: Yeshiva and Hebrew Union College. Again, no table could be made for the *Roman Catholic* denomination since it had eighty libraries at the $20,000+ level.

In summary, 188 libraries reached the highest level, $20,000+, and the leading denominations for Other expenditure were Baptist, Lutheran, Methodist, Other Denominations, Presbyterian, and Roman Catholic, with Christian and Independent following. Weakest were the Churches of Christ, Jewish, and United Church of Christ denominations. By state, lone star Texas led the way.

Total Library Expenditure

Total expenditure was obviously of great importance in enabling each library to meet the needs of its users, and this measure provides a way for us to gauge the library's potential for meeting these needs. As is true for all of the analyses described in this study, this one has the objective of ascertaining the characteristics of the variables being examined in each section of it. A summary will pull the findings together and describe their essence at the end of the analysis.

First, we will examine total expenditure by type of library, expenditure per student enrolled (and also per faculty member), and then we will examine it by region, by number of consortium memberships, per student, by chief librarian's gender, and finally by denomination. First we may look at *type of library* briefly and for 1978 only in table 4.177. This table shows total expenditure to have been higher by university libraries than by any other type, $348,400. Smallest type of library was convent/monastery, at only $4,682. Tables 4.178 for 1978 and 4.179 for 1988 show annual library expenditure by library type. The 1978 mean expenditure for scholarly libraries was $140,700, and the 1988 mean was $249,100. University and senior college libraries led the types in expenditures.

Next comes a more detailed analysis of 1988 tables. We start with *junior college* library table 4.180. These colleges did surprisingly well, four of them reaching the maximum level of $560,000+ in total expenditures—Ricks, Red Deer, and Vanier Colleges and Cégep de Jonquière. Half were Roman Catholic and almost half were Canadian (four were based in Quebec).

Senior colleges were well represented. Six of them reached the $560,000+ level, a good number: Ambassador, Loyola (Baltimore), Boston, Mercy, Bryn Mawr, and Swarthmore Colleges. All others on the list were at a relatively high level also. Almost half of them were Roman Catholic institutions and more than a third were located in Pennsylvania. Roman Catholic libraries were largest in terms of total expenditures.

University libraries were numerous at the maximum expenditure level, $560,000+ , one hundred of them, so no table was made. *Seminary* libraries can be seen in table 4.181. All thirteen of them scored at the top level, a fine showing. Almost a fourth of them were from the Independent denominational group, and there was much scatter by location. Largest number of volumes per library belonged to the Methodist and Independent groups. All of their 1978–88 longitudinal change percentages were high. *Convent/monastery* libraries generally had small expenditures, if any. However, the Passionist monastery spent $70,000. More than a fourth of these sequestered institutions were located in Virginia.

Denominational headquarters libraries can be seen in table 4.182. Only two libraries had major expenditures, both Southern Baptist. Other Denominations and Baptist libraries combined for almost two-thirds of the total, while geographic locations were scattered. The American Jewish Historical Society in Waltham, Massachusetts, led the table for *history/archive* libraries with a top level expenditure of $560,000+. The other libraries were strong in this variable also. Other Denominations and Mennonites were the strongest denominations and made up almost half of the list. A fourth of the libraries were located in Massachusetts.

Next comes an analysis of the mean annual total library expenditure *per student enrolled* and by library type. The two overall mean expenditures were $172 for 1978 and $349 for 1988, one about twice as large as the other. Largest expenditure was that of the seminary libraries in both cases, the 1988 figure reaching $848 per student. Ah, the rich seminaries! So expenditure rose much more quickly than enrollment. Smallest expenditure per student was in university libraries in both cases. A separate study was made of annual library expenditure *per faculty member,* and it showed much the same picture as student enrollment in which seminaries greatly outdistanced the other types of scholarly libraries.

In addition, we have two *special studies* of total expenditure. First table 4.183 for 1988 showed total annual library expenditure by *region* for matched pairs. It showed the West to lead the group through a $322,400 expenditure, with Canada next at $310,800. Smallest expenditure was Rocky Mountains at $237,300, with the Middle West next at $243,900. Table 4.184 shows total expenditure per student by region. Which region led this table? The Middle Atlantic and Rocky Mountains again led in 1988. The Southwest was the poorest region in both years.

The second special study showed total expenditure by number of consortium memberships. For those libraries with one consortium membership the mean expenditure was $207,000, but for libraries with six memberships the mean expenditure was $454,300 per library. So again the two variables correlated positively for these well-supported libraries.

Now we come to the detailed tables for the various denominations. Total annual expenditure by *denomination* was shown in the following series of tables. We may begin this series with the only *Baptist* table made, table 4.185 for 1978 libraries. Seven Baptist libraries reached the top level of annual support, even in that year, $560,000+, a good performance: Wake Forest, Southwestern Baptist Theological Seminary, Baylor, Richmond, Temple, Acadia, and McMaster. Most of the table's libraries were located in universities, but two were located in seminaries. Two of the libraries were located in Texas and two in South Carolina. The 1988 Baptist group listed nineteen libraries tied at the $560,000+ level.

For 1988 *Christian* libraries, three reached the top level of expenditure of more than $500,000 annually: Chapman, Lynchburg College, and TCU. Two libraries were located in Tennessee and two in Enid, Oklahoma. Short table 4.186 shows 1988 *Churches of Christ* libraries. Two of them, Pepperdine and Abilene Christian, reached the questionnaire's top level. The other libraries in the table were also old favorites from previous lists. Two of them were located in Tennessee.

Congregational libraries were taken from the 1978 database. Again there were three familiar libraries and again Washburn led the way. The expenditure levels were modest. *Episcopal/Anglican* libraries can be reviewed in 1988 table 4.187, where four of them reached the top level—Hobart and William Smith, Kenyon, University of the South, and Bishop's. Three of the list were located in New York State.

All eleven of the 1988 *Independent* libraries had expenditures at or above the highest category on the questionnaire. Independent libraries showed up well on this variable. These eleven libraries included four seminaries, five universities and two colleges. They were all located in California (2) and nine other states and provinces. *Lutheran* libraries are shown on the library list in table 4.188 for 1978. One of them, Wilfred Laurier University, made the top expenditure category even at that date. Three were university and four were college libraries. Two of them were located in Minnesota. The 1988 Lutheran list included sixteen libraries tied at the $560,000+ level, so no table was made.

Leading 1988 *Mennonite* libraries were listed in table 4.189. Eastern Mennonite College reached the top expenditure level, which was twice as large as the score of the next highest library. A very creditable accomplishment for a modestly funded denomination. We see an even greater concentration than before at libraries in Indiana and Kansas, totaling two-thirds of the table. Also, three of the libraries were located either in seminaries or history/archive centers. The 1978 *Methodist* library group contained seven libraries that reached the highest expenditure level. Again all but one were located in universities. Ten states were represented in this table. The 1988 Methodist list showed twenty-three libraries tied at $560,000+ for total expenditure, so no table was made.

Other Denominations libraries are represented in 1978 table 4.190. Even in that year seven of them reached the highest questionnaire category for total library expenditure, $560,000+. Again Quakers, Adventists, and Mormons were well represented. Three California, three Pennsylvania, and three Michigan libraries constituted the majority of the table. Another strong effort. The 1988 Other Denominations list showed nineteen libraries tied at the $560,000+ level.

Three *Presbyterian* libraries made the top questionnaire level in 1978—Tulsa, Trinity, and Queen's Universities. Two libraries were located in Pennsylvania, and five libraries were located in colleges. In 1988, the list of Presbyterian libraries showed seventeen libraries tied at the $560,000+ total expenditure level.

United Church of Christ libraries for 1988 are shown in table 4.191. Five libraries spent more than half a million dollars during the year.

Seven of these libraries were located in colleges. Three of them were located in Pennsylvania and two in Missouri to account for half of the total. A strong showing! To conclude this series of denominations, only two of the *Jewish* libraries for 1988 were located in universities. Three were located in colleges, two were history/archive libraries, two were seminaries, and one was a denominational headquarters library. Three were located in New York City and three in Massachusetts. Again no 1988 table could be produced for *Roman Catholics*, since eighty-five libraries were tied at the $560,000+ level.

To summarize these findings for annual total expenditure, 155 libraries reached the highest expenditure level, and the strongest denominations were the Independent, Methodist, Other Denominations, Presbyterian, and Roman Catholic, with the following coming next—Baptist, UCC, and Jewish. Weakest were the Congregational, Lutheran, and Mennonite. Those states with the most libraries were Pennsylvania, Tennessee, New York, and California.

Special Library Expenditure Analyses

The following section contains a large variety of specialized analyses of variables, primarily of total expenditures. They are designed to supplement and clarify the basic findings given in the preceding section. We will start with longitudinal growth tables that were made for type of institution and for denomination. They show growth in expenditures and other variables. By type of institution the leaders were seminaries and senior colleges and by denomination the leaders were Episcopal/Anglican and Roman Catholic libraries. Lowest growth scores were those for universities and Mennonites. Longitudinal table 4.192 summarizes the situation by *type of library*. Highest scores were made by universities and senior colleges. Longitudinal table 4.193 shows the primary longitudinal values for major scholarly library variables. It is a reference table of means useful for consultation.

For the four types of academic scholarly libraries we have four longitudinal tables that show total library expenditure by denomination, and each table shows a specific type of library. For junior colleges, the Ns were too small for use, however. For senior colleges longitudinal table 4.194 shows for most denominations the decennial means and the percentage change in the means. Lutheran and Episcopal/Anglican led the 1988 list with mean expenditures of $340,600 and $336,700. On the other hand percentages were highest for Jewish, Independent, and Roman Catholic libraries, all three above 110 percent. For university libraries again the Ns were too small to rely on.

Longitudinal table 4.177 shows annual library expenditures by library type. Scholarly libraries averaged $140,718 in 1978 and $249,076 in 1988, an increase in expenditure of 77 percent during the decade. The 1988 table was led by university libraries, and convent/monastery libraries were weakest.

By comparing three 1988 tables on total annual library expenditure by library type we can learn something. We will take total scholarly library mean expenditure for each one. The figures are $249,100 for the entire database, $267,700 for matched pairs and $127,500 for newly listed libraries. These figures suggest that the matched pairs figure was higher than the one for the entire database by 7.5 percent and that the newly listed library figure was lower than the entire database figure by 49 percent.

We see again that the matched pairs were the best library group with the entire database ranking second, the newly listed libraries poor (and youngest), and the no longer listed poorest. Let us now look at the same kinds of figures for 1978. Total mean scholarly library expenditure for the entire database was $140,700, for matched pairs was $150,800 and for no longer listed libraries was $46,270. We see the same pattern here as before. Matched pairs was 7.2 percent higher and no longer listed libraries were 67 percent smaller than the entire database figure. So we have evidence that matched pairs were larger in expenditure than the entire database, which suggests that matched pairs were somewhat stronger as a group than was the entire database. Again we find that both the no longer listed and the newly listed libraries were much smaller than either the matched pairs or the entire database groups.

We can study longitudinal table 4.195 for total annual scholarly library expenditures by library for their change percentage. Highest percentage change belonged to the convent/monastery group with 276 percent (probably it started with the lowest score), with history/archives next with 220 percent. Lowest percentage change was the property of the university libraries (it started highest) with 32 percent.

Longitudinal table 4.196 is one that shows total annual scholarly *library expenditure by denomination*. The denomination that changed most in the decade was Jewish at 104 percent and then Independent at 98 percent. The Christian denomination changed least at 43 percent. Mean total expenditure in 1988 was $249,100 (table 4.195). As usual, the matched pairs were somewhat larger in total expenditure than the entire database, and the lapsed and the newly listed groups were smaller in every way.[6] Incidentally, the lapsed seemed to be heavy with Roman Catholic and Other Denomination libraries here, also.

Now we can try a new type of analysis. In fact, we can look at several new analyses of library expenditures. First, we can analyze total *academic library expenditures,* not just by library but also *by faculty member* in a detailed picture *for each denomination.* The following tables, all for 1988, show the results of this analysis. For *Baptists,* table 4.197 for 1988 showed total expenditure per library with four libraries spending above $10,000 per faculty member, a strong showing, all of them seminaries. Central Baptist, Calvary Baptist, Eastern Baptist, and North American Baptist seminaries were the four institutions.

Table 4.198 shows *Christian* colleges that did well per faculty member. They were led at a high ratio by Phillips University Graduate Seminary at $26,500 per faculty member. Four colleges were above $10,000 per faculty member. The *Churches of Christ* had a short but first-class table display. Two libraries scored above the $12,750 level: Chicago Theological Seminary and Harding College Graduate School of Religion. *Episcopal/Anglican* colleges are seen in table 4.199, and more than half of them were not seminaries or Bible colleges. However, the table was led by Episcopal Divinity School in Cambridge with $36,000 spent per faculty member, a large investment!

Independent had six libraries above the $10,000 level, the Reformed Theological Seminary leading with a $26,500 expenditure. A third of these libraries did not belong to seminaries and a third were Canadian. *Lutheran* libraries in table 4.200 were led by the Lutheran Theological Seminary in Philadelphia with a fine $26,500 expenditure. More than half of them were seminary libraries.

We do not think of *Mennonite* libraries as having high expenditures, but their table showed two of them to be above the $10,000 level, led by the Associated Mennonite Biblical Seminary in Elkhart at $12,750 per faculty member. Two-thirds of these libraries were Canadian. Table 4.201 shows the St. Paul School of Theology in Kansas City to lead the *Methodists* with an $18,500 expenditure. In all, five libraries were above the $10,000 level. *Other Denominations* libraries were all above the $10,000 level, Bethany Seminary in Oak Brook, Illinois, leading the list with a fine $26,500 expenditure.

Presbyterian libraries were one-fourth liberal arts colleges and the rest seminaries. Almost half were located in Pennsylvania or Kentucky. Table 4.202 shows the Louisville Presbyterian Theological Seminary leading the way with a high $36,000 expenditure. *United Church of Christ* showed small expenditures, but the Lancaster Theological Seminary led with a $12,750 expenditure per faculty member. *Jewish* libraries presented a small list, but three libraries were above the $10,000 level in table 4.203. The leader was Hebrew Union College in Cincinnati, with a $18,667 expenditure. *Roman Catholic* institutions were strong in this area, also.

Two other detailed 1988 tables study highest total library expenditure per faculty member for *Roman Catholics*. The leaders in this table were mostly seminaries led by Mount Angel Abby in St. Benedict, Oregon, with $26,500 per faculty member spent. Another table did the same thing for the *Other Denominations* group. Again it was led at $26,500 per faculty member by Bethany Seminary in Oak Brook, Illinois. The other libraries in the table were mostly seminaries.

The next small set of tables shows scholarly libraries with the lowest annual total library expenditures *per faculty member*. This is another series of tables of poor-quality libraries. These are the libraries with the poorest income per faculty member. We begin with the *Baptist* table 4.204 for 1988, which ranges from $650 to $1,609 per faculty member, low. The corresponding *Methodist* table ranged down to $458 per faculty member. *Other Denominations* seen in table 4.205 for 1988 ranged from $400 up to $1,423 per faculty member per year, again small.

Presbyterians were seen in a short table. Scores were as low as $100 per year for Carver Bible Institute. At that rate, a college with fifty faculty members would spend only $5,000 per year on the library altogether, less than the cost of a clerk's salary. The table for *Roman Catholic* libraries, table 4.206 for 1988, shows low figures for all institutions, with a bottom figure of $100 per faculty member for Magdalen College in New Hampshire. With Catholic colleges we can hope that there was some donated staff service from nuns, priests, brothers, and laypersons to add personnel to what must have been a small institution. With Other Denominations institutions, however, we have no hope for such additional staff members.

Now for several per student and per faculty member tables. More discriminating than the total expenditure tables shown above are those detailed 1988 denominational tables that analyze highest total library expenditures on a per student basis. These are well supported libraries. We can see that table 4.207 for 1988 shows the *Baptist* table to be led by six seminaries, with three of them tied for the lead at $850 per student. A table for *Christian* libraries emphasizes seminaries and Christian colleges; its leader, Phillips University Seminary, spent $1,767 per student on the library.

Churches of Christ libraries in table 4.208 for 1988 have modest expenditures. *Episcopal/Anglican* showed three libraries with high expenditures led by the Episcopal Divinity School in Cambridge at $2,400 per student. An outstanding expenditure rate! *Independent* libraries in table 4.209 for 1988 reached even higher frequencies, with seven of them over $1,000 per student. The table was led by the Reformed Theological Seminary in Jackson, Mississippi. *Lutheran* libraries had four over $1,000 in expenditure with Trinity and Lutheran seminaries at the top.

Table 4.210 for 1988 for *Mennonite* colleges showed small totals but emphasized Bible and Christian colleges and seminaries. Iliff School of Theology in Denver led the *Methodist* libraries with a strong $2,400 expenditure per student. *Other Denominations* libraries were led by the Bethany Seminary just outside Chicago with a $1,767 expenditure in table 4.211 for 1988. Six libraries of the *Presbyterian* persuasion were above the $1,000 per student expenditure level and were led by the Union Theological Seminary in Richmond at the high rate of $3,733 per student. *United Church of Christ* libraries presented generally modest expenditures, but the Andover Newton Theological School in Massachusetts led with $1,767 per student (table 4.212 for 1988).

Only a few *Jewish* libraries were listed, but Hebrew Union College led them with a strong $3,733 per student expenditure. All ten *Roman Catholic* libraries in table 4.213 for 1988 spent over $1,000 per student on the library. They were led by St. Meinrad College in Indiana at $3,067. A fine table! Clearly both the per faculty member and per student tables were dominated by seminaries, Christian and Bible college libraries in unmistakable support of the idea that graduate and specialized higher education is more costly than undergraduate general education. No universities were represented in these tables.

Now we can look at yet another set of tables that present the underside of higher education libraries. They show the colleges and universities that spent *least* on the 1988 library per student. They formed a set of tables arranged by denomination showing the lowest library expenditure per student. They should be compared with the tables just discussed above for 1988 that show the opposite, those institutions spending the largest amount on the library per year.

The *Baptist* libraries chosen for this series of tables showed a range from $31 up to $121 per student for total annual library expenditure. Presumably the lower the figure the poorer the library service provided to students and faculty members. Almost half of these libraries are located in Missouri and Mississippi. As for *Christian* libraries, the lowest range was rather high, $156 up to $196 per student spent on the library in table 4.214 for 1988. These libraries show higher minimum expenditure rates than did the Baptist libraries. Note that 40 percent of the table contains Christian or Bible colleges.

Let us look at *Churches of Christ* table 4.215 for 1988 now. It shows a range from $52 up to $196 per student. Note that half of the table contains universities and that Texas and Tennessee libraries constitute half of the table. The reader who thinks this is a poor showing need only read further! Worse is coming! *Episcopal/Anglican* libraries have even higher minimum expenditures than do Churches of Christ libraries. Here we have one university library but no Christian or Bible colleges.

The *Independent* libraries ranged from $20 up to $196 per student. Note that a library with a $20 per student expenditure would have a total budget of only $10,000 (less than one full-time professional salary) even if it had as many as five hundred students. *Lutheran* scholarly libraries ranged from a low of $93 up to $196 total expenditure per student in table 4.216 for 1988. These libraries represent three universities. Note that Iowa and Minnesota constitute half of the table. *Mennonite* libraries were located in Kansas, 50 percent of them. Next are the *Methodists*. Table 4.217 for 1988 goes down to $31 per student, a low figure. The *Other Denominations* table contained no very low ratios, nor are the ones shown very high in table 4.218 for 1988. They include two Bible colleges, no universities, and seven colleges with under $100 per student annual expenditure.

We reach the lowest figure yet in table 4.219 for 1988 for *Presbyterian* institutions, $7 per student for Carver Bible Institute. This means that such an institution need spend only $7,000 on the library to serve a thousand students! The *United Church of Christ* table contains no Bible colleges but also no universities. The *Jewish* libraries table was short, and all four libraries' income was between $121 and $172 per year. They included two universities. The last table in this series, 4.220, contained another one of these very low institutions, one at $7 per student for *Roman*

Catholic libraries, Magdalen College in New Hampshire. Even the top end of this table is very low, only $72. In general, this set of tables portrays a series of apparently deplorable situations.

Table 4.221 for both 1978 and 1988 shows scholarly library expenditure per student by denomination. We may note first the approximate doubling of the mean total expenditure from 1978 to 1988. This is a substantial increase. Highest mean expenditure for 1988 was found in the Jewish group, which more than doubled the expenditures of most of the other denominations. Episcopal/Anglican was second, at $677 per student. Lowest expenditure was in the Baptist and Roman Catholic groups. Looked at by regional per student expenditure for scholarly 1978 and 1988 libraries, we see that their scores were similar but not the same. In any case for 1988 the largest expenditure was made by the Middle Atlantic group with Northeast second, $386 and $385 per student. Lowest was the Southwest at $292, not very much smaller.

Table 4.222 for 1978 and 1988 provides a new view of library expenditure in analyzing it by both student enrollment level and by library type, another variation. The table shows university libraries to have spent less per student than any other library type. While their expenditures were large, their enrollments were even larger, in a sense, as we have seen before. On the other hand, seminary expenditures were good sized and their enrollments were quite small, so their per student expenditures were by far the largest in the table. Senior college expenditures per student were somewhat larger than junior college expenditures.

Finally, we have a study of the library expenditure categories—material, personnel, and other—in percentages by denomination. Ratio patterns varied considerably. The division between the four kinds of library expenditures for each denomination is interesting though also perhaps inconsistent. Highest material expenditure ratio was that of the Presbyterians, 41 percent. Lowest was that of the Jewish group, 31 percent. Highest personnel expenditure was Jewish, 65 percent, and lowest was Presbyterian, 55 percent. Mennonite libraries spent the most on Other expenditures. However, differences between the denominations were small. Overall ratios were 36 percent (material), 59 percent (personnel), and 4 percent (Other): 36–59–4, or 9 to 15 to 1. See table 4.223 for 1988.

A final cumulative and longitudinal study was made of total annual expenditure by type of library. It cumulated the figures for material, personnel, Other, and total expenditure. By type of library the largest longitudinal changes were 301 percent for convent/monastery and 262 percent for history/archives, again. Smallest was 30 percent for university libraries, again. Junior and senior colleges were 125 percent and 87 percent while seminaries were 128 percent. See table 4.224 for 1988. By denomination the largest longitudinal expenditure changes were Independent at 100 percent and Jewish at 94 percent. Smallest was Christian at 44 percent and Episcopal/Anglican at 57 percent.

A further study was made to attempt to single out those variables on which the libraries grew fastest over the decade. This was a master longitudinal study and was carried out with matched pairs (the elite group) only. The results were interesting. By region the Southwest and West grew fastest for 1978–88 and Canada grew most slowly. A varied picture. As an added feature an analysis of growth was made by the gender of the chief librarian. In 1988 the change rate for the male to female ratio was 1.6 to 1.0, with males' frequencies growing fastest.

A further study was made that covered nine response variables for scholarly libraries.[7] It attempted to combine and examine the change in questionnaire response patterns of the libraries for all nine variables, change in chief librarian's gender ratios, in priests and nuns as chief librarians, and the other variables listed in longitudinal table 4.225. For the most part, positive scores were few and low. However, the Christian, Episcopal/Anglican, Mennonite, and Jewish groups responded with positive scores. The only group with a net negative score was the Roman Catholic due to a decrease in the number of religious serving as chief librarians.

Yet another set of tables was made to analyze institutional *educational activity* for matched pairs of scholarly libraries with small no response figures. In this study educational activity means the growth of higher educational institutions. Mean units were similar by region in table 4.226 for 1988, but Canada was the educational leader and Rocky Mountains was next. Smallest scores were made by the Southeast and the Middle West.

A special analysis was made of both the scholarly and popular databases to examine certain tables in order to study a total of twenty-seven variables for matched pairs. The purpose of the analysis was to study library growth from several directions as listed in each one of the tables reflecting the study results. Points were assigned for each evidence of growth on each table. The denomination or region with the largest number of points showed the most evidence of growth on a longitudinal basis; therefore, table 4.227 for 1978 and table 4.228 for 1988 show mean number of rating points for each region. They show Canada and the Northeast to lead the way in 1978 and the West and the Northeast again to lead in 1988. So, even though Canada and the Northeast had low scores on many tables, over a large number of variables their longitudinal growth picture was strong.

We have a further longitudinal table, 4.229, that examines the decade's growth points by denomination. These tables show the results of making a composite longitudinal study for the twenty-seven variables. Largest growth was that of the Mennonites and the Episcopal/Anglican groups in this case. Most stable by denomination were the Jewish and Methodist groups. A further longitudinal table, 4.230, examines the growth points by type of library. Largest growth was for the history/archives and senior college groups. Smallest growth was for convent/monastery and university groups with slow but steady progress. The similarity with other findings in this series was modest! About half of the numbers of college and university libraries were listed in the table.

Section Summary

To make a final summary for the four expenditure variables—material, personnel, other, and total—we must point out that there was much scatter in denominational emphasis, only the Baptist libraries standing out as leaders. However, the following denominations were strong in expenditure as a whole: Baptist, Independent, Methodist, Other Denominations, Roman Catholic, and United Church of Christ, and also to a lesser extent, Episcopal/Anglican and Presbyterian. Weakest showings were made by the Congregational and Mennonite groups. States with many leading libraries were Pennsylvania, California, and Texas.

More detail about expenditure summaries can be seen in the following paragraphs. For material expenditure, for 1978 the mean per library was $49,490 while for 1988 it was $81,500, a 65 percent difference. University libraries spent the most, $144,400 per year; the matched pairs figure was $88,530. No longer listed and newly listed had means that were 81 percent lower and 57 percent lower than the overall mean for the entire sample. By region, Middle Atlantic led with a mean expenditure of $94,300. Both history/archives and denominational headquarters expenditures increased in size by over 200 percent. Total expenditure and material expenditure correlated, positively and strongly. Male chief librarians headed libraries with significantly larger mean expenditures than those headed by females. Among the denominations Methodists led with a mean of $98,960.

For personnel expenditure the mean was $89,860 for 1978 and $141,325 for 1988, a 57 percent gain. University libraries were again largest at $265,400 per year. By region Canada was highest at $141,000. Total and personnel expenditure correlated positively and again male chief librarians headed much larger libraries than female chief librarians did. Jewish and Lutheran denominations had the largest personnel expenditures at about $140,000 for 1978 and $175,000 for 1988. For Other expenditure, there was the usual strong positive correlation between Other and total expenditure. Again university libraries were highest at about $20,000 and Baptists led this expenditure variable. There were 188 libraries that reached the expenditure level of $20,000.

For total expenditures, Roman Catholic were the largest (highest) among denominations. University libraries were largest in number at the top category, exactly one hundred of them at $560,000! By number of consortium memberships, there was again a strong positive correlation with total expenditures. For longitudinal growth, seminaries and Episcopal/Anglican grew fastest. Several special studies were made to learn more about total expenditures. Finally, several tables were made to identify libraries that appeared on the "highest" tables most frequently.

Denominational Characterizations and Cumulative Tables

As a kind of final summary, this section will describe the main characteristics of each denominational, type of library, and regional group and will list the leading libraries in the first ones of them. In so doing we will try to single out the strong and weak aspects of each group's performance. In a further section we will also list what seem to be the leading scholarly libraries in each denomination. All evidence is taken from chapters 3–4 and is usually based on the 1988 figures.

Denominational Characterizations

Specifically, the denominational characteristics will be based on library scores on the following variables: library denominational size, institutional degree level, accreditation, enrollment, faculty size, library age, professional, clerical, student and total staff size, volumes, periodical subscriptions, vertical files, microforms, media, maps, art reproductions, material, personnel, Other and total expenditures, consortium and OCLC memberships, and local automation projects.

Baptist scholarly libraries were strong in number of libraries, mean degree level, enrollment size, library staff size, book volumes, periodical subscriptions titles, vertical files, microforms, media, art reproductions, material expenditures, Other expenditures, consortium memberships, and OCLC memberships—fourteen variables. Baptists were weak in faculty size and local automation projects—two variables. On other variables the Baptists scored in the middle rank. This record left them ranking second out of the fourteen denominations (including both Congregational from 1978 and Mennonite from 1988), a strong showing.

Christian institutions were small and their libraries were strong in only a few variables. These were media holdings, art reproductions, material expenditure, and OCLC memberships—four variables. The libraries were weak in enrollment means, faculty size, and microform holdings—three variables. On a majority of variables Christian scholarly libraries were neither strong nor weak. This left them with a ninth-place ranking out of fourteen denominations.

Churches of Christ were at the same level as Christian church libraries, a group of small institutions. They were strong in degree level, enrollment, staff size, media, maps, and art reproductions—six variables. They were weak in number of libraries, faculty size, age (relatively young), number of volumes, and Other expenditures—five variables. They were mediocre in other areas. This left them with tenth place among the fourteen denominations.

The *Congregational* library group was small and weak in this context. It was strong in no area and weak in many—number of libraries, mean enrollment, faculty size, staff size, volumes, periodical titles, vertical files, microforms, maps, and personnel expenditures—ten variables. In other areas the Congregationalists were in the middle. This left them in fourteenth and last place among the denominations.

The small *Episcopal/Anglican* institutions came next. They were strong in mean degree level, age, material expenditures, and Other expenditures—four variables. They were weak in accreditation, enrollment level, faculty size, number of microforms, media and maps, and number of local automation projects—seven variables. These libraries were mediocre in other fields. This brought Episcopal/Anglican libraries the low ranking of eleventh out of fourteen denominations.

The unusual group of *Independents* ranked in the middle of the list of denominations, possibly because it did not represent any one coherent group. This group was strong in degree level, enrollment level, number of volumes, microforms, and Other expenditures—five variables. It was weak in accreditations, faculty size, age, art reproductions, and OCLC memberships—five variables. In all other variables it obtained a medium score. This gave the Independents the rank of eighth out of the fourteen denominations.

Lutheran institution libraries were another interesting group. They were strong in mean enrollment, faculty size, age, staff size, microforms, consortium, and OCLC memberships—seven variables. They were weak in no field (0 variables), a strong accomplishment in itself, and they were mediocre in all other variables. This yielded a ranking of sixth on the denominational list, a middle ranking group.

Mennonite was one of the two weakest denominations (along with the Congregationalists). The group consisted primarily of small colleges. Mennonites were strong in art reproductions only—one variable. They were weak in numbers of libraries, enrollment, faculty size, age, staff size, volumes, periodical titles, microforms, personnel expenditures, and local automation projects—ten variables. They were mediocre in the other factors. Their final rank was thirteenth out of fourteen denominations.

Now come in *Methodists,* the leading denomination. Methodists were strong in many areas—number of libraries, accreditation status, enrollment level, faculty size, age, staff size, volumes, periodical titles, art reproductions, personnel expenditures, consortium membership, OCLC membership and local automation projects—thirteen variables. Methodists were weak in no area, quite an accomplishment—0 variables. They were mediocre in all other categories, a very strong showing through which they ranked first out of all denominations.

The next denomination was *Other Denominations*. It was strong in staff size, volumes, periodical titles, vertical files, microforms, and personnel expenditures—six variables. It was weak in numbers of libraries, accreditation, faculty size and age—four variables. Other variables were present on a medium level. This left Other Denominations with a rank of seventh, in the middle.

We have the small colleges of the *Presbyterian* denomination next. Presbyterians were strong in number of libraries, mean degree level, accreditation, age, library staff size, microforms, personnel expenditures, consortium and OCLC memberships—nine variables. They were weak in faculty size and mediocre in the other variables. This gave them fifth place in the denominations, in the top third of the field.

The *United Church of Christ* denomination made a surprisingly strong showing. It was strong in degree level, accreditation, enrollment, age, media, maps, art reproductions, material expenditures, consortium and OCLC memberships, and local automation projects—eleven variables. This denomination was weak in number of libraries, however—one variable. All other variables were in the medium area. This denomination was weak in number of libraries, however—one variable. All other variables were in the medium area. This yielded the third highest rank, very good.

The *Jewish* denomination comes next and did poorly. It was strong in degree level, vertical files, and material expenditures—three variables. The young Jewish libraries were weak in accreditation, enrollment, faculty size, age, volumes, periodical titles, microforms, media, maps, OCLC membership, and local automation projects—eleven variables. All other variables were located at a medium level. Final rank was twelfth out of the fourteen denominations.

The last denomination was the *Roman Catholic*. It had several strengths: number of libraries, degree level, enrollment, faculty size, staff size, volumes, periodical titles, vertical files, microforms, art reproductions, consortium memberships, and local automation projects—twelve variables. The areas in which Roman Catholics were weak were accreditation and maps—two variables. Other variables were in the middle area. The final rank was good—fourth out of the fourteen scholarly denominations, in the top third.

Type of Library

This section will summarize the rankings by type of library. These rankings were based on a variety of tables, such as the series in which we count the number of tables on which each library appears (coming up soon!) and those on which we examined rankings on twenty-seven separate variables (just completed). All of these valuations were taken from mean values. They constitute an academic exercise and probably should not be taken as seriously as certain readers may wish; when looked at closely, many of the differences between regions or types were small. One group may rank high on one variable but low on a related one, so it is not always possible to make good sense of their rankings.

Junior college libraries were generally small and weak, fourth strongest among the four academic library types and the seven scholarly library types. They claimed several outstanding libraries, however. Fairly strong in media and student assistants (second), they were fifth in clerks and seventh in professionals. By total staff they ranked fifth out of seven types; by volumes they ranked fourth and by total expenditure they ranked fourth. Overall rank was fourth out of seven types.

Senior colleges constituted the largest library type in number and had many strong libraries. Some of them were stronger than certain universities. However, many of the poorest libraries in this study were senior colleges. Senior colleges and universities were well ahead of other types in table appearances. They were strong in all types of library material. However, they ranked only sixth on number of professionals, last on clerks, but first on student assistants and second on volumes. Overall rank was second out of seven types.

University libraries were usually the largest of all types in mean score. While they were large on mean, however, they were often small on longitudinal change scores, at least in part because their initial (1978) scores were relatively high. As a group their policies were stable. They were strong in everything—material, staff, and expenditure. However, they were only fifth in mean number of professionals, sixth in mean number of clerks, third in total student assistants, but first in total staff. Both expenditure and volumes reached first place. Overall rank was first out of seven types.

Seminary libraries were strong in per student scores of all kinds, but weak in media holdings. In staffing, they were fourth in professionals, fourth in clerks and student assistants, but third in total staff members. By expenditures and volumes they were third. Overall ranking was third out of seven types.

Convent/monastery libraries were seventh out of seven in most variables by quantity only. Their libraries were generally small and poorly supported. They scored high on certain longitudinal tables because they started very low, and their libraries had few table appearances. By mean number of professionals they ranked third, by clerks they ranked second, by student assistants they ranked sixth, and for total staff members they ranked seventh. For total expenditures they ranked seventh and for volumes they ranked sixth. Overall ranking was seventh out of seven types.

Denominational headquarters libraries were generally small and weak. Their libraries appeared on few tables. By mean staff they ranked first on professionals, first on clerks, seventh on student assistants, and sixth on total staff members. By expenditures they reached seventh and by volumes they ranked seventh. Overall rank was sixth out of seven types.

History/archives libraries varied, but several of them were well stocked with material. By staff members they were second in professionals, third in clerks, fifth in student assistants, and fifth in total staff members. By expenditures they reached fifth place and by volumes they ranked fifth also. Overall rank was fifth out of seven library types.

Region

We can conclude this series of ratings by examining the regions. How did they rank in this evaluation series? The *Northeast* region was second smallest. Its book collections seemed to be large, but its expenditures appeared to be small. As for educational activity Northeast ranked third, and in growth variables it ranked second. Ranking of staff total was fifth, on holdings was first. Overall ranking was first out of eight regions.

Middle Atlantic was a major region in gross size, the second largest of them all. It was a major factor in most tables. It was generally strong, especially with Jewish and Roman Catholic libraries. On staff size it ranked sixth, on holdings it ranked second, on educational activity it ranked third, and on growth variables it ranked second. Overall rank was second out of eight regions.

The *Southeast* region was the main center of Baptist libraries and was third largest of the regions. It was probably the fastest growing region also. It ranked first on staff total, seventh on holdings, eighth on educational activities, and fifth on growth variables. Overall ranking was fifth out of eight regions.

The *Southwest* was strong in Roman Catholic libraries and was another fast-growing region. It ranked fourth on total staff members, sixth on holdings, fifth on educational activity and fifth on growth variables. Overall rank was seventh out of eight regions.

The *Rocky Mountains* region was small in the *ALD*, in fact the smallest region in this study in number of libraries. However, it was surprisingly strong on certain variables, especially on mean scores. It ranked second on total staff members, third on library holdings, second on educational activities, and eighth on growth variables. Overall it ranked third out of eight regions.

The *West* was large in space but small in *ALD* libraries and generally lacked distinction. On total staff members it ranked seventh, on holdings it ranked fifth, on educational activity it ranked sixth, and on growth variables it ranked seventh. Overall it stood eighth out of eight regions.

The *Middle West* was the largest region in number of libraries and was a leader in many tables. It ranked third on total staff members, fourth on library holdings, seventh on educational activity, and seventh on growth variables. Overall its ranking was sixth out of eight regions.

Canada was male dominated and scored well on some longitudinal tables. Its scholarly library group was relatively large and strong. It ranked eighth on total staff members, eighth on holdings, first on educational activity, and third on growth variables. Overall Canada ranked fourth out of eight regions.

Cumulative Tables

Now we can move on to several lists of specific scholarly libraries that were leaders in the 1988 database. We have seen certain of these lists already. Table 4.231 for 1988 shows the cumulative table leaders, the "leaders among the leaders, the holiest of holies." These were the eighteen outstanding libraries among the scholarly library group, those libraries that were most often listed in the "highest" tables. All but one were large university libraries and almost half were Roman Catholic, though more than a quarter were Baptist and Methodist. No focus could be identified by location.

Other longitudinal tables show analyses of the tables in the section above. One shows the mean number of table listings achieved by the library for each denomination. For instance, the average Churches of Christ library was on twelve tables out of twenty. Another table shows much the same thing for type of library. Still another table shows the same thing but enables us to see that the larger the library expenditures the larger the number of tables on which the average library appeared.

Certain other tables provide the same view for each denomination separately. These tables show the ten or fifteen most often listed--the outstanding—libraries for each denomination. All were 1988 tables except the table for Congregationalists. Clearly the Congregational and Jewish groups were the weakest here also. How many scholarly libraries were listed on the "highest" tables by denomination? For scholarly libraries, 241 libraries appeared on ten or more of the "highest" tables, or would have if all of the possible variable tables had been generated and reprinted.

When broken down by type of library, senior colleges led in being listed on 110 tables; university libraries were second with 93. Convent/monastery libraries and denominational headquarters were on none of these "highest" tables. Look at the ten and above column of table 4.232 for 1988 of the 241 libraries listed. Roman Catholic led with thirty-two such libraries. Second was Lutheran with twenty-four and third was Independent with twenty-two libraries. Protestant scored lower than Jewish but higher than Roman Catholic in this table also.

Now we can look at a series of tables listing the libraries that were most often included in the tables showing the leaders in each field. Again, these libraries constituted "the best of the best," those libraries that were most often cited among the best in the various fields.

Let us consider them in detail. They listed most of the outstanding scholarly libraries in the 1988 database arranged by denomination. As usual, we will start with the *Baptist* group, table 4.233 for 1988. Wake Forest University led the table with eighteen out of nineteen possible appearances. Temple and Richmond Universities were next with seventeen out of nineteen possible appearances. The table contained two Texas and two Virginia libraries, a fourth of the total. Twelve universities, two seminaries, and one senior college constituted the entire list.

Christian libraries made a good showing in table 4.234 for 1988. Lynchburg and Tougaloo Colleges led this table, with strong scores. Three Missouri, two Oklahoma, and two Texas libraries made up the locations of 40 percent of these libraries. This was a list of colleges with a few universities and seminaries added. For *Churches of Christ* libraries in table 4.235 for 1988 the leaders were Oklahoma Christian College (with 19 listings altogether!), Lincoln Christian, and Freed-Hardeman, as well as Abilene Christian University. Four Tennessee, three Texas, two Florida, and two California libraries led in state locations, almost two-thirds of the total. Most of these institutions were colleges plus some universities and seminaries.

Table 4.236 showed the list of outstanding 1978 *Congregational* libraries, with two of them being listed in eighteen out of nineteen tables—Washburn and Olivet. *Episcopal/Anglican* table 4.237 for 1988 libraries was next, and was led by General Theological Seminary, Bishop's University, and the University of the South. More than a third of this group were seminaries but also half of them were colleges. New York with three and Tennessee with two led the location list.

Independent table 4.238 libraries were led by Brown University with seventeen listings. California with four, Illinois with two, and Kentucky with two led the location list for almost half of the total. *Lutheran* libraries were led by Valparaiso University with nineteen listings and by Wagner and Gettysburg Colleges. State location was two Ohio, three Pennsylvania, and four Minnesota, for more than half of the total, table 4.239. *Mennonite* libraries appeared in table 4.240 for 1988 with two nineteen-table libraries: Tabor College and Eastern Mennonite University. By state there were three libraries in Indiana, four in Kansas, and two in Maine, almost two-thirds of the total. Eleven college libraries dominated the table.

Methodist libraries can be seen in table 4.241 for 1988. The leader was Wesleyan University with sixteen table listings. A dozen universities dominated the table. In the *Other Denominations* table 4.242 BYU and Swarthmore led with seventeen and sixteen listings. By state and province, Pennsylvania had three listings, Michigan had three, and California had two, totaling half of the table.

The University of Tulsa and Trinity University led table 4.243 for 1988 for *Presbyterian* libraries, with eighteen and seventeen table listings. Two Pennsylvania and two Illinois libraries led by location. Most of these were libraries sponsored by colleges. The *United Church of Christ* group was led by four libraries: Elmhurst, Doane, and Catawba Colleges plus Pacific University with nineteen and eighteen listings. By state and province locations the leaders were Pennsylvania (3), Mississippi (2), Missouri (2), Ohio (2), North Carolina (2), for more than half of the table's libraries. Again most of these leading libraries were located in colleges. See table 4.244 for 1988.

In a surprisingly short table, 4.245 for 1988, *Jewish* libraries were led by Yeshiva University and Hebrew Union College, with seventeen and eighteen listings. By state, Massachusetts had three and New York had three libraries in the table. College and special libraries dominated the table. Lastly, the *Roman Catholic* table 4.246 for 1988. Two libraries led with sixteen listings apiece: Loyola and Notre Dame Universities. The table consisted of fourteen universities plus Boston College. By state, New York had two libraries, and Washington, D.C. had two.

It is not possible to provide a summary or conclusion for this section except to say that we have listed the leading scholarly libraries by denomination. The rating of the top libraries in each table was a measure of the strength of the competition as well as a measure of library strength.

Subject Areas for Further Study

It is obvious that these two scholarly library chapters have succeeded only in introducing the bare outlines of their subject fields. Additional studies are needed both to replicate this study and to make more intensive analyses of data in order to learn more about the scholarly religious library field. Studies are needed in each one of the major and minor subject areas of the two chapters. The following is a brief list of suggested additional research projects on these libraries.

1. A more intensive analysis is needed of the characteristics of the various denominations in the Other Denominations group. They must vary considerably among themselves on most variables, so it should be interesting to identify the strong and the weak library groups among them on each variable.
2. Though difficult to do, it would be desirable, perhaps for a handful of states or provinces, to compare directly the characteristics of a regional sample of the *ALD* scholarly religious libraries with a group of scholarly nonreligious libraries existing out in the field.
3. Certain additional analyses can be made of chief librarian's gender in a further longitudinal study in order to identify any changes in the ratios found here.
4. Through historical studies, it would be helpful to determine how certain denominations developed a strong scholarly library group, e.g., Methodist or Baptist. Such a study would probably need to go into the influence of the central denominational headquarters, of the seminaries, and of the people attracted to the faculties and administrative groups of these institutions.
5. If possible, an intensive analysis should be made to compare one large group of seminary libraries in a specific denomination with a group of seminary libraries in another denomination to identify the various kinds of differences.
6. The quality of scholarly religious book and periodical collections should be evaluated directly on a book and periodical title sampling basis.
7. A serious attempt should be made to determine the ways in which the religious university (or any other kind of scholarly) libraries of a particular denomination in twenty-five states

differ from nonreligious private and public university libraries in those states.

8. An attempt should be made to determine the quality and quantity of service provided by scholarly religious libraries in support of their religious material collections and for their religious clientele. Ultimately this study should attempt to describe and evaluate the special service for religion provided by religious scholarly libraries as compared with nonreligious scholarly libraries.
9. A series of detailed case studies should be made to describe the characteristics of (1) superior and (2) inferior scholarly libraries of the same type. The study should bring out the significant differences between the two groups.

Notes

1. The *ACRL University Library Statistics, 1987–1988* [100 large non-Association of Research Libraries libraries located in doctoral-granting institutions just below ARL size] (Chicago: Association of College and Research Libraries, 1989), was studied, particularly its mean figures, p. 6, to bring some evidence of the outer library world into the chapter for comparison with the *ALD* religious library figures used in this study.

The one hundred research libraries studied by the ACRL included nineteen university libraries that were part of the present study. They are listed here: Andrews, Baylor, Boston College, Brandeis, Catholic, Denver, Fordham, Loma Linda (Loma Linda, CA), Loyola (Chicago), Marquette, Ottawa, Pacific, Pepperdine, St. Johns (Jamaica), San Francisco, Southern Methodist, Texas Christian, Tulsa, and Yeshiva.

The reader may compare the ACRL with the *ALD* religious university library figures section by section. In all cases the scholarly *ALD* religious mean figures were significantly smaller than the religious and nonreligious ACRL university figures. This result was expected, since the ACRL report covered libraries that were well above average size in every category while the *ALD* libraries probably were only average on the whole. For example, in number of volumes held, the ACRL survey showed a mean of about 907,329 volumes compared with the 1988 *ALD* university library mean figure of 248,000 volumes (in accredited institutions). See table 4.247 for 1978–1988.

In addition, we can make a comparison between the 1978 *ALD* figures on certain variables and the corresponding figures for these variables taken from U.S. National Center for Education Statistics (NCES) National Survey report, *Library Statistics of Colleges and Universities Summary Data 1977,* by

Richard M. Beazley (Washington, D.C.: U.S. Government Printing Office, 1977). The NCES and ALD figures are shown in table 4.248 for 1977 and 1978. The table enables us to compare the entire 1977 U.S. academic library universe with the 1978 *ALD* religious academic figures. Apples, oranges, and accordions again! These are interesting comparisons, however.

2. Trevor Zweck, "The Future of Theological Libraries in Australia and New Zealand," *Australian and New Zealand Theological Library Association Newsletter,* 6 (December 1988): 3–10.
3. "Guidelines for Theological Libraries," *Association of British Theological and Philosophical Libraries Bulletin* 2 (June 1990): 1–31. And while we are at it, we might quote Peterson's 1984 figures on ATLA member library data. He said that these libraries increased their material collections by 2.7 percent per annum, increased their total expenditure 9.5 percent per annum, and contained 2.4 professionals per library. See John V. Howard, "North American Future," *Association of British Theological and Philosophical Libraries Bulletin,* 23 (March 1985): 9–14, which summarizes the Peterson report referred to in chapter 1.
4. Incidentally, the author assumed that any names using initials instead of a first name (and therefore with gender unidentifiable) belonged to males.
5. In certain cases, the failure of a library to repeat from the 1978 to thc 1988 table represents the failure of the library to return the questionnaire for the later year. In other cases, the library sent in the questionnaire but omitted a vertical file report; this was the most common fault in these tables. Wesleyan University in Connecticut was an example of this problem. In still other cases, the library's total score in 1988 was lower than that for 1978 (because of losses, perhaps) and was too low to permit inclusion in the 1988 table of highest ranking libraries.
6. The 1988 newly listed libraries showed higher scores on institutional faculty members than did the 1978 no longer listed libraries.
7. List of nine variables that are categorized simply as "questionnaire response variables": (1) Library type (scholarly), (2) religious affiliation, (3) questionnaire returned, (4) departmental library, (5) chief librarian named, (6) chief librarian's gender (7) religious order status, (8) circulation restrictions, and (9) reference service restrictions. Additional variables were devised for popular library analysis, which suffers from lower response rates. These variables show accurately the rate of change from 1978 to 1988 for the variables included in the compounds or cumulatives.
    1. Cumulative for expenditures: special formula maximizing on material, personnel, Other, and total expenditure values
    2. Cumulative for educational variables: enrollment, faculty members, and degree years offered
    3. Cumulative for library holdings: volumes, periodicals, vertical file drawers, and microforms

4. Cumulative for all media variables: media, maps, and art reproductions
5. Cumulative for restrictions variables: circulation to members only and reference service to members only
6. Cumulative for additional library activities variables: consortium memberships, OCLC membership, and automation projects
7. Cumulative for extended services variables: subject interest (1), religious subject interests (2), and special collections and publications

8. List of twenty-seven variables characterized as "growth" variables: age (shows no true growth), accreditation (any), degree years granted, professionals, clerks, student assistants, all staff, enrollment, faculty size, materials, personnel, other expenditures, total expenditures, periodicals, vertical file drawers, microforms, volumes, media, maps, art reproductions, automation projects, OCLC memberships, consortium memberships, subject interests, special collections, publications, religious subject interests (as separate from "subject interests"). These few tables are very accurate, since they are for *matched pairs only* and are *least* affected by varying reporting rates and changing sample compositions.

TABLE 4.1
1978 and 1988 *American Library Directory* Longitudinal Study of Scholarly Library Professional Staff Members by Library Type

Library Type	1978 Number of Libraries	1978 No Response	1978 Total Libraries	1978 Mean Members	1988 Number of Libraries	1988 No Response	1988 Total Libraries	1988 Mean Members	% Change 1978–88
Scholarly	759	616	1,375	3.8	896	535	1,431	4.0	5.3
Junior College	49	76	125	1.8	52	56	108	1.9	5.6
Senior College	433	217	704	3.5	500	205	705	3.6	2.9
University	115	39	154	8.0	156	33	189	7.9	−1.2
Seminary	105	128	233	2.4	113	117	230	2.6	8.3
Convent/ Monastery	7	28	35	1.4	6	19	25	1.3	−7.1
Denominational HQ	26	51	77	1.4	28	58	86	1.8	29.0
History/Archives	24	23	47	2.2	41	47	88	2.6	18.0

TABLE 4.2
1988 *American Library Directory* Senior College Libraries with the Largest Number of Professional Staff Members

Library	Denomination	Number of Professionals
1. Loyola-Notre Dame College, Baltimore, MD	Roman Catholic	13
2. Boston College, Chestnut Hill, MA	Roman Catholic	13
3. College of the Holy Cross, Worcester, MA	Roman Catholic	13
4. College of St. Benedict, St. Joseph, MN	Roman Catholic	13
5. College of St. Catherine, St. Paul, MN	Roman Catholic	13
6. College of St. Thomas, St. Paul, MN	Roman Catholic	13
7. Mississippi College, Clinton, MS	Baptist	13
8. Manhattan College, Riverdale, NY	Roman Catholic	13
9. Canisius College, Buffalo, NY	Roman Catholic	13
10. Mercy College, Dobbs Ferry, NY	Roman Catholic	13
11. Cedar Crest College, Allentown, PA	United Church of Christ	13
12. Muhlenberg College, Allentown, PA	Lutheran	13
13. Bryn Mawr College, Bryn Mawr, PA	Other Denominations	13
14. Lafayette College, Easton, PA	Presbyterian	13
15. Swarthmore College, Swarthmore, PA	Other Denominations	13
16. Meharry Medical College, Nashville, TN	Methodist	13
17. College of New Rochelle, New Rochelle, NY	Roman Catholic	9
18. Franklin and Marshall College, Lancaster, PA	United Church of Christ	9
19. Benedict College, Columbia, SC	Baptist	9

TABLE 4.3
1988 *American Library Directory* Convent/Monastery Libraries with the Largest Number of Professional Staff Members

Library	Denomination	Number of Professionals
1. Blue Cloud Abbey, Marvin, SD	Roman Catholic	3
2. Abbey of Regina Laudis, Bethlehem, CT	Roman Catholic	1
3. Blessed Sacrament Monastery, Yonkers, NY	Roman Catholic	1
4. Sacred Heart Monastery, Winchester, VA	Roman Catholic	1
5. St. Benedict's Abbey, Benet Lake, WI	Roman Catholic	1
6. St. Norbert Abbey, De Pere, WI	Roman Catholic	1

TABLE 4.4
1988 *American Library Directory* History/Archive Libraries with the Largest Number of Professional Staff Members

Library	Denomination	Number of Professionals
1. Yivo Institute for Jewish Research, New York, NY	Jewish	13
2. Church of Jesus Christ of Latter-day Saints, Salt Lake City, UT	Other Denominations	13
3. Presbyterian Study Center, Montreat, NC	Presbyterian	7
4. Shaker Library, Poland Spring, ME	Other Denominations	5
5. Shaker Museum, Old Chatham, NY	Other Denominations	4
6. Presbyterian Church Office of History, Philadelphia, PA	Presbyterian	4
7. Southern Baptist Convention Archives, Richmond, VA	Baptist	4
8. Goshen College, Goshen, IN	Mennonite	3
9. Concordia Historical Institute, St. Louis, MO	Lutheran	3
10. American Buddhist Archives, New York, NY	Other Denominations	3
11. Virginia Baptists Historical Society, Richmond, VA	Baptist	3

TABLE 4.5
1988 *American Library Directory* Total Scholarly Library Professional Staff Members by Region

Region	Professional Staff 1–4	%	5–8	%	9–12	%	13 and over	%	No Response	%	Number of Libraries	Mean Professionals
Northeast	29	38	12	16	1	1	6	8	28	37	76	4.7
Middle Atlantic	105	40	30	11	4	2	20	8	102	39	261	4.5
Southeast	130	49	43	16	1	0	8	3	84	32	266	3.8
Southwest	49	42	17	15	4	3	6	5	41	35	117	4.2
West	41	32	18	14	2	2	7	5	60	47	128	4.5
Rocky Mountains	7	33	1	5	0	0	3	14	10	48	21	5.1
Middle West	195	49	60	15	3	1	11	3	129	32	398	3.7
Canada	67	41	5	3	0	0	11	7	82	50	165	3.7
Total	623	44	186	13	15	1	72	5	536	37	1,432	4.5

TABLE 4.6
1988 *American Library Directory* Scholarly Library Professional Staff Membership by Denomination

	Professional Staff											
Denomination	1	%	2–3	%	4–5	%	6+	%	No Response	%	Number of Libraries	Mean Professionals
Baptist	27	18	36	24	24	16	20	13	45	30	152	3.9
Christian	8	20	11	27	4	10	3	7	15	37	41	3.0
Churches of Christ	6	22	10	37	1	4	4	15	6	22	27	3.0
Episcopal/Anglican	4	13	7	22	3	9	4	13	14	44	32	3.8
Independent	25	26	20	21	6	6	12	12	34	35	97	3.3
Lutheran	8	11	16	21	11	14	15	20	26	34	76	4.2
Mennonite	7	32	8	36	0	0	0	0	7	32	22	1.8
Methodist	15	10	49	33	23	15	25	17	37	25	149	4.2
Other Denominations	38	18	47	22	18	8	20	9	94	43	217	3.3
Presbyterian	8	9	26	29	13	14	12	13	31	34	90	4.0
U.C.C.	1	4	8	32	5	20	6	24	5	20	25	4.6
Summary												
Jewish	8	18	6	13	3	7	4	9	24	53	45	4.0
Roman Catholic	50	11	81	18	53	12	77	17	197	43	458	4.7
All Protestant	147	16	238	26	108	12	121	13	314	34	928	3.7
Total	205	14	325	23	164	11	202	14	535	37	1,431	4.5

TABLE 4.7
1988 *American Library Directory* Libraries with the Highest Number of Professionals by Denomination

Library	Number of Professional Staff Members
Baptist	
1. Samford University, Birmingham, AL	13
2. Mississippi College, Clinton, MS	13
3. Wake Forest University, Winston-Salem, NC	13
4. Temple University, Philadelphia, PA	13
5. Baylor University, Waco, TX	13
6. University or Richmond, Richmond, VA	13
7. Acadia University, Wolfville, NS	13
8. McMaster University, Hamilton, ON	13
Christian	
1. Texas Christian University, Fort Worth, TX	13
Churches of Christ	
1. Pepperdine University, Malibu, CA	13
Episcopal/Anglican	
1. University of the South, Sewanee, TN	13
Independent	
1. Graduate Theological Union, Berkeley, CA	13
2. Brown University, Providence, RI	13
3. McGill University, Montreal, PQ	13
Lutheran	
1. Muhlenberg College, Allentown, PA	13
2. Wilfred Laurier University, Waterloo, ON	13
Methodist	
1. University of the Pacific, Stockton, CA	13
2. University of Denver, Denver, CO	13
3. Wesleyan University, Middletown, CT	13
4. American University, Washington, DC	13
5. Emory University, Atlanta, GA	13
6. DePauw University, Greencastle, IN	13
7 . Boston University, Boston, MA	13
8. Duke University, Durham, NC	13
9. Meharry Medical College, Nashville, TN	13
10. Southern Methodist University, Dallas, TX	13
Other Denominations	
1. Loma Linda University, Loma Linda, CA	13
2. Bryn Mawr College, Bryn Mawr, PA	13
3. Swarthmore College, Swarthmore, PA	13
4. Brigham Young University, Provo, UT	13
5. Church of Jesus Christ of Latter-day Saints, Salt Lake City, UT	13
6. Church of Jesus Christ of Latter-day Saints, Library Archives, Salt Lake City, UT	13
Presbyterian	
1. University of Tulsa, Tulsa, OK	13
2. Lafayette College, Easton, PA	13

TABLE 4.7 (*continued*)
1988 *American Library Directory* Libraries with the Highest Number of Professionals by Denomination

Library	Number of Professional Staff Members
3. Trinity University, San Antonio, TX	13
4. Queen's University, Kingston, ON	13
United Church of Christ	
1. Cedar Crest College, Allentown, PA	13
Jewish	
1. Brandeis University, Waltham, MA	13
2. Yeshiva University, New York, NY	13
3. Yivo Institute for Jewish Research, New York, NY	13
Roman Catholic	
1. Loyola Marymount University, Los Angeles, CA	13
2. University of San Francisco, San Francisco, CA	13
3. University of Santa Clara, Santa Clara, CA	13
4. The Catholic University of America, Washington, DC	13
5. Georgetown University, Washington, DC	13
6. Loyola University, Chicago, IL	13
7. University of Notre Dame, Notre Dame, IN	13
8. Loyola University, New Orleans, LA	13
9. Loyola-Notre Dame College, Baltimore, MD	13
10. Boston College, Chestnut Hill, MA	13
11. College of the Holy Cross, Worcester, MA	13
12. University of Detroit, Detroit, MI	13
13. Saint Johns University, Collegeville, MN	13
14. College of St. Benedict, St. Joseph, MN	13
15. College of St. Catherine, St. Paul, MN	13
16. College of St. Thomas, St. Paul, MN	13
17. St. Louis University, St. Louis, MO	13
18. Fordham University, Bronx, NY	13
19. Manhattan College, Bronx, NY	13
20. Canisius College, Buffalo, NY	13
21. Mercy College, Dobbs Ferry, NY	13
22. St. John's University, Jamaica, NY	13
23. University of Dayton, Dayton, OH	13
24. Saint Joseph's University, Philadelphia, PA	13
25. University of Scranton, Scranton, PA	13
26. Villanova University, Villanova, PA	13
27. Marquette University, Milwaukee, WI	13
28. University of Ottawa, Ottawa, ON	13
29. University of Quebec, Chicoutimi, Chicoutimi, PQ	13
30. University of Montreal, Montreal, PQ	13
31. University of Quebec, Montreal, PQ	13
32. University of Laval, Quebec, PQ	13
33. University of Sherbrooke, Sherbrooke, PQ	13

1. 13 professional staff members represents 10 or over. Some of the institutions listed maintain many more than 10 professionals.

TABLE 4.8
1988 *American Library Directory* Scholarly Clerical Staff Members by Library Type

Type of Library	1 Staff Member	%	2–3 Staff Members	%	4–5 Staff Members	%	6+ Staff Members	%	No Response	%	Number of Libraries	Mean Clerks Per Library
Scholarly	151	11	254	18	186	13	267	19	574	40	1,432	5
Junior College	14	13	19	18	12	11	5	5	58	54	108	3
Senior College	75	11	143	20	124	18	130	18	233	33	705	5
University	2	1	17	9	16	8	114	60	40	21	189	10
Seminary	21	9	42	18	25	11	14	6	129	56	231	4
Convent/Monastery	5	20	3	12	0	0	0	0	17	68	25	0
Denominational HQ	19	22	11	13	3	3	1	1	52	60	86	2
History/Archives	15	17	19	22	6	7	3	3	45	51	88	3

TABLE 4.9
1988 *American Library Directory* Seminary Libraries with the Highest Number of Clerical Staff Members by Denomination

Library	Denomination	Number of Clerks
1. Graduate Theological Union, Berkeley, CA	Independent	13
2. Southwestern Baptist Theological Seminary, Louisville, KY	Baptist	13
3. Hebrew Union College, Cincinnati, OH	Jewish	13
4. Southwestern Baptist Theological Seminary, Fort Worth, TX	Baptist	13
5. Asbury Theological Seminary, Asbury Wilmore, KY	Independent	9
6. New York Theological Seminary, New York, NY	Independent	9
7. Lee College, Cleveland, TN	Other Denominations	9
8. Mid-America Baptist Theological Seminary, Memphis, TN	Baptist	9
9. Harvard University, Cambridge, MA	Independent	8
10. Southeastern Baptist Theological Seminary, Wake Forest, NC	Baptist	8
11. Dallas Theological Seminary, Dallas, TX	Independent	8
12. Yale University Divinity School, New Haven, CT	Independent	7
13. St. Vincent College, Latrobe, PA	Roman Catholic	7
14. Southern Methodist University, Dallas, TX	Methodist	7
15. New Orleans Baptist Theological Seminary, New Orleans, LA	Baptist	6

TABLE 4.10
1988 *American Library Directory* Denominational Headquarters Libraries with the Highest Number of Clerical Staff Members

Library	Denomination	Number of Clerks
1. Canadian Center for Ecumenism, Montreal, PQ	Roman Catholic	7
2. First Church of Christ Scientist, Boston, MA	Other Denominations	4
3. American Baptist Churches, Valley Forge, PA	Baptist	4
4. Southern Baptist Convention, Richmond, VA	Baptist	4
5. Jewish Federation Council, Los Angeles, CA	Jewish	3
6. Dominican Education Center, Sinsinawa, WI	Roman Catholic	3
7. Christian Science Monitor, Boston, MA	Other Denominations	2
8. Reorganized Church of Jesus Christ of Latter-day Saints, Independence, MO	Other Denominations	2
9. Mt. Saint Mary Research Center, Kenmore, NY	Roman Catholic	2
10. American Jewish Committee, New York, NY	Jewish	2
11. Anti-Defamation League, New York, NY	Jewish	2
12. Diocese of Pittsburgh, Pittsburgh, PA	Roman Catholic	2
13. United Methodist Publishing House, Nashville, TN	Methodist	2
14. American Atheist, Austin, TX	Other Denominations	2
15. Society of Jesus, St. Jerome, PQ	Roman Catholic	2

TABLE 4.11
1988 *American Library Directory* Clerical Staff Members by Region for Scholarly Libraries

Region	1–2	%	3–4	%	5–6	%	7 and over	%	No Response	%	Number of Libraries	Mean Clerks
Northeast	18	24	9	12	6	8	15	20	28	37	76	5
Middle Atlantic	49	19	32	12	23	9	47	18	110	42	261	6
Southeast	53	20	55	21	27	10	35	13	96	36	266	5
Southwest	22	19	18	15	9	8	17	15	51	44	117	5
West	21	16	15	12	7	5	21	16	64	50	128	6
Rocky Mountains	2	10	1	5	2	10	4	19	12	57	21	7
Middle West	99	25	76	19	32	8	55	14	136	34	398	5
Canada	36	22	14	8	9	5	29	18	77	47	165	6
Total	300	21	220	15	115	8	223	16	574	40	1,432	5

TABLE 4.12
1978 and 1988 *American Library Directory* Longitudinal Study
Student Assistants by Library Type

Library Type	1978 No. of Libraries	1978 No Response	1978 Total Libraries	1978 Mean Student Assistants	1988 No. of Libraries	1988 No Response	1988 Total Libraries	1988 Mean Student Assistants	% Change 1978–88
Scholarly	554	821	1,375	11	675	757	1,432	15	36
Junior College	33	92	125	6	39	69	108	8	35
Senior College	357	347	704	11	405	300	705	15	36
University	90	64	154	19	127	62	189	24	26
Seminary	72	161	233	4	75	156	231	7	82
Convent/ Monastery	1	34	35	2	4	21	25	2	0
Denominational HQ	1	76	77	12	9	77	86	2	−80
History/Archives	0	47	47	0	16	72	88	6	0

TABLE 4.13
1988 *American Library Directory* Seminary Libraries with the Largest Number of Student Staff Members

	Library	Denomination	Number of Student Assistants
1.	Graduate Theological Union, Berkeley, CA	Independent	33.5
2.	Southwestern Baptist Theological Seminary, Fort Worth, TX	Baptist	33.5
3.	Yale University Divinity School, New Haven, CT	Independent	25.5
4.	Winnipeg Bible College, Otterburne, MB	Independent	23.5
5.	Southeastern Baptist Theological Seminary, Wake Forest, NC	Baptist	19.5
6.	St. Vincent College, Latrobe, PA	Roman Catholic	19.5
7.	Garrett-Seabury Theological Seminary, Evanston, IL	Methodist	15.5
8.	Harvard University, Cambridge, MA	Independent	15.5
9.	Golden Gate Baptist Theological Seminary, Mill Valley, CA	Baptist	11.5
10.	St. Meinrad College, St. Meinrad, IN	Roman Catholic	11.5
11.	St. Mary's Seminary, Baltimore, MD	Roman Catholic	11.5
12.	College of St. Thomas, St. Paul, MN	Roman Catholic	11.5
13.	Reformed Theological Seminary, Jackson, MS	Independent	11.5
14.	Phillips University, Enid, OK	Christian	11.5
15.	Calvary Baptist Theological Seminary, Lansdale, PA	Baptist	11.5

TABLE 4.14
1988 *American Library Directory* Denominational Headquarters Libraries with the Largest Number of Student Staff Members

Library	Denomination	Number of Student Assistants
1. Naropa Institute, Boulder, CO	Other Denominations	7.5
2. Dominicans de St. Albert le Grand, Montreal, PQ	Roman Catholic	3.5
3. Reorganized Church of Jesus Christ of Latter-day Saints, Independence, MO	Other Denominations	1.5
4. Lutheran Church Missouri Synod, St. Louis, MO	Lutheran	1.5
5. Ecumenical Music and Liturgy, Lincoln, NE	Independent	1.5
6. Catholic Foreign Mission Society, Maryknoll, NY	Roman Catholic	1.5
7. Western North Carolina Episcopal Diocese, Black Mountain, NC	Episcopal/Anglican	1.5
8. Stevens Atheist Library, Austin, TX	Other Denominations	1.5
9. Diocese of Olympia, Seattle, WA	Episcopal/Anglican	1.5

TABLE 4.15
1978 and 1988 *American Library Directory* Longitudinal Study Student Library Assistants by Denomination

	-----------1 9 7 8-----------				-----------1 9 8 8-----------				
Library Type	No. of Libraries	No Response	Total Libraries	Mean Students	No. of Libraries	No Response	Total Libraries	Mean Students	% Change 1978–88
Baptist	79	144	223	11	104	119	223	15	36.0
Christian	23	36	59	8	28	30	58	13	73.0
Churches of Christ	14	13	27	13	17	12	29	14	7.7
Episcopal/Anglican	15	59	74	6	18	48	66	11	100.0
Independent	36	51	87	9	46	54	100	12	30.0
Lutheran	37	86	123	10	44	74	118	17	70.0
Mennonite	6	11	17	6	13	13	26	9	50.0
Methodist	69	133	202	13	107	106	213	16	23.0
Other Denominations	92	205	297	9	95	199	294	13	41.0
Presbyterian	63	142	205	10	60	127	187	13	30.0
U.C.C.	14	23	37	7	21	17	38	15	121.0
Summary									
Jewish	34	164	198	3	29	203	232	5	39.0
Roman Catholic	172	341	513	10	196	294	490	14	40.0
All Protestant	448	903	1,351	10	553	799	1,352	14	40.0
Total	654	1,408	2,062	10	778	1,296	2,074	14	44.0

TABLE 4.16
1978 and 1988 *American Library Directory* Longitudinal Study Size of Entire Staff for Scholarly Libraries

Position Level	1 Staff Member	%	2–3 Staff Members	%	4–5 Staff Members	%	6–9 Staff Members	%	10+ Staff Members	%	No Response	%	No. of Libraries	Mean Staff per Library
							1978							
Professional	183	13	270	20	155	11	105	8	46	3	616	45	1,375	4
Clerical	145	11	245	18	132	10	89	6	110	8	654	48	1,375	5
							1988							
Professional	205	14	325	23	164	11	130	9	72	5	535	37	1,431	4
Clerical	151	11	254	18	186	13	117	8	150	10	573	40	1,431	6
							Percentage Change							
Professional	12		20		6		24		57		−13		4	5
Clerical	4		4		41		31		36		−12		4	9

TABLE 4.16 (continued)
1978 and 1988 *American Library Directory* Longitudinal Study Size of Entire Staff for Scholarly Libraries

Position Level	1 Staff Member	%	2–3 Staff Members	%	4–5 Staff Members	%	6–9 Staff Members	%	10+ Staff Members	%	No Response	%	No. of Libraries	Mean Staff per Library
							1978							
Student Assistants	193	14	123	9	79	6	43	3	116	8	821	60	1,375	11
All Staff	149	11	151	11	111	8	90	7	274	20	600	44	1,375	16
							1988							
Student Assistants	161	11	110	8	98	7	56	4	250	17	756	53	1,431	15
All Staff	178	12	149	10	106	7	95	7	417	29	486	34	1,431	19
							Percentage Change							
Student Assistants	−17		−11		24		30		116		−8		4	36
All Staff	19		−1		−5		6		52		−19		4	19

TABLE 4.17

1978 and 1988 *American Library Directory* Longitudinal Study Total Scholarly Library Staff Membership by Library Type

Library Type	1978 No. of Libraries	1978 No Response	1978 Total Libraries	1978 Mean Members	1988 No. of Libraries	1988 No Response	1988 Total Libraries	1988 Mean Members	% Change 1978–88
Scholarly	775	600	1,375	16.0	945	486	1,431	19.0	19
Junior College	50	75	125	8.0	57	51	108	10.0	25
Senior College	440	264	704	16.0	513	192	705	20.0	25
University	115	39	154	32.0	157	32	189	36.0	13
Seminary	105	128	233	8.0	114	116	230	10.0	25
Convent/ Monastery	7	28	35	3.0	11	14	25	2.4	−20
Denominational HQ	33	44	77	3.6	41	45	86	3.2	−11
History/Archives	25	22	47	5.0	52	36	88	6.0	20

TABLE 4.18

1988 *American Library Directory* Entire Staff by Region for Scholarly Libraries

Region	Number of Libraries	Total Staff Members	No Response	Mean Staff Members per Library
Northeast	76	985	25	19
Middle Atlantic	261	3,080	93	18
Southeast	266	3,973	81	21
Southwest	117	1,515	38	19
West	128	1,396	51	18
Rocky Mountains	21	221	10	20
Middle West	398	5,518	118	20
Canada	165	1,261	71	13
Total	1,432	17,949	487	19

TABLE 4.19
1988 *American Library Directory* Total Library Staff Size by Total Annual Library Expenditure for Scholarly Libraries

	Total Library Staff Size											
Library Expenditures	1–4	%	5–8	%	9–12	%	13 & over	%	No Response	%	No. of Libraries	Mean Members
Under $1,500	3	25	0	0	0	0	0	0	9	75	12	2
$1,501–$20,000	31	48	7	11	0	0	2	3	25	38	65	3
$20,001–$95,000	48	24	35	17	26	13	22	11	73	36	204	7
$95,001–$220,000	26	9	46	16	34	11	113	38	77	26	296	15
$220,001–$410,000	2	1	27	12	27	12	129	59	33	15	218	22
$410,001–$510,000	0	0	1	2	3	6	34	69	11	22	49	28
$510,001 & over	1	0	3	1	2	1	174	85	24	12	204	39
No response	67	17	30	8	14	4	38	10	235	61	384	10
Total	178	12	149	10	106	7	512	36	487	34	1,432	19

TABLE 4.20

1988 *American Library Directory* Libraries with the Highest Number of Total Staff Members by Denomination

	Total Number of Staff Members
Baptist	
1. Samford University, Birmingham, AL	59.5
2. Wake Forest University, Winston-Salem, NC	59.5
3. Temple University, Philadelphia, PA	59.5
4. Southwestern Baptist Theological Seminary, Fort Worth, TX	59.5
5. Baylor University, Waco, TX	59.5
6. University of Richmond, Richmond, VA	59.5
Churches of Christ	
1. Pepperdine University, Malibu, CA	59.5
2. Abilene Christian University, Abilene, TX	59.5
Episcopal/Anglican	
1. University of the South, Sewanee, TN	59.5
Independent	
1. Graduate Theological Union, Berkeley, CA	59.5
2. Brown University, Providence, RI	59.5
3. McGill University, Montreal, PQ	59.5
Lutheran	
1. Muhlenberg College, Allentown, PA	59.5
Methodist	
1. University of the Pacific, Stockton, CA	59.5
2. University of Denver, Denver, CO	59.5
3. Wesleyan University, Middletown, CT	59.5
4. American University, Washington, DC	59.5
5. Emory University, Atlanta, GA	59.5
6. Mercer University, Macon, GA	59.5
7. University of Evansville, Evansville, IN	59.5
8. DePauw University, Greencastle, IN	59.5
9. Boston University, Boston, MA	59.5
10. Duke University, Durham, NC	59.5
Other Denominations	
1. Brigham Young University, Provo, UT	59.5
2. Church of Jesus Christ of Latter-day Saints, Salt Lake City, UT	59.5
Presbyterian	
1. Trinity University, San Antonio, TX	59.5
United Church of Christ	
1. Cedar Crest College, Allentown, PA	59.5
2. Franklin and Marshall College, Lancaster, PA	59.5
Jewish	
1. Brandeis University, Waltham, MA	59.5

TABLE 4.20 (*continued*)
1988 *American Library Directory* Libraries with the Highest Number of Total Staff Members by Denomination

	Total Number of Staff Members
Roman Catholic	
1. Loyola Marymount University, Los Angeles, CA	59.5
2. Loyola University, Chicago, IL	59.5
3. University of Notre Dame, Notre Dame, IN	59.5
4. Loyola University, New Orleans, LA	59.5
5. Boston College, Chestnut Hill, MA	59.5
6. College of the Holy Cross, Worcester, MA	59.5
7. Saint John's University, Collegeville, MN	59.5
8. College of St. Benedict, St. Joseph, MN	59.5
9. College of St. Catherine, St. Paul. MN	59.5
10. Fordham University, Bronx, NY	59.5
11. Mercy College, Dobbs Ferry, NY	59.5
12. St. John's University, Jamaica, NY	59.5
13. University of Dayton, Dayton, OH	59.5
14. Saint Joseph's University, Philadelphia, PA	59.5
15. University of Scranton, Scranton, PA	59.5
16. Villanova University, Villanova, PA	59.5
17. University of Montreal, Montreal, PQ	59.5
18. University of Quebec, Montreal, PQ	59.5

TABLE 4.21
1978 *American Library Directory* Scholarly Libraries with the Highest Number of Total Staff Members

	Library	Denomination	Total Number of Staff Members
1.	Georgetown University, Washington, DC	Roman Catholic	59.5
2.	Emory University, Atlanta, GA	Methodist	59.5
3.	DePaul University, Chicago, IL	Roman Catholic	59.5
4.	Duke University, Durham, NC	Methodist	59.5
5.	Wake Forest University, Winston-Salem, NC	Baptist	59.5
6.	Fordham University, Bronx, NY	Roman Catholic	59.5
7.	St. John's University, Jamaica, NY	Roman Catholic	59.5
8.	University of Dayton, Dayton, OH	Roman Catholic	59.5
9.	Temple University, Philadelphia, PA	Baptist	59.5
10.	Trinity University, San Antonio, TX	Presbyterian	59.5
11.	Brigham Young University, Provo, UT	Other Denominations	59.5
12.	Wheaton College, Wheaton, IL	Independent	55.5
13.	University of Evansville, Evansville, IN	Methodist	54.5
14.	College of the Holy Cross, Worcester, MA	Roman Catholic	54.5
15.	Baldwin-Wallace College, Berea, OH	Methodist	54.5
16.	Southwestern Baptist Theological Seminary, Ft. Worth, TX	Baptist	54.5
17.	Wesleyan University, Middletown, CT	Methodist	53.5
18.	The Catholic University of America, Washington, DC	Roman Catholic	53.5
19.	Brigham Young University, Laie, HI	Other Denominations	53.5
20.	Loyola University, Chicago, IL	Roman Catholic	53.5
21.	DePauw University, Greencastle, IN	Methodist	53.5
22.	Brandeis University, Waltham, MA	Jewish	53.5
23.	College of St. Catharine, St. Paul, MN	Roman Catholic	53.5
24.	Creighton University, Omaha, NE	Roman Catholic	53.5
25.	Wittenberg University, Springfield, OH	Lutheran	53.5
26.	Franklin and Marshall College, Lancaster, PA	United Church of Christ	53.5

TABLE 4.22
1988 *American Library Directory* Libraries with the Highest Number of Total Staff Members in Alphabetical Order by State/Province

	Library	Denomination	Total Number of Staff Members
1.	Samford University, Birmingham, AL	Baptist	59.5
2.	Graduate Theological Union, Berkeley, CA	Independent	59.5
3.	Loyola Marymount University, Los Angeles, CA	Roman Catholic	59.5
4.	Pepperdine University, Malibu, CA	Churches of Christ	59.5
5.	University of the Pacific, Stockton, CA	Methodist	59.5
6.	University of Denver, Denver, CO	Methodist	59.5
7.	Wesleyan University, Middletown, CT	Methodist	59.5
8.	American University, Washington, DC	Methodist	59.5
9.	Emory University, Atlanta, GA	Methodist	59.5
10.	Mercer University, Macon, GA	Methodist	59.5
11.	Loyola University, Chicago, IL	Roman Catholic	59.5
12.	University of Evansville, Evansville, IN	Methodist	59.5
13.	DePauw University, Greencastle, IN	Methodist	59.5
14.	University of Notre Dame, Notre Dame, IN	Roman Catholic	59.5
15.	Loyola University, New Orleans, LA	Roman Catholic	59.5
16.	Boston University, Boston, MA	Methodist	59.5
17.	Boston College, Chestnut Hill, MA	Roman Catholic	59.5
18.	Brandeis University, Waltham, MA	Jewish	59.5
19.	College of the Holy Cross, Worcester, MA	Roman Catholic	59.5
20.	Saint John's University, Collegeville, MN	Roman Catholic	59.5
21.	College of St. Benedict, St. Joseph, MN	Roman Catholic	59.5
22.	College of St. Catherine, St. Paul, MN	Roman Catholic	59.5
23.	Duke University, Durham, NC	Methodist	59.5
24.	Wake Forest University, Winston-Salem, NC	Baptist	59.5
25.	Fordham University, Bronx, NY	Roman Catholic	59.5
26.	Mercy College, Dobbs Ferry, NY	Roman Catholic	59.5
27.	St. John's University, Jamaica, NY	Roman Catholic	59.5
28.	University of Dayton, Dayton, OH	Roman Catholic	59.5
29.	Cedar Crest College, Allentown, PA	United Ch. of Christ	59.5
30.	Muhlenberg College, Bethlehem, PA	Lutheran	59.5
31.	Franklin and Marshall College, Lancaster, PA	United Ch. of Christ	59.5
32.	Saint Joseph's University, Philadelphia, PA	Roman Catholic	59.5
33.	Temple University, Philadelphia, PA	Baptist	59.5
34.	University of Scranton, Scranton, PA	Roman Catholic	59.5
35.	Villanova University, Villanova, PA	Roman Catholic	59.5
36.	Brown University, Providence, RI	Independent	59.5
37.	University of the South, Sewanee, TN	Episcopal/Anglican	59.5
38.	Abilene Christian University, Abilene, TX	Churches of Christ	59.5
39.	Southwestern Baptist Theological Seminary, Forth Worth, TX	Baptist	59.5

TABLE 4.22 (*continued*)
1988 *American Library Directory* Libraries with Highest Number of Total Staff Members in Alphabetical Order by State/Province

40.	Trinity University, San Antonio, TX	Presbyterian	59.5
41.	Baylor University, Waco, TX	Baptist	59.5
42.	Brigham Young University, Provo, UT	Other Denominations	59.5
43.	Church of Jesus Christ of Latter-day Saints, Salt Lake City, UT	Other Denominations	59.5
44.	University of Richmond, Richmond, VA	Baptist	59.5
45.	McGill University, Montreal, PQ	Independent	59.5
46.	University of Montreal, Montreal, PQ	Roman Catholic	59.5
47.	University of Quebec, Montreal, PQ	Roman Catholic	59.5

TABLE 4.23
1978 and 1988 *American Library Directory* Longitudinal Study
Scholarly Library Total Staff Members by Denomination

	1978				1988			
Denomination	No. of Libraries	No Response	Total Libraries	Mean Members	No. of Libraries	No Response	Total Libraries	Mean Members
Baptist	84	56	140	18.0	109	43	152	22.0
Christian	23	17	40	12.0	28	13	41	17.0
Churches of Christ	18	9	27	16.0	21	6	27	18.0
Episcopal/Anglican	16	16	32	11.0	20	12	32	16.0
Independent	46	36	82	14.0	65	32	97	16.0
Lutheran	38	32	70	17.0	53	23	76	23.0
Mennonite	11	3	14	7.9	17	5	22	11.0
Methodist	90	57	147	19.0	118	31	149	22.0
Other Denominations	108	97	205	14.0	131	86	217	15.0
Presbyterian	57	33	90	18.0	59	31	90	21.0
U.C.C.	15	9	24	14.0	20	5	25	25.0
Summary								
Jewish	20	15	35	9.7	25	20	45	8.5
Roman Catholic	249	220	469	16.0	279	179	458	20.0
All Protestant	506	365	871	16.0	641	287	928	19.0
Total	775	600	1,375	16.0	945	486	1,431	19.0

TABLE 4.24

1988 *American Library Directory* Denominations Having the Largest Number of Library Staff Members[1,2,3]

Denomination	Number of Libraries with Over 40 Staff Members	Percentage of Libraries with Over 40 Staff Members
Roman Catholic	42	29
Baptist	24	16
Methodist	19	13
Lutheran	13	9
Independent	12	8
Presbyterian	9	6
United Church of Christ	5	3
Churches of Christ	4	3
Episcopal/Anglican	3	2
Friends	3	2
Mormon	3	2
Adventist	2	1
Christian	2	1
Brethren	1	1
Christian Science	1	1
Jewish	1	1
Mennonite	1	1
Moravian	1	1
Total	146	100

1. These 146 libraries represented 7.0 percent of the entire 1988 sample.
2. Scholarly equaled 98.6 percent and popular equalled 1.4 percent of these libraries.
3. Number of large 1978 libraries still found in the 1988 edition equaled 50, or 34 percent of the number of, large 1988 libraries.

TABLE 4.25
1978 and 1988 *American Library Directory* Total Library Staff Size by Chief Librarian's Gender for Scholarly Libraries

Librarian's Gender	1–4	%	5–8	%	9–12	%	13+ and over	%	No Response	%	No. of Libraries	Mean Members
	Total Library Staff Size, 1978											
Male	70	10	82	12	52	7	231	33	266	38	701	18.0
Female	76	13	69	12	59	10	132	22	257	43	593	14.0
No response	3	4	0	0	0	0	1	1	77	95	81	4.1
Total	149	11	151	11	111	8	364	26	600	44	1,375	16.0
	Total Library Staff Size, 1988											
Male	89	12	69	9	53	7	306	40	252	33	769	21.0
Female	83	13	79	12	53	8	203	32	226	35	644	17.0
No response	6	32	1	5	0	0	3	16	9	47	19	12.0
Total	178	12	149	10	106	7	512	36	487	34	1,432	19.0

TABLE 4.26
1988 *American Library Directory* Total Staff Size by Library Type

Library Type	Total Library Staff Size: 1–4	%	5–8	%	9–12	%	13+ and over	%	No Response	%	No. of Libraries	Mean Members
Scholarly	178	12	149	10	106	7	512	36	486	34	1,431	19.0
Junior College	12	11	15	14	12	11	18	17	51	47	108	10.0
Senior College	57	8	77	11	64	9	315	45	192	27	705	20.0
University	4	2	6	3	8	4	139	74	32	17	189	36.0
Seminary	33	14	32	14	17	7	32	14	116	50	230	10.0
Convent/ Monastery	10	40	1	4	0	0	0	0	14	56	25	2.4
Denominational HQ	31	36	7	8	3	3	0	0	45	52	86	3.2
History/Archives	31	35	11	13	2	2	8	9	36	41	88	6.0

TABLE 4.27
1988 *American Library Directory* Scholarly Baptist Libraries with the Largest Number of Professional Staff Members

	Library	Number of Professionals
1.	Samford University, Birmingham, AL	13
2.	Mississippi College, Clinton, MS	13
3.	Wake Forest University, Winston-Salem, NC	13
4.	Temple University, Philadelphia, PA	13
5.	Baylor University, Waco, TX	13
6.	University of Richmond, Richmond, VA	13
7.	Acadia University, Wolfville, NS	13
8.	McMaster University, Hamilton, ON	13
9.	Benedict College, Columbia, SC	9
10.	Southwestern Baptist Theological Seminary, Fort Worth, TX	9

TABLE 4.28
1978 *American Library Directory* Scholarly Baptist Libraries with the Largest Total Number of Staff Members

	Library	Number of Staff Members
1.	Wake Forest University, Winston-Salem, NC	59.5
2.	Temple University, Philadelphia, PA	59.5
3.	Southwestern Baptist Theological Seminary, Fort Worth, TX	54.5
4.	Stetson University, DeLand, FL	51.5
5.	Tennessee Temple Schools, Chattanooga, TN	49.5
6.	Campbell University, Buies Creek, NC	48.5
7.	Mercer University, Macon, GA	46.5
8.	Benedict College, Columbia, SC	45.5
9.	Hardin-Simmons University, Abilene, TX	44.5
10.	Virginia Union University, Richmond, VA	44.5
11.	Carson-Newman College, Jefferson City, TN	41.5

TABLE 4.29
1988 *American Library Directory* Scholarly Baptist Libraries with the Largest Total Number of Staff Members

Library	Number of Staff Members
1. Samford University, Birmingham, AL	59.5
2. Wake Forest University, Winston-Salem, NC	59.5
3. Temple University, Philadelphia, PA	59.5
4. Baylor University, Waco, TX	59.5
5. University of Richmond, Richmond, VA	59.5
6. Southwestern Baptist Theological Seminary, Fort Worth, TX	55.5
7. Stetson University, DeLand, FL	54.5
8. Liberty University, Lynchburg, VA	54.5
9. Mercer University, Macon, GA	53.5
10. Furman University, Greenville, SC	53.5

TABLE 4.30
1988 *American Library Directory* Scholarly Christian Libraries with the Largest Number of Professional Staff Members

Library	Number of Professionals
1. Texas Christian University, Fort Worth, TX	13
2. Chapman University, Orange, CA	6
3. Lynchburg College, Lynchburg, VA	6
4. Atlantic Christian College, Wilson, NC	5
5. Hiram College, Hiram, OH	5
6. Columbia College, Columbia, MO	4
7. Jarvis Christian College, Hawkins, TX	4

TABLE 4.31
1988 *American Library Directory* Scholarly Christian Libraries with the Largest Number of Clerical Staff Members

Library	Number of Clerks
1. Texas Christian University, Fort Worth, TX	13
2. Chapman University, Orange, CA	8
3. Hiram College, Hiram, OH	8
4. Ozark Christian College, Joplin, MO	6
5. Lynchburg College, Lynchburg, VA	6
6. Transylvania University, Lexington, KY	4
7. Atlantic Christian College, Wilson, NC	4
8. Phillips University, Enid, OK	4
9. Jarvis Christian College, Hawkins, TX	4
10. Bethany College, Bethany, WV	4

TABLE 4.32
1988 *American Library Directory* Scholarly Christian Libraries with the Largest Total Number of Staff Member

Library	Number of Staff Members
1. Texas Christian University, Fort Worth, TX	47.5
2. Lynchburg College, Lynchburg, VA	45.5
3. Bethany College, Bethany, WV	39.5
4. Phillips University, Enid, OK	31.5
5. Atlantic Christian College, Wilson, NC	28.5
6. Chapman University, Orange, CA	27.5
7. Jarvis Christian College, Hawkins, TX	27.5
8. Culver-Stockton College, Canton, MO	26.5
9. Eureka College, Eureka, IL	23.5
10. Johnson Bible College, Knoxville, TN	22.5

TABLE 4.33
1988 *American Library Directory* Scholarly Churches of Christ Libraries with the Largest Number of Professional Staff Members

Library	Number of Professionals
1. Pepperdine University, Malibu, CA	13
2. Abilene Christian University, Abilene, TX	9
3. Harding University, Searcy, AR	6
4. David Lipscomb University, Nashville, TN	6
5. Freed-Hardeman University, Henderson, TN	4

TABLE 4.34
1988 *American Library Directory* Scholarly Churches of Christ Libraries with the Largest Number of Clerical Staff Members

Library	Number of Clerks
1. Pepperdine University, Malibu, CA	13
2. Abilene Christian University, Abilene, TX	13
3. Columbia Christian College, Portland, OR	7
4. Harding University, Searcy, AR	6
5. Great Lakes Bible College, Lansing, MI	6
6. David Lipscomb University, Nashville, TN	5
7. Lubbock Christian University, Lubbock, TX	4
8. Oklahoma Christian College, Oklahoma City, OK	3
9. Ambassador College, Big Sandy, TX	3
10. Amber University, Garland, TX	3

TABLE 4.35
1988 *American Library Directory* Scholarly Churches of Christ Libraries with the Largest Total Number of Staff Members

Library	Number of Staff Members
1. Pepperdine University, Malibu, CA	59.5
2. Abilene Christian University, Abilene, TX	55.5
3. Harding University, Searcy, AR	45.5
4. David Lipscomb University, Nashville, TN	44.5
5. Oklahoma Christian College, Oklahoma City, OK	22.5
6. Ambassador College, Big Sandy, TX	21.5
7. Lubbock Christian University, Lubbock, TX	19.5
8. Freed-Hardeman University, Henderson, TN	17.5
9. Ohio Valley College, Parkersburg, WV	14.5
10. Southwestern Christian College, Terrell, TX	9.5

TABLE 4.36
1978 *American Library Directory* Scholarly Congregational Libraries with the Largest Total Number of Staff Members

Library	Number of Staff Members
1. Washburn University, Topeka, KS	38.5
2. Olivet College, Olivet, MI	9.5
3. American Congregational Association, Boston, MA	7.0

TABLE 4.37
1988 *American Library Directory* Scholarly Episcopal/Anglican Libraries with the Largest Number of Professional Staff Members

Library	Number of Professionals
1. University of the South, Sewanee, TN	13
2. Kenyon College, Gambier, OH	7
3. Bishop's University, Lennoxville, PQ	7
4. Hobart and William Smith Colleges, Geneva, NY	6
5. Saint Mary's College, Raleigh, NC	4
6. Voorhees College, Denmark, SC	4
7. Saint Paul's College, Lawrenceville, VA	4

TABLE 4.38
1988 *American Library Directory* Scholarly Episcopal/Anglican Libraries with the Largest Number of Clerical Staff Members

Library	Number of Clerks
1. Hobart and William Smith Colleges, Geneva, NY	13
2. University of the South, Sewanee, TN	13
3. Bishop's University, Lennoxville, PQ	13
4. Kenyon College, Gambier, OH	9
5. Bard College, Annandale-on-Hudson, NY	5
6. Saint Mary's College, Raleigh, NC	5
7. Huron College, London, ON	5
8. George Mercer School of Theology, Garden City, NY	4
9. General Theological Seminary, New York, NY	4

TABLE 4.39
1988 *American Library Directory* Scholarly Episcopal/Anglican Libraries with the Largest Total Number of Staff Members

Library	Number of Staff Members
1. University of the South, Sewanee, TN	59.5
2. Bard College, Annandale-on-Hudson, NY	41.5
3. Voorhees College, Denmark, SC	40.5
4. Saint Paul's College, Lawrenceville, VA	29.5
5. Bishop's University, Lennoxville, PQ	23.5
6. Hobart and William Smith Colleges, Geneva, NY	22.5
7. Saint Mary's College, Raleigh, NC	20.5
8. Huron College, London, ON	16.5
9. Kenyon College, Gambier, OH	16.0
10. University of King's College, Halifax, NS	9.5

TABLE 4.40
1988 *American Library Directory* Scholarly Independent Libraries with the Largest Number of Professional Staff Members

Library	Number of Professionals
1. Graduate Theological Union, Berkeley, CA	13
2. Brown University, Providence, RI	13
3. McGill University, Montreal, PQ	13
4. Wheaton College, Wheaton, IL	8
5. Berea College, Berea, KY	8
6. Oral Roberts University, Tulsa, OK	8
7. Christian Broadcasting Network University, Virginia Beach, VA	8
8. Azusa Pacific University, Azusa, CA	7
9. Harvard University Divinity School, Cambridge, MA	7
10. Union Theological Seminary, New York, NY	7

TABLE 4.41
1988 *American Library Directory* Scholarly Independent Libraries with the Largest Number of Clerical Staff Members

Library	Number of Clerks
1. John Brown University, Siloam Springs, AR	13
2. Graduate Theological Union, Berkeley, CA	13
3. Biola University, La Mirada, CA	13
4. Wheaton College, Wheaton, IL	13
5. Brown University, Providence, RI	13
6. Bob Jones University, Greenville, SC	13
7. Christian Broadcasting Network University, Virginia Beach, VA	13
8. McGill University, Montreal, PQ	13
9. New York Theological Seminary, New York, NY	9
10. Columbia Bible College, Columbia, SC	9

TABLE 4.42

1988 *American Library Directory* Scholarly Independent Libraries with the Largest Total Number of Staff Members

Library	Number of Staff Members
1. Graduate Theological Union, Berkeley, CA	59.5
2. Brown University, Providence, RI	59.5
3. McGill University, Montreal, PQ	59.5
4. Wheaton College, Wheaton, IL	54.5
5. Bob Jones University, Greenville, SC	50.5
6. Berea College, Berea, KY	47.5
7. Azusa Pacific University, Azusa, CA	43.5
8. Biola University, La Mirada, CA	43.5
9. Westmont College, Santa Barbara, CA	42.5
10. Shaw University, Raleigh, NC	41.5

TABLE 4.43

1988 *American Library Directory* Scholarly Lutheran Libraries with the Largest Number of Professional Staff Members

Library	Number of Professionals
1. Muhlenberg College, Allentown, PA	13
2. Wilfred Laurier University, Waterloo, ON	13
3. St. Olaf College, Northfield, MN	8
4. Gettysburg College, Gettysburg, PA	8
5. Augustana College, Rock Island, IL	7
6. Concordia College, Moorhead, MN	7
7. Capital University, Columbus, OH	7

TABLE 4.44
1988 *American Library Directory* Scholarly Lutheran Libraries with the Largest Number of Student Staff Members

Library	Number of Student Assistants
1. Upsala College, East Orange, NJ	33.5
2. Lenoir-Rhyne College, Hickory, NC	33.5
3. Wittenberg University, Springfield, OH	33.5
4. Thiel College, Greenville, PA	33.5
5. Augustana College, Sioux Falls, SD	33.5
6. Susquehanna University, Selinsgrove, PA	13.5
7. Capital University, Columbus, OH	11.5
8. Valparaiso University, Valparaiso, IN	9.5
9. Luther College, Decorah, IA	9.5
10. Dana College, Blair, NE	9.5

TABLE 4.45
1988 *American Library Directory* Scholarly Mennonite Libraries with the Largest Number of Professional Staff Members

Library	Number of Professionals
1. Goshen College, Goshen, IN	3
2. Goshen College Mennonite Historical Library, Goshen, IN	3
3. Bethel College, North Newton, KS	3
4. Eastern Mennonite University, Harrisonburg, VA	3
5. Fresno Pacific College, Fresno, CA	2
6. Associated Mennonite Biblical Seminaries, Elkhart, IN	2
7. Tabor College, Hillsboro, KS	2
8. Lancaster Mennonite Historical Society, Lancaster, PA	2

TABLE 4.46
1988 *American Library Directory* Scholarly Mennonite Libraries with the Largest Total Number of Staff Members

Library	Number of Staff Members
1. Eastern Mennonite University, Harrisonburg, VA	40.5
2. Mennonite Brethren Church Bible Institute, Winkler, MB	20.5
3. Bethel College, North Newton, KS	18.5
4. Goshen College Mennonite Historical Library, Goshen, IN	14.5
5. Goshen College, Goshen, IN	12.5
6. Lancaster Mennonite Historical Society, Lancaster, PA	12.5
7. Mennonite Historical Library, Lansdale, PA	12.5
8. Columbia Bible College, Clearbrook, BC	12.5
9. Hesston College, Hesston, KS	9.5

TABLE 4.47
1978 *American Library Directory* Scholarly Methodist Libraries with the Largest Number of Clerical Staff Members

Library	Number of Clerks
1. University of the Pacific, Stockton, CA	13
2. University of Denver, Denver, CO	13
3. Wesleyan University, Middletown, CT	13
4. American University, Washington, DC	13
5. Emory University, Atlanta, GA	13
6. University of Evansville, Evansville, IN	13
7. DePauw University, Greencastle, IN	13
8. Boston University, Boston, MA	13
9. Duke University, Durham, NC	13
10. Ohio Northern University, Ada, OH	13
11. Baldwin-Wallace College, Berea, OH	13
12. Dickinson College, Carlisle, PA	13
13. Southern Methodist University, Dallas, TX	13
14. University of Puget Sound, Tacoma, WA	13

TABLE 4.48
1988 *American Library Directory* Scholarly Methodist Libraries with the Largest Total Number of Staff Members

Library	Number of Staff Members
1. University of the Pacific, Stockton, CA	59.5
2. University of Denver, Denver, CO	59.5
3. Wesleyan University, Middletown, CT	59.5
4. American University, Washington, DC	59.5
5. Emory University, Atlanta, GA	59.5
6. DePauw University, Greencastle, IN	59.5
7. Boston University, Boston, MA	59.5
8. Duke University, Durham, NC	59.5
9. University of Evansville, Evansville, IN	55.5
10. Dickinson College, Carlisle, PA	54.5

TABLE 4.49
1978 *American Library Directory* Scholarly Other Denomination Libraries with the Largest Number of Clerical Staff Members

Library	Number of Clerks
1. Loma Linda University, Loma Linda, CA	13
2. Loma Linda University, Riverside, CA	13
3. Brigham Young University, Laie, HI	13
4. Ashland University, Ashland, OH	13
5. Bryn Mawr College, Bryn Mawr, PA	13
6. Swarthmore College, Swarthmore, PA	13
7. Brigham Young University, Provo, UT	13
8. Church of Jesus Christ of Latter-day Saints, Salt Lake City, UT	13
9. University of Winnipeg, Winnipeg, MB	13
10. Mount Allison University, Sackville, NB	13

TABLE 4.50
1988 *American Library Directory* Scholarly Other Denomination Libraries with the Largest Total Number of Staff Members

Library	Number of Staff Members
1. Brigham Young University, Provo, UT	59.5
2. Messiah College, Grantham, PA	46.5
3. Aurora University, Aurora, IL	45.5
4. Moravian College, Bethlehem, PA	44.5
5. Earlham College, Richmond, IN	43.5
6. Whittier College, Whittier, CA	42.5
7. Bryn Mawr College, Bryn Mawr, PA	41.5
8. Southern College, Collegedale, TN	41.5
9. Principia College, Elsah, IL	40.5

TABLE 4.51
1988 *American Library Directory* Scholarly Presbyterian Libraries with the Largest Number of Clerical Staff Members

Library	Number of Clerks
1. Bloomfield College, Bloomfield, NJ	13
2. Davidson College, Davidson, NC	13
3. College of Wooster, Wooster, OH	13
4. University of Tulsa, Tulsa, OK	13
5. Columbia Christian College, Portland, OR	13
6. Lafayette College, Easton, PA	13
7. Presbyterian Church Office of History, Philadelphia, PA	13
8. Trinity University, San Antonio, TX	13
9. Queen's University, Kingston, ON	13
10. Coe College, Cedar Rapids, IA	8
11. Macalester College, St. Paul, MN	7
12. Westminster College, New Wilmington, PA	7

TABLE 4.52
1988 *American Library Directory* Scholarly Presbyterian Libraries with the Largest Total Number of Staff Members

Library	Number of Staff Members
1. Trinity University, San Antonio, TX	59.5
2. Queen's University, Kingston, ON	49.5
3. Lafayette College, Easton, PA	45.5
4. Millikan University, Decatur, IL	44.5
5. Lake Forest College, Lake Forest, IL	44.5
6. Coe College, Cedar Rapids, IA	44.5
7. Alma College, Alma, MI	44.5
8. University of Tulsa, Tulsa, OK	41.5
9. Hanover College, Hanover, IN	40.5
10. Buena Vista University, Storm Lake, IA	38.5
11. Beaver College, Glenside, PA	36.5

TABLE 4.53
1988 *American Library Directory* Scholarly United Church of Christ Libraries with the Largest Number of Clerical Staff Members

Library	Number of Clerks
1. Elmhurst College, Elmhurst, IL	13
2. Eden Webster University, St. Louis, MO	13
3. Cedar Crest College, Allentown, PA	13
4. Franklin and Marshall College, Lancaster, PA	13
5. Elon College, Elon College, NC	9
6. Doane College, Crete, NE	8
7. Pacific University, Forest Grove, OR	8
8. Drury College, Springfield, MO	6
9. Hood College, Frederick, MD	5

TABLE 4.54
1978 *American Library Directory* Scholarly United Church of Christ Libraries with the Largest Number of Student Staff Members

Library	Number of Student Assistants
1. Franklin and Marshall College, Lancaster, PA	33.5
2. Webster College Eden Theological Seminary, St. Louis, MO	15.5
3. Lakeland College, Sheboygan, WI	15.5
4. Elmhurst, College, Elmhurst, IL	3.5
5. Catawba College, Salisbury, NC	3.5
6. Heidelberg College, Tiffin, OH	3.5
7. Cedar Crest College, Allentown, PA	3.5
8. Lancaster Theological Seminary, Lancaster, PA	3.5
9. Northland College, Ashland, WI	3.5

TABLE 4.55
1988 *American Library Directory* Scholarly United Church of Christ Libraries with the Largest Number of Student Staff Members

Library	Number of Student Assistants
1. Elmhurst College, Elmhurst, IL	33.5
2. Hood College, Frederick, MD	33.5
3. Cedar Crest College, Allentown, PA	33.5
4. Franklin and Marshall College, Lancaster, PA	33.5
5. Fisk University, Nashville, TN	33.5
6. Heidelberg College, Tiffin, OH	25.5
7. Catawba College, Salisbury, NC	17.5
8. Huston-Tillotson College, Austin, TX	17.5
9. Drury College, Springfield, MO	15.5

TABLE 4.56
1988 *American Library Directory* Scholarly Jewish Libraries with the Largest Number of Professional Staff Members

Library	Number of Professionals
1. Brandeis University, Waltham, MA	13
2. Yeshiva University, New York, NY	13
3. Yivo Institute for Jewish Research, New York, NY	13
4. Hebrew Union College, Cincinnati, OH	9
5. Spertus College of Judaica, Chicago, IL	5
6. Hebrew College, Brookline, MA	4
7. Yeshiva University Gottesman Library, New York, NY	4
8. Baltimore Hebrew College, Baltimore, MD	3
9. American Jewish Committee, New York, NY	3

TABLE 4.57
1988 *American Library Directory* Scholarly Jewish Libraries with the Largest Number of Student Staff Members

Library	Number of Student Assistants
1. Brandeis University, Waltham, MA	33.5
2. Holocaust Library, San Francisco, CA	7.5
3. Hebrew Union College, Cincinnati, OH	7.5
4. Jewish Historical Society, Baltimore, MD	3.5
5. Baltimore Hebrew College, Baltimore, MD	1.5
6. Hebrew College, Brookline, MA	1.5

TABLE 4.58
1978 *American Library Directory* Scholarly Roman Catholic Libraries with the Largest Total Number of Staff Members

Library	Number of Staff Members
1. Georgetown University, Washington, DC	59.5
2. DePaul University, Chicago, IL	59.5
3. Fordham University, Bronx, NY	59.5
4. St. John's University, Jamaica, NY	59.5
5. University of Dayton, Dayton, OH	59.5
6. College of the Holy Cross, Worcester, MA	54.5
7. The Catholic University of America, Washington, DC	53.5
8. Loyola University, Chicago, IL	53.5
9. College of St. Catherine, St. Paul, MN	53.5
10. Creighton University, Omaha, NE	53.5

TABLE 4.59
1978 *American Library Directory* Scholarly Library Staff Categories in Percentages by Denomination

Denomination	Professionals	Clerks	Student Assistants	Total Staff	Cumulative Staff Members	Number of Libraries
Baptist	19%	25%	56%	100%	1,475	140
Valid Responses	83	77	68	84		
Christian	23%	28%	49%	100%	287	40
Valid Responses	23	20	19	23		
Churches of Christ	19%	20%	61%	100%	289	27
Valid Responses	18	14	14	18		
Congregational	20%	27%	53%	100%	55	5
Valid Responses	3	3	2	3		
Episcopal/Anglican	25%	36%	39%	100%	172	32
Valid Responses	16	15	11	16		
Independent	20%	27%	53%	100%	643	82
Valid Responses	43	44	36	46		
Lutheran	25%	30%	45%	100%	653	70
Valid Responses	38	38	27	38		
Methodist	22%	26%	51%	100%	1,747	147
Valid Responses	88	87	63	90		
Other Denominations	24%	24%	52%	100%	1,559	214
Valid Responses	112	101	82	116		
Presbyterian	20%	23%	57%	100%	1,013	90
Valid Responses	57	51	43	57		
United Church of Christ	28%	30%	43%	100%	210	24
Valid Responses	15	13	12	15		
Summary						
Jewish	37%	43%	21%	100%	194	35
Valid Responses	18	19	8	20		
Roman Catholic	26%	31%	43%	100%	3,950	469
Valid Responses	245	239	169	249		
All Protestant	22%	26%	52%	100%	8,103	871
Valid Responses	496	463	377	506		
Total	23%	28%	49%	100%	12,247	1,375
Valid Responses	759	721	554	775		

TABLE 4.60
1988 *American Library Directory* Scholarly Library Staff Categories in Percentages by Denomination

Denomination	Professionals	Clerks	Student Assistants	Total Staff	Cumulative Staff Members	Number of Libraries
Baptist	17%	22%	61%	100%	2,382	152
Valid Responses	107	97	87	109		
Christian	16%	17%	67%	100%	484	41
Valid Responses	26	23	25	28		
Churches of Christ	17%	20%	63%	100%	376	27
Valid Responses	21	19	16	21		
Episcopal/Anglican	21%	26%	53%	100%	321	32
Valid Responses	18	17	14	20		
Independent	20%	24%	55%	100%	1,031	97
Valid Responses	63	54	45	65		
Lutheran	17%	24%	59%	100%	1,208	76
Valid Responses	50	50	38	53		
Mennonite	14%	22%	64%	100%	190	22
Valid Responses	15	16	13	17		
Methodist	18%	21%	60%	100%	2,588	149
Valid Responses	112	111	89	118		
Other Denominations	21%	26%	54%	100%	1,946	217
Valid Responses	123	118	84	131		
Presbyterian	19%	22%	59%	100%	1,232	90
Valid Responses	59	56	48	59		
United Churches of Christ	18%	22%	59%	100%	495	25
Valid Responses	20	17	18	20		
Summary						
Jewish	39%	36%	26%	100%	215	45
Valid Responses	21	22	6	25		
Roman Catholic	22%	28%	50%	100%	5,480	459
Valid Responses	261	258	192	279		
All Protestant	18%	23%	59%	100%	12,253	928
Valid Responses	614	578	477	641		
Total	20%	24%	56%	100%	17,948	1,432
Valid Responses	896	858	675	945		

TABLE 4.61
1988 *American Library Directory* Scholarly Staff Categories in Percentages by Library Type

Denomination	Professionals	Clerks	Student Assistants	Total Staff	Cumulative Staff Members	Number of Libraries
Scholarly	20%	24%	56%	100%	17,946	1,432
Valid Responses	896	858	675	945		
Junior College	17%	30%	53%	100%	567	108
Valid Responses	52	50	39	57		
Senior College	18%	22%	60%	100%	10,046	705
Valid Responses	500	472	405	513		
University	22%	25%	53%	100%	5,705	189
Valid Responses	156	149	127	157		
Seminary	25%	31%	45%	100%	1,159	231
Valid Responses	113	102	75	114		
Convent/Monastery	31%	46%	23%	100%	26	25
Valid Responses	6	8	4	11		
Denominational HQ	37%	47%	16%	100%	133	86
Valid Responses	28	34	9	41		
History/Archives	33%	38%	28%	100%	310	88
Valid Responses	41	43	16	52		

TABLE 4.62
1988 *American Library Directory* Chief Librarian's Gender by Total Expenditures for Scholarly Libraries

	----Chief Librarian's Gender-----						
Library Expenditures	Male	%	Female	%	No Response	%	Number of Libraries
Under $1,500	3	25	8	67	1	8	12
$1,501–$20,000	30	46	35	54	0	0	65
$20,001–$95,000	100	49	100	49	4	2	204
$95,001–$220,000	146	49	147	50	3	1	296
$220,001–$410,000	129	59	88	40	1	0	218
$410,001–$510,000	38	78	11	22	0	0	49
$510,001 and over	147	72	56	27	1	0	204
No response	176	46	199	52	9	2	384
Total	769	54	644	45	19	1	1,432

TABLE 4.63
1988 *American Library Directory* Total Annual Expenditure by Library Type for Scholarly Matched Pairs

	Total Annual Library Expenditure										
Library Type	$1–7,500	%	$7,501–95,000	%	$95,001–220,000	%	$220,001 and over	%	No Response	%	Number of Libraries	Mean Dollars
Scholarly	16	1	180	15	265	23	448	38	263	22	1,172	26,770
Junior College	1	1	37	42	19	21	4	4	28	31	89	104,500
Senior College	3	0	79	13	176	29	254	42	98	16	610	260,400
University	1	1	3	2	13	7	139	79	21	12	177	462,700
Seminary	4	2	41	21	51	26	45	23	55	28	196	193,700
Convent/Monastery	2	12	2	12	0	0	0	0	13	76	17	8,875
Denominational HQ	4	9	7	16	0	0	2	5	30	70	43	87,480
History/Archives	1	3	11	28	6	15	4	10	18	45	40	133,500

TABLE 4.64
1988 *American Library Directory* Scholarly Institutional Degree Years Offered by Chief Librarian's Gender

	Institutional Degree Years Offered											
Librarian's Gender	1–2	%	3–4	%	5–6	%	7 and over	%	No Response	%	No. of Libraries	Mean Years
Male	34	4	225	29	190	25	134	17	186	24	769	4.9
Female	69	11	241	37	138	21	39	6	157	24	644	4.2
No Response	0	0	9	47	3	16	1	5	6	32	19	4.5
Total	103	7	475	33	331	23	174	12	349	24	1,432	4.6

TABLE 4.65
1978 and 1988 *American Library Directory* Scholarly Total Expenditure per Student by Chief Librarian's Gender for Academic Libraries Only

Librarian's Gender	Total Libraries	No Response	%	Mean Total Expenditure
		1978		
Male	634	154	24	$194
Female	533	147	28	148
No Response	49	39	80	109
Total	1,216	340	28	173
		1988		
Male	667	148	22	377
Female	548	177	32	311
No response	18	10	56	372
Total	1,233	335	27	350

TABLE 4.66
1988 *American Library Directory* Total Staff Members by Chief Librarian's Gender for Scholarly Libraries

Librarian's Gender	1–4 Staff Members	%	5–8 Staff Members	%	9–12 Staff Members	%	13+ Staff Members	%	No Response	%	Number of Libraries	Mean Staff Per Library
Male	89	12	69	9	53	7	306	40	252	33	769	21
Female	83	13	79	12	53	8	203	32	226	35	644	17
No response	6	32	1	5	0	0	3	16	9	47	19	0
Total	178	12	149	10	106	7	512	36	487	34	1,432	19

TABLE 4.67
1988 *American Library Directory* Institutional Faculty Membership Size by Chief Librarian's Gender for Scholarly Libraries

Librarian's Gender	1–60 Faculty Members	%	61–120 Faculty Members	%	121–180 Faculty Members	%	181+ Faculty Members	%	No Response	%	Number of Libraries	Mean No. of Faculty Members
Male	265	34	158	21	53	7	78	10	215	28	769	92
Female	257	40	116	18	40	6	33	5	198	31	644	73
No response	9	47	3	16	1	5	0	0	6	32	19	36
Total	531	37	277	19	94	7	111	8	419	29	1,432	83

TABLE 4.68
1978 and 1988 *American Library Directory* Scholarly Library Age by Chief Librarian's Gender

	Years of Library Establishment, 1978											
Librarian's Gender	1–15	%	16–25	%	26–60	%	61 and over	%	No Response	%	Number of Libraries	Mean Years
Male	11	2	52	7	194	28	401	57	43	6	701	89
Female	14	2	61	10	238	40	237	40	43	7	593	72
No response	1	1	3	4	30	37	10	12	37	46	81	56
Total	26	2	116	8	462	34	648	47	123	9	1,375	80

	Years of Library Establishment, 1988											
Librarian's Gender	1–15	%	16–25	%	26–60	%	61 and over	%	No Response	%	Number of Libraries	Mean Years
Male	27	4	61	8	201	26	402	52	77	10	768	86
Female	38	6	55	9	223	35	250	39	78	12	644	72
No response	1	5	5	26	5	26	4	21	4	21	19	56
Total	66	5	121	8	429	30	656	46	159	11	1,431	80

TABLE 4.69
1988 *American Library Directory* Scholarly Chief Librarian's Religious Order Status by Library Type

	Religious Order Status						
Library Type	Priest/ Brother	%	Nun/ Sister	%	No Response	%	Number of Libraries
Scholarly	19	1	87	6	1,325	93	1,431
Junior College	1	1	20	19	87	81	108
Senior College	5	1	45	6	655	93	705
University	0	0	4	2	185	98	189
Seminary	6	3	8	3	216	94	230
Convent/ Monastery	3	12	4	16	18	72	25
Denominational HQ	1	1	5	6	80	93	86
History/Archives	3	3	1	1	84	95	88

TABLE 4.70
1978 *American Library Directory* Scholarly Chief Librarian's Religious Order Status by Library Type

	---------------Religious Order Status---------------						
Library Type	Priest/ Brother	%	Nun/ Sister	%	No Response	%	Number of Libraries
Scholarly	29	2	120	9	1,226	89	1,375
Junior College	0	0	20	16	105	84	125
Senior College	9	1	79	11	616	88	704
University	2	1	4	3	148	96	154
Seminary	9	4	4	2	220	94	233
Convent/Monastery	8	23	8	23	19	54	35
Denominational HQ	1	1	4	5	72	94	77
History/Archives	0	0	1	2	46	98	47

TABLE 4.71
1978 and 1988 *American Library Directory* Longitudinal Study Scholarly Chief Librarian's Religious Order Status by Volume Holdings[1,2]

	----------------1 9 7 8------------------				----------------1 9 8 8---------------				
Number of Volumes	No. of Libraries	No Response	Total Libraries	Mean Responses	No. of Libraries	No Response	Total Libraries	Mean Responses	% Change 1978–88
Under 3,500 Volumes	2	9	11	1	4	14	18	2	50
3,501–20,000	20	35	55	2	18	25	43	2	6
20,001–100,000	89	155	244	2	51	152	203	2	0
100,001–240,000	21	68	89	2	23	99	122	2	5
240,001–440,000	3	11	14	1	2	31	33	2	50
440,001 and over	0	14	14	0	0	22	22	0	0
No response	11	31	42	2	4	13	17	2	−17
Total	146	323	469	2	102	356	458	2	6

1. This table shows religious order status as either priests, brothers, or sisters, and is for Roman Catholic libraries primarily. Three non-Roman Catholic libraries reported priests or sisters in 1978, and four non-Roman Catholic religious libraries in 1988. See tables 4.69 and 4.70
2. The percentage change column shows the composition change between nuns, priests, and laypersons.

TABLE 4.72
1978 and 1988 *American Library Directory* Longitudinal Study
Scholarly Volume Holdings by Library Type

	1978				1988				
Library Type	Mean 1978	No. of Libraries	No Response	Total Libraries	Mean 1988	No. of Libraries	No Responses	Total Libraries	% Change
Scholarly	93,384	1,258	117	1,375	112,610	1,382	50	1,432	21
Junior College	34,994	118	7	125	39,269	107	1	108	12
Senior College	87,293	666	38	704	107,652	696	9	705	23
University	246,560	147	7	154	276,238	187	2	189	12
Seminary	79,292	198	35	233	95,287	219	12	231	20
Convent/ Monastery	25,795	28	7	35	22,360	25	0	25	−13
Denominational HQ	15,663	63	14	77	15,023	76	10	86	−4
History/Archives	40,987	38	9	47	31,594	72	16	88	−23

Range: 0–640,000 volumes

TABLE 4.73
1988 *American Library Directory* Senior College Libraries with the Largest Number of Volumes

Library	Denomination	Number of Volumes
1. Boston College, Chestnut Hill, MA	Roman Catholic	590,000
2. Bryn Mawr College, Bryn Mawr, PA	Other Denominations	590,000
3. Swarthmore College, Swarthmore, PA	Other Denominations	590,000
4. Haverford College, Haverford, PA	Other Denominations	490,000
5. College of Holy Cross, Worcester, MA	Roman Catholic	390,000
6. Calvin College, Grand Rapids, MI	Other Denominations	390,000
7. St. Olaf College, Northfield, MN	Lutheran	390,000
8. Drew University, Madison, NJ	Methodist	390,000
9. Mercy College, Dobbs Ferry, NY	Roman Catholic	390,000
10. Wagner College, Staten Island, NY	Lutheran	390,000
11. Kenyon College, Gambier, OH	Episcopal/Anglican	390,000
12. College of Wooster, Wooster, OH	Presbyterian	390,000
13. Dickinson College, Carlisle, PA	Methodist	390,000
14. Lafayette College, Easton, PA	Presbyterian	390,000

TABLE 4.74
1988 *American Library Directory* Seminary Libraries with the Largest Number of Volumes

Library	Denomination	Number of Volumes
1. Union Theological Seminary, New York, NY	Independent	590,000
2. Graduate Theological Union, Berkeley, CA	Independent	390,000
3. Yale University Divinity School, New Haven, CT	Independent	390,000
4. Emory University, Pitts Theology Library, Atlanta, GA	Methodist	390,000
5. Garrett-Seabury Theological Seminary, Evanston, IL	Methodist	390,000
6. Princeton Theological Seminary, Princeton, NJ	Presbyterian	390,000
7. Hebrew Union College, Cincinnati, OH	Jewish	390,000
8. Southwestern Baptist Theological Seminary, Fort Worth, TX	Baptist	390,000
9. Jesuit-Krauss-McCormack Seminary, Chicago, IL	Independent	290,000
10. Southern Baptist Theological Seminary, Louisville, KY	Baptist	290,000
11. Harvard University, Andover-Howard Theological Library, Cambridge, MA	Independent	290,000
12. Jewish Theological Seminary, New York, NY	Jewish	290,000
13. Colgate Rochester Seminary, Rochester, NY	Independent	290,000
14. St. Vincent College, Latrobe, PA	Roman Catholic	290,000
15. Southern Methodist University, Bridwell Theological Library, Dallas, TX	Methodist	290,000
16. Union Theological Seminary, Richmond, VA	Presbyterian	290,000

TABLE 4.75
1988 *American Library Directory* Denominational Headquarters Libraries with the Largest Number of Volumes

Library	Denomination	Number of Volumes
1. Bibliothèque des Chatelets, Ottawa, ON	Roman Catholic	75,000
2. Dominicains de St. Albert le Grand, Montreal, PQ	Roman Catholic	75,000
3. Maison Bellarmin, Montreal, PQ	Roman Catholic	75,000
4. Society of Jesus, St. Jerome, PQ	Roman Catholic	75,000
5. Jewish Federation Council, Los Angeles, CA	Jewish	35,000
6. Jesuit Center, Los Gatos, CA	Roman Catholic	35,000
7. Seventh-day Adventists, Washington, DC	Other Denominations	35,000
8. Catholic Seminary Foundation, Indianapolis, IN	Roman Catholic	35,000
9. Review and Herald, Hagerstown, MD	Other Denominations	35,000
10. Lutheran Church Missouri Synod, St. Louis, MO	Lutheran	35,000
11. Jewish Federation, Omaha, NE	Jewish	35,000
12. American Bible Society, New York, NY	Independent	35,000
13. American Jewish Committee, New York, NY	Jewish	35,000
14. Southern Baptist Convention, Nashville, TN	Baptist	35,000
15. United Methodist Publishing House, Nashville, TN	Methodist	35,000
16. Charles Stevens American Atheist, Austin, TX	Other Denominations	35,000
17. Foreign Missions Society, Laval, PQ	Roman Catholic	35,000

TABLE 4.76
1988 *American Library Directory* History/Archive Libraries with the Largest Number of Volumes

Library	Denomination	Number of Volumes
1. Yivo Institute for Jewish Research, New York, NY	Jewish	290,000
2. American Congregational Association, Boston, MA	Congregational	200,000
3. American Jewish Historical Society, Waltham, MA	Jewish	200,000
4. Church of Jesus Christ of Latter-day Saints, Salt Lake City, UT	Other Denominations	200,000
5. Drew University, Madison, NJ	Methodist	130,000
6. Presbyterian Church Office of History, Philadelphia, PA	Presbyterian	130,000
7. Society of Friends, Providence, RI	Other Denominations	130,000
8. Concordia Historical Institute, St. Louis, MO	Lutheran	75,000
9. American Baptist Colgate Historical, Rochester, NY	Baptist	75,000
10. Institute for Advanced Studies, Stony Book, NY	Independent	75,000
11. Presbyterian Study Center, Montreat, NC	Presbyterian	75,000

TABLE 4.77
1988 *American Library Directory* Volume Holdings by Total Annual Expenditure for Scholarly Libraries

Library Expenditures	1–20,000	%	20,001–100,000	%	100,001–240,001	%	240,001 and over	%	No Response	%	Number of Libraries	Mean Volumes
Under $1,500	8	67	1	8	1	8	0	0	2	17	12	20,130
$1,501–$20,000	49	75	15	23	0	0	0	0	1	2	65	16,130
$20,001–$95,000	32	16	160	78	6	3	0	0	6	3	204	44,850
$95,001–$220,000	7	2	195	66	90	30	0	0	4	1	296	86,780
$220,001–$410,000	5	2	50	23	154	71	8	4	1	0	218	135,300
$410,001–$510,000	0	0	12	24	32	65	5	10	0	0	49	155,500
$510,001 and over	1	0	10	5	66	32	125	61	2	1	204	321,800
No response	148	39	152	40	43	11	7	2	34	9	384	52,010
Total	250	17	595	42	392	27	145	10	50	3	1,432	112,600

TABLE 4.78
1978 *American Library Directory* Volume Holdings by Denomination for Scholarly Libraries

Library Type	1– 20,000	%	20,001– 100,000	%	100,001– 240,000	%	240,001 and over	%	No Response	%	Number of Libraries	Mean Volumes
Baptist	23	16	72	51	24	17	9	6	12	9	140	92,610
Christian	12	30	18	45	7	18	1	3	2	5	40	69,850
Churches of Christ	8	30	14	52	2	7	2	7	1	4	27	71,220
Congregational	1	20	2	40	2	40	0	0	0	0	5	113,000
Episcopal/Anglican	5	16	15	47	6	19	1	3	5	16	32	75,210
Independent	22	27	38	46	12	15	6	7	4	5	82	84,700
Lutheran	8	11	29	41	23	33	3	4	7	10	70	99,120
Methodist	16	11	61	41	44	30	14	10	12	8	147	121,200
Other Denominations	57	27	102	48	26	12	7	3	22	10	214	66,850
Presbyterian	5	6	41	46	35	39	6	7	3	3	90	115,200
U.C.C.	1	4	10	42	11	46	2	8	0	0	24	120,700
Summary												
Jewish	9	26	10	29	5	14	4	11	7	20	35	107,200
Roman Catholic	66	14	244	52	89	19	28	6	42	9	469	94,980
All Protestant	158	18	402	46	192	22	51	6	68	8	871	92,060
Total	233	17	656	48	286	21	83	6	117	9	1,375	93,380

TABLE 4.79
1978 *American Library Directory* Scholarly Christian Libraries with the Largest Number of Volumes

Library	Number of Volumes
1. Texas Christian University, Fort Worth, TX	590,000
2. Hiram College, Hiram, OH	200,000
3. Chapman University, Orange, CA	130,000
4. Transylvania University, Lexington, KY	130,000
5. Tougaloo College, Tougaloo, MS	130,000
6. Atlantic Christian College, Wilson, NC	130,000
7. Phillips University, Enid, OK	130,000
8. Bethany College, Bethany, WV	130,000

TABLE 4.80
1988 *American Library Directory* Scholarly Churches of Christ Libraries with the Largest Number of Volumes

Library	Number of Volumes
1. Harding University, Searcy, AR	290,000
2. Pepperdine University, Malibu, CA	290,000
3. Abilene Christian University, Abilene, TX	290,000
4. Chicago Theological Seminary, Chicago, IL	130,000
5. Freed-Hardeman University, Henderson, TN	130,000
6. David Lipscomb University, Nashville, TN	130,000
7. Lincoln Christian College, Lincoln, IL	75,000
8. Cincinnati Bible Seminary, Cincinnati, OH	75,000
9. Oklahoma Christian College, Oklahoma City, OK	75,000
10. Harding College School of Religion, Memphis, TN	75,000
11. Lubbock Christian University, Lubbock, TX	75,000

TABLE 4.81
1988 *American Library Directory* Scholarly Episcopal/Anglican Libraries with the Largest Number of Volumes

Library	Number of Volumes
1. Kenyon College, Gambier, OH	390,000
2. University of the South, Sewanee, TN	390,000
3. Episcopal Divinity School, Cambridge, MA	290,000
4. Bishop's University, Lennoxville, PQ	290,000
5. Bard College, Annandale-on-Hudson, NY	200,000
6. Hobart and William Smith Colleges, Geneva, NY	200,000
7. General Theological Seminary, New York, NY	200,000
8. St. Augustine's College, Raleigh, NC	130,000
9. University of the South School of Theology, Sewanee, TN	130,000
10. Virginia Theological Seminary, Alexandria, VA	130,000
11. Huron College, London, ON	130,000

TABLE 4.82
1988 *American Library Directory* Scholarly Lutheran Libraries with the Largest Number of Volumes

Library	Number of Volumes
1. Wilfred Laurier University, Waterloo, ON	490,000
2. St. Olaf College, Northfield, MN	390,000
3. Wagner College, Staten Island, NY	390,000
4. Wittenberg University, Springfield, OH	390,000
5. Augustana College, Rock Island, IL	290,000
6. Valparaiso University, Valparaiso, IN	290,000
7. Luther College, Decorah, IA	290,000
8. Concordia College, Moorhead, MN	290,000
9. Muhlenberg College, Allentown, PA	290,000
10. Gettysburg College, Gettysburg, PA	290,000
11. Pacific Lutheran University, Tacoma, WA	290,000

TABLE 4.83
1988 *American Library Directory* Scholarly Methodist Libraries with the Largest Number of Volumes

Library	Number of Volumes
1. University of Denver, Denver, CO	590,000
2. Wesleyan University, Middletown, CT	590,000
3. American University, Washington, DC	590,000
4. Emory University, Atlanta, GA	590,000
5. Boston University, Boston, MA	590,000
6. Duke University, Durham, NC	590,000
7. Southern Methodist University, Dallas, TX	590,000
8. University of the Pacific, Stockton, CA	490,000
9. Ohio Wesleyan University, Delaware, OH	490,000

TABLE 4.84
1988 *American Library Directory* Scholarly Presbyterian Libraries with the Largest Number of Volumes

Library	Number of Volumes
1. University of Tulsa, Tulsa, OK	590,000
2. Trinity University, San Antonio, TX	590,000
3. Queen's University, Kingston, ON	590,000
4. Princeton Theological Seminary, Princeton, NJ	390,000
5. College of Wooster, Wooster, OH	390,000
6. Lafayette College, Easton, PA	390,000
7. Hanover College, Hanover, IN	290,000
8. Macalester College, St. Paul, MN	290,000
9. Davidson College, Davidson, NC	290,000
10. Lewis and Clark College, Portland, OR	290,000
11. Union Theological Seminary, Richmond, VA	290,000

TABLE 4.85
1988 *American Library Directory* Scholarly Jewish Libraries with the Largest Number of Volumes

Library	Number of Volumes
1. Brandeis University, Waltham, MA	590,000
2. Yeshiva University, New York, NY	590,000
3. Hebrew Union College, Cincinnati, OH	390,000
4. Jewish Theological Seminary, New York, NY	290,000
5. Yivo Institute for Jewish Research, New York, NY	290,000
6. University of Judaism, Los Angeles, CA	200,000
7. American Jewish Historical Society, Waltham, MA	200,000
8. Yeshiva University Gottesman Library, New York, NY	200,000
9. Hebrew Theological College, Skokie, IL	130,000
10. Hebrew Union College, New York, NY	130,000
11. Dropsie College, Merion, PA	130,000

TABLE 4.86
1988 *American Library Directory* Scholarly Christian Libraries with the Highest Number of Volumes per Student

Library	Ratio
1. Phillips University Rogers Graduate Seminary, Enid, OK	867
2. Atlanta Christian College, East Point, GA	500
3. Lexington Theological Seminary, Lexington, KY	500
4. Northwest Christian College, Eugene, OR	500
5. Christian Theological Seminary, Indianapolis, IN	289
6. Phillips University, Enid, OK	267

TABLE 4.87
1988 *American Library Directory* Scholarly Episcopal/Anglican Libraries with the Highest Number of Volumes per Student

Library	Ratio
1. Episcopal Divinity School, Cambridge, MA	1,933
2. General Theological Seminary, New York, NY	1,333
3. Episcopal Theological Seminary, Austin, TX	500
4. Nashotah House, Nashotah, WI	500
5. University of the South, Sewanee, TN	371

TABLE 4.88
1988 *American Library Directory* Scholarly Lutheran Libraries with the Highest Number of Volumes per Student

Library	Ratio
1. Trinity Lutheran Seminary, Columbus, OH	867
2. Lutheran Theological Seminary, Gettysburg, PA	867
3. Lutheran Theological Seminary, Philadelphia, PA	867
4. Lutheran Theological Southern Seminary, Columbia, SC	500
5. Wisconsin Lutheran College, Milwaukee, WI	500

TABLE 4.89
1988 *American Library Directory* Scholarly Methodist Libraries with the Highest Number of Volumes per Student

Library	Ratio
1. Iliff School of Theology, Denver, CO	867
2. Wesley Theological Seminary, Washington, DC	867
3. Garrett-Evangelical Seminary, Evanston, IL	867
4. United Theological Seminary, Dayton, OH	867
5. St. Paul School of Theology, Kansas City, MO	500
6. Methodist Theological School, Delaware, OH	500
7. Scarritt Graduate School, Nashville, TN	500

TABLE 4.90
1988 *American Library Directory* Scholarly Presbyterian Libraries with the Highest Number of Volumes per Student

Library	Ratio
1. Union Theological Seminary, Richmond, VA	1,933
2. Pittsburgh Theological Seminary, Pittsburgh, PA	867
3. Austin Presbyterian Theological Seminary, Austin, TX	867
4. Westminster Theological Seminary, San Marcos, CA	500
5. Louisville Presbyterian Seminary, Louisville, KY	500
6. Sheldon Jackson College, Sitka, AK	500
7. Covenant Theological Seminary, St. Louis, MO	500
8. Princeton Theological Seminary, Princeton, NJ	500
9. Memphis Theological Seminary, Memphis, TN	500

TABLE 4.91
1988 *American Library Directory* Scholarly Jewish Libraries with the Highest Number of Volumes per Student

Library	Ratio
1. Hebrew Union College, Cincinnati, OH	2,600
2. University of Judaism, Los Angeles, CA	1,333
3. Hebrew Theological Seminary, Skokie, IL	867
4. Hebrew Union College, New York, NY	867
5. Dropsie College, Merion, PA	867
6. Jewish Theological Seminary, New York, NY	644
7. Hebrew Union College, Los Angeles, CA	500

TABLE 4.92
1988 *American Library Directory* Scholarly Baptist Libraries with the Lowest Volume Holdings per Student

Library	Ratio
1. Selma University, Selma, AL	33
2. Palm Beach Atlantic College, West Palm Beach, FL	33
3. Missouri Baptist College, St. Louis, MO	33
4. Anderson University, Anderson, SC	33
5. Truett-McConnell College, Cleveland, GA	26
6. Brewton-Parker College, Mount Vernon, GA	26
7. Florida Baptist College, Lakeland, FL	15

TABLE 4.93
1988 *American Library Directory* Scholarly Independent Libraries with the Lowest Volume Holdings per Student

Library	Ratio
1. Azusa Pacific University, Azusa, CA	33
2. Logan College of Chiropractic, Chesterfield, MO	33
3. Briercrest Bible College, Caronport, SA	33
4. Vanderbilt University Divinity Library, Nashville, TN	25
5. Luther Rice Seminary, Jacksonville, FL	21
6. Biblical Theological Seminary, Hatfield, PA	15
7. Jordan College, Cedar Springs, MI	3

TABLE 4.94
1988 *American Library Directory* Scholarly Other Denomination Libraries with the Lowest Volume Holdings per Student

Library	Ratio
1. University of La Verne, La Verne, CA	35
2. East Coast Bible College, Charlotte, NC	33
3. Ricks College, Rexburg, ID	25
4. Latter-day Saints Business College, Salt Lake City, UT	9
5. Ottawa Theological Hall, Ottawa, ON	3

TABLE 4.95
1988 *American Library Directory* Scholarly United Church of Christ Libraries with the Lowest Volume Holdings per Student

Library	Ratio
1. Franklin and Marshall College, Lancaster, PA	149
2. Hood College, Frederick, MD	103
3. Drury College, Springfield, MO	103
4. Doane College, Crete, NE	100
5. Pacific University, Forest Grove, OR	96
6. Le Moyne-Owen College, Memphis, TN	71
7. Elmhurst College, Elmhurst, IL	62
8. Eden Webster University, St. Louis, MO	42
9. Elon College, Elon College, NC	40

TABLE 4.96
1988 *American Library Directory* Scholarly Roman Catholic Libraries with the Lowest Volume Holdings per Student

Library	Ratio
1. Marymount University, Arlington, VA	20
2. François-Xavier Garneau College, Quebec, PQ	20
3. Aquinas Junior College, Milton, MA	15
4. Our Lady of Lourdes School of Nursing, Camden, NJ	15
5. Ignatius College, Guelph, ON	15
6. Collège de Sainte-Foy, Ste. Foy, PQ	14
7. Diocese of Phoenix, Phoenix, AZ	6
8. Sacred Heart University, Fairfield, CT	3

TABLE 4.97
1978 and 1988 *American Library Directory* Scholarly Library Volumes per Faculty Member by Region

1978

Region	1–250	%	251–500	%	501–750	%	751 and over	%	No Response	%	Number of Libraries	Mean Volumes
Northeast	3	4	0	0	5	7	39	51	29	38	76	2,287
Middle Atlantic	1	0	8	3	16	6	148	56	91	34	264	2,641
Southeast	4	1	13	5	21	8	184	69	45	17	267	1,742
Southwest	2	2	8	7	5	4	70	63	27	24	112	1,770
West	1	1	4	3	12	10	69	58	33	28	119	1,756
Rocky Mountains	0	0	1	4	3	11	13	48	10	37	27	1,920
Middle West	4	1	19	5	21	5	282	68	86	21	412	2,065
Canada	2	2	1	1	4	4	26	27	65	66	98	2,115
Total	17	1	54	4	87	6	831	60	386	28	1,375	2,051

1988

Region	1–250	%	251–500	%	501–750	%	751 and over	%	No Response	%	Number of Libraries	Mean Volumes
Northeast	2	3	2	3	4	5	42	55	26	34	76	3,016
Middle Atlantic	2	1	5	2	13	5	153	59	88	34	261	3,255
Southeast	2	1	4	2	13	5	197	74	50	19	266	2,093
Southwest	0	0	2	2	3	3	82	70	30	26	117	2,169
West	0	0	5	4	8	6	73	57	42	33	128	2,492
Rocky Mountains	0	0	0	0	2	10	13	62	6	29	21	2,707
Middle West	2	1	12	3	18	5	281	71	85	21	398	2,444
Canada	2	1	7	4	9	5	48	29	98	60	164	2,079
Total	10	1	37	3	70	5	889	62	425	30	1,431	2,497

TABLE 4.98
1978 and 1988 *American Library Directory* Longitudinal Study
Scholarly Periodical Subscriptions by Library Type

Library Type	1978				1988				
	Mean 1978	No. of Libraries	No Response	Total Libraries	Mean 1988	No. of Libraries	No Reponses	Total Libraries	% Change
Scholarly	546	966	409	1,375	550	1,179	253	1,432	1
Junior College	218	78	47	125	228	94	14	108	5
Senior College	534	548	156	704	538	628	77	705	1
University	1,139	129	25	154	1,134	169	20	189	−0.5
Seminary	424	140	93	233	463	173	58	231	9
Convent/ Monastery	68	11	24	35	63	16	9	25	−7
Denominational HQ	164	35	42	77	149	54	32	86	−9
History/Archives	212	25	22	47	181	45	43	88	−15

TABLE 4.99
1988 *American Library Directory* Periodical Subscriptions by Denomination for Scholarly Libraries[1]

	------------Periodical Subscriptions-------------											
Denomination	1–200	%	201–600	%	601–1,400	%	1,401 and over	%	No Response	%	Number of Libraries	Mean Periodicals
Baptist	26	17	55	36	40	26	9	6	22	14	152	580*
Christian	11	27	13	32	7	17	1	2	9	22	41	414
Churches of Christ	8	30	11	41	5	19	2	7	1	4	27	469
Episcopal/ Anglican	6	19	7	22	3	9	4	13	12	38	32	650*
Independent	27	28	32	33	17	18	4	4	17	18	97	454
Lutheran	10	13	22	29	22	29	8	11	14	18	76	679*
Mennonite	7	32	8	36	4	18	0	0	3	14	22	334
Methodist	31	21	54	36	38	26	12	8	14	9	149	575*
Other Denomin-ations	71	33	61	28	36	17	11	5	38	18	217	448
Presbyterian	10	11	34	38	32	36	5	6	9	10	90	622*
U.C.C.	1	4	8	32	8	32	2	8	6	24	25	745
Summary												
Jewish	15	33	8	18	5	11	2	4	15	33	45	382*
Roman Catholic	102	22	131	29	88	19	45	10	93	20	459	590*
All Protestant	208	22	305	33	212	23	58	6	145	16	928	538
Total	325	23	444	31	305	21	105	7	253	18	1,432	550

1. Higher means for periodical subscriptions are quite obviously associated with older, larger mainstream denominations.
2. The means for larger mainstream denominations* versus newer, smaller denominations is, tellingly, 583 vs. 477, a difference of 22 percent.
3. The mean figure for total subscriptions, 550 titles, refers only to those libraries which reported subscriptions, those reporting none being excluded from these calculations.

TABLE 4.100
1988 *American Library Directory* Junior College Libraries with the Largest Number of Periodical Subscriptions

Library	Denomination	Number of Periodical Subscriptions
1. Red Deer College, Red Deer, AB	Lutheran	1,500
2. Lindsey Wilson College, Columbia, KY	Methodist	1,100
3. Vanier College, St. Laurent, PQ	Roman Catholic	900
4. Ricks College, Rexburg, ID	Other Denominations	700
5. Gwynedd-Mercy College, Gwynedd Valley, PA	Roman Catholic	700
6. Elizabeth Seton College, Yonkers, NY	Roman Catholic	500

TABLE 4.101
1988 *American Library Directory* Seminary Libraries with the Largest Number of Periodical Subscriptions

Library	Denomination	Number of Periodical Subscriptions
1. Graduate Theological Union, Berkeley, CA	Independent	1,700
2. Southwestern Baptist Theological Seminary, Fort Worth, TX	Baptist	1,700
3. Emory University, Atlanta, GA	Methodist	1,500
4. Southern Baptist Theological Seminary, Louisville, KY	Baptist	1,500
5. University of the South, Sewanee, TN	Episcopal/Anglican	1,500
6. Union Theological Seminary, Richmond, VA	Presbyterian	1,500
7. Jesuit-Krauss-McCormack Seminary, Chicago, IL	Independent	1,300
8. Trinity Evangelical Divinity School, Deerfield, IL	Other Denominations	1,300
9. Southeastern Baptist Theological Seminary, Wake Forest, NC	Baptist	1,300
10. Western Conservative Baptist Seminary, Portland, OR	Baptist	1,300

TABLE 4.102
1988 *American Library Directory* History/Archive Libraries with the Largest Number of Periodical Subscriptions

Library	Denomination	Number of Periodical Subscriptions
1. Presbyterian Church Office of History, Philadelphia, PA	Presbyterian	900
2. American Jewish Historical Society, Waltham, MA	Jewish	700
3. Friends Historical Collection, Swarthmore, PA	Other Denominations	500
4. Society of Friends, Providence, RI	Other Denominations	500
5. Archdiocese of San Antonio, San Antonio, TX	Roman Catholic	500
6. Goshen College, Goshen, IN	Mennonite	300
7. Bethel College, North Newton, KS	Mennonite	300
8. United Methodist Church, Madison, NJ	Methodist	300
9. Lutheran Council, New York, NY	Lutheran	300
10. Yivo Institute for Jewish Research, New York, NY	Jewish	300
11. Institute for Advanced Studies, Stony Brook, NY	Independent	300
12. Lancaster Mennonite Historical Society, Lancaster, PA	Mennonite	300
13. Southern Baptist Convention Archives, Richmond, VA	Baptist	300

TABLE 4.103
1988 *American Library Directory* Scholarly Christian Libraries with the Largest Number of Periodical Subscriptions

Library	Number of Periodical Subscriptions
1. Texas Christian University, Fort Worth, TX	1,700
2. Chapman University, Orange, CA	1,100
3. Christian Theological Seminary, Indianapolis, IN	700
4. Atlantic Christian College, Wilson, NC	700
5. Hiram College, Hiram, OH	700
6. Phillips University, Enid, OK	700
7. Emmanuel School of Religion, Johnson City, TN	700
8. Lynchburg College, Lynchburg, VA	700

TABLE 4.104
1988 *American Library Directory* Scholarly Congregational Libraries with the Largest Number of Periodical Subscriptions

Library	Number of Periodical Subscriptions
1. Washburn University, Topeka, KS	1,500
2. Olivet College, Olivet, MI	700
3. American Congregational Association, Boston, MA	150

TABLE 4.105
1988 *American Library Directory* Scholarly Independent Libraries with the Largest Number of Periodical Subscriptions

Library	Number of Periodical Subscriptions
1. Graduate Theological Union, Berkeley, CA	1,700
2. Oral Roberts University, Tulsa, OK	1,700
3. Brown University, Providence, RI	1,700
4. McGill University, Montreal, PQ	1,700
5. Maharishi International University, Fairfield, IA	1,300
6. Christian Broadcasting Network University, Virginia Beach, VA	1,300
7. Biola University, La Mirada, CA	1,100
8. Wheaton College, Wheaton, IL	1,100
9. Berea College, Berea, KY	1,100
10. Gordon-Conwell Theological Seminary, South Hamilton, MA	1,100

TABLE 4.106
1988 *American Library Directory* Scholarly Lutheran Libraries with the Largest Number of Periodical Subscriptions

Library	Number of Periodical Subscriptions
1. Concordia College, Ann Arbor, MI	1,700
2. Pacific Lutheran University, Tacoma, WA	1,700
3. Wilfred Laurier University, Waterloo, ON	1,700
4. Augustana College, Rock Island, IL	1,500
5. Concordia College, Moorhead, MN	1,500
6. St. Olaf College, Northfield, MN	1,500
7. Muhlenberg College, Allentown, PA	1,500
8. Red Deer College, Red Deer, AB	1,500
9. Valparaiso University, Valparaiso, IN	1,300
10. Gustavus Adolphus College, St. Peter, MN	1,300
11. Gettysburg College, Gettysburg, PA	1,300

TABLE 4.107
1988 *American Library Directory* Scholarly Mennonite Libraries with the Largest Number of Periodical Subscriptions

Library	Number of Periodical Subscriptions
1. Eastern Mennonite University, Harrisonburg, VA	900
2. Fresno Pacific College, Fresno, CA	700
3. Goshen College, Goshen, IN	700
4. Bluffton College, Bluffton, OH	700
5. Associated Mennonite Biblical Seminaries, Elkhart, IN	500
6. Tabor College, Hillsboro, KS	500

TABLE 4.108
1988 *American Library Directory* Scholarly Other Denomination Libraries with the Largest Number of Periodical Subscriptions

Library	Number of Periodical Subscriptions
1. Loma Linda University, Loma Linda, CA	1,700
2. Washburn University, Topeka, KS	1,700
3. Andrews University, Berrien Springs, MI	1,700
4. Calvin College, Grand Rapids, MI	1,700
5. Nazareth College, Rochester, NY	1,700
6. Bryn Mawr College, Bryn Mawr, PA	1,700
7. Swarthmore College, Swarthmore, PA	1.700
8. Brigham Young University, Provo, UT	1,700
9. University of Winnipeg, Winnipeg, MB	1,700
10. Mount Allison University, Sackville, NB	1,700

TABLE 4.109
1988 *American Library Directory* Scholarly United Church of Christ Libraries with the Largest Number of Periodical Subscriptions

Library	Number of Periodical Subscriptions
1. Franklin and Marshall College, Lancaster, PA	1,700
2. Cedar Crest College, Allentown, PA	1,500
3. Elon College, Elon College, NC	1,300
4. Eden Webster University, St. Louis, MO	1,100
5. Catawba College, Salisbury, NC	1,100
6. Elmhurst College, Elmhurst, IL	900
7. Drury College, Springfield, MO	900
8. Pacific University, Forest Grove, OR	900
9. Heidelberg College, Tiffin, OH	700
10. Ursinus College, Collegeville, PA	700

TABLE 4.110
1978 and 1988 *American Library Directory* Longitudinal Study
Scholarly Vertical File Drawer Holdings by Library Type

	1978				1988				
Library Type	No. of Libraries	No Response	Total Libraries	Mean Drawers	No. of Libraries	No Response	Total Libraries	Mean Drawers	% Change 1978–88
Scholarly	745	630	1,375	25.0	571	860	1,431	31.0	24.0
Junior College	65	60	125	14.0	51	57	108	20.0	43.0
Senior College	438	266	704	24.0	310	395	705	31.0	29.0
University	87	67	154	33.0	76	113	189	41.0	24.0
Seminary	87	146	233	19.0	69	161	230	22.0	16.0
Convent/ Monastery	11	24	35	26.0	6	19	25	28.0	7.7
Denominational HQ	26	51	77	42.0	29	57	86	31.0	−26.0
History/Archives	31	16	47	49.0	30	58	88	41.0	−16.0

TABLE 4.111
1988 *American Library Directory* Junior College Libraries with the Largest Number of Vertical File Drawers

Library	Denomination	Number of Vertical File Drawers
1. St. Mary's College, O'Fallon, MO	Roman Catholic	123.0
2. Salvation Army School for Officers, Suffern, NY	Other Denominations	108.0
3. Salvation Army School, Rancho Palos Verdes, CA	Other Denominations	93.0
4. Wood College, Mathiston, MS	Methodist	48.0
5. Northeastern Christian Junior College, Villanova, PA	Churches of Christ	48.0
6. Elizabeth Seton College, Yonkers, NY	Roman Catholic	35.5
7. Lees-McRae College, Banner Elk, NC	Presbyterian	35.5
8. Latter-day Saints Business College, Salt Lake City, UT	Other Denominations	35.5

TABLE 4.112
1988 *American Library Directory* University Libraries with the Largest Number of Vertical File Drawers

Library	Denomination	Number of Vertical File Drawers
1. Samford University, Birmingham, AL	Baptist	138
2. Loma Linda University, Loma Linda, CA	Other Denominations	138
3. Santa Clara University, Santa Clara, CA	Roman Catholic	138
4. Valparaiso University, Valparaiso, IN	Lutheran	138
5. Dillard University, New Orleans, LA	Methodist	138
6. Andrews University, Berrien Springs, MI	Other Denominations	138
7. Campbell University, Buies Creek, NC	Baptist	138
8. Johnson C. Smith University, Charlotte, NC	Presbyterian	138
9. Wake Forest University, Winston-Salem, NC	Baptist	138

TABLE 4.113
1988 *American Library Directory* Convent/Monastery Libraries with the Largest Number of Vertical File Drawers

Library	Denomination	Number of Vertical File Drawers
1. Franciscan Monastery, Washington, DC	Roman Catholic	123.0
2. Abbey of Regina Laudis, Bethlehem, CT	Roman Catholic	15.5
3. Sisters of the Immaculate Conception Convent, Putnam, CT	Roman Catholic	15.5
4. Carmelite Monastery, Barre, VT	Roman Catholic	8.0
5. St. Benedict's Abbey, Benet Lake, WI	Roman Catholic	2.5
6. St. Norbert Abbey, De Pere, WI	Roman Catholic	2.5

TABLE 4.114
1988 *American Library Directory* History/Archive Libraries with the Largest Number of Vertical File Drawers

Library	Denomination	Number of Vertical File Drawers
1. American Jewish Historical Society, Waltham, MA	Jewish	138
2. Evangelical and Reformed Historical Society, Webster Groves, MO	United Church of Christ	138
3. Goshen College, Goshen, IN	Mennonite	108
4. Hawaiian Mission Children's Society, Honolulu, HI	Independent	93
5. Shaker Library, Poland Spring, ME	Other Denominations	78
6. Presbyterian Study Center, Montreat, NC	Presbyterian	78
7. Lutheran Council, New York, NY	Lutheran	63

TABLE 4.115
1988 *American Library Directory* Scholarly Baptist Libraries with the Largest Number of Vertical File Drawers

Library	Number of Vertical File Drawers
1. Samford University, Birmingham, AL	138
2. Mobile College, Mobile, AL	138
3. Grand Canyon University, Phoenix, AZ	138
4. Southwest Baptist University, Bolivar, MO	138
5. Campbell University, Buies Creek, NC	138
6. Wake Forest University, Winston-Salem, NC	138
7. Judson College, Marion, AL	123
8. Temple University, Philadelphia, PA	123
9. Western Baptist College, Salem, OR	108
10. Ottawa University, Ottawa, KS	78

TABLE 4.116
1988 *American Library Directory* Scholarly Churches of Christ Libraries with the Largest Number of Vertical File Drawers

Library	Number of Vertical File Drawers
1. Freed-Hardeman University, Hendersen, TN	63.0
2. Northeastern Christian Junior College, Villanova, PA	48.0
3. Harding College, School of Religion, Memphis, TN	15.5
4. Pacific Christian College, Fullerton, CA	8.0
5. York College, York, NE	8.0
6. Oklahoma Christian College, Oklahoma City, OK	8.0
7. Ambassador College, Big Sandy, TX	8.0
8. Amber University, Garland, TX	8.0
9. Lubbock Christian University, Lubbock,TX	2.5
10. Southwestern Christian College, Terrell, TX	2.5

TABLE 4.117
1988 *American Library Directory* Scholarly Episcopal/Anglican Libraries with the Largest Number of Vertical File Drawers

Library	Number of Vertical File Drawers
1. General Theological Seminary, New York, NY	138.0
2. Anglican Church of Canada, Toronto, ON	48.0
3. Saint Paul's College, Lawrenceville, VA	15.5
4. Episcopal Diocese of Massachusetts, Boston, MA	8.0
5. St. George's Episcopal Mission, Holbrook, AZ	2.5
6. George Mercer School of Theology, Garden City, NY	2.5
7. Nashotah House, Nashotah, WI	2.5
8. Bishop's University, Lennoxville, PQ	2.5

TABLE 4.118
1988 *American Library Directory* Scholarly Lutheran Libraries with the Largest Number of Vertical File Drawers

Library	Number of Vertical File Drawers
1. Valparaiso University, Valparaiso, IN	138
2. Concordia Teachers College, Seward, NE	138
3. Lutheran Council, New York, NY	63
4. Concordia University, River Forest, IL	48
5. Wartburg College, Waverly, IA	48
6. Concordia Historical Institute, St. Louis, MO	48
7. Aid Association for Lutherans, Appleton, WI	48

TABLE 4.119
1988 *American Library Directory* Scholarly Methodist Libraries with the Largest Number of Vertical File Drawers

Library	Number of Vertical File Drawers
1. Asbury Theological Seminary, Wilmore, KY	138
2. Dillard University, New Orleans, LA	138
3. Drew University, Madison, NJ	138
4. LaGrange College, LaGrange, GA	123
5. Methodist College, Fayetteville, NC	93
6. Houghton College, Houghton, NY	78
7. North Carolina Wesleyan College, Rocky Mount, NC	63
8. Baldwin-Wallace College, Berea, OH	63

TABLE 4.120
1988 *American Library Directory* Scholarly Presbyterian Libraries with the Largest Number of Vertical File Drawers

Library	Number of Vertical File Drawers
1. Johnson C. Smith University, Charlotte, NC	138.0
2. Davidson College, Davidson, NC	93.0
3. Trinity University, San Antonio, TX	93.0
4. Bloomfield College, Bloomfield, NJ	78.0
5. Presbyterian Study Center, Montreat, NC	78.0
6. Carroll College, Waukesha, WI	63.0
7. Lindenwood College, St. Charles, MO	48.0
8. Waynesburg College, Waynesburg, PA	48.0
9. Lees-McRae College, Banner Elk, NC	35.5

TABLE 4.121
1988 *American Library Directory* Scholarly Jewish Libraries with the Largest Number of Vertical File Drawers

Library	Number of Vertical File Drawers
1. Spertus College of Judaica, Chicago, IL	138
2. American Jewish Historical Society, Waltham, MA	138
3. Jewish Educational Service, New York, NY	138
4. Jewish Federation Council, Los Angeles, CA	63
5. American Jewish Committee, New York, NY	63
6. Jewish Community Federation, Cleveland, OH	63
7. Midrasha College of Jewish Studies, Southfield, MI	48
8. Jewish Theological Seminary, New York, NY	48
9. Rhode Island Jewish Historical Association, Providence, RI	48

TABLE 4.122
1978 and 1988 *American Library Directory* Longitudinal Study
Scholarly Microform Holdings by Library Type

	1978				1988				
Library Type	Mean 1978	No. of Libraries	No Response	Total Libraries	Mean 1988	No. of Libraries	No Reponse	Total Libraries	% Change
Scholarly	27,658	622	753	1,375	46,925	777	655	1,432	70
Junior College	9,312	39	86	125	12,547	39	69	108	35
Senior College	18,139	367	337	704	37,177	439	266	705	105
University	92,717	100	54	154	121,679	143	46	189	31
Seminary	6,557	85	148	233	14,676	109	122	231	124
Convent/ Monastery	1,775	2	33	35	1,775	2	23	25	0
Denominational HQ	1,696	12	65	77	2,188	12	74	86	29
History/ Archives	19,441	17	30	47	18,821	33	55	88	−3

TABLE 4.123
1988 *American Library Directory* Junior College Libraries with the Largest Numbers of Microforms

Library	Denomination	Number of Microforms
1. Lindsey Wilson College, Columbia, KY	Methodist	150,000
2. Ricks College, Rexburg, ID	Other Denominations	100,000
3. Marymount College, Rancho Palos Verdes, CA	Roman Catholic	60,000
4. Faulkner University, Montgomery, AL	Churches of Christ	30,000
5. York College, York, NE	Churches of Christ	30,000
6. Young Harris College, Young Harris, GA	Methodist	15,000
7. Waldorf College, Forest City, IA	Lutheran	15,000
8. Lees College, Jackson, KY	Presbyterian	15,000
9. Red Deer College, Red Deer, AB	Lutheran	15,000
10. Villa Maria College, Buffalo, NY	Roman Catholic	7,500
11. Maria Regina College, Syracuse, NY	Roman Catholic	7,500
12. Elizabeth Seton College, Yonkers, NY	Roman Catholic	7,500

TABLE 4.124
1988 *American Library Directory* Seminary Libraries with the Largest Numbers of Microforms

Library	Denomination	Number of Microforms
1. Graduate Theological Union, Berkeley, CA	Independent	230,000
2. St. Meinrad College, St. Meinrad, IN	Roman Catholic	230,000
3. Jesuit-Krauss-McCormick Seminary, Chicago, IL	Independent	150,000
4. Union Theological Seminary, New York, NY	Independent	150,000
5. Westminster Theological Seminary, San Marcos, CA	Presbyterian	60,000
6. Assemblies of God Seminary, Springfield, MO	Other Denominations	60,000
7. Southeastern Baptist Theological Seminary, Wake Forest, NC	Baptist	60,000
8. Union Theological Seminary, Richmond, VA	Presbyterian	60,000

TABLE 4.125
1988 *American Library Directory* Denominational Headquarters Libraries with the Largest Numbers of Microforms

Library	Denomination	Number of Microforms
1. United Methodist Publishing House, Nashville, TN	Methodist	7,500
2. Review and Herald, Hagerstown, MD	Other Denominations	3,000
3. Christian Science Monitor, Boston, MA	Other Denominations	3,000
4. Reorganized Church of Jesus Christ of Latter-day Saints, Independence, MO	Other Denominations	3,000
5. American Bible Society, New York, NY	Independent	3,000
6. Anti-Defamation League, New York, NY	Jewish	3,000
7. Interchurch Center, New York, NY	Independent	3,000
8. Charles Stevens American Atheist, Austin, TX	Other Denominations	550
9. Lutheran Church Missouri Synod, St. Louis, MO	Lutheran	50
10. Moravian Music Foundation, Winston-Salem, NC	Other Denominations	50
11. Southern Baptist Convention Foreign Missions Board, Richmond, VA	Baptist	50
12. Anglican Church of Canada, Toronto, ON	Episcopal/Anglican	50

TABLE 4.126
1988 *American Library Directory* Scholarly Microform Holdings by Total Annual Library Expenditure

Library Expenditures	Microform Holdings: 1–5,000	%	5,001–20,000	%	20,001–80,000	%	80,001 and over	%	No Response	%	Number of Libraries	Mean Microforms
Under $1,500	1	8	0	0	0	0	0	0	11	92	12	50
$1,501–$20,000	14	22	1	2	0	0	0	0	50	77	65	2,067
$20,001–$95,000	78	38	13	6	8	4	2	1	103	50	204	8,600
$95,001–$220,000	94	32	57	19	39	13	5	2	101	34	296	16,110
$220,001–$410,000	42	19	54	25	42	19	30	14	50	23	218	44,260
$410,001–$510,000	2	4	12	24	13	27	11	22	11	22	49	68,120
$510,001 and over	7	3	23	11	41	20	91	45	42	21	204	124,400
No response	62	16	20	5	7	2	8	2	287	75	384	23,060
Total	300	21	180	13	150	10	147	10	655	46	1,432	46,920

TABLE 4.127
1988 *American Library Directory* Scholarly Library Microform Holdings by Denomination

	Microform Holdings											
Denomination	1–5,000	%	5,001–20,000	%	20,001–80,000	%	80,001 and over	%	No Response	%	Number of Libraries	Mean Microforms
Baptist	43	28	13	9	16	11	22	14	58	38	152	52,910
Christian	14	34	6	15	1	2	3	7	17	41	41	23,540
Churches of Christ	6	22	5	19	5	19	3	11	8	30	27	45,950
Episcopal/Anglican	9	28	1	3	5	16	1	3	16	50	32	16,800
Independent	19	20	15	15	6	6	10	10	47	48	97	48,820
Lutheran	12	16	12	16	11	14	10	13	31	41	76	55,900
Mennonite	8	36	1	5	3	14	0	0	10	45	22	17,150
Methodist	30	20	34	23	19	13	17	11	49	33	149	43,360
Other Denominations	50	23	20	9	22	10	17	8	108	50	217	40,910
Presbyterian	15	17	21	23	16	18	10	11	28	31	90	45,770
U.C.C.	6	24	7	28	4	16	5	20	3	12	25	45,480
Summary												
Jewish	6	13	1	2	3	7	0	0	35	78	45	14,310
Roman Catholic	82	18	44	10	39	8	49	11	245	53	459	55,330
All Protestant	212	23	135	15	108	12	98	11	375	40	928	44,260
Total	300	21	180	13	150	10	147	10	655	46	1,432	46,920

TABLE 4.128
1988 *American Library Directory* Scholarly Christian Libraries with the Largest Numbers of Microforms

Library	Numbers of Microforms
1. Lynchburg College, Lynchburg, VA	230,000
2. Atlantic Christian College, Wilson, NC	100,000
3. Texas Christian University, Fort Worth, TX	100,000
4. Phillips University, Enid, OK	30,000
5. Atlanta Christian College, East Point, GA	15,000
6. Tougaloo College, Tougaloo, MS	15,000
7. St. Louis Christian College, St. Florissant, MO	15,000
8. Phillips University Graduate Seminary, Enid, OK	15,000
9. Emmanuel School of Religion, Johnson City, TN	15,000
10. Chapman University, Orange, CA	7,500

TABLE 4.129
1988 *American Library Directory* Scholarly Independent Libraries with the Largest Numbers of Microforms

Library	Numbers of Microforms
1. Azusa Pacific University, Azusa, CA	230,000
2. Graduate Theological Union, Berkeley, CA	230,000
3. Wheaton College, Wheaton, IL	230,000
4. Oral Roberts University, Tulsa, OK	230,000
5. Brown University, Providence, RI	230,000
6. Christian Broadcasting Network University, Virginia Beach, VA	230,000
7. McGill University, Montreal, PQ	230,000
8. Union Theological Seminary, New York, NY	150,000
9. Bob Jones University, Greenville, SC	150,000
10. LeTourneau College, Longview, TX	100,000

TABLE 4.130
1988 *American Library Directory* Scholarly Mennonite Libraries with the Largest Numbers of Microforms

Library	Numbers of Microforms
1. Goshen College, Goshen, IN	60,000
2. Bluffton College, Bluffton, OH	60,000
3. Eastern Mennonite University, Harrisonburg, VA	60,000
4. Fresno Pacific College, Fresno, CA	15,000
5. Bethel College, North Newton, KS	3,000
6. Columbia Bible College, Clearbrook, BC	3,000
7. Conrad Grebel College, Waterloo, ON	3,000
8. Associated Mennonite Biblical Seminaries, Elkhart, IN	550
9. Tabor College, Hillsboro, KS	550
10. Bethel College Mennonite Library, North Newton, KS	550

TABLE 4.131
1988 *American Library Directory* Scholarly Methodist Libraries with the Largest Numbers of Microforms

Library	Numbers of Microforms
1. Hendrix College, Conway, AR	230,000
2. University of the Pacific, Stockton, CA	230,000
3. University of Denver, Denver, CO	230,000
4. American University, Washington, DC	230,000
5. Emory University, Atlanta, GA	230,000
6. University of Evansville, Evansville, IN	230,000
7. Boston University, Boston, MA	230,000
8. Millsaps College, Jackson, MS	230,000
9. Duke University, Durham, NC	230,000
10. Texas Wesleyan University, Fort Worth, TX	230,000
11. Seattle Pacific University, Seattle, WA	230,000

TABLE 4.132
1988 *American Library Directory* Scholarly Presbyterian Libraries with the Largest Numbers of Microforms

Library	Numbers of Microforms
1. University of Tulsa, Tulsa, OK	230,000
2. Presbyterian Church Office of History, Philadelphia, PA	230,000
3. Trinity University, San Antonio, TX	230,000
4. Austin College, Sherman, TX	230,000
5. Queen's University, Kingston, ON	230,000
6. College of Wooster, Wooster, OH	150,000
7. Grove City College, Grove City, PA	150,000
8. Davis and Elkins College, Elkins, WV	150,000
9. Hanover College, Hanover, IN	100,000
10. Tusculum College, Greenville, TN	100,000

TABLE 4.133
1988 *American Library Directory* Scholarly Jewish Libraries with the Largest Numbers of Microforms

Library	Numbers of Microforms
1. American Jewish Historical Society, Waltham, MA	230,000
2. Jewish Theological Seminary, New York, NY	30,000
3. Hebrew Union College, Cincinnati, OH	30,000
4. Yeshiva University Gottesman Library, New York, NY	7,500
5. Spertus College of Judaica, Chicago, IL	3,000
6. Baltimore Hebrew College, Baltimore, MD	3,000
7. Hebrew College, Brookline, MA	3,000
8. Anti-Defamation League, New York, NY	3,000
9. Yivo Institute for Jewish Research, New York, NY	3,000

TABLE 4.134
1978 and 1988 *American Library Directory* Scholarly Library Longitudinal Study Total Material Holdings (Cumulative) (Books, Periodicals, VFs, and Microforms) by Library Type

	1978				1988				
Library Type	No. of Libraries	No Response	Total Libraries	Mean Items	No. of Libraries	No Response	Total Libraries	Mean Items	% Change 1978–88
Scholarly	1,275	100	1,375	106,100	1,389	42	1,431	138,800	31
Junior College	118	7	125	38,220	108	0	108	43,640	14
Senior College	673	31	704	96,730	696	9	705	131,600	36
University	149	5	154	306,500	189	0	189	366,400	20
Seminary	203	30	233	80,380	219	11	230	102,900	28
Convent/ Monastery	28	7	35	25,960	25	0	25	22,550	−13
Denominational HQ	64	13	77	15,840	78	8	86	15,090	−4.7
History/Archives	40	7	47	47,370	74	14	88	39,260	−17

TABLE 4.135
1978 *American Library Directory* Scholarly Libraries with Audiovisual Media Holdings by Library Type[1]

Library Type	Libraries with Media Holdings	%	Libraries with No Media Holdings	%	Number of Libraries
Scholarly	958	70	417	30	1,375
Junior College	82	66	43	34	125
Senior College	554	79	150	21	704
University	123	80	31	20	154
Seminary	126	54	107	46	233
Convent/Monastery	9	26	26	74	35
Denominational HQ	32	42	45	58	77
History/Archives	32	68	15	32	47

1. All media is defined as any combination of art reproductions, maps or audiovisual media (or all three of them). This table refers to audiovisual media only.

TABLE 4.136
1988 *American Library Directory* Scholarly Libraries with Audiovisual Media Holdings by Library Type

Library Type	Libraries with Media Holdings	%	Libraries with No Media Holdings	%	Number of Libraries
Scholarly	1,006	70	426	30	1,432
Junior College	78	72	30	28	108
Senior College	557	79	148	21	705
University	141	75	48	25	189
Seminary	131	57	100	43	231
Convent/Monastery	9	36	16	64	25
Denominational HQ	39	45	47	55	86
History/Archives	51	58	37	42	88

TABLE 4.137
1978 *American Library Directory* Entire Sample Libraries with Audiovisual Media Holdings by Region

Region	Libraries with Media Holdings	%	Libraries with No Media Holdings	%	Number of Libraries
Northeast	57	50	57	50	114
Middle Atlantic	218	50	214	50	432
Southeast	218	61	140	39	358
Southwest	96	51	93	49	189
West	96	53	86	47	182
Rocky Mountains	20	54	17	46	37
Middle West	373	60	252	40	625
Canada	52	42	73	58	125
Total	1,130	55	932	45	2,062

TABLE 4.138
1988 *American Library Directory* Entire Sample Libraries with Audiovisual Media Holdings by Region

Region	Libraries with Media Holdings	%	Libraries with No Media Holdings	%	Number of Libraries
Northeast	60	54	51	46	111
Middle Atlantic	223	53	194	47	417
Southeast	237	66	122	34	359
Southwest	120	60	79	40	199
West	111	62	67	38	178
Rocky Mountains	17	59	12	41	29
Middle West	380	64	215	36	595
Canada	82	44	104	56	186
Total	1,230	59	844	41	2,074

TABLE 4.139
1978 and 1988 *American Library Directory* Scholarly Library Audiovisual Media Holdings by Denomination

Denomination	With Media	%	No Response	%	Number of Libraries
		1978			
Baptist	106	76	34	24	140
Christian	29	73	11	28	40
Churches of Christ	20	74	7	26	27
Congregational	3	60	2	40	5
Episcopal/Anglican	15	47	17	53	32
Independent	56	68	26	32	82
Lutheran	55	79	15	21	70
Methodist	113	77	34	23	147
Other Denominations	155	72	59	28	214
Presbyterian	72	80	18	20	90
U.C.C.	21	88	3	12	24
Summary					
Jewish	19	54	16	46	35
Roman Catholic	294	63	175	37	469
All Protestant	645	74	226	26	871
Total	958	70	417	30	1,375
		1988			
Baptist	124	82	28	18	152
Christian	34	83	7	17	41
Churches of Christ	23	85	4	15	27
Episcopal/Anglican	14	44	18	56	32

TABLE 4.139 (*continued*)
1978 and 1988 *American Library Directory* Scholarly Library Audiovisual Media Holdings by Denomination

	1988				
Denomination	With Media	%	No Response	%	Number of Libraries
Independent	70	72	27	28	97
Lutheran	57	75	19	25	76
Mennonite	16	73	6	27	22
Methodist	113	76	36	24	149
Other Denominations	147	68	70	32	217
Presbyterian	70	78	20	22	90
U.C.C.	20	80	5	20	25
Summary					
Jewish	19	42	26	58	45
Roman Catholic	299	65	159	35	458
All Protestant	688	74	240	26	928
Total	1,006	70	425	30	1,431

TABLE 4.140
1978 *American Library Directory* Scholarly Libraries with Map Holdings by Library Type

Type of Library	Libraries with Map Holdings	%	No Response	%	Number of Libraries
Scholarly	639	46	736	54	1,375
Junior College	52	42	73	58	125
Senior College	383	54	321	46	704
University	91	59	63	41	154
Seminary	70	30	163	70	233
Convent/Monastery	8	23	27	77	35
Denominational HQ	13	17	64	83	77
History/Archives	22	47	25	53	47

TABLE 4.141
1988 *American Library Directory* Scholarly Libraries with Map Holdings by Library Type

Type of Library	Libraries with Map Holdings	%	No Response	%	Number of Libraries
Scholarly	433	30	999	70	1,432
Junior College	30	28	78	72	108
Senior College	250	35	455	65	705
University	70	37	119	63	189
Seminary	39	17	192	83	231
Convent/Monastery	5	20	20	80	25
Denominational HQ	11	13	75	87	86
History/Archives	28	32	60	68	88

TABLE 4.142
1978 *American Library Directory* Scholarly Libraries with Map Holdings by Denomination

Denomination	Libraries with Map Holdings	%	No Response	%	Number of Libraries
Baptist	72	51	68	49	140
Christian	18	45	22	55	40
Churches of Christ	18	67	9	33	27
Congregational	2	40	3	60	5
Episcopal/Anglican	8	25	24	75	32
Independent	37	45	45	55	82
Lutheran	35	50	35	50	70
Methodist	73	50	74	50	147
Other Denominations	110	51	104	49	214
Presbyterian	42	47	48	53	90
U.C.C.	15	63	9	37	24
Summary					
Jewish	12	34	23	66	35
Roman Catholic	197	42	272	58	469
All Protestant	430	49	441	51	871
Total	639	46	736	54	1,375

TABLE 4.143
1988 *American Library Directory* Scholarly Libraries with Map Holdings by Denomination

Denomination	Libraries with Map Holdings	%	No Response	%	Number of Libraries
Baptist	51	34	101	66	152
Christian	17	41	24	59	41
Churches of Christ	11	41	16	59	27
Episcopal/Anglican	9	28	23	72	32
Independent	30	31	67	69	97
Lutheran	21	28	55	72	76
Mennonite	8	36	14	64	22
Methodist	51	34	98	66	149
Other Denominations	69	32	148	68	217
Presbyterian	26	29	64	71	90
United Church of Christ	6	24	19	76	25
Summary					
Jewish	9	20	36	80	45
Roman Catholic	125	27	334	73	459
All Protestant	299	32	629	68	928
Total	433	30	999	70	1,432

TABLE 4.144
1978 *American Library Directory* Scholarly Libraries with Art Reproductions by Denomination

Denomination	Libraries with Art Reproductions	%	Response	%	Number of Libraries
Baptist	32	23	108	77	140
Christian	7	18	33	82	40
Churches of Christ	7	26	20	74	27
Congregational	0	0	5	100	5
Episcopal/Anglican	3	9	29	91	32
Independent	9	11	73	89	82
Lutheran	9	13	61	87	70
Methodist	33	22	114	78	147
Other Denominations	43	20	171	80	214
Presbyterian	19	21	71	79	90
United Church of Christ	4	17	20	83	24
Summary					
Jewish	4	11	31	89	35
Roman Catholic	82	17	387	83	469
All Protestant	166	19	705	81	871
Total	252	18	1,123	82	1,375

TABLE 4.145
1988 *American Library Directory* Scholarly Libraries with Art Reproductions by Denomination

Denomination	Libraries with Art Reproductions	%	No Response	%	Number of Libraries
Baptist	16	11	136	89	152
Christian	5	12	36	88	41
Churches of Christ	3	11	24	89	27
Episcopal/Anglican	1	3	31	97	32
Independent	3	3	94	97	97
Lutheran	7	9	69	91	76
Mennonite	4	18	18	82	22
Methodist	21	14	128	86	149
Other Denominations	18	8	199	92	217
Presbyterian	8	9	82	91	90
United Church of Christ	3	12	22	88	25
Summary					
Jewish	3	7	42	93	45
Roman Catholic	55	12	404	88	459
All Protestant	89	10	839	90	928
Total	147	10	1,285	90	1,432

TABLE 4.146
1978 *American Library Directory* Scholarly Libraries with Art Reproductions by Library Type

Type of Library	Libraries with Art Reproductions	%	No Response	%	Number of Libraries
Scholarly	252	18	1,123	82	1,375
Junior College	29	23	96	77	125
Senior College	157	22	547	78	704
University	28	18	126	82	154
Seminary	20	9	213	91	233
Convent/Monastery	2	6	33	94	35
Denominational HQ	6	8	71	92	77
History/Archives	10	21	37	79	47

TABLE 4.147
1978 *American Library Directory* Entire Sample Libraries with Art Reproductions by Region

Region	Libraries with Art Reproductions	%	No Response	%	Number of Libraries
Northeast	15	13	99	87	114
Middle Atlantic	48	11	384	89	432
Southeast	71	20	287	80	358
Southwest	27	14	162	86	189
West	18	10	164	90	182
Rocky Mountains	7	19	30	81	37
Middle West	106	17	519	83	625
Canada	16	13	109	87	125
Total	308	15	1,754	85	2,062

TABLE 4.148
1978 *American Library Directory* Entire Sample Libraries with Any Kind of Media Holdings—Media, Art, Maps—by Denomination

Denomination	Libraries with Any Kind of Media Holdings	%	No Response	%	Number of Libraries
Baptist	131	59	92	41	223
Christian	34	58	25	42	59
Churches of Christ	20	74	7	26	27
Congregational	5	15	28	85	33
Episcopal	20	27	54	73	74
Independent	56	64	31	36	87
Lutheran	73	59	50	41	123
Methodist	126	62	76	38	202
Other Denominations	173	62	108	38	281
Presbyterian	98	48	107	52	205
United Church of Christ	26	70	11	30	37
<u>Summary</u>					
Jewish	68	34	130	66	198
Roman Catholic	301	59	212	41	513
All Protestant	762	56	589	44	1,351
Total	1,131	55	931	45	2,062

TABLE 4.149
1988 *American Library Directory* Entire Sample Libraries with Any Kinds of Media Holdings—Media, Art, Maps—by Region

Region	Libraries with Any Kind of Media Holdings	%	No Response	%	Number of Libraries
Northeast	60	54	51	46	111
Middle Atlantic	223	53	194	47	417
Southeast	237	66	122	34	359
Southwest	120	60	79	40	199
West	111	62	67	38	178
Rocky Mountains	17	59	12	41	29
Middle West	380	64	215	36	595
Canada	83	45	103	55	186
Total	1,231	59	843	41	2,074

TABLE 4.150
1988 *American Library Directory* List of Libraries Most Often Listed on Scholarly Tables[1,2]

Library	Denomination	Listings
1. Brown University, Providence, RI	Independent	17
2. University of Notre Dame, Notre Dame, IN	Roman Catholic	16
3. Loyola University, Chicago, IL	Roman Catholic	15
4. Boston University, Boston, MA	Methodist	15
5. Wake Forest University, Winston-Salem, NC	Baptist	15
6. University of Dayton, Dayton, OH	Roman Catholic	15
7. Temple University, Philadelphia, PA	Baptist	15
8. Baylor University, Waco, TX	Baptist	15
9. Brigham Young University, Provo, UT	Other Denominations	15
10. University of Ottawa, Ottawa, ON	Roman Catholic	15
11. American University, Washington, DC	Methodist	14
12. Georgetown University, Washington, DC	Roman Catholic	14
13. Boston College, Chestnut Hill, MA	Roman Catholic	14
14. St. Louis University, St. Louis, MO	Roman Catholic	14
15. St. John's University, Jamaica, NY	Roman Catholic	14
16. Duke University, Durham, NC	Methodist	14
17. Queen's University, Kingston, ON	Presbyterian	14
18. University of Montreal, Montreal, PQ	Roman Catholic	14
19. Santa Clara University, Santa Clara, CA	Roman Catholic	13
20. University of Denver, Denver, CO	Methodist	13
21. The Catholic University of America, Washington, DC	Roman Catholic	13
22. Brandeis University, Waltham, MA	Jewish	13

TABLE 4.150 (*continued*)
1988 *American Library Directory* List of Libraries Most Often Listed on Scholarly Tables[1,2]

Library	Denomination	Listings
23. Andrews University, Berrien Springs, MI	Other Denominations	13
24. University of Detroit, Detroit, MI	Roman Catholic	13
25. Fordham University, Bronx, NY	Roman Catholic	13
26. Yeshiva University, New York, NY	Jewish	13
27. University of Tulsa, Tulsa, OK	Presbyterian	13
28. Marquette University, Milwaukee, WI	Roman Catholic	13
29. McMaster University, Hamilton, ON	Baptist	13

1. This table lists the libraries appearing in the largest number of denominational tables and with the entire list of libraries considered as one list, not as a series of denominational lists.
2. The list was also compiled from the first fifteen libraries on each of the scholarly denominational tables.

TABLE 4.151
1978 and 1988 *American Library Directory* Longitudinal Study Library Expenditures on Material by Library Type

	----------------1 9 7 8--------------				----------------1 9 8 8----------------				
Library Type	Mean 1978	No. of Libraries	No Response	Total Libraries	Mean 1988	No. of Libraries	No Response	Total Libraries	% Change
Scholarly	49,489	748	627	1,375	81,501	1,057	375	1,432	65
Junior College	17,235	51	74	125	37,199	73	35	108	116
Senior College	46,298	435	269	704	82,179	579	126	705	78
University	113,108	113	41	154	144,352	169	20	189	28
Seminary	29,059	105	128	233	64,573	162	69	231	122
Convent/ Monastery	3,393	7	28	35	10,750	6	19	25	217
Denominational HQ	4,181	18	59	77	14,543	29	57	86	248
History/Archives	3,566	19	28	47	12,994	39	49	88	264

TABLE 4.152
1988 *American Library Directory* Junior College Libraries with the Highest Annual Expenditure on Material

Library	Denomination	Expenditure on Material
1. Ricks College, Rexburg, ID	Other Denominations	$175,000
2. Saint Mary's College, Raleigh, NC	Episcopal/Anglican	175,000
3. Kettering College of Medical Arts, Kettering, OH	Other Denominations	175,000
4. Red Deer College, Red Deer, AB	Lutheran	175,000
5. Elizabeth Seton College, Yonkers, NY	Roman Catholic	132,000
6. St. Mary's College, O'Fallon, MO	Roman Catholic	117,000
7. Cégep de Jonquière, Jonquière, PQ	Roman Catholic	99,000
8. Vanier College, St. Laurent, PQ	Roman Catholic	99,000
9. Lindsey Wilson College, Columbia, KY	Methodist	77,500
10. Upsala College, Sussex, NJ	Lutheran	57,000
11. Montreat College, Montreat, NC	Presbyterian	57,000
12. Peace College, Raleigh, NC	Presbyterian	57,000
13. Cégep de la Pocatière, La Pocatière, PQ	Roman Catholic	57,000

TABLE 4.153
1978 *American Library Directory* Senior College Libraries with the Highest Annual Expenditure on Material

Library	Denomination	Expenditure on Material
1. Ambassador College, Pasadena, CA	Other Denominations	$175,000
2. Boston College, Chestnut Hill, MA	Roman Catholic	175,000
3. Calvin College, Grand Rapids, MI	Other Denominations	175,000
4. Mississippi College, Clinton, MS	Baptist	17,5000
5. Manhattan College, Bronx, NY	Roman Catholic	175,000
6. Mercy College, Dobbs Ferry, NY	Roman Catholic	175,000
7. Davidson College, Davidson, NC	Presbyterian	175,000
8. Bryn Mawr College, Bryn Mawr, PA	Other Denominations	175,000
9. Lafayette College, Easton, PA	Presbyterian	175,000
10. Franklin and Marshall College, Lancaster, PA	United Church of Christ	175,000
11. Swarthmore College, Swarthmore, PA	Other Denominations	175,000
12. Benedict College, Columbia, SC	Baptist	175,000
13. College of the Holy Cross, Worcester, MA	Roman Catholic	152,000
14. College of Wooster, Wooster, OH	Presbyterian	152,000
15. Dickinson College, Carlisle, PA	Methodist	152,000
16. Gettysburg College, Gettysburg, PA	Lutheran	152,000
17. Westminster College, New Wilmington, PA	Presbyterian	152,000
18. Saint Joseph's University, Philadelphia, PA	Roman Catholic	152,000
19. Providence College, Providence, RI	Roman Catholic	152,000

TABLE 4.154
1988 *American Library Directory* Convent/Monastery Libraries with the Highest Annual Expenditure on Material

Library	Denomination	Expenditure on Material
1. Passionist Monastery, Jamaica, NY	Roman Catholic	$37,500
2. Gethsemani Monastery, Trappist, KY	Roman Catholic	8,000
3. St. Joseph's Abbey, Spencer, MA	Roman Catholic	8,000
4. Assumption Abbey, Richardton, ND	Roman Catholic	8,000
5. Abbey of Regina Laudis, Bethlehem, CT	Roman Catholic	1,500
6. Sacred Heart Monastery, Winchester, VA	Roman Catholic	1,500

TABLE 4.155
1988 *American Library Directory* Annual Material Expenditure by Total Annual Library Expenditure for the Entire Sample

Total Library Expenditure	Material Expenditure: 1–18,000	%	18,001–67,000	%	67,001–122,000	%	122,001 and over	%	No Response	%	Number of Libraries	Mean Dollars
Under $1,500	128	85	0	0	0	0	0	0	23	15	151	678
$1,501–$20,000	126	85	0	0	0	0	0	0	23	15	149	4,091
$20,001–$95,000	104	46	111	49	2	1	0	0	10	4	227	21,790
$95,001–$220,000	10	3	204	68	73	24	8	3	6	2	301	54,430
$220,001–$410,000	4	2	21	10	117	54	72	33	4	2	218	107,800
$410,001–$510,000	0	0	3	6	9	18	34	69	3	6	49	140,400
$510,001 and over	0	0	2	1	12	6	189	92	2	1	205	167,400
No response	25	3	20	3	9	1	4	1	716	93	774	37,790
Total	397	19	361	17	222	11	307	15	787	38	2,074	67,670

TABLE 4.156
1988 *American Library Directory* Scholarly Christian Libraries with the Highest Annual Expenditure on Material

Library	Expenditure on Material
1. Chapman University, Orange, CA	$175,000
2. Texas Christian University, Fort Worth, TX	175,000
3. Lynchburg College, Lynchburg, VA	175,000
4. Phillips University Seminary, Enid, OK	152,000
5. Atlantic Christian College, Wilson, NC	99,000
6. Hiram College, Hiram, OH	99,000
7. Phillips University, Enid, OK	99,000
8. Bethany College, Bethany, WV	99,000
9. Transylvania University, Lexington, KY	77,500

TABLE 4.157
1978 *American Library Directory* Scholarly Independent Libraries with the Highest Annual Expenditure on Material

Library	Expenditure on Material
1. Brown University, Providence, RI	$175,000
2. McGill University, Montreal, PQ	175,000
3. Graduate Theological Union, Berkeley, CA	99,000
4. Biola University, La Mirada, CA	99,000
5. Wheaton College, Wheaton, IL	99,000
6. Berea College, Berea, KY	99,000
7. Harvard University Divinity School, Cambridge, MA	99,000
8. Union Theological Seminary, New York, NY	99,000
9. Fuller Theological Seminary, Pasadena, CA	77,500
10. Westmont College, Santa Barbara, CA	57,000
11. Asbury College, Wilmore, KY	57,000
12. Bob Jones University, Greenville, SC	57,000

TABLE 4.158
1988 *American Library Directory* Scholarly Mennonite Libraries with the Highest Annual Expenditure on Material

Library	Expenditure on Material
1. Fresno Pacific College, Fresno, CA	$117,000
2. Goshen College, Goshen, IN	117,000
3. Eastern Mennonite University, Harrisonburg, VA	99,000
4. Associated Mennonite Biblical Seminaries, Elkhart, IN	37,500
5. Tabor College, Hillsboro, KS	37,500
6. Bethel College, North Newton, KS	37,500
7. Bluffton College, Bluffton, OH	37,500
8. Conrad Grebel College, Waterloo, ON	37,500

TABLE 4.159
1978 *American Library Directory* Scholarly Other Denominational Libraries with the Highest Annual Expenditure on Material

Library	Expenditure on Material
1. Ambassador College, Pasadena, CA	$175,000
2. Andrews University, Berrien Springs, MI	175,000
3. Calvin College, Grand Rapids, MI	175,000
4. Bryn Mawr College, Bryn Mawr, PA	175,000
5. Swarthmore College, Swarthmore, PA	175,000
6. University of Winnipeg, Winnipeg, MB	175,000
7. Loma Linda University, Loma Linda, CA	152,000
8. Brigham Young University, Laie, HI	117,000
9. Ricks College, Rexburg, ID	117,000
10. Nazareth College, Rochester, NY	117,000

TABLE 4.160

1988 *American Library Directory* Scholarly United Church of Christ Libraries with the Highest Annual Expenditure on Material

Library	Expenditure on Material
1. Elmhurst College, Elmhurst, IL	$175,000
2. Hood College, Frederick, MD	175,000
3. Eden Webster University, St. Louis, MO	175,000
4. Elon College, Elon College, NC	175,000
5. Ursinus College, Collegeville, PA	175,000
6. Franklin and Marshall College, Lancaster, PA	175,000
7. Pacific University, Forest Grove, OR	152,000
8. Cedar Crest College, Allentown, PA	117,000
9. Fisk University, Nashville, TN	117,000

TABLE 4.161

1988 *American Library Directory* Junior College Libraries with the Highest Expenditure on Personnel

Library	Denomination	Expenditure on Personnel
1. Ricks College, Rexburg, ID	Other Denominations	$325,000
2. Red Deer College, Red Deer, AB	Lutheran	325,000
3. Cégep de Jonquière, Jonquière, PQ	Roman Catholic	325,000
4. Vanier College, St. Laurent, PQ	Roman Catholic	325,000
5. Lindsey Wilson College, Columbia, KY	Methodist	117,500
6. Cégep de la Pocatière, La Pocatière, PQ	Roman Catholic	117,500
7. St. Mary's College, O'Fallon, MO	Roman Catholic	95,000
8. Villa Maria College, Buffalo, NY	Roman Catholic	95,000
9. Hilbert College, Hamburg, NY	Roman Catholic	95,000
10. Lees-McRae College, Banner Elk, NC	Presbyterian	95,000
11. Saint Mary's College, Raleigh, NC	Episcopal/Anglican	95,000
12. North Greenville College, Tigerville, SC	Baptist	95,000

TABLE 4.162
1988 *American Library Directory* Convent/Monastery Libraries with the Highest Expenditure on Personnel

Library	Denomination	Expenditure on Personnel
1. Assumption Abbey, Richardton, ND	Roman Catholic	$7,500
2. Gethsemani Abbey, Trappist, KY	Roman Catholic	2,500
3. Passionist Monastery, Jamaica, NY	Roman Catholic	2,500

TABLE 4.163
1988 *American Library Directory* History/Archive Libraries with the Highest Annual Expenditure on Personnel

Library	Denomination	Expenditure on Personnel
1. Presbyterian Study Center, Montreat, NC	Presbyterian	$212,500
2. American Jewish Historical Society, Waltham, MA	Jewish	177,500
3. Goshen College, Goshen, IN	Mennonite	145,000
4. Concordia Historical Institute, St. Louis, MO	Lutheran	145,000
5. Salvation Army Research Center, New York, NY	Other Denominations	145,000
6. Shaker Museum, Old Chatham, NY	Other Denominations	145,000
7. Disciples of Christ Historical Society, Nashville, TN	Christian	145,000
8. Southern Baptist Convention Archives, Richmond, VA	Baptist	145,000
9. Bethel College, North Newton, KS	Mennonite	95,000
10. American Congregational Association, Boston, MA	Congregational	95,000
11. Lutheran Council, New York, NY	Lutheran	95,000
12. Archdiocese of Boston, Brighton, MA	Roman Catholic	57,500
13. Virginia Baptist Historical Society, Richmond, VA	Baptist	57,500
14. Southern Baptist Convention, Atlanta, GA	Baptist	42,500
15. Episcopal Diocese of Massachusetts, Boston, MA	Episcopal/Anglican	42,500
16. Canadian Baptist Archives, Hamilton, ON	Baptist	42,500

TABLE 4.164
1988 *American Library Directory* Scholarly Christian Libraries with the Highest Annual Expenditure on Personnel

Library	Expenditure on Personnel
1. Chapman University, Orange, CA	$325,000
2. Texas Christian University, Forth Worth, TX	325,000
3. Lynchburg College, Lynchburg, VA	212,500
4. Hiram College, Hiram, OH	177,500
5. Atlantic Christian College, Wilson, NC	145,000
6. Phillips University, Enid, OK	145,000
7. Disciples of Christ Historical Society, Nashville, TN	145,000
8. Christian Theological Seminary, Indianapolis, IN	117,500
9. Transylvania University, Lexington, KY	117,500
10. Phillips University Seminary, Enid, OK	117,500
11. Northwest Christian College, Eugene, OR	117,500

TABLE 4.165
1988 *American Library Directory* Scholarly Episcopal/Anglican Libraries with the Highest Annual Expenditure on Personnel

Library	Expenditure on Personnel
1. Kenyon College, Gambier, OH	$325,000
2. University of the South, Sewanee, TN	325,000
3. Bishop's University, Lennoxville, PQ	325,000
4. Episcopal Divinity School, Cambridge, MA	247,500
5. General Theological Seminary, New York, NY	212,500
6. Voorhees College, Denmark, SC	145,000
7. Saint Paul's College, Lawrenceville, VA	145,000
8. Episcopal Theological Seminary, Austin, TX	117,500
9. Huron College, London, ON	117,500

TABLE 4.166
1978 *American Library Directory* Scholarly Lutheran Libraries with the Highest Annual Expenditure on Personnel

Library	Expenditure on Personnel
1. Luther College, Decorah, IA	$247,500
2. Concordia College, Moorhead, MN	247,500
3. St. Olaf College, Northfield, MN	247,500
4. Wittenberg University, Springfield, OH	247,500
5. Gettysburg College, Gettysburg, PA	212,500
6. Augustana College, Sioux Falls, SD	212,500
7. Augustana College, Rock Island, IL	177,500
8. Wagner College, Staten Island, NY	177,500
9. Capital University, Columbus, OH	177,500
10. Pacific Lutheran University, Tacoma, WA	177,500
11. Red Deer College, Red Deer, AB	177,500

TABLE 4.167
1978 *American Library Directory* Scholarly Methodist Libraries with the Highest Annual Expenditure on Personnel

Library	Expenditure on Personnel
1. University of the Pacific, Stockton, CA	$325,000
2. University of Denver, Denver, CO	325,000
3. Wesleyan University, Middletown, CT	325,000
4. American University, Washington, DC	325,000
5. Emory University, Atlanta, GA	325,000
6. Boston University, Boston, MA	325,000
7. Duke University, Durham, NC	325,000
8. Southern Methodist University, Dallas, TX	325,000

TABLE 4.168
1978 *American Library Directory* Scholarly Presbyterian Libraries with the Highest Annual Expenditure on Personnel

Library	Expenditure on Personnel
1. Trinity University, San Antonio, TX	$325,000
2. Queen's University, Kingston, ON	325,000
3. Lafayette College, Easton, PA	282,500
4. Macalester College, St. Paul, MN	177,500
5. Davidson College, Davidson, NC	177,500
6. College of Wooster, Wooster, OH	177,500
7. Lewis and Clark College, Portland, OR	177,500
8. Johnson C. Smith University, Charlotte, NC	145,000
9. Westminster College, New Wilmington, PA	145,000
10. Presbyterian Historical Society, Philadelphia, PA	145,000
11. Southwestern College, Memphis, TN	145,000

TABLE 4.169
1988 *American Library Directory* Scholarly Presbyterian Libraries with the Highest Annual Expenditure on Personnel

Library	Expenditure on Personnel
1. Lake Forest College, Lake Forest, IL	$325,000
2. Macalester College, St. Paul, MN	325,000
3. Princeton Theological Seminary, Princeton, NJ	325,000
4. Davidson College, Davidson, NC	325,000
5. University of Tulsa, Tulsa, OK	325,000
6. Lewis and Clark College, Portland, OR	325,000
7. Lafayette College, Easton, PA	325,000
8. Rhodes College, Memphis, TN	325,000
9. Trinity University, San Antonio, TX	325,000
10. Union Theological Seminary, Richmond, VA	325,000
11. Queen's University, Kingston, ON	325,000

TABLE 4.170
1988 *American Library Directory* Scholarly Jewish Libraries with the Highest Annual Expenditure on Personnel

Library	Expenditure on Personnel
1. Brandeis University, Waltham, MA	$325,000
2. Jewish Theological Seminary, New York, NY	325,000
3. Yeshiva University, New York, NY	325,000
4. Hebrew Union College, Cincinnati, OH	325,000
5. American Jewish Historical Society, Waltham, MA	177,500
6. Yeshiva University of Gottesman Library, New York, NY	145,000
7. Spertus College of Judaica, Chicago, IL	117,500
8. Hebrew College, Brookline, MA	95,000
9. Reconstructionist Rabbinical College, Wyncote, PA	57,500
10. Jewish Federation, Omaha, NE	27,500

TABLE 4.171
1988 *American Library Directory* Scholarly Library Annual Other Expenditure by Library Type

Library Type	Other Expenditure											
	1– 6,000	%	6,001– 12,000	%	12,001– 18,000	%	18,001 and over	%	No Response	%	Number of Libraries	Mean Dollars
Scholarly	45	3	63	4	30	2	437	31	857	60	1,432	17,280
Junior College	8	7	9	8	1	1	6	6	84	78	108	10,520
Senior College	26	4	35	5	21	3	236	33	387	55	705	17,180
University	0	0	5	3	3	2	126	67	55	29	189	19,450
Seminary	10	4	8	3	4	2	60	26	149	65	231	16,710
Convent/Monastery	0	0	0	0	0	0	0	0	25	100	25	0
Denominational HQ	0	0	4	5	0	0	3	3	79	92	86	13,140
History/Archives	1	1	2	2	1	1	6	7	78	89	88	15,200

TABLE 4.172
1978 *American Library Directory* Seminary Libraries with the Highest Annual Other Expenditures

Library	Denomination	Other Expenditures
1. Graduate Theological Union, Berkeley, CA	Independent	$20,000
2. School of Theology, Claremont, CA	Methodist	20,000
3. Fuller Theological Seminary, Pasadena, CA	Independent	20,000
4. Iliff School of Theology, Denver, CO	Methodist	20,000
5. Southern Baptist Theological Seminary, Louisville, KY	Baptist	20,000
6. Assemblies of God Graduate School, Springfield, MO	Other Denominations	20,000
7. Union Theological Seminary, New York, NY	Independent	20,000
8. Hebrew Union College, Cincinnati, OH	Jewish	20,000
9. Lutheran Theological Seminary, Columbus, OH	Lutheran	20,000
10. St. Vincent College, Latrobe, PA	Roman Catholic	20,000
11. Southwestern Baptist Theological Seminary, Fort Worth, TX	Baptist	20,000
12. Colgate Rochester Theological Seminary, Rochester, NY	Independent	17,000
13. St. John's Provincial Seminary, Plymouth, MI	Roman Catholic	15,000
14. Memphis Theological Seminary, Memphis, TN	Presbyterian	15,000

TABLE 4.173
1988 *American Library Directory* History/Archive Libraries with the Highest Annual Other Expenditures

Library	Denomination	Other Expenditures
1. Archdiocese of Boston, Brighton, MA	Roman Catholic	$20,000
2. American Jewish Historical Society, Waltham, MA	Jewish	20,000
3. Concordia Historical Institute, St. Louis, MO	Lutheran	20,000
4. Salvation Army Research Center, New York, NY	Other Denominations	20,000
5. Presbyterian Study Center, Montreat, NC	Presbyterian	20,000
6. Schwenkfelder Church, Pennsburg, PA	Other Denominations	20,000
7. American Baptist Colgate Historical, Rochester, NY	Baptist	13,000

TABLE 4.174

1978 *American Library Directory* Scholarly Baptist Libraries with the Highest Annual Other Expenditures

Library	Other Expenditures
1. Southern Baptist Theological Seminary, Louisville, KY	$20,000
2. Bethel College, St. Paul, MN	20,000
3. Campbell University, Buies Creek, NC	20,000
4. Wake Forest University, Winston-Salem, NC	20,000
5. Cedarville College, Cedarville, OH	20,000
6. Linfield College, McMinnville, OR	20,000
7. Temple University, Philadelphia, PA	20,000
8. Benedict College, Columbia, SC	20,000
9. Furman University, Greenville, SC	20,000
10. Southwestern Baptist Theological Seminary, Fort Worth, TX	20,000
11. University of Richmond, Richmond, VA	20,000
12. Acadia University, Wolfville, NS	20,000

TABLE 4.175

1978 *American Library Directory* Scholarly Churches of Christ Libraries with the Highest Annual Other Expenditures

Library	Other Expenditures
1. Oklahoma Christian College, Oklahoma City, OK	$20,000
2. Abilene Christian University, Abilene, TX	20,000
3. Lincoln Christian College, Lincoln, IL	13,000
4. Northeastern Christian Junior College, Villanova, PA	13,000
5. York College, York, NE	9,000
6. Freed-Hardeman University, Henderson, TN	9,000
7. Harding University, Searcy, AR	7,000
8. Northwest Christian College, Eugene, OR	3,000
9. Lubbock Christian University, Lubbock, TX	3,000
10. Columbia Christian College, Portland, OR	1,500

TABLE 4.176

1978 *American Library Directory* Scholarly Independent Libraries with the Highest Annual Other Expenditures

Library	Other Expenditures
1. Graduate Theological Union, Berkeley, CA	$20,000
2. Fuller Theological Seminary, Pasadena, CA	20,000
3. Maharishi International University, Fairfield, IA	20,000
4. Asbury College, Wilmore, KY	20,000
5. Union Theological Seminary, New York, NY	20,000
6. Shaw University, Raleigh, NC	20,000
7. Brown University, Providence, RI	20,000
8. LeTourneau College, Longview, TX	15,000
9. Westmont College, Santa Barbara, CA	11,000
10. Columbia Bible College, Columbia, SC	9,000

TABLE 4.177

1978 and 1988 *American Library Directory* Longitudinal Study Scholarly Total Annual Expenditures by Library Type

	1978				1988				
Library Type	Mean 1978	No. of Libraries	No Response	Total Libraries	Mean 1988	No. of Libraries	No Response	Total Libraries	% Change
Scholarly	140,718	969	406	1,375	249,076	1,048	384	1,432	77
Junior College	53,800	80	45	125	115,834	74	34	108	115
Senior College	130,044	572	132	704	248,029	570	135	705	91
University	348,398	130	24	154	458,750	166	23	189	32
Seminary	81,656	141	92	233	186,494	159	72	231	128
Convent/ Monastery	4,682	11	24	35	17,607	7	18	25	276
Denominational HQ	20,706	17	60	77	54,394	26	60	86	163
History/Archives	25,444	18	29	47	81,326	46	42	88	220

Range (Material) $0–$182,000
Range (Personnel) $0–$350,000
Range (Other) $0–$22,000
Range (Total P.A. Expenditure) $0–$610,000

TABLE 4.178

1978 *American Library Directory* Scholarly Total Annual Expenditure by Library Type

	Total Annual Library Expenditure											
Library Type	1–7,500	%	7,501–95,000	%	95,001–220,000	%	220,001 and over	%	No Response	%	Number of Libraries	Mean Dollars
Scholarly	60	4	443	32	286	21	180	13	406	30	1,375	140,700
Junior College	6	5	67	54	5	4	2	2	45	36	125	53,800
Senior College	18	3	248	35	226	32	80	11	132	19	704	130,000
University	4	3	11	7	25	16	90	58	24	16	154	348,400
Seminary	8	3	97	42	28	12	8	3	92	39	233	81,660
Convent/Monastery	9	26	2	6	0	0	0	0	24	69	35	4,682
Denominational HQ	8	10	8	10	1	1	0	0	60	78	77	20,710
History/Archives	7	15	10	21	1	2	0	0	29	62	47	25,440

TABLE 4.179

1988 *American Library Directory* Scholarly Total Annual Expenditure by Library Type

	Total Annual Library Expenditure											
Library Type	1–7,500	%	7,501–95,000	%	95,001–220,000	%	220,001 and over	%	No Response	%	Number of Libraries	Mean Dollars
Scholarly	38	3	243	17	296	21	471	33	384	27	1,432	249,100
Junior College	2	2	43	40	22	20	7	6	34	31	108	115,800
Senior College	6	1	107	15	194	28	263	37	135	19	705	248,000
University	2	1	3	2	14	7	147	78	23	12	189	458,800
Seminary	5	2	48	21	59	26	47	20	72	31	231	186,500
Convent/Monastery	3	12	4	16	0	0	0	0	18	72	25	17,610
Denominational HQ	12	14	12	14	0	0	2	2	60	70	86	54,390
History/Archives	8	9	26	30	7	8	5	6	42	48	88	81,330

TABLE 4.180
1988 *American Library Directory* Junior College Libraries with the Highest Total Annual Expenditures

Library	Denomination	Total Expenditures
1. Ricks College, Rexburg, ID	Other Denominations	$560,000
2. Red Deer College, Red Deer, IL	Lutheran	560,000
3. Cégep de Jonquière, Jonquière, PQ	Roman Catholic	560,000
4. Vanier College, St. Laurent, PQ	Roman Catholic	560,000
5. Cégep de Victoriaville, Victoriaville, PQ	Roman Catholic	460,000
6. Saint Mary's College, Raleigh, NC	Episcopal/Anglican	265,000
7. Kettering College of Medical Arts, Kettering, OH	Other Denominations	265,000
8. Lindsey Wilson College, Columbia, KY	Methodist	185,000
9. St. Mary's College, O'Fallon, MO	Roman Catholic	185,000
10. Elizabeth Seton College, Yonkers, NY	Roman Catholic	185,000
11. Anderson College, Anderson, SC	Baptist	185,000
12. Cégep de la Pocatière, La Pocatière, PQ	Roman Catholic	185,000

TABLE 4.181
1988 *American Library Directory* Seminary Libraries with the Highest Total Annual Expenditures

Library	Denomination	Total Expenditures
1. Graduate Theological Union, Berkeley, CA	Independent	$560,000
2. Yale University Divinity School, New Haven, CT	Independent	560,000
3. Emory University, Atlanta, GA	Methodist	560,000
4. Southern Baptist Theological Seminary, Louisville, KY	Baptist	560,000
5. Mount St. Mary's College, Emmitsburg, MD	Roman Catholic	560,000
6. Harvard University, Cambridge, MA	Independent	560,000
7. Princeton Theological Seminary, Princeton, NJ	Presbyterian	560,000
8. Jewish Theological Seminary, New York, NY	Jewish	560,000
9. Union Theological Seminary, New York, NY	Independent	560,000
10. Hebrew College, Cincinnati, OH	Jewish	560,000
11. Southern Methodist University, Dallas, TX	Methodist	560,000
12. Southwestern Baptist Theological Seminary, Fort Worth, TX	Baptist	560,000
13. Union Theological Seminary, Richmond, VA	Presbyterian	560,000

TABLE 4.182
1988 *American Library Directory* Denominational Headquarters Libraries with the Highest Total Annual Expenditures

Library	Denomination	Total Expenditures
1. Southern Baptist Convention, Nashville, TN	Baptist	$460,000
2. Southern Baptist Convention Foreign Missions Board, Richmond, VA	Baptist	265,000
3. Naropa Institute, Boulder, CO	Other Denominations	70,000
4. Seventh-day Adventists, Washington, DC	Other Denominations	70,000
5. Southern Baptist Home Missions, Atlanta, GA	Baptist	70,000
6. Reorganized Church of Jesus Christ of Latter-day Saints, Independence, MO	Other Denominations	70,000
7. Catholic Central Union, St. Louis, MO	Roman Catholic	70,000
8. Jewish Federation, Omaha, NE	Jewish	70,000
9. Society of Friends, Philadelphia, PA	Other Denominations	70,000
10. Maison Bellarmin, Montreal, PQ	Roman Catholic	70,000
11. Southern Baptist Convention Foreign Missions Board, Missionary Learning Center, Rockville, VA	Baptist	32,500
12. Canadian Center for Ecumenism, Montreal, PQ	Roman Catholic	32,500
13. Scripture Press Publications Library, Wheaton, IL	Other Denominations	13,750
14. Western North Carolina Episcopal Diocese, Black Mountain, NC	Episcopal/Anglican	13,750

TABLE 4.183
1988 *American Library Directory* Scholarly Total Annual Library Expenditure by Region for Scholarly Matched Pairs

	Total Annual Library Expenditure											
Region	1–7,500	%	7,501–95,000	%	95,001–220,000	%	220,001 and over	%	No Response	%	Number of Libraries	Mean Dollars
Northeast	2	3	10	17	6	10	27	45	15	25	60	299,900
Middle Atlantic	6	3	29	13	39	18	90	41	56	25	220	295,600
Southeast	2	1	33	14	75	31	88	37	41	17	239	245,600
Southwest	2	2	18	18	15	15	43	44	20	20	98	262,500
West	1	1	12	12	14	14	42	42	30	30	99	322,400
Rocky Mountains	0	0	2	12	5	29	3	18	7	41	17	237,300
Middle West	2	1	60	17	104	29	127	36	60	17	353	243,900
Canada	1	1	16	19	7	8	28	33	34	40	86	310,800
Total	16	1	180	15	265	23	448	38	263	22	1,172	267,700

TABLE 4.184
1978 and 1988 *American Library Directory* Scholarly Library Expenditure per Student by Region

Region	1–100	%	101–250	%	251–400	%	401 and over	%	No Response	%	Number of Libraries	Mean Dollars
						1978						
Northeast	11	14	23	30	2	3	2	3	38	50	76	157
Middle Atlantic	45	17	85	32	9	3	17	6	108	41	264	191
Southeast	73	27	101	38	11	4	18	7	64	24	267	165
Southwest	30	27	41	37	1	1	2	2	38	34	112	128
West	26	22	39	33	3	3	7	6	44	37	119	172
Rocky Mountains	6	22	6	22	0	0	2	7	13	48	27	189
Middle West	90	22	160	39	8	2	29	7	125	30	412	182
Canada	11	11	15	15	2	2	2	2	68	69	98	154
Total	292	21	470	34	36	3	79	6	498	36	1,375	172
						1988						
Northeast	2	3	18	24	10	13	10	13	36	47	76	385
Middle Atlantic	4	2	65	25	39	15	44	17	109	42	261	386
Southeast	14	5	85	32	45	17	53	20	69	26	266	333
Southwest	5	4	43	37	11	9	19	16	39	33	117	292
West	3	2	27	21	23	18	21	16	54	42	128	362
Rocky Mountains	1	5	5	24	1	5	5	24	9	43	21	435
Middle West	15	4	120	30	83	21	69	17	111	28	398	356
Canada	6	4	30	18	6	4	18	11	104	63	164	296
Total	50	3	393	27	218	15	239	17	531	37	1,431	349

TABLE 4.185
1978 *American Library Directory* Scholarly Baptist Libraries with the Highest Total Annual Expenditures

Library	Total Expenditures
1. Wake Forest University, Winston-Salem, NC	$560,000
2. Temple University, Philadelphia, PA	560,000
3. Southwestern Baptist Theological Seminary, Fort Worth, TX	560,000
4. Baylor University, Waco, TX	560,000
5. University of Richmond, Richmond, VA	560,000
6. Acadia University, Wolfville, NS	560,000
7. McMaster University, Hamilton, ON	560,000
8. Benedict College, Columbia, SC	460,000
9. Samford University, Birmingham, AL	360,000
10. Southern Baptist Theological Seminary, Louisville, KY	360,000
11. Furman University, Greenville, SC	360,000

TABLE 4.186
1988 *American Library Directory* Scholarly Churches of Christ Libraries with the Highest Total Annual Expenditures

Library	Total Expenditures
1. Pepperdine University, Malibu, CA	$560,000
2. Abilene Christian University, Abilene, TX	560,000
3. Harding University, Searcy, AR	360,000
4. David Lipscomb University, Nashville, TN	360,000
5. Oklahoma Christian College, Oklahoma City, OK	265,000
6. Freed-Hardeman University, Henderson, TN	185,000

TABLE 4.187
1988 *American Library Directory* Scholarly Episcopal/Anglican Libraries with the Highest Total Annual Expenditures

Library	Total Expenditures
1. Hobart and William Smith Colleges, Geneva, NY	$560,000
2. Kenyon College, Gambier, OH	560,000
3. University of the South, Sewanee, TN	560,000
4. Bishop's University, Lennoxville, PQ	560,000
5. Episcopal Divinity School, Cambridge, MA	360,000
6. Bard College, Annandale-on-Hudson, NY	265,000
7. General Theological Seminary, New York, NY	265,000
8. Saint Mary's College, Raleigh, NC	265,000
9. Huron College, London, ON	265,000

TABLE 4.188
1978 *American Library Directory* Scholarly Lutheran Libraries with the Highest Total Annual Expenditures

Library	Total Expenditures
1. Wilfred Laurier University, Waterloo, ON	$560,000
2. Concordia College, Moorhead, MN	460,000
3. Wittenberg University, Springfield, OH	460,000
4. St. Olaf College, Northfield, MN	360,000
5. Wagner College, Staten Island, NY	360,000
6. Gettysburg College, Gettysburg, PA	360,000
7. Pacific Lutheran University, Tacoma, WA	360,000

TABLE 4.189
1988 *American Library Directory* Scholarly Mennonite Libraries with the Highest Total Annual Expenditures

Library	Total Expenditures
1. Eastern Mennonite University, Harrisonburg, VA	$560,000
2. Fresno Pacific College, Fresno, CA	265,000
3. Goshen College, Goshen, IN	265,000
4. Goshen College Mennonite Historical Library, Goshen, IN	185,000
5. Bluffton College, Bluffton, OH	185,000
6. Associated Mennonite Biblical Seminaries, Elkhart, IN	127,500
7. Tabor College, Hillsboro, KS	127,500
8. Bethel College Mennonite Library, North Newton, KS	127,500

TABLE 4.190
1978 *American Library Directory* Scholarly Other Denomination Libraries with the Highest Total Annual Expenditures

Library	Total Expenditures
1. Loma Linda University, Loma Linda, CA	$560,000
2. Ambassador College, Pasadena, CA	560,000
3. Ricks College, Rexburg, ID	560,000
4. Andrews University, Berrien Springs, MI	560,000
5. Bryn Mawr College, Bryn Mawr, PA	560,000
6. Swarthmore College, Swarthmore, PA	560,000
7. University of Winnipeg, Winnipeg, MB	560,000
8. Loma Linda University, Riverside, CA	360,000
9. Brigham Young University, Laie, HI	360,000
10. Calvin College, Grand Rapids, MI	360,000
11. Haverford College, Haverford, PA	360,000

TABLE 4.191

1988 *American Library Directory* Scholarly United Church of Christ Libraries with the Highest Total Annual Expenditures

Library	Total Expenditures
1. Elmhurst College, Elmhurst, IL	$560,000
2. Eden Webster University, St. Louis, MO	560,000
3. Elon College, Elon College, NC	560,000
4. Cedar Crest College, Allentown, PA	560,000
5. Franklin and Marshall College, Lancaster, PA	560,000
6. Pacific University, Forest Grove, OR	460,000
7. Fisk University, Nashville, TN	460,000
8. Hood College, Frederick, MD	360,000
9. Drury College, Springfield, MO	360,000
10. Ursinus College, Collegeville, PA	360,000

TABLE 4.192

1978 and 1988 *American Library Directory* Longitudinal Study Institutional Educational Activity Variable by Library Type for Scholarly Matched Pairs[1]

	1978				1988				%
Library Type	Number of Inst's	No Response	Total Inst's	Mean Units	Number of Inst's	No Response	Total Inst's	Mean Units	Change 1978-88
Scholarly	1,015	154	1,169	1,146	1,006	165	1,171	1,298	13
Junior College	107	2	109	540	86	3	89	571	5.8
Senior College	615	11	626	1,037	596	14	610	1,126	8.5
University	140	10	150	3,018	166	11	177	3,185	5.6
Seminary	151	33	184	302	157	38	195	364	21
Convent/Monastery	2	14	16	4	0	17	17	0	−100
Denominational HQ	0	46	46	0	0	43	43	0	0
History/Archives	0	38	38	0	1	39	40	4	0

1. "Educational activity" is a composite variable consisting of three measures—student enrollment size, faculty membership size, and degree years awarded.

TABLE 4.193
1978 and 1988 *American Library Directory* Scholarly Library Longitudinal Study Table of Means for all Multivalue Variables (Master Table)

	Entire Sample			Matched Pairs			Residual Libraries		
	Scholarly	Popular	All	Scholarly	Popular	All	Scholarly	Popular	All
Library Expenditures on 'Other' Categories									
Edition 31	13,380	2,917	13,220	13,630	2,917	13,460	7,853	0	7,853
Active *N*	388	6	394	371	6	377	17	0	17
Edition 41	17,280	10,120	17,120	17,350	8,167	17,200	16,280	14,500	16,120
Active *N*	575	13	588	536	9	545	39	4	43
% Change 1978–88	29.1	246.9	29.5	27.2	179.9	27.7	107.3	0	105.2
Total Annual Library Expenditures									
Edition 31	140,600	4,973	121,900	150,800	4,509	131,400	46,270	7,929	39,330
Active *N*	970	155	1,125	875	134	1,009	95	21	116
Edition 41	249,100	12,140	203,100	267,700	10,720	226,000	127,500	15,440	87,890
Active *N*	1,048	252	1,300	909	176	1,085	139	76	215
% Change 1978–88	77.1	144.1	66.6	77.5	137.7	71.9	175.5	94.7	123.4
Library Volume Holdings									
Edition 31	93,380	6,282	68,430	101,600	6,040	74,710	38,090	7,651	28,410
Active *N*	1,258	505	1,763	1,095	429	1,524	163	76	239
Edition 41	112,700	6,789	79,940	126,800	7,227	92,660	41,780	5,516	26,970
Active *N*	1,381	618	1,999	1,152	460	1,612	229	158	387
% Change 1978–88	20.6	8	16.8	24.8	19.6	24	9.60001	−28	−5.1

TABLE 4.193 (continued)
1978 and 1988 *American Library Directory* Scholarly Library Longitudinal Study Table of Means for all Multivalue Variables (Master Table)

	Entire Sample			Matched Pairs			Residual Libraries		
	Scholarly	Popular	All	Scholarly	Popular	All	Scholarly	Popular	All
Library Periodical Subscriptions (Holdings)									
Edition 31	546	62	477	581	64	509	230	50	197
Active *N*	966	161	1,127	870	140	1,010	96	21	117
Edition 41	550	63	458	603	66	513	241	56	187
Active *N*	1,179	275	1,454	1,005	203	1,208	174	72	246
% Change 1978–88	.7	1.6	−4	3.7	3.1	.7	4.7	12	−5.1
Library Microform Holdings									
Edition 31	27,660	49,390	27,900	29,030	55,120	29,290	4,659	15,000	4,946
Active *N*	622	7	629	587	6	593	35	1	36
Edition 41	46,920	44,020	46,880	50,710	68,800	50,890	12,970	15,110	13,120
Active *N*	777	13	790	699	7	706	78	6	84
% Change 1978–88	69.6	−10.9	68	74.6	24.8	73.7	178.3	.7	165.2
Library City Population Size									
Edition 31	343,500	361,400	349,400	322,100	324,400	322,800	464,600	442,700	453,500
Active *N*	1,373	685	2,058	1,167	471	1,638	206	214	420
Edition 41	336,100	356,100	342,300	324,400	331,200	326,300	388,500	423,100	402,400
Active *N*	1,430	643	2,073	1,170	469	1,639	260	174	434
% Change 1978–88	−2.2	−1.5	−2.1	.7	2	1	−16.4	−4.5	−11.3
Institutional Faculty Size									
Edition 31	72	70	72	76	70	76	32	0	32

TABLE 4.193 (continued)
1978 and 1988 *American Library Directory* Scholarly Library Longitudinal Study Table of Means for all Multivalue Variables (Master Table)

	Entire Sample			Matched Pairs			Residual Libraries		
	Scholarly	Popular	All	Scholarly	Popular	All	Scholarly	Popular	All
Active *N*	1,028	2	1,030	936	2	938	92	0	92
Edition 41	83	40	83	86	50	86	47	30	46
Active *N*	1,013	2	1,015	923	1	924	90	1	91
%Change 1978–88	15.2	−42.9	15.2	13.1	−28.6	13.1	46.8	0	43.7
Institutional Student Enrollment									
Edition 31	1,065	250	1,063	1,134	250	1,131	379	0	379
Active *N*	1,056	3	1,059	960	3	963	96	0	96
Edition 41	1,196	300	1,195	1,255	450	1,254	641	150	636
Active *N*	1,076	2	1,078	974	1	975	102	1	103
%Change 1978–88	12.3	20	12.4	10.6	80	10.8	69.1	0	67.8
Library Expenditures on Material									
Edition 31	49,430	1,811	43,330	52,410	1,613	46,360	15,760	2,897	12,960
Active *N*	749	110	859	688	93	781	61	17	78
Edition 41	81,500	4,085	67,670	88,530	4,169	75,800	35,440	3,881	25,220
Active *N*	1,057	230	1,287	917	163	1,080	140	67	207
% Change 1978–88	64.8	125.5	56.1	68.9	158.4	63.5	124.8	33.9	94.5
Library Expenditures on Personnel									
Edition 31	92,460	6,029	88,320	96,290	5,667	92,180	37,560	8,750	35,160
Active *N*	676	34	710	632	30	662	44	4	48
Edition 41	141,500	21,990	132,300	149,900	19,180	141,800	79,110	28,500	70,260
Active *N*	995	83	1,078	877	58	935	118	25	143
% Change 1978–88	53	264.7	49.7	55.6	238.4	53.8	110.6	225.7	99.8

TABLE 4.193 (continued)
1978 and 1988 *American Library Directory* Scholarly Library Longitudinal Study Table of Means for all Multivalue Variables (Master Table)

	Entire Sample			Matched Pairs			Residual Libraries		
	Scholarly	Popular	All	Scholarly	Popular	All	Scholarly	Popular	All
Total Library Staff Size									
Edition 31	16	5.1	14	17	5.2	15	6.6	3.3	6.1
Active *N*	775	117	892	714	106	820	61	11	72
Edition 41	19	6.2	17	21	6.9	19	7.7	5.5	6.9
Active *N*	945	174	1,119	804	97	901	141	77	218
% Change 1978–88	18.7	21.5	21.4	23.5	32.6	26.6	16.6	66.6	13.1
Library Professional Staff Members									
Edition 31	3.8	1.7	3.6	4	1.7	3.8	1.8	1.1	1.7
Active *N*	759	80	839	703	73	776	56	7	63
dition 41	4	1.7	3.8	4.3	1.9	4.1	2	1.4	1.9
Active *N*	896	95	991	779	53	832	117	42	159
% Change 1978–88	5.2	0	5.5	7.5	11.7	7.8	11.1	27.2	11.7
Library Clerical Staff Members									
Edition 31	4.7	4.3	4.7	5	4.4	4.9	2	2.8	2.1
Active *N*	721	106	827	667	96	763	54	10	64
Edition 41	5.1	2.8	5	5.4	2.5	5.2	3.2	3.1	3.2
Active *N*	858	68	926	747	40	787	111	28	139
%Change 1978–88	8.5	−34.9	6.3	8	−43.2	6.1	60	10.7	52.3
Library Student Staff									
Edition 31	11	4.5	11	11	4.5	11	5.4	0	5.4
Active *N*	554	2	556	518	2	520	36	0	36

TABLE 4.193 (continued)
1978 and 1988 *American Library Directory* Scholarly Library Longitudinal Study Table of Means for all Multivalue Variables (Master Table)

	Entire Sample			Matched Pairs			Residual Libraries		
	Scholarly	Popular	All	Scholarly	Popular	All	Scholarly	Popular	All
Edition 41	15	7.2	14	16	8.7	15	6.7	5.7	6.2
Active *N*	675	103	778	601	54	655	74	49	123
%Change 1978–88	36.3	59.9	27.2	45.4	93.3	36.3	24	0	14.8
Library Age or Years Established									
Edition 31	80	44	73	83	43	75	63	51	60
Active *N*	1,252	319	1,571	1,097	270	1,367	155	49	204
Edition 41	80	41	71	85	43	76	44	36	41
Active *N*	1,272	373	1,645	1,113	298	1,411	159	75	234
%Change 1978–88	0	−6.9	−2.8	2.4	0	1.3	−30.2	−29.5	−31.7
Library Vertical File Drawers									
Edition 31	25	6.1	22	26	6.4	23	20	4	17
Active *N*	745	131	876	671	115	786	74	16	90
Edition 41	31	7.6	26	32	7.7	27	20	7.1	16
Active *N*	571	139	710	520	110	630	51	29	80
% Change 1978–88	24	24.5	18.1	23	20.3	17.3	0	77.5	−5.9
Library Consortium Memberships									
Edition 31	2	1	1.9	2	1	2	1.3	1	1.3
Active *N*	585	12	597	540	8	548	45	4	49
Edition 41	2.6	1.2	2.5	2.6	1.1	2.6	1.9	1.4	1.8
Active *N*	826	20	846	777	12	789	49	8	57
% Change 1978–88	29.9	20	31.5	29.9	10	29.9	46.1	39.9	38.4
Library Subject Interests									
Edition 31	1.4	2	1.6	1.4	1.9	1.5	1.8	2.3	1.9

TABLE 4.193 (continued)
1978 and 1988 *American Library Directory* Scholarly Library Longitudinal Study Table of Means for all Multivalue Variables (Master Table)

	Entire Sample			Matched Pairs			Residual Libraries		
	Scholarly	Popular	All	Scholarly	Popular	All	Scholarly	Popular	All
Active *N*	714	208	922	622	180	802	92	28	120
Edition 41	1.9	1.9	1.9	1.9	1.9	1.9	2	2	2
Active *N*	588	304	892	474	227	701	114	77	191
% Change 1978–88	35.7	−5.1	18.7	35.7	0	26.6	11.1	−13.1	5.2
Library Special Collections									
Edition 31	1.7	1.6	1.7	1.7	1.6	1.7	2.1	1.7	2
Active *N*	418	50	468	378	39	417	40	11	51
Edition 41	1.7	1.4	1.6	1.7	1.3	1.6	1.7	1.7	1.7
Active *N*	532	100	632	464	76	540	68	24	92
% Change 1978–88	0	−12.6	−5.9	0	−18.8	−5.9	−19.1	0	−15
Library Publications									
Edition 31	1.7	0	1.7	1.7	0	1.7	1.5	0	1.5
Active *N*	58	0	58	56	0	56	2	0	2
Edition 41	1.7	1.7	1.7	1.7	1.8	1.7	1.4	1.3	1.4
Active *N*	366	44	410	329	32	361	37	12	49
% Change 1978–88	0	0	0	0	0	0	−6.7	0	−6.7
Institutional Degree Years Awarded									
Edition 31	4.4	4	4.4	4.4	4	4.4	4.1	4	4.1
Active *N*	1,107	6	1,113	991	4	995	116	2	118
Edition 41	4.6	0	4.6	4.7	0	4.7	4.2	0	4.2
Active *N*	1,083	0	1,083	983	0	983	100	0	100
% Change 1978–88	4.5	−100	4.5	6.8	−100	6.8	2.4	−100	2.4

TABLE 4.194
1978 and 1988 *American Library Directory* Scholarly Library Longitudinal Study Total Annual Expenditure by Denomination

For Senior College Libraries Only

	1978				1988				
Denomination	Number of Libraries	No Response	Total Libraries	Mean Dollars	Number of Libraries	No Response	Total Libraries	Mean Dollars	% Change 1978-88
Baptist	59	13	72	106,700	59	19	78	184,200	73
Christian	19	9	28	95,250	25	5	30	144,900	52
Churches of Christ	10	3	13	97,000	10	3	13	128,400	32
Episcopal/Anglican	7	5	12	164,100	6	2	8	336,700	105
Independent	32	5	37	96,330	27	13	40	207,300	115
Lutheran	29	5	34	186,200	33	3	36	340,600	83
Mennonite	7	0	7	117,100	11	1	12	165,800	42
Methodist	69	9	78	131,500	70	11	81	258,100	96
Other Denoms.	84	28	112	122,900	94	24	118	225,700	84
Presbyterian	56	6	62	153,500	56	6	62	270,000	76
U.C.C.	15	1	16	152,200	15	0	15	311,500	105
Summary									
Jewish	3	3	6	57,500	2	7	9	127,500	122
Roman Catholic	182	45	227	134,100	162	41	203	281,500	110
All Protestant	387	84	471	128,700	406	87	493	235,300	83
Total	572	132	704	130,000	570	135	705	248,000	91

TABLE 4.195
1978 and 1988 *American Library Directory* Scholarly Library Longitudinal Study Total Annual Expenditure by Library Type

	1978				1988				
Library Type	Number of Libraries	No Response	Total Libraries	Mean Dollars	Number of Libraries	No Response	Total Libraries	Mean Dollars	% Change 1978-88
Scholarly	969	406	1,375	140,700	1,048	384	1,432	249,100	77
Junior College	80	45	125	53,800	74	34	108	115,800	115
Senior College	572	132	704	130,000	570	135	705	248,000	91
University	130	24	154	348,400	166	23	189	458,800	32
Seminary	141	92	233	81,660	159	72	231	186,500	128
Convent/Monastery	11	24	35	4,682	7	18	25	17,610	276
Denominational HQ	17	60	77	20,710	26	60	86	54,390	163
History/Archives	18	29	47	25,440	46	42	88	81,330	220

TABLE 4.196
1978 and 1988 *American Library Directory* Scholarly Library Longitudinal Study Total Annual Expenditure by Denomination

	1978				1988				
Denomination	Number of Libraries	No Response	Total Libraries	Mean Dollars	Number of Libraries	No Response	Total Libraries	Mean Dollars	% Change 1978-88
Baptist	105	35	140	142,300	121	31	152	236,500	66
Christian	26	14	40	117,000	34	7	41	166,800	43
Church of Christ	19	8	27	86,580	23	4	27	160,700	86
Episcopal/Anglican	19	13	32	148,900	20	12	32	235,800	58
Independent	54	28	82	118,800	60	37	97	235,600	98
Lutheran	53	17	70	168,600	59	17	76	305,700	81
Mennonite	13	1	14	78,770	18	4	22	134,000	70
Methodist	118	29	147	160,200	121	28	149	275,800	72
Other Denoms.	132	73	205	115,700	154	63	217	210,500	82
Presbyterian	80	10	90	149,300	79	11	90	265,600	78
U.C.C.	23	1	24	144,600	24	1	25	280,100	94
Summary									
Jewish	13	22	35	133,300	13	32	45	272,000	104
Roman Catholic	314	155	469	147,600	322	137	459	269,300	82
All Protestant	642	229	871	137,500	713	215	928	239,500	74
Total	969	406	1,375	140,700	1,048	384	1,432	249,100	77

TABLE 4.197
1988 *American Library Directory* Scholarly Baptist Libraries with the Highest Annual Total Expenditure per Faculty Member

Library	Ratio
1. Central Baptist Theological Seminary, Kansas City, KS	$12,750
2. Calvary Baptist Theological Seminary, Lansdale, PA	12,750
3. Eastern Baptist Theological Seminary, Philadelphia, PA	12,750
4. North American Baptist Seminary, Sioux Falls, SD	12,750
5. Florida Memorial College, Miami, FL	9,200
6. Southeastern Baptist Theological Seminary, Wake Forest, NC	9,200
7. Colgate Rochester-Bexley Hall-Crozer Theological Seminary, Rochester, NY	8,833
8. Western Conservative Baptist Seminary, Portland, OR	8,833
9. Mercer University, Atlanta, GA	8,000
10. Golden Gate Baptist Theological Seminary, Mill Valley, CA	7,200
11. Union University, Jackson, TN	7,200

TABLE 4.198
1988 *American Library Directory* Scholarly Christian Libraries with the Highest Annual Total Expenditure per Faculty Member

Library	Ratio
1. Phillips University Rogers Graduate Seminary, Enid, OK	$26,500
2. Northwest Christian College, Eugene, OR	12,750
3. Emmanuel School of Religion, Johnson City, TN	12,750
4. Johnson Bible College, Knoxville, TN	12,750
5. Atlanta Christian College, East Point, GA	7,000
6. St. Louis Christian College, Florissant, MO	7,000
7. Roanoke Bible College, Elizabeth City, NC	7,000
8. Chapman University, Orange, CA	6,222
9. Christian Theological Seminary, Indianapolis, IN	6,167

TABLE 4.199
1988 *American Library Directory* Scholarly Episcopal/Anglican Libraries with the Highest Annual Total Expenditure per Faculty Member

Library	Ratio
1. Episcopal Divinity School, Cambridge, MA	$36,000
2. General Theological Seminary, New York, NY	26,500
3. Episcopal Theological Seminary, Austin, TX	18,500
4. Saint Mary's College, Raleigh, NC	5,300
5. Huron College, London, ON	5,300
6. Hobart and William Smith Colleges, Geneva, NY	5,091
7. University of the South, Sewanee, TN	5,091

TABLE 4.200
1988 *American Library Directory* Scholarly Lutheran Libraries with the Highest Annual Total Expenditure per Faculty Member

Library	Ratio
1. Lutheran Theological Seminary, Philadelphia, PA	$26,500
2. Lutheran Theological Southern Seminary, Columbia, SC	12,750
3. Wisconsin Lutheran Seminary, Mequon, WI	12,750
4. Concordia Seminary, St. Louis, MO	12,000
5. Dana College, Blair, NE	9,200
6. Trinity Lutheran Seminary, Columbus, OH	8,833
7. Northwestern College, Watertown, WI	7,000
8. Roanoke College, Salem, VA	6,571
9. Lenoir-Rhyne College, Hickory, NC	6,222
10. Concordia College, Bronxville, NY	6,167
11. Lutheran Theological Seminary, Gettysburg, PA	6,167

TABLE 4.201
1988 *American Library Directory* Scholarly Methodist Libraries with the Highest Annual Total Expenditure per Faculty Member

Library	Ratio
1. St. Paul School of Theology, Kansas City, MO	$18,500
2. Garrett Evangelical Seminary, Evanston, IL	15,333
3. United Wesleyan College, Allentown, PA	12,750
4. Scarritt Graduate School, Nashville, TN	12,750
5. Iliff School of Theology, Denver, CO	12,000
6. School of Theology, Claremont, CA	8,833
7. Wesley Theological Seminary, Washington, DC	8,833
8. Boston University, Boston, MA	8,833
9. United Theological Seminary, Dayton, OH	8,833
10. Methodist Theological School, Delaware, OH	8,833

TABLE 4.202
1988 *American Library Directory* Scholarly Presbyterian Libraries with the Highest Annual Total Expenditure per Faculty Member

Library	Ratio
1. Louisville Presbyterian Theological Seminary, Louisville, KY	$36,000
2. Pittsburgh Theological Seminary, Pittsburgh, PA	26,500
3. Union Theological Seminary, Richmond, VA	18,667
4. Covenant Theological Seminary, St. Louis, MO	18,500
5. Westminster Theological Seminary, San Marcos, CA	12,750
6. Memphis Theological Seminary, Memphis, TN	12,750
7. Princeton Theological Seminary, Princeton, NJ	11,200
8. Alma College, Alma, MI	8,000
9. Geneva College, Beaver Falls, PA	7,200
10. Lees College, Jackson, KY	7,000
11. Reformed Presbyterian Theological Seminary, Pittsburgh, PA	7,000

TABLE 4.203
1988 *American Library Directory* Scholarly Jewish Libraries with the Highest Annual Total Expenditure per Faculty Member

Library	Ratio
1. Hebrew Union College, Cincinnati, OH	$18,667
2. Reconstructionist Rabbinical College, Wyncote, PA	12,750
3. Jewish Theological Seminary, New York, NY	11,200
4. Spertus College of Judaica, Chicago, IL	4,250
5. Hebrew College, Brookline, MA	4,250

TABLE 4.204
1988 *American Library Directory* Scholarly Baptist Libraries with the Lowest Annual Total Expenditure per Faculty Member

Library	Ratio
1. Temple University, Philadelphia, PA	$1,600
2. Baylor University, Waco, TX	1,600
3. McMaster University, Hamilton, ON	1,600
4. Clarke College, Newton, MS	1,375
5. Wayland Baptist University, Plainview, TX	1,262
6. Ottawa University, Ottawa, KS	650

TABLE 4.205
1988 *American Library Directory* Scholarly Other Denominations Libraries with the Lowest Annual Total Expenditure per Faculty Member

Library	Ratio
1. Point Loma Nazarene College, San Diego, CA	$1,423
2. Walker College, Jasper, AL	1,400
3. Manor Junior College, Jenkintown, PA	1,400
4. Catherine Booth Bible College, Winnipeg, MB	1,400
5. Cook Theological School, Tempe, AZ	1,375
6. Crowley's Ridge College, Paragould, AR	1,375
7. Oak Hills Bible College, Bemidji, MN	1,375
8. Friends World College, Huntington, NY	1,375
9. St. Stephen's Center for Continuing Education, Edmonton, AB	400

TABLE 4.206
1988 *American Library Directory* Scholarly Roman Catholic Libraries with the Lowest Annual Total Expenditure per Faculty Member

Library	Ratio
1. Marian College, Indianapolis, IN	$778
2. Heritage College, Toppenish, WA	778
3. Aquinas College, Nashville, TN	650
4. Gwynedd-Mercy College, Gwynedd Valley, PA	607
5. Queen of the Holy Rosary College, Fremont, CA	400
6. Marist College, Washington, DC	400
7. Sacred Heart Monastery, Winchester, VA	400
8. Magdalen College, Bedford, NH	100

TABLE 4.207
1988 *American Library Directory* Scholarly Baptist Libraries with the Highest Annual Total Expenditure per Student

Library	Ratio
1. Central Baptist Theological Seminary, Kansas City, KS	$850
2. Calvary Baptist Theological Seminary, Lansdale, PA	850
3. North American Baptist Seminary, Sioux Falls, SD	850
4. Golden Gate Baptist Theological Seminary, Mill Valley, CA	800
5. Colgate Rochester-Bexley Hall-Crozer Theological Seminary, Rochester, NY	589
6. Western Conservative Baptist Seminary, Portland, OR	589
7. Mercer University, Atlanta, GA	533

TABLE 4.208
1988 *American Library Directory* Scholarly Churches of Christ Libraries with the Highest Annual Total Expenditure per Student

Library	Ratio
1. Chicago Theological Seminary, Chicago, IL	$850
2. Columbia Christian College, Portland, OR	850
3. Harding College Graduate School of Religion, Memphis, TN	850
4. Michigan Christian College, Rochester, MI	467
5. Magnolia Bible College, Kosciusko, MS	467
6. Northeastern Christian Junior College, Villanova, PA	467
7. Southwestern Christian College, Terrell, TX	467

TABLE 4.209
1988 *American Library Directory* Scholarly Independent Libraries with the Highest Annual Total Expenditure per Student

Library	Ratio
1. Reformed Theological Seminary, Jackson, MS	$1,767
2. Yale University Divinity School, New Haven, CT	1,244
3. Harvard University, Cambridge, MA	1,244
4. Union Theological Seminary, New York, NY	1,244
5. Christian Broadcasting Network University, Virginia Beach, VA	1,244
6. Vancouver School of Theology, Vancouver, BC	1,233
7. Hawaii Loa College, Kaneohe, HI	1,022
8. King's College, Edmonton, AB	850
9. Logan College of Chriropractic, Chesterfield, MO	800
10. Ontario Bible College, Willowdale, ON	589

TABLE 4.210
1988 *American Library Directory* Scholarly Mennonite Libraries with the Highest Annual Total Expenditure per Student

Library	Ratio
1. Associated Mennonite Biblical Seminary, Elkhart, IN	$850
2. Eastern Mennonite University, Harrisonburg, VA	747
3. Columbia Bible College, Clearbrook, BC	467
4. Steinbach Bible College, Steinbach, MB	467
5. Mennonite Brethren Bible College, Winnipeg, MB	467
6. Conrad Grebel College, Waterloo, ON	467
7. Bluffton College, Bluffton, OH	411

TABLE 4.211

1988 *American Library Directory* Scholarly Other Denominations Libraries with the Highest Annual Total Expenditure per Student

Library	Ratio
1. Bethany Seminary, Oak Brook, IL	$1,767
2. Western Theological Seminary, Holland, MI	1,233
3. George Fox University, Newburg, OR	1,022
4. Salvation Army School, Rancho Palos Verdes, CA	850
5. Warner Southern College, Lake Wales, FL	850
6. Reformed Bible College, Grand Rapids, MI	850
7. New Brunswick Theological Seminary, New Brunswick, NJ	850
8. Winebrenner Theological Seminary, Findlay, OH	850
9. Canadian Nazarene College, Winnipeg, MB	850
10. Emmanuel Bible College, Kitchener, ON	850

TABLE 4.212

1988 *American Library Directory* Scholarly United Church of Christ Libraries with the Highest Annual Total Expenditure per Student

Library	Ratio
1. Andover Newton Theological School, Newton Center, MA	$1,767
2. Lancaster Theological Seminary, Lancaster, PA	850
3. Cedar Crest College, Allentown, PA	747
4. Fisk University, Nashville, TN	613
5. Bangor Theological Seminary, Bangor, ME	467
6. United Theological Seminary, New Brighton, MN	467

TABLE 4.213

1988 *American Library Directory* Scholarly Roman Catholic Libraries with the Highest Annual Total Expenditure per Student

Library	Ratio
1. St. Meinrad College, St. Meinrad, IN	$3,067
2. Cathedral College of the Immaculate Conception, Douglaston, NY	1,767
3. Athenaeum of Ohio, Cincinnati, OH	1,767
4. Mount Angel Abbey, St. Benedict, OR	1,767
5. St. Mary's Seminary, Baltimore, MD	1,233
6. College of St. Thomas Divinity School, St. Paul, MN	1,233
7. Maryknoll School of Theology, Maryknoll, NY	1,233
8. Pontifical College Josephinium, Columbus, OH	1,233
9. St. Charles Borromeo Seminary, Philadelphia, PA	1,233
10. University of Alberta Faculté St. Jean, Edmonton, AB	1,022

TABLE 4.214

1988 *American Library Directory* Scholarly Christian Libraries with the Lowest Annual Total Expenditure per Student

Library	Ratio
1. Atlantic Christian College, Wilson, NC	$196
2. Tougaloo College, Tougaloo, MS	170
3. Culver-Stockton College, Canton, MO	170
4. William Woods University, Fulton, MO	170
5. Bethany College, Bethany, WV	170
6. San Jose Bible College, San Jose, CA	156
7. Midway College, Midway, KY	156

TABLE 4.215

1988 *American Library Directory* Scholarly Churches of Christ Libraries with the Lowest Annual Total Expenditure per Student

Library	Ratio
1. Oklahoma Christian College, Oklahoma City, OK	$196
2. Lubbock Christian University, Lubbock, TX	170
3. David Lipscomb University, Nashville, TN	160
4. York College, York, NE	156
5. Freed-Hardeman University, Henderson, TN	137
6. Abilene Christian University, Abilene, TX	132
7. Harding University, Searcy, AR	126
8. Amber University, Garland, TX	121
9. Alberta Bible College, Calgary, AB	92
10. Faulkner University, Montgomery, AL	52

TABLE 4.216
1988 *American Library Directory* Scholarly Lutheran Libraries with the Lowest Annual Total Expenditure per Student

Library	Ratio
1. Grand View College, Des Moines, IA	$196
2. Wartburg College, Waverly, IA	196
3. Concordia College, Moorhead, MN	196
4. Texas Lutheran College, Seguin, TX	176
5. St. Olaf College, Northfield, MN	172
6. Pacific Lutheran University, Tacoma, WA	172
7. Capital University, Columbus, OH	160
8. Waldorf College, Forest City, IA	156
9. Valparaiso University, Valparaiso, IN	149
10. Suomi College, Hancock, MI	93

TABLE 4.217
1988 *American Library Directory* Scholarly Methodist Libraries with the Lowest Annual Total Expenditure per Student

Library	Ratio
1. University of the Pacific, Stockton, CA	$149
2. Simpson College, Indianola, IA	137
3. North Central College, Naperville, IL	136
4. Otterbein College, Westerville, OH	136
5. Methodist College, Fayetteville, NC	121
6. Central Methodist College, Fayette, MO	93
7. Oklahoma City University, Oklahoma City, OK	93
8. Andrew College, Cuthbert, GA	31

TABLE 4.218

1988 *American Library Directory* Scholarly Other Denominations Libraries with the Lowest Annual Total Expenditure per Student

Library	Ratio
1. Point Loma Nazarene College, San Diego, CA	$112
2. Evangel College, Springfield, MO	112
3. Southwestern Adventist College, Keene, TX	95
4. North Central Bible College, Minneapolis, MN	94
5. Walker College, Jasper, AL	93
6. Southwestern Assemblies of God College, Waxahachie, TX	93
7. Crowley's Ridge College, Paragould, AR	92
8. Oak Hills Bible College, Bemidji, MN	92
9. Friends World College, Huntingdon, NY	92

TABLE 4.219

1988 *American Library Directory* Scholarly Presbyterian Libraries with the Lowest Annual Total Expenditure per Student

Library	Ratio
1. College of Idaho, Caldwell, ID	$137
2. Queens College, Charlotte, NC	137
3. Carroll College, Waukesha, WI	137
4. University of Tulsa, Tulsa, OK	132
5. Lindenwood College, St. Charles, MO	95
6. Westminster College, Salt Lake City, UT	94
7. Pikeville College, Pikeville, KY	93
8. Waynesburg College, Waynesburg, PA	93
9. Tusculum College, Greeneville, TN	93
10. Missouri Valley College, Marshall, MO	67
11. Carver Bible Institute, Atlanta, GA	7

TABLE 4.220
1988 *American Library Directory* Scholarly Roman Catholic Libraries with the Lowest Annual Total Expenditure per Student

Library	Ratio
1. Ancilla College, Donaldson, IN	$72
2. Holy Cross Junior College, Notre Dame, IN	72
3. Aquinas College, Nashville, TN	72
4. College of St. Joseph, Rutland, VT	72
5. Marian College, Indianapolis, IN	67
6. Collège de la Sainte Anne, La Pocatière, PQ	67
7. Gwynedd-Mercy College, Gwynedd Valley, PA	65
8. St. Joseph's College, Edmonton, AB	42
9. Chatfield College, St. Martin, OH	31
10. Queen of the Holy Rosary College, Fremont, CA	27
11. Marist College, Washington, DC	27
12. Magdalen College, Bedford, NH	7

TABLE 4.221
1978 and 1988 *American Library Directory* Scholarly Library Longitudinal Study Annual Total Expenditure Per Student by Denomination

	---1978 Expenditure per Student---											
Denomination	1–100	%	101–250	%	251–400	%	401 and over	%	No Response	%	Number of Libraries	Dollar Ratio
Baptist	41	29	53	38	1	1	5	4	40	29	140	136
Christian	7	18	12	30	2	5	4	10	15	38	40	207
Churches of Christ	11	41	5	19	0	0	3	11	8	30	27	158
Congregational	1	20	1	20	0	0	0	0	3	60	5	149
Episcopal/ Anglican	2	6	8	25	2	6	6	19	14	44	32	300
Independent	19	23	22	27	3	4	6	7	32	39	82	176
Lutheran	8	11	35	50	1	1	3	4	23	33	70	189
Methodist	34	23	67	46	4	3	6	4	36	24	147	167
Other Denominations	49	23	61	29	5	2	9	4	90	42	214	166
Presbyterian	16	18	41	46	9	10	10	11	14	16	90	205
U.C.C.	4	17	13	54	2	8	3	13	2	8	24	201
Summary												
Jewish	4	11	4	11	0	0	1	3	26	74	35	390
Roman Catholic	96	20	148	32	7	1	23	5	195	42	469	159
All Protestant	192	22	318	37	29	3	55	6	277	32	871	175
Total	292	21	470	34	36	3	79	6	498	36	1,375	172

TABLE 4.221 (continued)
1978 and 1988 *American Library Directory* Scholarly Library Longitudinal Study Annual Total Expenditure Per Student by Denomination

	----1988 Expenditure per Student----											
Denomination	1–100	%	101–250	%	251–400	%	401 and over	%	No Response	%	Number of Libraries	Dollar Ratio
Baptist	7	5	55	36	22	14	21	14	47	31	152	269
Christian	0	0	15	37	8	20	9	22	9	22	41	369
Churches of Christ	2	7	11	41	2	7	7	26	5	19	27	312
Episcopal/ Anglican	0	0	4	13	4	13	7	22	17	53	32	677
Independent	3	3	16	16	8	8	25	26	45	46	97	458
Lutheran	2	3	17	22	19	25	15	20	23	30	76	418
Mennonite	0	0	3	14	3	14	7	32	9	41	22	408
Methodist	3	2	58	39	29	19	23	15	36	24	149	340
Other Denominations	7	3	38	18	40	18	37	17	95	44	217	345
Presbyterian	7	8	22	24	19	21	29	32	13	14	90	437
U.C.C.	0	0	9	36	7	28	6	24	3	12	25	389
Summary												
Jewish	0	0	4	9	0	0	3	7	38	84	45	911
Roman Catholic	19	4	141	31	57	12	50	11	191	42	458	287
All Protestant	31	3	248	27	161	17	186	20	302	33	928	369
Total	50	3	393	27	218	15	239	17	531	37	1,431	349

TABLE 4.222
1978 and 1988 *American Library Directory* Scholarly Library Longitudinal Study Annual Total Expenditure per Student by Library Type

Library Type	1–100	%	101–250	%	251–400	%	401 and over	%	No Response	%	Number of Libraries	Dollar Ratio
	---------1978 Expenditure per Student---------											
Scholarly	292	21	470	34	36	3	79	6	498	36	1,375	172
Junior College	40	32	31	25	1	1	4	3	49	39	125	137
Senior College	204	29	314	45	23	3	16	2	147	21	704	145
University	29	19	89	58	2	1	2	1	32	21	154	131
Seminary	18	8	36	15	10	4	57	24	112	48	233	363
Convent/ Monastery	1	3	0	0	0	0	0	0	34	97	35	92
Denominational HQ	0	0	0	0	0	0	0	0	77	100	77	0
History/ Archives	0	0	0	0	0	0	0	0	47	100	47	0
	---------1988 Expenditure per Student---------											
Scholarly	50	3	393	27	218	15	239	17	531	37	1,431	349
Junior College	15	14	30	28	8	7	16	15	39	36	108	248
Senior College	27	4	228	32	179	25	107	15	164	23	705	288
University	4	2	120	63	26	14	8	4	31	16	189	194
Seminary	3	1	15	7	5	2	107	47	100	43	230	848
Convent/ Monastery	0	0	0	0	0	0	0	0	25	100	25	0
Denominational HQ	1	1	0	0	0	0	1	1	84	98	86	234
History/ Archives	0	0	0	0	0	0	0	0	88	100	88	0

TABLE 4.223
1988 *American Library Directory* Scholarly Library Expenditure Categories in Percentages by Denomination[1]

Denomination	Material	Personnel	Other Spending	Total Annual	Cumulative in Dollars	Number of Libraries
Baptist	36%	60%	5%	109%	$26,173,500	152
Valid Responses	119	116	65	121		
Christian	35%	61%	5%	107%	$5,314,000	41
Valid Responses	34	34	17	34		
Churches of Christ	38%	58%	5%	99%	$3,746,000	27
Valid Responses	24	23	12	23		
Episcopal/Anglican	35%	62%	3%	122%	$3,873,500	32
Valid Responses	19	17	6	20		
Independent	36%	60%	5%	109%	$13,031,000	97
Valid Responses	64	56	35	60		
Lutheran	35%	61%	4%	114%	$15,879,750	76
Valid Responses	58	55	35	59		
Mennonite	32%	63%	6%	112%	$2,145,000	22
Valid Responses	20	19	9	18		
Methodist	38%	58%	4%	111%	$30,202,750	149
Valid Responses	120	120	73	121		
Other Denominations	36%	60%	5%	110%	$29,590,250	217
Valid Responses	156	147	84	154		
Presbyterian	41%	55%	4%	107%	$19,696,250	90
Valid Responses	81	76	50	79		
United Church of Christ	36%	60%	4%	112%	$6,002,750	25
Valid Responses	23	23	14	24		
Summary						
Jewish	31%	65%	4%	118%	$2,986,250	45
Valid Responses	16	11	7	13		
Roman Catholic	36%	60%	4%	111%	$78,244,000	458
Valid Responses	323	298	168	322		
All Protestant	37%	59%	4%	110%	$155,654,750	928
Valid Responses	718	686	400	713		
Total	36%	59%	4%	110%	$236,885,000	1,431
Valid Responses	1,057	995	575	1,048		

1. The "total annual" column as shown on this table was a separate questionnaire variable and did *not*, in many cases, equal the total "material," "personnel," and "other" expenses. On average, it ran about 110 percent of the totals of the three previously mentioned variables. Presumably, some libraries have budgets for book binding, etc.

TABLE 4.224
1978 and 1988 *American Library Directory* Scholarly Library Longitudinal Study Total Annual Expenditure (Cumulative) by Library Type

	1978				1988				
Library Type	Number of Libraries	No Response	Total Libraries	Mean Dollars	Number of Libraries	No Response	Total Libraries	Mean Dollars	% Change 1978–88
Scholarly	1,022	353	1,375	137,800	1,101	330	1,431	244,100	77
Junior College	87	38	125	51,670	78	30	108	116,100	125
Senior College	593	111	704	130,500	602	103	705	243,500	87
University	132	22	154	347,700	170	19	189	452,300	30
Seminary	149	84	233	81,040	166	64	230	184,900	128
Convent/Monastery	12	23	35	4,458	7	18	25	17,860	301
Denominational HQ	25	52	77	15,710	32	54	86	48,860	211
History/Archives	24	23	47	22,810	46	42	88	82,530	262

TABLE 4.225
1978 and 1988 *American Library Directory* Longitudinal Study Gross Library Rating Points Over Nine Response Variables by Denomination for Matched Pairs (Entire Samples)[1,2]

	1978		1988		
Library Type	Number of Libraries	Mean Points	Number of Libraries	Mean Points	% Change 1978–88
Baptist	187	13	186	13	0
Christian	50	12	51	13	8
Churches of Christ	25	11	24	11	0
Episcopal/Anglican	54	14	51	15	7
Independent	69	11	71	11	0
Lutheran	95	13	95	13	0
Mennonite	17	13	17	14	8
Methodist	177	12	179	12	0
Other Denominations	220	13	218	13	0
Presbyterian	172	14	173	14	0
U.C.C.	33	13	33	13	0
Summary					
Jewish	149	16	149	17	6
Roman Catholic	392	13	393	12	−8
All Protestant	1,099	13	1,098	13	0
Total	1,640	13	1,640	13	0

1. The nine response variables were the following:
   Library type
   Religious affiliation

TABLE 4.225
1978 and 1988 *American Library Directory* Longitudinal Study Gross Library Rating Points Over Nine Response Variables by Denomination for Matched Pairs (Entire Samples)[1,2] (continued)

Questionnaire returned
Departmental library
Chief librarian named
Chief librarian's gender
Religious order status
Circulation restrictions
Reference service restrictions

2. A brief examination of this table shows just how remarkably stable the matched pairs are in terms of these nine variables.

TABLE 4.226
1988 *American Library Directory* Institutional Educational Activity Variables by Region for Scholarly Matched Pairs[1]

	Enrollment Faculty Size and Degree Years Awarded											
Region	1–100	%	101–500	%	501–2,000	%	2,001 and over	%	No Response	%	Number of Libraries	Mean Units
Northeast	1	2	20	33	15	25	14	23	10	17	60	1,489
Middle Atlantic	4	2	55	25	71	32	43	20	47	21	220	1,486
Southeast	4	2	68	28	120	50	29	12	18	8	239	1,099
Southwest	3	3	24	24	40	41	20	20	11	11	98	1,376
West	3	3	32	32	30	30	23	23	11	11	99	1,374
Rocky Mountains	0	0	5	29	6	35	3	18	3	18	17	1,638
Middle West	10	3	95	27	161	46	52	15	35	10	353	1,147
Canada	7	8	17	20	11	13	20	24	30	35	85	1,882
Total	32	3	316	27	454	39	204	17	165	14	1,171	1,298

1. Variables included:
Degree years awarded
Student enrollment size
Faculty membership size

TABLE 4.227

1978 *American Library Directory* Entire Sample Gross Library Rating Points Over 27 Growth Variables by Region for Matched Pairs[1,2,3]

Region	Number of Libraries	No Response	Total Libraries	Mean Number of Points	Ratio of the Sample Mean
Northeast	84	2	86	250,400	1.15
Middle Atlantic	317	12	329	236,200	1.08
Southeast	301	6	307	191,700	0.88
Southwest	148	8	156	204,100	0.94
West	135	4	139	233,100	1.07
Rocky Mountains	23	2	25	212,900	0.98
Middle West	490	9	499	209,100	0.96
Canada	94	5	99	263,100	1.21
Total	1,592	48	1,640	218,200	1.00

1. A list of the twenty-seven growth variables is given in chapter 4, footnote 8.
2. The 1,640 matched pairs includes a total of 1,171 scholarly libraries for 1988, in other words, 71.4 percent of the table. The matching table for scholarly libraries differs in no significant way from the entire sample matched pairs distribution.
3. Canada has a larger ratio than might be expected partly, perhaps, due to the value of the Canadian dollar versus the U.S. dollar.

TABLE 4.228

1988 *American Library Directory* Entire Sample Gross Library Rating Points Over 27 Growth Variables by Region for Matched Pairs[1,2,3]

Region	Number of Libraries	No Response	Total Libraries	Mean Number of Points	Ratio of the Sample Mean
Northeast	84	2	86	362,700	1.05
Middle Atlantic	317	12	329	349,200	1.01
Southeast	301	6	307	345,300	1.00
Southwest	148	8	156	336,500	0.98
West	135	4	139	378,200	1.10
Rocky Mountains	23	2	25	287,000	0.83
Middle West	490	9	499	333,900	0.97
Canada	94	5	99	346,000	1.00
Total	1,592	48	1,640	344,600	1.00

1. A list of the twenty-seven growth variables is given in Chapter 4, footnote 8.
2. The 1,640 matched pairs includes a total of 1,171 scholarly libraries for 1988, in other words, 71.4 percent of the table. The matching table for scholarly libraries differs in no significant way from the entire sample matched pairs distribution.
3. This table seems to indicate that whereas the Southeast region appears to be drawing even to the rest of North America, the recession has been having a levelling effect on all other established libraries.

TABLE 4.229
1978 and 1988 *American Library Directory* Longitudinal Study Entire Sample Gross Library Rating Points Over 27 Growth Variables by Denomination for Matched Pairs[1]

Library Type	1978 Number of Libraries	1978 No Response	1978 Total Libraries	1978 Mean Points	1988 Number of Libraries	1988 No Response	1988 Total Libraries	1988 Mean Points	% Change 1978–88
Baptist	184	3	187	193,900	183	3	186	327,700	69
Christian	49	1	50	164,100	50	1	51	251,400	53
Churches of Christ	25	0	25	212,700	24	0	24	354,400	67
Episcopal/Anglican	51	3	54	117,500	48	3	51	202,300	72
Independent	69	0	69	232,500	71	0	71	378,400	63
Lutheran	93	2	95	241,700	93	2	95	408,800	69
Mennonite	16	1	17	165,100	16	1	17	311,500	89
Methodist	172	5	177	281,800	174	5	179	424,100	50
Other Denominations	211	9	220	192,300	209	9	218	303,100	58
Presbyterian	166	6	172	179,200	167	6	173	283,300	58
U.C.C.	32	1	33	267,100	32	1	33	447,800	68
Summary									
Jewish	139	10	149	58,050	139	10	149	77,500	34
Roman Catholic	385	7	392	300,700	386	7	393	462,400	54
All Protestant	1,068	31	1,099	209,300	1,067	31	1,098	336,800	61
Total	1,592	48	1,640	218,200	1,592	48	1,640	344,600	58

1. A list of the twenty-seven growth variables is given in chapter 4, footnote 8.

TABLE 4.230
1978 and 1988 *American Library Directory* Scholarly Library Longitudinal Study Gross Rating Points Over Twenty-Seven Growth Variables for Matched Pairs[1,2]

	1978				1988				
Library Type	Number of Libraries	No Response	Total Libraries	Mean Points	Number of Libraries	No Response	Total Libraries	Mean Points	% Change 1978–88
Scholarly	1,157	12	1,169	297,100	1,158	13	1,171	469,600	58
Junior College	108	1	109	92,850	88	1	89	139,800	51
Senior College	624	2	626	284,200	608	2	610	476,200	68
University	148	2	150	820,200	176	1	177	1,019,000	24
Seminary	181	3	184	171,500	191	4	195	285,900	67
Convent/Monastery	15	1	16	28,970	16	1	17	29,810	3
Denominational HQ	46	0	46	26,760	42	1	43	40,810	53
History/Archives	35	3	38	66,280	37	3	40	156,300	136

1. A list of the twenty-seven growth variables is given in chapter 4, footnote 8.
2. All libraries represented in this table were scholarly.

TABLE 4.231
1988 *American Library Directory* Libraries on the Largest Number of Specific Scholarly Library Tables[1,2]

Library	Denomination	Number of Tables on Which Library Appears
1. Brown University, Providence, RI	Independent	10
2. Loyola University, Chicago, IL	Roman Catholic	9
3. Wake Forest University, Winston-Salem, NC	Baptist	9
4. Temple University, Philadelphia, PA	Baptist	9
5. Brigham Young University, Provo, UT	Other Denominations	9
6. University of Denver, Denver, CO	Methodist	8
7. American University, Washington, DC	Methodist	8
8. University of Notre Dame, Notre Dame, IN	Roman Catholic	8
9. Boston University, Boston, MA	Methodist	8
10. Boston College, Chestnut Hill, MA	Roman Catholic	8
11. Fordham University, Bronx, NY	Roman Catholic	8
12. St. John's University, Jamaica, NY	Roman Catholic	8
13. Duke University, Durham, NC	Independent	8
14. University of Dayton, Dayton, OH	Roman Catholic	8
15. Trinity University, San Antonio, TX	Presbyterian	8
16. Baylor University, Waco, TX	Baptist	8

TABLE 4.231 (continued)
1988 *American Library Directory* Libraries on the Largest Number of Specific Scholarly Library Tables[1,2]

Library	Denomination	Number of Tables on Which Library Appears
17. McGill University, Montreal, PQ	Independent	8
18. University of Montreal, Montreal, PQ	Roman Catholic	8

1. The following "largest number" tables are covered here:
   1. Number of Professional Staff Members
   2. Number of Clerical Staff Members
   3. Number of Student Staff Members
   4. Total Number of Staff Members
   5. Material Expenditures
   6. Other Expenditures
   7. Total Expenditures
   8. Number of Volumes
   9. Library Age
   10. Number of Vertical File Drawers
   11. Number of Consortium Memberships
   12. Number of Microforms
   13. Subject Interests
2. The libraries listed above were highly placed on tables that considered all denominations together. Therefore, the eighteen libraries on this list were truly exceptional in terms of the thirteen listed variables.

TABLE 4.232
1988 *American Library Directory* Scholarly Libraries Listed on the Highest Number of Tables by Denomination

	----------Number of Table References--------											
Denomination	1–3	%	4–6	%	7–9	%	10 and over	%	No Response	%	Number of Libraries	Mean Tables
Baptist	65	43	38	25	13	9	15	10	21	14	152	5
Christian	5	12	9	22	5	12	20	49	2	5	41	10
Churches of Christ	0	0	3	11	5	19	19	70	0	0	27	13
Episcopal/ Anglican	7	22	4	13	2	6	16	50	3	9	32	10
Independent	42	43	18	19	3	3	22	23	12	12	97	6
Lutheran	18	24	15	20	9	12	24	32	10	13	76	8
Mennonite	1	5	1	5	5	23	14	64	1	5	22	12
Methodist	56	38	48	32	17	11	14	9	14	9	149	5
Other Denominations	90	41	52	24	15	7	18	8	42	19	217	5
Presbyterian	17	19	35	39	18	20	18	20	2	2	90	7
U.C.C.	2	8	0	0	2	8	20	80	1	4	25	14
Summary												
Jewish	13	29	9	20	5	11	9	20	9	20	45	7
Roman Catholic	193	42	103	22	22	5	32	7	109	24	459	4
All Protestant	303	33	223	24	94	10	200	22	108	12	928	6
Total	509	36	335	23	121	8	241	17	226	16	1,432	6

TABLE 4.233
1988 *American Library Directory* List of Scholarly Libraries Most Often Listed in Baptist Tables[1,2]

Library	Listings
1. Wake Forest University, Winston-Salem, NC	18
2. Temple University, Philadelphia, PA	17
3. University of Richmond, Richmond, VA	17
4. Southwestern Baptist Theological Seminary, Fort Worth, TX	15
5. Baylor University, Waco, TX	15
6. Samford University, Birmingham, AL	14
7. Mercer University, Macon, GA	13
8. Southern Baptist Theological Seminary, Louisville, KY	13
9. Furman University, Greenville, SC	13
10. Acadia University, Wolfville, NS	13
11. McMaster University, Hamilton, ON	13

TABLE 4.233 (continued)
1988 *American Library Directory* List of Scholarly Libraries Most Often Listed in Baptist Tables[1,2]

Library	Listings
12. Stetson University, DeLand, FL	12
13. Liberty University, Lynchburg, VA	12
14. Kalamazoo College, Kalamazoo, MI	11
15. Denison University, Granville, OH	10

1. This list was compiled from the top libraries listed on each of the scholarly Baptist tables.
2. The entire list of variables on which highest ratings could be evaluated included (1) professional staff size, (2) clerical staff size, (3) student staff size, (4) total staff size, (5) material expenditure, (6) personnel expenditure, (7) other expenditure, (8) total expenditure, (9) volume holdings, (10) periodical subscriptions, (11) microform holdings, (12) vertical file drawers, (13) library age, (14) number of consortium memberships, (15) number of subject interests, (16) number of special collections, (17) number of publications, (18) faculty membership size, and (19) student enrollment size.
A score or rating of 19, therefore, is considered perfect within each denomination.

TABLE 4.234
1988 *American Library Directory* List of Scholarly Libraries Most Often Listed in Christian Tables[1]

Library	Listings
1. Lynchburg College, Lynchburg, VA	18
2. Tougaloo College, Tougaloo, MS	17
3. Chapman University, Orange, CA	16
4. William Woods University, Fulton, MO	16
5. Atlantic Christian College, Wilson, NC	16
6. Phillips University, Enid, OK	16
7. Phillips University Rogers Graduate Seminary, Enid, OK	16
8. Texas Christian University, Fort Worth, TX	16
9. Bethany College, Bethany, WV	16
10. Eureka College, Eureka, IL	15
11. Transylvania University, Lexington, KY	15
12. Hiram College, Hiram, OH	15
13. Culver-Stockton College, Canton, MO	14
14. Christian Theological Seminary, Indianapolis, IN	12
15. Columbia College, Columbia, MO	12
16. Northwest Christian College, Eugene, OR	12
17. Jarvis Christian College, Hawkins, TX	12

1. This list was compiled from the top libraries listed on each of the scholarly Christian tables.

TABLE 4.235
1988 *American Library Directory* List of Scholarly Libraries Most Often Listed in Churches of Christ Tables[1]

Library	Listings
1. Oklahoma Christian College, Oklahoma City, OK	19
2. Lincoln Christian College, Lincoln, IL	18
3. Freed-Hardeman University, Henderson, TN	18
4. Abilene Christian University, Abilene, TX	18
5. Harding University, Searcy, AR	17
6. Pepperdine University, Malibu, CA	17
7. David Lipscomb University, Nashville, TN	17
8. Lubbock Christian University, Lubbock, TX	16
9. Chicago Theological Seminary, Chicago, IL	15
10. Harding College Graduate School of Religion, Memphis, TN	15
11. Ambassador College, Big Sandy, TX	15
12. York College, York, NE	14
13. Pacific Christian College, Fullerton, CA	13
14. Columbia Christian College, Portland, OR	13
15. Great Lakes Bible College, Lansing, MI	12
16. Cincinnati Bible Seminary, Cincinnati, OH	12
17. Amber University, Garland, TX	12

1. This list was compiled from the top libraries listed on each of the scholarly Churches of Christ tables.

TABLE 4.236
1978 *American Library Directory* List of Scholarly Libraries Most Often Listed in Congregational Tables[1]

Library	Listings
1. Washburn University, Topeka, KS	18
2. Olivet College, Olivet, MI	18
3. American Congregational Association, Boston, MA	11
4. Evangelical Congregational School of Theology, Myerstown, PA	5
5. Piedmont College, Demarest, GA	4

1. This list was compiled from the top libraries listed on each of the scholarly Congregational tables.

TABLE 4.237
1988 *American Library Directory* List of Scholarly Libraries Most Often Listed in Episcopal/Anglican Tables[1]

Library	Listings
1. General Theological Seminary, New York, NY	18
2. Bishop's University, Lennoxville, PQ	18
3. University of the South, Sewanee, TN	17
4. Episcopal Theological Seminary, Austin, TX	16
5. Saint Paul's College, Lawrenceville, VA	16
6. Nashotah House, Nashotah, WI	16
7. Bard College, Annandale-on-Hudson, NY	15
8. Hobart and William Smith Colleges, Geneva, NY	15
9. Kenyon College, Gambier, OH	15
10. Voorhees College, Denmark, SC	15
11. Huron College, London, ON	15
12. Saint Mary's College, Raleigh, NC	14
13. Episcopal Divinity School, Cambridge, MA	12
14. University of the South School of Theology, Sewanee, TN	12

1. This list was compiled from the top libraries listed on each of the scholarly Episcopal/Anglican tables.

TABLE 4.238
1988 *American Library Directory* List of Scholarly Libraries Most Often Listed in Independent Tables[1]

Library	Listings
1. Brown University, Providence, RI	17
2. Graduate Theological Union, Berkeley, CA	16
3. Wheaton College, Wheaton, IL	16
4. Berea College, Berea, KY	15
5. Union Theological Seminary, New York, NY	14
6. Azusa Pacific University, Azusa, CA	13
7. Biola University, La Mirada, CA	13
8. Oral Roberts University, Tulsa, OK	13
9. Christian Broadcasting Network University, Virginia Beach, VA	13
10. Moody Bible Institute, Chicago, IL	12
11. Maharishi International University, Fairfield, IA	12
12. Asbury College, Wilmore, KY	12
13. Dallas Theological Seminary, Dallas, TX	12
14. Westmont College, Santa Barbara, CA	11
15. Gordon College, Wenham, MA	11
16. Reformed Theological Seminary, Jackson, MS	11
17. Bob Jones University, Greenville, SC	11
18. McGill University, Montreal, PQ	11

1. This list was compiled from the top libraries listed on each of the scholarly Independent tables.

TABLE 4.239
1988 *American Library Directory* List of Scholarly Libraries Most Often Listed in Lutheran Tables[1]

Library	Listings
1. Valparaiso University, Valparaiso, IN	19
2. Wagner College, Staten Island, NY	17
3. Gettysburg College, Gettysburg, PA	17
4. Augustana College, Rock Island, IL	16
5. Concordia College, Moorhead, MN	16
6. Capital University, Columbus, OH	15
7. Wittenberg University, Springfield, OH	15
8. Susquehanna University, Selinsgrove, PA	15
9. Pacific Lutheran University, Tacoma, WA	15
10. Luther College, Decorah, IA	14
11. Muhlenberg College, Allentown, PA	14
12. Augustana College, Sioux Falls, SD	14
13. Augsburg College, Minneapolis, MN	13
14. St. Olaf College, Northfield, MN	13
15. Gustavus Adolphus College, St. Peter, MN	13
16. Wilfred Laurier University, Waterloo, ON	13

1. This list was compiled from the top libraries listed on each of the scholarly Lutheran tables.

TABLE 4.240
1988 *American Library Directory* List of Scholarly Libraries Most Often Listed in Mennonite Tables[1]

Library	Listings
1. Tabor College, Hillsboro, KS	19
2. Eastern Mennonite University, Harrisonburg, VA	19
3. Fresno Pacific College, Fresno, CA	18
4. Associated Mennonite Biblical Seminary, Elkhart, IN	18
5. Goshen College, Goshen, IN	17
6. Bluffton College, Bluffton, OH	17
7. Hesston College, Hesston, KS	16
8. Goshen College Mennonite Historical Library, Goshen, IN	14
9. Bethel College, North Newton, KS	14
10. Columbia Bible College, Clearbrook, BC	12
11. Steinbach Bible College, Steinbach, MB	12
12. Mennonite Brethren Bible College, Winnipeg, MB	11
13. Conrad Grebel College, Waterloo, ON	11
14. Bethel College Mennonite Library, North Newton, KS	10

1. This list was compiled from the top libraries listed on each of the scholarly Mennonite tables.

TABLE 4.241
1988 *American Library Directory* List of Scholarly Libraries Most Often Listed in Methodist Tables[1]

Library	Listings
1. Wesleyan University, Middletown, CT	16
2. University of the Pacific, Stockton, CA	15
3. Boston University, Boston, MA	15
4. Duke University, Durham, NC	15
5. American University, Washington, DC	14
6. DePauw University, Greencastle, IN	14
7. Drew University, Madison, NJ	14
8. University of Denver, Denver, CO	13
9. University of Evansville, Evansville, IN	13
10. Emory University, Atlanta, GA	12
11. Dickinson College, Carlisle, PA	12
12. Southern Methodist University, Dallas, TX	11
13. Baldwin-Wallace College, Berea, OH	10
14. Seattle Pacific University, Seattle, WA	10

1. This list was compiled from the top libraries listed on each of the scholarly Methodist tables.

TABLE 4.242
1988 *American Library Directory* List of Scholarly Libraries Most Often Listed in Other Denominations Tables[1]

Library	Listings
1. Brigham Young University, Provo, UT	17
2. Swarthmore College, Swarthmore, PA	16
3. Earlham College, Richmond, IN	15
4. Washburn University, Topeka, KS	15
5. Andrews University, Berrien Springs, MI	15
6. Calvin College, Grand Rapids, MI	15
7. University of Winnipeg, Winnipeg, MB	14
8. Loma Linda University, Loma Linda, CA	13
9. Nazareth College, Rochester, NY	13
10. Ashland University, Ashland, OH	13
11. Bryn Mawr College, Bryn Mawr, PA	13
12. Messiah College, Grantham, PA	12
13. Loma Linda University, Riverside, CA	11
14. Ricks College, Rexburg, ID	11
15. Hope College, Holland, MI	11
16. Mount Allison University, Sackville, NB	11

1. This list was compiled from the top libraries listed on each of the scholarly Other Denominations tables.

TABLE 4.243
1988 *American Library Directory* List of Scholarly Libraries Most Often Listed in Presbyterian Tables[1]

Library	Listings
1. University of Tulsa, Tulsa, OK	18
2. Trinity University, San Antonio, TX	17
3. Lafayette College, Easton, PA	16
4. Queen's University, Kingston, ON	16
5. Lake Forest College, Lake Forest, IL	15
6. Union Theological Seminary, Richmond, VA	15
7. Davidson College, Davidson, NC	14
8. College of Wooster, Wooster, OH	14
9. Macalester College, St. Paul, MN	13
10. Lewis and Clark College, Portland, OR	13
11. Hanover College, Hanover, IN	12
12. Westminster College, New Wilmington, PA	12
13. Rhodes College, Memphis, TN	12
14. Millikin University, Decatur, IL	11
15. Alma College, Alma, MI	11

1. This list was compiled from the top libraries listed on each of the scholarly Presbyterian tables.

TABLE 4.244

1988 *American Library Directory* List of Scholarly Libraries Most Often Listed in United Church of Christ Tables[1]

Library	Listings
1. Elmhurst College, Elmhurst, IL	19
2. Doane College, Crete, NE	19
3. Pacific University, Forest Grove, OR	19
4. Catawba College, Salisbury, NC	18
5. Eden Webster University, St. Louis, MO	17
6. Drury College, Springfield, MO	17
7. Heidelberg College, Tiffin, OH	17
8. Defiance College, Defiance, OH	16
9. Cedar Crest College, Allentown, PA	16
10. Ursinus College, Collegeville, PA	16
11. Franklin and Marshall College, Lancaster, PA	16
12. Hood College, Frederick, MD	15
13. Elon College, Elon College, NC	15
14. Fisk University, Nashville, TN	15
15. Andover Newton Theological School, Newton Center, MA	13
16. Lakeland College, Sheboygan, WI	13

1. This list was compiled from the top libraries listed on each of the scholarly United Church of Christ tables.

TABLE 4.245
1988 *American Library Directory* List of Scholarly Libraries Most Often Listed in Jewish Tables[1]

Library	Listings
1. Yeshiva University, New York, NY	18
2. Hebrew Union College, Cincinnati, OH	17
3. Spertus College of Judaica, Chicago, IL	16
4. Hebrew College, Brookline, MA	16
5. Brandeis University, Waltham, MA	16
6. Jewish Theological Seminary, New York, NY	15
7. Baltimore Hebrew College, Baltimore, MD	12
8. American Jewish Historical Society, Waltham, MA	11
9. Yivo Institute for Jewish Research, New York, NY	11

1. This list was compiled from the top libraries listed on each of the scholarly Jewish tables.

TABLE 4.246
1988 *American Library Directory* List of Scholarly Libraries Most Often Listed in Roman Catholic Tables[1]

Library	Listings
1. Loyola University, Chicago, IL	16
2. University of Notre Dame, Notre Dame, IN	16
3. St. Louis University, St. Louis, MO	15
4. St. John's University, Jamaica, NY	15
5. University of Dayton, Dayton, OH	15
6. Georgetown University, Washington, DC	14
7. Boston College, Chestnut Hill, MA	14
8. Fordham University, Bronx, NY	14
9. Marquette University, Milwaukee, WI	14
10. University of Ottawa, Ottawa, ON	14
11. University of Montreal, Montreal, PQ	14
12. Santa Clara University, Santa Clara, CA	13
13. The Catholic University of America, Washington, DC	13
14. Seton Hall University, South Orange, NJ	13
15. Saint Joseph's University, Philadelphia, PA	13

1. This list was compilied from the top libraries listed on each of the scholarly Roman Catholic tables.

TABLE 4.247
Analysis of Selected Variables of *Association of College and Research Libraries* (ACRL) University Libraries and Comparison with Basic Data in *American Library Directory* (ALD) University Library Data Tables[1]

	1988 ALD University Libraries					1988 ACRL University Libraries				
For the Year 1987–88	Number of Libraries	Highest	Mean	Median	Lowest	Number of Libraries	Highest	Mean	Median	Lowest
1. Professional staff members as a percentage of total library staff	156	100	26	23	5	100	54	27	26	16
2. Clerical staff members as a percentage of total library staff	149	76	30	27	5	100	72	45	46	17
3. Student assistant staff members as a percentage of total library staff	127	100	56	57	8	100	61	27	29	2
4. Ratio of professional staff members to clerical staff members (i.e., to nonprofessional staff and excluding student assistants)	149	13.0	1.1	1.0	0.1	100	2.3	0.7	0.6	0.3
5. Material expenditures as a percentage of total operating expenditures	169	100	37	35	17	100	64	38	38	13
6. Personnel expenditures as a percentage of total operating expenditures	163	83	61	64	33	100	70	49	48	28
7. Other operating expenditures as a percentage of total operating expenditures	134	13	5	5	2	100	34	11	9	1
8. Serial title holdings	169			550		100			8,072	
9. Microform titles	143			46,672		100		744,000		
10. Professional staff size	156			4		100		27.3		
11. Clerical and student assistant staff size	127			16		100			83.6	
12. Total staff size	156			19		100			112.9	
13. Material expenditure	169			$81,500		100			$1,983,365	
14. Personnel expenditure	163			$141,500		100			$1,859,736	
15. Total expenditure	169			$249,100		100			$3,794,979	

1. See chapter 4, footnote 1.

TABLE 4.248
1978 *American Library Directory* National Data Needed for 1977 *National Center for Education Statistics* (NCES) Comparison: Religious Academic Libraries Only[1]

	Mean Value per Library	No Response	Actual Libraries	Cumulative Variable Values	Mean Value per Library	Cumulative Enrollment	Mean Enrollment per Library
Canada							
1. Volumes per student	74.00	13	69	8,093,700	117,300.00	74,636	1,588
2. Periodical titles per student	0.37	33	49	28,910	590.00	74,636	1,588
3. Total staff members per library	15.00	40	42	630	15.00		
4. Total staff members per 1,000 students	9.40	40	42	630	15.00	74,636	1,588
5. Professional staff members per 1,000 students	2.50	40	42	168	4.00	74,636	1,588
6. Total library expenditures per 1,000 students	$146,159.00	40	42	$9,748,200	$232,100.00	74,636	1,588
United States							
1. Volumes per student	96.00	74	1,060	106,116,800	100,110.00	1,050,014	1,042
2. Periodical titles per student	0.55	288	846	486,840	575.00	1,050,014	1,042
3. Total staff members per library	17.00	466	668	11,363	17.00		
4. Total staff members per 1,000 students	16.30	466	668	11,363	17.00	1,050,014	1,042
5. Professional staff members per 1,000 students	3.80	474	660	2,599	3.94	1,050,014	1,042
6. Total library expenditures per 1,000 students	$137,020.00	253	881	$125,746,300	$142,731.00	1,050,014	1,042
Total libraries: U.S.A. and Canada	1,216.00	87	1,129				

TABLE 4.248 (continued)
1978 *American Library Directory* National Data Needed for 1977 *National Center for Education Statistics* (NCES) Comparison: Religious Academic Libraries Only[1]

	1977 National Center for Education Statistics (NCES) Data						
	Mean Value per Library	No Response	Actual Libraries	Cumulative Variable Values	Mean Value per Library	Cumulative Enrollment	Mean Enrollment per Library
1. Volumes per student	57.00	0	3,058	—	157,440.00	8,529,415	2,789
2. Periodical titles per student	0.55	0	3,058	—	1,527.00	8,529,415	2,789
3. Total staff members per library	18.00	0	3,058	—	18.00	8,529,415	2,789
4. Total staff members per 1,000 students	6.70	0	3,058	—	18.70	8,529,415	2,789
5. Professional staff members per 1,000 students	2.70	0	3,058	—	2.70	8,529,415	2,789
6. Total library expenditures per 1,000 students	$150,000.00	0	3,058	—	$150,000.00	8,529,415	2,789
Total libraries	3,058.00						

1. It appears that volumes per student were significantly fewer in the NCES than those in either the *ALD* United States or Canada. Staff membership per 1,000 students appears to be larger in the religious libraries. U.S. religious library professional staff memberships were larger than for the NCES. Periodical titles per student were low in religious libraries. Total library expenditures per thousand students were higher for NCES libraries than for either *ALD* U.S. or Canadian religious libraries.

APPENDIX A
ANNOTATED BIBLIOGRAPHY

Scholarly Religious Libraries

The literature of this subfield is sparse, especially on the research level. It is largely bibliographic and neither management nor service oriented.

American Library Directory. New York: R. R. Bowker Company. Annually. Lists about 1,550 scholarly (presumably fairly comprehensive) and 300–400 popular (only a small sample of the larger) religious libraries in the United States and Canada.

American Theological Library Association, Suite 300, 820 Church Street, Evanston, IL 60201-3707 USA. An association of leading Christian seminary libraries publishing

- *Conference Proceedings,* annually
- *Religion Index One,* a subject and author index to religious periodical literature
- *Religion Index Two,* an index to multi-author works
- *Newsletter,* quarterly
- *Statistical Records and Membership List,* annually
- *ATLA Scarecrow Press Series,* irregularly
- *ATLA Basic Bibliographies in Religious Studies,* irregularly
- *LIBRARYNET Directory*

Association of British Theological and Philosophical Libraries, Bible Society's Librarian, University Library, West Road, Cambridge, CB3 9DR, United Kingdom. Corresponds to the American ATLA. Publishes a three-times-a-year *Newsletter.*

A Book World Directory of the Arab Countries, Turkey and Iran, compiled by Anthony Rudkin (London: Mansell, 1986). Includes a variety of scholarly and a few popular religious libraries.

Canadian Library Association, 200 Elgin Street, Ottawa, ON K2P 1L5 Canada. Publishes the *Feliciter,* a news magazine. The Canadian Association of College and University Libraries forms one division of it.

Catholic Library Association, 1258 Pelham Parkway, Bronx, NY 10461 USA. Contains several sections of interest to both scholarly and popular level librarians. Now undergoing extensive reorganization and considerable budget reduction. Publishes

Books for Catholic Elementary Schools, 1987

Catholic Subject Headings, 1981

Dewey Decimal Classification, 200 Schedules Expanded for Use, 1988

Guide for the Organization and Operation of a Religious Resource Center, 1986

Handbook and Membership Directory, annually

Catholic Periodical and Literature Index, bimonthly

Catholic Library World, bimonthly

Christian Booksellers Association, Box 200, 2620 Venetucci Blvd., Colorado Springs, CO 80901 USA.

Conseil International des Associations de Bibliotheques de Theologie, 1961–1990. K. U. Leuven/Faculty of Theology, Bibliotheek Godgeleerdheid, St. Michielsstraat 2-6, B-3000, Leuven, Belgium. The International Association of Scholarly Theological Libraries. Has an annual conference and has member associations in several European countries.

A Guide to the Theological Libraries of Great Britain and Ireland, compiled by Emma R. M. Lea and edited by Alan F. Jesson (London: Association of British Theological and Philosophical Libraries, 1986). A directory of 397 libraries, now being revised.

Librarians' Christian Fellowship, Graham Hedges, 34 Thurlstone Avenue, Seven Kings, Ilford, Essex IG3 9DU, United Kingdom. A British association of Protestant and Catholic religious institution librarians and assistants. Carries out a variety of useful services, including conferences and cooperation with the Library Association. Publishes a newsletter and a magazine, *Christian Librarian.*

Heisey, Terry M. "Paradigm Agreement and Literature Obsolescence, A Comparative Study in the Literature of the Dead Sea Scrolls," *Journal of Documentation* 44 (December 1988): 285–301. Theology has an unusually low percentage of citations ten years old or less.

Presbyterian and Reformed Library Association, Pittsburgh Theological Seminary Library, 616 North Highland Avenue, Pittsburgh, PA 15206 USA.

Reference Works in the Field of Religion 1977–1985: A Selective Bibliography, by Elsie Freudenberger (Haverford, Pa: Catholic Library Association, 1986).

Slavens, Thomas P. *A Great Library through Gifts*. New York: K. G. Saur, 1986. The development of the Union Theological Seminary Library.

World Guide to Libraries. Munich: K. G. Saur, 1985. Presumably this is the most extensive world library directory.

World of Learning. London: Europa Publications, bienially. One of the more complete global lists of scholarly and certain popular libraries.

Popular Religious Libraries

Association of Christian Libraries, 910 Union Road, W. Seneca, NY 14224 USA. Publishes the *Christian Periodical Index.*

Association of Jewish Libraries, National Foundation for Jewish Culture, Room 1512, 122 E. 42nd Street, New York, NY 10168 USA. Has two sections: (1) Research and Special Libraries and (2) Synagogue, School and Center Libraries. Publishes

Newsletter, quarterly
Judaica Librarianship, a semiannual journal
Jewish Holiday Short Story Index
Weine Classification System, 1982
Basic Reference List for the SSC Library, 1989
Juvenile Judaica, 1985 plus updates
A Basic Periodical List for the Judaica Library, 1989
Membership Directory, 1982

In addition, the Temple Library, University Circle and Silver Park, Cleveland, OH 44106, USA, publishes useful Jewish library material.

Augsburg Publishing House, *Book Newsletter* (Minneapolis).

Berman, Margot S. *How to Organize a Jewish Library: A Source Book and Guide for Synagogue, School and Center Libraries.* New York: JWB Jewish Book Council, 1982.

Bowker Annual of Library and Book Trade Information. New York: R. R. Bowker. Contains directories of international and national library and publishers associations.

Church and Synagogue Librarians Fellowship, 3800 Donerin Way,

Phoenix, MD 21131 USA. Publishes a three-times-a-year newsletter, *Cross and Star*.

Church and Synagogue Library Association, P.O. Box 19357, Portland, OR 97219 USA.

An ecumenical association of two thousand congregational librarians. Ask for their publication list. Publishes

Church and Synagogue Libraries, a bimonthly bulletin

Twenty 10–50 page pamphlets

Five bibliographies

Five video cassettes

Newsletters are published by many CSLA chapters, also.

"The Church and Synagogue Library Association." In *Encyclopedia of Library and Information Science*. (New York: Marcel Dekker, 1971) 4: 674–76.

"Church and Synagogue Libraries." *Drexel Library Quarterly* 6 (April 1970). Entire issue.

Church of Christ, Scientist (Christian Science), 1 Norway Street, Boston, MA 02115 USA. Sponsors a network of public reading rooms in many nations where publications can be read or bought.

The Church of Jesus Christ of Latter-day Saints (LDS), E. North Temple Street, Salt Lake City, UT 84150 USA. Sponsors thousands of LDS genealogical and meetinghouse libraries around the world.

Church Library Association of Toronto, Flat 302, 10 Allanhurst Drive, Islington, ON M9A 4J5 Canada. Publishes a three-times-a-year newsletter, *Library Lines*.

Church Library Council, 5406 Quintana Street, Riverdale, MD 20237 USA. Publishes a quarterly newsletter, *News*.

Congregational Library Association of British Columbia, 38489 Old Yale Road, Abbotsford, BC V2S 4N2 Canada. Publishes a monthly newsletter, *Rare Bird*.

Evangelical Church Library Association, P.O. Box 353, Glen Ellyn, IL 60137 USA. Publishes a quarterly periodical, *Librarian's World,* containing many short book reviews.

Galfand, Sidney. "Organized Jewish Libraries." *Library Journal* 87 (January 1962): 31–34. An early description of synagogue libraries.

"Have a Church Library!" *International Journal of Religious Education* (October 1966). Entire issue.

Harvey, John F., and Shahr Azar Musavi. "Tehran Mosque Libraries and a Comparison with American Christian Church Libraries." *International Library Review* 13 (October 1981): 385–95.

Johnson, Marian. "Lutheran Church Library Association." In *Encyclopedia of Library and Information Science.* New York: Marcel Dekker, 1975, 16: 363–66.

Lutheran Church Library Association, 122 W. Franklin Avenue, Minneapolis, MN 55404 USA. Has eighteen hundred members and twenty-five chapters. Publishes manuals and booklists as well as *Lutheran Libraries,* a quarterly periodical.

McMichael, Betty. *The Church Librarian's Handbook.* Grand Rapids, Mich.: Baker Book House, 1984.

National Foundation for Jewish Culture, Room 1512, 122 W. 42nd Street, New York, NY 10168 USA. Publishes basic book and periodical lists.

Pacific Northwest Association of Church Libraries, P.O. Box Section 12379, Main Office Station, Seattle, WA 98111 USA. Publishes a quarterly newsletter, *The Lamplighter.*

"Periodicals to Assist Church Librarians." *Church and Synagogue Libraries* 23 (November/December 1989): 6.

Provident Library Associates Network, published quarterly by the Provident Bookstores of the Mennonite Publishing House, 616 Walnut Avenue, Scottdale, PA 15683 USA.

The Southern Baptist Convention Church Library Department, 127 Ninth Avenue North, Nashville, TN 37234 USA. Publishes several manuals and bulletins with information on library organization, and media and book selection, such as the quarterly *Church Media Library Magazine,* which contains articles, book and media reviews, and lists of books and media for Sunday school curriculum support.

Union Nationale Culture et Bibliothèques pour Tous, 63 Rue de Varenne, 75007 Paris, France. Operates an extensive religious public library system.

White, Joyce L. "Church Libraries." In *Encyclopedia of Library and Information Science.* New York: Marcel Dekker, 1970, 4: 662–73.

APPENDIX B
GLOSSARY AND ACRONYMS

See Appendix A for other addresses.

Academic Libraries
: This term is used generically to include all junior and senior college, seminary, and university libraries.

Accreditation
: Recognition of an educational institution as maintaining good quality standards in all operating areas thereby qualifying its graduates for admission to higher or more specialized institutions. In this study, institutions were recognized as being accredited by a regional college and university accrediting association, the Association of Theological Schools or the Association of Bible Colleges.

ACRL
: Association of College and Research Libraries, 50 E. Huron Street, Chicago, IL 60611 USA.

Active
: The libraries having a variable in some quantity as shown in a table as opposed to those libraries giving no response to a question asked about that variable.

Additional Activities
: A special analysis that obtained a total score by adding together the library's scores for consortium membership, OCLC membership, and local automation projects.

AJL
: Association of Jewish Libraries, c/o National Foundation for Jewish Culture, 330 Seventh Avenue, 21st floor, New York, NY 10001 USA.

ALA
: American Library Association, 50 E. Huron Street, Chicago, IL 60611 USA.

ALD

American Library Directory. New York: R. R. Bowker Company. Annually.

Archives

Official institutional records or correspondence in active storage.

ARL

Association of Research Libraries, 1527 New Hampshire Avenue, NW, Washington, DC 20036 USA.

ATLA

American Theological Library Association, Suite 300, 820 Church Street, Evanston, IL 60201-3707 USA.

Book

The term includes all types of printed and media library material.

Born

See Newly Born Libraries

CACUL

Canadian Association of College and University Libraries, 200 Elgin Street, Ottawa, ON K2P 1L5, Canada.

Cath LA

Catholic Library Association, 1258 Pelham Parkway, Bronx, NY 10461 USA.

Christian Science

Church of Christ, Scientist.

Circulation

Loaning of library material to a user.

City Population Level

The population of the city in which an institution was located.

CLA

Canadian Library Association, 200 Elgin Street, Ottawa, ON K2P 1L5, Canada.

Classification Scheme

The plan by which books are arranged in systematic order on the shelves, usually by subject.

Collection

The library's stock of print and nonprint material.

Congregational Library

A library serving a specific church, synagogue, mosque, or other house of worship, a popular religious library. The term should not be confused with the Congregational denomination or with the other kinds of popular religious libraries, i.e., religious parochial school and public libraries. Many congregations have a collection of book material which does not meet the definition of a library and so should not be called one.

To become a library, the collection should (1) be organized in a logical order, e.g., by author or subject, (2) have an appointed supervisor, librarian or committee, (3) actively provide circulation and reference service, (4) contain at least 100 volumes of library material, (5) be established in a dedicated room, space or other quarters having stack shelving, (6) have a recognized and clearly defined user group or clientele, (7) have a functional organization plan and set of objectives, and preferably (8) be supported with an annual income from the sponsoring institution. *See also* Library.

Consortium

An organized group of institutions banded together to carry out specific projects.

Convent

The house of a religious order or congregation where nuns and sisters live, work, and pray.

CSLA

Church and Synagogue Library Association, P.O. Box 19357, Portland, OR 97219 USA.

Data

While the words *data* and *information* are often used with separate meanings, in this book they are considered to have the same meaning.

Database

In this study, equals the entire sample at a given point in time, or all the questionnaires completed for one *ALD* edition.

DDC

Dewey Decimal Classification.

Dead Libraries

See No Longer Listed Libraries.

Degree, Highest

The highest level of academic degree awarded to students by a specific college or university.

Denomination

Christianity is a faith and Presbyterian is a denomination. A denomination is a religious organization uniting in a single administrative body a number of local congregations. As used in this book, the term *denomination* separates off each Protestant group from another.

Enrollment

The number of students attending classes at an academic institution at one time, usually expressed in full-time equivalent and covering both undergraduate and graduate credit students.

Extended Services and Collections

A special analysis that obtained a total score by adding together subject interests, religious subject interests, special collections, and publications for each library.

Faculty

Faculty members (teachers) are reported in full-time equivalent form for most of the academic institutions and their libraries that are represented in the *ALD*.

Faith

A system of beliefs: Buddhist, Christian, Hindu, Jewish, Moslem, etc.

FID

International Federation of Documentation, P.O. Box G0402, 2509 LK The Hague, Netherlands.

Finance

The library's income and expenditures of all kinds.

Founding

Starting date when the institution began work.

Gross Growth Library Rating

This special analysis was applied to numerous variables. It covers twenty-seven (scholarly) or twenty-two (popular) variables and shows the points earned by these variables by virtue of summing their growth percentages, table by table. The twenty-seven variables are total staff members, professional staff members, clerical staff members, student assistant staff members, volume holdings, periodical title holdings, vertical file holdings, microforms, media holdings, map holdings, art reproductions, material expenditures, personnel expenditures, other expenditures, total expenditures, consortium memberships, OCLC memberships, automation projects, subject interests, special collections, publications, library age, city population size, degree years offered, faculty size, students enrolled, and cumulative expenditure.

Holdings

A library's collection of reading and viewing material. Total holdings is a special analysis that shows the total adding together the volumes, periodical titles, vertical file drawers, and microforms for a specific library or group of libraries.

House of Worship

A generic term that refers to a church, synagogue, mosque, or other place of worship.

IFLA

International Federation of Library Associations and Institutions, The Royal Library, P.O. Box 95312, 2509 CH The Hague, Netherlands.

Independent

An institution that is affiliated with no denomination. In this study, the term carries a meaning similar to the words *interdenominational, ecumenical,* and *nondenominational,* though these terms are by no means synonyms. While these institutions are not affiliated with a denomination, this does not necessarily mean that they give no attention to religion. Some of them are permeated with religion, while others are not.

Junior College

The thirteenth and usually also the fourteenth year of formal schooling provided in an institution that commonly offers a program leading to an associate degree.

LCLA

Lutheran Church Library Association, 122 W. Franklin Avenue, Minneapolis, MN 55404 USA.

LDS

Church of Jesus Christ of Latter-day Saints.

Librarians

Narrowly, they are persons who have graduated from a library school, but broadly, and as used in much of this book, they are simply persons who are in charge of libraries. The narrow definition is used more often on the scholarly level and less often on the popular level.

Library

Should be interpreted in the widest possible sense to include all types of information activities and personnel. That institution in which such material as books, manuscripts, serials, documents, and media are collected and organized for use but normally not for sale. *See also* Congregational Library.

Library Age

Refers to the library's founding date.

Library Material

Includes books, bound and current issues of periodicals and continuations, documents, media, art reproductions, maps, vertical file material, and microforms.

LL
: Library Literature

Longitudinal
: A statistical term referring to a collection of data that covers a period from one to another point in time.

Matched Pair
: A library that appears in both the 1978 and the 1988 *ALD* editions.

Mean
: A statistical measure of central tendency, an average or the midpoint of a set of scores.

Media
: Includes films, filmstrips, video and audio cassettes, and many other audiovisual devices. Media holdings (cumulative) includes the book's measures of media, maps, and art reproductions. The total number is obtained by summing the scores of all three variables.

Median
: A statistical term denoting the figure that represents the midpoint in a range of numbers.

Micro
: Microform holdings. Microforms include microfiche, microfilm, microcards, ultrafiche—any printed material made available on film in miniaturized form.

Mode
: A statistical measure of central tendency, the most frequent value in a set of data.

Monastery
: The house of a religious order where priests, brothers, or monks live, work, and pray. Also may be called an abbey or a priory.

Mormon
: Member of the original or of the Reorganized Church of Jesus Christ of Latter-day Saints.

NCES
: National Center for Education Statistics, 400 Maryland Avenue, SW, Washington, DC 20202 USA.

Newly Listed Libraries
: These libraries appeared in the 1988 but not in the 1978 *ALD*, so presumably they were newly born in 1988 (as far as the *ALD* was concerned).

No Longer Listed Libraries
: These libraries were listed in the 1978 but not in the 1988 *ALD*. As far as the *ALD* was concerned, they did not reply to the 1988 questionnaire

nor could their information be located elsewhere, and so they were dead, at least temporarily.

No Response

A statistical term that refers to the number of libraries which did not respond to a particular item on the *American Library Directory* questionnaire.

North America

In this author's definition, North America is that Western hemisphere continent Northwest of South America that is bound by the Arctic, Atlantic, and Pacific oceans. This study omits Mexico and the Central American countries as well as the island countries constituting Cuba and the Caribbean area. That leaves Canada and the United States to be included. These two countries make up 80 percent of the land area and 70 percent of the North American population.

Number

Number is a term used in the study's tables (often shown simply as *N*) to show the total for libraries (or staff members, volumes, etc.) in that portion of the table. In the same context, the word *libraries* means *number* of libraries.

OCLC

Online Computer Library Center, Dublin, Ohio USA. A cooperative and computerized library consortium with a large number of academic library members.

Paired Libraries

See *Matched Pair*.

Parochial School

A private elementary or secondary school supervised and to some extent staffed by a religious group or church.

Percentage

A statistical and tabular term that shows the proportion of a whole represented by a part and expressed in hundredths, e.g., in the *ALD* 1978 study, 6 percent of the libraries were located in junior colleges, 125 of 2,062 libraries.

Periodical

A publication issued on a regular schedule two or more times a year.

Personnel

The library's staff members of all ranks. In this study they are divided among professional, clerical, and student assistants.

Popular or Popular-Level

Generally, popular religious libraries serve users primarily on an elementary or secondary school or a public library level with an appropriate material collection. Three types of religious libraries are classified at the popular level: congregational (church, synagogue, mosque, or other house of worship), parochial school, and public. More formally, a popular-level library is an organized and staffed collection that may include adult, children's, and young adult's material, religious periodicals, and other printed and media material. It provides educational and perhaps recreational reading and other library service primarily on religious themes and on a popular level for lay congregational members, friends, and for religious education centers, Sunday and synagogue school teachers and students, and in some cases, the general public.

Such libraries as the following are included in this group: (1) Roman Catholic church, parish, or community libraries and information centers; (2) synagogue, temple, or Jewish center libraries; (3) Jewish, Catholic, Lutheran, or other denomination parochial or private religious school libraries; and (4) Christian Science reading rooms and Church of Jesus Christ of Latter-day Saints meetinghouse and genealogical libraries. All faiths and denominations are included as found in all countries.

Private Public Libraries

In this context, a religious library that provides service to the general public rather than to a specific congregation, though its own congregation members may be among its heaviest users. These libraries constitute private public libraries. Such a library is sponsored by a specific congregation, society, or order and provides religious library material for borrower or for rental use.

Private School Libraries

A term that can be used in either a generic or a specific sense for a religious elementary or secondary school. Almost but not quite synonymous with a parochial or synagogue school. A parochial school is a private school directly sponsored by a house of worship or a diocesan headquarters. It is usually open to any student in its district who wishes to attend it. It may or may not be part of a city religious (usually Roman Catholic) school system. A private school (in the specific sense) is an independent school sponsored by a specific religious organization or board of trustees or religious order that may restrict its enrollment in any way it wishes. A synagogue school is a Jewish school at the elementary and secondary level that is sponsored by a specific synagogue or by a group of synagogues. Used in the generic sense, a private school is any school not publicly supported, so all parochial and synagogue (as well as nonreligious and nonpublicly supported) schools are private schools.

There are five kinds of religiously affiliated school libraries: (1) Catholic parochial school libraries, which are sponsored by a local parish or diocese and in certain large cities form part of a system of many such elementary and secondary school libraries; (2) private Catholic elementary and secondary school libraries, which are sponsored by an order of the clergy, brothers, or nuns or else are independent and have their own school board of trustees; (3) Lutheran, Episcopal, Quaker, Jewish, etc., elementary and secondary parochial school libraries, which may form part of a system of denominational school libraries; (4) Protestant or Jewish elementary and secondary schools, which are similar to those in (2) above; and (5) private part-time and independent synagogue or Jewish schools, which cover parts of both elementary and secondary school levels, concentrating on teaching the Jewish religion, culture, and life, which are sponsored by a specific synagogue or by a group of them.

Professional Librarian

A person who has graduated from a library school.

Publications

Serials or monographs published by the library.

Range

Represents the distance between the lowest and highest numbers in a group of figures.

Ratio

A statistical term in which two figures are juxtaposed in order to compare them closely and show their relative size. The number of 1978 U.S.: Canada libraries can be compared as 1930 to 116 or 16.6 to 1.0.

Reference Work

Answering reader's questions, helping them locate useful information.

Region

An area of the U.S. including several contiguous states. For Canada, the entire nation is put into one large region.

Religion

This word can be defined as the service and worship of a deity or god or else an institutionalized system of beliefs and practices relating to a supreme being.

Religious

This word is used in two distinct senses there. In general, it refers to any direct or indirect connection with a congregation or a religious denomination or faith. Specifically, it is used also to refer to the members of a religious order, such as Franciscan brothers or Dominican nuns, who may be referred to collectively by the phrase *the religious*.

Religious Administrative Office

Examples are a diocese or a denomination headquarters.

Religious History Libraries and Archive Centers

Libraries and archive centers that house and service religious historical and archive material, usually for a particular denomination, nationally or regionally. While table 1.1 calls for this category and data was collected on it from the *ALD*, relatively few of these libraries exist. A revised edition of the classification scheme may place this category under Organization or Institution Administrative Libraries.

Religious Libraries

Libraries that serve under an institution formally and officially or else informally sponsored by or affiliated or connected with a religious organization or institution, local, state or provincewide, national or international, such as a house of worship or a denominational headquarters. To put it in a somewhat different way, a library has a religious affiliation when its parent institution, e.g., college or university, house of worship, or religious order, has a formal and official tie (sponsorship or affiliation or connection) with a specific religious group. In other situations, a formal and official tie may not now exist, only an informal and friendly connection, but probably such a connection existed previously. Both cases are acceptable. Further, in this study, any library coded with an *R* in the *ALD*. Obviously this is a broad, flexible, and inclusive definition, which has been interpreted liberally here. In addition, many academic institutions that presently have or had in the past a connection with a religious institution or organization are included. No distinction was made between institutions that were sponsored formally and directly with financial support by a religious group vs. those affiliated with but without financial support by such a group. Nor was it important whether this affiliation was close or distant, presently existing or existing only in the past.

In other words, the definition of a religious library was sufficiently flexible to cover such examples as Canisius College in Buffalo, which was once officially sponsored by the Roman Catholic Society of Jesus but formally severed or at least revised that connection several years ago for reasons apparently relating to institutional eligibility for state and federal government student aid. Now, as a more-or-less independent college, Canisius is controlled by a primarily lay board of trustees but still has (and perhaps always will have) a Jesuit priest as president and other Jesuit priests as faculty members. Another questionable example is Temple University in Philadelphia, which is now clearly a state-government-sponsored and supported institution. However, in its earlier years it was under strong Baptist influence, and its president was a Baptist minister.

This definition may seem too loose and flexible to certain readers. However, under the present circumstances, the author thought he had no choice. Whether or not a particular religious denomination presently has influence on an academic campus (or at least did so in 1978 and 1988) was difficult for the author to ascertain without going there and studying the institution and its history closely, an impossibility. So he had to generalize. Many religiously marginal academic institutions were rejected on this basis, but others were accepted into the database. Finally, there is no implication intended here that a present or former religious connection necessarily implied any distinctive ideological, ethical, moral, or religious influence on the institution.

Repeat Question

This question asked if the library was included in both the 1978 and 1988 editions or merely in one of the two.

Rural

As used in this book, refers to a town or area with population of 25,000 or less.

Sample

Refers to the database. The questionnaires completed for each *ALD* edition.

Scholarly

Generally, scholarly libraries serve uses on a tertiary education or research level with material collections at that level. The author classifies several types of religious libraries at the scholarly level: (1) and (2) those affiliated with colleges of both junior and senior levels, (3) with universities, (4) with seminaries, with (5) convents or (6) monasteries, with (7) denominational or (8) religious order headquarters offices, and with (9) historical or archive collections. All religious libraries can be assigned either to the scholarly or popular category based on the educational level of the library's sponsoring organization as on the level of the user group.

Certain religious institutions' libraries were omitted from the *ALD* portion of this study. It deliberately excluded the many religious hospital libraries existing in these countries, for instance. Nor did the study include parochial elementary or secondary school libraries (except for a few). In the former case, the typical material collection contained few religious titles and the library's objectives did not involve religious material service. In the second case, the libraries were within the popular religious library classification, but only a few of them were listed in either the *American Library Directory* or the Church and Synagogue Library Association membership list.

Seminary

A school for education ministers, priests, and other religious workers. This word is used primarily in a generic sense to represent all schools or departments that educate persons for work in the ministry or religious education in any faith or denomination. So the reader may substitute such words as school or department of theology or divinity, hebrew college or rabbinical college for seminary if he or she wishes to do so.

Senior College

The thirteenth through the sixteenth years of formal schooling provided in an institution that commonly offers a program leading to a bachelor's and/or master's degree.

Service

Providing formal or informal advice and assistance directly to users through teaching, referring them to reference material or circulating material to them.

Small City

Cities with a population of 10,000 or fewer persons.

Special Collection

A library section in which are kept rare and unusual titles and narrowly focused subject collections, or the narrowly focused collection itself.

Student

Number of students (pupils) is reported for each academic institution represented in the *ALD* in full-time equivalent form.

Subject Interest

A topic of primary library collecting focus.

Sunday School Libraries

A synonym for the church or congregational library. Many of them serve primarily the church or Sunday school teachers and students and therefore resemble private elementary and secondary school libraries in certain ways. Generically the same as the synagogue library.

Synagogue Libraries

Among synagogue libraries there are two kinds: (1) synagogue libraries serving primarily the adult congregation and (2) synagogue or parochial school libraries serving private elementary and secondary school students and faculty members. Whenever there is a synagogue school library, there is often the primary library for any synagogue associated with it which probably has a part-time staff member in charge and regular service hours. This study treats all synagogue, temple, and Jewish center libraries as fitting the same definition.

University

A institution that provides at least five years of higher education and offers graduate degrees to students. In this study, also, any institution that calls itself a university.

Unmatched Pairs

Includes all libraries not in the matched pairs group, i.e., the dead and the newly born libraries.

U.S.A.

United States of America.

Variable

A factor or characteristic that is being studied here, e.g., student enrollment (fte), OCLC membership, or volumes in the library collection.

VF

Vertical file case or cabinet. A wood or steel cabinet in which pamphlets or papers are stored. This study counts the number of drawers held, not the number of cabinets.

APPENDIX C
SCHOLARLY LIBRARY STATISTICAL LIMITATIONS AND INTERPRETATION

by Jo Ann Mouridou

Qualifications

The statistics compiled on the 1978 and 1988 editions of the *American Library Directory* have been based on a number of common (although perhaps only partly justifiable) assumptions:

1. The *ALD* data collection activities used the same set of data definitions, i.e., data collected were comparable both *within* each edition and also *between* the two editions,

2. Growth projections made for all variables assume that change over time is approximately *linear*. That is, if a variable changes by a certain number of units in one year, then this change *in units per year* will be continued at more or less the same rate in subsequent years. Notice that the suggestion is that if a library adds five hundred books per year then this is the measure of *increase in units p.a.* The five hundred books may mean a 10 percent increase on a base of five thousand books for the year 1980 and only a 9 percent increase for the year 1981 (by which time the library has a base of fifty-five hundred books).

Nevertheless, the number of books added per year will tend to be constant.

The assumption of linear change in *units* rather than in *percentages* is probably quite reasonable for all variables except for financial measures such as expenditure on material, personnel, "other" categories and total annual library expenditure. For this set of variables it appears more likely that true change should be in the realm of a 10 percent increment in operating costs/expenditures p.a. The tendency toward percentage-oriented change is based on the practice of bodies to demand budgetary increases in terms of percentages (to cover both growth and inflation) rather than in terms of number of books, etc. However, there are several factors prohibiting accurate financial forecasts of growth as percentage-based rates. These include (1) the United States and Canada use different and incomparable currencies—they vary at different rates as well as being valued at differing rates of exchange; (2) although it is possible to calculate the past annual inflation rates, it is not possible to predict accurately the future rates of inflation for the United States and Canada; and (3) it is not safe to assume on the basis of the growth rates between 1978 and 1988 that annual financial change will take the form of an annual *percentage* increase. Total annual library expenditure between 1978 and 1988 "grew" by about 67 percent for all scholarly and popular libraries combined (see longitudinal table 4.178). If the average annual rate of inflation was 5 percent for this period of ten years, then more than 60 percent of the total increase of 67 percent was due to inflation alone! This means that *real* growth exclusive of inflation was between 3 percent and 5 percent for the entire decade! Contrary to appearances, it is unlikely that nearly all of the *actual* financial change was absorbed by inflation. This is obvious simply through examining the real change in volume holdings for all libraries: between 1978 and 1988 *actual* volume holdings "grew" by 21 percent for the scholarly libraries (see longitudinal table 4.73).

As the result of the contradictory trends concerning money, it has seemed wisest to project financial increases in the same way as for the other variables: change is calculated per annum in rates of dollars expected to be spent plotted against a *linear* curve, as for the other variables used.

3. The samples gathered as the foundation of the statistical analysis are representative of all the *ALD* religious libraries. Every effort has been made to ensure that this is the case.
4. The samples used for the 1978 and 1988 editions are representative, at least *to a somewhat lesser degree*, of all the religious libraries in the United States and Canada. No doubt this is true; however, it is also true that bodies responding to questionnaires tend to be those more inclined to group participation and less inclined to understaffing or inefficiency; therefore, there will be a distinct form of bias in the samples used, even though it is difficult to predict the exact *nature* or *direction* of the bias.
5. Data collection and publication in the *American Library Directory* does not systematically discriminate against any particular group of libraries. This assumption includes both that all libraries are treated equally in terms of data representation on paper *within* the two editions, and also that data publication policy is consistent *between* the publications for 1978 and 1988.
6. The system of data categorization used on the study questionnaires is reasonable (vis-á-vis category groups, midpoints, etc.) both in terms of the actual categories used, and also with reference to the top category for each one of the operative variables. This assumption is quite valid for most of the variables, i.e., for most of those with standard deviations of approximately one-sixth of the variable ranges. However, it is violated for some variables such as "other" expenditures. For this particular variable the top category was much too low to represent accurately the expenditure of many scholarly libraries on "other" categories.

   As a result, the SD for this variable runs between 25 percent and 32 percent of the variable range (see tables C-1, C-2, C-3) about 100 percent too much in the case of scholarly libraries (this phenomenon is the result of extreme skewness for scholarly libraries toward the *upper* end of the variable range).

Statistical Interpretation

For the purposes of future projections, a set of twenty-one variables, all using numeric ranges, were analyzed. This set is the group of variables on which it is possible to plot *means* and *standard deviations*. One further variable could have been used—number of library accreditations listed for each library. This variable, however, is not a variable in the true sense as it is a composite of the various types of accreditation claimed by the libraries in the samples.

Therefore, a library claiming accreditation with three separate bodies would be listed as having three times as many accreditations as another library with, say, regional accreditation only. Although this composite variable does in fact produce a mean value (at least for scholarly libraries—see table 2.84), it is an artificial mean as regional accreditation by itself may be more desirable than several other types of accreditation put together. Similarly, it seems unlikely that any library would wish to accumulate diverse accreditation statuses—often one such recognition is sufficient. Therefore, to predict a growing mean tendency toward more accreditations would be nonsensical. Hence, future projections are based on the original twenty-one numerical variables only. For the entire list, see tables 2.80, 2.83.

Scholarly Libraries: Entire Sample and Matched Pairs

For scholarly libraries generally the value of the average standard deviation over the twenty-one variables ran approximately 20 percent of the ranges of the variables (see tables 2.80, 2.84). This is a reasonable magnitude considering the size of the samples, the tendency of some of the variables toward bimodality, the category systems used (which were reasonable enough for the samples as groups but were inadequate for certain outstanding libraries), and the vastly differing types of libraries labeled as "scholarly." The libraries within the scholarly category did not usually approximate a normal curve for most of the variables. However, this is not surprising given that there are seven distinct subcategories that might themselves approximate normal distributions if there were sufficient cases in each subsample to allow us to study them effectively. The averages calculated for all scholarly versus scholarly: matched pairs were consistent. The largest difference is between the standard errors of the means: the matched pairs had an SD of the means 7.4 percent larger than for the entire scholarly sample. This is to be expected as the size of the latter group is proportionately larger than the former.

The SD of the mean statistic was calculated in order to estimate whether or not the two samples, 1978 versus 1988, were actually "different" and to assist in developing the future projection minima and maxima. Significance levels of 90 percent were calculated for these projection ranges (see tables 2.80, 2.83, C-3). In fact, the two samples, 1978 and

1988, *are* truly different—they are different samples even though they are largely composed of the same libraries. However, they have not changed as much over the ten intervening years as might be suspected. For example, the average SD of the means for the scholarly libraries is approximately 4,000 (see table 2.81). From tables 2.81 and 2.82 it can be seen that the difference between average actual mean 1978 and actual mean 1988 is approximately 10,700.

If a 99 percent significance test of the SD of the means is taken, then + −2.58 SDs of the Mean = + −10,135. This means, in principle, if not in fact, that the two samples 1978 and 1988 could almost have come randomly from the same larger sample! Note that 10,700 – 10,135 = 565, a small proportion relative to the base of 10,135. In terms of our study this finding is quite consistent with expectations: the two samples are largely (1,640) the same libraries at *different* points in time; they have changed somewhat over that period of time, but their basic variable configurations are still similar.

Statistically, they could *not quite* have been drawn from the same population at the same point in time—they are similar but "grown" larger by 1988.

A quick examination of table 2.81 shows that the scholarly libraries: matched pairs did slightly better on the average in 1978 than did the all scholarly group (0.7 percent difference and above the all scholarly group). By 1988 this lead was increased to 4.1 percent better than their counterpart. And by 1998 it is expected that the matched pairs will show an average differential of 6.2 percent higher than a similar all scholarly sample.

Statistical Comparison of the United States and Canada

Even a quick glance at table 2.83 shows that comparison of the United States versus Canadian distributions can proceed along only general lines. There are several profound problems arising out of a consideration of libraries from the two countries as comprising parts of the same sample; but there are even larger problems in considering them as separate, independent subsamples of the same whole. Most of the difficulties concern the Canadian libraries, of course.

It is questionable if the Canadian libraries listed by the *American Library Directory* are truly representative of Canadian libraries as a population. In addition, it is clear from a look at the mean ages of Canadian libraries in

1978 and 1988 (75 years and 68 years for scholarly) that the internal composition of the group is swinging toward younger establishments.

Canadian libraries show a *different profile* from their American counterparts. For example, Canadian popular libraries tend to locate increasingly in cities of over 500,000 persons. Canadian scholarly libraries are found in cities of well over 400,000 persons, although the mean is dropping slightly. American scholarly libraries, on the other hand, are located in increasingly smaller cities of approximately 325,000 persons, while American popular libraries are in cities of 350,000 on the average. Similarly, Canadian library spending has always been higher than that for the United States (in Canadian currency), but it is tending to level off, whereas the American library spending curves are on a sharp incline (well over a 40 percent rise for the United States, compared to less than a 20 percent increase for Canada—see the scholarly ten-year projection for 1998). The fact that the two countries show varying library profiles suggests strongly that these two groups ought *not* to be studied willy-nilly under the same sample curve.

The average variable response rates for Canadian libraries (over the 14 variables for which mean numeric projections to 1998 were calculated) is *fifty libraries for the scholarly subgroup* and only *7.1 for the popular libraries*. Although fifty libraries is a respectable (if small) sample, an average of seven responses is negligible and cannot be considered seriously as more than a token sample. Curiously enough, both of the Canadian groups are approximately 5 percent the size of their American counterpart groups (5.72 percent for scholarly). The rule for measuring the reliability of a sample is, "The size of the error is inversely proportional to the square root of the sample size." By this standard the American samples of 875 and 166 are stable, predictable, and reliable.

By contrast, the Canadian scholarly group is 4.2 times less reliable. When it is considered that the *American popular libraries* (the less stable of the two U.S. groups) are 2.3 times less reliable than their *scholarly* counterparts, this is a serious qualification indeed. However, the fact that the reduced reliability pattern displayed by the Canadian scholarly libraries is so closely replicated among that country's popular libraries suggests that the Canadian samples, if not overwhelmingly similar in profiles to the American samples, are at least *randomly representative of all Canadian libraries in the same proportions as are the U.S. scholarly and popular libraries*. This stands as one indicator that the *American Library Directory* is unbiased toward either scholarly or popular libraries within the U.S.-Canadian distribution.

Interpretation of the Statistics

Despite the limitations placed on interpretation as the result of the small Canadian sample sizes, the figures show distinct trends that will probably be continued into the future. Table 2.83 contains two columns of projection data which are valuable indicators of *present profiles* and *future developments*. For the two U.S. based samples, the column labeled "Projection 1998" shows how slowly or rapidly changes can be expected to affect the fourteen major variables listed.

For example, it can be predicted that total annual library expenditure will increase greatly in the next few years as scholarly institutional enrollment and faculty sizes both grow accompanied by an even greater increase in volume holdings (about 15–20 percent), a possibly enormous increase in microforms or their substitutes (depending on technological countertrends) and larger numbers of consortium memberships. A commensurate increase in subject interests, special collections, and library publications will round out this trend. Naturally, total library staff will also increase to handle the growth in services and holdings. The fact that the pattern of growth is generally consistent overall validates its predictive value (it is wise to bear in mind, here, that our samples also probably reflect the tendency of libraries, as with other human institutions, to suppress information [in this case questionnaire submission] if they are in significant operational or economic distress).

The second useful column is "10-year percentage change." This column shows American scholarly libraries as growing an average of 19.4 percent over the fourteen variables. The only variable which actually decreases in the set is city population size, by −3.9 percent. Canadian scholarly libraries show an overall or average one percent *decrease* over 1988. This figure is largely misleading as it is primarily the result of a *30 percent decline* in consortium memberships. If this figure is removed from the set of variables, then the rate of growth is reversed to show a 1.3 percent average *increase* over the ten years.

Whether the overall pattern for Canadian scholarly libraries ought to be considered as positive or negative is debatable. In fact, however, it is clear that the profile pattern is very mixed: seven (50 percent) of the fourteen variables register projected declines. These seven include library age, city population size, number of professionals, all types of library holdings, and consortium memberships. The suggestion is that the Canadian sample in 1988 picked up a number of smaller, younger libraries with their major bursts of growth yet to come.

If this is the case, then the pattern for 1998 may take one of two forms. *Either* it will reflect the forecast pattern as shown in table 2.83 as the outcome of the entry of yet another group of young, dynamic, small libraries, *or else* it will assume a different pattern entirely in which almost all of the major variables show significant growth, as in the American scholarly library profile. The second scenario should result as the younger entry group registering between 1978 and 1988 gain size and prominence. Whether the predominant pattern is the one or the other will depend on how many more young libraries are reported in 1998.

TABLE C-1
American Library Directory Statistical Summary for All Scholarly Libraries

	Variable Range from 0 –	Value of 1 Standard Dev'n	Percentage of Range	Value of 1 Standard Error of the Means
Library age	270	44	16	3
Library city population size	5,000,000	695,639	14	44,151
Institutional degree years offered	8	1	15	1
Total library staff size	69	14	20	2
Library professionals	16	3	19	1
Library clerks	16	4	25	1
Library student assistants	37	10	28	1
Faculty size	360	75	21	6
Students enrolled	5,500	1,193	22	90
Total annual library expenditure	610,000	141,375	23	12,242
Annual expenditure on material	182,000	48,488	27	4,269
Annual expenditure on personnel	350,000	84,902	24	7,747
Annual expenditure on "Other"	22,000	7,051	32	693
Library volume holdings	640,000	106,035	17	7,363
Library periodical subscriptions	1,800	433	24	33
Library microform holdings	280,000	59,209	21	5,885
Library vertical file drawers	145	29	20	3
Library consortium memberships	9	1	13	1
Library subject interests	7	1	14	1
Library special collections	12	1	9	1
Library publications	7	1	15	1
All variable total			418.9	
All variable mean			19.9	

TABLE C-2
American Library Directory Statistical Summary for All Scholarly Libraries: Matched Pairs

	Variable Range from 0 –	Value of 1 Standard Dev'n	Percent-age of Range	Value of 1 Standard Error of the Means
Library age	270	43	16	3
Library city population size	5,000,000	656,965	13	47,388
Institutional degree years offered	8	1	15	1
Total library staff size	69	14	21	2
Library professionals	16	3	19	1
Library clerks	16	4	25	1
Library student assistants	37	10	28	1
Faculty size	360	76	21	7
Students enrolled	5,500	1,217	22	96
Total annual library expenditure	610,000	144,364	24	13,051
Annual expenditure on material	182,000	49,232	27	4,531
Annual expenditure on personnel	350,000	86,183	25	8,160
Annual expenditure on "other"	22,000	6,951	32	702
Library volume holdings	640,000	110,378	17	8,288
Library periodical subscriptions	1,800	437	24	35
Library microform holdings	280,000	60,613	22	6,301
Library vertical file drawers	145	29	20	4
Library consortium memberships	9	1	13	1
Library subject interests	7	1	13	1
Library special collections	12	1	9	1
Library publications	7	1	15	1
All variable total			421.3	
All variable mean			20.1	

TABLE C-3
American Library Directory Statistical Information and Projections on All Major Variables: 1978, 1988, and 1998

Profile of Means and Mean Deviations All Scholarly Libraries: Matched Pairs	+−1.65 Standard Deviations (90% Accur.)	Percentage Growth (Ten Yrs.)	Projected Growth (1st Year)	P.A. Projected Unit Change	Projected Variable Minimum	Projected Variable Maximum	Actual 1978 Mean	Actual 1988 Mean	Extrapolated 1998 Mean
Library age	72	2.4	.2	.20	84	90	83	85	87
Library city population size	1,083,992	.7	.1	230.00	279,312	374,088	322,100	324,400	326,700
Institutional degree years offered	2	6.4	.6	.03	5	6	4	5	5
Total library staff size	23.5	19.0	1.9	.40	23.4	26.6	17.0	21.0	25.0
Library professionals	5.1	7.0	.7	.03	4.0	5.2	4.0	4.3	4.6
Library clerks	6.7	7.4	.7	.04	5.0	6.6	5.0	5.4	5.8
Library student assistants	17.2	31.3	3.1	.50	19.6	22.4	11.0	16.0	21.0
Faculty size	126.2	11.6	1.2	1.00	89.4	102.6	76.0	86.0	96.0
Students enrolled	2,008	9.6	1.0	12.00	1,280	1,472	1,134	1,255	1,376
Total annual library expenditure	238,200	43.7	4.4	11,690.00	371,549	397,651	150,800	267,700	384,600
Annual expenditure on material	81,232	40.8	4.1	3,612.00	120,119	129,181	52,410	88,530	124,650
Annual expenditure on personnel	142,202	35.8	3.6	5,361.00	195,350	211,670	96,290	149,900	203,510
Annual expenditure on "other"	11,469	21.4	2.1	372.00	20,368	21,772	13,630	17,350	21,070
Library volume holdings	182,124	19.9	2.0	2,520.00	143,712	160,288	101,600	126,800	152,000
Library periodical subscriptions	721	3.6	.4	2.20	590	660	581	603	625
Library microform holdings	100,012	42.8	4.3	2168.00	66,089	78,691	29,030	50,710	72,390
Library vertical file drawers	48	18.8	1.9	.60	34	42	26	32	38
Library consortium memberships	2	23.1	2.3	.06	3	4	2	3	3
Library subject interests	2	26.3	2.6	.05	2	3	1	2	2
Library special collections	2	.0	.0	.00	1	2	2	2	2
Library publications	2	.0	.0	.00	1	2	2	2	2
Total	1,842,267	372	37	25,970	1,198,639	1,375,785	767,808	1,027,510	1,287,212
Average	87,727	18	2	1,237	57,078	65,514	36,562	48,929	61,296

APPENDIX D *AMERICAN LIBRARY DIRECTORY* RELIGIOUS LIBRARY DATA FORM

1. Edition and lib number? (1) 31 ____ (2) 35 ____ (3) 36 ____ (4) 37 ____ (5) 41 ____ (6) 42 ____
2. Institution? ____________________
3. Library name? ____________________
4. Library type? (1) Scholarly _____: (2) Junior col ____ (3) Senior col ____ (4) University ____
   (5) Seminary ____ (6) Convent/Monastery ____
   (7) Denominational HQ ____ (8) History/Archives ____
   (9) Popular _____: (10) Congregational ____ (11) Parochial ____
   (12) Public ____
5. Accreditation status? (1) Regional ____ (2) Denominational ____ (3) Other ____ (4) AABC ____
   (5) ATLA ____ (6) ATS ____ (7) U.S. Dept. of Education ____
6. Formal religious denomination affiliation? (1) Yes ____ (2) No ____
7. Nation? (1) USA ____ (2) Canada ____
8. (1) State ____ (2) Province ____
9. Region? (1) NE ____ (2) MA ____ (3) SE ____ (4) SW ____ (5) W ____ (6) RM ____
   (7) MW ____ (8) Can ____
10. City? ____________________ 11. Repeat? (1) Yes ____ (2) ____ (3) ____
12. City popul? (1) 0–5000 ____ (5) 50001–100000 ____ (9) 700001–1000000 ____
    (2) 5001–10000 ____ (6) 100001–300000 ____ (10) 1–2 million ____
    (3) 10001–30000 ____ (7) 300001–500000 ____ (11) 2–3 million ____
    (4) 30001–50000 ____ (8) 500001–700000 ____ (12) 3+ million ____
13. Questionnaire returned? (1) Yes ____ (2) No ____
14. Departmental library? (1) Yes ____ (2) No ____
15. Age? (1) 0–1800 ____ (5) 1861–80 ____ (9) 1941–60 ____
    (2) 1801–20 ____ (6) 1881–1900 ____ (10) 1961–70 ____
    (3) 1821–40 ____ (7) 1901–20 ____ (11) 1971–80 ____
    (4) 1841–60 ____ (8) 1921–40 ____ (12) 1981+ ____
16. Highest degree? (1) Associate ____ (2) Bachelors ____ (3) Masters ____ (4) Doctors ____
17. Director named? (1) Yes ____ (2) No ____ 18. Director gender? (1) Male ____ (2) Female ____
19. Director religious order status? (1) Priest or brother ____ (2) Nun or sister ____ (3) Neither ____
20. Denomination?
    (1) Adventist ____ (12) Congregational ____ (23) Pentecostal ____
    (2) Assemblies of God ____ (13) Eastern Orthodox ____ (24) Presbyterian ____
    (3) Bahai ____ (14) Episcopal/Anglican ____ (25) Reformed ____

(4) Baptist ____
(5) Brethren ____
(6) Christian (D of C) ____
(7) Christian Science ____
(8) Church of Canada ____
(9) Church of Christ ____
(10) Church of God ____
(11) Church of Nazarene ____
(15) Friends ____
(16) Independent ____
(17) Jehovah's Wit ____
(18) Jewish ____
(19) Lutheran ____
(20) Mennonite ____
(21) Methodist ____
(22) Mormon ____
(26) Roman Catholic ____
(27) Sal Army ____
(28) Theosophy ____
(29) Unit Univer ____
(30) United Ch of Ch ____
(31) Unknown ____
(32) Other ____________________

21. Staff? *Profess* (1) 1 ___ (2) 2 ___ (3) 3 ___ (4) 4 ___ (5) 5 ___ (6) 6 ___ (7) 7 ___ (8) 8 ___ (9) 9 ___ (10) 10+ ___
22. Staff? *Clerk* (1) 1 ___ (2) 2 ___ (3) 3 ___ (4) 4 ___ (5) 5 ___ (6) 6 ___ (7) 7 ___ (8) 8 ___ (9) 9 ___ (10) 10+ ___
23. Staff? *Stud Asst* (1) 1–2 ___ (2) 3–4 ___ (3) 5–6 ___ (4) 7–8 ___ (5) 9–10 ___ (6) 11–12 ___ (7) 13–14 ___ (8) 15–16 ___ (9) 17–18 ___ (10) 19–20 ___ (11) 21–22 ___ (12) 23–24 ___ (13) 25–26 ___ (14) 27–28___ (15) 29+ ___
24. Enrollment? (1) 0–300 ____ (2) 301–600 ____ (3) 601–900 ____ (4) 901–1200 ____ (5) 1201–1500 ____ (6) 1501–1800 ____ (7) 1801–2100 ____ (8) 2101–2400 ____ (9) 2401–2700 ____ (10) 2701–3000 ____ (11) 3001–3500 ____ (12) 3501–4000 ____ (13) 4001–4500 ____ (14) 4501–5000 ____ (15) 5001+ ____
25. Faculty? (1) 0–20 ____ (2) 21–40 ____ (3) 41–60 ____ (4) 61–80 ____ (5) 81–100 ____ (6) 101–120 ____ (7) 121–140 ____ (8) 141–160 ____ (9) 161–180 ____ (10) 181–200 ____ (11) 201–220 ____ (12) 221–240 ____ (13) 241–260 ____ (14) 261–280 ____ (15) 281–300 ____ (16) 301–320 ____ (17) 321–340 ____ (18) 341+
26. Expenditures? *Material*
(1) $0–500 ____ (2) $501–1000____ (3) $1001–2000 ____ (4) $2001–6000 ____ (5) $6001–10000 ____ (6) $10001–18000 ____ (7) $18001–28000 ____ (8) $28001–47000 ____ (9) $47001–67000 ____ (10) $67001–88000 ____ (11) $88001–110000 ____ (12) $110001–122000 ____ (13) $122001–142000 ____ (14) $142001–162000 ____ (15) $162001+ ____
27. Expenditures? *Personnel*
(1) $0–5000 ____ (2) $5001–10000 ____ (3) $10001–20000 ____ (4) $20001–35000 ____ (5) $35001–50000 ____ (6) $50001–65000 ____ (7) $65001–85000 ____ (8) $85001–105000 ____ (9) $105001–130000 ____ (10) $130001–160000 ____ (11) $160001–195000 ____ (12) $195001–230000 ____ (13) $230001–265000____ (14) $265001–300000 ____ (15) $300001+ ____
28. Expenditures? *Other*
(1) $0–1000 ____ (2) $1001–2000 ____ (3) $2001–4000 ____ (4) $4001–6000 ____ (5) $6001– 8000 ____ (6) $8001–10000 ____ (7) $10001–12000 ____ (8) $12001–14000 ____ (9) $14001–16000 ____ (10) $16001–18000 ____ (11) $18001+ ____
29. Expenditures? *Total*
(1) $0–500 ____ (2) $501–1500 ____ (3) $1501–7500 ____ (4) $7501–20000 ____ (5) $20001–45000 ____ (6) $45001–95000 ____ (7) $95001–150000 ____ (8) $150001–220000 ____ (9) $220001–310000 ____ (10) $310001–410000 ____ (11) $410001–510000 ____ (12) $510001+____
30. Holdings? *Volumes*
(1) 0–1000 ____ (2) 1001–3500 ____ (3) 3501–10000 ____ (4) 10001–20000 ____ (5) 20001–50000 ____ (6) 50001–100000 ____ (7) 100001–160000 ____ (8) 160001–240000 ____ (9) 240001–340000 ____ (10) 340001–440000 ____ (11) 440001–540000 ____ (12) 540001+ ____

31. Holdings? *Periodicals*
(1) 0–100 ____ (5) 601–800 ____ (9) 1401–1600 ____
(2) 101–200 ____ (6) 801–1000 ____ (10) 1601+ ____
(3) 201–400 ____ (7) 1001–1200 ____
(4) 401–600 ____ (8) 1201–1400 ____

32. Holdings? *VF*
(1) 0–5 ____ (5) 31–40 ____ (9) 86–100 ____
(2) 6–10 ____ (6) 41–55 ____ (10) 101–115 ____
(3) 11–20 ____ (7) 56–70 ____ (11) 116–130 ____
(4) 21–30 ____ (8) 71–85 ____ (12) 131+ ____

33. Holdings? *Microforms*
(1) 0–100 ____ (5) 10001–20000 ____ (9) 120001–180000 ____
(2) 101–1000 ____ (6) 20001–40000 ____ (10) 180001+____
(3) 1001–5000 ____ (7) 40001–80000 ____
(4) 5001–10000 ____ (8) 80001–120000 ____

34. Holdings? *Other* (1) Media ____ (2) Maps ____ (3) Art Reproductions ____

35. Use? (1) Circulation to members only ____ (2) Reference service to members only ____

36. Consortium memberships? 37. Local automation projects? (1) Yes ____
(1) 1 ____ (2) 2 ____ (3) 3 ____ (4) 4 ____ (5) 5 ____ (6) 6 ____ (7) 7 ____ (8) 8+ ____
(9) OCLC? ____

38. Religious subject interests? (1) Relig studies ____ (2) Others ________________________
____ Number: (3) 1 ____ (4) 2 ____ (5) 3 ____
____ (6) 4 ____ (7) 5 ____ (8) 6+ ____

39. Religious special collections? (1) ____
__________________________ Number: (2) 1 ____ (4) 3 ____ (6) 5 ____ (8) 7 ____ (10) 9 ____
(3) 2 ____ (5) 4 ____ (7) 6 ____ (9) 8 ____ (11) 10+ ____

40. Publications? (1) ____
Number: (2) 1 ____ (3) 2 ____ (4) 3 ____ (5) 4 ____ (6) 5 ____ (7) 6+ ____

41. Notes ____
____

INDEX

LIST OF TABLES

About the Authors

John F. Harvey attended Dartmouth College, the University of Illinois, and the University of Chicago Graduate Library School (Ph.D., 1949). A former Presbyterian church deacon, he held several positions as a university library director and the dean or chairman of a graduate library school in such notable institutions as the University of New Mexico, Hofstra University, Drexel University, the University of Chicago, the University of Tehran, and Mottahedin University. He has published extensively and held office in several national and state library associations as well as several American university alumni associations. He founded the Church and Synagogue Library Association in the United States, the Iranian Documentation Centre, and the Tehran Book Processing Centre in Iran in the late 1960s. He has been listed in publications such as *Who's Who in America* and *Who's Who in the World.* Much of his time now is spent working on the Internet, on alumni association activities, in book editing, in book reviewing of library science and mystery and detective novels, and in library consulting. He has lived and worked in Cyprus since going there as a refugee in 1980.

Jo Ann Mouridou earned a master's degree in political science and research methods from Canada's most prominent Lutheran university. She followed with doctoral work in Edmonton, Alberta. Mouridou also holds formal U.K. qualifications in communications studies, marketing, advertising, and systems analysis and design. In addition to having worked in two large North American university libraries and as head of the business studies department of a local Cypriot senior college for five years, Mouridou has worked as accountant, program analyst, and researcher for several religious agencies. She designed and compiled the statistical analysis sections of Harvey's books *Scholarly Religious Libraries in North America* and *Popular Religious Libraries in North America* and is the author of several college-type study manuals, short articles, book reviews, and two unpublished volumes for children—one in verse and one in prose.

About the Authors

BOOKS EDITED OR WRITTEN BY JOHN F. HARVEY

The Library Periodical Directory, with Phillips Temple, Betty Martin Brown, and Mary Adele Springman (Pittsburg, Kans.: 1955 and 1967).

The Librarian's Career: A Study of Mobility, ACRL Microcard Series, no. 85 (Rochester, N.Y.: University of Rochester, 1957).

The Library College, with Louis Shores and Robert Jordan (Philadelphia: Drexel, 1964).

Data Processing in College and Public Libraries (Philadelphia: Drexel, 1966).

Comparative and International Library Science (Metuchen, N.J.: Scarecrow, 1977).

Church and Synagogue Libraries (Metuchen, N.J.: Scarecrow, 1980).

Librarians' Affirmative Action Handbook, with Elizabeth M. Dickinson (Metuchen, N.J.: Scarecrow, 1982).

Austerity Management in Academic Libraries, with Peter Spyers-Duran (Metuchen, N.J.: Scarecrow, 1984).

Internationalizing Library Education: A Handbook, with Frances Laverne Carroll (Westport, Conn.: Greenwood, 1987).

Scholarly Religious Libraries in North America: A Statistical Examination (Lanham, Md.: Scarecrow, 1998).

Popular Religious Libraries in North America: A Statistical Examination (Lanham, Md.: Scarecrow, 1998).

World Directory of Theological Libraries, 2d ed., 2 vols. (in process)